KU-039-908

ENGLISH PLACE-NAME SOCIETY   VOLUME LXIV/LXV

FOR 1986-7 & 1987-8

THE PLACE-NAMES
OF LINCOLNSHIRE

By

KENNETH CAMERON

PART TWO

LINCOLNSHIRE
LINDSEY
NORTH RIDING
THE WAPENTAKE OF YARBOROUGH

BERKSHIRE COUNTY LIBRARY

ENGLISH PLACE-NAME SOCIETY
1991

Published by the English Place-Name Society

© English Place-Name Society 1991

ISBN: 0 904889 16 5

Printed in Great Britain
by Woolnough Bookbinding, Irthlingborough.

ENGLISH PLACE-NAME SOCIETY   VOLUME LXIV/LXV

FOR 1986-7 & 1987-8

General Editor
KENNETH CAMERON

THE PLACE-NAMES OF LINCOLNSHIRE

PART TWO

ENGLISH PLACE-NAME SOCIETY

The English Place-Name Society was founded in 1923 to carry out the survey of English place-names and to issue annual volumes to members who subscribe to the work of the Society. The Society has issued the following volumes:

I. (Part 1) *Introduction to the Survey of English Place-Names.*
    (Part 2) *The Chief Elements used in English Place-Names.*
    (Reprinted as one volume).
II. *The Place-Names of Buckinghamshire.*
III. *The Place-Names of Bedfordshire and Huntingdonshire.*
IV. *The Place-Names of Worcestershire.*
V. *The Place-Names of the North Riding of Yorkshire.*
VI, VII. *The Place-Names of Sussex, Parts 1 and 2*
VIII, IX. *The Place-Names of Devon, Parts 1 and 2.*
X. *The Place-Names of Northamptonshire.*
XI. *The Place-Names of Surrey.*
XII. *The Place-Names of Essex.*
XIII. *The Place-Names of Warwickshire.*
XIV. *The Place-Names of the East Riding of Yorkshire and York.*
XV. *The Place-Names of Hertfordshire.*
XVI. *The Place-Names of Wiltshire.*
XVII. *The Place-Names of Nottinghamshire.*
XVIII. *The Place-Names of Middlesex* (apart from the *City of London*).
XIX. *The Place-Names of Cambridgeshire and the Isle of Ely.*
XX, XXI, XXII. *The Place-Names of Cumberland, Parts 1, 2 and 3.*
XXIII, XXIV. *The Place-Names of Oxfordshire, Parts 1 and 2.*
XXV, XXVI. *English Place-Name Elements, Parts 1 and 2.*
XXVII, XXVIII, XXIX. *The Place-Names of Derbyshire, Parts 1, 2 and 3.*
XXX, XXXI, XXXII. XXXIII, XXXIV, XXXV, XXXVI, XXXVII. *The Place-Names of the West Riding of Yorkshire, Parts 1-8.*
XXXVIII, XXXIX, XL, XLI *The Place-Names of Gloucestershire, Parts 1-4.*
XLII, XLIII *The Place-Names of Westmorland, Parts 1 and 2.*
XLIV, XLV, XLVI, XLVII, XLVIII *The Place-Names of Cheshire, Parts 1, 2, 3, 4, 5 I:i.*
XLIX, L, LI. *The Place-Names of Berkshire, Parts 1, 2 and 3*
LII, LIII. *The Place-Names of Dorset, Parts 1 and 2.*
LIV. *The Place-Names of Cheshire, Part 5 I:ii.*
LV. *The Place-Names of Staffordshire, Part 1.*
LVI, LVII. *Cornish Place-Name Elements.*
LVIII. *The Place-Names of Lincolnshire, Part 1.*
LIX, LX. *The Place-Names of Dorset, Part 3.*
LXI *The Place-Names of Norfolk, Part 1.*
LXII. LXIII *The Place-Names of Shropshire, Part 1.*
LXIV, LXV *The Place-Names of Lincolnshire, Part 2*

All communications concerning the Society and membership should be addressed to:

THE HON. DIRECTOR, English Place-Name Society,
The University, Nottingham, NG7 2RD.

READING CENTRAL LIBRARY
REFERENCE DEPARTMENT

CLASS   910.3 CAM

ADDED   16/11/91   PRICE

DISPOSED OF/FILED

This volume is dedicated to the memory of

Dorothy Whitelock, CBE, FBA

ACKNOWLEDGEMENTS

This collection of material, the preparation and printing of this volume have been greatly assisted by generous grants from the British Academy; for the collection of material from a grant from the University of Nottingham Research Fund; for the printing and publication by donations from the National Westminster Bank plc, from a gift to the University of Cambridge in memory of Dorothea Coke, Skjæret, 1951, and from two anonymous members of the Society.

The Camera-ready Copy of this volume
has been produced by Mrs Esmé Pattison
on equipment provided
by
Messrs Allied Breweries plc
and by
Messrs Advent Desktop Publishing Limited

CONTENTS

Preface   xi

Additions to Abbreviations and Bibliography in
    The Place-Names of Lincolnshire, Part I   xiii

Notes on Arrangement   xv

Addenda and Corrigenda to Volume 58   xviii

Phonetic Symbols   xxi

Map   xxiii

Lincolnshire   1

Lindsey   2

North Riding   7

Yarborough Wapentake   7

The Place-Names of Yarborough Wapentake   8

Index   313

PREFACE

The second part of *The Place-Names of Lincolnshire* covers one Wapentake in the North Riding of Lindsey, that of Yarborough. Again, I have to thank a number of friends in the Lincolnshire Archives Office, who have consistently helped me on my numerous visits there, particularly Mr Chris Johnson and Mr Nicholas Bennett for numerous suggestions they have made and for help in deciphering difficult spellings in medieval documents. Most of all, I thank Mr Nigel Colley for his constant attention and for his assistance in suggesting sources to search and Mr Peter Noon for his sheer efficiency in attending to my constant requests for documents, even when I have wrongly identified them! A glance through the text of this volume will show just how much material in the Archives I have searched and the time and energy on the part of the staff it has required to put it at my disposal.

Many Lincolnshire men and women have helped me in a variety of ways and to each I offer my warmest thanks. Some have provided me with lists of field-names, like Mr Rex C. Russell, others have commented on particular names, like Mr D.H. Appleby, Mr M.G. Border, Mr David Neeve and Mr R. Newton, or on the names of a particular parish, like Mr Raymond Cary and Mr Ifor Barton. Dr Rod Ambler has shown his friendship in many ways and has in addition enlisted the help of students in his Extra-Mural classes, like Mr and Mrs Anderson, Mrs Dinah Tyszka and notably Mrs Bettie Watkinson. Dr Paul Evison has always been ready to advise me about archaeological problems, while Captain M. Glover, formerly of the Earl of Yarborough's Estate Office, and his staff generously provided me with facilities to check Estate Plans which enabled me to locate two lost settlement sites.

I am indebted to my colleagues Mr Stanley Ellis, Professor Raymond Page, Dr Patrick Sims-Williams and Dr Veronica Smart for their help over particular problems, while Mr John Field prepared the first draft of each of the parish field-name lists and made numerous suggestions of etymology, based on his own considerable experience of the study of field-names. The immense task of setting these in alphabetical order can only be imagined. Above all, however, I am especially grateful to my friend and former student, Dr John Insley, who placed at my disposal his un-

rivalled expertise in the field of early personal names. His con-
tribution in this area is very considerable indeed and I trust I have
attributed to him all his suggested etymologies. Indeed I hope that
I have made due acknowledgement to all who have helped me in so
many ways and, if I have omitted any such, I trust I may be
forgiven.

The text itself has been prepared for press by our Secretary,
Mrs M.D. Pattison, whose experience and knowledge in handling
place-name material has earned the admiration of the Society's
editors over many years. I stand greatly in her debt once more.

University of Nottingham   Kenneth Cameron

ADDITIONS to the ABBREVIATIONS and BIBLIOGRAPHY printed in the PLACE-NAMES OF LINCOLNSHIRE, PART I

Adams	I.H. Adams, *Agrarian Landscape Terms: a Glossary for Historical Geography,* Institute of British Geographers Special Publication Number Nine 1976
BartonN	Robert Brown, *Notes on the earlier History of Barton-on-Humber,* 2 vols., London 1906
BC	Documents in the Broughton Castle Collection (LAO)
bdy	boundary
BH	Documents in the Brown, Hudson and Hudson Deposit (LAO)
Brad	Documents in the Earl of Bradford Collection (LAO)
Bry	A. Bryant, *Map of the County of Lincoln* 1828
BT	Bishop's Transcripts (LAO)
Btm, btm	Bottom (in f.ns. (a))
Census	The 1851 Census for Lincolnshire (Microfilm copy in LAO)
Cl(s), cl(s)	Close(s) (in f.ns. (a))
Deeds	Deeds in 4BM (LAO)
EDS	Publications of the English Dialect Society
FLDudd	Documents in the Dudding Collection in the Foster Library (LAO)
FLMisc	Miscellaneous documents in the Foster Library (LAO)
Gdn	Garden (in f.ns. (a))
Grd	Ground (in f.ns. (a))
Gt	Great (in f.ns. (a))
Ipm	Unpublished forms from Inquisitiones post mortem (PRO)
LCC	Lindsey Quarter Sessions documents (LAO)
LCL	Lincoln City Library documents (LAO)
LER	C.W. Foster, *Lincoln Episcopal Records* (LRS 2) 1912
LPR	*Protestation Returns 1641/2 -- Lincolnshire,* transcribed W.F. Webster, Nottingham 1984
Lr	Lower (in f.ns. (a))
LRA	Documents in the Lincoln River Authority Collection (LAO)
Lt	Little (in f.ns. (a))
LTR	Lindsey Quarter Sessions, Land Tax Returns (LAO)
MCD	Miscellaneous Copies of Documents (LAO)
Mdw	Meadow (in f.ns. (a))
Nr	Near (in f.ns. (a))
OSFacs	*Facsimiles of Anglo-Saxon Manuscripts I,* translated W.B. Sanders, O.S. 1878
OWScand	Old West Scandinavian
Pce, pce	Piece (in f.ns. (a))
Plant, Plnt	Plantation (in f.ns. (a))
PNITL	Margaret Gelling, *Place-Names in the Landscape,* London 1984
PN L	Kenneth Cameron, *The Place-Names of Lincolnshire,* Part 1 (EPNS 58) 1985

R1, R2	Regnal date, t. Richard 1, t. Richard 2
Rd	Road (in f.ns. (a))
Red	Documents in the Redbourne Hall Collection (LAO)
RIL	*The 1341 Royal Inquest in Lincolnshire*, ed. B.W. McLane (LRS 78) 1988
Scand.	Scandinavian
surn.	surname
Upr	Upper (in f.ns. (a))
vbl	verbal
Wd, wd	Wood (in f.ns. (a))
WMP	William of Malmesbury, *De Gestis Pontificum* (RS) 1970
WMR	William of Malmesbury, *De Gestis Rerum Anglorum* (RS) 1887-9
Yd	Yard (in f.ns. (a))

NOTES ON ARRANGEMENT

(1) Following the names Lincolnshire, Lindsey, The North Riding of Lindsey and Yarborough Wapentake, the parishes in the latter are set out in alphabetical order.

(2) Each of the parish names is printed in bold type as a heading. Within each parish the names are arranged as follows: (i) the parish name; (ii) other major names (i.e. names of sizeable settlements and names of primary historical or linguistic interest), each treated separately in alphabetical order; (iii) all minor names (i.e. the remaining names recorded on the 1906 edition of the O.S. 6" map, as well as some names that are 'lost' or 'local', *v. infra*), again treated in alphabetical order but in a single paragraph; (iv) field-names (which include other unidentified minor names) in small type, (a) modern field-names, normally those recorded since 1750, with any older spellings of these names in brackets and printed in italics, (b) medieval and early modern field-names, i.e. those recorded before about 1750, printed in italics, the names in each group being arranged alphabetically.

(3) Place-names no longer current, those not recorded on the editions of the 1" and 6" maps are marked '(lost)'. This does not mean that the site to which the name refers is unknown. Such names are normally printed in italics when referred to elsewhere.

(4) Place-names marked '(local)' are those not recorded on the 1" and 6" O.S. maps but which are still current locally.

(5) The local and standard pronunciations of a name, when of interest and not readily suggested by the modern spelling, are given in phonetic symbols in square brackets after the name.

(6) The early spellings of each name are presented in the order 'spelling, date, source'. When, however, the head-form of a name is followed only by a 'date and source', e.g. BARNETBY MILL, 1824 O, 1828 Bry, the spelling in 1824 O and 1828 Bry is the same as that of the head-form.

(7) In explaining the various place-names and field-names summary reference is often made, by printing the elements in bold type, to the analysis of elements which will appear in the final volume of the Lincolnshire County Survey, and more particularly to *English Place-Name Elements* (EPNS 25,26) and to *Addenda and Corrigenda* to these volumes in *English Place-Name Society Journal* 1. In many of the minor names and field-names the meaning is so obvious as to need no comment or so uncertain as not to warrant

it. For personal-names which are cited without authority, reference should be made for Old English names to Redin, Searle and Feilitzen, for Old (Continental) German to Förstemann PN and Forsner, and for English surnames to Bardsley and Reaney (for details of these sources *v.* Abbreviations and Bibliography in *The Place-Names of Lincolnshire*, Part 1 (EPNS 58).

(8) Unprinted sources of the early spellings of place-names are indicated by printing the abbreviation for the source in italics. The abbreviation for a printed source is printed in roman type. The exact page, folio or membrane is only given where the precise identification of an entry is of special importance or value, as e.g. under MAUSOLEUM in Brocklesby parish *infra.*

(9) Where two dates are given for a spelling, e.g. Hy2 (e13), 1190 (m13), the first is the date at which the document purports to have been composed and the second the date of the copy that has come down to us (in many cases the latter is a Cartulary, ecclesiastic or lay). Sources whose dates cannot be fixed to a particular year are dated by century, e.g. 11, 12, 13, 14 etc. (often more specifically e13, m13, l13 etc., early, mid and late 13th century respectively), by regnal date, e.g. Ed1, Hy2, Eliz, Jas1 etc., or by a range of years, e.g. 1150-60, 1401-2 etc., although this last form of date may alternatively mean that the spellings belong to a particular year within the limit indicated.

(10) The sign (p) after the source indicates that the particular spelling given appears in that source as a person's surname, not primarily as a reference to a place.

(11) When a letter or letters (sometimes words or phrases) in an early place-name form are enclosed in brackets, it means that spellings with and without the enclosed letter(s), words or phrases occur. When only one part of a place-name spelling is given as a variant, preceded or followed by a hyphen, it means that the particular spelling only differs in respect of the cited part from the preceding or following spelling. Occasional spellings given in inverted commas are usually editorial translations or modernisations and whilst they have no authority linguistically they have chronologically.

(12) Cross-references to other names are given with *supra* or *infra*, the former referring to a name already dealt with, the latter to a name dealt with later in the text.

(13) Putative forms of personal names and place-name elements

which appear asterisked in the concluding volume of this survey are not always asterisked in the text, although the discussion will often make it clear which are on independent record and which are inferred.

(14) In order to save space in presenting the early spellings of a name, *et passim* and *et freq* are sometimes used to indicate that the preceding form(s) occur respectively from time to time or frequently from the date of the last quoted source to that of the following one, or to the present day.

xii   s.n.   Brunner, For Halle 1948, read Tübingen 1965.

xiv   s.n.   Camden. Read W. Camden, *Britannia* 1590,
Britain, translated Philemon Holland, 1610.

xxxix   s.n.   Yougn. Read Young.

48   s.n.   ALMA TCE. *Alma* must, of course, com-
memorate the battle of that name in the Crimean
War which took place in 1854 and not 1864 as in
the text.

58   Add. CHOLLERGATE (SMart). Dr Kathleen Major
draws my attention to several references to this
lost street, (*venelle que vocatur*) *Chollergate* 113,
1298, 1302, 1305, 1320, 1359, 1364 (c. 1380)
Welbourne, 'the street of the beggars, vagrants',
from ME *chullere* 'a vagrant, a beggar', *v.* MED
s.v., and **gata**.

68   Add. GLOVERS ROW (SMart). Again Dr. Major
draws attention to this lost row, the references being all in Latin -- in   *Rengia crote-*
cariorum 1298, *-Cirotecariorum* 1302,
-Cirothecariorum 1304, *-Cirot*(*h*)*e- car'* 1305
(c. 1380) *Welbourne*, from MedLat
cerotecarius 'a glover', and note the occurrence
of the surn. in the same parish, Richard
Cirotecarius, Richard *Glouer* 113 (c. 1380)
Welbourne. Unfortunately, the English form of
the name has not so far been noted.

126   s.n.   ST MARGARET IN WIGFORD. Mrs Mary
Lucas draws my attention to the following affix
not previously found for this church -- *sancte*
margarete down the towne, sanct margaretes
down ye towne 1558 *Wills* (LCC Wills 1558/3,
ff. 10 and 11).

132   s.n.   ST PETER AT GOWTS. Mrs Mary Lucas
has also found the following affix to the church
name, not noted before -- *the churche off sancte*
petyre the more, ye cherche of sanct pet' of
lincoll' ye mor' 1558 *Wills* (LCC Wills 1558/3
ff. 10 and 11).

162-63   s.n.   BLACK BOY (lost, Castle Hill). Mr J.

Ketteringham points out that I misunderstood the
footnote, Hill iv, 24n. The Black Boy was still a
Public House in the early 1920s, as Mr Tom
Baker confirms, and is today the Castle Hill Club.

205 s.n. *Gybonvelethyng.* Mr A.D. Mills, 'Some Alternative Analyses of Medieval Field-Names' in *Studies
in Honour of Kenneth Cameron*, Leeds Studies in
English 1987, p. 205, brilliantly suggests that the
otherwise obscure *-vele-* represents the ME surn.
Vele (Reaney s.n. *Veal*), so *Gibbon*, a diminutive
of *Gibb*, a pet-form of *Gilbert*, is a Christian
name, hence 'Gibbon Vele's possession, property'. This interpretation, for which analogical
examples are known, is without doubt correct.

210 line 14. For Stangeways, read Strangeways.

219 s.n. the Beaths or Banks. Mr John Field draws
attention to the discussion of Beetham in PN
We 67-68, where it is shown that there must
have been an ON **beð* meaning 'an embankment' or the like. This could well be the source
of *Beath*, with lengthening of the vowel in an
open syllable, giving ME **bēthe*, ModE *beath*.
Since the 1682 form, like that for 1754, suggests
that it must have been understood to have been
identical with *Banks*, the proposed sense of
*beð seems eminently suitable here.

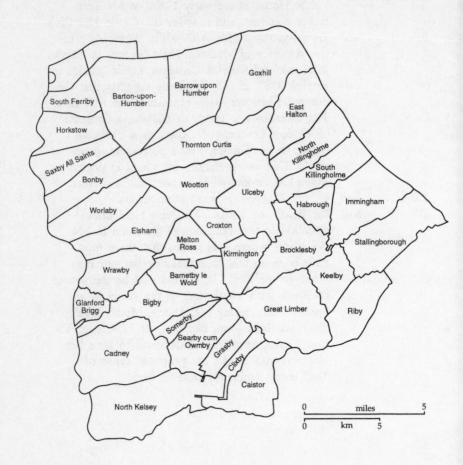

Goxhill

South Ferriby

Barton-upon-Humber

Barrow upon Humber

East Halton

Horkstow

Thornton Curtis

North Killingholme

South Killingholme

Saxby All Saints

Bonby

Wootton

Ulceby

Habrough

Immingham

Worlaby

Elsham

Croxton

Brocklesby

Stallingborough

Melton Ross

Kirmington

Wrawby

Barnetby le Wold

Keelby

Glanford Brigg

Bigby

Great Limber

Riby

Somerby

Cadney

Searby cum Owmby

Grasby

Clixby

Caistor

North Kelsey

0   miles   5

0   km   5

YARBOROUGH WAPENTAKE

Based upon the 1963 Ordnance Survey four miles to one inch map, with the permission of the controller of Her Majesty's Stationery Office. © Crown Copyright.

PHONETIC SYMBOLS

p	pay	j	you	ɔ	pot
b	bay	x	loch (Scots)	ɔ:	saw
t	tea	h	his	ɔi	oil
d	day	m	man	e	red
k	key	n	no	ei	flay
g	go	ŋ	sing	ɛ	jamais (Fr.)
ʍ	when	r	run	ɛ:	there
w	win	l	land	i	pit
f	foe	ʧ	church	i:	bead
v	vote	ʤ	judge	ou	low
s	say	ɑ:	father	u	good
z	zone	ɑu	cow	u:	boot
ʃ	shone	a	mann (German)	ʌ	much
ʒ	azure	ai	fly	ə	ever
þ	thin	æ	cab	ə:	bird
ð	then			?	water (Cockney, glottal stop)

Phonetic symbols are enclosed in square brackets: [   ].

LINCOLNSHIRE

Lindcolnescire s.a. 1016 (m11) ASC C

Lincolne scire s.a. 1016 (p1050) ASC D, s.a. 1016 (c. 1121) ib E,
Lincolna scire s.a. 1065 (?l12) ib D, s.a. 1065 (c. 1121) ib E,
Lincolenscire 1091-92 (12) Eyns

Lincole scire 1086 DB, *-scira* 1101, c. 1101, 1123-33, 1120-33 RA
i, *Lincolescire* 1132 (1403), Stephen (1464) Pat, *-scir* 1138-39
(1329) Ch, *-scr'* 1171 P

Lincolescyra, -scyre, -scire, -scira 1086 DB, *-syre* 1129 HH,
Lincolascira 1096-1100 France, Wm2 (13-14) Selby, *Lincolia
scira* 1100-15, 1101-15, a1107, 1110-22, 1114-16 RA i,
Lincoliescira 1130, 1156 P, *Lincolie siria* 1155-58 RA i,
Lincoliesiria 1155-58 (1329) Ch, *-scr'* 1157, 1158 *et passim* to
1168 P, *-sira* 1158-63 (1329) Ch

Lincol'scira c. 1107, 1123-33, 1135-39, 1140-44, 1141, 1147-52,
1155, 1155-62, 1163 RA i, 1187, 1188 P, *-scir'* 1155-58 AC,
-scire 1157 LRCh, *-scr'* 1162, 1165, 1170, 1172 *et passim* to
1183 P, *-sira* 1155-58 RA i

Lincolscyre 1075-92 (12) Eyns, 1154-89 (1329) Ch, *-scyr* Hy2
(1437) Pat, *-scyra* 1158-62 (1329) Ch, *-scire* 1155-58 (Ed3)
YCh i, Hy2 BC, Hy2 (1427) Pat, *-sira* 1154-66 (1329) Ch

Lincoll'sira 1154-60 RA i, *-scira* 1186, 1188 P, *-scir'* 1197 *et
passim* to 1215 ib, *-scr'* 1190, 1193, 1194 ib, *-sir'* 1205, 1207,
1209, 1211 ib, *-sr'* 1191, 1192 ib, 1196 ChancR, *-schir'* 1207,
1230 P, *-schire* 1212 ib

Lincolnescira 1100-35 (13-14) Selby, c. 1128 (12) ChronPetro,
1136-40 (1464) Pat, 1137 (1329), 1189 (1332), Hy2 (1301)
Ch, 1202 Ass, *-scire* 1155-58 (1329) Ch, 12 HC, *-shir'* c. 1151
(14) RA i, *-scyre* 1155-58 (1329) Ch, *-scir'* 1195 P, *-scr'* 1175
ib, 1178 ChancR, *-sira* 1101-9 (13-14) Selby, 1156, 1156-57 *et
passim* to 1199-1200 RBE, Hy2 (1397) Pat, R1 (1318) Ch,
1221-30, 1237 Fees, *-sire* 1154-55 RBE, *-sir'* 1194 P, R1 Cur,
-syra 1201-12 RBE

Lincolnie scira 1120-22 (1308), Stephen (1330), Hy2 (1316) Ch,
Lincolnisira 1154-65 (1329) ib

Lyngcolne chyre (sic) Stephen (m14) *HC*

Linc' scira 1121-23 RA i, 1121-33 RS, 1129-33, 1146, 1153-54 RA
i, *-Scira* 1185 Templar, *-scire* c. 1160 RA i, *-scyra* 1155-58 ib

i, *-sira* 1155 ib i, *-sire* 1155-66 ib i, *-sir'* 1194 CurP
Lincolnschire 1099 (15) ArchÆl 4th, vi, *-scire* 1146 Dugd i, 1154-
   79 BC, *-scira* 1156-57 (14) YCh i, 1166 RBE, 1184, 1185 P,
   1185 RotDom, 1211-12 RBE, *-sira* 1160-62 ib, *-scr'* 1176 P,
   -sire Hy2 (1301) HMCRep, 1262 LRCh, *Lincoln' scire* Hy2
   LN, *-scir'* 1194 P, *-sir'* 1199 Memo, *Lincollnsir'* 1202 Ass
Lincolnshire 1371, 1376, 1382, 1413, 1424, 1479 Cl *et passim*,
   Lyncolnshire 1364 ib, 1478 WillsPCC, *Linccolne shire* 1470
   ChronReb
Sudlincolia 1086 DB
Nicholasira 1126 RA i, *nicolasira* 1126 (e13) *LincCart, Nicolseira*
   1163-72 Kirkst, *Nicholescr'* 1169, 1170 P, *-sir'* Hy2 Kirkst,
   1212 Cur, *Nichol'scira* Hy2 (1314) Ch
le Counte de Nichole 1335 *MiD*

Forms from spurious AS charters have not been included.

Lincolnshire denoted a district (*v.* scīr) comprising the Parts of
Lindsey, Kesteven and Holland. It was an English creation after
the reconquest of the Danelaw in the earlier 10th century and must
have included at least the areas under the control of the Danish
armies of Lincoln and of Stamford. *v.* further, F.M. Stenton,
Anglo-Saxon England, 3rd ed. 1971, p. 338. Forms in *N-* are due to
AN influence.

Lindsey

LINDSEY
   in prouincia Lindissi (4x), *in Lindissi prouincia, de Lindissi* (*reuer-
      sum*) 731 Bede, *iuxta Lindissi urbe* l10 (e11) Æthelweard,
      Lindissi 1127-35 (e14) Brid (p), *de-* 1129 HH, *super Lind-
      issim* 1093 RA i, *-issiam* 1093 (Ed3) YCh i, and note also
      *man ge halgode Lindis warum to biscope Eadhed. se wæs on
      Lindissi ærost biscopa* s.a. 678 (c. 1121) ASC E
   eiusdem lindissae provinciae 731 Bede, *Lindissae* (gen.sg.) l8
      Alcuin (*Monumenta Germaniae Historia, Poetae* 1, 177)
   in prouincia lindisi 731 Bede, *parochiam Lindisi* 1061 RA i, *in
      pago qui dicitur Lyndisi* 1082 (1303) Pat, *Lindisia* a1135 (c.
      1240) Whit

in prouincia(m) ..... *Lindisfarorum* (2x), *episcopatum gentis* ....-
Lindisfarorum episcopatus 731 Bede, *landesir* .... *Lindesfarona*
l8 (l10) Tribal Hidage (EHR x1), *biscup* ..... *Lindesfarena,*
biscopdom ..... *Lindesfearena, -fearona bisceop* c.
890 (10) OEBede, *in provincia Lindisfarorum* 1129 HH
on Lindesse s.a. 838, s.a. 873, *from Lindesse* s.a. 874 all (c. 900)
ASC A, *in Lindesse* (4x), *of Lindesse* (2x) c. 890 (10)
OEBede, *on lindesse lande, in lindesse mæʒþe* c. 890 (10)
ib, *in urbe Lindesse* l10 (e11) Æthelweard
in Lindisse, -londe, -mægðe c. 890 (10) OEBede, *a Lindisse* c.
1125 Ord, *provincia Lindisse* 1129 HH, note also *Paulinus*
bodad fulluht on Lindisse s.a. 627 (c. 1121) ASC E
on Lindesie s.a. 838 (m11) ASC C, *Lindesi* 1086 DB, 1156-57
(Ed2) YCh i, *in Lindesium* 1103 France, *Lindesiam* 1126 RA
i, *Lindesia* 1139 ib, 1142-53, c. 1150, c. 1155 Dane, 1181,
1185 P *et passim* to 1212 (l13) Guis, Hy2 LN, c. 1180 Bly
(p), 1202 P (p), 1219 Ass
on Lindese (2x) c. 890 (10) OEBede, *de partibus Lindese* 1226
Pat, 1254 (14) Percy, *Lindese* 1322 Pat
on Lindesige s.a. 838 (c. 1050) ASC D, *on-* (2x), *in Lindesige* c.
890 (m11) OEBede, *in Lindesige* 973 (14) ECEE, *on*
Lindesige s.a. 933 (c. 1121) ASC E, s.a. 993 (m11) ib C,
Lindesig c. 1000 Asser, *on Lindesige* c. 1000 Saints, s.a. 1013,
s.a. 1014, s.a. 1016 (m11) ASC C, *Lindissig* c. 1000 Asser,
in lindisige 973 (13) ECEE, and note also *in lindes iglande*
c. 890 (m11) OEBede
in-, of-, on lindes ege, of lindesege, inn lindes ege landes c. 890
(m11) OEBede, *on Lindesege* s.a. 1066 (11) ASC C
Lindeseia 1040-41 (l13) RamsChron, 1115 YCh iii, c. 1124 RA
iii (p), c. 1128 (12) ChronPetro, 1200 P *et passim* to c.
1250 Crone, *Lindesei* 1100-16 (c. 1240) Whit, R1 (1308) Ch,
1145-66 YCh iii, c. 1150 (c. 1310) Werb, 1185 Templar, 1194
(Hy4) YCh iii, *Lindeseie* 1129 HH, 1314 Pat, *in partibus-*
1338 Hosp
Lindissei 1 Cur
Lindesey 1096-1101 (c. 1310) Werb, 1100-15 (m13) YCh ii, 1147-
66 (1409) Gilb (p), 1175-78 (e14) YCh x, 1249 Ipm *et passim*
to 1568-70 MinAcct, Hy *Lindesey* 1535-43 Leland, *Lyndesey*
1329, 1331 Pat, 1359 Cl, (*in partibus de*) 1360 Peace, c. 1360
Gough *et freq* to Lowe *Lyndesey* 1538 LP xiii, *Lyndeseye*

1123-47 RA iv, 1210-12 RBE, 1235-36 Fees, 1237 Lib, 1242
Pat, 1260 Lib *et passim* to 1554 Pat, *Lyndeseye* 1294, 1301,
1304, 1305 ib, 1314 Fine, 1315 Cl *et freq* to 1405 Pat,
Lindeseya 1166 RBE, 1200, 1201 ChR, 1274 Ipm, *Lyndesaya*
112 RA ii, 1253 Abbr, 1258 Cl, 1298 Ipm, *Lyndesay* 1446
Fine
Lindesaya a1070, c. 1078, 1090-96, Hy1 all (c. 1240) Whit, *-aye*
1145-48 (c. 1240) ib, 1336 (e14) Guis, *Lyndesaye* 1359 Misc,
Lindesay 1250, 1346 Ipm, 1351, 1391 Cl
Lindsey 1326 Cl, 1332 Pat *et passim*, *Lynsey* 1338 Fine, 1509 Pat,
Linsey 1491 ib, 1579-87 ChancP, *Lynsay* 1536 LP xi

Forms from spurious Anglo-Saxon charters are not included.

According to Rivet and Smith, PNRB 393b, Lindsey is derived
from "Lindenses, an ethnicon formed from the name of the *colonia*
(plus Anglo-Saxon *ēg* 'island')". The development of the name is
discussed twice by Jackson, LHEB 332 and 543. At p. 332, he
states "Brit. Lat. **Lindẹses* (<**Lindeneses* ....) >Pr.AS. *Lindẹs* >AS.
Lindes, Lindessē". Later, p. 543, in discussing the development of
Latin *ns* in "Brittonic", he points out that the Britons "heard the
Latin sound with the *n* lost and with compensatory lengthening" and
he goes on "Hence the W. [i.e. Welsh] suffix for tribal and district
names, *-wys* < Lat. *-ensēs*. This is to be seen in an AS. loan in
*Lindenses **Lindẹs* > Pr.AS. **Lindẹs* .. > *Lindesse*, etc.". So, the
PrW name must have meant 'the people around Lincoln' or 'the
people around the pool' (Brit **lindo-*, PrW **linn*), cf. Lincoln, PN L
1, 1-2. The Latinised forms *Lindisfarorum* in Bede and the later
OE *Lindisfarena* represent the gen.pl. of OE *Lindisfaran* 'the
Lindsey people', while *Lindis warum* in the annal s.a. 678 reference
is the dat.p. of *Lindisware* 'the Lindsey dwellers or people'. The
editor of Æthelweard, xxxv n.3., takes *urbs* to mean 'region', but it
has been shown that this was not his normal usage and that it
should be interpreted 'town'.

The OE forms of the name, suggested above by Jackson, are
well represented in the collection of early spellings presented here,
as well as by *Lindisse*, but Bede's *Lindis(s)i* is puzzling. It has
been explained by Ivar Dahl, *Substantival Inflexion in Early Old
English: Vocalic Stems*, 102, as the gen. of a Latin nom. *Lindissum*,
but Bede has also *eiusdem lindissae provinciae*, as has Alcuin too,

which suggests that *Lindis(s)i* can hardly be from the Latin neuter gen.sg..

Dr Patrick Sims-Williams points out, in a personal communication, that no ancient form from **Lindenses* had come down to Bede in Latin tradition. He further notes that the final syllable of Brit. **Lindǣses* was presumably reduced to some form of [ə] "before the stage **Lindǣs* was reached, but he believes that Bede's *Lindissi/Lindissae* can hardly be regarded as a reflection of such an intermediate stage. He comments further that the OE starting point could well be Brit. **Lindǣs*, a form which would seem to demand the addition of a recognisable ending, whether in OE or Latin. He concludes however, that *Lindissi/Lindissae* "have no obvious import" so far as Brit. is concerned. Dr Sims-Williams then makes the interesting point that if Bede and his sources were constructing Latinized forms, principally for use in the gen.sg. after *prounicia* etc., that would explain his *-ae* beside *-i*, the former also occurring in Alcuin. He notes a parallel for such a variation in declension and gender in Gregory 1's *Lundoniae ciuitatis* (quoted in Bede 1.29) instead of *-ii* and adds "presumably such formations were *ad hoc* adaptations".

Dr Margaret Gelling (*Anglo-Saxon England* xviii, 31-32) draws attention to Bede's form for Leeds. This is assumed by Jackson (*Antiquity* xx, 209-10) to be derived from a comparable British-Latin folk-name formation -- **Lātenses*, later *Lōdǣses* (and presumably **Lōdǣs*) -- which then appears in Bede as *Loidis* not *Loidissi*. Had a similar development taken place in *Lindsey* one would have expected *Lindis* in Bede not *Lindissi*. Clearly, Bede's forms for Lindsey cannot be readily explained.

Dr Gelling draws attention to the fact that Bede's *Lindissi* "appears to have been current until the late 9th century". Indeed, the forms above show that this tradition persisted till the 12th century, while forms from ASC etc. in *Lindesse, Lindisse* are clearly later developments of *Lindissi* itself. At the same time in ASC, OEBede and Asser another basic form occurs with variant spellings, *Lindesige, Lindisige, lindes ege* etc.. The earliest of these has a purported date of 838 in ASC D, a manuscript believed to have been compiled in York, and it is from these forms that the current name *Lindsey* itself has developed. It should be noted that other versions of ASC have *Lindesse* in the annal for 838. Now, the *-i* in *Lindissi* cannot be taken as a variant or reduced form of OE īg, ēg 'an island, etc.', for this OE word regularly appears in an archaic form *-eu* in Bede.

Dr Gelling argues that "it seems probable that a form with *-īg*, 'island', was current together with *Lindesse*", as indeed the forms quoted above suggest. Already, W.H. Stevenson, Asser 242, had noted that *Lindesig* was not the same name as Bede's *Lindissi* and the *Lindesse* of the ASC, and he suggested that it was a later form "the name having been wrongly connected with OE *īeg, īg*". While conceding that Stevenson's explanation is possible, she claims that this would "at least be confirmation of the view that the *Lindissi, Lindesse* forms have a final element, and are not simply derivatives of a folk-name **Lindes-*". If this *is* so, then we have no idea what that final element was. Cf. also Sims-Williams' comments above.

It would appear that OE īg was added to a form without final *-si*. The exact significance of OE īg, ēg 'an island, land partly surrounded by water, a piece of dry ground in fen' here is also uncertain. Already in Bede it is described as a *prouincia* and for 12th century historians, Lindsey seems to be looked upon as a district similar in extent to its modern boundaries, cf. HH 86, and *Giraldi Cambrensis Opera* VII, 19. But, the detailed examination of īg, ēg in p.ns. by Margaret Gelling, PNITL 34-40, has clearly demonstrated that the word was used to denote a *small* piece of land. There is no comparable example to the use of Lindsey as the name of a division of Lincolnshire.

In the latest work on the subject, 'Lincoln and the Anglo-Saxon See of Lindsey', *Anglo-Saxon England* xviii, 1-32, Steven Bassett has examined the evidence afresh, and argues that *Lindesse/Lindesig* originally denoted a specific settlement and not a region. His arguments are detailed and cannot be easily summarized. He sees the location of *Lindsey* (pp. 121-8) as lying south of the Roman walled area of Lincoln and the 'island' as comprising the small promontory "defined on its western and northern sides by the present course of the Witham (including Brayford Pool), and on the east by what seems to be a former course, now dry", outlined by the five metre contour south and east of the Witham. He goes on to argue that though it may no longer have been surrounded by water in historical times "the feature is entirely appropriate for a place-name in ēg, which 'most frequently refers to dry ground surrounded by marsh when it occurs in ancient settlements'. No other piece of land in the vicinity of Lincoln has these characteristics". *v.* his Fig. 1, p. 13. If this is so, then *Lindsey* was originally the name of a settlement and that this name was subsequently extended to denote a district. For the ecclesiastical history of Lindsey, *v.* further Bassett 1-6, 18-29.

The most sensible interpretation of *Lindsey* is 'the island of the *Lindēs*', in which *Lindēs* means 'the people of Lincoln or of the pool', *v.* Brit. *lindo-, PrW *linn.

North Riding

NORTH RIDING, *Nort Treding, Norttreding, Nort Tred', Nortreding* 1086 DB, *Nortriding* c. 1115 LS, *Nortrihing'* 1212 Fees, *Northrehinga* Hy3 (1409) Gilb, *Nortreyng* 1272-73 Misc, *Northtrithing* 1275 RH, *in ... Northrithingo* 1316 FA, *Northrything'* 1276 RH, *Northtrehyng* c. 1300 *AncPet, Northrething* 1318 Pat, *Northtrethyng* 1318 ib, *Northridyng* 1349 *Cor, le Norththrithyng* 1356 *ib, Northeredyng'* 1360 *ib.* The division of Lindsey, like the county of Yorkshire, was divided into three parts - North, South and West Riding. Riding is derived from ON þriðjungr, late OE þriðing 'a third part'; it should be noted that initial þ- has become *t-* through AN influence, cf. IPN 109, and was absorbed by the final ð of norð to give *Riding*.

Yarborough Wapentake

YARBOROUGH WAPENTAKE
  Gereberg 1086 DB
  Gereburg 1086 DB, *-burc* 1162, 1163 P, *Gerburc* 1183 ib, *Gierburc'* 1202 Ass
  Ierburc c. 1115 LS, 1179 P, *Yerburc* 1166, 1170, 1171 ib, 1196 ChancR 1197, 1198, 1199 P, 1204 ChancR, 1209 P, *-burch'* 1178 ChancR, *-burc* 1202, 1206, 1207, 1210 P, *-burg* 1203, 1204, 1205 ib, *-burgh* 1428, 1431 FA
  Yereburc 1167, 1168, 1169 P *et freq* to 1194 ib, *-burg* 1184 ib, *-burch* 1191, 1192 ib, *-burgh* 1465 Pat
  Yeresburc 1185, 1186, 1187 P
  Jareburg 1185 RotDom
  Yerdeburga 1202 Ass, *-burg* 1265 Misc, Hy3 *AddCh,* 1287 Ipm, *-burgh* 1298 Ass, *Ierdeburg(')* 1254 ValNor, 1271-72 *Ass*

Jerdebrug' (sic) 1219 Fees, *-burg'* 1242-43 ib, *-burgh* 1338 Pat
Jorburg' 1238-43 Fees, lHy3 *NCot, -burgh*(') 1375 Works, 1378 Cl,
    1535 VE iv
Jortheburg' 1246 *NCot, -burgh* 1296 Ass, 1298, 1305 Ass
Jordeburg' 1271, 1273 *NCot,* 1281 QW, 1290 *NCot,* 1290 RSu,
    1303 *NCot, -burg*(') 1281 QW, 1291 Tax, 1305 Ass
Yordeburg' 1274 *NCot,* 1305 *LCCA, -burgh*(') 1304 *DCAcct,* 1316
    FA, 1327, 1332 *SR,* 1343 NI *et freq* to 1404 RRep
Yordburgh(') 1338 Misc, 1373 (*hundredi de*) Peace
Yardeburg 1288 Ipm, *-burgh* 1428 FA, *Yardburgh* 1517 ECB
Yarburgh 1446 Pat, 1526 Sub, 1562-67 LNQ v, 1585 SC, *-bourgh*
    1456 Pat, *-brough*(*e*) 1610 Speed, 1604 SC, 1652 *ParlSurv*

The forms are preceded or followed by some form of Latin
wapentacium etc., though some later forms refer to Yarborough
Deanery.

Anderson 50 suggests that this is derived from ON *jarð-borg* 'an
earthwork' or less likely from the cognate OE eorð-burg, with a
similar meaning. However, both Ekwall (DEPN s.n.) and
Fellows-Jensen (SSNEM 383-84) rightly take the name to be from
the OE form, though some spellings have clearly been influenced by
the ON word. The latter points out that the early spellings are
consistently in *-burc, -burg* which reflect *burh* rather than *borg.* She
also notes that there are a number of p.ns. showing a shift of stress
to the second element of an initial diphthong and claims, therefore,
that it is unnecessary "to postulate a Scand first el. to explain the
spellings in *Gere-, Ier-* and *Jer-*". The wapentake (ON vápnatak,
lOE wæpengetæc 'a sub-division of a county') is named from
Yarborough Camp in Croxton *infra* and Yarborough itself is
identical in origin with Yarburgh LSR, which has very similar
forms.

Barnetby le Wold

BARNETBY LE WOLD
    Bernodebi 1086 DB (3x)
    Bernedebi 1086 DB
    Bernetebi 1086 DB, c. 1115 LS, c. 1160, lHy2 Dane, 1188, 1190,
        1191 P (p) *et passim* to 1338 Pat with spellings in *-by,*

Bernetteby 1190 (1301) Dugd vi, 1202 Ass, 1219 Welles *et passim* to 1288 *Ass*, 1330 Ch

Bernethebi 1143-47 Dane, *Bernettheby* 1219 Welles, *Bernetheby* 1228 ib, *Bernethby* 1327 *SR*, 1343 NI

Brenetebi (sic) 1158 France

Bernetby 1180-90 RA x (p), 1210 FF, 1268 Ch, 1269 *HarlCh*, 1289 Cl, 1291 Tax *et freq* to 1431 FA

Barnebi 1185 Templar, *-by* 1428 FA, *Barnaby* 1504 Pat, 1505 Ipm, 1624 HMCRep, 1700 *Terrier*, *-be* 1519 Wills ii, 1536-7 Dugd vi, *-bee* 1548-9 ib, *-bye* 1545 LP xx, 1547 Pat, *-bie* 1557 InstBen

Barneteby 1203 Cur, *Barnetby* 1375 Peace, 1388 Cl, 1394 Pat, 1398 Cl, 1428 FA *et passim*, *-bye* 1576 Saxton, 1610 Speed, *-bie* 1576 LER

Barnetby Hall 1695 Morden

Barnetby le Wold 1824 O

The three DB forms in *Bernodebi* suggest that the name means 'Beornnōð's farm or village', *v.* by, the explanation given by Ekwall (IPN 69-70 and DEPN s.n.) and accepted by Fellows-Jensen (SSNEM 35), who does not, however, comment on the fact that this OE pers.n. has not the OE gen.sg. inflexion *-es*. Its early forms have a consistent *-e*. The most likely explanation of this *-e* is that it is a weakened form of a Scandinavian gen.sg. *-a*, earlier *-ar*, as first suggested by Ekwall (IPN 69-70) and this would presumably indicate that the name was formed by Scandinavian speakers. The numerous spellings in *Bernede-*, *Bernete-* etc. would, if the first el. is OE *Beornnōð*, presumably be explained as weakened forms due to weak stress in the second syllable of the name. However, Dr John Insley points out that there are very many such spellings, and goes on to suggest that the first el. is rather an unrecorded hypocoristic OE pers.n. in *-ede*, that is **Beornede*, parallel to the recorded *Lēofede*. He further proposes that forms in *-t(h)*, *-tt(h)* represent "contamination by OE *bærnet(t)*, ME *bernet, barnet* 'a place cleared by burning, burnt-over ground', facilitated by the fact that the pers.n. **Beornede* would inevitably have been unfamiliar in the ME period". If this is the case, then the name would mean 'Beornede's farm or village', *v.* by, and the DB forms *Bernodebi* would simply reflect confusion with the common pers.n. el. *-nōð*. The affix *le Wold*, found only very late, refers, of course, to the situation of the village on the Lincolnshire Wolds, *v.* **wald**, and note also the occurrence of the name in the f.ns. First -, Second -, Third Wold in f.ns. (a) *infra.*

GLEADOW PLANTATION, cf. *Gleedow* 1601, *Gleadhow(e)* 1626, 1634, *Glead(-)How* 1662, 1690 *et passim* to 1742 all *Terrier, Gleadhoe Lane* 1828 Bry, *Bottom -, First -, Second Gleadow* 1820 *MiscDep 204.* Although the forms are late this appears to be identical with Gledhow PN YW 4 136 and means 'kite hill', *v.* **gleoda, haugr.**

BACK LANE (lost), 1828 Bry. BARNETBY MILL, 1824 O, 1828 Bry, *ye Mill* 1671 *Terrier.* BARNETBY WOLD FM is *Abraham F^m* 1828 Bry, named from the family of John *Abram* 1762 *Terrier.* For the later name, cf. the name of the parish and *v.* First -, Second -, Third Wold in f.ns. (a) *infra.* COSKILLS, *Costels* 1690, *(the) Costales* 1697, 1700, 1742, 1762, *ye-, the Costals* 1709 *et passim* to 1748 all *Terrier, Costhills* 1768 *EnclA. Casthills* 1820 *MiscDep 240, Cottagers Coskills* 1828 Bry. It is *Barnetby Gorse Hills* 1824 O. Earlier forms are needed to suggest a certain etymology, but the name may perhaps be comparable to Costall, Costoll PN O 437, where other examples of the compound are quoted. The source would be OE **cot-stall** 'the site of a cottage', in the present case in the pl. The late spellings in *-hills* and *Gorse Hills* are obviously rationalisations. GALLOWS COVERT, *v.* Gallows Covert in Melton Ross *infra.* GLEBE FM is *Parsonage Farm* 1828 Bry. KNAB'S HILL, *nab Hill* 1671 and cf. *ye far Nab* 1601, *-high Nabb* 1638, *ye Nabb Close* 1638, *Nab-Close (Side)* 1690, 1700, *Nab Close* 1724 all *Terrier, the Nabbs Closes* 1768 *EnclA,* 'the knoll, the hill', *v.* **nabbi** and note the added *Hill.* LOW FM. LOW WOOD, 1832 *Yarb,* 1848 *TA* (Melton Ross), *Melton Low Wood* 1824 O, *-W^d* 1828 Bry, from its situation in comparison to Melton High Wood in Melton Ross *infra.* MALTHOUSE. MANOR HO, 1842 White. NEW BARNETBY. OLD HALL (lost), 1828 Bry. PROSPECT HO, perhaps a reference to the view from the site. SKEGGER BECK, 1824 O, on the boundary with Bigby and Melton Ross both *infra.* STONECLIFFE. STONECROFT HO. VICARAGE, *the Vicaradge house* 1626, *- vicaridge house* 1634, *The Vicarage house* 1638 all *Terrier.*

Field-Names

The principal forms in (a) are 1820 *MiscDep 204* (note: all the f.ns. recorded in this document are to be found on the 1820 Plan in *Aspects of the History of Barnetby-le-Wold 1766-1901*, Barnetby Branch, W.E.A., 1983, p. 11). Forms dated 1768 are *EnclA;* those dated 1577, 1601, 1626, 1634, 1638, 1662, 1664, 1668, 1671, 1690, 1700, 1709, 1724, 1733, 1748, 1762 (Bigby), 1781 (Bigby) are *Terrier;* forms marked + are modern names collected by the late Canon Henry Thackrey and supplied by Dr F. Henthorn.

(a) Ash Cl (... *Ash* ... *Close(s), the Ash or Holy Well Close* 1768, *v.* **æsc** and cf. Holywell Lane in (a) *infra*); Barn Walk; Barnetby Cl 1762, 1768, 1820 (1671, 1700, 1709, 1733, 1748, *Barnetbye Close* 1662, *Barnetby-Close* 1690); the Beck 1762, Beck's Cl, Barnetby beck 1762, 1781 (*barnabie becke* 1577, *barnaby beck* 1601, *ye becks* 1626, *the beck* 1634, *-Beck* 1700, 1733, *-Bek* 1709 and *-Beck side* 1662, *v.* **bekkr** 'a stream'); Bigby Rd 1768 ('the road to Bigby' and cf. *Bigbie headings* 1638, for which *v. ye headings* in f.ns. (b) *infra*); Burdall Cl, Burdale Closes 1768, Birdall 1820; Brick Kilns; Brigg Rd 1768 ('the road to Brigg'); Burton Leys (Common) 1768 (*Binton leas* (sic) 1601, *Burtland leas* (sic) 1626, *Burntland leas* 1638, *Burton Leas* 1662, 1671, *-Leayes* 1690, *-Leys* 1700, 1709, 1724, 1733, 1762, cf. *Burton Ings* 1748 (*v.* **eng**); all the forms are from Terriers and in spite of the variant spellings they all seem to refer to the same piece of land, but what the original form was is impossible to say; for *Leys,* etc., *v.* Leys Fm in Barrow upon Humber *infra*); First -, Second Caster Gate (*Cayster gate* 1626, *Caister gate* 1634, 'the road to Caistor', *v.* **gata**; it is recorded as *Caster Road* 1768); First -, Second -, Third Chalks adjacent to which are Melton -, Milk -, Torr's Calks (cf. *ye Caulkes* 1626, *the long calkes* 1634, *-Caulkes* 1638, *ye Long Chalkes* 1671, *The Long(-)Cawkes* 1700, 1733, *ye Long Caukes* 1709, *the Long Cawks* 1748, *the short Caulkes* 1626, *ye short calks* 1634, *-Caulkes* 1638, *-Calkes* 1664, *-Short Cawks* 1690, *the short Chalkes* 1671, *ye short caukes* 1709, *the short Caukes* 1733, *the Short Cawks* 1748, 'the chalky land', *v.* **calc**; Torr may be from an unidentified family); Church Lane 1768 (cf. *ad eccl'iam de Bernetteby* 1288 *Ass* (p), *atte Chirch* 1294 *ib* (p)); the Church Yard Cl 1768; First -, Second -, Far Clay Pits (*Clay-pitts* 1664, 1668); the Commons 1762; Cottagers Pasture 1768 (pasture let to the *cottagers*); Croft; the Cross of the Wold 1762 (*the crosse of ye wold* 1664, *ye Crosse of ye Wold* 1668, 1671, *ye Cross of ye Would* 1690, *the Cross of the Wowld* 1700, *-would* 1733, *v.* **cros, wald** amd cf. the affix to the parish name); Dials, + Dyles Cl (*v.* **dial** 'a sun-dial carved in the turf'); + Dike Cl (*v.* **dic, dīk**); Drift Road called Limber Road 1768, *v.* dial. **drift** 'a lane or road along which horse or

cattle are driven', cf. *the cowe drift* 1638); the East Lands 1768 (*v.* ēast, land);
Fir Cl (*the fur close* 1601, *y^e -*, *the furr Close* 1626, 1634, *ye Furre Close* 1638,
Furr Close 1662, 1724, *ye Fur close side* 1664, *the Furre Close* 1671, *ye Fure Close*
1690, *the Fir-Close* 1700, *ye Fir close* 1709, *the Firr Close* 1748, cf. *Furre Leas*
1671 (*v.* lǣs) (a fairly common f.n. in LNR, probably from OE feor, ME *furre*,
cf. dial. *fur* 'far, distant', and so easily confused with *fir*); Fourteen Acre; Far -,
First -, Second Fox Cover; Gareings, + Three Cornered Garings (this is
presumably an unrecorded derivative of ON geiri 'a gore, a triangular plot of
ground', corresponding to ME *gōring* (*v.* MED s.v.), itself from ME *gōre* (OE
gāra), both having the sense 'a triangular strip of ground'); the Gate Marfar
1762 (*Gate marfer* 1601, *gate mar-furre* 1662, *gate Marfur* 1664, *ye Gate Marfar*
1690, *the Gate Marfare 1700, 1733, 1748,* cf. *the gate close* 1634, from gata 'a
road' and marfur 'a furrow marking a boundary' (*v.* EDD s.v. *mear*, 5), itself
representing OE *mǣrfurh, from (ge)mǣre 'a boundary' and furh 'a furrow';
marfar is used as an appellative in 1762 and frequently appears as a noun in
north L documents); Goose Hole (*ye Gooshooles* 1638, *Goose holes* 1662, *ye
Goose-Holes* 1690, (*the*) *Goose Holes* 1700, 1709, 1724, 1748 ('the hollows
frequented by geese', *v.* gōs, hol[1]; it is *the Gorse Holes* 1768); The Gorse or
Furze Cl, the Furze Cl, The Gorse Cl (cf. *furz close* 1733, *v.* gorst, fyrs,
clos(e)); Gosgerdale Hill, + Gosgodale Fd (cf. *goss-gar-dale* 1662); the Headland
1762 (*ye headland* 1626, *the Headland* 1634, *Head Land* 1664, *Headland* 1671, *ye
Headeland* 1709, *the Head Land* 1748, cf. *two lands ... the headland & his fellow*
1601, - *and the fellows* 1634, *Two lands ... a headland & ye fellowe, headland
fellow* (sic) both 1638 (*v.* hēafod-land; *fellow* is perhaps in the sense 'a
counterpart, a match', *v.* NED s.v. 4b); the Hemp Pleck or Croft 1768 ('a small
plot used for growing hemp', *v.* hænep, plek, croft, and cf. *the Hempe-pitt* in
f.ns. (b) *infra*); the Hill Side 1762, the Hill Cl 1768, Hills, Hillside (*the hill*
(*side*) 1601. 1626. 1634, *aboue ye hill* 1626, *the hill side* 1638, *ye Hill side* 1690,
1790, 1724, *the Hill-side* 1700); + Hilly Nabs (*v.* nabbi); the Holmes 1762, 1768
(-*holmes* 1626, 1634, -*homes* 1638, *ye Holmes* 1662, 1690, 1709, *v.* holmr 'a
water-meadow, higher ground amidst marshes', the next field to the south is in
fact called Marshes *infra*); Hollywell Lane, - Closes 1768, Holy Well 1820, +
Holy Well; Ings Common 1768, Ings Corner (cf. *the Inges* 1601, 1662, -*Ings* 1626,
1634, 1700, 1733, *y^e -*, *ye Ings* 1638, 1671, 1690, 1709, 1724, *the Inggs* 1748, *v.* eng
('meadow, pasture', as elsewhere in this parish); Kermington Rd 1768 ('the road
to Kirmington', and cf. *Kirmington heads* 1638, *v.* hēafod in pl.); Kettleby Rd
('the road to Kettleby (in Bigby parish)'); Lane; Leas Mdw (*v.* lēah; *leas* is
common as an appellative in north L); Lime Pit Wold; (the) Lings 1768 (*y^e
Linges* 1601, *the linges* 1626, - *lings* 1634, *ye lings* 1638, *y^e -*, *ye Lings* 1671, 1690,
1709, 1724, *the Lings* 1700, 1733, 1748, cf. *ling(e)furlanges* c. 1160 (Ed1) *Newh*,

the Ling ends 1664, 'the place(s) where ling, heather grows', *v.* **lyng**); Low Cl; low Fd 1768, Low Fd (*the lowe feilde* 1634, - *Low field* 1662, (*ye* -) 1664, 1671, *ye low field by ye towne side* 1638 (self-explanatory); Marshes; Mealing Hill, + Mealands Hill; Melton Btm (-*bottome* 1626, 1634, -*bothom* 1638, *v.* **botm**; the field is on the Melton Ross boundary); Mill Cl; the North Fd 1768 (*in aquilon' campo* c. 1160 (Ed1) *Newh, the north fielde* 1626, *North Feild* 1634, *the Northfield* 1662, - *north field* 1638, - *North Field* 1664, 1671, 1700, 1748, *ye North-field* 1690, - *North field* 1709, *v.* **norð, feld**, one of the open fields of the village); the Oat Close(s) 1768, Oats Cl (cf. *Oate close* (*nooke*) 1638, *the lower oat Close* 1671); Orchard (*the* - 1634, 1638); Out Leys 1768 ('outlying pasture', *v.* **ūt, lǣs**); Little Saint Foin (*v.* **sainfoin**, probably referring to the leguminous plant *Onobrychis viciifolia*, and for variant spellings *v.* Field 190); the Shaw Ings 1768, Shaws (*v.* **sceaga** 'a copse, a small wood', eng); First -, Second Sixty Acre; Sleightings 1768, Great Sleightings ('level meadows', *v.* **sléttr**, eng); Small Cl 1768; Smallend Cl 1768; South Cl; (the) South Fd 1762, 1768 (*in australi campo* c. 1160 (Ed1) *Newh, the south fielde* 1626, *South Feild* 1634, (*y^e*) *south field* 1638, 1662, *the South Field* 1664, 1724, 1748, - *South*(-)*field* 1700, 1733, self-explanatory, *v.* **sūð, feld**, one of the open fields of the village); Stone Hill 1762, - Hills (*Stonehill* 1626, 1634, 1638, *Stone hill* 1662, - *Hill* 1664, 1697, 1700, 1709, *the* - 1733, 1748, *Stoney Hill* 1690, self-explanatory, *v.* **stān, hyll**; the 1690 form refers to the same place); the Stone Pits 1768 (*ye stone pittes* 1638, *v.* **stān, pytt**); Teatherings 1768, Tetherings (*ye tetherings* 1638, 'pasture for tethered animals, *v.* **tethering**); Thirty Acres; Thornhills; (the) Thorns 1762, 1768 (*ye Thorns* 1690, *the Thornes* 1700, - *thorns* 1733, - *Thorns* 1748 (presumably named from prominent thorn-bushes, *v.* **þorn**); the Town's End 1762, Town End Cl (*the townes end* 1634, *ye Towne end* 1664, *ye Towns-end* 1690, *the Towns end* 1700, *ye Town's end* 1709, *Townes end* 1724, *the Townsend* 1733, cf. *ye towne side* 1638, *ye towns-side* 1690, - *Towns Side* 1700, - *Town's Side* 1709 and *ye townes end Becke* 1671 (*v.* **bekkr**), *v.* **tūn, ende**¹ and **sīde**); Townend and Smallend Closes 1786 (cf. Smallend Cl *supra*); North -, South Townend Lane 1768; Twenty Acres; Wellams (probably from **wella** 'a spring' and **holmr**); Bottom -, Top West Fd (one of the great fields of Barnetby); Willow Holt (*v.* **holt**); the Wind Mill 1768; Woulds Cl 1768, First -, Second -, Third Wold (cf. *ye wold Bottom* 1671, *the Wowlds* 1700, *v.* **wald, botm** and the affix to the parish name); Woodside.

(b) *ye acredikes* 1638 (cf. *Akerdik* PN Nt 279; this is a fairly common minor name in L, derived from **æcer** 'a plot of arable or cultivated land', later 'a measure of land (an acre)' and **dīc** or **dīk**; the exact sense is uncertain but it may be noted that Kristensson, SMETT 47, translates the name 'ditch in or by the field'); *in campis de Bernetebi* c. 1160 Dane, - *bernetby* c. 1160 (Ed1) *Newh* (*v.* **feld**); *Blackmandale* 1601, *Blackman dale bottome* 1626, *Blacmandale bottom* 1634, *Blackmandale bottome* 1638, *Blackmelldale Bottom* (sic) 1662, *Blackmay-dale Bothom* (sic) 1690 (probably from the ME surn. *Blakeman, Blacman* (OE *Blæcmann*) and **dæl, dalr** 'a valley', since Bottom has been added, though the second el. could be **deill** 'a share of land'); *ye Bull piece* 1690 (self-explanatory); *the corne field* 1671; *ye flour pits* 1690; "the grange of" *Barnabye* 1545 LP xx, *y*^{e} *Grange meadowe, the Grange land* 1638 (*v.* **grange**, a grange of Newstead Priory as indicated in 1545 LP xx); *the Hall Land* 1671 (*Barnetby Hall* is named on Morden's map of 1695); *haluedailes* c. 1160 (Ed1) *Newh* ('the half shares of land', *v.* **half deill**); *y*^{e} *headings* 1638 (cf. *Bigbie headings* under Bigby Rd in (a) *supra*; note its appellative use in *3 headinges* 1601 and elsewhere in north L; this may be the pl. of ME *heved* (OE **hēafod**) with the noun suffix -**ing**[1], perhaps with much the same sense as OE **hēafod-land**, ME *hevedland*, so denoting places at the end of a ploughed field where the plough is turned, *v.* also MED s.v. *hed* 8b. This sense does not seem to be recorded in Dictionaries, though NED s.v. *heading* 10 notes the use of *headings* in *The Hevedinges of Spalding*, quoting 1662 Imb, and suggests a meaning '? a bank or dam'. This can hardly be the sense in the f.ns. here. It would seem likely, lacking additional evidence at present, that *headings* could well have the meaning suggested above); *the Hempe-pitt* 1671, *ye Hemp pits* 1690, cf. *ye vicaridge Hempe-pitt* 1668 (*v.* **hænep, pytt**, and cf. the Hemp Pleck in (a) *supra*); *y*^{e} *land end* 1638 (*v.* **land** 'a strip of land in the common field', **ende**[1]); *lamare* 1332 SR (p) (*v.* **(ge)mǣre**); *Melton Oat close, - Shopp* 1668 (from the neighbouring parish of Melton Ross; *Shopp* is, no doubt, ultimately OE **sceoppa** in the sense 'a shed'); *the Sandes* 1601, *y*^{e} *sandes* 1638, *ye Sand*(-)*Lands* 1690, 1733; *Scarbrough Gate* 1638, *Scarbrow Gate* 1690 (probably from the surn. *Scarborough* and **gata**); *the common sewer* 1638; *y*^{e} *stintings* 1738 (*v.* **stinting** 'a portion of common land set apart for one man's use', as in ModE dial, and common in north L as an appellative, sometimes in the pl. with a number as first el.); *Stubble heads* 1638; *the Turmers* 1601 (the reading is doubtful); *T.yahoudale* c. 1160 (Ed1) *Newh* (*v.* **haugr, deill**, the first letter is doubtful and the second is illegible); *Wate deile* c. 1160 Dane, *Wattedaile c. 1160 (Ed1) Newh* (perhaps 'the wet share of land', *v.* **vátr, deill**; if so, the form from *Newh* shows confusion with *Wat*(*t*), a pet form of *Walter*, as Dr John Insley points out); *Watlandes* c. 1160 (Ed1) *Newh, Wettlands* 1626, 1634, 1638 (if these later forms represent the same name as *Watlandes*, the latter is presumably 'the wet strips of land' from **vátr**, replaced by *wet* (OE **wēt**); *wray bottom* 1668 (*v.* **vrá** 'a nook, a corner', **botm**).

Barrow upon Humber

BARROW UPON HUMBER

in loco qui dicitur Adbaruae (variant *Adbearuae*) 731 Bede
Bearuwe 737-40 (11) BCS 165 (S 99), *æt Bearuwe* 971 (12)
    PetLN, bearuwe in lindisige 973 (13) ECEE (S 792), *Bearuwe*
    973 (15) BCS 1297 (S 792)
in þære stowe þe is nemned Æt Bearwe c. 890 (10) OEBede
to Baruwe 971 (12) *PetLN* (S 782), *Baruue* 972 (12) *ib* (S 787),
    Beruwe in Lindesige 973 (14) ECEE (S 792), 793 (15) BCS
    1297 (S 792)
Barwe 972 (s.a. 963) (1121) ASC E, 972 (12) BCS 1281 (S 787),
    972 (16) BCS 1258 (S 787), *Barwa* c. 1115 LS, c. 1160 Dane
    (p), 1163 RA i, 1190 (1301) Dugd vi, 1268 RRGr
Barewe 1086 DB, 1183, 1184, 1185, 1186 P, 1190 (1301) Dugd vi,
    1190, 1191, 1192 P *et passim* to 1368 Pat, - *upon Humbre*
    1371 ib, - "*by Barton upon Humber*" 1324 ib, - *in Lyndeseye*
    1368 ib, *Bareuua* 1096-1100 France, *Bareue* 1198 FF, *Barew'*
    1202 Ass (p), 1203 ib, p1220 WellesLA
Barua c. 1115 LS, 1143-47, c. 1160 Dane, Hy3 (1301) Ch, 1312
    (e14) Brid, *Barva* c. 1150 (Ed1) *Newh, Barue* 1195 P, 1200
    Cur (p), 1203 ib, 1252 Ch, 1265 Misc, 1268 Ch, 1268 FF,
    1312 Pat, 1346 FA
Baruua 1196-1100 France, *Barruve* 1096-1100 ib, *Baruue* 12 HC
Barowa 1115 YCh iii, *Barow* 1160-62 (1287) ib, 1287 *Ass*, 1287
    Ipm, 1332 *SR*, 1428 FA, *Barowe* 1303 ib, "- *upon Humbre*"
    1317 Pat, "- *by Barton*" 1318 ib, 1320 Cl, 1320 Ipm *et freq*
    to 1576 LER, - *juxta Barton* 1325 Inqaqd, - *iuxta Barton'*
    1357 Cor, - *iuxta Barton sup' Humbre* 1418 *FF*, - *besyd*
    Barton up on Humber BRA 866
Barou 1150-70 YCh iii
Barawra (sic) c. 1155 Dane
Barew 1160 Dudg vi, 1191, 1192 P
Barwe c.1160 Dane, 1206 FF, 1206 Ass, 1220 Cur *et passim* to
    1388 Misc
Baaruhe 112 Dane
Baruwe 1212 Fees, 1291 Tax
Baru 1238-43 Fees, 1276 RH, *Barw* 1288 Ipm
Barrowe 1342 *AD*, 1541 *AOMB 213*, 1548 Pat *et passim* to 1584
    AD, Barrow 1535 VE iv, 1552 Pat *et passim*

Barugh' 1412 RRep, *Barogh* 1446 Fine
Baroo 1428 FA

The forms in Bede and in the translation of Bede (OEBede)
show that the name means 'at the grove', *v.* **æt, b(e)aru**, dat.sg.
b(e)arwe, all subsequent forms retaining the *-w-* of the dat.sg. case.
It is variously described as *in Lindsey, by Barton upon Humber* and
upon Humber.

NEW HOLLAND, 1828 Bry, *the modern hamlet of the New
Holland, where a large Inn was built on the Humber bank about ten
years ago* 1842 White. A note in LNQ ii, no. 96, quotes from the
Hull Advertiser, Dec. 8th, 1848, which it is claimed throws light on
the origin of the name "On the 4th instant, at Caister [died], Mr.
Thomas Lumley ..... from whom New Holland first received its
name, he having landed there a cargo of smuggled goods .....".

TARRYGARTH QUARTER (lost), - *quarter* 1609, 117, *tarrigarth
quarter* 1683 all *BPD, Tarrygarth Quarter* 1649 *ParlSurv,* 1779 *BPD,*
1785 *Map,* - *garthes quarter* 1651 *BPD, Tarry Garth Quarter Field*
1729 *ib,* cf. (*common Field called*) *Tarrygarth field* 1649 *ParlSurv,*
1822, 1876 *Terrier, Tarry Garth Field* 1734 *LRMB 256,* 1796 *BPD
Tarry Dale* 1715 BarrowTB, 1734 *LRMB 256* (*v.* **deill**), *Tarrygate*
1649 *ParlSurv* (*v.* **gata**) and also *iuxta curiam Tyrri* Hy3 *HarlCh.*
'*Tyrri's enclosure'*, *v.* **garðr**, the pers.n. being OFr *T(h)ier(r)i,* the
man from whom the name is derived being presumably the one
named in the Hy3 charter. *Quarter* is used here in the sense 'a
quarter, a division of, or locality in, a larger area', three other
quarters having been noted in the parish, i.e. Beck Lane *infra,*
Stonepit and Watermill, recorded in f.ns. (a) *infra.*

WELHAM (local), (*to, fram*) *willum* 971 (12) *PetLN, ad Wellum*
Hy3 *HarlCh, Wellam dale* 1649 *ParlSurv, Wellam marfar* 117 *BPD* (*v.*
marfur 'a boundary furrow'), *Welham Dale* 1734 *LRMB 256,
Wellham Close, -Hole* 1817 *Map,* 'at the springs', from the dat.pl.
wellum of **wella, well(e)**. The name occurs in the bounds of the
Barrow AS charter and the site is approximately TA 067190, as Mr
Paul Everson informs me. He has also reported that there were
three springs here, Top Wellum, Middle Wellum and Wellum, and
that the last was still running within recent memory.

WORTH (lost), (*to, fram*) *wyrðe* 971 (12) *PetLN, pratum vocatur* ....
Wirth 1190 (1301) Dugd vi, and derived from it, *Worthynges* 1549
Yarb, Worthings m16 *Cragg, Worthinges* 1552 Pat, *Worthyng* Eliz
ChancP, *Worth ings* 1648 *MiscDon 251*, - *Ings* 1713 BarrowTB, 1785
Map, 1803 *EnclA*, 1822 *Terrier* (*v.* **eng** 'a meadow, pasture') and
Worthecott 1552 Pat, *Worthecotegarth* 1549 *Yarb, worth cotis garthe*
m16 *Cragg, Worthcotegarth* 1550 Pat (*v.* **cot** 'a cottage, a shed', with
garðr 'an enclosure'). This name is also found in the Barrow AS
charter and means 'the enclosure', *v.* **worð, wyrð**. It is map
reference TA 097242, as Mr Paul Everson informs me.

BARNBY HO, presumably named from the *Barnby* family, cf.
Thomas *Barnby* 1775 *BT.* BARROW FERRY, 1830 Gre, *the Ferry*
1803 *EnclA*, cf. *Ferry Road* 1803 *ib*, 1822 *Terrier, Ferry Road or
New Barrow* 1828 Bry. BARROW GRANGE, for **grange**, cf.
Croxton Grange in Croxton *infra.* BARROW HALL, 1824 O, 1828
Bry. BARROW HANN, HANN FM, (*the*) *Hann* 117 *BPD*, 1822,
1827 *Terrier.* BARROW HANN COVER (lost), 1824 O, 1830 Gre,
- *Ann Cover* 1828 Bry. EAST HANN FM, 1649 *ParlSurv*, 1715
BarrowTB, (*the*) - 1796 *BPD*, 1803 *EnclA*, 1827 *Terrier, East Hanne*
1683 *BPD, east Hanne* 117 *ib, East hand* 1692 *ib, East Han* 1785
Map. WEST HANN FM, *West Hann* 1649 *ParlSurv, West-hann*
1624 *BPD, West Han* 1683 *ib*, 1785 *Map, West hand* 1692 *BPD, West
Hann* 1803 *EnclA*, 1855 *MiscDon 82.* HANN LANE, cf. *Little Hann
gate* 1649 *ParlSurv, Han Gate* 1785 *Map.* Although there is almost
a complete consistency of spelling, the forms are too late to suggest
an etymology. BARROW HAVEN, *portum de Barewe* 1190 (1301)
Dugd vi, *Barowehaven* 1371 Cl, *Barrowe Haven* Philip & Mary Lanc,
the old Haven 1695 *Foster*, (*the*) *haven* 1709, 1715 BarrowTB, *Haven*
1785 *Map*, 1803 *EnclA*, and cf. *the old -, the new haven chaps* 1715
BarrowTB, *v.* **hæfen**; *chaps* is the mouth of an estuary or harbour.
BARROW HAWK, *hawk thinge* m16 *Cragg, Common ground called
Hawke* 1649 *ParlSurv, Hawk* 1715 BarrowTB, 1785 *Map*, probably
from ME **halke** 'a corner, a nook', with a similar development as in
Hawk Mill PN C 139, Hawkwood PN Ess 20. BARROW MERE,
Barrowe Meare 1621 *MiscDon 251*, - *meere* 1649 *ParlSurv, the Meare*
1662 *Terrier, Barrow meere*, - *meare* 1666 *BPD*, - *Meare* 1674 *ib*, -
meare 1676 BartTB, - *Meere* 1685, 1694 *ib*, - *Meir* 1720 *ib*, - *Mear*
1761 *ib*, 'Barrow boundary', *v.* **(ge)mære**, on the parish boundary
with Barton upon Humber. BARROW MILLS (lost), *New Barrow*

Mills 1828 Bry. BARROW VALE, cf. *the valley* 1803 *EnclA*.
BARTON LANE, *Barton gate* 1649 *ParlSurv*, *(the) Barton Road*
1803 *EnclA*, 1822 *Terrier*, 1843 *MiscDon 82*, v. **gata**, leading to
Barton upon Humber. THE BECK, *Barrow beck* 1715 BarrowTB,
the Beck 1803 *EnclA*, cf. *the Beck drain* 1827 *Terrier* and *Crofti voc'*
Beckarthe 1589-91, 1605-7 *MinAcct* (probably for *Beckgarthe*), v.
garðr, 'the stream', v. **bekkr**. BECK LANE, *Beck' lane* 1649
ParlSurv, *(the) Beck Lane* 1729 *BPD*, 1803 *EnclA*, cf. *becklane*
quarter 1609 *BPD*, *Becklane quarter* 1649 *ParlSurv*, *Becklaine Quarter*
1683 *BPD*, *Becklane quarter* 1692 *ib*, *the beck lane quarter* 117 *ib*
(for *Quarter*, v. *Tarrygarth Quarter supra*), and *the Becklane Field*
1715 BarrowTB, *Beck Lane Field* 1734 *LRMB 256*, 1796 *BPD*, 1822
Terrier, 1843 *MiscDon 82*, v. prec. BUTFORTH DRAIN, - LANE,
(*ad pontem de*) *Budeford* Hy3 *HarlCh*, *Budfurth* 1624 *BPD*, *Budford*
(*gate*) 1649 *ParlSurv*, 1683 *BPD*, *butforth* 1692 *ib*, *(the) Budforth*
1715 BarrowTB, 1729 *BPD*, 1785 *Map*, *Budforth Drain* 1803 *EnclA*,
1855 *MiscDon 82*, *Budforth Road* 1803 *EnclA*, perhaps 'Budda's
ford', v. **ford**, with the same OE pers.n. *Budda* as occurs in
Budbrooke PN Wa 204-5. CARFAX HO. THE CASTLES, *juxta*
castellum de Barwew 1190 (1301) Dugd vi, *(the) Castles* 1715
BarrowTB, 1785 *Map*, 1803 *EnclA*, 1822 *Terrier*, *(the) Castle Hills*
1715 BarrowTB, 1828 Bry, v. **castel(l)**; for a late 19th century
description, v. AASR xix, 358-60. This is a Motte and Bailey
Castle, described by P&H 180 as having "a large, low motte and
two very large baileys" and covering a large area. CHERRY
LANE, 1803 *EnclA*, 1822 *Terrier*, - *lane* 1649 *ParlSurv*,
self-explanatory; cf. *Chery garth* 1605-7 *MinAcct*, *Cherrygarth(e)* 1607
Rental, *The Cherrigarth* 1633 *AOMB 390*, *Cherry garth* 1649 *ParlSurv*,
v. **chiri**, **garðr** 'an enclosure'. COLLEGE RD, *(the)* - 1803 *EnclA*,
1822 *Terrier*, 1843 *MiscDon 82*, leading to Thornton College in
Thornton Curtis parish *infra*. DOWN HALL, *le Down hall* m16
Cragg, *Downehall'* 1568-70 *MinAcct*, "a manor in Barowe called
Downhall" 1569 Pat, *manerj de le downhall* 1580 *Terrier*, *Maner'*
vocat' ... *Dounhall'* 1589-91 *MinAcct*, *Downehall* 1601 *Terrier*, *down*
hall 1649 *ParlSurv*, *the Mannor of Downe Hall* 1662 *Terrier*, *a farme*
called downe hall 1668 *ib*, *Down Hall* 1709 BarrowTB *et passim*,
and note *the Common Right House called Downhall* 1803 *EnclA*. It
is no doubt 'down' from its situation in the village, v. **dūne**. ELM
TREE HO. GOXHILL RD, 1785 *Map*, 1803 *EnclA*, cf.
Gouxhillgate 1649 *ParlSurv*, *Goxhill gate* 117 *BPD*, - *Gate* 1729 *ib*,

'the road to (the neighbouring parish of) Goxhill', *v.* **gata.**
GROVE HO. HIGH ST, *the Highstreete* 1649 *ParlSurv,*
self-explanatory. INGS HO, cf. *le Inges de Barrowe* 1589-91, 1605-7
MinAcct, 1607 *Rental, ye Inges* 1671 *Terrier, the Ings* 1709
BarrowTB, 1803 *EnclA,* 1822 *Terrier, the late Ings of Barrow* 1843
MiscDon 82 and *the great Inges* 1601 *Terrier,* 1609 *BPD, (of Barrow)*
1611 *Terrier, the Great-Ings* 1624 *BPD, Great Inges* 1649 *ParlSurv,*
the great Ings 1651 *BPD,* 1662 *Terrier,* 1671 *BPD, the Great Ings*
1790, 1804 *MiscDon 82,* 'the meadows, pastures' *v.* **eng.**
KEYHOLME. THE LAWNS, *Close* .... *called the Lawnes* 1649
ParlSurv, the Homestead .... *called the Lawns* 1803 *EnclA,*
presumably from the pl. of ME **launde** 'a glade, a woodland
pasture'. LEYS FM, *Leys* 1785 *Map,* - *Fm* 1824 O and it is
Barrow Ann F^m 1828 Bry, presumably from the plural of **lēah** in
the later sense of 'an open pasture'. *Leys* is common in many
parts of L as an appellative. LORD'S LANE, *the Lordes Lane*
1649 *ParlSurv,* self-explanatory. MANBY HO, named from the
Manby family, cf. David *Manby* 1804 *BT.* MARSH FM, cf.
marescis de barue c. 1150 (Ed1) *Newh, Barrow marsh* 1576 *BPD,*
the Marshes of Barrowe 1649 *ParlSurv, Barrow Great Marsh* 1729
BPD, Barrow Marshes 1824 O, 1830 Gre, *v.* **mersc.** MARSH
LANE, *Marsh Road* 1828 Bry. MIDBY (local), *The sewer or drain*
called Midby 1715 BarrowTB, *the ancient watercourse called* - 1803
EnclA, a Drain or Sewer called the Midby 1822 *Terrier,* the forms
are late, but this may be a partial anglicisation of Scand. *miðr ı bȳ*
literally 'middle in the village' and comparable to *Northiby* and
Suthiby from *norðr ı bȳ* and *suðr ı bȳ*, respectively 'north in the
village' and 'south in the village', recorded elsewhere in L. MOUNT
PLEASANT. NEW BARNS (lost), 1828 Bry. OXLEY (lost), 1830
Gre. OXFORD GRANGE is *Marsh Road Ho* 1828 Bry; for
Oxford, perhaps cf. Scholar Dale in f.ns. (a) *infra.* OXMARSH FM,
Ox Marsh Fm 1824 O, cf. *Oxmarsh dike* 1649 *ParlSurv, Barrow Ox*
Marsh dicke 1685 *LindDep 67, Oxmarsh Banks* 1709 BarrowTB, *Ox*
Marsh 1785 *Map, (the) Oxmarsh* 1803 *EnclA,* 1804 *MiscDon 42,*
1822, 1826 *Terrier,* self-explanatory, *v.* **oxa, mersc.** OXMARSH
LANE, *(the) Oxmarsh Road,* 1803 *EnclA,* 1822 *Terrier.* PALMER
LANE, named from the *Palmer* family, cf. William *Palmer* 1803
EnclA. PARK FM, cf. *Park* 1817 *Map.* PEPLO LANE, cf.
Peplow(e) 1649 *ParlSurv, Pepolley* (sic) 1715 BarrowTB, *Pople Hall*
(sic) 1734 *LRMB 256, Pepley* 1785 *Map, the Peplow* 1803 *EnclA;* the

forms are too late to suggest an etymology, though the second el. would appear to be hlǣw 'a mound, a hill, a tumulus'. PROVIDENCE COTTAGE & PLACE. ROWLAND HILL, *Rowlandhill F^m* 1828 Bry. ROYAL OAK, 1842 White, cf. *Royal Oak Lane* 1803 *EnclA*. ST CHAD, *Cottage .... called St Chadds* 1649 *ParlSurv, a certain Street .... called Saint Chad* 1798 *BPD, St Chad's* 1803 *EnclA, a place called Saint Chad* 1848 *MiscDon 82*, no doubt named from the 'lost' church of St Chad's, on which *v. St Chad's, Barrow-on-Humber. report of excavations 1976-8*, ed. J.B. Whitwell, Humberside Heritage Publication no. 17, forthcoming. SAND PIT FM. SANER'S COTTAGES. SIX BELLS, 1842 White. SMITHY LANE, cf. *Smithy Green* 1624 *BPD*. STRAWBERRY COTTAGE. SUMMERCROFT FM, cf. *Somercroft(e)* 1549 Pat, 1549 *Yarb*, 1584 *AD, - crofts* 1631 (1649) *ParlSurv, Sommercrofts* 1633 *AOMB 390, Somercroftes* 1645-7 *Rental,* 1649 *ParlSurv, Summercrofts* 1713 BarrowTB, *the Somercrofts* 1734 *LRMB 256, Summercrofts* 1785 *Map,* 1803 *EnclA,* 1822 *Terrier,* 'the croft(s) used in summertime', *v.* sumor, croft. THORNEY'S FIELD. THORNTON RD, 1803 *EnclA,* 'the road leading to Thornton Curtis'. WATERCRESS BEDS (several). WESTCOTT FM, *le Manor Place alias Westecorte* 1541-3 LDRH, *West Courts* 1542 LP xvii, "*manor of" Westcote* 1549 Pat, *le Westcote* m16 *Cragg, Maner' vocat Westcote* 1589-91 *MinAcct, Mannor of Westcote* 1633 *AOMB 390, Messuage .... called Westcote house* 1649 *ParlSurv, (the) Westcote* 1709, 1713 BarrowTB, *the West Cote Homestead* 1803 *EnclA*. The first two spellings suggest that the second el. is court 'a large house, a manor-house', while all the rest are from cot 'a cottage, etc.'. It is impossible to be certain, therefore, whether the original meaning is 'the west manor house' or 'the west cottage', *v.* west, court, cot, especially when the different forms are almost contemporary. WEST MARSH, *the West Marshe* 1633 *AOMB 390, West Marsh* 1785 *Map, the late West Marsh* 1843 *MiscDon 82, the West Marsh* 1848 *ib,* cf. *Westmarsh-heades* 1624 *BPD, the Westmarsh heades* 1649 *ParlSurv* (*v.* hēafod in the sense 'headlands, strips of land left unploughed for the plough to turn on'), *Westmarsh Close alias the dovecote-close* 1649 *ParlSurv, West Marsh Close* 1695 *Foster, Westmarsh Close* 1803 *EnclA,* self-explanatory, *v.* west, mersc. WESTOBY LANE, named from the family of Thomas *Westoby* 1803 *EnclA*. WINDMILL, cf. *Barrow West Milne, Winde Mill Hill* 1629 *BPD, a Wynd mill, the Wyndmill gate* (*v.* gata) 1649 *ParlSurv, the wind Mill* 1692 *BPD, ye Wind Mill* 1762 *Terrier, Mill* 1824 O.

Field-Names

The principal (undated) forms in (a) are 1803 *EnclA*; those dated 1541 and 1633 are *AOMB 213-14* and *390*, 1549[1], 1550, 1552 Pat, 1549[2] *Yarb*, m16 *Cragg*, 1580, 1601, 1662, 1671, 1712, 1718, 1724, 1745, 1762, 1797, 1822, 1826[2], 1827, 1876 *Terrier*, 1589-91, 1605-7 *MinAcct*, 1604[2], 1609, 1624, 1631, 1649[2], 1651, 1671, 1676, 1677, 1679, 1683, 1685, 1686, 1692, 117, 1719, 1729, 1779, 1796 *BPD*, 1607 *Rental*, 1649[1] *ParlSurv*, 1709, 1713, 1715 BarrowTB, 1734 *LRMB 256*, 1785, 1817 *Map*. 1790 forms and dated 19th cent. spellings not otherwise ascribed are *MiscDon 82.*

(a) Abbey Gate 1785 (*the Abbye gate* 1659[1], presumably 'the road to (Thornton) Abbey', *v.* **gata**); Barrow Lane, - Rd; Bartle Lane (Rd) 1803, 1822 (from the *Bartle* family, cf. John *Bartle* 1709); Beck Carr ((*the*) *Beck carr(e)* 1649[1], 1715, 1785, *v.* **kjarr** and The Beck *supra*); the Black Mold, Blackmould Gate 1803, Barrow Black Moulds 1833 *Yarb* (*two sheepewalkes within the feilds of Barrow cawled blackemoldes* ... 1574 *Nelthorpe, Blackmo(u)ld* 1649[1], *Blackmold field* 1676, *v.* **blæc molde** 'earth, soil' and *middel hille* in the bounds of the AS charter *infra*; it is as the extreme southern point of the parish boundary); (the) Bogs 1803, 1879, the Boggs 1817, 1827; Bowman Garth (cf. *Beamond thinge* m16, from the *Beaumond* family, cf. Hugh *de Beaumond* 1332 *SR, uxor Beamond* m16, with **garðr** 'an enclosure' and **þing** in the later sense 'possession, property', as elsewhere in the f.ns. of this parish); Bowmers Garth (1649[1], from a surn. and **garðr**, cf. Edmund *Bawmer* 1592 *Inv*); Bracken Dear Pit 1817 (cf. *Brackandale Marfurr* 1624 (*v.* **marfur** 'a boundary furrow, a furrow marking a boundary', as elsewhere in the f.ns. of this parish), *Brakendale* 1649[1], *Brackon Dale* 1704, *v.* **brakni, deill** rather than **dæl, dalr**); The Brick Cl, Brick Close Drain (cf. *ye brick Mill* 1762); (the) Brigg Rd 1803, 1822, 1826 ('the road to Brigg'); Bully Croft (*Bul(l)iercrofts* 1589-91, 1605-7, *Bullercroft* 1633, - als. *Bullygarth, Bullygarth pitt* 1649[1], *one cottage called Bullen* 1654 WillsPCC, probably from the surn. *Bull(i)er* with **croft** and **garðr**); Burnham Gate 1785, 1796 (*Burnhame gate* 1609, *Burn(e)ham Gate* 1649[1], 1734, 'the road to Burnham (in Thornton Curtis)', *v.* **gata**); Castles Drain (named from The Castles *supra*); Castor Rd (leading to Caistor); Chapel Cl 1844 (cf. *le Chaplehouse* 1605-7, *le Chappell howse* 1607, - *House* 1589-91, *v.* **chapel(e)**); Cow Cl 1817; the Headland by the Crossing of the Gates 1796 (*the Crossinge of the gate* 1624, *the crossing of the gate* 1692, 'the road junction', *v.* **crossing, gata**, and **hēafod-land**); the Deep Carr, Deep Carr Drain (*Deep Carr* 1715, *v.* **dēop, kjarr**); the Delph (within the -, next to Humber Bank) ('the pit, the quarry', *v.* **(ge)delf**); Dogdale Head 1785 (*dockdale* 1649[1], *v.* **docce, deill**); the East Hall 1796, 1822; the East Wold (1734, - *Wolde* 1633, *East*

Would 1649[1], 1729, *the Easte* - 1683, *v.* **wald**, cf. the West Wold *infra*); the Farr
Heads 1785 (for *Heads*, cf. West Marsh *supra*); Fleet 1796 (*the* - 1729, *the Fleete*
1649[1], *v.* **flēot** in the sense 'a stream'); the Foundry; Frith Heads 1785 (*le Frith*
1299 Ipm, *the Furth heade(s)* 1649[1], 1683, *the Furth* 1683, 1715, *Furth bridge* 1715,
v. **fyrhð** 'a wood, woodland'); Garth 1817 (*v.* **garðr** 'an enclosure'); (the) Grass
Garth (*the gersegarth* 1633, *Grassegarth* (*close*) 1649[1], self-explanatory, *v.* **gærs**,
garðr, cf. prec.); the Gravel Pit (in The Hawk) (for The Hawk, *v.* Barrow Hawk
supra); the Grimesgate Road (cf. *Grimes'gate'dale* 1649[1], *Grimesgate* 117, 1822,
Grimes Gate Dale, - *Pitt* 1734, from the surn. *Grime* and **gata**, cf. *Christobell*
Gryme 1601 *BT*, John *Gryme* 1606 *ib*); Gypsie Hall (a messuage); Half Crown
Hill 1817 (perhaps a nickname type from the rent or value); Hall Garth (*v.*
garðr); the little Hann & Castles, Hann and Castles Rd (*the Littlehand* 1633,
Little Hann gate 1649[1], *little Hann* 1729, *the Little Hann* 1796, *v.* Barrow Hann
and The Castles *supra*); Hann Drain (cf. *Han Close* 1683, - *Heads, Stubble Hann*
1715, cf. prec.); (the) High Gate 1796 (1729, cf. the Low Gate *infra, v.* **gata**);
Holland Cottage (cf. *Hollande Garth* 1549[1], from the *Holland* family and **garðr**,
cf. John *Holland* 1589 *BT*); Inhams 1803, East -, Old Inghams 1817 (*Hynnames*
Hy3 (1301) Ch, *the old Inhams, old Inham steighe* 1609, *Old Innams* 1624, *East*
Old -, *West Old Inham(s)* 1649[1], *the west ould* -, *the east old Inhams, old Inhams*
stigh 117, *the old Enholm's* 1729, (*the old*) *Inhams* 1734, *v.* **innōm** 'a piece of
land taken in or enclosed', and **stīg**); the Lawns Well Cl (*v.* The Lawns *supra*);
Lings 1785, 1803 ('heather-covered land', *v.* **lyng**); the Low Gate 1796 (*the lowe*
gate 117, *yᵉ Lowgate* 1729, *Low Gate* 1734, *v.* **gata**); Maggot Dale 1803, 1804 (*that*
plat or Dale of Meadow Ground commonly Called - 1790, perhaps from the
feminine pers.n. *Mag(g)ot* and **deill**; noteworthy is the appellative use of *Dale*
in the 1790 form, though this is common in LNR); the Main Drain; Marams
Drain (*Mareham* 1609 (a place), *Marum* 1624, *Mare ham, Mareham* (*End*) 1649[1],
perhaps *v.* **(ge)mære** 'a boundary' and **hamm** 'an enclosure, a water-meadow, land
in the bend of a river' or **holmr** 'an island, a water-meadow, etc.', since the
latter develops various forms, such as *ham* in north L); Mickledale (*Mikell dall'*
m16, *Mikkell* -, *Mykell Dale* 1541, 1549[1], *Mykyldale* 1549[2], *Mickledaleheadland*
1609, *Mickel-, Mickledale* 1709, 'the big share or portion of land', *v.* **mikill, deill**,
a Scand. compound); Mic(k)lemere Rd 1803, 1822 (*Mickle meere* 1649[1], *the gote*
or drain going along Micklemer 1715, 'the great boundary', *v.* **mikill, (ge)mære**);
Middle Cl 1817; the Mill 1796 (1649[1], *molendino juxta castellum de Barewe* 1190
(1301) Dugd vi, *v.* **myln**); Mill Cl 1817, - Fd 1803, - Hill 1785 (cf. *a way called*
Milstowe gate 1609, *the Mildale, the Mill headland,* - *leaze,* - *Marfurre* 1649[1],
mildale marfare 1683, *Mill Carr* 1715, - *Dale,* - *Headland,* - *Hill* 1734, 1734, cf.
prec. and *v.* **myln-stōw** 'the site of a mill', **gata, deill, hēafod-land, lǣs, marfur,
kjarr**); Mill Rd (cf. *the Millgate* 1649[1]), *yᵉ Millway, the common way to the Mill*

.... *thaforesaid Millway* 1649, *v.* **gata, weg**; Millers Cl (presumably named from the *Miller* family, first noted so far with Elizabeth *Miller* 1851 *Census*); the Nursery; Papist Hall (a messuage); the Pingle (*v.* **pingel**); Piking Green (*pytinge thinge* m16, *Pyethinge greene, - thinge* 1649[1], *Piking Green* 1779 *BPD, v.* **grene**[2], **þing**); Pook Creek (sic) (perhaps an error for foll.); (the) Pool Creek (Drain) 1803, 1855; Roes Cl, ancient Inclosure called Roo's Close (cf. *Rowsgarth Marfurr* 1649[1], perhaps from a surn. with **garðr**); a lane then or then lately (sic) called Rhodes Lane 1880 (*an ancient lane called Thomas Rhode's Lane* 1803); Scholar Dale 1796 (*v.* **deill**, and cf. *the Schollers meadowe, the College alias Schollers Meadowe*, and *the Colledge Meadowe* all 1649[2], alluding to the holdings of New College, Oxford); Shaw Briggs 1803, 1804; Sluster Gate 1785; Spring Well Cl 1817; Stone Pit Cl 1817 (*Stone pitt quarter* 1609, *Comon feild* .... called *Stonepitt quarter* .... *a stonepitt in the said Feild* 1649[1], *Stone pitt Quarter* 1683, *Stonepitt Quarter Field* 1729, *-pit Quarter* 1779, - *Pitt Field, little Stone Pitt* 1734, (*the*) *Stone Pit Field* 1796, 1803, self-explanatory; for *Quarter v. Tarrygarth Quarter supra*); the Street Rd 1803, 1843 (cf. *Streetgate, the Streetegate* 1649[1], *Street Gate* 1734, *v.* **gata**), *Streete headland* 1649[1] (*v.* **hēafod-land**), *Streetdale* 1683, - *Dale* 1734 (*v.* **deill**), *v.* **strǣt**; to be identified with the road heading NW-SE in the south of the parish, as Mr Paul Everson points out to me. It is a pre-Roman trackway, known also as Barton Street); Summer-Crofts Rd, Summercrofts Drain (*v.* Summercroft Fm *supra*); Swanland Dale Mearfur (the forms are too late to decide the etymology of Swanland, *v.* **deill, marfur**); Thorn Garth, Thorngarth Cl, Thorngarth Lane, an ancient lane called Thorngarth Rd (*Thorn(e)garth* m16, 1633, *v.* **þorn, garðr**); Thorn Tree Cl 1817; Three Corner Cl 1803, 1822; Tilban Garth (sic) (*Tyl-, Tiltongarth* 1589-91, 1605-7, 1607 *Rental*, 1633, - *Garth* 1682 *Lamb, Tylton garth* 1649[1], from the surn. *Tilton* and **garðr** 'an enclosure', cf. *Magdaleyn Tylltone* 1561 *BT*); Toast Ings 1796, 1803 (*Tosteng* 1190 (1301) Dugd vi, i, *Toftinge* m16, *Tostyng(es)* 1541, 1549[1], 1549[2], 'Tósti's meadow, pasture', *v.* **eng**, a Scand. compound. The form, dated m16, is no doubt due to confusion with the common **toft** 'the site of a building, a curtilage, etc.', since *Tósti* appears to be a rare pers.n. in L, as Dr John Insley points out, cf. SPNLY 291); Town Side (Rd) 1803, 1843 (*Townside* 1734, and cf. *Arrable abutting vppon the Towne* 1633); Town St 1803, 1843, 1850; Wakefield Cl (from the surn. *Wakefield* and **clos(e)**, cf. John *Waykefeld* 1525 Wills i): Walkhouse Lane (cf. *Walkmilne* in f.ns. (b) *infra*); the Watermill 1762, Barrow Watermill 1822; Watermill Clough (*v.* **clōh**); Barrow Water Mill Fd 1762, Watermill Fd 1803, 1817, 1843, 1848, 1879 (*Barrow water Mill-field* 1712, - *mill field* 1718, *Water Mill Field* 1724, 1734, 1745); Water Mill Quarter 1785 ((*the*) *Watermill Quarter* 1662, 1683, - *quarter* 1692, 1683, 1713, - *quarter* 1692, for *Quarter v. Tarrygarth Quarter supra*); Waterside Fd; Well Cl 1803, - Nook 1796 (*Well Close* 1734, cf. *the Wellgarth* 1633, *v.* **wella, clos(e)**, garðr); the West Wold 1796, 1803, 1843, (1734, *the East and West Wolde* 1633, (*the*) *West Would* 1683, 117, 1729, cf. the East Wold *supra* and the Wold *infra*); the wide Furlong 1796 (*v.* **wīd, furlang**); the Wold of Barrow 1826 (*vppon the wolde* 1633, *the Would* 1683, and cf. *Lowewould -, the Low Would Gate* 1649[1], *v.* **wald**); Wold Inhams (*the wold Inholmes* 1633, *the Westwould Inhams* 1683, *v.* **wald, innōm**); Wood Garth Cl 1803, (the) Woodgarth Close Rd 1804, 1850 (perhaps the same as *Watgarth(e)* 1633, *v.* **garðr**).

(b) *the acre dike* 1649[1] (*v.* **æcer, dīc, dik** and f.ns. (b) in Barnetby le Wold *supra*); *Annabelle -, An(n)able(s) lande* m16, 1589-91, 1605-7, 1607 *Rental* (from the pers.n. *Anabel* or the derived surname (*v.* Reaney s.n. *Annable*) and **land**); *Atkinson land* m16, *Atkinsons Land* 1649[1], *- land* 1679 (from the family name *Atkinson* and **land**, cf. Robert *Atkinson* m16 and Robert *Atkynson*, probably the same person, 1554 *Inv*); *Baldwyns buttes* 1649[1], *Baldwin Butts* 1734 (from the family name *Baldwin* and **butte**, cf. Roger *Baldwin* 1584 Admin); *in campis de Barwe* c. 1160 Dane, *- de Barue* Hy3 *HarlCh, in campo de Barwa* 1268 RRGr, *the feilde of Barrowe* 1609, *Barrow Field* 1662, *- feild* 1671 (*v.* **feld**); (*mess' cum crofto voc'*) *Barrowland(e)* 1589-91, 1605-7, 1607 (*v.* **land**); *Barton Meare* 1609, *- Meere* 1649[1], *- meare* 1683, *- Meer* 1734 ('the boundary with Barton (upon Humber)', *v.* **(ge)mǣre**)); *Barton Lowe way, - streete* 1649[1]; *The bean field* 1715 (*v.* **bēan, feld**); *Beckham Close, Beckhams garth* 1633, *Beckham(s) close* 1649[1] (perhaps from a surn. *Beckham*, though this has not been noted in the sources searched); *Bell land* 1604[2], 1649[1] (probably an endowment for the support of the church bell(s)); *Besby Manor* 1715 (named from the *Beesby* family, cf. John *Beisbye* m16); *Blod hou* Hy3 *HarlCh* (more forms are needed to suggest a certain etymology, but, as Dr John Insley points out, it could be derived from ON *blóthaugr* 'a sacrificial mound'); *Bray gate* 1649[1], *Tenement .... called Bray house .... on the southside of Bray Lane* 1649[1] (from the surn. *Bray*, cf. Richard *Braie* 1586 BT); *Braytoft thinge* m16 (no doubt from the surn. *Braytoft* and **þing** 'possession, property', though no example of the surn. has been noted in the parish; it is less likely that it is to be associated with the prec.); *the Bull Pieces* 1715 (*v.* **bula, pece**); *Burnham Feild* 1649[1], *- Field* 1662, *- feild* 1671, *- ffield* 1734 LRMB 256, *Burn(e)ham Headland* 1649[1], *- headland* 117, *- Headland* 1734 LRMB 256 (*v.* **feld** and **hēafod-land**, named from Burnham in Thornton Curtis *infra*); *Burstall Gars* 1633, *- garthes* 1649[1] (probably from a family name and **garðr**); *le Buttes* 1604[2], *at the Bute* 1633, *the Butts* 1649[1] (*v.* **butt**[2] 'an archery butt'); *Cargarth* m16, 1633, *Car garth house* 1633, *Carre garth* (*house*), *Carrgarth on the north side of Cherry lane* 1649[1] (perhaps from the surn. *Car(r)* and **garðr**, though it has not been noted earlier than Robert *Carr* 1728 BT, *v.* also Cherry Lane *supra*); *Carvers ffurres* 1649[1] (probably from the surn. *Carver* and the pl. of **furh** 'a furrow'); *Clefteng* 1190 (1301) Dugd vi, i (*v.* **eng**); *Clerreng* 1190 (1301) ib (*v.* **eng**); *the great Cleypitt* (*in Watermill Quarter*) 1649[1], *Clay Pitt* 1729; *Clough* 1725 (*v.* **clōh**); *Coggan land* 1631 (from the family name and **land**, cf. Henry *Coggan* 1609); *Cornercrofte heads* 117; *Crosby Close* 1633 (from the surn. *Crosby* and **clos(e)**, cf. John *Crosbe* 1542 *Inv*); *The Crossehouse* 1633, *the Cross house* 1649[1]; *Dale-gate* 1624 (*v.* **deill, gata**); *Disney als Pilching Lane* 1728; *dovecoate lane* 1649[1] (cf. West Marsh *supra*); *Dow-croftes* 1624, *Dovercrofts* 1715 (prob. for *Dove-*) (*v.* **dūfe** 'a dove', **croft**, but the surn. *Dove* is also possible); *drabble headland* 1649[1] (no doubt from the surn. *Drabble* and **hēafod-land**); *Duffeld land* m16 (from the surn. *Duffield* and **land**); *the East End* 1647 *MiscDon 251*; *Edlington thinge* m16 (from the surn. *Edlington* and **þing**); *xi acr' dale, 11 acre dalle* m16 Cragg (*v.* **deill**); *terr' vocat Ellerdale* 1624 (*v.* **elri**, **deill**, a Scand. compound); *mes*(*suag'*) *voc*(*at'*) *Fishertinge* 1589-91, *-thing* 1633, *messuage called ffishers thinge* 1649[1] (from the surn. *Fisher* and **þing**, cf. Robert *Fisher* 1606 *BT*); (*the*) *Fleedales* 1609, 1729, *Fleedale bancke* 1609, *Fleet Dale bank* 1624, *fleedale* (*banck*(*e*)) 1649, *Fleedale*(*s*) *bank*(*s*) 1709, 1715 (probably from Fleet in (a) *supra* and **deill**); *le foldecourse* 1549[1] ('the sheep-walk', *v.* NED s.v. *fold-course*); *Forbienge* 1589-91, *terr' vocat' Forbyenge* 1605-7, *Meadowe called Forebinge* 1633 (this is presumably a compound of *forby* and *eng*, cf. *forbyland*, NED s.v., and Adams 87, 93, 'land cultivated separately from the common field in which it lay', and *v. forby land* in Worlaby f.ns. (b) *infra* for a full discussion); *iiii acre dale* m16; *fouretene acre Dale* 1541, 1549[1], *Fourtene acre dale* 1549[2] (*v.* **deill**); *Frawaredale* 1609, *Franard dale* 1709; *Gagg house* 1649[1] (presumably from a surn., but no references to a *Gagg* family have been noted in the sources searched); *Three lands call'd Gare and Goldings* 1734 (the first is probably from **geiri** 'a triangular plot of ground', the second is uncertain); *Golflete* 1536-43 Leland ('the gold stream', *v.* **gold, flēot**, but the exact sense of *gold* cannot be determined); *Garmound close* m16, *Gamon Close* 1549[1] (probably from the ME surn. *Garmo*(*u*)*nd* and **clos(e)**); *Gell house* m16, *Close* .... *called Gells* 1633, *an ancient cottage called Gells house* 1662 (named from the *Gell* family, cf. John *Gell* 1575 *Inv*); *Gildons Dale* 1734 (*v.* **deill**); *Gil*(*le*)*sdale* (*gate*) 1649[1] (from the surn. *Gilles* and **deill**, cf. Anthony *Gilles* m16); *cotage* .... *in a lane* .... *called Goodwynns Lane* 1649[1] (named from the *Goodwin* family, cf. Richard *Goodwyne* 1592 *BT*); *Gosewich* Hy3 *HarlCh* ('the goose farm', *v.* **gōs, wīc**); *Gouxhill Furres, - Hedge, - meere* 1649[1], *- mill stigh* 117, *- bank, - hedge, - pales* 1715, *- leazes* 1683, *- Leazes* 1729 (all named from the neighbouring parish of Goxhill with **furh** 'a furrow' in the pl. (cf. *shooteing furrs* in Barton f.ns. (b) *infra*), **hecg, (ge)mǣre, myln, stīg, stigr** 'a path, etc.', **banke** and **lǣs**); *Grandsire-farme, Grandsires farme* 1624, *Messuage* .... *called Gransier Farme* 1649[1] (apparently self-explanatory); *Graby oxgange* m16, *Graybyes Oxgange* 1649[1] (from the surn.

Graby and **oxgang**); *greendale Marferrs* 1651 (*v.* **grene**[1], **deill**, **marfur**); *Green(e)gate* 1649[1], *greene gate* 1651, 1692, *Greengate* 1683, 1729 (probably 'the green road', *v.* **grēne**[1], **gata**, rather than 'the road to the village green', but cf. *Attegrene* 1281 *Ass* (p), *v.* **grēne**[2]); *Greenway* 1649[1]; *(a Midforeland vppon the Topp of) Groundhill* 1649[1] (cf. *the Middforlande infra*); *Haddingham Marfarr* 1729 (probably from the surn. *Haddingham* and **marfur**); *the half swaths* 1715 (*v.* **healf**, **swæð**, ME **swathe** 'a strip of grassland'); *Hambercoata* 1541 (the same as *Humber cote infra*); *Harnes Tofte* 1549[1] (from the *Harnes* family and **toft**, cf. John *Harnis* 1601 *BT*); *the Hay Garth* 1715 (*v.* **heg**, **garðr**); *the Heades* 1624 (*v.* **hēafod**); *the headland* 117 (*v.* **hēafod-land**); *Hekelinghil* Hy3 *HarlCh* (probably from a surn. derived from Healing LNR and **hyll**); *Hills house* 1649[1], *Hill House* 1649[2], 1676, 1685 (from the surn. *Hill*, cf. William *Hyll* m16); *Holmar* 1729; *marmaduke Hodgson' House* 117; *Honberdale* (sic) 1649[1]; *Hookedale* 1649[1], *Hook Dale* 1734 (from the surn. *Hook* or **hōc** 'a hook, a projecting piece of land' and **deill**); *a lane* .... *called Howle lane* 1649[1], *(a certain street or lane anciently called) Howle-Lane* 1676, 1686, *the Howle Lane* 1694, *Howle Lane bridge* 1715, *How Lane Dale* 1734, cf. *Howle Meere, Howlemeere Dale* 1649[1] (without early spellings it is impossible to suggest an etymology for *Howle*); *Humber banks* 1709, 1715; *Humber cote* m16, *humbercote* 1574 *Nelthorpe* (the name of a sheepwalk) ('the (sheep)cote by the R. Humber', *v.* **cot**); *King garth* 1683, *Kingland* 1649[1], *King's Pinfold* 1715, *Kings-Streete* 1624 (perhaps from the *King* family, well-represented in the parish, cf. Richard *King* 1597 *BT*, but the Crown had substantial interests in Barrow); *Kirkgarth lane* 1649[1] ('the enclosure belonging or near to the church', *v.* **kirkja**, **garðr**, a Scand. compound, cf. Simon *atte Kirke* 1328 Banco); *Kitchen Acre* 1649[1], 1734 (*kitchen* is common enough in f.ns. denoting land on which vegetables for immediate use were grown, *v.* Field 118-9); *the knowle of the hill* 1624 (*v.* **cnoll**); *Lammas Piece* 1713, 1715, 1734 (cf. *Midsummer Piece infra*); *Ladie Crosse headland* 1624, *lady crosse way* 1649[1], *Lady Crosse* 1683 (presumably a cross dedicated to Our Lady); *land cotegarthe* 1605-7, 1649[1], *Land-, landcotegarthe* 1589-91, 1607 (*v.* **land**, **cot**, **garðr**); *ditch called Land dike als Lowdike* 1649[1], *Low Dike* 1734 (**land**, **lágr**, **dīc**, **dík**); *The Lars* 1715; *laurenc thinge* m16 (named from the *Laurence* family and **þing**, cf. *hered Willī laurance* m16); *the Laverack Goat* 1715 (from the *Laverock* family and **gotu** 'a watercourse, a stream', cf. John *Lauerocke* 1546 *Inv*); *parcell of Meadowe ground* .... *in* .... *great Inges called Leave and Want* 1649[1] (a somewhat cryptic nickname, perhaps enjoining moderation, cf. the proverb 'Leave with an appetite'); *Leman dale* 1649[1], *Lemon Dale Pitt* 1734 (presumably from the surn. *Leman, Lemon* (Reaney s.n. *Loveman*) and **deill**); *terr' vocat' linwoode* 1589-91, 1605-7, *Linwoodthing* 1633, *Linwood garth, - thinge* 1649[1] (it is impossible to say whether this is an original p.n., identical with the two Linwoods in L, 'the lime tree wood', *v.* **lind**, **wudu**, or more probably a surn. *Linwood*, though none has been noted in the sources searched, *v.* þing and garðr); (*the*) *Little Carr* 1715 (*v.* kjarr); *Loftbrige* c. 1160 Dane (*v.* loft, brycg); *Longlande* 1649[1] ('the long strip of arable land in the common-field', *v.* lang, land); *Lupton Acre* 1729 (from the *Lupton* family, cf. John *Lupton* 1649 Admin); *the marfer end* 1715 ('the end of the boundary furrow', *v.* marfur); *George Marriss Farm* 1715; *the Middforeland,* y*e* *Midd Furlonge* 1649[1], *the middle furlong* 1692, *the mid furlong* 117, *Midfurlong* 1729; *the Middleland furlonge, a Midland furlong* 1649[1]; *Middle-dale headland* 1624; *Middlestigh gate* 1649[1] (*v.* middel, stīg, stīgr 'a path', with gata); *Midsummer Piece* ("*is common for kine upon Lammas day*") 1715, 1734 (cf. *Lammas Piece supra*); *Widow Mighills Close* 1729; *milesbergh gate* 117; *Milner Farme* 1633 (from the *Milner* family, cf. Edward *mylner* m16, Richard *milner* 1587 *BT*); *milnesteigh gate* 117 (*v.* stīg, stīgr and gata and the Mill, Mill Rd in (a) *supra*); *Minster gate* 1649[1], -*Gate* 1734 (*v.* mynster (its exact sense is uncertain), gata); *Morlay Acre* 1729 (from the *Morley* family, cf. George *Morley* 1681 *BT*); *Nelhouse* 1633, *Neale close, Neales house* 1649[1], *Neeles House* 1679, 1719 (from the *Neale* family, cf. Robert *Nele* 1531 Wills iii, Robert *Neylle* 1537 *Inv*); *the sure* (i.e. 'sour') *banks near the new haven chaps* 1715 (*v.* Barrow Haven *supra*); *le New-close* 1624; *Newland Heades* 1649[1], -*heads* 1683, -*Heads* 1709 (no doubt newly claimed land, *v.* hēafod in pl.); *North cote* 1549[2] (*v.* cot); *le olde peys* 1549[2] (*v.* pece); *the Oxdales* 1633, 1715, *Oxdale(s)* 1649[1] (*v.* oxa, deill); *Parsonage Barne* 1633; *Pedderdale* 1649[1] (presumably from the surn. *Pedder* and deill); *Pethery Dale* 1734; *pynder howse* m16, (*cotag' voc'*) *Pinder House, Pinderhowse* 1605-7, 1607, 1633, *Pinder house,* -*thinge* 1649[1] (named from the *Pinder* family, cf. John *Pynder* m16, *v.* also þing); *Pittdale .... abutting on a great Pitt* 1649[1] (*v.* deill); *Potterdale slacke* 1649[1], -*slack* 117 (apparently from the surn *Potter* (cf. Miles *Potter* 1642 *PR*) and deill, with slakki 'a small shallow valley, a hollow in the ground', an OWScand word, rare in the East Midlands); *Messuage .... in Poynter Lane* 1649[1] (Thomas *Poynter* was the tenant); *pontis vocati Prestbrygge de Barugh'* 1412 RRep ('the priests' bridge', *v.* prēost, brycg); (*terr' vocat'*) *Rawlinclose* 1589-91, 1605-7 (named from the *Rawlin* family and clos(e), cf. George *Rawline* 1585 *Inv*); *Scarborough headland* 1649[1] (presumably from a family not so far noted before John *Scarborough* 1851 *Census*, and cf. *Scarbrough Gate* in Barnetby le Wold f.ns. (b)); *Sea Banks at haven* 1709; *Serowhute* (*infra le Inges de Barrowe*) 1605-7, 1607; *Seton thinge* m16 (from a family frequently mentioned in late 16th century sources and þing, cf. *Alicia Seatone* 1571 *BT*); *Seven acre dale* 1709 (*v.* deill); *several lane ends* 1715 (*v.* several); *le shepecote* 1549[1], 1549[2]; *Shepe course* 1549[2] ('the sheep fold-course', *v.* course and further *le Abbotescourse* in Thornton Curtis f.ns. (b) *infra*); *le shepe gate* 1549[1] ('pasturage for sheep', *v.* shep-gate, sheep-gate NED, s.v. sheep 8 and for a 13th century example, *v.* Nettleton f.ns.

(a) *infra*); *pastur' ouilem voc' a Shepegarthe* 1541 ('the sheepfold', *v.* garðr and NED s.v. *sheep* 8); *shippendicke Marfar* 117 (*v.* scypen, dīc, dīk, marfur); *shippenstallgate, Shippenstall hill* 1649[1] ('the site of a shippen', *v.* scypen, stall with hyll); *Shoare gate* 1649[1]; *Shorby headland* 1624 (presumably from a surn. though it has not been noted in the sources searched); *Sixacredale* 1609, - acre dale 1709 (*v.* deill); *a place called Skindols* 1609, *Skindale* 1649[1], *Skin Dale Hill* 1734; *the Slad Dike* 1715 (*v.* slæd, dīc, dīk); *Sladhil* Hy3 HarlCh (*v.* hyll); *the greate Pitt at Smithy lane end* 1649[1], *a certain Street or Lane anciently called smithy Lane* 1698 (self-explanatory); *Sokomer thinge* m16 (presumably from a family name and þing); *Somercloses* m16 (*v.* sumor, clos(e)); *Somercotes* 1549[2] ('sheds used in summer', *v.* sumor, cot); *Sontercroft* (*n*=*u*) 1190 (1301) Dugd vi, i (from the occupational name, or derived surv., *sutere* 'a shoemaker' and croft); *Sparrow cote* m16, *Sporow cote* 1589-91, 1605-7, 1607, *Sheepecoate or Spurrow-coategarth* 1633, *Sparrow cote garth* 1633, *Sparrow cote garth* 1649[1] (perhaps from the surn. *Sparrow* and cot; in the m16 reference it is described as a *Sheppcot*); *Spencer land* m16 (no doubt from the surn. *Spencer*, but none has been noted in the early sources examined); *Spicers headland* 1649[1], *Spicer Headland* 1734 (from the surn. *Spicer* and hēafod-land, cf. *Aliccia Spycar* 1587 BT, Cuthbert *Spicer* 1588 *ib*); *Spillesby Land* 1549[1] (from the *Spilsby* family and land, cf. William *Spillesby* 1504 Wills i); *the Spring Heads* 1715; *the Springs* 1715; *Spur Howk* 1709; *Staynhouse* m16 (the first el. is Scand. steinn 'stone'); *Steinholm* c. 1146 Dane (*v.* steinn, holmr, a Scand. compound); *certaine little Holes called Stintholes* 1649[1] (the same name is found in the neighbouring parish of Barton f.ns. (b) *infra*); *Stoop Lands* 1734 (*stoop* is probably from ON stolpi 'a stake, a stump, a post'); *The stubble Wold* 1715 (*v.* the Wold of Barrow in (a) *supra*); *Stokbrig' de Barowe* 1385 Peace (p) ('the bridge made of logs', *v.* stocc, brycg, identical with Stockbridge PN YW 1, 25); *Sukkabur Land* 1549[1]; (*the*) *Swyneholes* 1649[1], *Swyneholmes* 117 (it is quite uncertain whether the two forms represent the same name, *v.* swīn[1], hol[1], holmr); *Tenacre Dale* 1541, *tenne acre dale* 1549[2], *tenne acr' dale* m16, *Ten acre dale* 1709 (*v.* deill); *thirtene acre Dale* 1541, *Thirtene Acre Dale* 1549[1], - *acre dale* 1549[2], *Thirteen acre dale* 1709, 1729 (*v.* deill); *Thirty acre dale* 1649[1] (*v.* deill); *Thomson land* m16 (named from the *Thompson* family, cf. Thomas *Thomson* m16, Robert *Thompson* 1644 Admin); *Thornton meare* 1609, *Thorn(e)ton Meere* 1649 ('Thornton Curtis boundary', *v.* (ge)mǣre); *Thorppe wraye* m16, *Thorphall Wray* 1604[2], *Thropehallwray* 1633, *Thorpe hall wray* 1649[1] (named from the *Thorpe* family, cf. John *Thorppe* m16; *wray* is probably from vrá 'a nook, a corner of land', with the same development as in Wray PN YW 4, 82); *three stonges* 1624 (*v.* stong, used as a standard of measure 'a pole', freq. in L); *Touthilldale* 1649[1] ('the look-out hill', *v.* tōt-hyll, with deill); *Towsdale* 1729 (perhaps from the surn. *Towes*, from Great & Little Towes in

Ludford LSR, and **deill**); *two common Marfurrs* 1649[1] (from **marfur** 'a boundary furrow', as elsewhere in this parish); *Tuppcotgarth* m16, *Tupcotegarthe* 1589-91, 1605-7, 1607. *Tupcott garthe* 1604[2] ('the shed for tups', *v.* **tup, cot**, with **garðr**); *Twelve acre dale* 1709 (*v.* **deill**); *the vicarage grounde* 1580; *Wakendale* 1649[1]; *Walkemilne* 1580-91, 1605-7 ('the fulling mill', *v.* **walke-milne**); *a Comon waye called the watermilne gate* 1609, *Watermill gate* 117, *The watermill gate* 1715 (*v.* **gata** and the Watermill in (a) *supra*); *Well Close* 1649[1], 1715; *Whitton lane* 1630, 1682; *Wilsonhouse* 1633 (from the family name *Wilson*, cf. William *Wylson* 1562 *Inv*); *a way called the wouldgate* 1609, *Wouldgate* 1624, *- Gate* 1729, *wo*(*u*)*ld gate* 1734, *the* (*High*) *Would gate* 1683, 117, *the Highwould gate* 1649[1], *- would gate* 1683, *- High Wold Gate* 1715 ('the way to the Wold', *v.* **wald, gata** and the Wold of Barrow in (a) *supra*); *Wotwate Close* 1715; *Wreght thinge* m16 (presumably from the surn. *Wright* and **þing**, cf. Steven and Richard *Wright* 1561 *BT*); *Wyntergate* 1549[2] ('the way usable in winter', *v.* **winter, gata**); *Yardmarr* 1729; *ykelmere* Hy3 *HarlCh* (the second el. is apparently **mere**[1] 'a pool', but the first is uncertain).

THE ANGLO-SAXON CHARTER
FOR
BARROW UPON HUMBER

The bounds of the AS charter for Barrow upon Humber, dated 971 (12) *PetLN* (S 782), have been checked from the manuscript. Mr Paul Everson, in "The Pre-Conquest Estate of *Æt Bearuwe* in Lindsey", in *Studies in Late Anglo-Saxon Settlement*, ed. Margaret L. Faull, Oxford 1984, pp. 123-37, especially Fig. 1 for a plan on which the boundary-names are marked, has convincingly demonstrated that these bounds follow in part the modern boundary of Barrow itself, but also in part that of Barton upon Humber. A detailed discussion of the individual names will appear in Paul Everson and G.C. Knowles, "The Anglo-Saxon Bounds of *Æt Bearuwe*", as Chapter 12 of *St Chad's, Barrow-on-Humber. Report of Excavations 1976-8*, ed. J.B. Whitwell, Humberside Heritage Publication. no. 17, forthcoming. Mr Everson has kindly allowed me to read the chapter in typescript.

The bounds are as follows: *þis syndon þa land ge mæro to Baruwe. Ærest up of humbre* (R. Humber) *andlanges þere ealdan dïc* ('the old dyke', *v.* **ald, dïc**, the first el. perhaps in the sense of long used or formerly used) *þæt it cymeð to wyrðe* (*v. Worth supra*) *fram wyrðe to heope bricge* ('the bridge where hips grow', *v.* **heope, brycg**

and Middendorf 70) *fram heope bricge to merce mot.* (probably 'the
meeting of the boundaries', *v.* **mearc, mōt** and Middendorf 93-4 and
95) *fram merce mote to Cumbre hole.* ('the hollow, depression of the
Welsh', *v.* **Cumbre, hol**[1]) *fram cumbre hole to willum* (*v.* Welham
supra) *fram willum to micle hoh.* ('the big heel, hill-spur, etc.', *v.*
micel, hōh) *fram micle hohe to middel hille* ('the middle hill', *v.*
middel, hyll, tentatively identified by Everson 125a as "the height
formerly known as Black Mould Hill", *v.* the Black Mold in f.ns. (a)
supra) *to mere dīc. swa andlang mere dic eft up on humbre* (*mere
dic* is 'the boundary dyke', *v.* **(ge)mǣre, dīc,** following the western
boundary of Barton upon Humber. Everson, 125a, notes that this is
marked in places by a substantial linear bank, formerly a striking
feature and forming "part of the remarkable continuous north-south
boundary line along the highest point of the western edge of the
Wolds, that serves unbroken a total of thirteen parishes over a
distance of at least 10 miles ... south from the Humber" .... "clearly
an ancient and obvious feature in the landscape". It has been
identified as an early routeway, perhaps also a Roman road).

Barton upon Humber

BARTON UPON HUMBER
    Bertune 1086 DB, *-tuna* c. 1115 LS, *-tone* 1086 DB (4x), *-tona*
        c. 1190 (1402) Dugd iv, Hy2 Lane, *-ton* c. 1090 (1402) Dugd
        iv, 1228 Cl, 1458 WillsPCC
    Bartuna c. 1115 LS, eHy2, l12 Dane, 1178 (p1269) *Bard, -tun*(')
        l12 Dane (p), 1166 RBE (p), Hy2 LN (p), c 1210 RA iv,
        1230 P, 1250 YD x, *-tona* 1100-14, 1125 (p1269) *Bard,* c.
        1140 Dane, c. 1145 (p1269) *Bard et passim* to 1226 (p1269)
        ib, -tonie 1147-67 (m13) Pontefract, *-tunie* c. 1150 (m13) ib
    Barton' 1115 (14) *Bard,* 1176 (p1269) *ib,* 1180, 1181, 1185 P (p),
        1185 Templar, 1186 P *et freq* to 1332 *SR,* 1382, 1385
        Peace, *Barton* 1156 (p1269) *Bard,* 1184-5 YCh ii, Hy2, l12
        (e14) Brid, 1206 Ass, 1219 FF, 1227 Ch *et freq* to 1638
        VisitN
    Barton' iuxta Humbriam l12 (p1269) *Bard,* 1256 RA ii, *- super
        Humb'* 1202 ChancR, *- super Humbram* 1203 P, 1213 Cur,
        - super Humbre a1213 RA iv, *- super Humbriam* 1214 FF
    Barton "upon-, on- Humber" 1245 Ch, 1298 Fine, 1307 Cl, 1313

Pat *et freq* in printed texts to 1552 ib, "on-, upon" *Humbre*
1275 Fine, 1289 Pat, 1304 Ipm, 1317 Pat, 1317 Cl *et freq* in
printed texts to 1510 LP, "by Humber" 1331 Ch, *Barton
upone Humber* 1578 *Terrier*, - *upon Humber* 1657, 1664, 1686
BPD *et freq*

Barton super Humbre 1275 Orig, 1304 *AD*, 1319 YearBk, 1345
Cragg et passim to 1539 *AD*, - *super Humbr'* 1331 Abbr,
1377 *AD*, 1424 IBL, 1517 ECB, - *super Humber* 1314 Inqaqd,
1373 Peace, 1553 Pat, 1660 *BPD*, 1697 *MiscDon 136*, - *juxta
Humber'* 1284 Abbr, - *iuxta Humber* 1374 Peace

Bareton' 1202 FF

Barthon' 1207 FF, 1223 Cur, *-thona* 1209-35 LAHW, *-thon* 1239,
1245 FF, 1257, 1272, 1273 Ipm, 1303 FA

The numerous forms in *Bar-* indicate that this is OE bær-tūn 'a
barley farm, corn farm' in the developed sense 'the outlying grange'.
The 971 AS charter for Barrow *supra*, the bounds of which include
Barton as well as Barrow, suggests that Barton was an outlying
grange of Barrow.

GASCRICK (lost), *Gastecrike* (sic) eHy3 (p1269) *Bard, Gascrike*
1250 FF, 1250 (p1269) *Bard* (copy of prec.), *Gascrik* Hy3 *HarlCh*
(p), 1297 Cl (p), 1302 *Nelthorpe* (p), 1313 Pat (p), *Gascrike* 1318
AddCh (p), *Gaskryk* 1332 *SR* (p), *Gayskerik* 1334 Cl (p), recorded
from at least 1332 *SR* as an hereditary surn. in Robert *Gascrik'*. In
spite of the spelling of the first form, it would appear that this is a
Scandinavian compound of gás 'a goose, a wild goose' and kriki 'a
nook, bend', ME crike 'a creek' (cf. MED s.v.), hence 'the creek of
the wild geese' or the like, with a similar diphthongisation in the
1334 form as occurs in Gaisgill, PN We 2, 50, and Gazegill, PN
YW 6, 176. According to LNQ vi, 204-6, "Gascrike .... was the
original name of the Haven of Barton".

SHADWELLS (local, represented today by the st.n. Shadwell Rise),
Schadewelle m12, eHy3 (p1269) *Bard*, Hy3 *HarlCh, stagnum
molendini de Scadewelle* l12-e13 (p1269) *Bard, Shadwells* 1621
MiscDon 251, 1676 BartTB, 1704 *BPD*, cf. *Schadewelledal(e)*, *-dam*
eHy3 (p1269) *Bard* (v. dammr), *Schadewalledale* (sic) Hy3 (p1269)
ib, Schadewel dale 1294 *Foster, Schadewelledale, in valle de
schadewelle* Hy3 *HarlCh* (v. dæl, dalr), *Shadwell dry pitt* 1658 BPD,

shadwell drie Acre pitt 1666 *ib*. There does not seem to be a known or suspected boundary here, so it is unlikely to be identical with Shadwell Spring, PN O 10, 'the spring on or near a boundary', from scēad and wella. The most likely explanation would, therefore, appear to be 'the spring in a shady place', *v.* sceadu, wella, as in Shadwell, PN YW 4, 102, and PN Gl 2, 254. *v.* Blow Wells Plantation *infra*.

BARDNEY HALL, *Bardenayhall* 1391 Pat, *Bardney Hall* 1535 VE iv, 1538-9 Dugd i, *Bardney Halle* 1538-40 LDRH, *Bardney Hall* 1842 White; the earliest reference above is to the death of "Richard Carter of Bardenayhall *alias* John, servant of the abbot of Bardenay", the hall being named from Bardney Abbey. BARTON CLIFF, CLIFF HO. BARTON FIELD FM, cf. *in campis Bartonie* 1147-67 (m13) Pontefract, *in campo Bartone* 1185-91 (e14) YCh v, *in campis de Barton* 112 (m13) Pontefract, *in campis de Barton' iuxta Humbriam* 112 (p1269) *Bard, in campis de Barton'* eHy3 (p1269) *ib, in Campo Bart'* Hy3 (p1269) *ib, in camp' de Barton* 1276 RH, *Barton Feild* 1614 *Nelthorpe, Berton feild* 1671 *Terrier* (Barrow upon Humber), *Barton feald* 1692 *Nelthorpe, - Fields* 1697 Pryme, *v.* feld. BARTON GRANGE, *The Grange* 1799 Young, *Grange F.* 1824 O, cf. *Grange Lane* 1779 *Nelthorpe,* and *in uno muro ... super quod grangia lapidea & nouum stabulum sita sunt* Hy3 (p1269) *Bard,* a grange of Bardney Abbey, *v.* grange. BARTON HAVEN, *inter portum eiusdem uille* (i.e. Barton) 1250 (p1269) *Bard, del Haven* "of Barton" 1343 Cl (p), *the Haven* 1633 *AOMB 390,* 1676 BartTB, 1795 *BPD,* 1796 *EnclA,* 1822 *Terrier,* self-explanatory, *v.* hæfen[1], hafn and *Gaskrick supra,* said to be an earlier name for Barton Haven. BARTON HILL FM, *Hill F.* 1824 O, and cf. *toftum Will'i de Hille* e13 (p1269) *Bard, supra montem de Bartona* Hy3 (p1269) *ib* (p), *del Hull'* 1294 *Ass* (p), *the hill* 1621 *MiscDon 251, v.* hyll. BARTON LODGE, 1824 O, *Lodge* 1826 White. BARTON VALE, cf. *the Valley* 1796 *EnclA.* BARTON WATERSIDE, *water-side* 1709 *Terrier, the Waterside House* 1822 *ib, Barton Water Side* 1824 O. BARTON WOLD FM (lost), *Barton Wold F.* 1824 O. BAYSGARTH, - PARK, *basegarth* 1537 *Nelthorpe, Base garthe* 1585 *FLMisc, Basegarthe* Eliz ChancP, *Bayes Garth* 1614, *FLMisc*; since the same name occurs in East Halton and in Brocklesby f.ns. (a) *infra,* it is very unlikely that the first el. is the surn. *Base* (cf. Reaney s.n. *Bass*). The forms for all three examples are late, but it is possible that they are each Scand. compounds of **báss** and **garðr** 'the enclosure with a cowshed'. BEACON HILL, 1824 O, cf. *Beacon gate* 1658, 1694 *BPD, Becon gate* 1681 *MiscDep 166, Beacongate* 1707 *Terrier,* 1761 *BPD, Beacon Gate* 1719 BartTB, *Beakon Gate* 1720 *BPD* and *the Beacon* 1697, 1700 *Terrier,* 1733 *BPD, yᵉ Beaken* 1709 *Terrier,* self-explanatory, *v.* **běacon, gata** 'a road', as frequently in this parish. BEAUMONTCOTE FM, *mesuagium domini de bello Monte* 1415 *AddCh, Bemon Cotts* 1535 VE iv, *Beamont Coate* 1707 *Terrier, Beaumont Court* 1765 *ib,* - *Cote* 1796 *EnclA,* 1822 *Terrier,* named from the *Beaumont* family and **cot**. For the family, lords of the manor, *v.* Barton 16ff and 62-4, and note "the messuage which Robert Houke held of Sir John de Bello Monte" 1343 Cl, "land held of the lord of Beaumont (*de Bello Monte*)" 1350 Ipm, "John de Beaumond lord of Barton upon Humbre" 1289 Cl, "All that manor of Beaumond-fee alias Beaumont-fee" 1699 Barton. BEECH GROVE, - *grove* 1842 White. BLACK BULL, *the Black Bull* 1777 *LindDep 67.* BLOW WELLS PLANTATION, cf. *Blow Wells Drain* 1796 *EnclA, Blow Well* 1824 O, the earlier name of which was *Shadwells supra,* as Mr David Neave points out. BLUE BELL INN, *Blue Bell* 1842 White. BLUE COAT CHARITY FM. CHAPEL FM. CHOWDER NESS, 1824 O. CLAY PIT. CORNHILL FM. DEEPDALE, *Depedal'* Hy2 (15) Bridl, *Depedale* lHy2, eHy3, Hy3 (p1269) *Bard, Depedal'* Hy3 (15) Bridl, *Depedalelith* eHy3 (p1269) *Bard* (probably from **hlið¹** 'a slope'), *deepdale stintinge* 1621 *MiscDon 251* (*v.* **stinting** 'a portion of meadow set apart for one man's use', a word occurring as an appellative in north L), *a valley ... called deepdale* 1649 *ParlSurv, Deepedale* 1658, 1694 *BPD, Deepdale* 1697 *Terrier et passim,* self-explanatory, *v.* **děop, dæl, dalr**. DUDMANDALE (lost), *v. Warren Fm infra.* EASTFIELD FM, cf. *In campo uersus orientali* l12 (p1269) *Bard, in orientali Campo de Bartona* Hy3 (p1269) *ib, in campo oriental'* 1294 *Foster, in orientali camp'* 1302 *Nelthorpe, the East feild* 1621 *MiscDon 251, the East(e) feilde* 1633 *AOMB 390, the Eastfeild* 1649 *ParlSurv,* 1658 *BPD, the East Feild* 1666 *ib, the eastfield* 1668 *ib, the East Field* 1674 *ib et freq,* and note *the former east field* 1795 *ib* and *the East Field* 1822 *Terrier,* self-explanatory, *v.* **ěast, feld,** one of the open fields of Barton. FERRY (lost), 1824 O, where Barton Haven is marked on the modern map, cf. *the waterfferry .... hyt is knowen ... as .. a dystincte place of yt self* Ed6 *CtAugm, the ferry* 1649 *ParlSurv,* and *that Fery*

boate .... *comonly called Barton Boate* 1649 *ib, Barton Bote* c. 1638
Monson. It is *Hasyll fery alias Barton fery* 1536 LP xi, *Barton Ferry*
1537 ib xii, where *Hasyll* is Hessle on the opposite side of the
Humber. FIELD FM, FIELD HO (2x), *v.* Barton Field Fm *supra.*
GEORGE HOTEL, *(the) George Inn* 1796 *EnclA*, 1842 White.
GLEBE FM. GREEN GATE, *the* - 1614 *Nelthorpe, Grene Gate*
1704 *BPD*, cf. *Greengate Hill* 1826 White, 'the green road', *v.*
grēne[1], gata. HOE HILL BRICK WORKS. KINGSFORTH, 1658,
1733 *BPD*, 1824 O, 1842 White, *King furth* 1658 *BPD, Kingsfurth*
1703 *MiscDon 251, Kingsforth House* 1826 *MiscDon 82*, cf. *Kingforth*
meerfurr 1666 *BPD, Kings forth Marefurr* 1674 *ib, Kinsfurth Meerefurr*
1685 *ib, Kingforth Marfur* 1761 *MiscDon 251* (*v.* **marfur** 'a furrow
marking a boundary'). The forms are too late to suggest a
convincing etymology. MARSH FM, *per medium Marisscum* (sic)
e13 *HarlCh, usque ad mariscum* eHy3 (p1269) *Bard*, Hy3 *HarlCh,*
the Marsh 1676 BartTB, *Barton Marsh* 1670, 1683, 1696, 1728 *Yarb*,
1799 Young, *y*[e] *Marshe* 1700 *Terrier*, self-explanatory, *v.* **mersc.**
Note also LITTLE MARSH (lost), *Lytylmerche* 1115 (?14) *Bard*,
Litellmersk' m12 (p1269) *ib, Litelmerse* 1184-5 YCh ii, *-mers* 1202
FF, *Litlemerhs* (sic) 1250 ib, *Littilmersk* 1304 Ipm, *Litelmersk* 1331
Ch, *the little Marsh* 1676 BartTB, 1724, 1765, 1788 *Terrier*, *- of*
Barton 1691 *Dudding, the little Marsk* 1737 *BPD, the littel Marsh*
1745 *Terrier*, cf. *Little Marsh Lane* 1827 *MiscDon 82*, *v.* **lytel, mersc,**
said in LNQ vii, 204-6, to be land east of The Haven from Butts
Rd to the Humber Bank, bounded on the east by the Cow Pasture
(for the latter *v.* f.ns. (a) *infra*). The occasional spellings in *-sk* are
noteworthy as Scandinavianised forms. MERE PLANTATION, cf.
the meare 1621 *MiscDon 251, y*[e] *Mear* 1681 *ib 166, the Meer* 1697
Terrier, 1707 *ib, y*[e] *mear* 1709 *ib, Barton Meer* 1712, 1718, 1724 *ib*
(Barrow upon Humber), *the Mear* 1733 *BPD*, *v.* **(ge)mǣre** 'a
boundary', that with Barrow upon Humber, giving name also to
Barrow Mere in Barrow upon Humber parish *supra.* MOUNT HO,
1842 White, 1877 *BPD*, adjoining which was *Mount Close* 1778, 1784
FLDudd, 1824 O, 1877 *BPD*. MOUNT PLEASANT (lost), *Mount*
pleasant 1826 White, presumably a complimentary nickname. NESS
END FM, named from Chowder Ness *supra.* NUT HILL (lost), -
hill 1826 White. ST JAMES CROSS (local), *S*[ct] *James Crosse* 1621
MiscDon 251, S[t] *James Crosse* 1658 *BPD*, 1697 *Terrier, St James*
cross 1681 *MiscDep 166*, 1700 *Terrier, S*[t] *James Cross* 1709 *ib, S*[t]
James's Cross 1788 *BPD*, a medieval cross dedicated to St James,

situated at the point where the Thornton and Burnham roads meet, TA 043206, as Mr Paul Everson informs me. Mr R. Newton comments "said to have replaced a wayside shrine. The foundations of the shrine were exposed when the Home Guard dug a defensive trench there at the beginning of the last war. Foundations destroyed by a bomb." SOUR HILL (lost), *Sowerhill* 1621 *MiscDon 251*, *sourehill* 1658 *BPD*, *Soure hill* 1668 *ib*, *sourhills* 1694 *ib*, *Sore-hill* 1702 *MiscDon 251*, *Sore hill* 1704, 1733 *BPD*, *Sorehill* 1755 *MiscDon 248*, *v.* sūr, hyll, the first el. being used of coarse, worked-out or acid soil. Mr David Neave suggests its location is TA 038208. SOUTH CLIFF, 1842 White. SOUTHFIELD (Kelly), "South field" 1598 AD v, (*the*) *Southfeild* 1621 *MiscDon 251*, 1649 *ParlSurv, the South feild* 1664 *BPD et freq* to *South Feild* 1720 *ib et freq, Barton south Field* 1761 *ib*, self-explanatory, one of the three open fields of Barton. SUMMERDALE. SWAN HILL (now the name of a modern house, as pointed out by Mr R. Newton), *Swanhill* 1633 *AOMB 390*, and cf. *Swanland* 1652 *Foster*, though the forms are late, they may well be self-explanatory. TYRWHITT HALL, *that Capitall mesuage or Tenement called or knowne by the name of Tirwhite Hall* 1624 *BRA 1587*, named from the family of that name, cf. Robert *Turwhite* 1508 Cl, Margaret *Tirwhit* 1590 *Foster*, and cf. also *Tirwhitgarth* 1633 *AOMB 390* (*v.* garðr). WARREN FM (lost) is earlier *Dudmandal* 112 (15) Bridl, *Dudemandale* 112 (l13) Stix (p), eHy3 (p1269) *Bard, Dudmandale alias Barton* (sic) 1537 LP xii, ii, *Dudnamsdale* (sic) 1538-40 LDRH, *Dudmandale* 1633 *AOMB 390, Dudman dale* 1716 *Hill, Dudman Dale or Warren Farm* 1796 *EnclA*, 1822 *Terrier*, and cf. "the king's warren at Barton" 1300 Pat. The earlier name is 'Dudemann's valley', *v.* dæl, dalr, the first el. being the OE pers.n. *Dudemann*, which, it may be noted, occurs as a surn., cf. Geoffrey *Dudman* 1332 *SR*, in the adjacent parish of South Ferriby. The later name is self-explanatory and is in the extreme southern corner of the parish. It is shown on the maps in Rex C. Russell, *The Enclosure of Barton-upon-Humber 1793-6*, Barton Branch, W.E.A., 1968. WESTFIELD HO, cf. *in campo occident' de Barton'* 1294 *Foster, in occidentali campo* 1302 *Nelthorpe, - de Barton* 1586 *BPD*, "West field" 1598 AD v, *the west feild* 1621 *MiscDon 251*, (*the*) *Westfeild* 1649 *ParlSurv*, 1658, 1663 *BPD et freq* to y^e *west feild* 1709 *Terrier, West Feild* 1720 *BPD, the westfield* 1685 *ib, the West Field* 1685 *ib*, 1697 *Terrier, the westfield* (*of Barton*) 1722 *Nelthorpe et passim*,

self-explanatory, *v.* **west, feld,** one of the three open fields of
Barton. WHITE LION, 1842 White. WHITE SWAN, 1842 *ib,*
White Swan Inn 1685 *MM,* cf. *the Inne called the Swanne* 1633
AOMB 390, Swan Inn 1708, 1718 *Foster.* WHITING MILL
BOTTOM. WINDMILL, *Mill* 1824 O.

STREETS, LANES and ROADS

EAST ACRIDGE, 1676 BartTB, *East acridge* 1633 *AOMB 390,* 1649
ParlSurv, (Slipp of Common ground called), the East Accridge 1666,
1877 *BPD.* WEST ACRIDGE, 1676 BartTB, 1780 *MiscDon 111.*
Cf. *the accridge* 1621 *MiscDon 251, - Acridge* 1662 *Terrier,* 1633,
1684, 1685, *BPD,* 1697 *Terrier, ye akrig* 1681 *MiscDep 166, - acreg*
1681 *ib, the Aceridge* 1700 *Terrier,* ackerige 1709 *ib, the acridge* 1717
BPD, originally a topographical p.n., probably 'the oak ridge', *v.* **āc,**
hrycg; the two streets are separated by the High St., Burgate and
Beck Hill. ADLUMSTY (lost), cf. *adlumstig'* l12-e13 (p1269) *Bard,*
from the OGerm pers.n. *Adalhelm, Adelelm* and **stīg, stīgr** 'a path,
a narrow road'. BARROW RD, 1796 *EnclA, superiorem -,*
inferiorem uiam de Barue l12 (p1269) *Bard, uiam -, uie de Barue*
eHy3 (p1269) *ib, a superiore via de barue* Hy3 *HarlCh, Barugate* Hy3
(p1269) *Bard, Barrow high way* 1703 *MiscDon 251, Barrow Lane End*
1719 BartTB, 'the road to Barrow (the adjoining parish)'. BECK
HILL, 1796 *EnclA, - Road* 1822 *Terrier, Beck hill* 1826 White, cf. *le*
Beckefeld 1568-70 *MinAcct, le beckside* 1589-91 *ib, - Beckside* 1605-7
ib, 1607 *Rental, le Backside* (sic) 1618-20 *MinAcct, ye Water Mill*
called ye beckmill 1719 BartTB, *the Beck Mill* (a watermill) 1785
MiscDon 248, the Beck, Beck Drain 1796 *EnclA,* from **bekkr** 'a
stream'. BOWMANDALE, 1668, *(a place called)* 1761 *BPD,*
Bowman dale 1756 *ib,* cf. *the Bowman Dale Drain* 1796 *EnclA.*
According to Barton ii, 31, this is to be identified with *Baunedale* in
f.ns. (b) *infra,* but there does not seem to be anything to indicate
that this is the case. Presumably it is derived from the surn.
Bowman and **deill** 'a share of land'. BRIGG RD, 1796 *EnclA, -*
road 1761 *BPD, the Brigg Road* 1822 *Terrier,* 'the road to Brigg'.
BURGATE, *le Burghgate de Barton'* 1318 *AddCh, Burgate* 1354 Ipm,
1458 WillPCC, *via voc' Burgate Waye* 1535-46 *MinAcct, in quodam*
vico ... vocat Burgait 1565 *BPD, Burgateway* 1576-7 *MinAcct,*
"Burgate street" 1586 AD v, *a certayne street .... called Burgate* 1590

Foster, Burgate waye 1597-8 *MinAcct, via vocat' Burgate Waye* 1613-5 *ib, a certaine street there called Burgate* 1627 *BPD, Burgate* 1796 *EnclA,* 1822 *Terrier,* a common name in towns, derived from OE **burh-geat** 'the town-gate', extended to refer to a street. BURNHAM RD, *Brunnumgate* l12 (p1269) *Bard, uie-, uiam de Brunham* eHy3 (p1269) *ib, Burnam gate* 1621 *MiscDon 251, Burnham gate* 1649 *ParlSurv,* 1658, 1694 *BPD,* 1700 *Terrier, Burnamgate* 1681 *MiscDep 166, Burnholme Gate* 1694, 1704 *BPD, Burnham Gate* 1697 *Terrier,* 1719 BartTB, 1761 *BPD, burnhame gate* 1709 *Terrier, Burnholm gate* 1729 *MiscDon 248, Burnhamgate* 1755 *ib,* 'the road to Burnham (in the neighbouring parish of Thornton Curtis)', *v.* **gata.** BUTCHERY (lost), 1796 *EnclA,* 1826, 1842 White, and note *Market Place or Butchery* 1746 *MiscDon 82.* BUTTS RD, 1827 *MiscDon 82, Butt's road* 1826 White, cf. *a close .... whereupon the butts stand* 1633 *AOMB 390, Butt close* 1652 WillsPCC, - *Close* 1681 *Cragg, the Butts, Butts Close, the Butts Drain* 1796 *EnclA,* the explanation being given in the 1633 reference, which must be to archery butts, *v.* **butt**^{2}. CAISTOR RD, 1796 *EnclA,* self-explanatory. CASTLEDYKE, *Casteldyke* 1458 WillsPCC, *Castledykes* 1633 *AOMB 390, the Castledikes* 1649 *ParlSurv, the highway called Castle dikes* 1651 *BPD, Castle Dykes* 1700 *Terrier, - dikes* 1713 *ib,* y^e *Castle Dike* 1719 BartTB, *Castle Dikes* 1755 *BPD, - dikes* 1797 *Terrier, Castle-Dikes* 1842 White, cf. *castellum in eadem uilla* (i.e. *Barton*^{a}) m12 (p1269) *Bard, castellum .. de Barton*^{a} Hy2 (p1269) *ib, Castellum in eadem uilla* (i.e. *Bartona*) l12, e13 (p1269) *ib, v.* **castel, dīc, dīkr.** The situation of the Norman Castle is shown on Fig. 8 (c) in Warwick Rodwell, "Churches in the Landscape; aspects of topography and planning", in *Studies in Late Anglo-Saxon Settlement,* ed. Margaret L. Faull, Oxford 1984, pp. 1-23. It is possible that Castledyke was part of the bailey of the Castle. CATHERINE ST., cf. *S*$^t.$ *Catherin's well* 1697 Pryme, *v.* Newport St. *infra.* CHANTRY LANE, cf. perhaps *one hous called Chantrey* 1709 *Terrier.* VE iv 69 (1535) records two chantries in Barton - Cantaria de Barton (2x). Presentation was made *ad cantariam sancti Thome martiris infra ecclesiam pochialem* (*sic*) *beate Marie virginis de Barton'* 1492 *Presentation Documents 1492 20* (LAO) and reference has been noted to the *Cantar' voc' Ouresbie chauntrey* 1607 *Rental, v. Owesby land'* (sic) in f.ns. (b) *infra.* CHAPEL LANE, 1796 *EnclA,* 1877 *BPD,* presumably named from *le Chapell de le well* 1565 *BPD, le Chappell on the well* 1590 *Foster,* the site of which is shown on Fig. 8 (c) quoted under Castledyke *supra*. DAM RD, cf. *the damm* 1621 *MiscDon 251*, 1694 *BPD*, - *Damm* 1694 *ib*, - *dame* 1658, 1685 *ib*, - *dam* 1658 *ib*, - *Dam* 1676 BartTB, 1684, 1694, 1761 *BPD*, 1796 *EnclA*, y^e *dam* 1681 *MiscDep 166*, *meadowe called Milldam* 1649 *ParlSurv*, *Barton Mill Dam* 1824 O, and may be identified with *Schadewelledam* eHy3 (p1269) *Bard*, presumably the mill-dam associated with the *stagnum molendini de Scadewelle* l12-e13 (p1269) *Bard* (*v.* Shadwells *supra*), *v.* **dammr**. FAR INGS LANE, cf. *the Farr Innges* 1624 *BRA 1587*, *Farings* 1633 *AOMB 390*, *the farre Inges* 1649 *ParlSurv*, *the far Ingg'* of *Barton* 1650 WillsPCC, *the Farre Inges* 1673 *BPD*, *farr Ings* 1676 BartTB, *the Farr Ings* 1684, 1699, 1720, 1761 *BPD*, and cf. *le ynge* 1535-46 *MinAcct*, - *Inge* 1613-5 *ib*, *the Inges* 1633 *AOMB 390*, - *of Barton* 1649 *ParlSurv*, *Barton Ings* 1676 BartTB, (*the*) *Ings* 1724, 1822 *Terrier*, 'the meadow(s), the pasture(s)', *v.* **eng**. FERRIBY RD, 1796 *EnclA*, cf. *ab inferiori uia de feriby* l12-e13 (p1269) *Bard*, *in transuerso superioris uie de feriby* eHy3 (p1269) *ib*, *Ferrebie highway* 1666 *BPD*, *Fereby hye way* 1681 *MiscDep 166*, *Ferriby high way* 1703 *MiscDon 251*, *le Ferebie Lowe waye* 1586 *BPD*, *Ferraby low way* 1694 *ib*, the road to South Ferriby. FINKLE LANE, 1704 *BPD*, 1796 *EnclA*, *Finkill Lane* 1717 *BPD*, *a place called Finkill Lane* 1794 *MiscDon 248*, cf. *Finkle St.* in Lincoln, PN L 1, 65-6, where it is pointed out that Ekwall, Studies[3] 47-53, has plausibly suggested that this is an obscene name for a 'lovers lane'. *Finkle* cannot be derived from Dan. *vinkel* 'a corner', since this would have given *winkle*. FLEET GATE, "a road called" *Fletgate* 1406 Cl, *via que vocatur*- 1415 *AddCh*, *ffletegate* 1419 LNQ iv, *Fletegate* 1458 WillsPCC, *Fleitgate* 1555 *Foster*, *Fletegate* "Street" 1598 AD v, *Fleetgate* 1676 BartTB, 1731 *LindDep 67*, 1772 *Foster*, 1780 *MiscDon 111*, 1796 *EnclA*, *Fleet-Gate* 1708, 1718 *Foster*, 'the road to the estuary, inland creek', *v.* **flēot**, **gata**, no doubt to what is now known as Barton Haven. GRAVEL PIT RD, cf. *Gravel Pit* 1796 *EnclA*. GREEN LANE, perhaps to be identified with *ad virid' viam* 1302 *Nelthorpe*, self-explanatory, but cf. Green Gate *supra*. HAWTHORN LANE (now East Field Rd, cf. Eastfield Fm *supra*), *uersus uiam Haketorn'* lHy2 (p1269) *Bard*, *uiam* -, *uie de Haketorn'* eHy3 (p1269) *ib*, *uiam que uocatur Haketorne* eHy3 (p1269) *ib*, *semita de Haketorn'* eHy3 (p1269) *ib*, *uiam de Haketornegate* Hy3 (p1269) *ib*, *uia de achetorn* Hy3 *HarlCh*, *viam de Hacyhthorn* (sic) 1302 *Nelthorpe*, *Haketornestich'* (sic), *Haweporpstich* (sic) Hy3 (p1269) *Bard*, *a Way* *called Hawthorne Stigh* 1649 *ParlSurv, Hawthorne Stigh* 1685, 1686, 1704 *BPD, Hothorn Stye* 1719 BartTB, *Hathorn Steigh* 1733 *BPD* and note also *hawthorne* 1668 *ib, Hawthorn(e)* 1697, 1700 *Terrier* and *Haketornhil* eHy3 (p1269) *Bard, Haghthornhill* 1294 *Foster* (*v.* **hyll**). It would appear that *Hawthorn* was originally a p.n., presumably from OE **haca-þorn** ' a thorn' of some kind, this being replaced by **hagu-þorn** 'the hawthorn, the whitethorn'. To this in one instance was added **gata** 'a road', but the rest of the spellings are from **stīg, stīgr** 'a path, a narrow road'. HIGH ST., *Highstreete* 1649 *ParlSurv,* (*the*) *High Street* 1733, 1748 *BPD,* 1778 *FLDudd,* 1798 *Foster,* with *High* in its usual sense in st.ns. of 'chief, important'. HOLYDYKE, - *lane* 1826 White, - *Road* 1877 *BPD.* HORKSTOW RD, 1796 *EnclA, uia de horkestoue* Hy3 (p1269) *Bard, viam de Horkestau* 1302 *Nelthorpe, Horkstow(e) gate* 1621 *MiscDon 251,* 1658, 1685 *BPD,* 1703 *MiscDon 251,* 1729 *ib 248, Horkstoe gaite* 1697 *Terrier, Horkstow Gate* 1719 BartTB, 1720 *BPD,* 1755 *MiscDon 248, horstow gait* 1709 *Terrier,* 'the road to Horkstow', *v.* **gata.** HUNGATE, *terram Hug' de Hundegate* eHy3 (p1269) *Bard, in vico qui appellatur* - Hy3 (p1269) *ib,* - *de Barton* 1302 *Nelthorpe* (p), *venellam de* - 1318 *AddCh, Hundegate* 1327 *SR* (p), *Hundgate* 1354 Ipm, *Hungate* 1458 WillsPCC, (*a certaine streete ... called*) *Houndgate* 1651, 1693, 1713, 1748 *BPD, Hound Gate* 1699 *ib, the street called Hound gate* 1755 *ib,* 'the street of the dogs', *v.* **hundr** (gen.pl. **hunda**), **gata,** cf. Hungate in Lincoln, PN L **1,** 75. MALTBY LANE is *Maltkiln Lane* 1796 *EnclA,* self-explanatory, the modern name being presumably from the *Maltby* family, cf. John *Maltby* 1796 *EnclA.* MARKET LANE, 1817 *MiscDon 82,* "the way called" *Marketgate* 1343 Cl, *the Markett Laine* 1681 *BPD, the market lane* 1700 *Terrier, Markittlain* 1709 *ib.* MARKET PLACE, 1796 *EnclA, the Market(t) place* 1633 *AOMB 390,* 1684, 1719 *BPD,* 1777 *LindDep 67, the Markett stead* 1699 *BPD, the Market Stead* 1748 *ib, Market Place or Butchery* 1746 *MiscDon 82,* (*v. Butchery supra*), and cf. *Mercatum de Barton'* 1202 Ass, *in foro de Barton'* 1305 ib, "Barton market" 1369 Ipm. The market is referred to as *mercatum* in 1086 DB. MARSH LANE, cf. Marsh Fm *supra.* NEWPORT ST, *a certaine street ... called Newport* 1720 *MiscDon 251, a street there called* - 1732 *BPD, a certain Street or place there called Saint Catherine's or* - 1771, 1790 *MiscDon 248, a certain Street ... called* - 1785 *ib,* cf. *Neuport* 1185-91 (15) YCh v, 'the new town, market', *v.* **nīwe, port**[2] and cf. Newport in Lincoln, PN L **1,** 30 and Catherine

St. *supra.* PASTURE RD, *the* - 1796 *EnclA.* PRESTON LANE, presumably named from the family of John *Preston* 1826 White. PRIESTGATE, 1684 *BPD*, 1796 *EnclA*, "a street called" *Prestegate* 1386 Cl, *Preistgate* 1697 *BPD*, "the street of the priest(s)', *v.* prēost (probably in the gen.pl. prēosta), gata. ROBINSON ROW (lost), 1796 *EnclA*, - *row* 1826 White, no doubt named from the family of Thomas *Robinson* 1676 BartTB. SOUTERGATE, 1655, 1657, 1674, 1684 *BPD*, 1796 *EnclA*, 1826 White, *Sootergate* 1697 *BPD*, *Souther-gate* 1700 *Terrier, Southergate* 1707, 1709 *ib*, though the forms are late this would appear to be 'the street of the shoe-makers', *v.* sūtere, gata, and cf. dial. *souter.* SOUTHGATE, now Whitecross St. *infra.* It is *Southgate* 1458 WillsPCC, 1643 (1648), 1653, 1713, 1755 *BPD, South gate* 1688 *ib*, - *Gate ib*, *Southgatestreete* 1624 *BRA 1587, a street called Southgate* 1654 WillsPCC, *Southgate Streete* 1660 *BPD, a certain Street there comonly called .... Southgate and sometimes ... Whitecross Street* 1779 *BPD*, self-explanatory, *v.* sūð, gata. TOFTS RD, *the* - 1796 *EnclA*, 1877 *BPD*, cf. *the Tofts* 1694 *ib*, 1697 *Terrier, y^e* - 1700 *ib*, - *tofts* 1709 *ib*, 'the building sites, the curtilages, the messuages', *v.* toft. WATERSIDE RD, 1796 *EnclA*, cf. *the Waterside* 1693 BartTB. WATERSLACKS RD, - *Lane* 1796 *EnclA*, cf. *water slackes* 1621 *MiscDon 251, the great Waterslacke* 1664 *BPD, water slacke* 1666 *ib, the Water Slackes* 1697 *Terrier, ye water-slacks* 1700 *ib, Water Slacks* 1761 *BPD.* This appears to be a compound of wæter 'water', probably in the sense 'wet', and slakki 'a shallow valley, a hollow in the ground', a Scand. word rare in eastern England, cf. the comments in PN Nt 290 s.v. slakki. WESTFIELD RD, *West Field Road* 1796 *EnclA*, cf. Westfield Ho *supra.* WHITECROSS ST., 1796 *EnclA*, formerly Southgate *supra*, cf. *a certain Street there comonly called .... Southgate and sometimes .... Whitecross Street* 1779 *BPD*, presumably a reference to a stone cross. WILLOWTREE LANE. WINSHIP RD (lost), - *road* 1826 White, *a lane called Winshipplane* 1713 *BPD, Winship Lane* 1755, 1761 *ib*, 1796 *EnclA*, and cf. *Winship pit* 1719 BartTB, *Winship Farm* 1777 *BPD*, named from the *Winship* family, cf. George *Winshoppe* 1607 *BT*, Edward *Winship* 1653 *ib.*

Field-Names

Principal forms in (a) are 1796 *EnclA*. Spellings dated 1565, 1586, 1643 (1648), 1651[1], 1653, 1655, 1657, 1658, 1663, 1664, 1665[1], 1666, 1673, 1674[2], 1678, 1684[1], 1684[2], 1685, 1688, 1692[1], 1693, 1694, 1695, 1696, 1699, 1704, 1713[1], 1715[1], 1717, 1720, 1732, 1733, 1737, 1738, 1745[1], 1748, 1752, 1755, 1756, 1760, 1761[1], 1774, 1788[1], 1795, and 1877 *BPD*, 1568-70, 1589-91, 1605-7, and 1618-20 *MinAcct*, 1578, 1606[1], 1671[1], 1674[1], 1697, 1700, 1707, 1709, 1712, 1718[1] (Barrow upon Humber), 1724, 1730, 1745[2], 1765, 1788[2], and 1822 *Terrier*, 1590, 1606[2], 1652[1], 1671[2], 1684[3], 1708, and 1718[2] *Foster*, 1607 *Rental*, 1621, 1703, and 1761[2] *MiscDon 251*, 1624 *BRA 1587*, 1633 and 1649[2] *AOMB 390*, 1649[1] *ParlSurv*, 1651[2] and 1652[2] WillsPCC, 1665[2] *Nelthorpe*, 1681[1] *MiscDep 166*, 1681[2] *Cragg*, 1676, 1715[2], and 1719 BartTB, 1698 *MiscDon 92*, 1713[2] BarrowTB, 1729, 1742, 1755, 1785, and 1789 *MiscDon 248*, 1778 and 1784 *FLDudd*, and 1817[2] and 1827 *MiscDon 82*. Other sources are noted.

(a) a Building called the Bell Foundry; Bradwell Cl (*Bradewelle* 1233 (p1269) *Bard*, *Bradwells* 1658, v. **brād, wella**); Breck hill 1842 White; the Brick Cl 1795, 1796; Close late called Bryans Cl (*Bryans close* 1624, *Brian -* 1633, named from the *Brian* family and **clos(e)**, cf. *Elenor Bryan* 1540 *Inv*); Burnham pit 1784; Burnham Stigh 1761 (1649[1], 1685, - *Steigh* 1658, 1694, 1720, - *steigh* 1665, - *stigh* 1674[2], *Burnholm stigh* 1666, *Burnholme Stigh* 1694, v. **stīg, stigr** and cf. Burnham Rd *supra*); Burnthouse Farm 1795; (the) Common 1765, 1788[2]; Constable Cl 1795, 1796 (*The Constable Close in the East Acridge* 1719, *the Constable close* 1737, cf. East Acridge *supra*); the Cowpasture 1795, 1822, the late Cow Pasture 1817[2] (cf. *the Cowplat* 1621, *the Cow platt* 1676, (*platt ... commonly called*) - 1678, *the Cowplatt* 1717, 1755 (v. **plat[2]** 'a small piece of ground'), and *the Cowphill* (sic) 1691 *Dudd*); Cottage House ... formerly Dobson's 1788[2] (- *Dobsons* 1730, 1745, named from the *Dobson* family, cf. *Mr Dobson* 1666, Mr William *Dobson* 1676 BartTB); Dobson's Hedge 1761[2] (cf. prec.); Dovecot Cl (*dovecote close* 1693, *dovecoat Closes* 1713, *dovecoate Close* 1755, cf. *one Close with a dovehouse called or knowne by the name of the dove house Close* 1624, v. **douve-cote, douve-hous**); Messuage and Homestead called East Cote (cf. West Cote in (a) *infra*); the East Lanes of Barton upon Humber 1788[1] (1748, *the East laines of Barton* 1684[1], - *Laines of Barton* (*upon Humber*) 1699, 1745[1], 1755, *the East Lane Close* 1745[1], *East Laines Close* 1755, presumably ME **leyne, lain** 'a layer, a tract of arable land'); Ferris Cl 1774 (1666, 1719, named from the *Ferris* family, cf. *Henry Ferris* 1681[2]); Football Cl 1796, 1822 (1696, *Foot Ball Close* 1738); the fore Ings Road ((*the*) *fore Inges* 1621, 1624, 1658, - *Ings* 1676, 1755, (*the*) *Fore* - 1666, 1733, *the foreings* 1633, *v.* **fore** 'in front', **eng**, cf. Far Ings Lane *supra* and Middle Ings *infra*); Froggot(t)s Land 1778, 1784 (presumably from the surn. *Froggot*); Gallow Dale Cl (*Gallowdale* (*Close*) 1649[1], 1697, y^e *galedal Close* (sic) 1709, *gallow-dale Close* 1733, *the Gallowdale close* 1737, *Gallow daile Close* 1685, - *close* 1707, 'the share of land near the gallows', *v.* **galga, deill**); Gorrie hill half Acre 1788[1]; Grimesgate Rd (in Barrow *supra*); Hobson's House 1765, 1788[2], 1822 (*Hobsons house* 1724 (it was given to the church in 1626), named from the *Hobson* family, cf. John *Hobson* 1628 *Inv*); the Home Cl 1877; the Horse Pasture; Houlegate Swarth 1755 *MiscDon 248* (*Houlgate* - 1729, and cf. *the Hole Marsh* 1676); the Humber Bank; Ings Drain (*the Inge*(*s*)) dike 1663, 1666, cf. Far Ings Lane *supra*); the Intack Lane 1795, 1822 (*the Intack* 1737, *v.* **inntak** 'a piece of land taken in or enclosed', as elsewhere in the parish); the Little Intack 1795, 1796, *v.* **inntak**); Knot Hill 1822 *v.* **knǫttr** 'a hillock, etc.'); the Lings 1765 (1707, 1724, 1745[2], *v.* **lyng** 'heather', presumably in the sense 'places where heather grows'); the little Close 1877; long Close part of the East Field (*the longe close* 1666, *the Long* - 1707, y^e *long Closis* 1709, *the long Closes* 1733); Markhams Cl 1788[2] (named from the *Markham* family, cf. John *Markham* 1610 Admin); the Middle Ings 1761[1] (1676, 1684[1], 1694, 1755, (*the*) *middle* - 1676, 1733, *the Middle Inges* 1621, 1649[1], *Middle Inges wathstead, the middleing*(*e*)*s* 1633, 1658, *the mid Inge* 1621, cf. Far Ings Lane *supra*); Miller Cl 1761[1] (either from the occupational name or the derived surn., but the earliest reference to such a family so far noted is Thomas *Miller* 1842 White); old Millhill 1761[1] (... *wheron a Mill heirtofore stood called the Broken Mill* 1649[1], *Mill-hill* 1703, *the Mill hill* 1756, cf. *molendinus Bartonye* 1115 (?14) *Bard, ex meridionali parte molendini monachorum de Bard'* eHy3 (p1269) *ib*, *de tribus molendinis Bartonis* m12 (p1269) *ib*, *de molendino de fonte de Barton* 1202 Ass, *v.* **myln, hyll**; there were a number of mills in Barton); Morrel Cl 1785 (no doubt from a surn.); the Outgangs Rd (*the Outgangs* 1733, 'roads to the outer pasture', *v.* **ūt, ggang**); Paradise Cl near the Beck (*Paradise Close* 1614 *FLMisc*, - *close* 1684[3], *one close calld Paradise* 1700, *one Close Called Parradis* 1709, presumably a complimentary name, but ME *paradis*(*e*) also denoted 'a garden, an orchard, a pleasure-garden', *v.* **paradis(e)**); Paragon terrace 1842 White; Parker Cl (named from the *Parker* family, cf. Richard *Parker* 1578 *BT*); the Pasture Drain; Pasture Lane 1822; Pasture South Road; Pond Cl (1681[2], - *close* 1652[2], *the pond Close* 1719, cf. *a Close ... called Pond Garth* 1785 (*v.* **garðr**), *ad stagnum* e13 (113) *Stix* (p), cf. Sedge Cl, *infra*); Poors Watermill; Prospect Place 1842 White; Providence House 1877 (between Chapel Lane & Holydyke); Queens Leys, - Leas (- *Leaz* 1761 *MiscDon 251*, *v.* **lǣs**); Quickset Cl; (in the West Field opposite to) Saint Trunnion's 1774 (*St Tronians* 1665[1], 1694, *St Trunions tree* 1681[1], *St Troynian's* 1691, *St Trunyon's Tree 1697 Pryme*; trunnion is recorded in a single example in NED, where it is queried as a "perversion of Trin-union or Tri-union, used as an asseveration or oath", *v.* also NED s.v. *trinune, trin-une* referring to the Trinity. It seems likely that the forms here represent variations of this word, and that this is the meaning of the f.n.); Saxby Gate ("a certain Gate or Road") (- *gate* 1652[2], *Saxby gate* 1658, *Saxby g[t]* 1666, *Saxby-Gate* 1703, *saxebigategreines* lHy2 (p1269) *Bard, Saxby gate, - meere* 1649[1], *Saxby gait -, - gate grainings* 1681[1], 1700, 1709, 1733, 'the road to Saxby', *v.* **gata**; *-greines* in the lHy2 form is presumably from the pl. of ON **grein** 'a small valley forking off from another', while the later *grainings* is presumably from **grein** and the pl. of **eng** 'meadows, pastures', a Scand. compound, an earlier example of which occurs as *le Grayninges* in Goxhill f.ns. (b); for a comparable name, cf. *Graynings* 1558, PN YW 7 196); Saxby Road Pit; Thomas Scriveners Acridge Cl (cf. East, West Acridge *supra*); Sedge Cl (*the Segge Close* 1664, *the Segg* - 1745[1], - *close* 1760, *Close of Meadow or Passture Ground ... heretofore called or known by the Name of Pond close and now commonly called or known by the name of Seg Close* 1789, *v.* **secg** and cf. Pond Cl *supra*); the Seeds Cl 1827; the Sheep Dike 1822, Sheep dike 1842 White; Shields Cl 1788[1] (1748, *Sheilds Close* 1699, named from the family of Richard *Sheildes* 1617 *BT*); Shoulder of Mutton (alluding to the shape); Spittle Stigh Gate 1761[1] (- *stigh gate* 1621, *spittle steigh gayt* 1664, *Spittle Steigh* 1697[1], 1720, 1729, - *gate* 1703, - *Gate* 1761, *spittle steigh* 1665, *Spittle Stigh* 1666, 1685, 1694, 1700, *Spitell* - 1719, *Spitlestegh* 1709, 'path to or beside a hospital', cf. *a crofto Hospital'* eHy3 (p1269) *Bard, v.* **spitel, stīg, stīgr, gata**, presumably that referred to as "the hospital of St Leonard, Barton on this side Humber" 1259 Pat); Sugar Cl 1796, 1877 (1715, presumably a complimentary nickname for sweet land); Tangarth; Thornton Rd (*uiam que ducit ad Thornton* 1115 (14) *Bard, - dirigit' uersus Thorentona* e13 (p1269) *Bard, Thornetonmerstig* Hy3 (p1269) *ib* (*v.* **(ge)mǣre** 'a boundary', **stīg, stīgr**), *Thornton(-)gate* 1621, 1658, 1685, *-Gate* 1697[1], 1761[1], *thornton gate* 1709, 'the road to Thornton Curtis', *v.* **gata**); the Town's Intack (cf. the Intack Lane *supra*); Town end Rd (cf. *the Townes end of Barton* 1649[1]); Tythe Acre 1788[2] (*Tithacre* 1765, *v.* **teoða, æcer**); the Vicarage Cl 1788[2] (cf. *ye Vicarage* in f.ns. (b) *infra*); the Vinegar Hill 1877; Waddle hill 1761, - Cl 1817 *Map*, Waddel hill 1842 White (*Waddlehill* 1658, *Waddle Hill* 1697, *Wadle* - 1700, (*the*) *waddle hill* 1621, 1666, 1715, - *gate* 1703 and cf. *Waddelholegates* e13 (p1269) *Bard*, in which *holegate* is presumably 'the road running in a hollow', *v.* **hol**[2], **gata**; *Waddle* is obscure, but Dr John Insley makes the interesting suggestion that it might be an unrecorded OE *wædel* or *wadol*, late diminutives formed with an *-il* or *-ul* suffix from OE **(ge)wæd** 'a ford', hence 'the little ford')); Water Mill Cl; Waterslades Drain; messuage or Tenement called Watmans 1752 (*the Messuage comonly called Watmans grounde* 1651[1], presumably from a surn.); Messuage and

Homestead called West Cote (cf. Westcott Fm in Barrow *supra*); the White House 1795 (1737); Willow Cl 1789; Common Wold (*v.* **wald**).

(b) *Alkazedail* 1250 FF, 1250 (p1269) *Bard* (copy of FF) ('Alcaz' share, portion of land', *v.* **deill**, the first el. being an obscure pers.n. or surn. found in *terra que fuit Rogeri Alcaz* eHy3 (p1269) *Bard*); *the Alms dale, - peas Dale* 1676 (cf. "Persons to sow their Alms Peas within the time limited by the Jury and good peas" BartTB 17, *v.* **ælmes(se), pise, deill**); *Arnolds Tenement* 1655, *a Toft or Tenement ... formerly called by the name of Arnolds ground* 1657 (from the family of Leonard *Arnolde* 1546 *Inv*); *Atkinson Lands* 1698 (from the family of Thomas *Atkinson* 1649 *FLMisc*); *one Barne called the Backlath* 1652[1] ('rear barn'. *v.* **back, hlaða**); *Baldwine Gaire* Hy3 (p1269) *Bard* (from the pers.n. or surn. *Baldwin* (OGerm *Baldwin*), cf. John *Baldewyn* 1332 *SR*, and ON **geiri** 'a triangular plot of ground'); *the barnard hutt* 1666, *y*[e] *great Bernard Hut* 1681[1]; *Baunedale* 112-e13 (p1269) *Bard* (a Scand. compound of **baun** 'a bean' and **deill** 'a share or portion of land'); *Beggar bush* 1703 ('scrubland frequented by beggars', cf. PN Gl 2 53, PN O 428, *v.* **beggere, busc**); *Beley milne* 1632-3 *MinAcct* (presumably from the surn. *Beeley* and **myln**); *Belt(e) land* 1633 (perhaps referring to a line of trees, *v.* **belt**); *blackman stigh* 1621, *Blackman steigh* 1658, - *stigh* 1666, *Blackeman Stigh* 1685, - *Steigh* 1694 (from the ME surn. *Blacman* (OE *Blǣcmann*) and **stīg, stīgr** 'a path, a narrow road'; the same name occurs in f.ns. (b) of Barnetby le Wold *supra*); *Blac sic* 1233 (p1269) *Bard, the black Syke* 1666 (*v.* **blæc, sīc, sīk**); *Blakemoldes* (sic) eHy3 (p1269) *Bard* (to be identified with the Black Mold in f.ns. (a) in Barrow upon Humber, *supra*, *v.* **blæc, molde**); *Bondebigate graungys* lHy2 (p1269) *Bard* (*v.* **grange**), *Bonbie gate* 1621, *Bon(d)by gate* 1649[1], *Bonby* - 1658, 1681[1], 1694, 1697[1], - *Gate* 1695, 1719, *Bondby g*[t] 1666, cf. *uiam de Bondeby* e13 (p1269) *Bard, uie de -* Hy3 *HarlCh* ('the road to Bonby', *v.* **gata**); *Bondelbridge* 1653, *Bondell Brigge* 1658 (in Southgate); *Braddewat* e13 (p1269) *Bard* (in spite of the *-dd-*, this is probably 'the broad ford', *v.* **brād, vað**); *Brindtoft* 1298 Ipm, *Brend-* 1301-2 IpmR, 1301-2 Inqaqd ('burnt messuage', *v.* **brende**[2], **toft**); *Broadacre* 1649[1] (*v.* **brād, æcer**); (*de*) *Brok'* a1213 RA iv (p) (*v.* **brōc**); *the farme called Brownes farme* 1624, *Guy Brown's Ground at the Waterside* 1693 BartTB, *Browns meadow* 1713[1] (for an earlier reference to the family name, *v.* Edward *Browne* 1575 Admin); *Bucks acre* 1684[2] (from the family of William *Buck* 1642 *BT*); *Buterhawes* eHy3 (p1269) *Bard, Butter-* e13 (p1269) *ib*, Hy3 (p1269) *ib* (*v.* **butere, haga**[1], probably denoting an enclosure with rich pasture which produced good butter); *Chequer land* 1633 (*v.* **cheker**); *Cocke boat pitt* 1695, *Cockboat Pit* 1720 ('pool in which a small boat was moored', *v.* **pytt** and *cockboat* NED s.v.); *the Common* 1676; *Cony garth* 1666 ('rabbit warren', either an altered form of **coningre** or *v.* **coni, garðr**; it is noteworthy that Coney Garth is very common in this wapentake, so that derivation from *coni* and **garðr** seems more likely); *the Copieholdyard* 1652[1], *unum Croftam* (sic) *vocat le Coppihold yard* 1671[2] (cf. *Customs for the Copyhold lands* 1719, *v.* ME **copie-hold, geard**); *the Corn Field* 1676; *Cotegarth* 1458 WillsPCC, *Coategarthland* 1633 (*v.* **cot, garðr, land**); *Creake Close* 1684[2] (*v.* ME **crike** 'inlet' and cf. *Gascrick supra*); *Cuckstoole dike* 1684[2] (*v.* ME **cuk-stol, dīc, dīk**); (*de*) *Dene de Barton* 1368 *FF* (p) (*v.* **denu**); *the dike Acre* 1658 (*v.* **dīc, dīk, æcer**); *Driescharthe* e13 *HarlCh* (possibly 'the dry gap', *v.* **drȳge, sceard**); *drunken peece* 1658 (perhaps either 'awkwardly shaped close' or 'land on which malting barley was grown'); *the Eastermostlong Close* 1733 ('most easterly part of Long Close', cf. Long Close in f.ns. (a) *supra*); *the Estliteldale in orientali Campo de Bartona* Hy3 (p1269) *Bard* (*v.* **ēast, lȳtel, deill**, and cf. *Suthelit(t)eldale* and *liteldale infra*); *the Farr Meerfurr* 1694 (*v.* **marfur**); *Feribie acres* 1633, *Ferrebie headland* 1621, *Fer(r)eby meere* 1649[1], *Ferrebie meer* 1666, *Ferrabymear* 1676, *Ferriby Meer* 1697[1], *Ferryby mear* 1700 (named from South Ferriby with **æcer, hēafod-land** and (**ge)mǣre**); *finnesacra* (probable reading) eHy3 (p1269) *Bard* (Dr J. Insley suggest that this is 'Finn's field', *v.* **æcer**, the first el. being ON *Finnr*, ODan *Fin*); *Forkedal'* 1185-91 (e14) Bridl, *forkedales* eHy3 (p1269) *Bard*, e13 (l13) *Stix* (presumably from OE *forca* 'a fork', in some topographical sense, and **deill**); *the four nooked close* 1633; *foxedale* eHy3, Hy3 (p1269) *Bard*, *foxendale gate* 1621, *Foxendale gate* 1649[1], *Foxendale* 1733, *Fosendale* (sic) 1742 (*v.* **fox, deill**, the suffix -*en*- being adjectival or dial. pl.); *foxelstig(h')* e13 (l13) *Stix*, *Folkesstiye* (sic) Hy3 (p1269) *Bard* (perhaps *v.* **fox-hol, stīg**); *the Furlong* 1720 (*v.* **furlang**); *Goldburgh Wra* 1415 *AddCh* (from the fem. pers.n. *Goldburg* with **vrá** 'a nook or corner of land'); *Gosemer* eHy3 (p1269) *Bard*, *Gosemere* Hy3 (p1269) *ib*, *the gose myers* 1621, *goosemire gate* 1658, *Goosemire* - 1733, (*the*) *Goos(e)mire(s)* 1649[1], 1703, 1733, *Goosemire lane* 1733 ('the goose pool', *v.* **gōs, mere**, in the later forms *mere* being replaced by *mire* (ON **mýrr**)); *Gospellane end(e)*, *Gospell lane* 1633 (referring to the Rogationtide ceremony of beating the bounds, *v.* **gospel**); *the Gowle alias Cowslipp Hill* 1649[1], *the Goole* 1673 ('the ditch', *v.* **goule**); *del Grene* 1344 Cl (p) (*v.* **grēne**[1]); *Grimesacra* eHy3 (p1269) *Bard* ('Grīm's plot of arable or cultivated land', *v.* **æcer**, the pers.n. being probably ODan *Grīm* and note *iii bouatas terre in Bartona que fuerunt Radulfi filii Grim* c. 1140 Dane, *troftum quod Grim quondam tenuit* e13 (p1269) *Bard* and *terre quam Rad' fil' Grijm dedit* eHy3 (p1269) *ib*); *Gunnildedaile* Hy3 (p1269) *Bard* ('Gunnhild's allotment', from the ON fem. pers.n. *Gunnhildr* and **deill**, a Scand. compound); *Hallclose* 1633, *the Hall Close* 1719; *Halledaile* l12-e13 (p1269) *Bard* (*v.* **hall, deill**); *handle pit* 1719; *Hauerflat* 1185-91 (e14) Bridl (from **hafri** 'oats' and **flat**); *Hingingdale* 1658, *Hing-, hingindale* 1666, 1704, *Hingingdale bottome* 1664 ('steep valley', *v.* **hangende, dalr**, with **botm**); *Horkstouhawes* eHy3 (p1269) *Bard* (from

the neighbouring parish name Horkstow and the pl. of **haga**[1] 'an enclosure');
Horstowe meere 1649[1], *Horstow meere* 1666 ('the boundary with Horkstow', *v.*
(ge)mǣre); *houedland* Hy3 (p1269) *Bard, the headland* 1621, *the Headland* 1665,
1673, 1704, *One Acr called the headland* 1666 (*v.* **hǫfuð, hēafod-land**, Scand.
hǫfuð having been replaced by the corresponding English word); Huckback Hill
1733 ('the hump-backed hill', cf. NED s.v. *huck*[1]); *Humbre mylne* 1394 Pat, *the
Humber Mill* 1676, *one water-milne called Humber Mill* 1700 (self-explanatory);
Law garth 1652[2] (*Law* is a freq. spelling for *Low* in LNR); *Leddegrindels* e13
(p1269) *Bard, Lethgrindles* eHy3 (p1269) *ib* (obscure); (*a Way called) Lincoln(e)
gate* 1621, 1649[1], 1658, 1700, - *gayt* 1664, - *g^t* 1666, - *Gate* 1704, - *gait* 1709,
Lincolne gate 1665[1], cf. *a uia qua itur ad linc'* lHy2 (p1269) *Bard, a uia Linc'*
eHy3 (p1269) *ib, inter uiam Linc' & uiam de Bondeby* e13 (p1269) *ib, super
communem viam Lincolnie* e13 *HarlCh, a uia Lincolnie* Hy3 *ib* ('the road to
Lincoln', *v.* **gata**); *litteldale* e13 (p1269) *Bard* (*v.* **lytel, deill**); *Mr Long Folly Close*
1719 (one of several examples in LNR where *folly* is used of a piece of land
and not of a building); *the lowe waye* 1621, *the low way* 1658, 1700, *the lowe -*
1663, *ye low -* 1681[1], *the Low -* 1694, 1704, 1733, *the Lowway of Barton* 1692[1]
(self-explanatory); *above the Loweside, shott called Lowside* 1649[1]; *two closes called
the Mayden head* 1611 WillsL (the significance of ME **maidenhede** 'virginity' in
f.ns. has not so far been properly explained); *le meare gate* 1665[2] (*v.* **(ge)mǣre**,
gata and Mere Plantation *supra*); *ye litle merfer* 1681[1] (*v.* **marfur**); *place called
Mewith* 1591 AD iv, *Mewyth* 1684[3] (obscure); *middle hill(gate)* 1666, 1681[1]; *y^e
Midle way* 1681[1], *the Middle way* 1697[1], 1700; *Mikelden lande* 1633 (perhaps *v.*
micel, mikill, denu, though the latter is very rare in north L); *cottage called the
mill ground,* 1651[2]; *mushaudale* e13 (p1269) *Bard* (*v.* **mūs, haugr** 'a (burial)
mound, a hill', **deill**); *uiam que uocatur Nautmarket* Hy3 (p1269) ('cattle market',
v. **naut, market** and cf. Market Lane, Market Place *supra*); *Neuland* 1382, 1384
Peace, 1386 Cl all (p) (*v.* **nīwe, land**); *James Nicholson land* 1703; *One Close ...
called Nine acres* 1678; *the Northallstint* 1666 (*v.* **stint** 'allotted share of
pasturage'); *Owesby land'* 1568-70, *Owresbye landes* 1589-91, 1605-7, *Owresby
landes* 1607, *Owesbie landes* 1618-20 (referring to the *Owresbye Chauntrey* 1587-91,
Cantar' voc Ouresbie chauntrey 1607, cf. Chantry Lane *supra*); *Ox pasture Ings*
1676 (*v.* **eng**); *Parkers close* 1624 (the surn. has not been noted in the sources
searched); *the Parsonage Hall* 1700, *the Parsonage house* 1713[1], *the Parsonage
Hutt* 1733; *peninghil* e13 (p1269) *Bard* (Dr John Insley suggests that this is a
compound of ON *penningr* 'a penny, a silver coin' and **hyll**, perhaps with
reference to rent); *pigeon land' apud le Beckfeld'* 1568-70, *Pigeon landes* 1589-91,
1607, 1618-20, *pigeon -* 1605-7; *the great pitt* 1633 (*v.* **pytt**); *Rafeneshaudale* e13
(p1269) *Bard, Raueneshaudale* e13, eHy3, Hy3 (p1269) *ib,* 'Hrafn's mound', from
the ON pers.n. *Hrafn* and **haugr** with **deill**, a Scand. compound); *Ratten Rowe*

1643 (1648) (a derogatory term, usually for delapidated, rat-infested dwellings, v. raton, räwc); *Ravonscrosse* 1652[2], *Ravens Cross* 1658, *Raines cross* 1715[1] (cf. *Rafeneshaudale supra*, v. cros); *Redcliffe* 1370-1 IpmR, *Radclif* 1371 Cl ('the red cliff or bank', v. rēad, clif); *Redfleth* lHy2 (p1269) *Bard* (perhaps 'the red stream', v. flēot); *Safendaile* 1719 (v. deill); *Salmuddale* (sic) eHy3 (p1269) *Bard* (p) (prob. 'Salmund's share of land', v. deill, the first el. being ON *Salmundr*, ODan *Salmund*, with nasalizing stroke of the -u- omitted, for which v. *Insley* 3, f.n.2); (*de*) *Saltemars* 1352 *Cor* (p), (*de*) *Saltmerks* 1381 Ipm (p) ('the salt marsh', v. scalt, mersc, the metathesised second el. in the 1381 spelling showing Scand. influence); *Sandy-lane* 1700, *Sande lane* 1709; *Scurpit* lHy2 (p1269) *Bard*, 1331 Ch (possibly 'the polluted pool, covered with algal or other scum', v. sceorf, scurf, pytt, cf. Shurlach PN Ch 2 210); *Shepecote close* 1606[2], *sheepcote* - 1614 (v. shep-cote); *shooteing furrs* 1658, *Shutting Furrow, Shooting furrowes* 1697[1] ('furrows extending beyond the ends of adjacent ones', v. shooting and for *furr* 'a furrow', EDD s.v. *fur(r)* sb1); *Skrempholm* 1354 Ipm, v. holmr, the first el. may be, as Dr John Insley agrees, the Scand. byname *Skrœmir*, *Skrœma, proposed by Ekwall (DEPN) for Scremby and Scremthorpe, both L; the latter has the forms *Skrempthorp* 1503 and - alias *Skerenthorp* 1571); *Smytheg^i mholme* (sic) eHy3 (p1269) *Bard*; *ye South End* 1719; *one Stagg Garth* 1707, *One Stack garth* 1724, 1745[2] ('the rickyard', v. ME stakgarth (ON stakkgarðr)); *little Holes called Stintholes* 1649[1] (the sense of *stint* here is uncertain, and note that the same name occurs in the neighbouring parish of Barrow f.ns. (b) and v. comment at end of this Section); *ye Stone Gate* 1719, *Stone gate end* 1658, v. stān, gata); *the Stonepitts* 1649[1], *Stone pitt* 1694 (v. stān, pytt); *cotage ... called Stowes garth* 1649[1] (from the family of *Jennet Stowe* 1574 *BT* and garðr); *Sutheli(t)eldale, suthlitteldale* eHy3 (p1269) *Bard* (v. sūð and cf. *Estliteldale* and *litteldale supra*); *Swainesdaile* eHy3 (p1269) *Bard* (perhaps 'Sveinn's share of land', v. deill, the first el. would then be the ON pers.n. *Sveinn* and a further Scand. compound); *The Swath* 1694, *the Swarth* 1697, *ye Swarth aker* 1709 (v. swæð); *ten acre land* 1658; *Theuestih* l12 HarlCh ('path infested by thieves', v. þēof, stīg); *thingau-, Thinghaudale, Ting-, tynghoudale* eHy3 (p1269) *Bard, Tingaudale* eHy3 (p1269) *ib*, *Tinghaudale* Hy3 (p1269) *ib* ('the moot mound', v. þing, haugr, with deill 'a share of land'); *Tiruelhou* l12 Dane (obscure); *Goddard Tripps land* 1664, *John Tripp's Close* 1719 (cf. also Mr John *Tripp* 1668); *Twygrayn* 1371 Cl, *Twigraynes* 1370-1 IpmR ('the double forks', v. twī, grein, in which grein presumably refers to the forks of a stream, or perhaps it is in the dial. sense of *grain* 'a small valley forking off from another'. Cf. also the f.n. *Twyngreyn* 1190 (PN YE 324)); *valterdalvelles, -dalewelles* e13 (l13) Stix (perhaps 'the springs belonging to a man called *Walter Dale*', v. wella); *vicarage* 1606[1], *The vicarage house was burnt downe in (or about) the yeare of our Lord (god)*

1642 (& was never since rebuilt) 1671[1], *A New built Viccaridge House* 1724; *Wadthekersting* (sic) e13, (p1269) *Bard* (obscure); *le Wale* 1349 *Cor* (perhaps from OE **walu** 'a ridge of earth or stone', perhaps 'a ditch, and embankment'); *Mesuage or Tenement called Wallers ferme* 1624 (from the family of Ellen *Waller* 1588 *BT*); *Wardal* 1185-91 (e14) Bridl; *Westaby Garth* 1614 *FLMisc* (from the family of Robert *Westeby* 1529 Wills ii and **garðr**); *Westenges* 1250 FF (*v.* **west**, **eng**); *the West Milne* 1621; *A Windmillhill where A windmill stood wch is blowen downe* 1633; *Woods Lande* 1633.

Note on *Stintholes* by John Field: This seems to have a mining connexion.   NED, s.v. *stint, sb*[1]. (10), has *stint-holer,* 1897 quot. "the man who undercuts the coal by 'piece'", where *stint* means probably 'piece', cf. NED entry for *holer,* 1891 quotation, "*Holer's Day or Stint,* the measure of undercutting, undermining, or curving a length of seam" (from the Glossary of Commission Report). The lateness of the citations does not argue against their relevance to the 1649 example, as these technical terms might well have a long history in colloquial usage, without finding their way into land records.

Bigby

BIGBY
> *Bechebi* (3x) DB, c 1115 LS, Hy2 (1409) Gilb (p), 1233 Welles
> *Bekebi* 1191, 1192, 1193, 1194, 1195, 1197, 1198, 1199 all P, 1212
>   Fees, 1219 Ass, 1238-43 Fees, *-by* c. 1200 HMCRutl, 1219
>   Fees, 1220 Cur (p), 1242-3 Fees, 1245 FF, 1248 Cl, 1254
>   ValNor, 1273 AD iv *et freq* to 1576 Saxton, *-bye* 1610 Speed,
>   *-be* 1346 FA
> *Becby* 1303 FA, *Bekby* 1425 Pat, *Beckby* 1329 *Ass,* - als *Beakby*
>   1661 *Elw, Beakeby* 1634-42 Holles
> *Bigby* 1526 Sub, 1608, 1621, 1663, 1691 *BT et passim,* - als *Beckby*
>   1656, 1674 *ib, -bie* 1576 LER, 1577, 1601, 1634 *Terrier,*
>   *-bey* 1687 SP, *Bygby*(*e*) 1535 VE iv, 1553 Pat, 1562,
>   1566, 1604 *BT, -be* 1539 LP xiv

This is very probably 'Bekki's farmstead or village', *v.* **by**, the first el. being the ODan pers.n. *Bekki*, as suggested by Ekwall (DEPN s.n.). Fellows-Jensen (SSNEM 36) proposes as an alternative etymology for the first el. the gen.pl. of Scand. **bekkr** 'a brook', but a local search and enquiry suggests that there is only one stream here which, as Mr Ifor Barton points out, runs down beside the vicarage and along Smithy Lane, and is sometimes referred to as Bigby Water. DB spellings in *-ch-* are AN forms. In the 16th century a raising of *-e-* to *-i-* had taken place, as well as a development of [k] to [g], found also in Bigbury PN D 266-7 etc.

KETTLEBY

Kitlebig, Kytlebig 1066-8 (12) ASWills

Chetelbi DB (3x), *Chetlebi* c. 1115 LS

Ketelbi 1196 P, 1238-43 Fees, *-by* 1225, 1231 Cur, 1242-3 Fees, 1259 Cl, 1262, 1271 FF, 1294 Ipm *et freq* to 1509-10 LP i, *Kettelby* 1281 QW, *-bye* 1553 Pat

Ketilby 1347 *Cor*, 1359 Ipm, 1388 Cl *et passim* to 1513 LP i, *Ketylby* 1405 Pat, 1428 FA, *Kettylby* c.1520 Brasses, 1550 Pat, *-be* 1539 LP i

Kettlebie 1561 InstBen, *-bye* 1576 Saxton, *-by* 1610 Speed *et passim*, *- hall* 1695 Morden, 1696 Pryme (*has been a very fine structure, but they are now pulling it down*)

Ketlesby 1210-18 RA iv (p), *Ketelesbi(a)* 1212 Fees, *Kettlesbia* 1212 ib, *Ketelesby* 1230 P, *Ketelsby* 1316 FA, 1332 *SR* (p), *Ketylsby* 1428 FA, *Ketilsby, Ketlesby* 1509-10 LP i

'Ketill's farmstead, village', *v.* **bȳ**, the first el. being ON *Ketill*, ODan *Ketil*, very common in England as a pers.n. Both Ekwall (DEPN) and Fellows-Jensen (SSNEM 56) comment on the fact that the vast majority of forms appear in the stem form without a gen.sg, but point out that there are many analogous p.ns. with uninflected pers.ns. It may be noted that this contrasts dramatically with the forms for Ketsby in South Ormsby LSR, a name of identical origin, where the spellings with an inflected pers.n. outnumber those with the stem forms by nine to one.

KETTLEBY THORPE

Torp 1086 DB, c.1115 LS, 1166, 1168 *et freq* in P to 1188, 1212

Fees, 1268 Ch

Thorp(') 1232 Cur, 1238-43, 1242-3 Fees, 1276 RH, 1303 FA, 1327, 1332 *SR* both (p) *et passim* to 1732 *Elw*

Thorp' iuxta Kettelby 1306 *FF, Thorpe iuxta Ketelby* 1402 Inqaqd

Thorp in Mora 1316 FA, *Thorp' in the More* 1386 Peace

Thorp "by" *Bekeby* 1331 Ipm, - *iuxta Bekeby* 1408 *FF*, - *in Beghby* 1448 Pat

Thorpp Ketelby 1431 FA, *Thorpe als Kettleby Thorpe als Thorpe in the Moore* 1661, 1674 *Elw*

Ketelby Thorp' iuxta Ketelby 1375 Works, *Kettlebie thorpe* 1605 Terrier, *Kettleby Thorpe als Thorpe in the Moore* 1655 *Elw*, *Kettleby Thorpe als Thorp als Thorpe in the Moore* 1674, 1704 *ib*

'The outlying, dependent farmstead, belonging to Kettleby', *v.* þorp. It is noteworthy that this is the only major p.n. in LNR derived from þorp and recorded in DB.

ASH HOLT (lost), 1828 Bry; it was situated in the extreme northern corner of the parish. BENTLEY FM, named from the family of *M*^{r} *George Bentley* 1776 *BT*. BIGBY COMMON (lost), 1828 Bry, *the commons* 1577, 1601, 1626, *y*^{e} - 1605, 1668, *y*^{e} -, *the Common* 1674, 1700, 1762, 1781 all *Terrier*, 1800 *Elw*, 1840 *TA*, *y*^{e} *Comon* 1697, 1712 *Terrier*, self-explanatory. BIGBY HILL, *y*^{e} *hill* 1668, 1674 *Terrier*, cf. - *side* 1668, 1690 *ib*, - *Side* 1700 *ib*. BRIDGE FM. CANDLEY BECK. DONKEY PARK. KETTLEBY BECK, 1844 *TAMap* (Cadney); it is *Kettleby Dike* 1768 (1791) *LindDep Plans*, - *Dyke* 1824 O, *v.* bekkr, dīc, dīk. KETTLEBY CARRS, 1824 O, 1830 Gre, *carr* 1674 *Elw*, *Carr* 1732, 1795 *ib*, *the Carrs at Kettleby* 1767 *Stubbs*, *v.* kjarr, no doubt in the sense of 'boggy land'. KETTLEBY COVERT. KETTLEBY PARKS, *Kettleby parke* 1639 *Inv*, *the Park*(*e*) *of Kettleby* 1656, 1695 *Elw*, *Kettleby Parke* 1693, - *park* 1703, - *Park* 1707, 1745, 1762 all *Terrier*, *the said Mannor Parke* 1656 *Elw*, *Kettleby Deere park* 1662 *Terrier*, *the Deere Parke* 1664, 1668 *ib*, *y*^{e} *Deer parke* 1671 *ib*, *the parke of Ketleby* 1674 *Elw*, *Parke* 1680, 1682, *the* - 1718 *ib*, self-explanatory, *v.* park. MIDDLEGATE LANE, *the middle gate* 1605, *y*^{e} *midle gate* 1624, 1662, (*the*) *Middlegate* 1668, 1781, *y*^{e} - 1690, *y*^{e} *middell-gate* 1674, *middle Gate* 1700 all *Terrier*, 'the middle road', v. **middel, gata**. This is the name of the way which follows the line of the scarp slope of the Wolds from South Ferriby southwards to Caistor and is recorded from a number of parishes. It is an ancient ridgeway, and according to Margary 240 "it was clearly used for Roman traffic". From Caistor to Horncastle it is known as High Street. PINFOLD HO (lost), 1828 Bry, v. **pynd-fald**. It was in Kettelby. PINGLEY FM, -LANE. POOL END, 1768 (1815) *LRA*, 1824 O. RECTORY, *the Rectory* 1762, y^e *parsonage house* 1605, - *Parsonage* - 1697, 1700 all *Terrier, Parsonage House* 1824 O, y^e *Mantion house* 1712, *the Manse house* 1745, *the Mansion house* 1800, - *is newly erected* 1822 all *Terrier*. SMITHY LANE (local). WELLHOLMES HOLT, *Welhams* 1731 *EstMap*, 1840 *TA*, - *Cover* 1828 Bry, *Well-holmes* 1824 O, the forms are late, but this is likely to mean 'the dry grounds in marsh with a spring', v. **wella, holmr**, the latter often being represented by spellings in *ham* in north L; a small stream rises in the Holt. WESTRUM, 1674, 1732 *Elw*, 1800 *Terrier*, 1824 *TA*, -*ram* 1692 *Elw*, it is impossible to determine the source of the final el. with the existing material. Cf. Postrum in f.ns. (a) *infra*. WHITE HALL FM.

Field-Names

The principal forms in (a) are 1840 *TA* 38, supplied by Mr Rex C. Russell. Forms dated 1655, 1661, 1674[1], 1680, 1682, 1704, 1708, 1732, 1795, and 1799 are *Elw*, 1674[2], 1800, and those dated between 1577 and 1864 are *Terrier*, unless otherwise noted; forms marked 1674[3] are *Cragg*. Forms from 1731 *EstMap* have been supplied by Dr F. Henthorn.

(a) The Acre-dike 1762, 1781 (*le Akerdyk* 1276 HMCRutl, y^e *Acar ditch* 1605, *Akar dike* 1662), Acre dike hedge 1781 (*the Akerdike Hedge* 1577, y^e *acardicke hedge* 1624, *the acer-dicke hedge* 1626, y^e *Akadike-* 1668, (y^e) *Acre Dyke-* 1697, - *dyke hedge* 1745, - *Dike hedge* 1700, - *dyke* - 1712, v. **æcer, dīc, dīk**, and the same name in Barnetby le Wold f.ns. (b) supra); All Ale (1732, the first el. is possibly **ald** 'old', and the second perhaps **halh**, but the forms are too late for certainty); Anthony Cl 1799, 1840 (1732, prob. from the surn. *Anthony*); Averams (*close called Abrahams or Averrams* 1655, *that Close called the Averame* 1661, *Averholmes* 1674[1], 1674[3], 1682, 1704, possibly from **hafri** 'oats' with **holmr**); Backside(s) 1799, Backside (1732, *the Backside* 1682, 1704, *backside, the backsyde* 1674[1], v. **bak-side** 'a backyard', 'a field at the back of a house', etc.); Bailey Cl 1799, Bayley hill 1762 (*the -*, y^e *bayly close* 1601, 1605, *Bailey Close* 1731 *EstMap*,

the Bayley hill 1624, *Bayley Hillside* 1700, y^e *Baily Hill* 1712, from **baillie** 'a bailiff'
or the derived surn.); Barley Cl 1799, - Hill (*v.* **bærlic, clos(e), hyll**); Barnetby
Fd 1762 (- *feild* 1662, *barnaby field* 1601, - *feeld* 1626, *Barnabye feild* 1672^2,
Barnaby Field 1697, 1700, - *Feild* 1712, alluding to land abutting on the open
fields of the adjoining township of Barnetby le Wold); Blacksmith Cl 1795
(1732), Blacksmiths - 1840; Bogg; South Bottom 1795 (1732), North & South -
1840 (*Bottom* 1732, *North* - 1732, *v.* **botm**); Bownum 1799, Bowman South
(*Bandam closse* 1655, *Bondham close* 1661, *a close called Bownam* 1674, 1682,
(*the*) *High bownam* 1674, 1682, 1704); Brook Cl 1795, 1799, 1840 (*v.* **brōc**); the
buck pits 1762, the Buckpit 1781 (*the bucke pit* 1624, *v.* **pytt**); (the) Short Bulls
1762, - bulls 1781, (*shorte bulles* 1577, *the short* - 1601, 1624, y^e *short Bulls* 1668,
1690, (y^e, *the*) *Short* - 1700, 1712, 1745); the But hole 1781 (*the butt hole* 1624,
y^e *Butts hole* 1690, *Butt* - 1697, 1712, perhaps 'the hollow place among outlying
pieces of land', *v.* **butte, hol**^{1}); the long Calkes, the short - 1762 (y^e *longe* -,
the short Calkes 1601, 1700, 1712, *the longe* -, *the Shortte calkes* 1577, *the long* -,
ye -, *the longe* -, *the short calkes* 1624, 1626, y^e *long* -, y^e *short Caukes* 1697,
Long Cauks 1731, *Short* - 1745, *ye long* -, *ye short Cawk(e)s* 1662, 1668, *Long* -
1745, y^e *long* -, y^e *Short chalkes* 1605, cf. y^e *kaukes, kaukegate* 1674^2 (*v.* **gata**), y^e
Caulkes 1697 probably 'the chalky places', showing a similar range of forms to
Calke PN Db 626-7, *v.* **calc** and note *the Calke pytt* in (b) *infra*); Carr (2x),
Carr Cl, - Garth (*Care close* 1655, (*the*) *Carr close* 1661, 1674^3, *the Car Close*
1674^1, 'the marsh', *v.* **kjarr, garðr** 'an enclosure', as elsewhere in this parish);
Cary Cl (perhaps named from William *Cary,* Rector of Bigby, 1746-90, *v. BT*
from 1746); Chappel Cl (*the Chappel(l) Close,* - *close* 1655, 1661, 1732, it is
recorded as *Chapel close* 1752 *BT,* the name of a Burial Ground); Common
Marfer 1762 (y^e *Common Marfore* 1668, y^e *Comon marforow* 1690, *common
Marfar* 1745, 'the common boundary furrow', *v.* **marfur**, cf. PN YE 323);
Composition 1799, 1840 (*the Composicon Close* 1674^1, *the Composition Close* 1682,
Compositōn Close 1704, perhaps land conveyed in payment of a debt); Canch
1795, Conch 1840 (*a close called the Cantch* 1674^1, 1682, *Canch* 1732, from dial.
canch (*v.* EDD s.v.) in some such sense as 'a water channel', cf. *The Canch* in
Thornton Curtis *infra,* referred to as *one water called the Canche* 1587 *Yarb,*
etc.); Coney Garth 1795 (1732, *Conygarth* 1674^1, 1682, 1704, *Cony Garth* 1680, *the
Little Cony Garth* 1674^1, *the Little Connygarth* 1682, 1704, 'rabbit warren', *v.* **coni,
garðr** 'an enclosure', as elsewhere in this parish); Corn Cl (cf. *Cornfield* 1697);
Cottagers Ings 1799, 1840 (cf. *Cottager* - 1732, *the Cottagers Close* 1674^1, 1682,
1704, the heading reads 'Lands let to the Cottagers' 1799, *v.* **eng** and **clos(e)**);
Cow Cl 1795, 1840 ((*the*) - 1682, 1704, 1732, *the Cowe Close* 1674^1, cf. *the
Cowzgarth* (sic) 1674^1); the cow common 1822 (cf. y^e *Cow pasture* 1662, y^e *Cow
paster* 1674^2, y^e *Cowpaster* 1690); Crow Wd 1795, 1840 (1682, *Crowwood* 1674^1,

cf. *Crow Garth* 1732, *v.* **cräwe, wudu, garðr**; it lies on the parish boundary); Dikes End (1732, *Dike end closes* 1661, *the dykes close* 1655, *v.* **dīc, dīk**); Englands 1799 (*england(e)s* 1601, 1605, *England(e)s* 1624, 1690, *England* 1697, *Englands Land* 1700, *Inglands* 1731, perhaps from **eng, land**, but spellings in -(*e*)*s* and the 1700 form may suggest a derivation from the surn. *England* noted in the parish, cf. William *England* 1681 *BT*); (Gt & Lt) Far Field Ho; Feeding Pasture; Ferraby Cl 1795, 1799, 1840 (*Ferreby Close* 1732, held by George *Ferreby*); Ferry Gate Btm (*v.* **ferja, gata, botm**); Fotherby Hill 1795 (probably from the surn. *Fotherby*); Fox Cover (on bdy); Garth 1799 (cf. *the garth endes* 1601, *y*ᵉ *Garth Ends* 1690, *v.* **garðr**); the Gaules 1762, - Gauls 1781 (- *Gawlles* 1577, *y*ᵉ *galles* 1605, *y*ᵉ *gaules* 1624, *y*ᵉ -, *the Gaul(e)s* 1668, 1697, 1700, 1712, *y*ᵉ *Gaulls* 1690, *Gawls* 1745, 'the wet places', *v.* **galla**); Glebe; Green Fd 1799, 1864, the green field 1822, Green Fds 1840; Guild Houses 1799, Gild Houses 1840 *Stubbs* (*Great Gildhouse* 1731, shown on this map near Somerby bdy, and it may refer to land held by a Guild House, *v.* **gildi-hús**); Headgates 1762, Head-Gates 1781 (1697, 1700, *the head gate* 1601, *-gatis* 1605, *head gates* 1624, 1662, 1668, 1712, *v.* **hēafod, gata**); *y*ᵉ Headland 1781 (1712, *the headland* 1624, *v.* **hēafod-land**); Hemp dikes 1781 (cf. *hemp croft* 1708, *v.* **hænep, dīc, dīk**); *y*ᵉ high gate 1762 (1697), High - 1781 (*the high(-)gate* 1624, 1626, *y*ᵉ *highgate* 1690, *The High Gate* 1697, *v.* **hēah¹, gata**); Home Fd; Hop Garth 1799, 1840 (*Hopp* - 1732, cf. *hopp yard* 1674¹, *Hoppyard* 1682, *Hopp Yard* 1704, *v.* **garðr, hop-yard**); North & South House Moor; How hills, How hill beck 1781 (*howes, howels* 1601, *howel* 1605, *howhilles, the howhill becke* 1624, *howhills, howhilles beck* 1626, *y*ᵉ *How Hills* 1712, *How hill feild* 1712, *v.* **haugr** 'a hill', **hyll** with **bekkr**); Ings (1732, *the* -, *The Ings* 1655, 1674¹ (- *in Kettleby Thorpe*), 1674³, 1704, *y*ᵉ *Ings in Kettleby Thorpe, The Inggs* 1682, *East* -, *upper Ings Intacke* 1655, *Middle* -, *the Lower Ings, - Upper Inges* 1661, *v.* **eng** 'the meadow, pasture'); Intake 1795, Intack 1840 (1732, *the East Intacke* 1661; it lies on the bdy, *v.* **inntak** "land taken in'); (Low) Jane Brown 1795, Jenny Brown (cf. *Brownes Close* in f.ns. (b) *infra*); Kettleby Lane Cl 1795, 1840 (1732); Kirk Fd (1732, poss. from the surn. *Kirk*, or *v.* **kirkja**); Land Croft; Lawns 1799 (1674¹), Lawnes 1840 (1680, 1682, 1704, 1732, *v.* **launde**); East -, West Limekiln 1799 (- *kilns* 1732), East & West Lime Kiln Cl (*the Great* -, - *great* -, *the little Lyme Kilnes* 1674¹, 1680, 1682, 1704, *y*ᵉ *little Lyme Kilne* 1674¹); Little Cl (2x) (1732, *the* - 1682, 1704); Long Carr 1790 *Monson* (*v.* **kjarr**); Low Cl 1795, 1799, 1840 (2x) (1732); the Low Fd 1762, *y*ᵉ Low fd 1781 (*the lawe feilde* 1577, *the lowfeeld* 1624, *the low-feeld* 1626, *y*ᵉ *low feild* 1674, - *field* 1690, *y*ᵉ *Low Feild* 1712, *y*ᵉ *North Low Field, y*ᵉ *South Low field* 1700, self-explanatory); Lower Cl; Man Cl 1785 (*v.* **(ge)mǣne** 'common'); *y*ᵉ Marfer 1781 (*y*ᵉ *Marfarr* 1662, *v.* **marfur** 'a boundary furrow' and Common *Marfer supra*); Maw Cl (1732, named from the family of William *Maw*

1703 *BT*, Mr Mathew *Maw* 1732); Meadow Moor (1732, cf. *medow* 1668); Mill Fd 1795, - Cl, - Fd 1799, 1840 (*the Milne Close* 1674[1], 1682, 1704, *Mill Field* 1732); the Mill Marfer 1781 (*the mereffurre called the mylne mearfurre* 1577, y^e -, *the milne marfur* 1601, 1605, *the millen marfour* (sic) 1624, *Milln Marforow* 1690, y^e *mill Marfurs* 1697, *Mill: marfur* 1700, *v.* **myln, marfur**, and note the use of *marfur* as an appellative); the Moor heads 1762, 1781 (*the more head* 1601, - *heades* 1624, *v.* **mōr**[1], **hēafod**); Gt, Lt Oak Wood 1795, 1840; Ox Cl 1795, 1799, 1840 ((*the*) - 1682, 1732, *the Oxe close* 1674[1]); Paddock (1732); Low-, Upr Park 1795 (*Old Parke* 1674[1], 1682, 1704); Park Hill 1795, Park Hill Cl 1840 (*Parkehill close* 1674[1], *Parke(-)hill Close* 1682, 1704, different from Kettleby Park); Parsons Carr 1767 *Stubbs* (*the Late Parson Close* 1674[1], 1674[3], *v.* **kjarr**); Parsonage Cl 1795, 1840 (1680, 1682, 1704, 1732, *parsonage-* 1674[1], y^e *Parsonage Swarth* 1668 (*v.* **swæð**, dial. *swarth* 'a strip of grassland, etc.'; *v.* Rectory *supra*); Pingle 1795, 1840 (1732, *v.* **pingel**); Pissy Bed (*Pissey-* 1732, *Pissy Bed(d)* 1674[1], 1682, 1704, this is perhaps 'the place where dandelions (or some similar plants) grow', from dial. *pissy-bed v.* EDD s.v. *piss-a-bed*. The dial. word denotes the dandelion, *Leontodum taraxacum*, or some similar plant. It is also recorded of the ox-eye daisy, *Chrysanthemum leucanthemum*); the Pits 1762, the Pitts 1781 (- *pites* 1624, - *Pittes* 1626, *v.* **pytt**); Postrum 1795 (1732), Postrum (Cl) 1840 (the forms are comparable to Westrum *supra*, but the origin of *-rum* is not clear. It may be noted that Isaac *Post* is named in the 1732 document); Pry Cl 1799, 1840 (2x) (1732, *two Prycloses* 1655, *the Two pry closes* 1661, *the further Pry Close* 1655, *The Great* -, *The Little Pry Close* 1674[1], *the Great* -, *Little Prye Close* 1704, probably from dial. *pry*, recorded from Nt, *v.* EDD s.v., "a variant species of the carex grass, especially *Carex glauca* and *Carex panicea*" and **clos(e)**); The Sands 1762, 1781 (- *sandes* 1605, (y^e) *Sands* 1712, 1745); Sand Crofts 1799, - Croft 1840 (*sand Close* 1674[1], *Sand* - 1682, 1704, *v.* **sand**); Scrub Close Btm (*Scrub Closes* 1674[1], *Scrubb Close* 1704, 1732, *v.* **scrubb**); Somerby hedge 1762, 1781 (*Somerbie hedg* 1601, 1605, *Somerby hedge* 1624, 1662, *Sommerby* - 1668, *Sumerby Hedge* 1674[2], *Summerby hedge* 1697, *Sum'erby Hedge* 1700, *Som'erby hedge* 1712, from the adjoining parish of Somerby and **hecg** 'a hedge'); South Cl 1795, South Close (Btm); (the) South Fd 1762, 1799, 1840 (1732, (*the*) *Southfeild(e)* 1577, 1662, 1690, *the South filde* 1601, *the South field* 1605, y^e *south feeld* 1624, y^e *Southfield* 1668, *the Southfeild Bottom*, *the Southfeilds* 1674[1], y^e -, *The South field* 1697, 1745, - *Field* 1712, self-explanatory, one of the open fields of Bigby); Stonepit 1762; Sweet Hill 1795, 1799, 1840 (poss. a complimentary name, alluding to rich pasture); Thorn Wd 1795, 1840 (1732, *v.* **þorn, wudu**); (North) Thorpe Walk (*Thorp Walk* 1732, (*v.* **walk**); cf. *Thorpe feild* 1661, i.e., Kettleby Thorpe); Three Nook Carr 1790 *Monson*; Timothy Cl (1732), - Ings (1732) (perhaps 'land on which cat's-tail grass grows', referring to the native British plant, *Phleum* *pratense*, cultivated in the US by *Timothy* Hanson, c. 1720 and cf. Timothy Plat in Wootton f.ns. (a) *infra*); Tunnel Cl 1795, Tunnil Cl 1840 (*Tunnell Close* 1732, possibly from the surn. *Tonnell*, Reaney 324); Upper Cl 1795, 1840 (2x) (cf. *the upper Round Close* 1674); Walk End (1732, - *Nook* 1732, cf. Thorpe Walk *supra*); Warley Carr 1767 *Stubbs*, 1790 *Monson*, 1840 - Car 1799, 1800 *Stubbs* (*Warley Hill & Carr* 1674[1], 1704, *Warley Hill and Car* 1682, probably from a surn. and **kjarr**); Willow Garth 1799, 1840 (*Willowgarth* (*and backside*) 1674, 1732, *v.* **wilig, garðr**); Wilson Cl 1799, Willason Cl (*Wilson Close* 1732, named from the family of *Jno Wilson* 1732); The Would 1781, the Wold 1800, 1822, Wolds 1840, Wouldgate 1762, the Wold gate 1781 (*The Would* 1577, *the would* 1624, 1626, *ye-* 1662, *ye Wold 1668*, *ye Wowld* 1690, *Woulds* 1745, *the would gate* 1626, *Would Gate*, *woldgate* 1700, 1712, *ye wowld gate* 1690, *v.* **wald, gata** 'a road'); Wright Cl 1799, 1840 (1732, named from the family of Edward *Wright* 1666 *BT*).

(b) *barnaby beck* 1601, *Barnaby becke* 1624, *barnabie-* 1690 (*v.* **bekkr** and for the same name *v.* the Beck, etc. in Barnetby le Wold f.ns. (a) *supra*); *Barnaby Gate* 1700, *Barnetby gate* 1668 (*v.* **gata**), - *Mere* 1668 (*v.* **(ge)mǣre** 'a boundary'), - *way* 1668, *Barnabye pits* 1674[2] (cf. Barnetby Field in (a) *supra*); *Bigby Field* 1664 ('the open fields of Bigby', *v.* **feld**); *Blew Gates* 1732; *Bloom dale* 1745; *brend milnedam* Ed1 *HarlCh* (probably 'the burnt mill' with **dammr** or perhaps 'the burnt mill-dam', *v.* **brende**[2], **myln, dammr**); *ye Brick Pitt* 1712; *Brownes Close* 1674[1], 1674[3], 1704, - *close* 1682, named from the family of John *Browne* 1376 Cl, John *browne* 1607 *BT*, and cf. the f.n. in (a) (Low) Jane Brown, no doubt a member of the same family); *Brumby's Close* 1674[1], *Brumbys* - 1682, *Brumbyes* - 1704 (no doubt from a surn. *Brumby*); *ye bull-park* 1674[2], *ye bul peice* 1662, (*y^e*) *Bull*(-)*peice* 1668, 1690; *Butts* 1745, *Short Butts* 1731 (*v.* **butte**); *Calf Close* 1732; *the Calke pytt* 1577, *ye Cawkpits* 1668, *ye Cawke Pitt* 1690, *Calke pitt* 1700, *ye Kauke pite* 1674[2], - *pitt* 1712, *the chalkepit* 1624 (self-explanatory, *v.* **calc, pytt** and cf. the long Calkes in (a) *supra*); *Clover Close* 1732; *Common Grass* 1731; *the common more* 1601, 1624, *ye Common Moor* 1712, *the more* 1626, *ye moor* 1668, - *Moor* 1700 (*v.* **mōr**[1], cf. the Moorheads in (a) *supra*); *the common pittes* 1601 (*v.* **pytt**, cf. the Pits in f.ns. (a) *supra*); *Craiks* 1731; *Creame Poake Nooke* 1674[1] (probably a complimentary nickname); (*in the*) *Croftes* 1332 SR (p); *ye fallow feild* 1662, *fallow field* 1668, - *Field* 1697, *ye fallow gate* 1662, *ye fallow heade* 1674[2], - *heads* 1690, *ye Fallows* 1668 (*v.* **falh**); *the Fox close* 1674[1], 1682, - *Close* 1704 (named from the *Fox* family, cf. James *Fox* 1704); *the garth endes* 1601 (*v.* **garðr, ende**[1]); *Le Gayre, Gereford 1276* HMCRutl (*v.* **geiri** 'a triangular piece of ground', **ford**); *Habmershe* 1553 Pat (*v.* **mersc**, the first el. is uncertain); *Healy's Close* 1674[1], *Healeys-* 1674[3], 1704, *Healey-* 1732 (named from the *Healey* family, cf. Robert *Healey* 1639 *Inv*, 1661); y^e *Highfeild* 1674[2], y^e *North High Field* 1700, *South High Field* 1700; *the high marfur* 1605, y^e *high marfarr* 1662 (v. **marfur**, as elsewhere in this parish); *Hill Thornes* 1700; *le Hob* (sic) 1276 HMCRutl (perhaps from **hobb(e)** 'a tussock, a hummock'); *Houlton Close* 1732 (held by *Tho. Houlton*); *lambcotes* Ed1 HarlCh (v. **lamb, cot**); *lane ends* 1674[1], *Lane - * 1674[3], *- Ends* 1682, 1704; *Leuchmilne* c.1200 HMCRutl, *te're ex est parte molendini de Schuch* (sic) Ed1 HarlCh (obscure); y^e *Middle of* y^e *Wold* 1668 (cf. Wolds in (a) *supra*); *mikelwode* Ed1 HarlCh ('great wood', v. **mycel, mikill, wudu**); *the nether fild* 1601, *- field* 1605 (v. **neoðera, feld**); *Nevil Dale* 1731, *Nevildale* 1745 (the first el. presumably commemorates the holding of one fee in Bigby by the *Neville* family, cf. Hugo *de Nevill'* 1242-43 Fees; the second is **deill**); *Noddles Closes* 1674[1], *the Neddles Closes* 1682, *Neddles Close* 1704 (probably from a surn.); *the north feeld* 1624, y^e *North field* 1668, 1674, *- Feild* 1690, 1697, 1712 (one of the great fields of Bigby); *the old Garden* 1674[1], *- Old - * 1682, 1704; *old orchard* 1674[1], *old Orchard* 1680, 1682, 1704; *the ponds* 1674[1], *- Ponds* 1682, 1704; *the Posternehill* 1674[1], *- Posterne hill* 1682, *- Hill* 1704 (the sense of *postern* is unclear, but the same name has been noted in the f.ns. of Wingfield, PN Berks 42); *the Rate-dickes* 1624; *Salmon welles* 1577, *Samon Wells* 1605 (v. **wella**, the first el. probably being the surn. *Salmon*); *Segwad* c.1200 HMCRutl ('the sedge ford', v. **secg, (ge)wæd**); *the common meare Furre called the sheperd lodge* 1577, *the shepard - * 1601, *sheppherd - * 1624, *Sheppard(s) - * 1690, 1697, *Shepherd Marfare* 1668 (v. **loge, marfur**, again its use as an appellative is noteworthy); y^e *Sikes* 1624 (v. **sic, sík**); *Spencers Close* 1682, 1704 (no doubt from the surn. *Spencer*); *the streete* 1577, *the high street* 1605 (cf. *regiam stratam Linc'* Ed1 HarlCh); *Stubblefield* 1668; *swinegraue* Ed1 HarlCh ('the wood used as a swine pasture', v. **swīn, græfe**); *Thorpe Moore* 1655, 1661, (v. **mōr**[1] and Kettleby Thorpe *supra*); *towell thorn* 1601, *Towelthorne* 1668, *Towell-Thornes* 1674[2]; *Welbeck marfarr* 1662 (v. **marfur**), *Well(e)becke* 1697, 1700 (presumably 'the stream running from a spring', v. **wella, bekkr**, v. for the same name, Welbeck Spring in Melton Ross *infra*, and Welbeck PN Nt 103-4).

Bonby

BONBY

Bundebi 1086 DB (2x), 1200 ChR, 1212 Fees, 1219 Ass, *-by* 1228, 1229 Cl, 1230 Welles, 1231 Cl, 1232 FF, 1291 Fine, 1291 Orig

Bondebi c.1115 LS, 1156-84 YCh ii, 112 Dane, 1200 ChR, 1211 P, 1238-43 Fees, 1268 FF, *-by* 1200 CartAnt, 1208 FF, 1221 *AD*,

1230 P, 1242-3 Fees, 1247 Lib, 1247 Cl, 1254 ValNor, 1256
FF *et freq* to 1535 VE iv, - *alias Bondby* 1461 Fine, (*juxta
Wolfrikby*) 1316 Orig, ("by" *Worliby*) 1366 Cl
Bondby 1294 *Ass*, 1317 Ipm, 1342, 1344, 1347 Pat, 1385 Peace,
1402 Cl *et passim* to 1723 SDL, - *alias Bondeby* 1451 Fine,
-*bye* 1536-7 Dugd vi, -*bey* 1577 *Yarb*, -*bie* 1580 *ib*, 1601, 1606
Terrier
Boundeby 1474, 1475, 1478 Pat, *Bowndbye* 1545 LP xx
Bonby 1383 Cl, 1428 FA, 1455 Cl, 1530 Wills iii *et passim*, -*be*
1526 Sub, -*bye* 1553 Pat, 1576 Saxton, 1579 *Terrier*, 1610
Speed, -*bie* 1562-7 LNQ v, 1576 LER, 1582 *Yarb*, 1611
Terrier, - *otherwise Bondby* 1827 *Brad*

According to Ekwall (DEPN s.n.) this is 'Bondi's farmstead,
village', *v.* bȳ, the first el. being the ON pers.n. *Bóndi*, ODan *Bundi*.
The pers.n. is very common in England, but it is comparatively rare
in L as compared, for instance, with Nf, where it is extremely frequent (*v. Insley* 198-218). However, an alternative interpretation is
to take the first el. as the gen.pl. of the Scandinavian appellative
bondi, *bunde* 'a farmer, a peasant proprietor', from which the
pers.n. is itself derived. No certainty is possible since the gen.sg. of
the pers.n. and the gen.pl. of the appellative would give identical
forms in ME. Given the comparative infrequency of the name in
L, Insley (*ib.* 217) believes that Bonby represents an OSc *Bōndaby*
which he translates 'the village of the peasant proprietors' and
compares this with the p.n. Bondeby in Denmark and Sweden. A
meaning 'Bondi's farmstead, village', however, must remain a
possible alternative.

It should be noted that the form *Bodebi* 1086 DB f. 363a may
well refer to Bonby.

BONBY CARRS, *the Carrs in Bonby* 1632 *Yarb*, *Bondby Carrs*
1767 *Stubbs*, *Bonby Water Carrs* 1824 O, 1830 Gre, *v.* kjarr, in the
sense 'boggy land', as elsewhere in this parish. BONBY INGS, *the
Ings* 1808, 1832 *Yarb*, 1841 *TA*, cf. *one cloase Called Ings* 1667 *Yarb*,
one close called the Inges 1670 *ib*, from the pl. of eng 'the
meadows, pastures', as elsewhere in this parish, and *v.* also Carr
Lane *infra*. BONBY LODGE, *Bonby Lodge, Stables, and Paddock*
1841 *TA*. BONBY WOLD FM, *Bonby Wold F.* 1824 O, self-
explanatory and *v.* f.ns. (a) *infra*. CARR LANE, cf. *the Carlane*

Inges 1631 *Yarb*, - *Carr Lane Inges* 1632 *ib*, cf. Bonby Carr and Bonby Ings *supra*. CRAVEN CLOSE COVER (lost), 1824 O, 1830 Gre, cf. *Craven carr*, - *Hard ings* 1810 *Yarb*, v. **kjarr, heard** 'hard to till', **eng**; named from the family of John *Craven* 1739 *Yarb*. GORSE COVER (lost), 1830 Gre. GOULTONS COVER (lost), 1828 Bry, named from the family of Thomas *Goulton* e19 *Yarb*. HALL FM, cf. *Bonby Hall* 1770 *Yarb*, *the Hall Closes* 1631, 1632 *ib*, - *Close* 1832 *ib*. MIDDLEGATE LANE, *Middle Gate Road* 1839 *TAMap*, v. the same name in Bigby *supra*. OLD STONE PIT, cf. *Stonepit Hill* e19 *Yarb*, *Stone Pit Wold* 1832 *ib*, 1841 *TA*, *Stone Pit and Waste* 1841 *ib*. THE VICARAGE, *the Vicaridge* 1606 *et freq* to 1671, *the vicaridge* 1679, - *Vicarage* 1697, 1709, 1712, 1745, y^e *Vicarage* 1703, *the Vicarage House* 1825 all *Terrier*, it is also *a mansyon howsse* 1579 *ib* and note too *the parsonage* 1579, 1601 *ib*, *Rectorie and Parsonage* 1624, *the Rectory or Parsonage* 1631, *the parsonage house* c.1806 all *Yarb*.

Field-Names

Principal forms in (a) are 1841 *TA* 44. Spellings dated 1579, 1601, 1606, 1611, 1638, 1662, 1671, 1679, 1690, 1697, 1703, 1709, 1712, 1745, and 1825 are *Terrier*, and the remainder are *Yarb* unless otherwise noted.

(a) Acre pce c.1806; Ancholme Bank; Ancholme Navigation 1839 *TAMap* (a canal, a reference to New River Ancholme); Bank 1851; Barton Street Cl (leading to Barton upon Humber); Beacocks Cl 1832, 1841 (from the family name *Beacock*, cf. David *Beacock* 1783 *LTR*); Bean carr 1810; Becky carr 1810, - Car 1832, 1841 (v. **kjarr**; presumably *Becky* is the common fem. pet pers.n.; note all the f.ns. in - car(r) *infra* are parts of Bonby Carrs *supra*); Bottom pce (v. **botm**); (North -, South) Bottoms 1832, 1841 (v. **botm**); Brough (sic) 1810, e19, Brough Cl 1832, 1841 (*Brough* is usually a modern reflex of *burh* 'a fortification', etc., but so far no archaeological evidence appears to have been reported from the area); Bull hill 1810, - Hill 1817, 1832, 1841 (*the* - 1632, *the bull hill* 1631); Calf Cl 1832; First -, Second -, Bottom -, Middle Car 1841, Fourth -, Middle -, North -, South -, West Carr 1851 (v. **kjarr** and Bonby Carrs *supra*); Carrot Cl; Catch Water Drain e19; Clay pit pce; Cliffs e19, 1810, (North -, South) Cliff 1832, (Bottom -, Gt -, Middle -, Narrow -, North -, South -, Top) Cliff 1841 (v. **clif**); Coopers Car, - Ings (presumably from the surn. *Cooper*, cf. John *Cooper* 1783 *LTR*, and **kjarr, eng**); Cottagers Meadow Carr 1770, Cottagers Cl 1832,

1841 (pieces of land allotted to the *cottagers*); Cover Pce, - Wold (*v.* **pece, wald**); Cow Cl 1810, - Cl 1832, 1841 (*the Cow(e) Close* 1631, 1632); Danns or Danis Lairs 1757, 1758, 1761, 1767 (*the Dams Laires* (sic) 1724, *Dann's or Danis Lairs* 1739, obscure); Drain Car Bank 1832[2], Drain Bank, - Car 1841; Drury Car 1832 (named from the family of *Georg Drury of Bonby* 1633 *Inv* and **kjarr**); Duncan Car 1832, 1841, - Ings, - Moor e19, 1810, 1832, 1841, Duncans homestead 1806 (from the surn. *Duncan* and **kjarr, eng, mōr**[1], **hām-stede**); East or Sleights Garth 1805 (*v.* **slæget** 'sheep pasture', **garðr**); Espin Carr 1810 (cf. Espin Cl in Brocklesby f.ns. (a); it is just possible that *espin* is an unrecorded dialectal form of *aspen*); Faulding cl 1810, Folding Cl e19, 1832, 1841; First Cl; Firth Carr 1806, 1810, 1832, Frith Car 1841 (*the Forth Carr(e)* 1631, 1632, cf. *one Clase* (sic) *called Fourth* 1667, *one other close called the Furth* 1670, *v.* **kjarr**, the first el. is uncertain); Forty Acre Carr 1810 (*v.* **kjarr**); Fox Cover (Pce) 1832; Gatelands 1851 (*two closes of pasture called gateland closes* 1670, 'roadside lands', *v.* **gata, land**); Far Green Carr 1810, Far -, Nr Green Car 1832, 1841 (*v.* **kjarr**); Hall ings 1810; Hard Ings c.1806, 1851 (*v.* **heard** 'hard to till', **eng** 'meadow', as elsewhere in this parish, and cf. *Craven Close Cover supra*); Healey Car 1832, 1841 (from the surn. *Healey* and **kjarr**); Hill Cl e19, 1832, 1841, - *close* 1810, Hillside Cl (cf. *Attenhull* 1271 *Ass* (p), *v.* **hyll**); Home Cl (2x); Home Pce; Hop garth 1810 (*v.* **hoppe, garðr**); Horse Car(r) 1806, 1832, (Low -, Top) Horse Car 1841, Horse Carr 1810, 1851 (*the horse carre* 1635 (c.1900) *LindDep 78, v.* **hors, kjarr**); Horse Cl 1832 (*the Horseclose* 1631, 1632); Btm -, Top Ings 1832, 1841 (cf. *twenty Inges* 1631, *Twentie-* 1632, *v.* **eng** and *Bonby Ings supra*); Kings Garth 1805 (*v.* **garðr**, the first el. probably being a surn., cf. William *Kinge* 1594 Admin); Kirk - 1810, Kirks Mdw Car(r) 1832, 1841 (*v.* **kjarr**), Kirk Summer eater Carr 1810 (*v.* **summer-eater** 'pasture used in summer' and **kjarr**, the noun does not seem to be recorded in Dictionaries, but cf. EDD s.v. *summer-eat* 'to use land as a summer pasture' and cf. Summer-eaten Marsh in Habrough f.ns. (a) and for *Kirk atte Kirk'* 1332 *SR*, *atte Kirke* of *Bondeby* 1338 *Misc*, *atte Kyrke* 1402 Cl all (p), *v.* **kirkja**); Line Garth Cl (formerly two closes and called Middle Moor and low Moor Closes) 1808, Line-Garth 1832 ('the enclosed plot on which flax was grown', *v.* **līn, garðr**, cf. the Moor-duke Cl *infra*); Little pce 1806, 1810 (*v.* **pece**); Far -, First Low Car(r) 1832, 1841 (*v.* **kjarr**); Matt Foy carr 1810, Foys Cl e19 (perhaps *Matt Foy* is for *Mathew Foy*, though no such person has been noted in the source searched); Meadow Car 1832, 1841 (*v.* **mǣd, kjarr**); Middle pce; Midgley Cl, - Ings e19, Midgeley cl 1810 (probably from the surn. *Midgley*); Mitchel Carr, Mitchell Cl, - Water Ings 1810, Garth later Mitchell 1810 (named from the family of John *Mychell* 1576 *Inv* with **kjarr, water** 'wet', **eng** and **garðr**); Moor Cl c.1806, the Moor-duke Cl (formerly two closes called the Middle Moor and Low Moor Closes) 1832, (Near) Moor Cl 1841 (cf. Line

Garth Cl *supra*); Morley's Cl 1832, Morley - 1841 (named from the family of William *Morley* 1842 White); Narrow Cl; Narrow Grds 1832, 1841; Narrow Row; New Causey 1810 (*v.* **caucie**); North Cl e19 (*the North Closes* 1632); North Ings e19, 1832, 1841 (*v.* **eng**); Phillipson carr 1810, - Car 1841, Philipson Car 1832 (named from the family of John *Phillipson* 1676 *Inv* and **kjarr**); Prate Duke Cl 1808, 1832 (cf. the Moor-duke Cl *supra*); Road Cl; Round cl 1810; Rundall Carr (probably from **rynel** 'a small stream, a runnel'); (Little) Sainfoin e19, Sain foin cl 1810, Saintfoin Cl 1832, 1841 (*v.* **sainfoin**); Sam Car 1810, 1832, 1841 (*v.* **kjarr**) - Ings 1832, 1841; Sam Hard Ings 1810, - Water Ings e19, 1810 (alluding to dry and wet pasture land respectively, *v.* **heard, wæter, eng,** the Water Ings (cf. Water Ings *infra*) being low by a Catch Water Drain, with Hard Ings higher up, cf. Hard Ings *supra*); Sam Moor Cl e19, 1810, - Moores Cl 1832, Sam Moors - 1841; Saxby Side Cl (from the adjoining parish of Saxby All Saints); Second Cl; Seed Car 1832, Far -, Near Seed Car 1841 (*v.* **sǣd, kjarr**); Shift Car c.1806, Shift Car Wend 1810, Shifts Car 1841 (*v.* **kjarr, wende** 'a bend'; for a discussion of *shift, v. a shifte Acre* in South Ferriby f.ns. (b)); the Sixth Car 1770; Stephenson - e19, Stevenson's - 1832, Stevensons Cl (cf. *Ann Stephenson Carr 1810, Close Nanny Stephinsons* (sic) 1810); Stone dale 1810, - Dale 1832, North -, South Stone Dale 1832, Far, Nr - 1841 (*v.* **deill**); Far -, First -, Middle Stones Cl; 10 Acres 1832; Thirds; Top Cl e19; Turnip Cl; 12 Acres 1832; Twelve & Eight Acres (sic) 1832; 20 Acre Car 1832, 1841; Waggon Garth & Plant' 1832; Water Ings c.1806, 1851, - ings 1810 ('the wet pasture(s)', (either by natural inundation or by managed irrigation) *v.* **wæter** often used in the sense 'wet' as a first el., **eng**); West Side Carr 1832, - side Car 1841; West Cl e19; Wheat Cl; Wilkin Ings 1810 (named from the family of Richard *Wilkin of Bondby* 1705 *Inv* and **eng**); (Low -, North -, South) Wold 1832, (Lt -, Low -, First -, 2nd -, 3rd -, 4th -) Wold (*v.* **wald**); North -, South Worlaby Rd Wold (*v.* **wald**, the road leading to the adjacent parish of Worlaby).

(b) *Atkinsons Carr, - Ings* 1724 (from the surn. *Atkinson*, the earliest noted so far being Thomas *Atkinson* 1832, with **kjarr, eng**); Becks gate 1724 (cf. perhaps cf. *Atte Becke* 1327 *SR, atte Bek'* 1332 *ib* both (p)); *Boynton place* 1402 Cl (from the surn. of John *Boynton* 1402 *ib*, *v.* **place**); *Braddaylle* 1402 Cl (*v.* **brād, deill**); *the broade Leas, the broad leas Inges* 1632 ('the broad pieces of meadow', from **brād** and the pl. of **lēah** in its later sense 'a meadow, an allotment of meadow, an open pasture', in common use in L, as in *one lea, two leas,* with numerous variants like *ley, leyes* especially in 17th century Terriers; here the pl. of **eng** also 'meadow, pasture' has been added); *Conyngarthdaylle* 1402 Cl, *cony Warren* 1631, *Connye* - 1632 (*v.* **coni, garðr, deill, warçine**); *darnelle Carre* 1631, *darnell Carrs* 1632 (alluding to darnel, *Lolium temulentum,* a troublesome weed, from ME darnel and **kjarr**, though the surn. *Darnel(l)* is equally possible); (*de*) *Dene* 1385 Cl (p) (*v.* **denu**, but this may not be a local name since **denu** is very rare in north L); *the doggarth* 1631, *One close ... called the Doggarth* 1632 (probably 'dock-infested enclosure', *v.* **docce, garðr**); the *Gaunoke* 1402 Cl (no doubt for *Gannoke, v.* **gannok**; suggesting that this may allude to an outlying pig-farm, Mr John Field draws attention to 113-14 records of payments made to a Keeper and a *porcarius* of *le Gannok* at Lynn, in the cellarers' accounts of Norwich Cathedral Priory, *v.* H.W. Saunders: *An Introduction to the Obedientiary and Manor Rolls of Norwich Cathedral Priory*, Norwich 1930, p. 100 n.1); y^e *hempland* 1601 (*v.* **hænep, land**); *Holbekgarth* 1402 Cl (presumably from the surn. *Holbeck* and **garðr**); *one Cloase called House Carr* 1667, *one other close called the house carre* 1670, (*v.* **hūs, kjarr**); *Howlfleet* m16 *Cragg* (*v.* **flēot**); "divers tenements called" *Kentfee* 1402 Cl; *the land ditch* 1632 (*v.* **land, dīc**); *the Lane Cloase* 1667 (*v.* **lane**); *Mikylgat* 1402 Cl ('main street', *v.* **mikill, gata**, but perhaps for *Midylgate, v.* Middlegate Lane *supra*); *the newlayne* 1606, *Newlayne* 1611, *the new-layne* 1638, *the new layne* 1671, *the New-lane* 1662, *the -*, y^e *new lane* 1679, 1690, 1697, 1709, y^e -, *the New(-)lane* 1703, 1745, *the new laine* 1712 (perhaps 'freshly prepared arable land', *v.* **leyne**); *the North Closes* 1632; "the north field" 1385 Cl; *the North Moore Close* 1631; *the Northwest Carre* 1631; (*del*) *Park' de Bondeby* 1287 *Ass* (p); *Pergarth, -daylle* 1402 Cl ('the pear orchard', *v.* **pirige, garðr**, with **deill** 'a portion or allotment of land'); *atte Reke* (sic) 1402 Cl (p) (perhaps an error for *Roke*, from OFr **roke**, ME **rokke** 'a rock'); *Sadcroft* 1402 Cl; *Schordaylle* 1402 Cl (probably 'the short allotment of land', *v.* **sceort, deill**); *Shepewalke* 1631, *the Sheepe Walke* 1632 (*v.* **shepe-walk**); "the south field" 1385 Cl; *atte wode* 1402 Cl (p) (*v.* **wudu**).

Brocklesby

BROCKLESBY

   Brochelesbi 1086 (5x), *Brokelesbi* 1200 Cur, *-by* 1238, 1256 (e13)   *NCot,* 1276 RH, 1298 Pat

   Brachelesbi 1086 DB (*Brchelesbi* 1086 (13) *DB Abbreviatio*)

   Brochesbi (sic) c.1115 LS, *Brokesby* 1254 FF, 1566 Pat, *Brockesby*   1353 Pap

   Broclesbi c.1115 LS, 1143-47, c.1155, 1155-60, 1157-63, 1190-95   all Dane, 1238-43 Fees, *-bia* 1212 ib, *-by* R1 (1318) Ch, 1232   Cur, 1235 Dugd ii, 1242-3 Fees, 1441 *Yarb, Broklesby* 1226   FF, 1429, 1565 *Yarb, Brocleseby* 1205 Cur

   Broclousebi 1143-7, a 1150, c.1150, 1160-66 all Dane, 1269 RRGr,

Brocklouseby 1254 ValNor

Broclousbi c.1150, p1182 Dane, John *HarlCh*, *-by* 1242-3 Fees,
    1276 RH, 1338 Pat, *-bia* 1190 (1301) Dugd vi, *-by* 1274
    RRGr, *-lowsby* 1268 Ch

Broclausebi 1150-60 Dane, *-by* 1181-5 (e13) *NCot*

Broclausbi c.1150, p1182 Dane, 1159-81 (e13) *NCot*, 1195-6, R1
    Dane, l12, e13 *HarlCh*, *-by* c 1155, 1160, 1189 (e13) *NCot*,
    1291 Tax

Broclosbi c.1115 LS, a1155, p1182, 1186-1200 Dane, 1271
    HarlCh, *-by* eHy2, 1160, Hy2, l12 (e13) *NCot*, R1 (1318)
    Ch, 1204 P *et passim* to 1327 *SR*, *Brocclosbi* a1147 Dane,
    Broklosby 1305 Pat, 1305 *HarlCh*, 1349 Fine

Broclosebi l12 Dane, 1218 Ass, *-by* 1281 QW, *Brochloseby* 1263
    HarlCh

Brouchelossebi 1171-5 Dane

Brockeleseby 1205 FF, *Brockelesseby* 1281 QW

Broclawesbi 1200 Cur

Brotelbi (*-t-* for *-c-*) 1166, 1167 P, *Brocelby* 1233 Cl, 1322, 1344
    Pat, *Brocilby* 1233 Cl, *Broccelby* 1325, 1330, 1332 Pat

Broclusby 1303 *HarlCh*, 1345 Misc

Brokelesby 1303 FA, 1317 Pat, 1338 Cl, 1343 NI, 1346 FA *et*
    passim to 1535 VE iv, 1536 *Yarb*, *-bye* 1551 Pat, *Brokelysby*
    1428 FA

Brokelsby 1316, 1428 FA, 1543, 1553 *Yarb*, *-bie* 1554 InstBen,
    1576 LER, *-bye* 1549 Pat, 1576 Saxton, 1610 Speed,
    Brokylsby 1428 FA, 1443 *Yarb*, *Brokilsbie* 1552 Pat,
    Brokkelsby 1544 *AOMB 216*, *Brockulesbye* 1566 Pat

Brocclesby 1328 Banco, *Broklesby* 1331 Ipm, 1332 *SR*, 1336,
    1341, 1346, 1348 Pat, 1348 Orig, 1385 Pat, 1472 WillsPCC,
    1526 Sub, *Broclesby* 1335, 1338 Pat, 1373 Peace (p),
    Brokklesby 1378 Pat, *Brocklesby* 1339 ib, 1372 Misc *et passim*

'Bróklauss' farmstead, village', *v.* **bý**, as suggested by Ekwall
(DEPN s.n.) and Fellows-Jensen (SPNLY 65, SSNEM 39). The
first el. is an unrecorded ON pers.n. *Bróklauss, a nickname
meaning 'breechless'. It is recorded TRE in DB in L as *Broclos* in
Middle Rasen and as *Brocles* in Maltby le Marsh, and later in
Grainthorpe, cf. *terram Rogeri Broclaus* R1 (1409) Gilb, *toftum quod*
fuit (*Rogeri*) *Broclaus* mHy2 (1409) ib. It has also been noted in
Theddlethorpe in the f.n. *Broclousdail* c 1200 RA vi 'Bróklauss'

share of land', *v.* **deill**. Spellings in *-c-* and *-ch-* are due to AN influence and those in *-les-* to anglicisation, with OE *lēas* replacing ON *lauss.*

COATHAM NUNNERY (site of), NUN COTHAM (local), also NUNCOTON

Cotes 1086 DB, 1218 Ass

Cotum c.1150, 1154-79, 1156-85, 1160, 1170, 1180, 1181-5, 1187, 1189, Hy2 (e13) *NCot,* 1190-1207 *HarlCh,* c.1190 Dane, 1212 Fees, 1219 FF, 1225 FineR *et passim* to 1345 Ipm, *Cottum* l12 (e13), 1259, 1260, eEd1 *NCot*

Cotun c.1115 LS, p1182 Dane, 1185 P, p1186, Hy2 (e13) *NCot,* 1203 P, 1219 Ass *et passim* to 1290 RSu, *-tuna* c 1150, 1153-4, 1159-81, a1180, 1201 (e13) *NCot,* a1183 Dane, *Cottuna* Hy2 (1292) Ch, 1275 *NCot*

Cotona 1159-81, eHy2, Hy2, 1187 (e13) *NCot, Cottona* Hy2 (1292) Ch, *-ttone* 1211-2 RBE, *Cotoun* 1354 Ipm

Cothum 1197, 1198 P, *Chotum* (sic) eHy2 Dane (p)

Norcotum a1180 (e13) *NCot*

Nuncottum 1268, 1278 *NCot, Nunnecotum* 1290 *ib,* 1291 Tax, 1295 *NCot,* 1308, 1392 Cl, *Nun-* 1275 RH, 1326 *NCot,* 1370 Inqaqd, 1428 FA, 1457 *NCot, None-* 1307 Pat, *Nonn-* 1326 *NCot, Nune Cotum* 1309 Ipm, *Nonne -* 1310 *HarlCh, Nunnecotom* 1438 Cl, *Nuncotom* 1428, 1431 FA, 1448 *DCAcct, Nuncottome* 1519 DV

Nunnecotun 1269 RRGr, 1314 Pat, *- Cotun* 1298 Ipm, *Noncotun* 1282 RSu, *Nun-* 1368 Pat, *Nunne Coton* 1303, 1317 Pat, *Nunecoton* 1361 Cl, *Nun-* 1342 ib, 1346 FA, 1360, 1370 Pat, 1401-2 FA, 1404, 1563 Pat, *-cotone* 1440 Visit, *Nuncotton* 1526 Sub, 1535 VE iv, 1553, 1566 Pat, *Nonne-* 1536-7 Dugd vi, 1550 Pat, *Nonne Cotton* 1553 ib

Nonnecotham 1540 LP xi, *Nuncottham* 1632 *MiscDep 65, Nuncotham* 1635 *Foster, - als Nuncotton* 1639 *ib, Nun Cotham als Nun Cotton* 1639 *ib*

Note also *æt Lehcotum* 852 (12) ASCharters (S 1440), *Cotum* 1066-8 (12) ASWills. Both have been tentatively identified with Nun Coton or Cotham, and the identification is reasonably certain.

'At the cottages, sheds or shelters', *v.* **æt, cot.** dat.pl. **cotum,** and for the variation in the forms, *v.* Ekwall, Studies[3] 31-2. It is *Nun* from the Cistercian Priory of Nuns founded c.1150. *v.* also FF ii, lxv and DB liv.

LITTLE LIMBER

Limberge 1086 DB

parua Limbergia c.1155 Dane, 1269 *HarlCh, Parva Limberga* 1200 ChR, *Parua -, Parva Limberg'* 1190 (e13) *NCot,* 1238-43 Fees, *-berge* 1211 FF, 1212 Cur, 1242-3 Fees, *-berg* 1303 FA, 1364 Pat, "Little" *Limberg(e)* 1251, 1253, 1257 FF, 1268, 1301 Ch

parua Limbergh' 1287 *Ass, parua -, Parva Lymbergh(')* 1305 *HarlCh,* 1316, 1346 FA, 1359 *Cor,* 1401-2, 1402, 1428 FA, 1436 Pat, *Lymbergh Parva* 1382 Pat, *-berge parua* 1440 Visit, *-bergh parua* 1576 Saxton, "Little" *Lymbergh* 1305, 1430, 1447 Pat, *Little Lymbergh* 1610 Speed

Parva Lumberge 1242-3 Fees, *-bergia Parva* 1539 LP xiv, 1571 Pat

Lymburgh Parva 1423-4 Lanc, *Litell Lymborough* 1557 Pat

Parva Linberga c.1115 LS, *Parva Linbergh'* 1281 QW, *parva Linberg'* 1291 RSu

paruam lindbergiam (acc.) 1246 *NCot, parua Lindbergh'* 1288 *Ass, Parva Lyndeberg* 1304-5 RA ix

Little Lymber 1472 WillsPCC, *Lymber Parva* 1536-7 Dugd vi, *parva lymber* 1538-9, 1576-7 *AD, Limber Parva* 1653 WillsPCC, 1824 O, *Lytle Lymber* 1530 Wills iii

For additional forms, including those for Limber, *v.* Great Limber *infra,* where the meaning of the name is discussed.

NEWSHAM ABBEY (site of), the name is represented on the modern map by NEWSHAM LODGE

Neuhuse 1086 DB (5x)

Neuhus 1143-7 Dane (4x), 1143-52 (Ed1) *Newh,* a1147, c.1150 Dane, 1153-4 (Ed1) *Newh,* c.1155, 1155-60, 1160-66, 1177 Dane *et freq* to 1349 Pap, *-husa* a1150 Dane, *-hous (iuxta Vlsebiam)* 1236-47 *HarlCh,* 1275 Cl, 1291 Tax, 1296 Cl, 1335 Pat *et freq* to 1431 FA, *-house* 1325 Cl, 1327, 1333 Pat, 1433 Visit, *-hows* 1409 Pap

Neuahus 1143-47 Dane

Nehus c.1150, c.1155, eHy2, 1177 Dane *et passim* to 1283 Pat,

Neus a1155 Dane, 1200 OblR

Newehus c.1141 BMFacs, 1190-5 Dane, 1191, 1192, 1193, 1194,
1195, 1197, 1199 P *et passim* to 1271 FF, *-huse* 1199 CurR,
to 1303 Pat, *-house* 1311 Pat, *-hous* 1334 Cl, 1348 Pat, 1364
Cl, *Newhus* 1196 ChancR, 1224 Cur, 1271 FF, 1292 RSu,
-house 1201 Abbr, *-hous* 1305 ib, 1375 Works, 1382 Cl *et
passim* to 1428 FA, *-hows* 1451 *DCAcct,* (*aliter Newsom*)
1509 *HarlCh,* 1519 ECB, *-howse* 1535 VE iv

Niewehus 1177 Dane, *Niwehus* 1177, 1190, 1205 ChancR, *Niehus*
1205 P

Neosum c.1115 LS

Neuhusum lHy2 Dane

Neusum 1222 Cur, 1256 Pat, 1257 Ch, 1316, 1317 Cl, 1320 Pap,
1347 Cl, *-om* 1310, 1312, 1316 Cl, 1316 FA, 1323 Pat, 1334
Cl, 1343 NI *et passim* to 1450 LDD, - alias *Neuhouse* 1495
IBL, *-ome* 1382 Gaunt, 1450 LDD, *-am* 1316 Pat

Nusum 1363 Ipm, 1375 Works, 1428 FA

Newsum 1318, 1400 Pap, *Newe-* 1327 *SR* (p), *Newsom* 1417 Cl,
1509-10 LP i, 1526 Sub, 1536 *HarlCh* (*scitum nuper
monasterii de*), 1538 LP xiii, 1547 Pat, - alias *Newsham*
1570 ib, *-ome* 1538 LP xiii, 1552 FCP, 1556 AASR xxxvii,
1564 Pat, - *sive Newsham* 1609 *Foster, Newesom* 1395 Cl,
1395 Pat, 1401-2 FA, 1410 Cl, *-ome* 1527 *HarlCh*

Neusun 1261 Cl, *New-* 1279 Pat, *Neweson* 1323 Cl, *Newson*
1535 VE iv

Newesonhouse 1383 Gaunt

Newesham 1571 *Yarb, Newshame als Newsome* 1628 *ib, Newsham
ab*: 1576 Saxton, *Newsham Abbye* 1610 Speed

There are two alternative forms of this name. Ekwall, Studies[3]
33, would presumably interpret the DB *Neuhuse* as the nom.pl. of
hūs 'a house', though all the rest in *-hus, -hous(e), -hows* appear to
represent the nom.sg., hence 'the new house(s)', *v.* **nīwe, hūs.**
The alternative form, represented by the LS *Neosum* and forms in
-um, -om(e), -on, is from the dat.pl. *æt nīwan hūsum* 'at the new
houses'. It is the latter which has given *Newsham*, the weakly
stressed ending having been interpreted in the 16th century as *-ham*,
and this would suggest that this was the form most commonly used
locally. The same development has taken place in Howsham (in
Cadney) *infra*, also from the dat.pl. of **hūs.** Ekwall, DEPN s.v.

hūs, points out that this word "is mostly found in Scandinavian England and chiefly in the (dat.) plur." Fellows-Jensen, SSNEM 136-7, points out that *hūsum* is a type of name common in Denmark and suggests that "it seems reasonable to accept Howsham as being of Scandinavian origin". The dat.pl. form of Newsham is probably to be interpreted in a similar way. Newsham is once described as *iuxta Vlsebiam* 'next to, by Ulceby'.

ALDER CARR WOOD. ALDER WOOD. BELL PIT, - *pit* 1810 *Yarb*, cf. *Bellpit(t) Field* 1765, 1774, *ib*, *Bell pit close* 1824 *ib*, probably from the *Bell* family, well-evidenced in the Brocklesby PR, cf. Margaret *Bell* 1593, William *Bell* 1753. BLUEGATE WOOD. BROCKLESBY HALL, 1697 Pryme. BROCKLESBY PARK, 1824 O, *The Park* 1765, 1774 *Yarb* and cf. *leparcdich* Hy3 *HarlCh*, *v*. **park**, **dīc**. CARR LEYS WOOD, cf. *the carre leyes* 1587 *Yarb*, cf. *the Carres* 1587 *ib*, **kjarr**; *ley(e)s* is sometimes a later spelling for OE **læs** 'a meadow, pasture', but in the sg. *ley* and pl. *ley(e)s* are also later forms from **lēah**, in its developed sense 'a meadow, a piece of meadow, an open pasture'. Spellings in *lea* and *ley* are common as appellatives in L documents, particularly in 17th and 18th century Terriers, e.g. *two leyes, two pasture lease, a two acre Ley*, etc. It is, therefore, difficult to determine the etymology of minor names and f.ns. in *Ley(es)*, but the pl. of **lēah** in its later sense is probably most likely. COTTAGERS DALE WOOD, *Cottagers Dales* 1828 Bry, *v*. **deill** 'a share of land', presumably let to the cottagers. DAM BOTTOM, cf. *Dammesdale* Ed2 *HarlCh* (*v*. **deill**), *Dam Paddock* 1765 *Yarb, Dampaddock* 1774, 1779 *ib*, self-explanatory, *v*. **dammr**. GRANNY WOOD. IRONGATE WOOD. LAMBERT HILL COTTAGE & POND, 1774, 1779, 1780, 1810 *Yarb*, cf. *Lambertmare* c.1200 *HarlCh, lamberdemare* e13 *ib, Lamberdmare* e13, eHy3, m13, Hy3 *ib*, -*mar'* 13 (Ed1) *Newh, Lambert mare* Hy3 *HarlCh*; *Lambert* is the ME pers.n. from OGerm, OFr *Lambert*, ultimately OGerm *Landbert*; the second el. is **(ge)mǣre** 'a boundary, land on or forming a boundary'. LITTLE LIMBER CHAPEL (lost), *Lytle Lymber chapell* 1530 Wills iii and note "there is a chantry in honour of God and the Virgin Mary ... founded ... at *Parva Lymbergh* out of a messuage and a small portion of land, the value of which messuage and land does not in modern times suffice for the reasonable sustenance of a chaplain, the king has granted licence for them, for the surer maintenance of that chantry, to assign in mortmain land and rent, not held in chief, to the value of *4l.* yearly to a chaplain to celebrate service daily at the said chantry ..." 1356 Pat xxiv, 417-8. The chapel belonged to Newsham Abbey and the earliest reference to it so far noted is *G. abbas & conuentus de Neuhus concessimus Roberto capellano ut seruiat in tota uita sua capelle parue Linberge* eHy3 *HarlCh* 44 G 22 and 23. LITTLE LIMBER GRANGE, 1842 White, apparently a late example of **grange**, as elsewhere in north L. MAJOR WOOD. MAUSOLEUM, 1786 *Yarb*; this document, *Yarb* 5/2/17/2, contains *Accounts of Stone from Doncaster for the Mausoleum* and the text states *Began the 7th August 1786.* According to P&H 201, it was completed by 1792 and commemorated Arabella Aufrère. MERE HILL, cf. *Mere Hill Plat* 1832 *Yarb*, presumably named from the pool there, *v.* **mere**[1]. MILLER'S WOOD. NEW BECK DRAIN, 1824 O. THE NURSERY, *Nursery* 1830 PR Brocklesby. THE PADDOCKS. PRIMROSE HILL. ROUGH PASTURE WOOD. SPUR PLAT WOOD, *Spur plat (wood)* 1832 *Yarb*, cf. *Spur platt* 1779 *ib*, named from the family of John *Spur* 1721 PR Brocklesby and **plat**[2] 'a plot, a small piece of ground'. THOMAS WOOD. WASHDYKE WOOD. WATERHILL WOOD, cf. *Warlot de Wat'hil, Wat'hilgote, Waterhilgote* eHy3 *HarlCh, Waterhilgote, Waterhil Warlot* Hy3 *ib, Wat'hilgote* 13 *ib, The Greate -, The lesser watter hille* 1587 *Yarb, Uttermoor watrilles* 1543 *Anc* ('outer moor'), *The Water Hills Close Meadow* 1762 *Monson.* Waterhill is derived from **wæter** and **hyll**, in which **wæter** is presumably used in the sense 'wet'. *v,* also **gotu** 'a water-channel, a stream' and **warlot**. The latter, common in north L, is defined by NED s.v. *warlott*, as 'some kind of waste or common land'. However, the late Professor M.T. Löfvenberg, in a personal letter, doubted the meaning given there. Indeed, the three references quoted in NED, two of which are in fact from north L, give no clue at all to the meaning of the word and NED's interpretation appears to be really a guess. The editors of NED associate the first el. of *warlott* with *warland* 'agricultural land hend by a villein', that is OE **waru** and Professor Löfvenberg pointed out that, among other meanings, it had the sense 'defence, protection, guard'. If the OE form of *warlott* was indeed **warhlot* or the like, then *etymologically* it would seem to refer to a lot, a share or an allotment of land subject to some form of defence or protection. It seems likely that *warlot* should be associated with *warland,* as Dr John Insley suggests, drawing attention to YCh ii, p.

vii, where the editor states "Each carucate or bovate had a parcel
of meadow appurtenant to it, assessed to geld and other burdens,
and occasionally denominated "warlot", possibly from this
circumstance". A *warlot* would seem to have been a piece of land
assessed to a specifically defined payment of geld. WILLOW
HOLT.

Field-Names

Forms dated 1762 are *Monson*; those dated 1516, 1587, 1765, 1774, 1779,
1810, 1824, and 1832 are *Yarb*, 1578, 1634, 1638, and 1724 are *Terrier*, 1629 are
Ipm (forms supplied by Dr R. Ambler). Other sources are noted. The
reference PR is to *The Parish Register of Broklesby 1548-1837*, ed. C.W. Foster,
1912.

(a) The Abbey Homestead 1824 (the reference is to Nun Cotham Priory);
Abby Close 1779 (*sic*) (cf. *curiam -, viuariam ... abbacie* e13 *HarlCh*, the
reference is to Newsham Abbey); The Ash Close Mdw 1762 (*Ashe Cloase
replenyshed with yung Aishes* 1587, and cf. *Ash Spring Close* 1629, *v.* æsc); Base
Garth 1765, Bacegarth 1779 (the same name survives as Baysgarth in Barton
upon Humber *supra* and East Halton *infra*); Backhouse dale 1824 *v.* bæc-hūs
(ME *bak(e)-hous*) 'a bake-house', deill); Beck Cl 1765, 1774 (*v.* bekkr);
Brocklesby Cl 1765, 1774; Brocklesby Fd 1779 (*ad campum de Broclosby* eHy2
(e13) NCot, *in campis de Broclosbi* p1182 Dane, *campum de broclousbi* John
HarlCh, in campis de - Hy3 *ib,* - *de Broclosby* 113 *ib, Brockelsbie feild, the great
field* 1587, *Brocklesby feild* 1634, *Brocklesby-feild* 1637 both *Terrier* (Great Limber),
v. feld); But Field Paddock 1765, Butfield - 1774, Buttfield - 1779 (*v.* butte); The
Chappell Close Mdw 1762 (*v.* chapel(e)); Colt Cl 1779; Coney Green 1765, 1774
(cf. (*The) Conny garth(e)* 1587; the 18th century forms are from coningre 'a
rabbit warren', while the 1587 spelling is from coni and garðr, with a similar
meaning); the Corne Fields 1762; Cotham wd 1824; Cressy cl 1810, - Cl 1824
(from the family of James *Cressy* 1723 PR); Cuthbert cl 1824; Enfield 1824;
Espin Cl 1765, 1774, 1810 (cf. Espin Carr in Bonby f.ns. (a)); the fallow fds
1762; Far Platt 1774, - platt 1779 (*v.* platt² 'a plot, a small piece of land',
frequent in this parish); Fox Cover pce 1832 (cf. *Foxgraues* p1182 Dane, perhaps
'the groves, copses where foxes are found', *v.* fox, grāf, græfe); Gibsons Cl 1765,
Gibson - 1774, 1779 (from the family of John *gybson* 1542 PR); Glebe Cl 1779;
Habrough Lane 1832 PR (leading to the neighbouring parish of Habrough);
South Hardings 1765, 1774 (cf. *hardhenges* 1294 *HarlCh, Neusum Hardenges* 1364

Misc, *The hardings, Harding carre* 1587, *Hardinges Close* 1629, 'the meadows hard to till', *v.* **heard, eng**); Farr Hog Fd 1765, Far hog - 1774, Farr Hoggfield 1779, (The) Near Hogg Fd 1765, 1779, Nearhog - 1774, Hog field 1810 (*v.* **hogg**); Hoggards Cl 1765, 1774 (from the family of William *Hogherd* 1730 PR, William *Hoggard* 1752 ib); Horse Close 1765, 1774, 1779; The Great Inham Mdw 1762 (*v.* **innäm** 'a piece of land taken in or enclosed'); Jenny Platt 1774, Jenny or Oat platt 1779 (from the family of Joseph *Jenny* 1819 PR and **platt²**); Kermington Seed Plat 1832 (*v.* **sæd, platt²** and the adjacent parish of Kirmington); Lees Cl 1765, 1774, 1779; The Ley Close Pasture 1762 (*le High ley -, the high leys -, long ley Cloase, The ley Cloase behind the barne* 1587, *Ley Close* 1724, perhaps 'the fallow close(s)', *v.* **læge, clos(e)**); Limber-lane-end 1755 PR (*vie* (gen.) *que ducit ad magnam Limbergiam* Hy2 (e13) *NCot, the lane towards great Limber* 1638, *v.* **lane**); little Cl 1765, 1774; (The) Lowfield 1762, 1779, Low Fd 1765, 1774; Mares Cl, Mare Close Mdw 1762; Marshalls Cl 1765, 1774 (*marshall Cloase* 1587, presumably named from an ancestor of Robert *Marshall* 1765); Six Meadow Closes 1762; The Millfield Mdw 1762, Mill Fd 1765, 1774, 1779 (cf. *The wynd myll in Brock: field, one windmyll in the South Field, the wynde mill neere to newsham close* 1587, *the Mill* 1632 *MiscDep 65* (in Nun Cotham), *the myll howse garthe* 1587, *a molendino vent'* eHy2 (e13) *NCot, - ven'* Hy2 (e13) *ib*); Milner cl 1810, 1824, - wood 1810 (from the family of Thomas *Millner* 1781 PR); New Close 30 Acres 1765 (*new closse 1543 Anc*); North Fd 1774, Northfield 1779 (*in aquiloni campo* Hy3 (Ed1) *Newh, in Aquilonali Campo de Broclosbi* 1271 *HarlCh,* 14 *ib, in bor' campo de Broclosby* Hy3 (Ed1) *Newh,* 'the north field' of Brocklesby); The Old Beast Pasture 1762; Old Scales 1779 (*Aldeschaldes, Aldescales* p1182 Dane, 'old sheds or huts', *v.* **ald, skáli,** 'a temporary hut or shed', the second el. being common in NW England, but rare in the East Midlands, cf. *Walgerscales* in Immingham f.ns. (b) *infra*); Parsons Platt 1774, - platt 1779 (*v.* **persone, plat²**); Pinfold 1762 (*v.* **pynd-fald**); Ride and plantation 1779 (*v.* **ride** 'bridle-path'); Rye Cl 1774, 1779; Saint foyn Platt 1774, Sainfoin platt 1779 (*v.* **sainfoin, platt²**); Sandhills 1774, 1779 (cf. *Sandhil gate* Hy3 (Ed1) *Newh* (*v.* **gata**), self-explanatory, *v.* **sand, hyll**); 70 Acres 1832; Sharps Cl 1765, 1774, 1779 (from the family of Roger *Sharpe* 1578); Smith fd 1824 (from the family of Robert *Smythe* 1546 PR, Anthony *Smithe* 1578 *Inv*); The Sooslow 1762; Stone pit Walk 1832 (*v.* **walk**); Stones Cl 1765, 1774; Sweet Willow Carr 1779 (alluding to the sweet-bay willow, *Salix pentandra, v.* **wilig, kjarr**); Taylors Cl 1762 (from the family of Benjamin *taler* 1633 PR); Tenpound Cl 1774, 1779 (possibly referring to a rent); The Watering Dike close Mdw 1762 (cf. *ab aque ductu de Broclousby* Hy3 *HarlCh*); Westcote wd 1810 (cf. *The west Coatt or three South Cloases* 1587, *v.* **west, cot, wudu**); Wold Head 1832 (*v.* **wald, hēafod**); Wood Cl 1765, 1774, 1779 (*v.* **wudu**).

(b) *Bacyorindeile* Hy3 (Ed1) *Newh* (y = þ) (perhaps for *Blacþorn-*, v. **blæc-þorn, deill**); *Baddocwelle* Hy3, c.1270, *Badek Welle* m13 *ib* (probably from the OE pers.n. *Baduca* or alternatively the ME surn. *Baddok* (Reaney s.n. *Baddick*), as suggested by Dr J. Insley; the second el. is **welle**); *The north barely* -, *The South Barely Cloase* 1587, *North* -, *South Barly Close* 1629 (v. **bærlic, clos(e)**); (*a via*) *iuxta bercharia* eHy2 (e13) *NCot*, *Iuxta sedem bercharie* (*apud Cot'*) eHy2 (m13) *NCot*, *iuxta* - Hy2 (m13) *ib*, *Boyouedlande* p1182 Dane, *Boyheuedland* Ed2 *HarlCh*, *Boitoft* 112 Dane ('Boia's headland and toft', from OE pers.n. *Boia*, v. Feilitzen 205, or (less probably) from **boi(a)** 'boy, servant'; *-ouedland* shows replacement of OE **hēafod** by ON **hǫfuð**, v. **hēafod-land**, toft); *bounetoft'* Hy3 (Ed1) *Newh*, *Bounetoft'* m13 *HarlCh*, *Bowntoft 1516*, the *bonde tofte headlandes* 1578, ('bean enclosure', v. **baun, toft**, a Scand. compound, with **hēafod-land**); *iuxta marascum ad bramadeila* Hy2 (e13) *NCot* (probably v. **brōm** 'broom', **deill**); *Bramhil* p1182 Dane ('broom hill', v. **brōm, hyll**); *Braythenges* 1294 *HarlCh* (a Scand. compound of **breiðr** 'broad' and the pl. of **eng** 'a meadow, pasture'); *Broode nooke* 1587, *Broode noke* 1629 (self-explanatory); *Casse garth* m13 *HarlCh*, 1578 (Dr J. Insley suggests that the first el. is the ME fem. pers.n. *Casse*, a pet form of *Cassandra*, the second is **garðr**); the *Castell garth* 1587 (v. **castel, garðr**, but the sense of castle is apparently not known); *The Caulfe Cloase* 1587 (v. **calf**, cf. *the lesser Willingham infra*); *Cawodes Cloase* 1587 (from the family of James *cawood* 1564 PR); *Chalke pitt Cloase* 1587, *the Chalke Pit Close* 1629 (v. **calc, pytt**); *the Chauntrie head lande* 1578 (v. **chaunterie, hēafod-land**; there is no note of a Chantry here in ChantCert, but in A.K. McHardie, *Clerical Poll Tax Assessment in the Diocese of Lincoln, 1377-81*, LRS in preparation, there is a reference under Brocklesby to "John subwarden of the Chantry"); *cultura que uocatur Coc* c.1200 *HarlCh*, Hy3 *ib* (perhaps from **cocc**[1] 'a hillock'); *Cokket landes* 1516 (v. **land**; *Cokket* is prob. a surname); *Coldesdaila* Hy2 (e13) *NCot* (this may be 'Kolr's share of land', v. **deill**, the first el. being ON *Kolr* with excrescent *-d-*); *Cornheade* 1578 (v. **corn, hēafod**); *Cotesick* m13 *HarlCh*, *-sike* Hy3 (Ed1) *Newh* (v. **cot, sīc, sīk**); *ad campum de Cotum* Hy3 *HarlCh*, Hy3 (Ed1) *Newh*, *viam de Cotum* Hy3 (Ed1) *Newh*, *Cotome hedge* (sic) 1516 (named from Nun Cotham); *The Cowe Cloase* 1587; *terram vocat' Craneland* 1516 (v. **land**, the first el. being OE **cran** 'crane, heron', or a surn. derived from it); *crophil* Hy2 (m13) *NCot* (3x) (identical with Cropwell Bishop and Butler PN Nt 234-5, from **crop(p), croppa** 'mound, hill', and **hyll**); *croxton' gate* e13 *HarlCh*, *croxtungate* 13 *ib*, *croxton' Gate* Hy3 *ib*, ('the road to Croxton', v. **gata**, cf. *uiam que ducit ad Croxtonam* c.1200, Hy3 *HarlCh*, *vie* (gen.sg.) *de Croxtun* John *ib*); *viam de Cyrnington'* 1271 *HarlCh* ('the road to Kirmington'); *the dabar Cloase* 1587; *Dabbs Close* 1724 (named from the *Dabbs* family, cf. Thomas *Dabs* 1625 PR, and **clos(e)**); *Daledaile* c.1200, Hy3 *HarlCh* ('allotment in the valley', v. **dalr**,

deill); *The north -, the south deare Cloase* 1587 (probably 'the deer enclosure', *v.*
dēor, clos(e)); *dicfur langes* 112 (Ed1) *Newh,* Hy3 (Ed1) *ib,* Ed1, 113 *HarlCh,* -
furlonges Hy3 *ib* (*v.* dīc, dīk, furlang); *Dikeshil* 1271 *ib* (*v.* dīc, dīk, hyll, though
the gen. form suggests the surn. *Dike*); *terram Rad' Dounibi* 1271 *HarlCh,* Donyby
1332 *SR* (p) ('down in the village', *v.* dūne, ī, bȳ, cf. Midby in Barrow upon
Humber *supra*); *in orient' campo de broclosby* Hy3 (Ed1) *Newh, in campo orient'*
1516 ('the east field (of Brocklesby)'; *le efedes* Ed1 *HarlCh* (*v.* hēafod in the pl.);
Emersons Close 1724 (from the family of Thomas *Emerson* 1604 PR); *Estibyi* 1327
SR (p) (*v.* ēast, ī, bȳ, and cf. *Douniby supra* and *Northiby infra*); *Ferehermere*
(sic) 1516; *super forarium usque ad mariscum* 1262-3 *HarlCh,* Forster *Close* 1629
(*Forster* is presumably a surn.); *tres selliones ... inter duos Fraunchereys* 1271
HarlCh (probably 'between two freeholds', taking *Frauncherey* to be from OFr or
AN *frauncherie 'a freehold'; the same name occurs in Killingholme f.ns. (b)
and in Nettleton f.ns. (b) *infra*); *the fure Cloase with the Carres, the furre Cloase*
1587, *Furr Close* 1629 (perhaps from ME *furre* (OE *feor*) 'far, distant' and kjarr,
cf. ker-, kirfurlonges infra); *the fyfth garthe* Ph&M *Dep* (*v.* garðr); *Grenegate hende*
Hy3 *HarlCh,* grengate *hende* Hy3 (Ed1) *Newh* (possibly alluding to land near a
green lane or occupation road, *v.* grēne[1], gata, ende[1]); *Grenhylle* m13 *HarlCh*
(self-explanatory, *v.* grēne[1], hyll); *Gunheuedland* e13, 13 *HarlCh,* Guneheuedland
Hy3 *ib* ('Gunni's headland', from the pers.n. *Gunni,* with hēafod-land, or the
fem. ON *Gunna,* as Dr J. Insley points out); *Gypitt gate* 1516, *gye pitte -* 1578
(*v.* pytt, the first el. being perhaps OFr *gui* 'a guide', one of the sources of the
surn. *Guy* (Reaney s.n. *Guy*), as Dr J. Insley suggests); *Hagelmar* Hy2 (e13)
NCot (perhaps a mistake for *highelmar' infra*); *Haremare* eHy2 (e13) *NCot,* Hy3
HarlCh, de Haremare strip uersus occidentem Hy2 (e13) *NCot, in tota haramara*
112 (e13) *NCot* (*v.* hara 'a hare', (ge)mǣre, with what appears to be a rare
medieval use of strip 'narrow tract of land' possibly even 'individual holding in
the common fields'); *Hargraves Close* 1724 (from the family of Thomas *Hargrave*
1620 PR); *harmers butt'* 1516, *Armers Close* 1724 (presumably from the surn.
(*H*)*armer,* though this might be a later development of *Haremare supra*);
haufurlanges eHy2 (e13) *NCot,* Hy2 (e13) *ib* (2x) (probably *v.* haugr, furlang);
The haver Cloase 1587 (*v.* hafri 'oats'); *highelmar'* 112 (Ed1) *Newh* (2x),
Highelmare 113 *HarlCh,* Ed1 *ib, Igelmar', ygeldmar', ylemar'* Hy3 *Newh*
(possibly from hygel 'hillock' and (ge)mǣre); *hil-, Hilgerehou* R1 (Ed1) *Newh,*
1262-3 *HarlCh,* hilgerhou eHy3 *ib, Hildegarhou* John, e13 *ib, Hildegarthou* (sic)
e13 (Ed1) *Newh* (probably 'Hildegar's mound, hill', *v.* haugr, with the first el.
OE *Hildegār,* which occurs in *hilgaringdoun* 843 (m9) (S.293) recorded from
Kent); *Hilderholm'* m13 *HarlCh* (Dr J. Insley suggests that the first el. is perhaps
the gen.sg. *Hildar* of the ON fem. pers.n. *Hildr,* the second is holmr); *Holemere*
Hy3 *HarlCh* (perhaps 'the pool lying in a hollow', *v.* hol[2], mere[1]); *Holegraue*

dich Hy3 *HarlCh, Holgrauedic* 1271 *HarlCh,* Hy3 (Ed1) *Newh* (this may be 'the deep ditch', *v.* **hol²**, **grafa¹**, with **dīc** added); *Hommer pitt* 1587 (*v.* **pytt**); *Howsham Cloase* 1587; *hundemar'* 13 (Ed1) *Newh, hu'demare* m13 *HarlCh* (perhaps 'Hundi's boundary', *v.* **(ge)mǣre** and SPNLY 144); ... *tenuit de feodo Hurthequarter* Hy3 *HarlCh* (*v.* **quarter**, the first el. being uncertain); *Huttons Close* 1724 (from the family of Francis *Hutton* 1639 PR); *tres bouates ad Hutware* Ed2 *HarlCh* (Adams 30 defines ME *utware* as 'an incident of tenure imposed on landowners, demanding defence away from home'. The word has been noted as an appellative in *a utware* (in Sixhills LSR) and *a utteware* (in Nettleton *infra*) both c.1150 (1409) Gilb. This legal term is discussed in some detail by Stenton (Dane cxxxiii-cxxxv) who gives examples of land granted *ad utwara* (spelt also *ad hutware*). He states "The utwara of the twelfth century represents the *utwaru* of pre-Conquest documents; it denotes the permanent charges incumbent on an estate in respect of the king's service. The word is normally employed in a context which shows that it refers to fiscal burdens."); *Huuerpittes* p1182 Dane ('the upper pits', *v.* **uferra**, **pytt** and cf. *Netherpittes supra*); *in mora que vocatur Indelesmore* 1303 *HarlCh* (*v.* **mōr¹**, the first el. being possibly the Scand pers.n. *Ingjaldr* or *Ingolfr*, though the development is unusual); *ker-, kirfurlanges, le Kergate* Hy3 (Ed1) *Newh, kerfurlanges* m13, Ed1 *HarlCh, In le Ker de Neuhus* Ed1 *HarlCh, the Carre* (*bottom*), *the carre Cloase* 1587, *the Carr Close* 1629, *Carredyk* 1559 *Anc* (*v.* **kjarr**, **gata**, **furlang**, **dīc**, **dīk**, cf. *iacet propinquarem Kerrie sue* Hy2 (e13) *NCot* and *the fure Cloase supra*); *le kirkestie* John *HarlCh,* (*del*) *kyrkegate* e13 *ib* ('path or road to the church', *v.* **kirkja**, **stīg**, **stīgr**, **gata**, cf. *ad ecclesiam* m13 *HarlCh,* ad Ecclesiam, atte Kyrke 1327 SR, atte Kirk' 1332 *ib* all (p)); *le kylne House* 1549 *Pat* (*v.* **cylen**, it was in Little Limber); *Langeberg* eHy2 (e13) *NCot, langeb'ge* Hy2 (e13) *ib, Langhebergh* c.1155 Dane, *Langeberge* l12 *ib, Langberc* Hy3 *HarlCh, Langberggate* 1271 *ib, langeberg', langberggate* Hy3 (Ed1) *Newh* (*v.* **gata**), *Langberg'* m13, Ed1 *HarlCh* ('the long hill, mound', *v.* **lang**, **be(o)rg**); *le Land'dik'* l12 (Ed1) *Newh* (*v.* **land**, **dīc**, **dīk**, as elsewhere in LNR); *langdic* c.1260 (Ed1) *Newh* (*v.* **lang**, **dīc**, **dīk**); *Leffled-, Leffletdeile* p1182 Dane, *-daile* Hy3 *HarlCh,* Hy3 (Ed1) *Newh, Le Fletdaile* (sic) Hy3 (Ed1) *ib* ('Lēofflǣd's share of land', from the OE fem. pers.n. *Lēofflǣd* and **deill**); *Limberge sich* Hy3 *HarlCh* (*v.* **sīc**); *ad campum parue Limberg'ie* 1271 *HarlCh,* ad -, *uersus campum de parua limbergia, de campo de parue limberg'* Hy3 (Ed1) *Newh, super campum de parue Limberg'* c.1290 *HarlCh, Little Limber field* 1674, - *Field* 1690 both *Terrier* (Great Limber) (self-explanatory); *Lingmare* p1182 Dane, *the Lyngemere headland* 1578 (*v.* **lyng** 'ling, heather', **(ge)mǣre** with **hēafod-land**); *Ludhestrete* John *HarlCh, super Ludei stratam* e13 *ib, Lidhestret* (sic) m13 *ib, ludestrete* l12 (Ed1) *Newh,* Hy3 13 (Ed1) *ib, Ludestrete, Luthestrethe* Hy3 *HarlCh,* l12 *ib, Luetstrete* Hy3 (Ed1) *Newh,* (*de*)

Luthestrete m13, 1271, Ed1, Ed2 *HarlCh, Luyestret(e)* (y = þ) eHy2, Hy2 (e13) *NCot*, 'the road to Louth', *v.* **strǣt**, cf. *Lude stratam* p1182 Dane, *a strata Lude* l12 ib, Hy3 (Ed1) *Newh, super ledestratam* (sic) 13 *HarlCh, apud stratam lude* 13 ib, *ad stratam Lude* Ed1 *ib*); *ad maladerie* Hy2 (e13) *NCot* (*v.* **maladerie** 'infirmary'); *mantell dalle* 1587 (probably from the surn. *Mantel(l)* and **deill**); *marfure* eHy2, Hy2 (e13) *NCot*, Hy2 (e13) *NCot* (*v.* **marfur** and note its appellative use in *ii Marfure* 1578; this is a very early example of a f.n. derived from this word); *a marisco de cotum* Hy3 *HarlCh* (*v.* **mersc**); *middeldaile* l12 (Ed1) *Newh, Middeldayle* Ed1, l13 *HarlCh* ('the middle allotment', *v.* **middel, deill**); *Midfurlang* 1271 *HarlCh* (*v.* **mid** 'middle', **furlang**); *Musemare* e13 *HarlCh, musmare* 13 *ib* (apparently 'the boundary infested by mice', *v.* **mūs, (ge)mǣre**); *The midell Cloase* 1587 *Yarb; Netherpittes* p1182 Dane (self-explanatory, *v.* **neoðera, pytt** and cf. *Huuerpittes supra*); *le fosse qe est apele le Newe dik* e14 *HarlCh* (OFr document), *le Neudik inter Vlseby et Broclosby* 1312 *ib* (cf. *Nouum fossum* e13 *HarlCh, super nouum fossum* Hy3 *ib, v.* **nīwe, dīc, dīk**); *in campo de Neuh'* R1 (Ed1) *Newh,* (*ad*) *campum de Neuhus* Hy3 *HarlCh,* Hy3 (Ed1) *Newh,* Ed2 *HarlCh, in campo de* - 1262-3 *ib; Neuh' Wra* l12 (Ed1) *Newh, Neuhus Wra* Ed2 *HarlCh* (*v.* **vrá** 'a nook, a corner of land'); *The little Cloase called newsham cloase, Newsham Cloase* 1587; *The Watter myll* 1587, *ad molendin' aquaric'* 1559 *Anc, nesham myll* (sic) 1629 *Inv, Newsham mill* 1629 Admin, *Newsham Milne* 1711 PR, *Newsham Water Mill* 1723 *Inv,* (*culture ... que iacet*) *ante portam nordmolendini* c.1200 *HarlCh, le Northmylnes de Nusum* 1375 Works, *one water mylne* 1543 *Anc* (*v.* **myln**); *in aquilon(al)i campo* John, e13 *HarlCh,* - *de Nehus* e13, 13 *ib, le North chaump de Neuhus* e14 *ib* (Fr document) ('the northfield of Newsham'); *Normannemare* Hy3 *HarlCh,* -*mar'* Hy3 (Ed1) *Newh* (presumably 'Norðmann's boundary', *v.* **(ge)mǣre**, the pers.n. being OE *Norðmann*, recorded from the second half of the 10th cent., *v.* Feilitzen 331-2); *Northyby* 1327 SR (p), *Northibi* 1332 *ib* (p) ('north in the village', *v.* **norð, í, bý**, and cf. *Douniby, supra*); *the Northest feilde* 1578 (cf. *the South est feld infra*); *The old inges* 1587 (*v.* **ald, eng**); *the orchard* 1587; *The medow Cloase ... called osgarbs Cloase* (sic) 1587, *Osgarby Close* 1629 (no doubt from the surn. *Osgarby*); *the Oxhand Close* (sic) 1629; *the Parsonage* -, *parsonage house* 1634, 1638 (cf. *partem de Mara que iacet iuxta domum que fuit Joh'is presbiteri* e13 *HarlCh*); *pawmer close* 1543 *Anc, The Palmer Cloase* 1587, *Palmer Close* 1629 (presumably from the surn. *Palmer* and **clos(e)**); *the pease Cloase* 1587, *Peese Close* 1629 (*v.* **pise, clos(e)**); (*una*) *cultura q' vocat' pek* eHy2, Hy2 (e13) *NCot,* - *peke* Hy2 (e13) *ib* (*v.* **pēc** 'a knoll, a hill, a peak'); *Pitgate* 1271 *HarlCh* ('the road to the pit', *v.* **pytt, gata**); *via de magna porta* Hy2 (e13) *NCot, Ridale* Hy2 (e13) *NCot* (*v.* **ryge, deill**); *the round Cloase* 1587; *Rudefleth* l12 Dane (checked from the original, *v.* **flēot**); *Sandholm, Sandpitte* c.1200, Hy3 *HarlCh* (*v.* **sand, holmr, pytt**); *Scortebuttes* p1182

Dane, *skorte-, Skorte-* Hy2 (e13) *NCot, scorte-* Hy3 *HarlCh, scort-* Hy3 (Ed1) *Newh* (*v.* **sc(e)ort, butte** with the first el. apparently in a Scandinavianised form); (*of*) *the seler(e)* 1327 *SR* (p) ('the store-house, granary', etc. from ME *celer, seler*); *cultura ... que uocatur Settecoppe* c.1200, Hy3 *HarlCh* ('the seat-shaped hill' i.e. flat-topped, *v.* **set-copp***); Shepcote garth* 1543 *Anc* (*v.* **shep-cote, garðr**); *siward toft filing* e13 *HarlCh, Siwardetoffilling* (sic) 13 ib, *siwardtoftfiling* Hy3 ib ('Siward's toft', from the ME pers.n. or surn. Siward (OE *Sigeweard,* ODan *Sigwarth*) and **toft**; it may be purely coincidental that a *Siuardus litel* witnesses Brocklesby charters c.1155 Dane; *fil(l)ing* is obscure, but the reading is correct); *in australi campo* (*de Neuhus*) John, e13 *HarlCh* ('the south field'); *the South est feld* 1578 (of Brocklesby); *the South west f(i)eld* 1578 (of Brocklesby); *sponhil* John *HarlCh,* e13 *CottCh, sponebil* (sic) e13 *HarlCh, sponhil* Hy3 ib, *sponehil* 13 ib, *Sponhille* m13 *HarlCh* ('hill where shingles for tiling were obtained', *v.* **spōn, hyll,** cf. Spondon PN Db 605, which has **dūn** 'a hill' as second el.); *stagnum de Broclosbi* p1182 Dane (checked from original); *les Styntyngges* 1312 *HarlCh* (*v.* **stinting;** this is an early example of *stinting,* noted as an appellative in 16th and 17th century Terriers in north L, *v.* NED sb.2 with a quotation dated 1889, and EDD s.v.; both give the same meaning "a portion of common meadow set apart for the use of one person"); *Sykes close* 1724 (probably from the surn. *Sykes,* cf. *Annas Sikes* 1593 PR); *the Thorne Cloase* 1587; *yornhill* (y = þ) 13 (Ed1) *Newh,* Hy3 (Ed1) *ib, Thornhil* 1271 *HarlCh* (self-explanatory, *v.* **þorn, hyll**); *tvamar' gate* Hy3, 13 (Ed1) *Newh, tuamargat* m13 *HarlCh, viam ... voc' Twomergate* 1516 '(road by and to) the two boundaries', *v.* **twegen, (ge)mǣre, gata**); *Tudmargat* Ed1 *HarlCh, twentiaccre* (sic) c.1200 *HarlCh,* (*forariam de*) *twentiacres* e13, 13, Hy3 *ib, twentiacres* eHy3 *ib, twenti acre* 1294 *ib, Twentiaker* 1297 *ib* (self-explanatory, *v.* **æcer**); *Tyrwytt or spring Cloase* 1587 (from the surn. *Tyrw(h)itt*); *the Viner garth* 1587 (from the surn. *Viner* and **garðr**); *Wadecroft* 112 (e13) *NCot* (presumably 'Wade's croft', *v.* **croft,** the first el. being ME *Wade,* OE *Wada* on which *v.* Feilitzen 407, s.n. *Wada* and Reaney s.n. *Wade*); *ad Walchort* Hy2 (e13) *NCot; the Watter Cloase* 1587; *atte Welle* 1341 RIL (p) (Little Limber), *Attewell* 1343 NI (p), *ad Fontem, ad fontem* 1327, 1332 *SR* (p) (*v.* **wella**); *Wendinges* e13, Hy3 *HarlCh* ('the bends (in a road)', *v.* **wending**); *West Close* 1629; *the west corne heade* 1578 (cf. *Cornheade, supra*); *Westda'm* e13 *HarlCh, Westdam* Hy3 *ib* (selfexplanatory, *v.* **west, dammr**); *in occid' campo* 1516 ('the west field'); *Westfurlanghes* John *HarlCh* (*v.* **west, furlang**); *westhenges* 13 (Ed1) *Newh* (*v.* **west, eng**); *the wheat Cloase* 1587; *le Wilekegarth* e13 *HarlCh* (from an unrecorded OE pers.n. **Wileca* or perhaps preferably ON *Vigleikr* and **garðr**); *the greater Willingham, the lesser Willingham or Caulfe Cloase* 1587, *Willingham Close* 1629 (note that Thomas *Willingham* held land in Habrough, apparently of *The Mannere Howse* of Brocklesby 1587, p.12v.);

the windmyll 1587 (in Brocklesby), *the wynde mille neere to newsham cloase* 1587 (cf. *newsham cloase, supra*); *Withmare* eHy2 (m13) *NCot* (the same name occurs in Killingholme and Stallingborough f.ns. (b); for a possible explanation *v. Withemare* in Killingholme f.ns. (b)); *the woodhouse* 1715 PR.

Cadney

CADNEY

Catenai 1086 DB (2x), *Catenase* (sic) 1086 ib (2x)

Cadenai c.1115 LS, 1204 P, *-aie* a1189 Semp, *-aia* 1212 Fees, *-ay* 1238-43 Fees, 1276 RH (p), 1305 Orig, 1318 Cl, 1318 Pat *et passim* to 1428 Fine

Cadenei Hy2 (1319) Dugd vi, 1253 Pap, *-eia* 1201 Dugd vi, 1260 RRGr, *-eie* 1218 Ass, *Cadeney* 1209-35 LAHW, 1253 Abbr, 1275 RH *et passim* to 1526 Sub, *-eye* 1210-12 RBE, 1272 FF, 1294 Pat, 1296 *Ass*, 1303 Pat, 1328 Banco, 1359 Cl, *-eya* 1278 PRGr, 1291 RSu

Kadenai 1157-63, c.1160 Dane, 1194 Cur(P), *-ay* a1219 Welles, 1351 *Cor*, 1375 Peace, 1375 Works, 1391 Cl, *-aye* 1259-78 RA iv

Kadenei Hy2 (1319) Dugd vi, *-eia* eHy3 CollTop (*insula de*), *-eya* 1229 Welles, *-eye* 1240-45 RA iv, 1281 Ipm, *-ey* 1242-3 Fees, 1281 QW, *-ei* 1255 Pap

Cadney 1318 Pat, 1431 Fine, 1461 Pat, 1477 Cl *et freq, Cadney and Howsonne* 1552 Pat, *Cadney cum Housham* 1789 *SocFr, Cadney cum Howsham* 1824 0

Cadnay 1330 Ch, 1375 Works, 1383 Misc, 1384 Cl, 1395 Pat, 1426 Cl *et passim* to *Cadnaye* 1556 LNQ xiv, *Cadnay Housom* 1417-8 Inqaqd

Kadnay 1351 *Cor*

Caddenay 1402 FA

The following forms, *Ceden ac* s.a. 675 (c.1121) ASC E, *Cedenac* 680 (12) BCS 48 & 49 (S 72), given as *Cadanac* ECEE no. 146, and *Cedenan Ac* 675-92 (12) BCS 843 (S 1804), have been associated by Hart with Cadney. He states, ECEE 99, "could be 'Cada's oak'. Cadney was 'Cada's island'". It would appear that this relationship is based purely on the superficial similarity of the two names.

The name means ' Cada's island of land', *v.* ēg and note that in eHy3 it is described as *insula* 'island'. The place lies low east of the R. Ancholme on a raised piece of land.

HOWSHAM
Usun 1086 DB (3x)

Husum c.1115 LS, 1159-81 (e13) *NCot,* Hy2 (1319) Dugd vi, 1177 P, 1196 ChancR, 1199 P, 1201 ChancR *et freq* to 1343 Pat, *Cadenay Husum* 1319 ib, *Cadenayhusum* 1328 Banco, 1343 Pat

Hussum 1201 P, 1539 LP xiv

Husom 1316 FA

Housom 1281 QW, 1303 FA, 1327 *SR,* 1329 *Ass,* 1332 *SR et passim* to (*juxta Someretby*) 1437-8 Inqaqd, *-ome* 1384 Cl, *Cadeney Housom* 1384 Pat, *-um* 1294, 1305, 1329 Pat, 1330 Ch *et passim* to *-um'* 1395 Peace, *-ume* 1402 FA, *Cadeney Housum* 1329 Pat, *Cadeneyhousum* 1408 Cl, *-oum* 1362 Pat

Howsom 1375 Works, 1408 RRep, 1530 Wills iii, 1525 VE iv, *-ome* 1553 Pat, *Howesome* 1391 Cl, 1504 Ipm, *-um* 1444 Pat ("by" *Someretby*), (*juxta Somerby*) 1444-5 Inqaqd

Housam 1408 Cl

Howesame 1570 Pat, *Howsam* Eliz ChancP

Howsham 1566 Pat *et passim*

'At the houses', from the dat.pl. of either OE **hūs** or ODan **hús** , since both have forms in **hūsum**. Ekwall (DEPN s.n.) draws attention to the fact that *Husum* is a common name in Denmark, and Fellows-Jensen (SSNEM 149) points out that "this type of name is mostly found in the areas of England where there was Scand. settlement and it is very common in the Scand homelands". It is, therefore, highly likely that the name is derived from the ODan form. *v.* also Newsham in Brocklesby parish, *supra.* It is described as next to, by Somerby, the adjacent parish to the east.

NEWSTEAD PRIORY, the name surviving as NEWSTEAD
PRIORY FM
in insula de Rucholm, in territorio de Cadenei, quæ Novus Locus dicitur Hy2 (1319) Dugd vi, *Rockholm'* 1407 RRep
de Novo -, Nouo Loco 1199 ChR, 1199 CartAnt, (*in Lindeseya*) 1201 ChR, 1203, 1204, 1206, 1207, 1208, 1209, 1210 all P,

1210 Cur *et passim* to (*near Ancolm*) 1557 InstBen, (*super Ancolme*) 1215 (m15) CNat, (*juxta pontem Glanford'*) 1281 RSu, (*super Anckolm'*) 1281 QW, (*juxta Ancolm'*) 1291 RSu, (*super Ancolne*) 1318 Pat, (*juxta Ancolm*) 1346 FA, (in Lindesey) 1383 Gaunt, (*on Anckeholm*) 1555 HMCRep
Novus Locus 1254 ValNor
Novel Lieu 1310 Cl
Newsted(e) 1227 Ch, ("on" *Ancolm*) 1327, 1333 Pat, ("by" *Ancolne*) 1369, 1408 Cl, ("upon" *Ancolm*) 1434 Pat, 1450 LDD *et passim, Newestede* "on" *Ancolme* 1453, 1557 Pat
Neusted(e) c.1265 RA ii, ("upon" *Ancoln*) 1385 Fine, 1391 Cl, ("on" *Ancoln*) 1397 Pap, ("on" *Ancolne alias Ancolm alias Acolme*) 1442 Pat, 1450 LLD
Nusted 1462 Pat
Newfeld 1610 Speed
Newstrop hall 1675 Ogilby

Sandred 108 takes this as an example of **stede** in the sense 'holy place, church establishment, monastery', as also does Ekwall, DEPN s.n. The meaning is indeed 'the new monastery', *v.* **nīwe**, **stede**, from the Gilbertine Priory founded by Henry II at a place called *Rucholm* 'the rough island of land', *v.* **rūh**, **holmr**. This must have been a perfect description of the site, and note that it *is* described as an *insula* 'island' in the first reference, cf. North and South Ruffham in f.ns. (a) *infra*. It is referred to as near Glamford Brigg and on the R. Ancholme. The 17th century forms are clearly errors, while the Latin spellings are normally preceded by *prioratus* and/or *conventus*.

BEGGARTHORN (lost), 1824 O, 1830 Gre, *Beggar thorne* 1629 *Yarb, Beggor Thorne* 1687 *Inv, Beggarthorne* 1720 *Yarb, Beggar Thorn Farm* 1795 *ib, Beggarthorne walk* 1844 *TA.* On 1824 O, *Beggarthorn* occupies the site of the modern Pepperdale Fm *infra*, Pepperdale itself being marked to the south of the farm. *Beggar* is found among minor and f.ns., where it is often used in a transferred sense of 'worthless', *v.* the examples quoted in Field 17-18. BLACK BANK (lost), 1824 O, (*the*) *black banke* 1634, 1638 *Terrier, Black bank* 1844 *TA*; 1824 O shows it as an extension of the modern Faraway Drain. BRANDICARR, *Brandicar* 1711 *Inv, Brandy Carr* 1720 *Yarb*, 1723 *BT* (Elsham), 1753 *SocFr*, 1795 *Yarb*, 1808 *SocFr*,

Brandey Carr 1723 *Inv*, the forms are too late to suggest a plausible etymology, but the final el. is **kjarr** 'marshy, boggy land'. BRANDICARR COVERT. BURNT WOOD. CADNEY BRIDGE is *Redcar Br.* 1824 O, - *Bridge* 1830 Gre, cf. Redcar *infra.* CADNEY CARRS, 1765 *Yarb*, cf. *Carre grounde* 1538 *AOMB 211, ye Car* 1687 *Inv, the Carr* 1780 (1819) Red, *Cadney Carr* 1817 ib and *weste karre* 1525 Wills i. *Stubbs* 4/1/1 1767 is *A Survey of Carrs,* from **kjarr** 'boggy, marshy land'. CADNEY CAUSEWAY (lost), 1828 Bry, cf. *the Cawsie* 1587 *Yarb, v.* **caucie.** CADNEY GRANGE (local), *grang' suis de Cadney* 1535 Val iv, cf. *Grainge Platt* 1767 *Stubbs, Grange platt* 1795 *Yarb* (*v.* **plat^2**); it was a **grange** of Thornholme Priory. CARR FM is *Chrissey Hills* 1720 *Yarb, Cressy Hills* 1767 *Stubbs, Cresey hills* (*or Criss Wife hills*) (sic) 1795 *Yarb, Criss Wife Hills* 1824 O, 1830 Gre, *Chrissey hills* 1844 *TA.* This is probably named from the family of Henry *Cressye* 1540 *Inv* and William *Cressie* 1639 *BT*; the alternative *Criss Wife Hills* is presumably due to popular etymology. EDLINGTON HO (local), presumably named from the family of William and Thomas *Edlington* 1842 White. FARAWAY DRAIN, 1768 (1791) *LindDep Plans,* 1824 O, 1828 Bry, *Farraway Dike* 1635 (c.1900) *LindDep 78, Farroway Dike* (sic) 1640 *Monson,* self-explanatory. FOX COVERT, *Howsham Fox Cover* 1828 Bry, *Fox Cover* 1844 *TA.* FROGHALL, 1824 O, *Frog Hall* 1830 Gre, 1844 *TAMap,* a name found elsewhere in this county, *v.* Field 84; it is almost certainly used ironically of boggy pieces of land, *v.* **frogga, halh,** cf. foll. FROGHALL CARRS, *Frog Hall Carr* 1767 *Stubbs,* 1790 *Monson, Frogghall Carrs* 1795 *Yarb, v.* **kjarr** 'marshy, boggy land' and cf. prec. GORBET BRIDGE, 1824 O, perhaps from a local surn., but note EDD s.v. *gorbit,* used figuratively of 'a child'. HOWSHAM BARFF, *Bragh* (sic) 1587 *Yarb, Barffe* 1633, 1637 *Inv, Howsham Barfe* 1720 *ib,* - *Barff* 1824 O, cf. *Bargh Cloase, Bragh Bottome* 1587 *Yarb,* from **beorg** 'a hill, a mound', dial. *barf, bargh* (EDD) 'a long low ridge or hill'. HOWSHAM GRANGE, 1537-9 LDRH, *Howsham, firma grang'* 1538-9 Dugd vi, *Howsham graunge* 1542 *AOMB 214, the Grange* 1633 *Yarb,* a **grange** of Newstead Priory. LONG SCREED, presumably *screed* 'a narrow strip of land', NED sb I, 1 b. LOW BARFF, 1830 Gre, - *Barf* 1824 O, *v.* Howsham Barff *supra.* NEWSTEAD DRAIN. NORTH CARR BANK, 1824 O, cf. - *dike* 1632 *Yarb, North carre dale* 1635 (c.1900) *LindDep 78, North Carre, North Carr Lane* 1640 *Monson, North Carr* 1765 *Yarb* and is also

North Dyke Lane 1828 Bry, - *lane* e17, 1709, 1724, *northdike lane*
1634, 1674, 1697, *Northdike lane* 1638, *-dike land* 1679, *nordicke
Laine* 1668, *nor dike lane* 1700, *Nordike lain* 1703, *Northdyke Lane*
1712, *north-dyke lane* 1890 all *Terrier, v.* norð, kjarr and dīc, dík.
OAK WOOD is *Weather Platt* 1720, 1795 *Yarb, Wether Plat* 1824 O,
1830 Gre, *weather plat* 1844 *TA,* 'the plot, small piece of ground for
wethers', *v.* veðr, weðer, plat². PARK WOOD, 1824 O, 1830 Gre,
cf. *Parks* 1720 *Yarb.* PENNY CARRS (lost), 1828 Bry, perhaps
from a local surn. or a rent, *v.* kjarr. PEPPERDALE FM, cf.
Peper dalle 1587 *Yarb, Pepperdale* 1720 *Yarb,* 1828 Bry, named from
the family of Robert *Pepper* 1594 *Inv,* Thomas *Pepper* 1638 *BT* and
deill 'a share of land'. PEPPERDALE COVERT is *Barf(f) Cover*
1824 O, 1830 Gre, *v.* Howsham Barff *supra.* POOLTHORNE, 1720
Yarb, Pool-thorn 1762 *Terrier* (South Kelsey), *Poolthorn* 1763 *Inv,*
1824 O, 1830 Gre, cf. *Pule hedlandes* 1530 Wills iii (*v.* hēafod-land),
'the thorn-bush by the pool', *v.* þorn, pōl¹; there is a small pool
close to the farm. POOLTHORNE COVERT, *Poolthorn Cover*
1824. 1830 Gre. PYE HO, named from the family of Thomas *Pye*
1687 *Inv.* REDCAR, *Red Carr* 1767 *Stubbs, - Car* 1844 *TA,* cf.
Redcar dalle (*v.* deill), *Littel Redd Carre* 1587, *the great read carr,
little readcarr* 1615, *Little Redcar* 1720, *Great -, Little Red Carr* 1795
all *Yarb, Redcare laine* 1668, *Redcar(r) lane* 1674, 1690, *red carr lane*
1700, *Red Carr(e) lane* 1709, 1724, *- Lane* 1762, 1822, 1890, *Redcarr
lain* 1748, *Reede Car laine* 1697 all *Terrier, Thoroughfare Red Car*
(sic) 1790 *Monson,* probably 'the marshy ground where reeds grow',
v. hrēod, kjarr, the place lies low by the R. Ancholme; but it is
possible that it is 'the red marsh', *v.* rēad, kjarr and not far away is
Sand Hills. ROSCAR DIKE, *Ross Carr Dyke* 1824 O, perhaps to
be identified with *Rossiter Carre* 1635 (c.1900) *LindDep 78, Rositer
Carre* 1640 *Monson,* which is named from the family of Richard
Rossetter 1587 *Yarb* and kjarr. SAND HILLS, (*the*) *Sandhills* 1632,
1720 *Yarb,* 1844 *TA, Sandhill* 1795 *Yarb, Sand Hill* 1824 O, 1830
Gre, self-explanatory. SOUTH BANK (lost), 1824 O, 1830 Gre,
part of Roscar Dike. THIRTY FOOT DRAIN, *30 Feet Drain* 1768
(1791) *LindDep Plans, 30 Fᵗ Drain* 1824 O, *Thirty Foot* 1828 Bry,
30 Feet Drain 1844 *TAMap.* THORN COVERT.

Field-Names

Principal forms in (a) are 1844 *TA* 72 (Cadney-cum-Howsham and Newstead). Spellings dated 1545, 1587, 1615, 1626, 1628, 1629, 1632, 1720, 1765, and 1795 are *Yarb,* 1606, 1634, 1638, 1668, 1674, 1679, 1690, 1697, 1700, 1703, and 1709 are *Terrier,* 1640 and 1790 are *Monson* and 1767 are *Stubbs.*

Other sources are noted.

(a) The Acres 1790; Ancholme banke, Old Ancholme Bank (*Anckon bankes* 1587, *v.* foll.); Old River Ancholme 1844 *TAMap;* Ancholme Navigation 1844 *TAMap* (a reference to New River Ancholme, cf. the same n. in Bonby *supra*); Back Cutt 1767, 1795, - Cut 1790 (*v.* **cut** 'a water-channel'); Barley Carr 1765, 1767, 1790, 1795 (1720), - Car 1844 (*v.* **kjarr**, all the f.ns. in - *Car(r)* in this list are parts of Cadney Carrs *supra*); Barr Syke 1795, Barsike (and Smelford cl) 1844 (*Barsike* 1720, cf. *Bersicke dalle* 1587, *v.* **sīc, sík**); Bedford Carr 1765, 1767, 1790, 1795 (1720), - Car 1844 (probably from the surn. *Bedford* and **kjarr,** though only one instance of the name, Nathaniel *Bedford* 1659, has been noted in *BT*); Bell Dale 1795 (1720), - dale 1844 (perhaps named from the *Bell* family, cf. Robert *Bell* 1587, though it could of course be a share of land endowed for the upkeep of a church bell); Black Root 1767, 1795 (- *Roott* 1720); Blacksmith cl; Boat dike Bank; Bottoms (3x), Fore bottoms (*Bottom* 1720, *v.* **fore** (cf. *the fore garth* in f.ns. (b) *infra*), **botm**); Bower Carr 1767, 1790 (named from the family of Thomas *Bower* 1671 *Inv* and **kjarr**); Bratlings cl 1844, Batline cl (sic) 1795 (*Brett Land Cloase* 1587, *Bratlins Close* 1720, cf. perhaps *Bretterne dalls* 1587); Bull Hill 1767 (the reference states "Bylawmen for keeping a bull"); Butler Carr 1767, 1790 (named from the family of Anthony *Butler* n.d. *Inv* and **kjarr**); Butter Carr 1765, 1767, 1790, 1795, 1844 (2x) (1720, from the *Butter* family, cf. Anthony *Butter* 1587 *BT*, and **kjarr**); Calf cl 1795 (- *Close* 1720, *the Calfe Close* 1629, *v.* **calf**); Car (2x), Car heads (2x) (*v.* **kjarr**, **hēafod** and Cadney Carrs *supra*); Chapel cl 1795, 1844 (*Chappill Close* 1720, *v.* **chapel(e)**); Checker btm 1795, 1844 (- *Bottom* 1720, *v.* **cheker, botm,** presumably referring to the chequered appearance of the ground); Chicken btm 1795; Brook -, Lr -, Upr clint 1795, - Clint 1844 (*the Clinte* 1615, *ye Klint close* 1679, *Brooke -, Low -, Upper Clint* 1720, *v.* **klint** 'steep bank, projecting rock'); Far -, Neather Coat Dale 1767, Nether Cote Dale 1790, (far) nether Coat Dale 1795, Nether Coat dale 1844 (*Neither Coat Dale* 1720, *v.* **cot(e), deill**); Corner Car (*v.* kjarr); Cottager Cl 1767, 1790, 1795, Cottagers cl 1795, 1844 (3x) (- *Close* 1720, *the Cottagers Close* 1632, *the cotchers* - 1635 (c.1900) *LindDep 78, Cotchers close* 1640; *cotcher* is a common dial. form in L for *cottager,* this was land let to the cottagers); Cottager west carr 1795 (*v.* **kjarr** and prec.); Cow cl 1795, 1844 (3x), Lr -, Lt -,

Upr Cow cl (- *Close* 1720); Cow Hills 1767, 1790 (1720), Cowhills 1795; Cream poke 1795, 1844 (- *Poke* 1720, 'cream bag', probably as elsewhere, a complimentary term for pasture producing good cream); Cullam (sic) nook (probably an error for *Pullam* -, which it follows in *TA*, v. Pullam dale *infra*); Dalton Carr 1765, 1790, 1795, Far -, Near Dalton - 1767, Daunton Carr 1795, Danton -, Daunton Car 1844 (the 18th and 19th cent. forms appear to refer to the same carr, so it is probably named from the *Dalton* family, well evidenced in the parish, cf. Edward *Dalton* 1670 *BT* and Thomas *daulton* 1716 *Wills*); Daunton cl 1765, 1844 (cf. prec. f.n.); Gt -, Lt Duke Penny 1767, 1790, Duke penny Carr 1795, - Penney Car 1844 (*Duke Penny Carr* 1720, v. **kjarr**); Dyking hard ground 1795, Dyking hill 1795, Diking hills 1844 (6x) (*Dikeing Hill* 1720, the fields are on both sides of North Carr Bank and presumably refer to where *diking* has taken place); East fd; East Wd 1795 (1720, *The East woode cloase* 1587, *the east wood* 1629, v. **ēast, wudu,** cf. West wood *infra*); Eb(b)warr 1795, Btm -, Top Ebbwarr 1844 (*meadowe called Ebwarre* 1629, *Ebwarr* 1720, perhaps, as suggested by Mr John Field, alluding to an *ebbing-weir* 'weir for detaining fish at the ebb-tide', NED s.v. *ebbing* 2, but here, if so, in an extended use of the term, in water-meadow management, v. **ebba, wer, wær**); First -, Second -, Third -, Fourth eight acres; Far Car (v. **kjarr**); Far cl; Far Fd 1795, - fd 1844 (3x) (- *Field* 1720, cf. Near fd *infra*); Far garth (v. **garðr**); Fen car (cf. *le ffenne* 1538 *AOMB 211,* v. **fenn, kjarr**); Field (*Cadney felde* 1538 *AOMB 211,* - *feild* 1587); fifteen acre Carr 1765; Fifteen Acres 1767, 1790; First Car (v. **kjarr**); Fish Cl 1795 (no doubt named from the *Fish* family, cf. Richard *Fishe* 1586 *BT*, frequently recorded in the parish); Five acres (- *Acres* 1720); five pound cl 1795, Five - 1844 (*Five Pound Close* 1720, cf. ten pound close *infra*); Flagg Carr 1765, 1767, Flag Car 1790, 1844, - Carr 1795 (*Flagg Carr* 1720, cf. *the flags Cloase* 1587, 'land growing with irises or rushes', v. **flagge, kjarr**); Fogg cl 1795, (Lt) Fog - 1844 (*fogg Cloase* 1587, *the fog close* 1711 *Inv*, *Fogg Close* 1720, v. **fogga** 'the long grass left standing during winter, aftermath', **kjarr**); Fold Yd & Stack Yd; fore Car, Fore Carr 1765, 1767, 1790, 1795 (1720), - Car 1844 (v. **fore** 'in front', **kjarr** and cf. *the fore garth* in (b) *infra*); Forty Acres 1767, 1795, The - 1790, Forty acres 1795, 1844 (1720); Four Acres 1767 (1720), The - 1790; Fourteen acre Car; Fure Carr (sic) 1790 (cf. perhaps *furre grounde* 1538 *AOMB 211,* from ME *furre* (OE *feor*) 'far, distant'); Furze (2x) (v. **fyrs**); Garden Leys; Garth 1795, Far Garth, Garths (*the garth* 1711 *Inv, Garth(s)* 1720 (several), v. **garðr**); Gate ends (- *Ends* 1720); Goat Car 1767 (v. **gotu** 'a water-course, a stream', **kjarr**); Grainge Platt 1767, Grange Platt 1790 (1720), - plat (4x) - platt 1795, - plat 1844 (this must be a plat or plot of land (v. **plat**^{2}) belonging to a grange, since it is east of Cadney, at some distance from Howsham Grange); Cow cl & Gravel pit, Gravel pit Garden; Great Car (v. **kjarr**); (Btm) Great cl

(*Great Close* 1720); Green Carr 1767, 1790 (*v.* grēne[1], kjarr); Green Garth 1795 (perhaps cf. *Othe Grene* 1327 *SR, atte Grene* 1332 *ib, atte Grene of Housham* 1343 *Pat, de Grene de Housu'* 1396 *Pat* all (p), *v.* grēne[2], though it could of course be the colour green); Low Greets 1795, Upr & Lr Greets 1844, (*Low -, Upper Greets* 1720, *v.* grēot in the pl., presumably in the sense of gravelly places); Gullis Carr 1765, North Gulliss - 1767, North Gullis - 1790, (Farr) Gulliss carr 1795, (Far) Gullis Car 1844 (1720, *v.* kjarr; the first el. is probably a surn.); Hagg 1795, 1844 (1720, *v.* hogg 'cutting, a part of a wood marked off for cutting); Hall Carr 1795, - Car 1844 (- *Carr* 1720); Hall Cl 1767, 1790, Hall cl (Car) 1844 (*Hall Close (Carr)* 1720, cf. *the Hall* 1587, *v.* hall); Hall Garth (1720, *hall garth* 1587, *v.* hall, garðr); South Helcliff 1765, Furr -, North Hell Cliff 1767, Far -, North Hell Cliff 1790, Farr -, Hither hell Cliff 1795, Far -, Hither hell cliff 1844 (*the great hellcliffe* 1629, *Hellcliffe* 1635 (c.1900) *LindDep 78, Helcliffe* 1640, *Far -, Higher Hellcliff* 1720 (*v.* clif; hell is perhaps used in a derogatory sense, but the forms are late); Hill btm, Hill cl, Buildings Stackyard etc. (*Hill Close* 1720); Hills 1767, 1790, Far hills, Fore hills & plantn 1844; Hither Fd 1795, - fd and Ozier holt 1844 (cf. Ozier Holt *infra*); Home cl (*-Close* 1720); Home pce; Hopyard 1795, Hop yard 1844 (- *Yard* 1720, *v.* hop-yard); Horse cl (- *Close* 1720, *the horse Close* 1711 *Inv*); Howsham cl, Howsham Lane (1720); Huggans Platt 1795, - hill 1844 (cf. *Huggans Platt* 1720, possibly from the surn. *Huggons* or *Huggins*, cf. Reaney s.nn. *Huggin, Huggon*); Hundred Acres 1767, 100 Acres (sic) 1790, Hundred acres & bank (a common ironic name for a small field, here an enclosure with an area of 2 roods, 23 perches); Hutton Leas 1765, - Leys 1767, 1790, 1844 (1720), - leys 1795 (named from the family of Robert *Hutton* 1602 *BT* and lea, the pl. of lēah, common in north L and which appears as *Leas, Leys,* etc.); Island 1767, 1790, 1844 (1720; this is a small isolated piece of ground between the New and Old River Ancholme); Kelk Car (*Kelk Close* 1720, named from the family of Edward *Kelke* 1587 and kjarr); Knabb 1767, Knab 1790, Nab 1795 (1720), - fd 1844 (*Nabb Cloase* 1587, *v.* knabbe 'hill top'); Leg Car (2x) (*v.* kjarr, perhaps named from its shape; the fields abut on Soak Drain); Ley cl; Little cl (- *Close* 1720); Little Fd 1795; Long cl 1795, 1844 (*the long Cloase* 1587, *the Long close* 1629); Low cl (- *Close* 1720); Meadow cl (& fold yard); Melton Cl 1795, 1844 (1720; perhaps a close held by Melton Ross parish, but note the family name *Melton* in the parish, e.g. Thomas *Melton* 1605 *BT*); Mew platt (the first el. is obscure, *v.* plat[2]); Middle Carr 1765, 1790 (1720), - Car 1844; Middle pce; Middle Toft (1720, *v.* toft); Mill fd (- *Field* 1720, cf. *The Parrock or newe myll cloase* 1587, *v.* pearroc 'a small enclosure, a paddock'); Mount Bank 1795; Narrow closes; Near fd (- *Field* 1720); New fd 1795, 1844, Newfield (3x) 1844 (*New Field* 1720); Nine Acres 1795 (1720), - acres 1844; Nine Riggs 1767, 1790, 1795, - riggs 1844 (2x) (*the Nine riggs* 1632, (*Low*) *Nine Riggs* 1720, literally 'nine strips of the common field', with *Riggs* from the Scand. form **hryggr**); North bottom (*v.* **botm**); North cl; North Fd 1795, - fd 1844 (- *Field* 1720, and *no: S: and west feildes* (sic) 1587); North Leys (cf. South Leys, West Leys *infra*); Oaks & Stable (*Oaks* 1720); Oat Carr 1765, 1790 (1720), 1795 (2x), (Great) - 1767, (Great) Oat car 1844, (*v.* **kjarr**); Ox Cl 1767, 1790, 1795 (1720), - cl 1844 (5x) (*Oxcloses* 1635 (c.1900) *LindDep* 78, *The Greate Gled and Oxcloses* 1635 (c.1900) *ib, great Eawes* and *Oxeclose* 1640); Ozier bank (3x), Ozier holt (2x); Paddock 1767, 1790, Far -, Fore -, Lt Paddock; Padnook 1765, Pad Nook 1767, 1790, 1795, - nook 1844 (- *Nooke* 1720, *v.* **padde** 'a toad'); Paley Carr 1765, 1767, 1790 (1720), - Car 1844 (from the surn. *Payley,* cf. *Jo' Payley* 1631 *Inv,* and **kjarr**), Paley Traynam 1765, 1767, - Traneum 1795, - Trancum 1844 (1720, cf. prec. n. and Traynam *infra*); Park Carr 1795 (*v.* **kjarr**), Gt -, Lt Park 1767, 1790, Parks 1795, 1844 (2x) (1720, cf. *north parkes Padocke* 1629 and South Park *infra*); pear tree cl 1795, Pear tree - 1844 (*the peare tree Cloase* 1587, *Pear Tree Close* 1720); Pen cl; Pennel Car 1765 (named from the *Pennel* family, cf. M^{rs} *An Pennell* 1702 *Inv,* and **kjarr**); Home -, Middle -, South pce (*v.* **pece**); Pingle (*the pingels* 1587, *v.* **pingel**); Gt Pippinwells 1795, (Lt -, Upr) Pippinwells 1795, 1844 (*Pippinwells* 1720, *v.* **wella**); Pissey bed 1767, 1844, - Bed 1790 (1720), - bed Carr 1795 (alluding to the dandelion, cf. Pissy Bed in the f.ns. (a) of Bigby *supra*); Pisster Hills 1767, Pisster - 1790 (*Pister Hills* 1720, obscure); Plantation (freq); Pullen Dale, (Low) Pullam Dale 1795, (Lr -, Upr) Pullam dale (3x) 1844 (1587, - *Dale* 1720, *Pulham dale Close* 1629, the first el. is probably a surn.); Ram Carr 1795; Rans Carr 1767, 1790 (1720), Rands Car 1844 (named from the family of William *Rands* 1627 *BT,* Richard *Rans* 1767 and **kjarr**); Resle Garth 1795, Ressle Garth 1844 (*Resle Field,* - *Garth* 1720, named from the family of Robert *Wresle* 1638 *BT* and John *Wressel* 1683, 1686 *BT* with **feld** and **garðr**); Reste Fd 1795; River Car (*v.* **kjarr**); North -, South Ruffham 1767, 1790, - Rougham 1795 (1640, 1720, cf. *Rougham Cloase* 1587; this is almost certainly the same as *Rucholm,* the earlier name of the site of Newstead Priory; *-ham* is a frequent 16th century reflex of **holmr** in LNR. On the Plan, 1720 *Yarb,* the two fields are separate from one another, but *North Rougham* is situated immediately south of the Priory grounds at approximately TA 004035, though the fields themselves cover a wider area. The 1587 form is from a Survey of Newstead Priory land); Rush Carr 1767, 1790; Rye Cl 1795, - cl 1844 (- *Close* 1720, *The rie Cloase* 1587, *the Rye close* 1629, cf. *the East Cloase formerly rie cloase* 1587, *East Close* 1720, *v.* **ryge**, **clos(e)**); Sallow Holt 1767, 1790, wood or Sallow Holt Low Land 1795 (cf. *the sallowe Cloase* 1587, *v.* **salh** 'willow', **holt**); Sand Cl 1795 (1720), - cl 1844; Scaman - 1767, Scaman Carr 1890 (*Scamin* - 1720 probably from a surn.); Scorbur Carr 1767, 1790, - Car 1844 (*Scorber Carr* 1720, no doubt named from an ancestor of John *Scorborough* 1767 and **kjarr**); North -, South Scott Carr 1767, North -, South Scot - 1790, Scot Carr 1795, - Car 1844 (*Scott Car, Near Scott Carr* 1720, named from the surn. *Scott*, cf. Richard *Scotte* 1686 *BT*, and **kjarr**); Searby Cl (from the neighbouring parish of Searby); Second Car; Sedwick Carr 1765, Sedgwick Carr 1767, 1790, Sedgick Carr 1795 (*Sedgeick Carr* 1720, from the family of Thomas *Sedgwicke* 1656 *BT* and **kjarr**); Seeth Car (and ozier bank) (*v.* perhaps **sēað** '(brine) pit' or the surn. *Seath*, **kjarr**); Seg Carr 1767, 1790, Sedge Carr 1795 (*Segg Carr* 1720, *v.* **secg**[1], **kjarr**; the forms in *seg(g)* are Scandinavianisations); Seven acres 1844 (2x) (- Acres 1720); Sheep cl (- *Close* 1720), Sheep dike pingle (*v.* **dīc, pingel**); Shipman Cl 1767, 1790 (perhaps the same as foll.); Shipton Cl 1795, - cl 1844 (*Shipston Close* 1720, presumably from the surn. *Ship(s)ton*); (Long) Six Acres 1767, 1790; Six acre Car (- *Acre Car* 1720); Sixteen Acre Car 1765; Sixteen Acre Cl 1795 (1720), (North -, South) Sixteen acres 1844; Sluice Carr 1765; Smelford Cl 1795 (1720, cf. Barsike *supra*); South Carr (Bottom) 1790 (*south carre* 1587, *South Carre* 1635 (c.1900) *LindDep* 78, 1640, - *Carr* 1720); South cl; South Fd 1790 (1720), (Low) South Fd 1795, 1844 (*v.* North fd *supra*); South Leys; South & West bank; South Park 1765 (*south parkes* 1630); South pce; Gt -, Lt Spring Well Dale 1795, (Lt) Springwell dales 1844 (*Springwell dale* 1629, *Great -, Little Springwell* (*Dale*) 1720, the first el. being presumably *spring* 'a plantation', the second **wella** 'a spring'); Square cl (- *Close* 1720, *the square close* 1711 *Inv*); Stackyard & home cl; Stiddy Cl 1795 (1720, possibly alluding to a forge, cf. dial. *stiddy* 'a smithy', *v.* ON **steði** 'anvil'); Stone cl; Stone Dale (btm) 1795, 1844; Stripe ('narrow tract of land', *v.* **strīp**); Sweet Leys (1720, a complimentary name for good meadow or pasture; for *Leys* cf. Hutton Leas *supra*); Tayler Car hill (*Taylor Carr Hill* 1720, from the surn. *Taylor*, cf. *Richard taylor* 1545 *Inv*, and **kjarr**); Taylor Carr Nooking 1767, 1790 (1720, cf. prec. f.n.); Ten acres; ten pound cl 1795, Ten - 1844 (*Ten Pound close* 1720, cf. five pound cl, *supra*, which adjoins, both alluding to the purchase or rental value of the land); Tesh close Bottom (*Tesh Close* 1720, the first el. being no doubt the surn. *Tesh*); Thirteen Acres 1790, - acres 1844; Thirteen Acre Carr 1767, 1790, 1795 (1720), (Pt of) Thirteen acre Car 1844; Thirteen acre cl; Thirty foot Bank (cf. Thirty Foot Drain *supra*); Thirty three acres Car; Thompson Car (2x) 1844 (*Tompson Carr* 1720, from the surn. *T(h)ompson*, cf. William *Tomson* 1587 *Inv*, and **kjarr**); Thorney Carr 1765 (*v.* **þorn, -ig, kjarr**); Thorough Fair Red Carr 1767 (cf. Redcar *supra*), Thorough Farr fd 1795, Thorough fare Car, Thorough fare fd 1844 (*Thorough Far Field* 1720, *v.* **thoroughfare, kjarr**); Three acre cl (- *Acre Close* 1720); Three acres (2x) - *Acres* 1720); Three Corner pce; Three Nooks 1767, 1790, 1795; Top Car (*v.* **kjarr**); Town end cl (- *End Close* 1720, *Townes end close* 1635 (c.1900) *LindDep* 78, 1640, 'close at the end of the village', and cf. *the Townes Ende* 1587, *v.* **tūn**,

ende[1]); Traynam 1765, Furr - 1767, Middle and Nook Traynam 1767, 1790, Nook
Carr - 1795, Hither -, Middle Tranum 1795, Hither -, Middle -, Nookt Trancum
(sic) 1844 (*the greater and lesser tranehams* 1629, (*a parcel of ground ... called*)
Treynham 1635 (c.1900) *LindDep 78*, 1640, *Higher -, Middle Trancum* (sic) 1720,
perh. 'the water-meadow frequented by herons', *v.* **trani, holmr,** with *-ham, -um*
for *-holme*, as frequently is the case in LNR, cf. Paley Traynam *supra*); Pt of
Twelve acres (2x) (*Twelve Acres* 1720); Twelve Acre Carr 1765, 1790 (1720), -
acre Car 1844; Twenty Acres 1767, 1790; Twenty acres Car (*Twenty Acre Carr*
1720, *v.* **kjarr**); Twenty five acres Car; Two four acres (sic); Under Thorn(e)s
1767, - Thorne 1795, - thorns 1844 (*a place called under thornes* 1668 *Terrier,
Under Thorns* 1720, *v.* **under, þorn,** '(place) beneath, under the thorn-bushes');
Upr & Lr close (*Upp' Close* 1720); Ureby Carr 1767 ('in South Ferreby Carrs');
Vicarage Carr 1767 (1720), Vicarage Cl 1790 (1720); the walk 1844, Walk 1795,
1844 (*the Walk* 1711 *Inv*, (*Little*) *Walk* 1720, from **walk** denoting land used for
the pasture of animals, especially of sheep, hence the common *Sheepwalk*); Ward
Carr 1767, 1795 (1720), - Car 1790, 1844 (doubtless from the surn. *Ward*, cf.
William *Ward* 1700 *BT*, and **kjarr**); (Lt) Warlotts (cf. *The East warlottes* 1587, *v.*
warlot, and the discussion s.n. Waterhill Wood in Brocklesby parish *supra*); West
Carr 1765, 1767, 1790, 1795, Gt West - 1767, 1844 (- Car), Nook - 1767, (Far)
West -, Gt West -, Middle West -, Nookt West Car(s) 1844 (*weste karre* 1525
Wills i, *weste Carre* 1587, *West Carre* 1640, *Wescarr, Far -, Gt -, Middle -, Nooke
Wescar* 1720, *v.* **west, kjarr**); West fd (*v.* North fd *supra*); West Holme Cl 1795
(- *Close* 1720), - Home cl 1844 (*v.* **west, holmr**); West Leys (1720); West wd (-
Wood 1720, *the west wood* 1629, *v.* **west, wudu**); Willgoat Carr 1765, Wells Goat
Carr 1767, 1790, - Car 1844, Wells gate cl 1795 (- *Gote Carr* 1720, *v.* **gotu**);
Willow Car (*v.* **wilig, kjarr**); Willow Garth 1795 (*v.* **wilig, garðr**); Winship Carr
1765, 1767, 1790 (from the surn. *Winship*, cf. Robert *Winship* 1719 *BT*, with
kjarr); Wood cl (cf. *the wood, the littel woode Cloase* 1587); Wott Carr 1767,
1790; Wright Carr 1767, 1790, 1795, (1720), - Car 1844 (named from the *Wright*
family, cf. John *Wryght* 1572 *Inv*, and **kjarr**); Yew platt 1795, - plat 1844 (- *Platt*
1720, *v.* **īwc, plat**[2]).

(b) (*in*) *the bayle* 1332 *SR* (p) (*v.* **bail** perhaps in the sense 'a palisade', but
it may not, of course, be a local surn.); *Bennet house* 1530 Wills iii (from the
surn. *Bennet(t)*, but the earliest so far noted is Thomas *Bennett* 1767); *the blynd
mans closse* 1545; *the borden bridge* 1629 (the first el. is apparently an
unrecorded OE **borden* 'made of planks' from **bord** and **-en**[2] adjectival suffix,
hence 'planked bridge', *v.* **brycg**, the same name being found in North Kelsey
f.ns. (a) and the reference may well be to the same bridge); *Brighills* 1629
(presumably 'the hill(s) by the bridge', *v.* **brycg** (in a Scandinavianised form),
hyll); *Buner Carr* 1720; *the Byrde cloysse* 1545; *Constable cloose* 1545 (from the

family of Robert *Constable* 1545 and **clos(e)**); *Corne Close* 1720; *Costhead* 1695 *Inv*, *Damon Carr* 1720; *the east close* 1629, *East Close* (*v*. Rye Cl *supra*); *the fallowe Cloase* 1587; *Five Acre Close* 1720; *the fore garth* 1587 (*v*. **fore** 'in front', **garðr** and cf. its appellative use in a *foregarth* also 1587); *the garner dick* 1587 (from the surn. or occupational name and **dīc, dīk**); *Grovie-acre* (sic) Hy2 (1319) Dugd vi; *Hamma lande* 1530 Wills iii; *one dale ... in west carre called Haslopp dale* 1587 (Henry *Haslopp* held a cottage, also 1587, cf. West Carr (a) *supra*); *le Hallf Dicke* 1588 *Ipm* (*v*. **dīk**); (*Low*) *Holmes Close* 1720 (*v*. **holmr**, cf. West Holme Cl (a) *supra*); *Great* -, *Little Horse Backs* 1720 (perhaps named from its shape); *Howsham low feild, the low feild* 1629; *the Kirke hedge* 1632 (cf. *ad ecclesiam* 1327 *SR*, *atte Kirke of Housom* 1329 Pat, *atte Kirke* 1332 *SR*, *atte Kirk'* 1351 *Cor* all (p), *v*. **kirkja**); *the land drean* 1690, *ye Land Drean* 1703 (i.e. 'land drain'); *the litell Cloase* 1587, *Little Close* 1720; *littelham hill* 1587, *Litleham* - 1629 (probably from **lȳtel** and **holmr**, with *-ham* for *-holme*, as elsewhere in LNR); *the Lordys closse* 1545 (self-explanatory); *Marlings* 1720 (probably from ME **marling** 'a marl pit', cf. PN Berks 35, 890); *Middle Toft* 1720 (*v*. **toft**); *Mouse Lane* 1606, *mouse lane* 1700; *in nether carre one dale called Peripitt dalle* 1587, *Nether carre dale* 1635 (c.1900) *LindDep* 78, 1640 (*v*. **neoðera, kjarr, perige, pytt, deill**); *New Close* 1730 Red; *Newstead causey* 1640 (*v*. **caucie** and cf. *Cadney Causeway supra*); *North'by* 1332 *SR*, 1359 *Cor* (both (p)) ('north in the village', *v*. **norð, i, bȳ**, cf. *Southiby, Westiby infra*); (*Great* -, *Little*) *North Platt* 1720 (*v*. **plat²**); *Oglesby Garth* 1720 (named from the *Oglesby* family, cf. Robert *Oglesby* 1671 *Inv*, and **garðr**); *paine hill* 1587; *peache hill* 1587; *the pound Cloase* 1587 (*v*. **pund**); *Ranby Garth* 1720 (presumably from the surn. *Ranby* and **garðr**); *Round Close* 1720; *the saffrone garth* 1587 (*v*. **saf(f)roun, garðr**); *Sheepe Coatt Cloase with the Sheep Coatt* 1587, *Sheepestall Close* 1635 (c.1900) *LindDep* 78, *Sheepestalle close* 1640 ('sheep shelter', *v*. **scēap, cot, stall**); *the South feild of Howsham* 1626; *Southiby* 1327 *SR* (p), *Suthiby* 1332 *ib* (p) ('south in the village', *v*. **sūð, i, bȳ**, cf. *North'by supra*); *the Stone Bridge* 1626 (in Howsham, perhaps the one referred to in *Brighills supra*); *Tharroll Carrs* 1720 (named from the family of Mr *Jessop Tharrald* 1767 and **kjarr**); *Well cloysse* 1545, *Well garth* 1720 (cf. *ad Fontem* 1327 *SR*, *at Welle* 1388 Peace both (p), *v*. **wella, clos(e), garðr**); *Westcott Cloase* 1587 (*v*. **west, cot**, it adjoins *west towne* 1587); *Westiby* 1327 *SR* (p), *Westeby* 1332 *ib* (p) ('west in the village', *v*. **west, i, bȳ**, and cf. *North'by supra* and *the west towne* 1587, *a peece of ground their called the west towne* 1615); *Whittam Hill* 1634 (named from the family of John *Whitamme* 1587 and **hyll**); *Wrendocke dalle* 1587 (*v*. **deill**, the plant alluded to being perhaps *Polygonum bistorta*, taking the first el. to be from ***wrēo**, or some other *wr-* word with a sense of 'twisting', or the word may simply mean 'the little dock', from the bird-name *wren* (OE **wrenna**); the term does not seem to occur in plant-vocabularies).

Caistor

CAISTOR
  CASTR 975-8 ASCoins, CAZT 978-9 ib (forms supplied by Dr
    Veronica Smart)
  Castre 1070-87 RA i, 1086 DB (3x), 1138-9 RA i, 1146 ib,
    c.1150 *TYR,* c.1155 (e13) *NCot,* 1157-63 Dane, 1158-9 RBE,
    a1180 (e13) *NCot,* 1195 P *et freq* to 1556 CA
  Castra 1090, 1093-1100, 1100-15, 1110 RA i, 1130 P, 1135-6 RA
    i, 1135-54 (1384), 1138-9 (1329) Ch, 1139, 1146, 1147-53 RA
    i, 1154-8 (1329) Ch, c.1155 Dane, 1155-61 RA i, c.1160
    Dane *et freq* to 1254 ValNor
  Castr' 1159, 1160, 1161, 1166, 1167, 1169, 1171, 1173 P *et
    passim* to 1329 Pat, 1343 NI, 1393 Works
  Castor c 1275 LNQ vi, 1392 Works, 1555 Pat, - *Saxonice
    Ðuangcaster & Thongcaster* 1587 Camden, 1695 Pryme, - *alias
    Thong Castor* 1741 *PT,* 1824 O
  Caster 1276 (1409) Gilb, 1331 Pap, 1491 Pat, 1509 Ipm, 1526
    Sub *et passim* to 1697 LNQ viii
  Castur 1443 Fine, *Kastur* 1536 LP xi
  Castyr 1445 AASR xxix
  Caestre 1472 WillsPCC
  Caister 1485, 1548, 1550, 1557 Pat, 1569 SP, 1576 LER, *Caistre*
    CA, *Cayster* 1537-8 Dugd iv, *Kayster* 1539 LP xiv, *Keyster*
    1526 Sub
  Caistor 1634 SP *et passim*
  Kester 1536 LP xi
  Thwancastr(e) 1190 (e13), 1291 *NCot,* 1329 *Ass,* 1337 Pat, 1338
    Misc, 1342 Ipm, 1356 Pat, 1373 Peace, 1391 *FF, Thuancast'
    als Castor* 1576 Saxton
  Thwangcastr(e) 1298 *Ass,* 1303 Ipm, 1303 Cl, 1310 *Extent,* 1316
    Pat *et passim* to 1465 *Dixon*
  Thwongcastre 1345 *FF, Thowncaster* (sic) 1538-44 ECP
  Twangcastre 1316 Pat, *Twancastre* 1318 Cl
  Thangcastr' c 1275 LNQ vii, *Thaungkastre* 1346 FA
  Yongcastr' 1275, *Yoncastre* 1276 (with *Y-* for *þ-*) RH, *Thong
    Caster* 1610 Speed, - *Castor* 1799 Young

'The Roman station', *v.* cæster, ceaster. The prefix *Thwang-* etc.
is clearly from **þwang** 'a thong' in some transferred topographical

sense, though it is not clear what this is. Caistor has been identified with *Bannovalum* 17 (13) Ravenna 24a. Rivet and Smith RB 265b suggest either Caistor or Horncastle, and it seems more likely that it should be identified with Horncastle.

CAISTOR SOKE, *de sokna de Castre* 1143-52 (Ed1) *Newh, socam* - 1155-60 Dane, *soca* - 1195 P, 1196 ChancR, 1197, 1199, 1201 P *et passim, socha de Castra* 1170, 1171, 1172 *et freq* in P to *soca de Castra* 1197, *Soka de Castre* 1231 Cl *et passim* with spellings similar to those of the parish name, *Castersoke* 1510 LP 1, *soka de thwancastr'* 1190 (m13) *NCot, soka de Thancastra* 1200 ChR, *Swang cast' soca* (sic) 1317 Inqaqd, from **socn**, ME *soke* 'a district over which a right of jurisdiction was exercised, an estate'.

AUDLEBY
  Aldulve- (2x), *Alduluebi* 1086 LB
  Aldolbi c.1115 LS
  Aldolfbie c.1150 *TYR, -by* 1299 *FF*, 1316 FA
  Aldelfbiam (sic) 1190 (1301) Dugd vi
  Aldolby 1288 Ass (p), 1301 Ch, 1327, 1332 *SR, Aldelby* 1331
      Ipm, 1343 NI, *Aldalby* 1390 Cl
  Alfdolby (sic) 1313 Cl
  Adolfbi 1212, 1238-43 Fees, *Adolsfby* (sic) 1535 VE iv
  Audelbi 1160-62 (1287) YCh iii, *-by* 1547 Pat, *Awdelbye* 1546 LP
      xxi, 1587 *Yarb, -bie* 1567 Pat
  Audleby(e) 1556 CA, 1562-7 LNQ v *et passim*

'Aldwulf's farmstead or village', *v.* **bỹ**, the first el. being the OE pers.n. *(E)aldwulf.* It is noteworthy that there is no trace of the OE genitival *-es* in the forms for Audleby and it is likely that the name was given by Scandinavians. Indeed, Ekwall, *Selected Papers* 66, assumes that the DB form in *Adulve-* presupposes the Scandinavian genitive *-a-* < *-ar-*. In any case the name itself suggests a preponderent Danish population in the area. See further Dorothy M. Owen, "Thornton Abbey and the Lost Vill of Audleby", LAAS vii, 113-6.

FONABY
  Fuldenebi 1086 DB
  Fulmedebia 1177 P

Folmodebi 1204 P
Felmetheby 1226 Fees
Folmetby 1316 FA, 1354 *Cor* (p), 1378 *Foster, Folmethby* 1343 NI
Folnetby l12 (Ed1) *Newh,* 1294 *Ass,* 1431 FA, *Folnetheby* 1364
    Foster
Folneby iuxta Castra 16 (endorsement) *Foster*
Fonneby 1562-7 LNQ v, *Fonnabye otherwise Fulnabie* 1574 AASR
    xxvii
Fonaby 1720 *Foster et passim*
Furneby F^m 1828 Bry

The inconsistency in the early spellings makes it difficult indeed
to suggest any etymology. The preponderance of *-m-* seems to indicate that this is original, and so Ekwall's tentative suggestion
(DEPN s.n. Follingsby) that the first el. is OScand *full-nautr* 'one
who has a full share' can hardly be correct. No convincing
etymology can be suggested and this name is better considered
unexplained, till additional material is available.

HUNDON MANOR
    Humendone 1086 DB
    Hundidune 1086 DB
    Hauendona 1110 RA i (*Hauedon'* in margin, checked from MS)
    Huneduna c.1115 LS, l12 Dane, *-dune* l12 (1409) Gilb, l12 (m13)
        NCot, *-dun* 1212 Cur, *-don'* 1193, 1194 P (p), a1218 RA iv (p)
    Hunduna 1187 (1409) Gilb, *-dun* e13 (1409) ib, 1212, 1238-43
        Fees, *-dune* 1275 RH, *-done* c.1240 *R, -don'* 1242-3 Fees, 1298
        Ass, e14 *KirkstInv* i, 1327 *SR,* 1329 *Ass* (p), 1373 Peace (p),
        -don 1303, 1316 FA, 1331 Ch, 1347 Cl, 1347, 1349, 1373, 1374
        Fine all (p) *et passim*
    Hondon 1282 Ipm, 1327 *SR,* 1354 *Cor,* 1535 VE iv
    Honton 1316 FA
    Hunden 1556 CA

'Hūna's hill', *v.* **dūn,** with the same OE pers.n. as occurs in
Hundon (Sf), where the second el. is **denu** 'a valley', *v.* DEPN s.n.
Presumably the DB and 1100 RA i forms are erratic in view of the
overwhelming evidence of all the later spellings.

ANGEL (lost), 1826, 1842 White. AUDLEBY SQUARE WOOD

is *Audleby Top Cover*, 1824 O, 1830 Gre. AUDLEBY TOP is *Audleby Clump* 1828 Bry. BACK WOOD. BLACK SWAN (lost), *Dwelling house* .... *heretofore a Farmhouse known by the Name of the Black Swan* 1785 *MiscDon 140*. BRICK KILNS (lost), 1828 Bry, 1830 Gre, cf. *Brick Kiln Close* 1783 *LTR*; it was between Fonaby and Hundon. BRIGG ROAD, *Brigg road* 1834 Red. BUTTER MARKET, *Butter market* 1826 White. CAISTOR MOOR, *la Mora* 1219 Ass (p), *quoddam molendinum situm in La More de Castre* 1229-45 RA iv, *la More de Castre* 1239-44 ib iv, *mora de Castre* 1275, 1276 RH, *mora de Castr'* 1281 QW, *Castre More* 1537 LP xii, *Caster moore* 1664 *Terrier*, - *Moor* 1671 *ib*, *Cayster Moor* 1674 *ib*, *Caister moor* 1679 *ib*, *Caster Moore* 1685 *Nelthorpe*, *Caistor Moor* 1707 *Terrier*, self-explanatory, *v.* mōr[1]. CANADA, CANADA LANE, CANADA WOOD, near to the east boundary of the parish, a nickname of remoteness. CASTLE HILL, *There is a place by the fold south-west of the church still Call'd Castl-hill* 1724 Stukeley, the exact nature of the "castle" is not known. CORNHILL, 1826 White. FALCONER'S ARMS (lost), 1842 ib. FAR FM. FLEECE INN, 1828 Bry, 1830 Gre, 1841 *TAMap*. FONABY TOP, 1841 *ib*. FOX DALE (partly in Great Limber also), *uallem quandem que a uulgo Foxedale uocatur* c.1150 *TYR*, self-explanatory, *v.* **fox**, **dæl**, **dalr**. GEORGE HOTEL, *George Inn* 1826, 1842 White. GOLDEN FLEECE (lost), 1826, 1842 ib. GRIFFIN (lost), 1826, 1842 ib. GROVE HO, *Grove hs.* 1826 ib. HORSE MARKET, *a certain Street or place called the Horse Markett* 1727 *MiscDon 140*, *the Horse Markett* 1730 *ib*, *Horse market* 1826 White. HOUSE OF INDUSTRY (lost), 1823 *PR* (Caistor), 1824 O, 1826, 1827, 1828 *PR* (Caistor), 1828 Bry, 1830 *PR* (Caistor), 1830 Gre, 1832, 1833 *PR* (Caistor), 1842 White, *We* ... *Do hereby consent and agree to the erecting a House of Industry upon a certain part of the said Common Mor not exceeding Ten Acres* (i.e. Caistor Moor) 1801 *Lamb*. HUNDON WALK HO, cf. *Hundon Walk* 1825 *BC*, cf. *East -*, *West Side Walk* 1829 *TA*, for *walk*, *v.* Cadney f.ns. (a) *supra*. JOINER'S ARMS (lost), 1826, 1842 White. KING'S ARMS (lost), 1826 ib. KING'S HEAD (lost), 1826, 1842 ib, *the Inn Called* .... *the Kings Head* 1733 *MiscDon 140*. LOW FONABY, *Low-Foneby* 1638 *Inv*, *Lowfonebie* 1664, 1667 *BT*, *Low fonaby* 1670 *Inv*, *Low Fonaby* 1776 *Tur*. MARKET PLACE, 1826 White, 1829 *MiscDon 292*, *fori de Castra* 1182 P, *fori de Castre* 1197, 1198 P *et passim* to *fori de Castr'* 1210 ib, *ex orientali parte fori* 1210-20 RA iv, *viam fori de Castre*

1220-30 ib, *Castre* "market" 1370 Pat, "the market place" 1536 LP xi, self-explanatory. MARQUIS OF GRANBY (lost), 1826 White. PLOUGH (lost), 1826, 1842 ib. NAVIGATION LANE, 1864 *Terrier.* NETTLETON RD, *Nettleton way* 1677 *ib,* - *gate* 1679 ib, - *Gate* 1706, 1707 *ib, Nettleton road* 1828 *PR* (Caistor), 'the road to Nettleton', *v.* **gata.** OLD VICARAGE, *the vackarige house* 1671 *Terrier, Vicarage* 1826 White. OLD WINDMILL, cf. *the Windmill* 1734 Foster. PAPER MILL (lost), *Elizabetha vxor Roberti Howel de paper Mill caster* 1668 *BT, The paper Milne* 1677, y^e *paper miln* 1679, *the paper Millnes* 1700, *where ye paper mill was standing* 1703, and cf. *Paper Milne Closes* 1700, *paper-milne close* 1706, *ye paper mill closes* 1707 all *Terrier.* RED HILL (lost), 1828 Bry, between Fonaby and Hundon. RED LION HOTEL, 1842 White, *Red Lion Inn* 1826 ib, 1838 *Lamb.* REIN DEER (lost), 1826 White. SANDBRAES, *the Sand Brays on Caistor Moor* 1825 *BC, Sand Brays* 1828 Bry, *The Sand Braes Plantation* 1854 *MiscDon 140,* presumably 'the sandy slope', the second el. being ME *bro, bra* 'a slope, a bank', dial. *brae,* chiefly Scots and North Country. SHAW WOOD, cf. *Shaw Wood Close* 1825 *BC.* SHOOTERS DALE. SLOOP (lost) 1826 White. SPA SPRING, 1841 *TAMap.* SUDDELL HO. TALBOT HOTEL, *Talbot* 1826, 1842 White. THORNEY BOTTOM WOOD. VICTORIA (lost), 1842 White. WATER HILLS, 1825 *BC,* 1829 *TA.* WATER MILL (lost), 1828 Bry. WEST MOOR FM. WHITEGATE, *White gate* 1733 *Nelthorpe.* WHITEGATE HILL, *White gate Hill* 1864 *Terrier.* WHITE HART, 1842 White. WHITE HORSE (lost), 1826, 1842 ib. WIND MILL P. H. (lost), *Wind Mill* 1826, 1842 ib, and cf. *Old Windmill supra.*

Field-Names

The undated forms in (a) are 1839 *TA* 74 (covering Audleby, Hundon and Fonaby only). Spellings dated 1587 and 1832 are *Yarb,* 1649 are *ParlSurv,* 1733 are *Nelthorpe.* 1800 and 1829 are *MiscDep 292,* 1825 are *BC,* 1834 are *Red,* and the remainder are *Terrier,* unless otherwise noted.

(a) Ash Holt (*v.* **æsc, holt**); the Back Street 1800 (*Back Lane* 1748 *BPD*); Barn Plat (2x, *v.* **plat**^{2} 'a plot of ground', as elsewhere in this parish); Beck Cl, - Plat (cf. *atte Bek of Castre* 1342 Cl, *Atte Bek* 1343 NI both (p), *v.* **bekkr,**

plat^2); Bog Cl 1789 *LTR*; Brick Yd, Kiln, Sheds and Pasture Land, Brick Yard
Cl; Burnt Mill Cl 1783 *LTR*; Part of New Calkers; Cave's Cl 1825 (from the
family of William *Cave* 1659 BT and **clos(e)**)); Chapel Cl 1825, 1839 (*Chappell* -
1677, 1679, - *Closes* 1700, - *close* 1703, *chappell close* 1706, *Chappele* - 1707);
Church Cl 1825 (*the church close* m17, *Church Closes* (*Hundon*) 1734 *Foster*); Clay
Pit(t)s, Clay Plat (*v.* **clæg, pytt, plat**^{2}); Coarse Plot 1825; Cow Cl 1825 (*Cowe*
cloase 1587); Cuckolds Gap 1832, Cuckold - 1839 (probably a secluded piece of
land by an opening in a hedge, *v.* **gappe**); Cundiff (cf. *Conduit Closes* 1700, -
close 1707, y^e - 1703, 1706, *v.* **conduit**); Dyke Cl (cf. *the old Dikebottom* 1733, *v.*
dīc, dīk); Nr -, Far East Cl; Pt of East Walk (cf. the walk in f.ns. (a) of
Cadney, and Hundon Walk *supra*); Five Acres (*v.* **æcer**); Fold Yd and Stack
Yd; Forty Acres 1825, Pt of Forty Acres (5x); Forty five Acres (*v.* **æcer**); Fox
Cover 1832 (cf. *the Fox Hall* 1733 *MiscDon 140*, near King's Head *supra*); Pt of
Gales Cl, North Side Gales Cl (from the surn. *Gale*); Garden Cl, Garden Fd
(2x); Goose Hills 1832, 1839; Haddlesey's Cl 1825 (from the family of Robert
Haddelsey 1755 *BT*); Hall Cl 1783 *LTR*; Harbour Hill 1825, 1839, - Hills 1832,
1839, Top Harbour Hill 1839; The Hills 1825, 1832, 1839, Gt -, Lt Hills Cl 1825,
Great Hill(s) 1839 (cf. *Hill'* 1327 *SR* (p), *Caster* -, *Castre Hill* 1536, 1537 LP xi,
v. **hyll**); Home Cl 1825, 1839 (2x); Hundon cl 1825; Hundon Moor 1825,
Hundon Moor otherwise Hundon Low Grds otherwise the Old Race Course
1854 *MiscDon 140*; Iron Gate Plat (*v.* **plat**^{2}); Joseph Hills 1825, Joseph's Hill
1839; (North) Kirby Cl (named from the family of John *Kirbie* 1666 *BT*);
Limber Road Cl; Long Hill 1839, - Cl 1825; Lords Cl 1825; Malt Kiln 1783
LTR; Mill Plot 1825 (cf. *ye milne closes* 1703, *middle mill close* 1733, *v.* **myln**);
Moor Close 1832, 2 moor closes 1834, Far -, First -, Second -, Third Moor
1839; Nine Acres; (Far -, Nr) North Cl; North Walk (*v.* **walk**); (Low) Oak Tree
Plat (*v.* **plat**^{2}); Ozier Holt 1825, 1839 (*v.* **holt**); The Paddock 1829; Lt Paradise,
Paradise Mdw 1825, Paradise (*v.* ME **paradis(e)** 'an orchard, a garden'); Pinfold
Cl 1864 (*v.* **pynd-fald**); Plantation Pce; Race Course 1829, Part of - 1839 (cf.
Hundon Moor *supra*); Red Hill 1825, - Hills 1839 (2x); Round (Plantation) Cl;
Sand cl 1825, (Far -, Near) Sand Cl 1829, 1839 (cf. *Sandgate* 1677); Sans Cl
1832, Part of - 1839 (perh. for *Sands*-); Scrivener Cl 1790 *LTR* (1679, *Scrivenars*
close m17, *Scrivener close* 1686-90, - *Closes* 1703, *Scriveners close* 1706, from the
surn. *Scrivener*); Seven acres; Sixty acres (*v.* **æcer**); East -, West Side Walk;
South Cl (- *close* 1733); Spring Borough; Stack Yard Cl; Stile Cl 1825, - Plat
1839 (*v.* **stigel, clos(e), plat**^{2}); Stone Stack Wold 1825, 1839; Swallow Road Cl
1832, 1839 (leading to Swallow); Sweeting Pce 1832, (Far) Sweeting Pce 1839
(named from the family of Mathew *Swetyng* 1561 *BT* and **pece**); Thirty five
Acres; Toll Bar 1823, 1826 *PR* (Caistor); Turnpike Gate 1826 *PR* (Caistor);
Water Hills (2x, *v.* **wæter, hyll**, and cf. Waterhill Wood in Brocklesby *supra*);

(Far -, Nr) West Cl; Walk Cl 1825, Pt of West Walk 1839 (cf. East Walk *supra*); Wheat Cl; White Hill Cl 1825, White Hills 1839; Willow Holt 1825 (cf. Ozier Holt *supra*); Middle -, North -, South Wold 1825, 1839, Wold Plot 1825 (*Castre wold* 1537 LP xi, *v.* **wald**); Near wood cl 1832, close over the wood 1834, (Lt -, Nr) Wood Cl 1839 (*v.* **wudu**).

(b) *campis adolfbie* c.1150 *TYR*, *Audelbie Field* 1671 *Terrier* (Great Limber); *Awdelbie Corner*, *Awdlebie dalle* 1587 (from Audleby *supra*); *Austin Yard* 1734 *Foster*, *in Ballio* 1327 *SR* (p) (*v.* **bail** 'a palisade, etc.', but the surn. may well not be a local one here); *Beanhills* 1679, 1686-90 (*v.* **bēan, hyll**); *Bogger Furlong* 1649 (probably alluding to a secluded spot, supposedly haunted by a *boggart*); *Branhills* 1733 (probably in Caistor); *brochau* c.1150 *TYR* (*v.* **haugr**); *Cabourn Hedge* 1696 *Haigh* (on the boundary with Cabourn); *Caister Warren* 1733 (*v.* **warcine**); *Calfe Close* 1677, 1679, *calf close* 1703, (*the*) *Calve Closes* 1700, 1706, *the Calf closes* 1707; *Cant green close* 1686-90; *Carleswathe* (Audleby) 1190 (1301) Dugd vi, i (the first el. is either *carl* (ON *karl*) 'a man, a fellow of humble status' or the ON pers.n. *Karl(i)*, recorded in L in DB, the second is **vaδ** 'a ford'); *in campis de Cast'* 13 *HarlCh*, *- de Castre* Hy3 *ib*, *the filde at Castre called Castre filde* 1536 AASR xxvii (*v.* **feld**); *Caster Ings* m17, *the Ings* 1733 (*v.* **eng**); *the church lane* m17; *the clock peices* m17 (probably an endowment for the maintenance of the church clock); *the Common meerfurrow* 1733 (*v.* **marfur** 'a boundary furrow'); *Cressebec* 13 *HarlCh*, Hy3 *ib* ('cress stream', *v.* **cærse, bekkr**); *Croe garth* 1700, *crow -* 1703, *Crow -* 1706, 1707 (perhaps 'the enclosure frequented by crows', *v.* **crāwe, garðr**, but it may well be named from the family of *James Crow* 1686 *BT* and **garðr**); *Cuntebecsic* Hy3 *HarlCh* (the apparent combining of **sīc, sīk** and **bekkr** is puzzling; if the first el. here is **co(u)nte** topographically used, the name may refer to a small stream feeding another called **Cuntebec* 'stream flowing through a cleft'); *dighton Cloase* 1587 (from the surn. *Dighton* and **clos(e)**); *the drift Cloase* 1587 (for *drifte*, *v.* Drift Rd in Barnetby f.ns. (a) *supra*); *the Fallow Feild* 1649; *The fogg Cloase* 1587 (alluding to tall thin grass, aftermath, *v.* **fogga**, cf. Fogg cl in Cadney f.ns. (b) *supra*); *The furre Cloase* 1587 (perhaps 'the far, distant close', *v.* **fur (feor), clos(e)**); *Grene* 1327 *SR* (p), 1332 *ib* (p), (*v.* **grēne**[1]); *Green's meadow* 1733 (probably in Caistor, and named from the family of George *Greene* 1675 *BT*); *the Hatters Stalls* 1748 *BPD*, *Hoggs ground* 1665 Cust ii (probably belongs here; it is from the surname *Hogg*, cf. *Mr Luddington was to hold, with those he hath allready at Funnabie, if Hogg leave his* 1665 *ib*); *Hundon lane end* m17; *kilnehouse close* 1677, *Kilne house Close* 1679, *kilnehouse close* 1686-90 (self-explanatory, and note *Brick-kiln Closes, Lime kilnfurlong* 1733); *Kokyswode juxta Cayster* 1537-8 Dugd iv (probably from the ME surn. *Cōk* 'a cook' and **wudu**); *Lillys close* 1686-90, *Lilly's Closes* 1733 (from the surn. *Lilly*); *the Lowfield* 1733 (self-explanatory); *Mawdson's Nook* 1735 (from the family of Richard *Maudson* 1647 *BT* and **nōk**); *Milners closes* (probably named from the family name *Milner*); *in Campo borali* 13 *HarlCh*, *in aquilonali campo* Hy3 *ib, North field, North and South Fields* 1626 LNQ iii, *the North Feild* 1649, *the Northfield* 1732 (one of the open fields of Caistor, cf. *in campo australi infra*); *Northiby* 1327, 1332 *SR* both (p) ('north in the village', cf. the same form in the f.ns. of Cadney (b) *supra, v.* **norð, i, bȳ**); *Otbye close* 1686-90, *Ottby & Lilly Closes* 1700 (presumably named from the surn. *Otby*, and cf. *Lillys close supra*); *the Poor House* 1717 *BT*; *pratum d'ni Regis* 13 *HarlCh* ('the king's meadow'); *Sayntmariland de Caster* 1276 (1409) Gilb 17 (p), - *in Castre* 1328 Banco (p), *Stayntyngriland* (sic) 1327 *SR* (p) (presumably endowed land dedicated to the Blessed Virgin, *v.* **land**, the same name occurring in Nettleton (f.ns. (b)), the adjoining parish, so probably referring to the same family, but the name may not be local; this name has also been noted as *Seyntmaryland* PN C 336); *a platt called the Southdales* 1733 (*v.* **sūð, deill**); *in Campo australi* 13 *HarlCh*, *in australi campo* Hy3 *ib, the South feild* m17, *ye Southfield* 1677, 1697, *ye South Feild* 1697, - *feild* 1703, 1706, *the -* 1707, - *Feild* 1700, 1709, *the Southfield* 1733, *the Southside or feild of Castor* 1663 (cf. *North field supra*); *Springarth Close* 1677, 1679 (*v.* **spring, garðr**); *Stoll crofts close* 1686-90, *Stoll crofts* 1703, 1706, *Stole crofts* 1707 (possibly an endowment for the provision of stoles for use in the church, or a surn. *Stoll, v.* **croft**); *Stotwall close* 1686-90; *Streett Furlong* 1649, *streetfurlong* 1733 (cf. *infra magnam uiam qua de Castra itur ad Kirningt*(*unam*) c.1155 Dane, *ad viam de Castre* 1202 FF, *v.* **strǣt**); *Taylordale* 1733 (named from the family of Thomas *Tailer* 1602 *BT* and **deill**); *Tenter hill* 1733 (from **tentour** 'a frame for tenting cloth' and **hyll**); *The Thorne Cloase* 1587; *Thornhil'* 13 *HarlCh*, *Thornhil* Hy3 *ib* (*v.* **þorn, hyll**); *Tollcroft* 1733; *the Towne Furlong* 1649 (*v.* **furlang**); *Warthgate* (sic) 1733 (apparently 'the way, road to *Warth*', *v.* **gata**. *Warth* is from OE **waroð**, ME *warth*, probably in the sense 'a flat piece of land or meadow along a stream, marshy ground near a stream'); *Westfield* m17 (cf. *North field supra*).

Clixby

CLIXBY (now in the parish of Grasby)

Clisbi 1086 DB, 1199 P, 1238-43 Fees, *-by* 1268 *NCot*, 1342 Cl, 1380 Fine, 1383 Peace, ("by" *Gresby*) 1320, 1321, 1342 Pat, (*juxta Grosby* (sic)) 1333 Orig, (*juxta Gresseby*) 1341-2 IpmR, (*juxta Gresby*) 1342 Orig, *Clysby* 1303 FA, (*juxta Gresby*) 1321 Orig, ("by" *Gresby*) 1333 Pat

Clissebi 1177 P, 1202 Ass, *-by* 1242-3 Fees, 1247, 1259 Ipm, 1259

FineR, 1270 Pat, (- *alias Clixseby*) 1273 Ipm, *-by* 1276 ib, *et freq* to 1384 Pat, (*iuxta Gresseby*) 1293 *Ass, Klisseby* 1281 QW, *Clysseby* (*iuxta Gresseby*) 1292 *FF*, 1298 Cl, 1332-3 IpmR, 1354 *Cor*, 1368, 1369 Ipm, *Clyseby* 1226-8, 1244 Fees

Clipsebi 1196 ChancR, 1203 *et passim* to 1214 P, 1230, 1231, 1232, 1234, 1253 Cl, 1256 FF

Clipesbi 1206, 1230 P, *Clypesby* 1237 Cl

Clifsebi c.1115 LS, 1202 Ass, *Clifsbi* 1150-60 Dane

Cliffeby 1210-12 RBE

Clessebi 1192 P (p), *Clesby* 1504 Ipm

Clestebi (sic) 1209 P (p), *Clestesbi* (sic) 1210 ib (p)

Clixby 1300 FF, 1311 Fine, 1311 Orig, 1316 Cl, 1316 Fine, 1327 *SR*, 1338 Banco *et freq*, *-bi* 1548 *Anc*, *-bye* 1576 Saxton, *Clyxby* 1368, 1382 Pat, 1398 Fine, 1401-2, 1431 FA *et passim* to 1453 Fine

Clixheby 1275 RH, *Clixeby* 1275 ib, 1312 Ipm, *-bie* 1276 RH, *Clyxeby* 1276 ib

Clexby 1369 *AD*, *-be* 1539 LP xiv

This is a very difficult name. Ekwall (DEPN s.n.) takes the spellings in *-ps-*, *-pes-* as indicative of the original form and assumes the name to be identical with Clippesby Nf and means 'Klypp's farmstead or village', *v.* **bỹ**. The first el. would then be the Scand. pers.n. *Klyppr*, which he assumed occurred here in the 10th century as the name of a moneyer in the form *Clip*. Dr Fellows-Jensen (SSNEM 41), however, points out that *Klyppr* is not found independently in L. She takes the forms in *-fs(e)-* to reflect the original spelling and suggests that the first el. is "Scand *klif* n. "steep slope or bank", perhaps replacing OE *clif* n., used of the steep slope on which C. stands", though, in fact, the slope is steeper at a number of places with names in **bỹ** along the scarp slope. It may be objected that there are fewer such instances in the large collection presented above than in *-p(e)s-*, and that it is certainly possible that *-fs-* is an error for *-ss-*, due to the similarity of *f* and *s* in medieval script. It should also be noted the form with *-ss-* is very common from the 12th to the late 14th century in the spellings for Clixby, and are most likely to be explained as the result of the assimilation of *-ps-* to *-ss-*. The *-ff-* form in RBE looks very much like an error for *-ss-*. In his discussion of ON *Klyppr, Insley* 533-36 notes first that the name is "sparsely attested and seems to have

been a side-form of ON *Kleppr* (personal name and byname)", and
points out that the Scandinavian evidence "might be taken to suggest
that ON *Klyppr* is, in fact, merely a scribal variant of ON *Kleppr*".
He goes on to suggest that it might be better to regard Clixby and
Clippesby, as well as Clipston (PN Nt 232, PN Nth 111) and
Clipstone (PN Nt 73, and Bd, PN BdHu 122) as containing an
OScand pers.n. **Klippr*, corresponding to ON *Kleppr* in the same
way as the Danish appellative **klip(p)* corresponds to ON *kleppr*,
ODan *klæp(p)* 'a lump', used also to denote the top of a hill.
Insley, further, takes *Clip*, the name of a moneyer of the reign of
King Edward the Elder, as being derived from **Klippr*, since, as he
rightly points out, it appears in an OE source at too early a date
for the late OE unrounding of [y] to have taken place. Following
Insley, we may then suggest that Clixby in fact means 'the
farmstead, village of Klip', *v.* **by**, the first el. being the Scandinavian
pers.n. *Klippr*.

AUDLEBY LOW COVERT, *Audleby low Cove* (sic) 1830 Gre,
named from Audleby in the neighbouring parish of Caistor.
CLIXBY LODGE, 1824 O, 1828 Bry, 1830 Gre. CLIXBY
MANOR. HALL CROSS (lost), 1828 Bry, 1830 Gre. HONEY
CLOSE PLANTATION (lost), *Honey Close Pl.*[n] 1828 Bry, no doubt
a nickname for good land, *v.* Field 107-8. LAWRENCE FM (lost),
Lawrence F.[m] 1828 Bry, no doubt from a family name, perhaps cf.
William *Lawrence* 1778 *BT* (Caistor). MOOR HO, cf. *Clixby Moor*
1824 O, *the Moor* c.1832 *Yarb*, *Moor* 1839 *TA*. SOUTH VIEW.

Field-Names

Principal forms in (a) are 1839 *TA* 92. Dated forms are *Terrier* unless otherwise
noted, except for those for 1717 which are *LCC*.

(a)   Bottom Cl (cf. Long Cl *infra*); Bracken Platt *v.* **brakni**, **plat**[2] 'a plot of
ground', as elsewhere in this parish); Bromley Marsh (apparently identical with
Ranby Marsh 1717 and *Romley Marsh* 1745 *LCC*, which certainly denote the same
place; this variation makes an interpretation difficult, though each is likely to be
from a surn.); Chalk pitt Platt (*Chalke pitt furlong* e17, *v.* **pytt**, **plat**[2]); Church
Yd (cf. *atte Kyrke* 1327 SR, *ad ecclesiam* 1332 *ib*, *ad ecclesiam* 1354 *Cor* all (p));
Clover Cl, Clover Plantation, - Platt Plantation; Cotchers Moor (2x) (i.e.

'cottagers' moor', for the dial. form *v.* Cottager Cl in the f.ns. of Cadney (a) *supra*); Cottage & Gdn; Cow Cl (3x) & Rd; Cuckhold Platt (*sic*) (2x) (*cuckold* usually refers to a secluded piece of land, *v.* **plat²**); Dake Cl (*sic*, corrected from *Drake*); Dike Platt (*v.* **dic, dik, platt²**); (Middle -, Top) Drill Cl; Eighteen Acres (3x); Eleven Acres; Fifty Acres dale (3x) (*v.* **deill**); Furze Pce (*v.* **fyrs, pece**); Garden (2x); Home Cl; Homestead etc.; Hop Garth (amended from Hoop -), Hop Yd (*v.* **hoppe, garðr, hop-yard**); Horse Cl (2x) & Rd; Howe (3x) (*the How* 1717, 'the (burial) mound', *v.* **haugr**); Hunters Cl (from the occupational name or the derived surn., though the latter has so far not been noted here); Kennington Corner (probably from the surn. *Kennington*, cf. William *Kennington* 1791 *BT* (Caistor, which includes Clixby names)); Ling Pce (2x) & Rd (*v.* **lyng**); Long Cl (*Long close* 1717; adjacent to Long Cl in *TA*, are Bottom Cl, Middle Cl and New Cl); Middle Cl (cf. Long Cl); Gt -, Lt Millin Cl (cf. *the Mill* 1671, *The Mill furland* 1664 (*v.* **furlang**), *Mill -* 1671, *Mill Hill Close* e17, 1700, 1717, *the Mill hill Close* 1706, *the Mill-hill close* 1709, *- Close* 1715, *Mills hill close* 1690, *milne hil close* 1697, *Miln hile clos* 1703, y^e *same dale called* y^e *milne dale* 1703 (*v.* **deill**), *v.* **myln** 'a mill'); New Cl (*new close* 1717, cf. Long Cl *supra*); Oat Platt (*v.* **platt²**, cf. Platts, Rye Platt, Wheat Platt *infra*); Occupation Rd; Paddock (3x); Plantation (*freq*) & Rd; Platts (4x) (*v.* **plat²**); Potatoe Gdn; Ringdam Cl (*Ringdam* 1717; this is obscure, for there is no stream or pool here; it is No. 40 on *TAMap*); Russle Pce and Rd (*sic*) (perhaps from the surn. *Russel*, cf. Thomas *Russel* 1768 *BT* (Caistor)); Rye Cl, *- Platt* (2x) & Rd (*v.* **ryge, plat²**); Sainfoin Cl (*v.* **sainfoin**); Seed Platt (*v.* **sæd, plat²**); Sixteen Acres; Thirty two Acres (*v.* **æcer**); Thistle Plot; Three Corner Pce (alluding to its triangular shape); Twenty Acres (2x); Twenty one -, Twenty two - (2x), Twenty Four -, Twenty five -, Twenty six Acres (*v.* **æcer**); Wheat Cl (2x), Wheat Platt (*v.* **hwǣtc, plat²**).

(b) *Bennetts Yard* 1717 (no doubt named from the *Bennett* family, cf. Thomas *Bennitt* 1641 LPR); *Brigg gate* e17 ('the road to Brigg', *v.* **gata**); *the Castle Feild* 1700 (there appears to be no evidence as to the exact nature of *Castle* here); *Clixby feild* 1606, *- field* 1697, 1703, 1707 (*v.* **feld**); *Collop Monday close* 1717 (from *Collop Monday* 'the day before Shrove Tuesday, on which fried bacon and eggs still form the appropriate dish in many places', *v.* NED s.v. *collop* 1c, though the exact significance of this in a f.n. is uncertain); *the Corne feild* 1664; *the Crook dale* 1664 (probably a share or portion of land in a 'crook' of land, *v.* **crōc, deill**); *Dallison Leas, Dallisons close* 1717 (no doubt from the surname *Dallison* with the pl. of **lea** (OE **lēah**) and **clos(e)**); *the Dove Cote close* 1717; *the East feild* 1697, 1700, *the Eastfield* 1690, y^e *East field* 1703, *the - * 1715, *the east -* 1709, *the East Field* 1706 (*v.* **ēast, feld**, cf. *Northfield infra*); *the eight acre deal* (sic) 1671 (*v.* **deill**); *the Fallow feild* 1664; *the Fen closes* 1717; *the* *foureteene acre* 1671; (*at*(*te*)) *Grene* 1293 *Ass* (p), 1332 *SR* (p) (*v.* grēne²); *the headland* e17, 1671, 1690, 1700, 1709, *the head land* 1697, *yᵉ head Land* 1702, *the - 1706* (*v.* hēafod-land); *the hole bodham* 1671, *yᵉ houlbottom* 1697, *the houl bottome* 1700, *- Bottom* 1706, *Houle bottome* 1703, *the houle bottom end* 1690, *houl bottom end* 1709, *the whole bottom End* 1715 (*v.* hol¹ 'a hollow', botm, ende¹); *the Ings* 1717 (*v.* eng); *yᵉ Land mark* 1697, 1703, *the land - 1700, the Land Mark* 1706 ('the land boundary', *v.* land, mearc); *Lilly farme* 1671 (perhaps from the surn. *Lily,* cf. *Lillys close* in Caistor f..ns. (b) *supra*); *the long lands* 1671 (*v.* lang, land); *low platts* 1717 (*v.* plat²); *the Marferr* e17 ('the furrow marking a boundary', *v.* marfur); *Marigold parke* e17, *the Merrigold Park* 1717; *the Marrowes Platt, Marrows close* 1717; *the upper meadow close* 1664; *Northfield* e17 (self-explanatory; one of the open fields of Clixby and cf. *the East feild supra*); *the Sank Sale* 1717; *Scott gate* e17, *the Scotgate* 1664, 1671 (the same name occurs in Croxton f.ns. (b) and in East Halton f.ns. (a) and is discussed in the former s.n. *Scotgate*); *the sheepe walke, the Sheepe walk leas* 1671 (*v.* shepe-walk, lea, the pl. cf. lēah in the later sense 'meadow, pasture'); *the short acres* 1671, *short Acres* 1690, 1715, *Short acres* 1697, *the Short acre* 1706 (*v.* sceort, æcer); *Short grasse leas* 1671 (*v.* lea); *the Six Acres* 1664, *six acres* 1671, *Six acars* 1697, *a dale Called six Akers* 1703, *yᵉ Six Acre daile* 1690, *Six Acres dale* 1706, *the 6 acre dale* 1709, *the six Acres* 1715 (*v.* æcer, akr with deill); *the Southfield* e17 (cf. *Northfield supra*); *Stone Horse Paddock* 1717 (a *stone horse* is 'a stallion', cf. *the Stone horse close* in Thornton Curtis f.ns. (b) *infra*); *two stonges* e17 ('two roods of land', *v.* stong); *the street* 1671 (*v.* strǣt); *Towne end Closes* 1717; *the wain gappe* 1671 ('an opening (in a hedge) to allow the passage of a wagon or cart', *v.* wægn, gappe); *the West field* 1690, *- Field* 1706, *west feild* 1697, *- field* 1709, *the West-Field* 1715 (*v.* west, feld and cf. *Northfield supra*); *the Willows close* 1717; *the wold bottome, the woldgate* 1664, *the wolde gate* 1671 (*v.* wald, botm, gata); (*in the*) *wro* 1293 *Ass* (p) (*v.* vrá 'a nook, a corner of land', dial. 'a nook, a secluded spot, a cattle shelter').

Croxton

CROXTON
   Crocestone (3x) 1098 DB, *Crokestun* lHy2 Dane (p), -*ton'* 1190,
      1191, 1192, 1193 P (all p), 1194 ib, 1234 Cl, *Crokeston* "by"
      Newshus 1293 Ipm, *Crokastun* 1159-81 (e13) *NCot* (p)
   Crochestune 1086 DB, -*tone* 1086 ib, -*tuna* c.1115 LS, -*tun*(*e*)
      c.1150 Dane, lHy2 ib (p), -*ton'* 1086-8, 1088, c.1143 (l13)
      Blyth, 1166, 1167 P (both p)

Crocston' 1194 CurP (p), 1195 P, 1196 ChancR
Croxston c.1150 (Ed1) *Newh*, 1284 *FF*, 1428 FA, 1539 *AD*
Croxtune 1155-60 Dane, *-tuna* 1166-75 Fulstow (p), *-tun*(')
    1157-63 Dane (p), c.1180 (e13) *NCot*, e13 *HarlCh*, 1219
    (e13) *NCot*, 1220-30 *HarlCh*, 1224, c.1235 (e13) *NCot*,
    1238-43 Fees, *-ton*(') 1188 P (p), 1190 (e13) *NCot*, 1196
    ChancR, 1197, 1198, 1199 P, 1200 ChancR, 1202 Ass, 1212
    Fees, 1227 Ch, 1238 *HarlCh*, 1241 (e13) *NCot*, 1242-3 Fees
    et freq
Croketon' 1218, 1219 Ass
Crokton(') 1231 Cur, 1353 Inqaqd, 1535 VE, *Crocton'* 1232 Cur
Croston 1325 Inqaqd, 1408 Cl
Crowston 1697 Pryme

This is to be compared with Croxton (St) and Croxton Kerrial
and South Croxton (Lei), all four being interpreted as 'Crōc's
farmstead or village', *v.* tūn by Ekwall (DEPN s.n.). The same first
el. seems to occur in Croxall (now St, but *v.* PN Db 631-32) and
Croxden (St). The OE occurrences of the per.sn. have been
collected by *Insley* 558, and two l12-e13 century examples from L
are noted in SPNLY 181. There seems general agreement that
Crōc represents an original byname ON *Krókr*, ODan *Krōk*.
However, Dr Fellows-Jensen objects that this "pers.n. only makes
infrequent appearances in England, however, and I would tentatively
suggest that the first el. of the six p.ns. is in fact the OE topographical el. **crōc* m. "crook" perhaps "nook" .... It should be noted
that there is no trace of Scand gen. *ks* in the DB forms of the
p.ns." It may be objected that it would be remarkable in the
extreme to find six p.ns. in genitival composition with the same
hypothetical OE appellative. So, on balance of probabilities it
would seem more reasonable to accept that the first el. is indeed
the pers.n. *Crōc*, from ODan *Krōk*, which is probably also found in
Croxby (LNR), Croxley Green (PN Hrt 81), Croxteth (PN La 114),
Croxton (PN C 158) and Croxton (Nf 2x). It may be noted that
Croxall is first recorded in a 13th century copy of an AS charter
dated 942 *Peniarth* (S 1606), *v.* PN Db 631, and this led Ekwall
(DEPN) to remark "The Scandinavian name here appears remark-
ably early". As is pointed out in PN Db 632, however, there is
good evidence for such early settlement in South Derbyshire. In all
probability, then, Croxton is to be interpreted as 'Crōc's farmstead,

village'.

YARBOROUGH CAMP, 1824 O, 1828 Bry, 1842 White, *Yerborowe Hill* 1536 LP xi, *yarbarrow Hill* 1601 *Terrier*, *Yarbrough Hill* 1601 *ib*, *yearbrough hill* 1631, 1634 *ib*, *Yarborough hill* 1664 *ib*, *Yarbrow Hill* 1690 *ib*, *Two mile west of Thornton is a great roman camp call'd Yarborough which surveys the whole hundred denominated from it* 1724 Stukeley. It is called *Fort Hills* 1697 Pryme. This must have been the site of the meeting place of Yarborough Wapentake (for which see early forms and etymology), which takes its name from it. It is described as a "small, possibly Iron Age fort", *v.* Jeffrey May, *Prehistoric Lincolnshire*, 1976, p. 182. On a Plan, c.1810 *Yarb* 4/11/1, the next field to the Camp is called *Brough Hill Plot* for which cf. *Burghil* 1240, m13 *HarlCh*, *Broughe Hill* 1577, *brough hyl* 1662, *Brough Hill gate* 1690, - *hill Gate* 1707, *broughill Gate* 1769, *brough Hill Gate* 1762 all *Terrier*, 'the hill with a fortification', *v.* **burh, hyll**, with **gata** 'a road, way'.

CROXTON GRANGE, 1877 *MiscDon 82*; it is earlier *Parsonage Fm* 1824 O, 1830 Gre (cf. The Parsonage House in f.ns. (a) *infra*) and *Tithe F*ᵐ 1828 Bry. This appears to be a late example of **grange**; for which *v.* EDD s.v.2 'a homestead, small mansion or farm-house, esp. one standing by itself remote from others', a sense quoted from L. CROXTON PLANTATION, *Croxton Plantations* 1824 O, 1830 Gre. CROXTON WOLD (lost), 1828 Bry, cf. *the wouldehill* 1577, *Waude hill bottome* 1601, 1664, - *bottume* 1631, *Would hill bottom* 1662, *the Wold Sheep Walk* 1707, 1762 all *Terrier*, *the Wold or Sheep Walk* c.1810 *Yarb*, *v.* **wald**, as elsewhere in this Wapentake. LONG CLOSE PLANTATION is *Croxton Long Close* 1824 O, 1830 Gre, cf. *bugden or long close* 1631, *at longe close or at Bugdon close* 1634, *Long close or Bugden close* 1664, *longe close* 1662, *ye Long Close* 1697, 1700, *Croxton Long Close* 1707, 1769, - *long Close* 1762 all *Terrier*, *Long close* 1796 *Yarb*, - *Close* c.1810 *ib*, and *bugden close* 1601, 1631, *Bugton close* 1662, *Bugdale close side* (sic) 1690 all *Terrier*. Long Close is self-explanatory, *v.* **lang, clos(e)**, but the alternative name is obscure, unless it is a family name, though no such has been noted either in *Terrier* or *BT*. POND CLOSE WOOD, *Pond Close W*ᵈ 1828 Bry, cf. *pond closes*

1662, *Pond Closes* 1707, *Pond Close* 1762 all *Terrier*, 1796, c.1810 *Yarb*, self-explanatory.

Field-Names

Principal forms in (a) are 1796 *Yarb*; those dated c.1810 are from a Plan in *Yarb*. Spellings dated 1220-30, c.1240, 1240, Hy3, and m13 are *HarlCh*; the remainder are *Terrier* unless otherwise noted.

(a) Atkinsons cl, - Cow Cl 1796, Atkinson Cl c.1810 (from the surn. *Atkinson*, cf. Robert *Atkinson* m16 *Cragg*, John *Atkinson* 1571 *Inv*); Barrow Gate 1762, 1769, c.1810 (*Bareuegate* 1220-30 (Ed1) *Newh*, *Barwewgate* c.1240, *Barrow gate* 1690, *barowe gate bottome* 1577, *barrow gate bottom* 1601, *Barrow gate bottome* 1631, *barrowgat* - 1662, *Barrowgate* - 1664, *a Small road Called Barrow Gate* 1707, 'road to Barrow' v. **gata**); Barton Gate 1762, 1769 (1707, - *gate* 1631, 1662, 1664, 1690, *the hygh way called the Barton* - 1601, *barton gate* 1577, 'road to Barton', v. **gata**); Bracken Cl 1796, Braken Cls c.1810 (v. **brakni**); Brigg Gate 1762, - gate 1769 (1707, *Briggate* 1577, 'road to Brigg', v. **gata**); Butt Cl (*but Close* 1601, - *close* 1631, *But close* 1690, *the buts* 1631, 1662, y^e *buts* 1664, v. **butte**); Clay Pit Plott 1796, - Pitt Platt c.1810 (*clapit dalle* (sic) 1631, v. **clei-pit**, **plot**, **plat**^{2}, **deill**); Cotham Dales 1796, c.1810 (presumably commemorating the holdings of Coatham Nunnery here); Cottagers Moor 1796, c.1810; Cow Pasture; Croxton Fd 1762 *BM* (*in campo de Croxton*', *in campis de Croxton*' Hy3 (Ed1) *Newh*, 1395 *Peace*, *campus de Croxtun* 1241 (e13) *NCot*, v. **feld**); Croxton Mill 1762 *BM*, Mill flg 1796, - Flg c.1810 (cf. *iuxta molendinum* 1220-30, y^e *Mill dale(s)* 1577 (v. **deill**), *myll gate* 1601, *myll gate or betwen gate* 1631, *myllgate* 1664 (v. **gata**), y^e *mill pit* 1577 (v. **pytt**), *the mylle stigh* 1601, *the Mylle stigh* 1631, *milne stigh* 1662, *myll stigh* 1664, *the olde myll steigh* 1601, - *stigh* 1631 (v. **stīg**, **stigr** 'a path, a narrow road'); Dam c.1810 (y^e *damme furlonge* 1577, *the dame* - 1601, *the water in the dame* 1631, *the dame* 1634, *the dam* (*furland*) 1662 (v. **furlang**), *the dam hedg* 1690, *mickeldames* 1634, *Mickelldame* 1664, cf. *attedam de Croxton*' 1285 FF, *atte Dam* 1327 SR, *atte Dame* 1332 ib, *atte Dam* 1350, 1357 Cor all (p), v. **dammr**, ME **damme** 'a pond'); Croxton East Fd 1769, the East Fd 1762, East Fd 1796 (*in orientali campo* 1220-30, c.1240, 1240, m13, *in orient*' - c.1240 (Ed1) *Newh*, y^e *east fielde* 1577, *the easte felde* 1601, - *Easte feilde* 1631, *the Easte feild* 1662, *East Feild* 1690, y^e - 1697, - *feild* 1700, v. **ēast**, **feld**, one of the great fields of Croxton); Garth (v. **garðr**); Green Hutt Plott, - platt c.1810 (y^e *greene hurst* (sic) 1577, *the greene hu(t)* 1601, *greene huts* 1631, 1662, *green* - 1664, v. **grēne**^{1}, **hut**, **plat**^{2} 'a plot of ground', as elsewhere in this parish, **plot**);

Hall Dales 1796, c.1810 (*v.* **hall, deill**); Humber Btm 1796, c.1810 ((*a furlong called*) *Humber bottome* 1601, 1631, - *bottom* 1662, 1664, *v.* **botm**, the reference to *Humber* is uncertain; the fields are immediately north of Yarborough Camp); Kirmington (West) Flg 1796, Kermington flg c.1810 (cf. *Kirminghton mere* 1577, *Kirlinton meare* 1601, *Kirlington mear*(*e*) 1631, 1664, *Kirlington* - 1631, *Kirmington meare* 1662, *Kerninton Mear* 1690, 'the boundary with Kirmington (the neighbouring parish)', *v.* **(ge)mǣre**); Leys c.1810 (*v.* **lǣs** or the pl. of **lēah**); Marris's Fm (Mrs *Marris*, Tenant); Melton Flg (*melton close* 1601, *Melton* - 1634, - *Close* 1690, alluding to Melton Ross); New Cl c.1810; new Ride c.1810 (a road); Old Leys c.1810 (*v.* **lǣs**); Orchard; Parsonage Dale 1762, parsonage - 1769 (*Parsonage dale* 1707, cf. *y*[e] *parsones close* 1577, *the Parson close ende* 1601, *y*[e] *Parsons close* 1690, *the Parsonne garth ende* 1631, *y*[e] *parsonage garth* 1664, *the Personage close* 1631, *v.* **deill, clos(e), garðr** and foll.); The Parsonage House 1762, The parsonage house 1769 (*the Parsonage* 1631, - *house* 1634, *the parsonage* 1664, *ye Parsonage* 1697, 1700, and cf. Croxton Grange *supra*); Pingle 1796, c.1810 (*v.* **pingel**); Reed cl (*v.* **hrēod**); Rud Cl c.1810 (perhaps an error for the prec.); Sand Flg 1796, c.1810 (cf. *y*[e] *Sandes* 1577, - *sands* 1664, *the Sands* 1631, - *sandes* 1662); Seed Plott 1796, - platt c.1810 (*v.* **plat²**); the Sheep Walk 1762, c.1810, *y*[e] - 1769 (1707, *v.* **shepe-walk** and cf. the forms under Croxton Wold *supra*); Shop cls 1796, - Cls c.1810 (the meaning of *shop* here is probably 'shed'); Stone Dale Plott (cf. *the stone furlonge* 1601); Three Stong Flg 1796, - flg c.1810 (*three stongs* 1662 'three roods of land', *v.* **stong**); Town End Plott 1796, - platt c.1810 ('plot at the end of the village', *v.* **toun, ende¹, plat², plot**); Ulceby Flg 1796, c.1810; Ulceby Sneaks 1796, - Snecks c.1810 (from dial. *sneck* 'a small piece or tongue of land abutting on or intersecting an adjoining field' NED s.v. *sneck* sb¹, 3; this may be the same land as *Ulcebie headland* (b) *infra*, named from the neighbouring parish of Ulceby); the West Fd 1762, Croxton West feild 1769, West Fd 1796 (*in occidentali campo* 1220-30, m13, *In* - c.1240, *West fielde* 1577, *Weste felde* 1601, (*the*) *weste feild* 1631, 1662, *y*[e] *west field* 1664, *West Feild* 1690, *y*[e] - 1697, 1700, - *field* 1707, *v.* **west, feld** and cf. Croxton East Fd *supra*); Yellow Dales 1796, c.1810 (perhaps to be identified with *Yaldehaudale* 1240, *yaldehaudale* m13, from **jalda** 'a mare, a nag', **haugr** 'a mound, a hill', **deill**; the same name occurs in Killingholme f.ns. (b) *infra*).

    (b) *in aquilonali Campo* Hy3 ('the north field', cf. *in australi campo infra*, evidently later renamed *East* and *West Fields* (a) *supra*, as *North* and *South* do not appear in later f.ns.); *in capite australi* eHy3 (m13) NCot; *in australi campo de Croxton* Hy3 (Ed1) Newh ('the south field', *v.* prec.); *Cole pite bottome* 1601, *cole pit bottume* 1631, *Cole pit* (*bottom*) 1662, *Colepit bottom* 1664, *Culpit* - 1690 (self-explanatory, *v.* **botm**); *the Copy Hill or Stacke Stede* 1601, *Coppy Hill dall* (sic) 1601, *the Copie hill* 1631, *Copie hill* 1664 (cf. *Stacke steade infra*, *v.* **copis**); *ye Corn Feild* 1697, - *feild* 1700; *Croxton Drain* 1626 LH ii 8 (cf. *Croxton sich* c.1150 (Ed1) *Newh*, *v.* **sic**); *ad Crucem* 1327 *SR* (p) (*v.* **cros**); *dumbkarlcroft* e13 (e13), *dumkarlecroft* eHy3 (e13), *dumcarlecroft* c.1235 (e13) all *NCot* (as Dr John Insley points out, the first el. is a compound of ON *dumbr* 'dumb, silent' and ME *carl* (ON *karl*) 'a man, a fellow of humble status', perhaps denoting 'a simpleton', the second is **croft**); *Ferebe* -, *feribe stigh* 1601, 1662, *ferebye* -, *ferrebe* - 1631, *Fereby stigh* 1662, *Ferebie Stigh* 1664 ('the path to South Ferriby', *v.* **stig, stigr**); *atte Gape* 1350 *Cor* (p) (*v.* **gap** 'a gap, an opening', ME *gappe* 'a breach or opening in a wall or fence'); *gawberpitt furlonge* 1577 (probably *gawber* is identical with Gawber PN YW 1 316 and means 'gallows hill', *v.* **galga, beorg**, with **pytt** and **furlang**); *atte Grene* 1327 *SR*, 1332 *ib* both (p) (*v.* **grēne^2**); *Grenehil* Hy3 (Ed1) *Newh*, c.1240 (*v.* **grēne^1, hyll**); *hamondale* 1577 (probably from the ME pers.n. or surname *Hamon(d)* and **deill**); *de Hoke* 1327 *SR* (p) (if this is a local name, it is presumably **hōc** 'a hook, an angle', used in some topographical sense); *Leisingwang* (2x) eHy3 (e13) *NCot* ('in-field of the freedman', from **leisingi** 'a freedman' or the byname derived from it, though this is hardly found in L (SPNLY 186f.), and **vangr**); *viam de meltun'* 1220-30, *meletungate* 1240, *Meltun(e)gate* c.1240, *Meltongate* m13, *melton gate* 1601, 1631, *Melton Gate* 1664, 1690 (*v.* **gata**), *Melton meare, melton stighe* 1577, *Melton Stea* 1690 (*v.* **(ge)mǣre, stig, stigr**; all named from Melton Ross); *the mere furlonge* 1577 (*v.* **(ge)mǣre**); *super moram* Hy3 (Ed1) *Newh*, - *Moram* Hy3, *ye Moore* 1697, 1700 (self-explanatory); *Northcroft* c.1240 (*v.* **norð, croft**, and cf. *terram ... que fuit Will'i North* c.1240); *Northiby* Hy3 (Ed1) *Newh* (p) ('north in the village', *v.* **norð, í, bý**, cf. *Oustiby, Suthiby, Westiby infra*); *Oustiby* 1357 *Cor* (p) ('east in the village', *v.* **austr, í, bý**, cf. *Northiby supra, Suthiby, Westiby infra*); *Parsonage Stackstead* 1690 (cf. *Stacke steade infra*); *scam lands furlonge* 1631, *Scamlands* 1634, 1664, *Scramlands* (sic) 1662 (probably from **skammr** 'short' and **land**); *uia que uocatur Scotgate usque ad campum de Wtton'* (i.e. Wootton) eHy3 *NCot* (the same name occurs in Clixby f.ns. (b), recorded from the 17th century and in East Halton f.ns. (a) from the 18th century, though the latter is probably from a local family called *Scott*, the more likely explanation of *Scotgate* in Lincoln, PN L 1 98. It is also recorded as *Scotgate* PN YN 326, where the first el. is taken to be **Scot(t)** 'a Scot', hence 'the road of the Scots', *v.* **gata**. Four other examples have been noted in the wapentake, which appear to have the same first el., *Scothil* in Keelby f.ns. (b), *Scosteholm* (sic), *Scotholme, Scozholme* in Stallingborough f.ns. (b), *Scothow* in Habrough f.ns. (b) and *Schothoudale, Scohthowdale* in Great Limber f.ns. (b). It is suggested under the last that the first el. is indeed **Scot(t)** 'a Scot, a Gael' and this seems to be the most likely interpretation of *Scot-* in these four names too. So, we appear to have **Scot(t)** occurring in six of the seven names noted above, and if this is correct, then this group indicates the presence of Scots in a comparatively restricted area of north-east L. Besides 'the road of the Scots', we have 'the hill, the raised land in marshes and the mound of the Scots' respectively, *v.* **hyll, holmr** and **haugr**, though *Scotholme* and *Scozholme* seem to indicate a variation between sg. and pl. forms); *Skylegates* Hy3 (Ed1) *Newh*, *Skylegates* c.1240 (the first el. is obscure, the second is **gata**); *Stacke steade* 1577, *the stacke stede* 1601, *- steade* 1631, *The Stack* - 1662, y^e *Stack Stead* 1664, *the Stackstead* 1690 (cf. *the Copy Hill supra; Stackstead* must mean 'the site of a stack of rick', and for a discussion *v. Stakstede* in Nettleton f.ns. (b) *infra*); *Stayngrafgate* Hy3 (Ed1) *Newh* ('(the road to) the stone pit', *v.* **steinn, grafa**[1] or **græf**, with **gata**; the same name occurs in Ulceby f.ns. (b) and no doubt refers to the same road); *Suthiby* Hy3 (Ed1) *Newh*, *Southiby* 1327, 1332 *SR*, *de Sotheby* "of Croxton" 1395 Fine, *Sotheby de Croxton'* 1400 *FF* all (p) ('south in the village', *v.* **sūð, í, bÿ**, cf. *Northiby, Oustiby supra*); *thorne-, tornecroft* 1159-81 (e13) *NCot* (*v.* **þorn, croft**); *three thorne pittes* 1577, *the 3 thornes* 1601, *the three -* 1631, *le three thorns* 1662, *the three -* 1664 (self-explanatory, *v.* **þrēo, þorn**); *John Turners Close* 1601, *- close* 1631; *Ulcebie headland* 1662, *Vlsby -* 1664 (*v.* **hēafod-land** and cf. Ulceby Sneaks in (a) *supra, ad semitam de Vlseby* Hy3 (Ed1) *Newh*, c.1240 ('the path to Ulceby' (an adjoining parish)); *Wakehou* Hy3 (Ed1) *Newh*, c.1240 (Dr John Insley suggests that the first el. is perhaps a byname from ON *vakr* 'watchful' (cf. Reaney s.n. *Wake*) and **haugr** 'a (burial) mound, a hill'); *Walrike meres* 1577, *Wolrike furlonge* 1601, *walricke -* 1631, *Walricke furelong* 1664 (from the OE pers.n. *Wulfíc* or the derived surn. and **furlang**); *toftum in Croketon' quod vocatur Wardnoth* 1219 Ass (this is almost certainly **toft** held by *warnoth* tenure. Stenton (Dane cxxxv-cxxxvii) points out that *warnoth* is not recorded before the Conquest, but occurs sporadically in DB denoting some unspecified kind of render or service, not defined there. In a Lincolnshire Plea Roll of 33 Ed1, 1304-5, it denoted "a form of rent which if not paid on the appointed date was exacted two-fold on the following day, three-fold on the third day" and so on. Though the authority is late, Stenton states that there is no reason for questioning the accuracy of its interpretation and he points out that "there are parallels to such multiplied renders in pre-Conquest law". He further quotes a number of examples of land held *de warnothe. Wardnoth* here would appear, therefore, to have been transferred as the name of a **toft** held by payment of such a rent. Two further examples of the use of this term as a f.n. have been noted: *i selionem terræ ... nomine Warnot* 1428 AASR xxix in Osgodby (Kirkby cum Osgodby) LNR and *certas terras in Caborne* (Cabourn LNR) *nomina warnott* 1445 ib); *ad fontem* 1327 *SR*, *atte Welle* 1332 *ib* both (p) (*v.* **wella** 'a spring, a well'); *west coalepittes* 1577, cf. *Cole pite bottome supra*); *Westiby* Hy3 (Ed1) *Newh*, m13, 1327, 1332 *SR* all (p) ('west in the village', *v.* **vestr**, **í**, **bý**, cf. *Northiby* etc., *supra*); *upper West Leyes* 1651 WillsPCC (probably from the pl. of **lēah** in the later sense of 'meadows'); *Wotton brats* or *meare* 1601, *wotton brats* 1631, *Wooton brates* 1662 (*meare* is no doubt from **(ge)mǽre** 'a boundary', while *brats* is from ON **brot** 'a small piece of land'), *witton stighte* 1577, *Wotton Steighe* 1601, - *steigh* 1631, *Wootton stigh* 1662, - *Stigh* 1664, *Wotton Stea* 1690 (*v.* **stīg, stīgr** 'a path'), *witton mere* 1577, *wotton meare* 1631, *Wotton Mear* 1690 (*v.* **(ge)mǽre** and cf. *Wotton brats supra*) (these are all named from the adjoining parish of Wootton); *the Wrays furlonge* 1577 (probably a furlong in nooks of land, *v.* **vrá** , **furlang**).

Elsham

ELSHAM

   Eleham (2x) 1086 DB

   Elesham (2x) 1086 DB, c.1115 LS, Hy2 (1409) Gilb (p), 1190 P (p), c.1190 RA viii, 1238-43 Fees *et passim* to 1382 Peace, *Elseham* 1242-3 Fees, 1382 Cl, 1504 Ipm, *Elesaham'* 1242-3 Fees

   Helesham c.1115 LS, 1170-75 YCh iii, 1202 SelectPleas (p)

   Ellesham c.1160 Dugd vi, c.1162 RA ii, 1169 P (p), l12 Dane, l12 (l13) Blyth, 1204 P, 1208 FF, 1210-12 RBE, 1212 Fees *et freq* to 1529 Wills ii, *Ellisham* c.1167 RA vi, 1210-12 RBE, 1242-3 Fees *et passim* to 1534 LP vii, *Ellysham* 1428 FA, 1535 LP vii

   Elleshaim c.1160 Dane (p)

   Hellesham 1157-63 Dane, 1163 RA i, 1181 P (p), l12 Dane, 1208 FF, 1212 Fees, p1220 WellesLA

   Elsham 1247-8 RRG, 1281 QW, 1291 Fine, 1303 Pat, 1303 FA, 1307 Cl, 1316 FA, 1316 Pat, 1322 Cl, 1327 *SR et freq*, - *alias Ellesham* 1571 Pat, *Ellsham* 1291 Tax

   Helsam c.1160 Dane

   Elsam 1242-3 Fees, 1293 Blyth, 1330 Ipm, 1330 Cl, 1330 Ipm *et passim* to 1450 *LDD, Elssam* 1354 *Cor, Elsame* 1539 LP xiv, *Elsom* 1653 WillsPCC, 1746 LNQ xviii

   Ailesham 1206 Ass, *Heylesham* 1267 Pat

   Helfesham 1208 FF, *Eluesham* 1218 Ass, *Elnesham* 1218 FF, 1219 Ass (the last two presumably have -*n*- for -*u*-)

The 13th century spellings in *Ailes-, Heyles-, Helfes-, Elues-* are

out of line with the rest of the large collection of forms for Elsham
and are presumably to be regarded as errors. Ekwall (DEPN s.n.)
is, therefore, no doubt right in interpreting the name as 'Elli's
homestead', *v*, **hām**, the first el. being the OE pers.n. *Elli*. Initial
H-, found in a number of 12th and 13th century spellings is intrusive. The isolated c.1160 form in *-haim* is noteworthy as a
Scandinavianised spelling.

BRICK YARD (lost), 1824 O. CARR SIDE PLANTATION, cf. *le
Kerside* 1416 *HarlCh*, *ye Carre-side* 1668 *Terrier*, *Carreside* 1679, 1697,
ye Carre side 1700 *ib*, *the Carr-side* 1706 *ib* '(land) alongside the
marsh', *v*. **kjarr, sīde**. CHURCH GARTH HOLT (lost), 1624 O,
1830 Gre, *v*. **garðr** 'an enclosure'. CHURCH LANE (lost), *y^e
church Lane* 1674 *Terrier*, *- lane* 1679 *ib*, *Church-lane* 1703 *ib*, *the
Church Lane* 1712, 1724, 1762 *ib*, cf. *ad ecclesiam* 1271-2 *Ass*, 1327,
1332 *SR* all (p). COURT CLOSE (lost), 1824 O. DECOY
COVERT, a fox covert. DEEPDALE PLANTATION, cf. *great
deepe daile* 1601 *Terrier*, *deepdale* 1611 *ib*, *deep daile hole* 1625 *ib*,
Deepedale 1638 *ib*; in spite of the spellings in *daile*, which suggest
deill 'a portion or share of land', the topography clearly suggests
that this is 'the deep valley', *v*. **dēop, dæl, dalr**. DOLL LANE.
EAST PLANTATION. ELSHAM CARRS, ELSHAM CARR FM
(now RENNISON'S CARR FM), *the Carre, the Common Carres*
1638 *Terrier*, *Carrs* 1767 *Stubbs*, *Elsham Carrs* 1824 O, *v*. **kjarr**, and
cf. Carr Side Plantation. ELSHAM HALL, *Elsom hall* 1675
Ogilby. ELSHAM HILL, 1824 O. ELSHAM MAY BANK.
ELSHAM TOP. ELSHAM WOLDS, cf. *Lower -, Upper Wold F^m*
1828 Bry. ELSHAM WOOD (lost), 1830 Gre, *- W^d* 1828 Bry.
FOX HILLS (lost), 1828 Bry. LITTLEWORTH FM (lost), 1830
Gre, *- F^m & W^d* 1828 Bry. LONG HOLT (lost), 1828 Bry. LOW
MOOR DRAIN, *Low Moor Dam* 1830 Gre. MALTKILN LANE.
MARSHALL'S COVERT, named from the *Marshall* family, cf.
Francis *Marshal* 1671 *BT*, John *Marshall* 1842 White.
MIDDLEGATE LANE, *middle gate* 1601 *Terrier*, *midle gate* 1611,
1638 *ib*, *midlegate syde* 1625 *ib*, *v*. Middlegate Lane in Bigby *supra*.
MOOR PLANTATION, cf. *Moor Cover* 1828 Bry, cf. *Mora* 1332 *SR*
(p), 1338 *Misc* (p), *of the More de Elsam'* 1381 *Peace* (p), *ye
Common more* 1638 *Terrier*, *ye Moore* 1668, 1700 *ib*, *Elsham Moore*
1674 *ib*, *the Moore* 1690 *ib*, *the Moor of Elsham* 1706 *ib*.
NEWLAND HILL, cf. *Newelande* 1327 *SR*, *Neulant* 1338 *Misc*,

Neulond 1343 NI all (p), 'land newly brought into cultivation', *v.* **nīwe, land.** NEW PLANTATION. OLD LANE HOLT. POPLAR WALK, 1828 Bry. ROOKERY (lost), 1828 Bry. SHEEP LANE PLANTATION (lost), 1824 O, 1830 Gre. SHEPHERDS HO (lost) 1828 Bry, probably from the family name *Shepherd*, cf. Thomas *Shepherd* 1746 *BT.* SMITH'S PIECE, named from the *Smith* family evidenced in Elsham from at least the 14th century, cf. *Iohannes filius Thome Smyth' de Elsham* 1381 Peace, Henry *Smyth* 1527 Wills ii, Edward and Thomas *Smith* 1638 *Terrier.* SOUTHSIDE PLANTATION. STEEP HILLS (lost), 1828 Bry. TWEEDMOOR PLANTATION, named from the *Tweed* family, cf. William *Tweed* 1732 *BT.* VICARIDGE, *the Vicaredge* 1601 *Terrier, the Vicarige* 1606 *ib, the vicarage* 1611, 1625 *ib, ye vicaridge* 1664, 1700 *ib.* WASHDYKE LANE is *Folly Lane* 1828 Bry. WIRE PLATT PLANTATION.

Field-Names

Forms dated 1767 are *Stubbs*; other dated forms are *Terrier*, unless otherwise marked.

(a) Elsham's common Drain 1762 (*Elsham draine* 1679, *Elshams common draine* 1707, *Elsham common Drain* 1745 (all the forms are from Wrawby Terriers, in which it is described as a boundary)); Pingle 1767 (*the Pingle* 1601, 1606, 1611, *the Pingles* 1638, *v.* **pingel**); the Sworth 1767 (1611, 1638, *a place called the Swords* 1635 (c.1900) *LindDep* 78, *Elsham Swath* 1724, 'strip of grassland, grass-grown track', *v.* **swæð** (ME *swathe*), cf. its use as an appellative in a *pingle and a Sworth* 1625).

(b) *the abbey land* 1638 (probably a reference to Thornton Abbey); *Barton way* 1638 ('road to Barton on Humber', *v.* **weg**); *the Beacon* 1601 (*v.* **(ge)bēacon**); *Atte Bek' de Ellesham* 1308 FF (p), - *Becke* 1327 SR (p), *atte bek* 1354 *Cor* (p) (*v.* **bekkr**); *ultra cokebec* m13 *HarlCh* (possibly 'the stream frequented by wild birds', *v.* **cocc²**, **bekkr**); *Coopers close* 1638 (from the surn. *Cooper*, though no member of a family of that name has so far been noted here); *Crispyn Maner* 1441 Pat, *Crispynemanere* 1441 Cl (named from the *Crispin* family, cf. Thomas *Crispyn* of Elsham 1343 Pat); *the far croftes* 1601, *the Croftes* 1611, *the Crofts* 1635 (c.1900) *LindDep* 78 (*v.* **croft**); *Crosse daile* 1601, *Cross dales* 1611 ('shares of land near the cross (i.e. perhaps *the Stumpe Crosse infra*), *v.* **cros, deill**); *Elshamcotes* 1395 Peace (*v.* **cot**); "a certain dike which is called" *Ellesham dik'* 1256 FF (*v.* **dīk**, cf. *yᵉ Inges infra*); *Ferriby gate* 1601 ('the road to South Ferriby', *v.* **gata**); *Forby Lande* 1553 Pat, *forby land* m16 Cragg ('an odd piece of land taken out for rent', *v.* Adams, 87, 93 and, for a discussion, *forby land* in Worlaby f.ns. (b) *infra*); *Fromundland* 1364 Misc, 1368 Pat, *Fromond-* 1367 ib, 1369 Misc ('Fromund's land, strip of land in the common field', from the OGerm pers.n. *Fromund,* OFr *Fromont* and **land**); *Hav‹er›dale close* 1638 (tear in MS) ('the allotment of land used for growing oats' *v.* **hafri, deill** with **clos(e)**); *yᵉ Inges, the Inges* 1601, 1625, *the Ings* 1638, 1697, 1700, *yᵉ Ings close* 1700, *the Ings-close* 1706 (*v.* **eng** 'meadow, pasture', as elsewhere in the parish, and *Water Ings* and *Whinnings infra*); *the Kilbye Crofte, Kilby dicke* 1606, *Kilby croftes* 1611, *Keelby Croft* 1638 (named from the surn. *Keelby, Kilby,* though it has not been noted so far in the parish); *lady Crofts, Lady crofts* 1638 (possibly an endowment dedicated to the Virgin, *v.* **hlǣfdige, croft**); *the leas* 1638 (from the pl. of **lēah** in its later sense 'the meadows, pastures'); *in marisco de Elesham* 13 (l14) Gox (*v.* **mersc**); "the prior's [i.e. of Elsham Priory] own pasture called" *Midledale* 1370 Pat, *v.* **middel. deill**); *Newgate close* 1668, *New Yate -* 1674, *New yate -* 1679 (cf. *ad Portam* 1321 Misc (p), *v.* **geat** 'a gate'); *Northclif* m13 HarlCh (*v.* **norð, clif**); *longe Norlandes* 1625, *the north lands* 1638 (*v.* **norð, land**); *the Northe feilde* 1601, *- feild* 1606, *the North feild* 1611, 1625, *- northfield* 1638 (one of the open fields of Elsham); *Nunnery close* 1638; *le Oxpasture* 1416 HarlCh (*v.* **oxa, pasture**); *ad Pontem* 1332 SR (p) (*v.* **brycg**); *Rale Cr(oft)* 1638 (tear in MS) (probably 'the enclosure with a rail fence' *v.* **raile**); *rose crofte* 1611, *the Rosse Croft* 1638 (named from *the Rosse manner,* referred to in 1638, and **croft**; the *Ross* family held land in Elsham before 1462, cf. Thomas *Roos* 1462 Pat); *Sargeants closes* 1638 (from the frequently occurring surname *Sargeant,* cf. William *Sargant* 1604 *Inv,* Thomas *Sergeant* 1697*); the south Croft* 1638 (*v.* **croft**); *the Southe feild* 1601, *the South feilde* 1611, *yᵉ South field* 1638, *the Southfeild* 1625 (cf. *the Northe feilde supra*); *Stowe gate* 1601, *stowe -* 1611, *the Stowe -* 1625, *Stow -* 1638 (it is not clear what place *Stowe* refers to, *v.* **gata**); *the Stumpe Crosse* 1611 (a common name for a cross which has lost its top); *atte Tounend* 1327 SR (p), *the towne ende* 1611 *v.* **toun, ende**[1]); *the towne feild of Elsham* 1606; *the up Croftes* 1606 ('higher crofts', *v.* **upp, croft**); *yᵉ -, the Vicaridge close* 1668, *- Close* 1706, *the vicaridge close* 1679, *yᵉ vicaridge closes* 1697 (*Vicaridge Close was layd to the vicaridge by Sʳ Samuel Oldfield Lord of yᵉ Mannour & Patron of yᵉ Vicaridge in lieu of yᵉ gleab Lands which he took in when he inclosed yᵉ Lordship* 1668 (enclosure said in 1679 *Terrier* to be '1635 or 1636' and in 1690 *Terrier* '1634 or 1635', cf. Vicaridge *supra*)); *Warlates* (sic) 1601, 1611, *a parcell of land called three Warlets* 1638 (*v.* **warlot** and the discussion s.n. Waterhill Wood in Brocklesby *supra*); *yᵉ*

-, *the water Ings* 1638, 1668, 1697, 1700, *the water-Ings* 1706, y^e *great Water Ings* 1674, *the greater water Ings* 1679 ('water meadows', *v.* **wæter, eng**); *Atte Welle* 1327 *SR* (p), *atte* - 1348, 1354 *Cor* (p), *atte Well'* 1332 *SR* (p) (*v.* **wella**); *Three achres of medowe in the Eings called the Whinens* 1611, *a place of the Ings called the Whinnings* 1638, *whinning close* 1679 ('gorse-covered pasture', *v.* **hvin, eng,** a Scand. compound); *Wirlobye headeland* 1601, *Worletby field* 1638 (named from the neighbouring parish of Worlaby and **hēafod-land**); *Woutten meare* 1601 ('the boundary with Wootton (the neighbouring parish)', *v.* **(ge)mǣre**); *Wrawebigate* 1416 *HarlCh* ('road to Wrawby', *v.* **gata**).

South Ferriby

SOUTH FERRIBY

> *Ferebi* 1086 DB (3x), c.1115 LS, Hy2 Dane (p), Hy2 (1397) Pat, 1202 Ass (p), *-by* 1088-93 YCh i, 1207, 1239 FF, 1275 Cl, 1351 *Cor*, 1275 Ipm, 1457 WillsPCC, 1566 Pat, *-bie* 1576 LER
> *Feribi* 1156-67 (14-15) YCh i, 1175-81 Dane, 1180-85 (e14) YCh ii, l12 RA ii, l12 Dane, (*iuxta Humbre*) c.1210 RA iv, 1214 Cur, 1219 Ass, 1238-43 Fees, *-by* 1167 (l13) *Stix*, 1180-85 (e14) YCh ii, 1180-96 (l13) ib ii, 1185-91 ib v (p), l12 (m13) Pontefract, 1214 FF (p), 1219 (e14) Bridl, 1226, 1231 FF *et freq* to 1431 FA, *Feryby* c.1230 Bodl, 1233 FF, 1276 RH, 1303 FA, 1312 Pat *et passim* to 1431 FA, 1517 ECB, 1537 LP vii, *-be* 1535 VE iv
> *Feriebi* Hy2 Dane, *-by* 1212 Cur (p)
> *Ferreby* 1281 QW, 1291 Tax, 1526 Sub, *-bye* 1566 Pat
> *Sutferebi* 1125-30 (e14) YCh ii
> *Suth feriby* Hy1 (e14) Bridl *Suth Feriby* 1202 (e14) YCh xii, 1285 RSu, *Suthferiby* 1145-53, 1155-57 (e14) YCh ii, c.1160 (m13) Pontefract, 1165-75, 1190-95 (e14) YCh ii (p), 1231 FF *et passim* to 1309 Orig, *Suth Feribi* 1147-67 (m13) Pontefract, 1215-19 *HarlCh, Suthferibi* c.1150, 1155-58, (m13) Pontefract, 1153-54 (m13) YCh iii, *South Feriby* 1192-1218 (l14) ib xii 1327, 1339 Pat, 1340 Ipm *et passim* to 1409 Cl, *Southferiby* 1309 Inqaqd, 1319 Pat, 1327 Ipm, 1327, 1346 Pat, 1361 Ipm, 1364 Pat, 1394 Cl, *Southferibi* 1312 (e14) Bridl, *-feryby* 1339 Cl, 1357, 1559 Pat, *-ferybe* 1553 *Nelthorpe, Southe Feryby* 1531 Wills iii
> *Suthfereby* 1135-39 (e14) YCh ii, 1155-58 (m13) ib iii, Hy2

(1230) Ch, 1255 Pap, *Suth fereby* 1229 Welles, *Suth Fereby*
1278 RRGr, *Suthferebi* 1253 Pap, 1268 RRGr, *Southfereby*
1555, 1566 Pat, 1576-77 *MinAcct,* *Southefereby* 1506 Ipm,
Southeferebye 1580-81 *AD, South Fereby* 1612 AD, *Southferebe*
1527 Wills ii, *Sowth Fereby* 1522 *Nelthorpe, Sowthfereby* 1555
Pat, *-ferybye* 1560 ib
Suth ferribi 1155 (m13) Pontefract
Suhdferibi (sic) Hy2 Dane, *Sudferibia* eHy2 ib, *-feribi* Hy2 ib
South Ferreby 1657, 1779 *Nelthorpe,* - *Ferraby* 1788, 1792 *ib*
South Ferriby 1685 *Nelthorpe et passim*

'The farmstead, village beside the ferry', *v.* **ferja, by**, a Scand.
compound. It is *South* in contrast to North Ferriby on the opposite
bank of the Humber, *v.* PN YE 214. There are numerous
references to the ferry itself, as in *passagium de Suth Feriby* 1147-67
(m14) Pontefract.

FARRISHES LANE (local), *the strete called the ferrysies* 1576, *una
venella vocat le Farrissees* 1577, *communem viam vocat Faresses*
1587, *the street called Pharisees* 1640 all *Nelthorpe.* It would appear
that this name was as obscure in 1640 as it is today, for *Pharisees*
must be an example of popular etymology. FERRIBY BRIDGE
(lost), "the bridge of" *Feryby* 1312 Pat, - *Feryby* 1313 ib, *Feribybrigge*
1345 ib, *Feribrigge* (sic) 1457 WillsPCCC, *Ferybe Bryggez* 1535 LP vi,
Ferrabie Bridge 1573 *Monson, Ferriby brigg* 1638 (1662) Imb, self-
explanatory. FERRIBY HILL, *del Hyll'* 1327 *SR* (p), *the hill* 1580,
1625 *Terrier,* - *Hill* 1803 *EnclA, ye hill* 1612 *Terrier, ye hilles* 1604
Nelthorpe, the hills 1634, 1665 *ib,* 1638 *Terrier,* - *Hills* 1640
Nelthorpe, cf. *mikelhill* e13 (l13) *Stix, mikill hill* 15 *ib,* self-
explanatory. FERRIBY SLUICE, 1830 Gre, *The great sluce* .... *at
Ferriby* 1696 Pryme, *Feriby sluice* 1724 Stukeley, *the Sluice* 1803
EnclA; this must be the sluice referred to in a Commisioners of
Sewers document raising money *for makeinge a sufficient Sluce or
clowe neare the outfall of the said river of Anckholm* 1625 *Monson*
3/IX/130. For a description of the Sluice, *v.* Pryme 115, who states
This I had from several old men. FERRY BOAT, 1826, 1842
White. FIELD HO, cf. *in campo de South Feriby* 1192-1218 (15)
YCh xii, *in campis de feriby* Hy2 (l13) *Stix, in camp' de Sowth
Ferebie* 1587 *Nelthorpe, the Feyldes* .... *of South Feribe* 1544 *ib,* the

modern name commemorating the open fields of the village.
FULSOAR DRAIN (local), 1824 O, 1830 Gre, cf. *(the) fullseȝes
closse, Fulseȝes Closse* 1603, *the little Fullseyes, great Fulls(e)yes*
1614, *Fullseye close, the great -, the little Fullseys* 1640, *little full seas,
the great full seas* 1665, *the fulseys, yᵉ little fulses* 1692, *Fulseas* 1703
all *Nelthorpe, Fulseas Drain, the little Fulseas* 1803 *Encl*, the forms
are late but it might be suggested that this is 'the foul, dirty marsh',
v. **fūl, sǣge**, though the latter is rare in p.ns. Mr Raymond Carey
informs me this is locally called Fulches Drain. THE GRANGE,
grangie sue in feriby l12 (l13) *Stix, le Southegrange* 1538-40 LDRH, *le
Southfereby grange al's South grange* 1576-77 *MinAcct, The
Southgrange* 1580 *Terrier, le graunge ... al's Southgraunge* 1596-97
MinAcct, the sowth grange 1640 *ib, South Grange* 1803 *EnclA*, 1824
O, 1830 Gre; it was a grange of Stixwould Priory, *v.* **grange** and
North Grange infra. HOPE & ANCHOR, 1826, 1842 White.
MIDDLEGATE LANE, *Middlegate* 1640, 1686 *Nelthorpe, Middle
Gate* 1665 *ib, the Middlegate* 1703 *ib, v.* the same name in Bigby
supra. NELTHORPE ARMS, 1842 White, *Nelthorpe's Arms* 1826
ib, named from the *Nelthorpe* family, lords of the manor. NORTH
GRANGE (lost), *Northgraunge* 1535-46 *MinAcct, Northegrange*
1535-37 LDRH, *northgrange de Southferibie* 1579 *Nelthorpe, the farm
.... called North Grange* 1596 WillsL, *le Northgraunge de South
Ferriby* 1600 *Nelthorpe, le northe grange de South Ferebye* 1601 *ib,
North Grange* 1659, 1667, 1734 *ib*; it was a grange of Thornholme
Priory, *v.* **grange** and The Grange *supra.* READ'S ISLAND (mostly
in Winteringham parish), "About 200 acres of this bank has been
recently warped and embanked, and is now called *Read's Island*,
being taken on a long lease from the Crown, by Mr. R.A. Read, of
Burton Stather" 1842 White. THE RECTORY, *the Parsonage* 1580,
1612, 1640, *the parsonage* 1668, 1709, *Parsonage house* 1679, *The
Parsonage House* 1800 all *Terrier*, cf. *Parsonagehill* 1665, *Parsonagehill* 1686 both *Nelthorpe.* ST CHAD'S or CADWELL (local),
Cadwell 1614 *Nelthorpe*, 1638 *Terrier*, 1658, 1666 *Nelthorpe, Cadwells*
1665, 1683 *ib*, cf. *Chadwell Close(s)* 1803 *EnclA*; the forms are late
but this may be 'Cada's spring', *v.* **wella**, identical with Cadwell PN
O 121, and perhaps *viam de Sadewell'* 1207 FF, in f.ns. (b), is an
error for *Cadewell'.* Mr Raymond Carey points out that this is a
blow-well and is on the site of an Iron Age and Romano-British
settlement. SOUTH FERRIBY CLIFF, *the Cliff* 1828 Bry.
SOUTH FERRIBY HALL, *Ferriby Hall* 1824 O, 1842 White,

Ferraby Hall 1828 Bry, cf. *the Hall Farme* 1707, 1712, 1731, - *Farm* 1735 and *the Hall land* 1640, - *Land* 1703 all *Nelthorpe*.

Field-Names

Principal forms in (a) are 1803 *EnclA*; those dated 1580, 1601, 1612, 1625, 1626, 1638, 1640[1], 1664, 1668, 1671, 1679, 1707, 1709, 1724, 1800, 1822 are *Terrier*; forms marked *RC* are from Manorial Rolls in the PRO, kindly supplied by Mr Raymond Carey; all others are *Nelthorpe* unless otherwise marked.

(a) Barton Gate 1788, - Road 1803 (*Barton gate* 1638, 1640, 1703, v. **gata**); Barton Low Way 1788 (*viam voc. le law waye* 1587, *ye law way* 1604, *the low* - 1614, *the lowe* - 1634, *The low* - 1638, *Lowe* - 1683, *Loweway* 1686, *the low way* (*to Barton meare*) 1639, 1640, 1692, *lowway* 1665, *the Low way* 1703, - *Way* 1739, self-explanatory); Barton Mere 1788 (*Barton meare* 1583, 1614, 1638, 1665, 1692, - *meer* 1634, - *Meare* 1639, 1640, 1686, 1703, - *meere* 1692 ('the Barton (upon Humber) boundary', v. **(ge)mǽre**); Caistor Rd; Church Hill Rd 1803, 1822; Church Land 1788 (*bouate ecclesie* 1202 (e14) Bridl 344, *ye Church land* 1604, *the* - 1625, 1626, *Church land* 1665, 1682, *church* - 1679, *the church lands* 1634, *the Church* - 1639); Coney Garths (*Coniegarth mouldrome* 1602 *RC*, v. **coni**, **garðr**); the Far Marsh (v. The Marsh in (a) *infra*); Ferriby Carr 1786 (v. **kjarr**); Field Rd (cf. Field Ho *supra*); a certain Lane in South Ferraby ... (sometimes) called or known by the Name of Joseph Galloway's Lane 1779, 1788, 1790; Gibsons Lane (named from the *Gibson* family, John *Gibson* being named in 1803, and note also Christopher *Gibson* 1603, 1614); Grange Lane 1779 (*the Grainge lane* 1640, (*a Laine called*) *Grainge Laine* 1698, 1722, 1727, 1738, v. The Grange and North Grange *supra*); Gravel Pit; Green Gate 1788 (*the Grene Gate* 1614, v. **grēne**[1], **gata**); an ancient Inclosure called the Hermitage (cf. perhaps *Harmit* (sic) 1599 *RC*, v. **ermitage**); the High Street (*the common waye ... called ye Highe strete* 1583); the Hill side (*le hill side* 1579, *y^e* - 1601); the Hill Top 1788 (both this and the prec. are named from Ferriby Hill *supra*); Horkstow Rd (*uiam de Horkestoue* Hy3 (in a late hand) Stix, *Horstow High way* 1614, cf. *Horkstow(e) low(e) way* 1614, *Horkstow low way* 1692, leading to the adjoining parish of Horkstow); the Marsh (Drain) 1803, the Marsh Rd 1803, 1822 (cf. *exteriori parte ville uersus mariscum* p1167 (l13) Stix, *the south marsh lyeing between the new and old rivers* (i.e. R. Ancholme), *the north marshe* 1635 (c.1900) LindDep 78, v. **mersc**); the middle Fd 1788, 1822, the Middle - 1803 (*in medio campo* 1587); the Navigation Canal; the New River Ancholme (v. *supra*); the North Fd 1788, 1803 (1683, 1686, 1703, *in borial' campo* 1587, *in campo borial' de South Feribie* 1592, *ye north feilde* 1604, *- feald* 1692, *The north feild, he North Feild* 1614, 1634, *The Northfield* 1665, *the -* 1638, 1640, *v.* **norð, feld**, one of the open fields of South Ferriby); a Plantation Inclosure made to the said Sir Henry Nelthorpe; the Poors House; Saintfoin Cl (*v.* **sainfoin**); the South Fd (1683, 1686, 1703, *the Sowth feild* 1614, *the South Feild* 1639, *- feild* 1665, *South field* 1692, *the Southfeild* 1634, 1638, 1640, *in australi campo* 1587, *v.* **sūð, feld** and cf. the North Fd *supra*); the Stone Pit (*ye stone pits* 1692, *the stone pitt* 1703); the late a Waste Lane (so called several times); the late West Fd (no other reference has been found for this); Sir Rowland Winns Drain; Winterton Rd.

(b) *tofta Adgari* 1207 FF ('Ēadgār's tofts', from the OE pers.n. *Ēadgār* and **toft**); *akerheuede* e13 (l13) *Stix (v.* **æcer, hēafod**); *Aldegate* 1192-1218 (114) YCh xii, *Haldegate* e13 (113) *Stix* ('old road', *v.* **ald, gata**); *aliwelle* 112 (113) *Stix, Halliwell becke* 1665 (*v.* **halig** 'holy', **wella, bekkr**); *anlepihaudale* 112 (113) (2x) *Stix,* Hy2 (113) *ib, anlepihoudale* Hy3 (in a late hand) *ib* ('the single, solitary mound', *v.* **ānli(e)pig, haugr**, with **deill** 'a share, a portion of land' added); (*the) Ash Close* 1665, 1682, 1683, 1724, 1735; *Barton stight comonly called the mylln' stight* 1614 (*stight* appears to be a local form, found elsewhere in LNR, of **stīg, stīgr** 'a path'); *the Beeck* 1602 RC (forms in *-ee-* have been noted in north L in names derived from **bekkr** 'a stream'); *bonecrofte* 1580 (the first el. is perhaps the ME surn. *Bon(e)* (*v.* Reaney s.n. *Bone*), the second being **croft**); *Botsworth garthe* 1580 (named from the family of Agnes *bottesworthe* 1560, *John Bottesworthe* 1562 and Richard *Botsworthe* 1579 all *PR* and **garðr** 'an enclosure'); *Burnamgate* 1604, 1665, *Burnomgate* 1614, *burnham gate* 1642, *Burneholme gate* 1602, 1604, 1614, 1634, 1638, 1639, *Borneholm gate* 1614, *Burnholme gate* 1640, *Burnhamgate* 1665, *Burnham gate* 1692, *- Gate* 1703 ('the road to Burnham' (in Thornton Curtis parish), *v.* **gata**); *a place called Crayne Hause otherwise called Crayne Sause, Crayns Hause* 1573 Monson (presumably from a family name with an unintelligible *Hause/Sause*); *Checkerheade* 1602 (*v.* **cheker, hēafod**); *Church headland* 1665 (*v.* **hēafod-land**, cf. Church Land (a) *supra*); *the cockstonge* 1614 (perhaps from **cocc²** 'a cock' or rather the ME surn. *Cock* and **stong** used of a measure of land, 'a pole', common in L); *the Common* 1640¹, 1685, *the Comon* 1683; *Common lane* 1579 (a p.n.); *coper dale* e13 (l13) *Stix* (a compound of the ME occupational name or derived surn. *Copere* 'a cooper' and **deill**); *cowhowes* Hy2 (p1167) (113) *Stix* (perhaps 'the mounds where cows are found', *v.* **cū, haugr**); *Cow Pasture* 1602 RC; *Crowkmearegate* 1604, *Croked-, Crokt meare gate* 1614, *Crookemarr gate* 1634, *Crookmer -* 1639, 1640, *Croockmeare -* 1638, *crooke meargate* 1665, *Crookmore gate* (sic) 1683, *Crookmire gate* 1692, *Crooke meare* 1703 (the exact semse is uncertain, though the elements are clear - **krókr** 'a crook, a bend' and **(ge)mǣre** 'a boundary, land on a boundary' with **gata** 'a road', with

the frequent confusion of *mear* with *moor* and *mire*, as elsewhere in north L; it
is interpreted in 1614 as 'crooked'); *dikesdale* Hy2 (113) *Stix* (the gen.sg. *dikes*
suggests that this is the surn. *Dike* (as in *atte Dike*) with **deill** 'a share, a
portion of land'); *the dovecote garth* 1614 (*v.* **douve-cote, garðr**); *dovecothows*
1572 (referred to as a toft), *le dovecote house* 1624 (is a house), *All that Toft
builded or Cotage Commonly Called the dovecote house* 1624 (cf. the prec. name);
dridayle 112 (113) *Stix* ('dry allotment of land', *v.* **dryge, deill**); *uno tofte qd dr
estcroft* (sic) 112 (113) *Stix* (*v.* **east, croft**); *the Est Feild* 1614, *the Eastfeild* 1634,
1638, *the East feild* 1640, 1665, *the East Field* 1683, 1686, 1703, y^e *east feild* 1604,
East field 1692 (cf. the North Fd in (a) *supra*; Mr Raymond Carey informs me
that this was alternately, called Middle Field or Miln Field); y^e *East hills* 1683;
farrflet dyke 1614, *Fauflett dike* 1640 ('the far, distant inlet or stream', *v.* **feor,
flēot**, with **dīk**); *Flaxlet* 1602, *Flaxlighte dick* 1604, *Flexlight dike* 1639 (possibly 'a
conduit where flax was prepared', *v.* **fleax, (ge)lǣt**, dial. *leat* 'a conduit of
water'); *Gaire* 1207 FF (*v.* **geiri**); *Le gatelandes* 1592, *gate landes* 1604, *gatelands*
1634 (a furlong), *the* - 1638, *gate lands* 1639, *the Gatelands* 1683, *Gate lands*
1640, - *Lands* 1692 (*v.* **gata, land**); *Goodlake garthe* 1580 (named from the
family of *Agnes* and *Michael Goodlake* 1559 *PR* and **garðr**; it may be noted that
no member of the family has been noted later than May 1559, when over 90
deaths were recorded, as Mr Raymond Carey points out); *the grange marfer*
1614, y^e *Grange marfar* 1692, *v.* **marfur** and Grange Lane in (a) *supra*); *the
growes* 1614, *Groves* 1634, *the* - 1703 (probably eModE dial. *grove* 'a ditch, dike,
or watercourse', *v.* **grafa**, EDD s.v. *grove* sb[1] quotes from north L without
identifying the place "Four fields immediately adjoining the Humber embankment
are called the Groves", cf. *Feribie Inges infra*); *tedgate* (sic, perhaps for *atte
hedgate*) Hy3 (in a late hand) *Stix*, *viam voc. hedgate* 1587, *headgate* 1604,
Headegate 1614, *Headgate* 1634, 1639, *headegate* 1665, *head gate* 1692 (the precise
sense of *head* here is uncertain; the second el. is **gata** 'a road', cf. the 1587
form); *the headland* 1614, 1634, 1638, 1639, 1640, - *headlands* 1638, y^e *head land*
1692, *Ferryby Headland* 1739 (*v.* **hēafod-land**); *Head Spout* 1602 *RC* (from ME
spoute 'a spout, a gutter'); *Hempe Crofte* 1580-81 *AD*; *le Hempe Garthe* 1555 Pat,
duabus garthes vocat hempgarthes 1577, *the hempgarthe* 1580, *le hempgarth* 1587,
1588 (cf. prec. and *v.* **hænep, garðr**, *hempyard* is used freq. in *Nelthorpe* as an
appellative and note also the use of the appellative *garthes*); *Hendalle* 1614 (*v.*
henn, deill); "in the" *Hirne* "of" *Southferiby* 1327 Pat (p) (appears to be the
same as *in Angulo* 1327 *SR* (p), - *angulo* 1332 *ib* (p), *v.* **hyrne**); *the hye* -, *the
hygh close* 1614, *the high Close* 1665, *High* - 1688 (cf. *the low close infra*);
Holgatesti' 1192-1218 (114) YCh xii (probably 'the road running in a hollow', *v.*
hol[2], **gata**, with **stīg, stīgr**); *the hopgarth* 1580 ('the enclosure where hops are
grown', *v.* **hoppe, garðr**); *Horkstow marfur* 1692 (presumably 'the boundary furrow

belonging to Horkstow (the neighbouring parish)', *v.* **marfur**. Mr Raymond Carey informs me that this is nowhere near Horkstow and is sited at the north end of the old coastline); y^e *meadow cauled Horxstow alias Horstow* 1602 (cf. prec.); *Howbery land* 1580, *Howbraye Lane* 1583 (presumably from a surn., not noted independently in the parish); *the Howcrofts* 1738; *Howthersgarth* 1553 Pat (apparently from a surn. and **garðr**); *Humber Bankes* 1665 (self-explanatory); *Feribie Inges* 1602, *Feriby* - 1603 (3x), *the inges* 1614, - *Inggs* 1634, y^e *Inges & growes* 1604, (*the*) *Ings & groues* 1639, 1640, *the Inggs* 1634, *Ings, Ingbanck* 1638, *the Ings* 1640, 1665, 1672, 1683, 1703, 1712, y^e - 1692, *the Ings of Ferriby* 1731, *the Fore Inges* 1703 (*v.* **fore** 'in front') ('the meadows', cf. perhaps *in pratis de Feriby* e13 (l13) *Stix, v.* **eng** and cf. *the growes supra*); *dale of medow calld Jondale* 1672 (Mr Chris Johnson suggests that the first el. may be the name of the *Ion* family, recorded from 1570-1611 in the adjacent parish of Barrow, *v.* A.R. Maddison, *Lincolnshire Pedigrees,* Harleian Soc. vol. 51, 540); *the kilnehouse garthe* 1580 (*v.* **garðr**); "meadow called" *lee Kynges fee* 1506 Ipm (cf. *yorkes landes infra*); *Landflett dike* 1592, *Landfletdike* 1599, 1602 RC, *lanflet dick* 1604, *lanflit, lanflight dike* 1614, *Lanflettdike, Lanfleet Dik* 1634, *landflett dike* 1638, *Landflett* - 1639, *Landflitt* - 1640, *Landflit(t)dike* 1665 (possibly alluding to an irrigation ditch, cf. ME *lond-flode* 'flood caused by the overflowing of a river', *v.* **land, flēot** with **dīc, dīk**); *Langfurlanges* 1192-1218 (l14) YCh xii, *langfurlangs* l12 (l13) *Stix, -furlanges* e13 (l13) ib, y^e *long furlonge* 1604, *The long furlong* 1614, *longe Furlong* 1634, *long furlong* 1639, *the* - 1665 (*v.* **lang, furlang**); *Leclose* (sic) 1600 RC, *inter Litelgates et foreram* 1192-1218 YCh xii, *viam voc. littellgate* 1587 (*v.* **lytel, gata**); *the Little Closes* 1703; *the low close* 1614 (cf. *the hye close supra*); *molendinum ... de feriby* 1167 (l13) *Stix, molendinum de feriby* Hy2 (l13) ib, *usque ad molendinum meum de Feriby* l12 (l13) ib, *molendini de Feriby* 1232 Cur, *milnecrofte* 1580 (*v.* **croft**), *milnefeild* 1587, y^e *mylne feilde* 1602, y^e *milne feald* 1692 (*v.* **feld**, referring to a Windmill at the top of Ferriby Hill, as suggested by Mr Raymond Carey), *the milln marfer* 1614 (*v.* **marfur** 'a boundary furrow'), *milnegate* 1665, *Millgate* 1686 (*v.* **myln, gata**) (Mr Raymond Carey suggests that more than one mill is referred to in this collection of forms, cf. also *Barton stight supra*); *Neudic* e13 (l13) *Stix* (*v.* **nīwe** 'new', **dīc, dīk**); *Newclose* 1604 RC, *Northeferrybie close* 1576, *north Ferrebe close* 1577, *north feriby* 1614, *north Ferriby* 1665 (a piece of land), *North Fereby* 1686 (this presumably commemorates the holdings of North Ferriby Priory in South Ferriby); y^e *north headland* 1692 (*v.* **hēafod-land**); *the North hills* 1683; *the parsons close* 1614; *Polgraves house* 1580 (named from the *Polgrave* family, cf. Thomas *Poulgrave* 1591 BT); *Pontefracte house* 1580, *Pontefrete* 1614, *Pomfrete* 1638 (the last two in the bounds of pieces of land) (presumably commemorating the holdings of Pontefract Priory); *the Lane called Raskellgate* 1583 (from the surn. *Raskell* and **gata**; this surn. is perhaps earlier *Raskelf*, as in Emma *Raskelf* 1332 *SR*); *the rectorye* 1601, - *Rectorie* 1625, 1626, - *Rectory* 1664, 1671, y^e - 1707 (this appears to be an alternative name for Parsonage House in Terriers, *v.* f.ns. (a) *supra*); *Riskedale* e13 (113) *Stix, inter duas Ryskedales* Hy3 (in a late hand) *ib, Rushdaile* 1703 ('rushy allotment(s) of land', the two earliest spellings being Scandinavianised with -*sk, v.* **risc, deill**); *viam de Sadewell'* 1207 FF (2x) (perhaps an error for *Cadewell', v.* St Chad's Well or Cadwell *supra*); y^e *Sandie lane* 1580; *the Sands* 1640; *pontem de Saxfortesflet* Hy2 (113) *Stix, Saxfardflet* e13 (113) *ib* (Dr John Insley agrees that this is 'Saxfriŏ's inlet, creek', *v.* **flēot**; for the first el. *v.* Feilitzen 51-2, s.n. *Seaxfriŏ*); *sciterdale* Hy2 (113) *Stix* ('allotment of land beside a sewer', *v.* **scitere, deill**, with *sc-* probably a Scandinavianised form); *Semperingham lande* 1587, *Sempringham* 1614 (in the bounds of a piece of land) (there is no evidence that Sempringham Priory held land in the parish, though Bullington Priory, a Gilbertine house, was granted the advowson of half the Church (Hy2 Dane) and also held land there); *a shifte Acre* 1603, *one acre of meadow ... caulde or knowen by ye name of a shifte acre* 1603, *Shift Acre* 1633 RC, (*shift* is here recorded over a hundred years earlier than the first reference in NED s.v. 11, in the sense "each of the successive crops in a course of rotation". It is also recorded in EDD s.v. 11 as "the division of land arranged with a view to the rotation of crops; any division of land", the likely meaning here being one of those given in EDD); y^e *South lane* 1580; y^e *South stones* 1604, *the South -* 1634, 1639; *Stibbyng'* (sic) 1332 *SR* (p) ('the clearing', *v.* **stybbing**); *Stintings* 1634, 1639 (for an early example of **stinting**, *v.* Brocklesby f.ns. (b) *supra*); *a place called the stones* 1642, 1665, *ye stones* 1683; *Stump Crosse* 1665 (a common name for a cross which has lost its top; the same name occurs in Elsham f.ns. (b) *supra*); *tadewelle* (2x) 112 (113) *Stix* (probably 'spring where toads are found', *v.* **tāde, wella**; the readings are correct, but could be errors for Cadwell *supra*); *tedgate* Hy3 (*in a late hand*) *Stix* (*v.* **hedgate** *supra*); *the Towne end* 1665; *the towne streete* 1655, y^e - 1658, *the Town Street* 1738 (probably to be identified with the High Street in (a) *supra*); *Wellhouse* 1633 RC, - *House* 1686 (self-explanatory); *whitegate(s)* 1614, *Whitegate* 1638, 1640 (*v.* **hwīt, gata**); *the white house* 1658, 1666, *Whitehouse* 1659, 1667, *the -* 1734; *Wind Mill* 1682 (cf. *milnefeild supra*); y^e *landes of ye kinges majesties cauled yorkes landes* 1604, *the kings Maties landes called york lands* 1634, *Yorke lands* 1639 (cf. *the grange marfer between S^t maryes of York on the Sowth & Yorke on the North* 1614, cf. also *Kynges fee supra*).

Glanford Brigg

GLANFORD BRIGG
  Glanford' 1183, 1184 P
  Glaunford 1314 Pat
  pontem de Glamford 1203 P
  punt de Glanford' 1218 Ass, *pontem de -* 1235 FineR, 1237
    RRG, *Glanford Brigg* 1235 Ch, *- Brigge* 1329 Pat, *-brig*
    c.1360 Gough, *-brigge* 1442 Inqaqd, *-brige* 1509-10 LP i,
    Glannford Brigge 1374 Peace, *Glannforde Brigge* 1375 ib,
    Glannfordbrigge 1376 ib, *Glannforthbrigge* 1373 ib
  "the bridge of" *Glaunford* 1256 FF, 1312, 1313 Pat, *pontem de
    Glaunford'* 1259 Cl, 1276 RH, *pontem Glaunford* 1276 RH,
    Pont' de - 1281 QW, *ponte de -* 1332 SR, *Pons Glaunford*
    1316 FA, *Glaunford Brigge* 1318 Pat, *Glaunfordbrigge* 1318
    ib, 1328 Banco, 1375 Peace, 1380 Pat, 1387 Misc, 1465
    Pat, *-brigg* 1330 Cl, 1332, 1349 Pat, 1351 Cl *et passim* to
    1462 Pat, *- Brigg* 1329, 1462 ib, *-brygge* 1329 Ass, 1381
    Misc, *-brig* 1356 ib, "the bridge and causeway of" *-* 1362
    Ipm, *Glaunfordebrigge* 1330 Ipm, 1335 Misc, 1535 VE iv,
    Glaunforthbrig 1337 Pat, *-brigge* 1393 Cl, *-bryg* 1395 Works,
    Glaunforthebrigge 1382 Cl
  Glamfordbrigges 1331 Pat, *-brig* 1367 Misc, 1383 Pat, 1398 Cl,
    1475 Pat, *- Brygg* 1494 Ipm, *Glamforthbrig* 1374 Pat,
    1538-9 Dugd vi, *Glamfurthbriges* 1519 LP iii, *Glamfordbridge*
    1576 Saxton, *- Bridge* 1600 Hall, *-brigges* 1610 Speed,
    - Briggs 1638, 1662, 1664, (*a Market towne*) 1668, 1671
    Terrier
  ponte de Glaumforde 1327 SR, *Glaumfordbrigg* 1359 Pat, 1375
    MiD, *-brig* 1379 Ipm, *-brigge* 1432 Fine, 1441 Pat, *-brygg*
    1449 Fine, *Glaumforthbryg* 1338 Cl, *-brige* 1417 Cl, *-brygg*
    1431 FA
  Glauntfordbrig 1359 Ipm
  Glaymfordbrigg 1405 Pat
  Glamysforthe Bridge 1536 LP xi
  Clamforthbrigges (sic) 1537 LP xii, *- Brigges* 1555 Pat
  Brigg alias Glanford Brigg 1674 Elw, *Brigge* 1681 BT, *Brig*
    1682 ib, *Brigg* 1734 Foster

Glanford is almost certainly derived from OE **glēam** 'revelry, joy, merriment' and **ford**, probably in the sense 'the ford where sports are held', as suggested by Ekwall (DEPN, s.n. Glandford). The forms in *Glaum-* and *Glaun-* are Scandinavianised, showing the influence of ON *glaumr*, cognate with **glēam**, while spellings in *-forth(e)-* are similarly Scandinavianised forms of **ford**. To this was added Brigg, from ON **bryggja** 'a jetty, a quay', but which here refers to a bridge over the R. Ancholme, as the Latin forms clearly show - note also the 1362 Ipm reference to "the bridge and causeway of *Glaunfordbrig*" and also "Hugh *atte Brigge* of *Glamforthebrigge*" 1313 Pat. The parish is known as Glanford Brigg, formerly a part of Wrawby; the town is called Brigg.

ANCHOLME TAVERN (lost), 1842 White. ANGEL HOTEL, *the Angel Inn, Brigg* 1820 *MiscDep 204, Angel Inn* 1826, 1842 White. BACCHUS (P.H.) (lost), 1826 ib. BIGBY ST., 1826, 1842 ib, leading to Bigby. BLACK BULL HOTEL, *Black Bull* 1826, 1842 ib. BRIDGE END (lost), *Bridge end* 1826, 1842 ib. BRIDGE ST., *Bridge street* 1826, 1842 ib. BROCKLESBY OX INN, *Brocklesby Ox* 1842 ib. BUTCHERY (lost), 1826 ib. COACH & HORSES (P.H.) (lost), 1826, 1842 ib. COAL DYKE END, 1768 (1815) *LRA, Coal Dike Bank near the Bridge at Glanford Bridge* 1795 *Elw.* CROSS KEYS (P.H.) (lost), 1842 White. THE CROWN (P.H.) (lost), *The Crown Public House* 1795 *Elw.* DYING GLADIATOR, *Gladiator* 1842 White.   GEORGE & DRAGON (P.H.) (lost), 1826 ib. GRAMMAR SCHOOL, *yᵉ Grammar scool at Brigge* 1681 *BT* (Elsham), *yᵉ Freeschool at Brig* 1682 *ib* (Elsham), *School House* 1824 O. GRAMMAR SCHOOL RD, *School Ho. Lane* 1824 O, *School lane* 1826 White. HAMMER-IN-HAND (P.H.) (lost), 1826, 1842 ib. HOPE (P.H.) (lost), 1826, 1842 ib. HOPE YARD (lost) 1826 ib. ISLAND CARR, 1824 O, self-explanatory, *v.* **kjarr**, situated between New and Old River Ancholme. LAMB (P.H.) (lost), 1826, 1842 White. LION HOTEL (lost), 1838 *Nelthorpe, 1842* White, *White Lion Inn* 1826 ib. LITTLE LANE (lost), *Little lane* 1826 ib. LORD NELSON HOTEL, *Lord Nelson* 1826, 1842 ib. MARKET PLACE, 1826, 1842 ib, *forum de Glannford Brigge* 1374 Peace. MILL LANE, cf. *Molendinum de Pont' de Glaumfordbrig'* 1357 *Cor, Mill place* 1826, 1842 White. NELTHORPE ARMS HOTEL, - *Inn* 1829 *Nelthorpe.*

NICHOLSON'S YARD (lost), *Nicholson's yarde* 1826, 1842 White, named from the *Nicholson* family, cf. John *Nicholson* 1826 ib. PARADISE PLACE, *Paradise row* 1826 ib, - *place* 1842 ib, often a complimentary nickname, though sometimes in towns it is given ironically. REDCOMBE RD, cf. *Redcome* 1767 *Stubbs*, 1824 O, -*combe* 1790 *Monson*, -*com* 1795 *LLHS*. RED LION, 1842 White. ROBINSON'S ROW (lost), *Robinson's row* 1826 White, *Robinson row* 1842 ib, named from the *Robinson* family, cf. William *Robinson* 1826 ib. ST HELEN'S WELL, 1697 Pryme, cf. *Saint Hellens-wells-dale* 1707 *Terrier* (Wrawby), *S.t Helings well dale* 1724 ib (Wrawby), *S.t Helen's Well Dale* 1745 ib (Wrawby), *S.t Hellen's Wells Dale* 1762 ib (Wrawby), *St Helens Fox Cover* 1828 Bry. SHIP (P.H.) (lost), 1826 White. SUN (P.H.) (lost), 1842 ib. TEMPERANCE HOTEL (lost), 1842 ib. WHEAT SHEAF (P.H.) (lost), 1826, 1842 ib. WHITE HART, 1826, 1842 ib. WHITE HORSE, 1826 ib. WILLIAM IV (P.H.) (lost), 1842 ib. WOODBINE COTTAGE, 1824 O. WOOLPACK HOTEL, *Woolpack* 1826 White, *Wool Pack* 1842 ib. WRAWBY ST., 1795 *Elw*, leading to Wrawby.

Field-Names

(a) Brigg Pitts 1768 (1791) *LindDep Plans* (*Brige* - 1588 *Stubbs*, meadow called *Brigg pitts* 1707 *Terrier* (v. **pytt**)).

(b) *Briggfield* 1700 *Terrier, Brigg Field* 1703, 1745 ib, - *field* 1707 ib, 1724 ib (for additional forms v. Brig Fd in Wrawby f.ns. (a); *Grene de Gloumfordbrig* 1381 Peace (p) (v. **grēne**[2] 'a village green, grassy spot'); *hospitalis de ponte Glanford* 1236-7 RRG.

Goxhill

GOXHILL
> *Golse* 1086 DB (5x), 1175 P (p), 1182, 1183, 1184, 1185, 1190 ib, 1191, 1192 ib both (p)
> *Golsa* 1086 DB, c.1115 LS, c.1141 BMFacs (p), 1142-51 Dane (p), 1143-47, a1150 ib, 1164 P (p), 1165 ChancR (p), 1166, 1167, 1171, 1172 ib all (p) *et passim* to 1178 ib (p)

Gausa 1148-52 LAAS vi, c.1150 Dane (p), *Gousa* 1143-7 ib
  (p), *Goussa* c.1155 ib (p), *Gouse* 1203 P (p)
Gosla 1135-39 (e14) YCh ii (p), c.1145 Dane (p), 1155-57 YCh
  ii, 1193, 1194 P, *Gosle* 1199 FF, 1267 Pat, 1312 (e14) Brid,
  1312 Pat
Gosel 1194 CurP
Goxa 1147-68 YCh iii, *Gossa* 1165 P (p)
Gousle 1135-40 (e14) YCh ii (p), 1194 (e14) Bridl, Hy2 Dane
  (p), 1200-12 (e14) YCh iii (p), e13 *HarlCh*, 1204 P (p), 1205
  Cur (p), 1209, 1210, 1211 P (p), 1212, 1213, 1214 Cur *et
  freq* to 1311 (e14) Bridl, *Gousle alias dict' Goxhill* 1549
  LindDep 67, *Gouslee* 1214 Cur, *Goussle* a1147 Dane (p)
Gousla 1143-47 Dane (p), 1149-50 (e15) YCh iii (p), 1152 ib
  iii (e14) (p), 1179-89 (e14) ib iii, 1182 ib iii (p) *et passim* to
  1304 Pap
Gousel 1127-35, 1189-1217 (e14) YCh iii both (p), a1202 RA
  viii (p), 1210-12 RBE, 1238-43 Fees, 1254 ValNor *et freq* to
  1314 YearBk, *Gousell* 1286 Ipm, 1376 Orig, 1376 Pat, 1471
  Fine, *Goussell* 1475 Pat
Gousele 1163 RA i, 1185-87 Dane (p), 1212 Fees, 1213 Cur,
  1230 P, *Gousel'* 1185 RotDom (p), 1210-11, 1256 FF, 1265
  RRGr, *Goussell'* 1281 QW
Gausle c.1150 (e14) Guis (p), 1150-60 YCh ii (p)
Gausla 1154-68 (e14) YCh iii, c.1155, 1157-63. c.1160 Dane all
  (p), 1160-66 ib, e13 *HarlCh*, 1260 *NCot*
Gausel Hy2 Dane (p), *Gausal* (sic) c.1160 ib (p)
Gausele 1145-60 YCh iii (p), 1150-60 Dane (p)
Gousil 1242-3 Fees, 1268 Ch, (*in Lyndeseye*) 1303 Pat, 1314
  YearBk, 1316 FA, 1329 Inqaqd, *Gousill* 1353, 1363 Ipm,
  1392 Pat, 1428 FA, *Gousyl* (*in Lindesay*) 1301 Pap, 1303
  FA, *Gausill* 1398 Cl
Gowsill "or" *Gouxill* 1349 Ipm, *Gowsill otherwise Gowxill* 1681
  Yarb, *Gowsyll* 1422 Cl, 1557 Pat, *Gowshill otherwise Gowxhill*
  1720 *Yarb*
Gowesell 1465 Pat, *Gowsell* 1545 LP xx
Goushill 1263 FF, 1291, 1294 Ipm, 1312, 1314 Cl, 1314 Ipm *et
  passim* to 1440 Pat, *goushill* 1601 *Terrier*, *Goushille* 1314
  YearBk, 1386 Cl, *Goushyll* 1340 Ipm, *Goushill(e)* 1399 Pat,
  1399 Cl, *Goweshill in Lyndeseye* 1401 Pat, *Gousehill* 1358 Pat
Goushull 1287 Ipm, 1292, 1294 Pat, 1295 Cl, 1312 Inqaqd *et*

passim to 1428 FA, *-hulle* 1313-14 Inqaqd, *-ul* 1242-3 Fees
Goushill ("on" *Humbre*) 1331 Ch, 1338 Ipm, 1341 Pat, 1346 FA,
    1347 *Cor*, 1378 Pat *et passim* to 1566 ib, *Gowxhyll* 1539 LP
    xiv, *Gouxhyll* 1549 Pat
Gouxull' 1332 *SR*, *Gouxhull*(') 1332 *ib*, 1346 Pat, 1346 FA,
    1541 LP xvi, 1549 Pat, *Gouxshull* m16 *Cragg*
Gouxill 1462 Pat, 1528 Wills ii, (*alias Gouxhill*) 1564 *LindDep*
    67, 1566 *BT*, 1576 LER, (*alias Goxhill*) 1604 *LindDep 67*,
    Gouxyll 1519 DV
Goxhill 1462, 1550 Pat, 1576 Saxton, 1577 *BT*, (*alias Gowsell*)
    1582 AD v, 1610 Speed *et passim*, *-hyll* 1547 Pat, *-hull*
    1535 VE iv, 1653 WillsPCC
Gowksell alias Gouxhill 1562 *BPD*

The full list of forms presented here shows that Goxhill is
identical in origin with Goxhill (PN YE 66-7), where numerous
alternative derivations are considered. This is a very difficult name,
and the most satisfactory explanation seems to be that it was
originally OE **Gēaceslēah* 'the cuckoo's wood or glade', from OE
gēac 'a cuckoo' and **lēah** 'a wood, glade', though the first el. might
alternatively be the unrecorded OE pers.n. **Gēac*, cognate with ON
Gaukr, and adduced by Ekwall (DEPN s.n.) for Yaxham Nf. It
has also been suggested that the second el. might be OE **hyll** 'a
hill' in an early weakened form, though this does seem somewhat
less likely. There are, of course, many spellings in *-hill* etc. from
the 13th century onwards, so that at least later the second el. was
associated with **hyll**. The numerous forms in *-ou-* and *-au-* indicate
that the first el. was similarly associated with or replaced by ON
gaukr 'a cuckoo' or the derived pers.n. *Gaukr*, well-evidenced in L
in the 12th and 13th centuries (SPNLY 96-7). The spellings with
final *-a* are simply Latinisations. Without OE forms, however, no
certainty is possible, and only what appears to be the most satisfactory explanation can be offered.

CHAPEL FIELD RD, *the Chappelfield road* 1775 *BPD*, cf. *Chappell
Field* 1685 *ib*, *- Feild* 1693 *Foster*, *- field* 1706 *ib*, *Chapel -* 1777
LindDep 77, *Chappel Field* 1775 *EnclA*, *the Chapel -* 1822 *Terrier*,
Chapel field (a farm) 1842 White, (*ye feild called*) *Chappell quarter*
1601, 1611 *Terrier*, 1631 *Dudd*, 1638 *Terrier*, 1648 *Foster*, 1667
MiscDon 14, 1679 *Terrier*, 1682 *Dudd*, 1700 *Terrier*, *- Quarter* 1690,

1697 *ib*, 1700 *LindDep 67*, 1728 *BPD*, 1730 *Foster*, 1749 *Dudd*, *Chapple quarter* 1606 *Terrier*, *Chappel Quarter* 1648 *LindDep 67*, 1662, 1668 *Terrier*, 1669 *LindDep 67*, 1718, 1724 *Terrier*, *Chapel quarter* 1671, 1745 *ib*.   In 1601 *Terrier* it is stated that the parish is divided *in foure feildes or quarters as they ar called*, and note *y*[e] *foure fields of goxhill viz.* .... *Horsegate quarter* .... *Chappell quarter* .... *Swallowmyln quarter* .... *Hallands quarter* 1611 *Terrier*. The name is self-explanatory, *v.* **chapel(e)**, **quarter** 'a quarter division of land'. A similar division of the parish into quarters is found in Barrow upon Humber *supra*.

EAST MARSH, *in orientali marisco* m13 *HarlCh*, *in est marisco de Gouxl'* 1260 (l14) *Gox*, *in oust marisco* lHy3 (l14) *ib*, *Gouxhull Estmershe* 1541 LP xvi, *le Estmershe de Gouxhill* 1549 *LindDep 78*, *le Estmershe* 1549 Pat, *in orientali marisco de Gouxhill* 1549 *Yarb*, *Gouxhill Estmarche* 1550 Pat, *the Est marshe* m16 *Cragg*, *le Eastmarshe* 1613 *BPD*, *the Eastmarsh* 1631 *Dudd*, 1667 *MiscDon 14*, 1678 *Dudd*, 1682 *LindDep 67*, *the East Marsh(e)* 1633 *AOMB 390*, 1648 *Foster*, 1682 *Dudd*, 1693 *Foster et freq*, - *marsh* 1648 *LindDep 67*, 1709 *Dudd*, (*of Goxhill*) 1730 *Foster*, *le east marsh* 1700, 1728 *LindDep 67*, *le East Marshe* 1713 *ib*, cf. *Estmersh(e)bridge* 1589-91, (*pro nova factur' de*) 1605-7 both *MinAcct*, *the East marsh Bridge* 1649 *ParlSurv*, self-explanatory *v.* **ēast**, **mersc**, and note that the lHy3 form is derived from ON **austr** cognate with **ēast**. Cf. *maresco de Gousla* c.1150 (Ed1) *Newh*, 1155-60 *Dane*, R1 (1318) *Ch*, - *Gausla* 1160-66 *Dane*, *marisco de Gousel* lHy3 (l14) *Gox*, - *de Gousill'* 1329 *Ass*, *Gouxhyll Mersshe* 1549 Pat, *the marshe(s)* m16 *Cragg*, *le Marshe* 1589-91 *MinAcct*, 1607 *Rental*, *Gouxhill Marshe* 1589-91 *MinAcct*, *Goxhill Marshes* 1598 *Yarb*, *le mershe* 1605-7 *MinAcct*, *the Marsh* 1648 *Foster*, *y*[e] *Marshes of Goxhill* 1649 *ParlSurv*, *Goxhill Marsh* 1657, 1675 *FLMisc*, 1736, 1737, 1745 *Foster*, 1765 *Yarb*, - *marshes* 1799 *Young*, - *Marshes* 1824 O.   Cf. also West Marsh Lane *infra*.

GOXHILL HALLANDS, *Haland* 1309 (e14) *Bridl*, *Hallands* 1638 *Terrier*, (*a certaine place called*) 1667 *MiscDon 14*, 1668, 1674 *Terrier* (Thornton Curtis), *Goxhill Hallands* 1824 O, presumably 'land belonging to a hall', *v.* **hall**, **land**.

HALLAND'S FIELD, *Hallands Field* 1685, 1775 *BPD*, 1775 *EnclA*,

Hollands Field 1749 Dudd, (*ye Feild called*) *Hallands quarter* 1601,
1611, 1638 *Terrier,* 1648 *LindDep 67,* 1662 *Terrier* (Thornton Curtis),
1667 *MiscDon 14,* 1671, 1679, 1690 *Terrier, - Quarter* 1662, 1668,
1700 *ib,* 1702 *Dudd,* 1724 *Terrier,* 1728 *BPD,* 1730 *Foster, Halland
quarter* 1606 *Terrier, Hallons -* 1631 *Dudd, Hallonds -* 1682 *ib,
Hallans Quarter* 1695 *LindDep 67,* 1697 *Terrier, Hallams -* 1693
Foster, Hollande quarter 1648 *ib, Hollands -* 1687 *LindDep 67,
Holland field Quarter* 1703 *BPD, Halland's -* 1718, 1745 *Terrier,* and
Goxhill hallons quarter feild 1697, *goxhill Hallands Quarter feld* (sic)
1712, *Goxhill's Halland's Quarter-Field* 1745, *Goxhills Hallands
Quarter Field* 1825 all *Terrier* (Thornton Curtis). For Halland's *v.*
prec. and for *quarter* Chapel Field Rd *supra.*

HORSEGATE FIELD RD, cf. *Horsegate road* 1775 *BPD, - Road*
1775 *EnclA,* 1822 *Terrier, Horsegate Field* 1775 *BPD,* 1775 *EnclA,*
1822 *Terrier, ye Feild called Horsgate* 1606 *ib, the feild called
Horsegate* 1611 *ib, a Feild called Horsegate quarter* 1700 *LindDep 67,
Horsegate Field* 1685 *BPD, a certaine Field called horse gate quarter*
1687 *LindDep 67, horsgate -* 1601 *Terrier, horsegate -* 1611 *ib,* 1648
LindDep 67, Horsegate - 1638 *Terrier,* 1631 *Dudd,* 1633 *AOMB 390,*
1648 *Foster,* 1695 *LindDep 67,* 1679, 1700 *Terrier, Horsgate Quarter*
1662, 1668 *ib, Horsegate -* 1706 *Foster,* 1728 *BPD,* 1730 *Foster, Horse
gate quarter* 1671 *Terrier,* 1682 *Dudd,* 1690 *Terrier, - Quarter* 1693
Foster, Horse-gate - 1697 *Terrier, Horse-Gate -* 1724, 1745 *ib,* and
horsgate 1601 *ib, Horsgate* 1638, 1679, 1700 *ib, horsegate* 1648
LindDep 67, (*y^e*) *Horsegate* 1662 *Terrier,* 1685 *BPD,* 1697 *Terrier,
horse-gate* 1690 *ib, Horse gate* 1693 *Foster, Horse Gate* 1718, 1724,
1745 *ib,* 'the road for horses', *v.* **hors, gata**. Horsegate Quarter was
one of the four fields of Goxhill, for which *v.* Chapel Field Rd
supra.

LANGLEYS (lost, approximately TA 113237), 1824 O, 1830 Gre,
Langley Holme 1549 Pat, *langley cote* 1549 *Yarb, Langley* 1775
EnclA, 1822 *Terrier, Langly* 1693 *Foster, Langley Sick*(*e*) 1607 *Rental,
Langly Sykes* 1633 *AOMB 390, Lanley heads* 1682 *Dudd, Langly
head, - Dike* 1693 *Foster, Langley Drain* 1775 *EnclA,* 1822 *Terrier* (*v.*
holmr, cot, sīc, sīk, hēafod, dīc, dīk). The situation, near to the
Salt Marsh, hardly supports a meaning 'the long wood or glade', *v.*
lang, lēah, so perhaps it is to be identified with *Langgney* 1268 Ch,
langhenaie, langnaye (2x) lHy3 (114) *Gox, langnaycroft* 1273 (114) *ib,*

Langmay (sic) *holm* m16 *Cragg, langney holme* 1549 *LindDep 78*,
langney 1685 *ib 67*, which seems to be 'at the long piece of dry
ground in marsh', *v.* **lang** (dat.sg. **langan**), **ēg**, forms with medial *-n-*
clearly indicating that the name is a dat.sg. formation. Cf. Langney
PN Sx 447, where the local pronunciation and 18th century forms
indicate a similar replacement by *Langley*. This identification is
almost certainly correct, for at the site of the lost *Langleys* there is
a long and slightly raised, but quite distinct piece of land in the
otherwise level marsh.

NEATGANGS FM, cf. *le Netgange, netegonges, Nautegangedike* lHy3
(l14) *Gox, placea q' vocat' Nouteganges* 1273 (l14) *ib, les Neteganges
de Gouxhill* 1381-82 *AddR 37683, a pasture called the neitgatth* m16
Cragg (*v.* **gata**), (*the*) *Neatgangs* 1648 *LindDep 67*, 1685 *BPD*, 1723
LindDep 67, 1730 *Foster et passim, Neat Gangs* 1683 *BPD* and *Neat
Gang dike* 1693 *Foster,* 'the track(s) or road(s) for cattle', from OE
nēat and **gang,** cf. dial. *gang* 'a road, a track, a cattle-walk'. The
earliest forms in *-ou-* and *-au-* are from the cognate ON **naut**.

RUARD RD, 1775 *EnclA,* cf. *Ryward, -he* (*v.* **ēa** 'a river, a
stream'), *Rywardedall'* lHy3 (l14) *Gox, Reward* 1309 (e14) *Bridl*
(checked from MS), *Ruerdaile gate* 1601 *Terrier, Rewerdale -* 1638 *ib,
Ruardgate. Ruarddaile gate* 1648 *LindDep 67, Reward -, Reward dale
-* 1668 *Terrier, Reward -* 1669, 1700 *LindDep 67, Ruard -, Ruard
dale* 1679 *Terrier, Ruhard dale gate* 1671 *ib, Ruardale -* 1700 *ib,
Ruard-dale -* 1690 *ib, Ruard Dale* (*gate*) 1693 *Foster,* 1697 *Terrier, -
Dalegate* 1730 *Foster, Rewerd stigh end* 1631 *Dudd, Reward Stiegh*
1669 *LindDep 67, - Steigh* 1700 *ib, Ruard -* 1724 *Terrier,* 1728 *BPD,*
1730 *Foster,* 1745 *Terrier, Ruard* 1775 *EnclA.* The basic name is
represented by the modern *Ruard,* to which has been added **deill** 'a
portion, share of land', **gata** 'a road' and **stīg, stīgr** 'a path, narrow
road'. Dr John Insley agrees that the second el. of Ruard is ME
ward (OE *warod*) 'low-lying land, marsh', on which *v.* Löfvenberg
220, and this is perfectly appropriate topographically. The earliest
spelling suggests the first el. is **ryge** 'rye', but the subsequent
development is obscure. Perhaps, however, the name does mean
'the low-lying land, the marsh where rye grows'.

SWALLOW MILL QUARTER (lost), *Swallowmyln quarter* 1606,
1611 *Terrier, Swallow mill -* 1648 *LindDep 67,* 1682 *Dudd,*

Swallow(e) Mill - 1648 *Foster*, 1671, 1679 *Terrier*, 1687, (*a Feild called*) 1700 *LindDep 67*, 1700 *Terrier*, - *Quarter* 1662 *ib*, 1693 *Foster*, 1697, 1718, 1724 *Terrier*, 1730 *Foster*, 1745 *Terrier*, *swallow Mill quarter* 1685 *LindDep 67*, in all probability named from an ancestor of Thomas *Swallow of Beasby*, who held land in Goxhill 1676 *MiscDon 14*. It is the same as *the Feild called Show bridgquarter* 1601 *Terrier*, *Shawbridge quarter* 1638 *ib*, *Shaw Bridge Quarter* 1668 *ib*, cf. *Scobrigmar* 1309 (e14) Bridl (*v.* **(ge)mǽre** 'a boundary'), *Shawbriggs* 1631, 1702 *Dudd*, 1718, 1724, 1745 *Terrier*, *Shawbridges* 1679 *ib*, *Shaw Briggs* 1693 *Foster*, 1697 *Terrier*, 1775 *EnclA*, *Shaw-brigge* 1690 *Terrier*, *Shaw-Briggs* 1697 *ib*, *Shawbrigs* 1700 *ib*, *Shaw bridge* 1730 *Foster*, *Shoebridge* 1648 *LindDep 67*, *Shoebridgs* (sic) 1649 *ib*, and also *the Shaw* 1702, 1707 *Dudd*, 1775 *EnclA*; the 1309 form *Scobrig-* is apparently a Scand. compound from **skógr** 'a wood' and **bryggja**, with the English meaning 'a bridge', and it is noteworthy that the majority of the later forms are in *-brigg*. The first el. of these later spellings is from OE **sceaga** 'a small wood' and it is impossible to be sure of the exact history of the name, which could originally have been **Sceagbrycg* 'the bridge near a small wood', which was Scandinavianised, as in the *Scobrig-* form. On balance this seems more likely than that the name was a Scand. compound, subsequently with a replacement of **sceaga** for **skógr**. The same quarter appears once as *Sherriff Mill quarter* 1690 *Terrier*, named from the family of James *Sheriffe* 1630 *BT* and James *Sherife* 1665 *Inv*. This was one of the four fields of Goxhill and for *quarter*, *v.* Chapel Field Rd *supra*.

WEST MARSH LANE, 1828 Bry, cf. "the West Marsh of" *Gousle* e13 (e14) Bridl, *in occidentali marisco, in Westmarisco* lHy3 (l14) *Gox*, - "of" *Goushill* 1291 Ipm, *Coxhill Westmersshe* (sic) 1546 LP xxii, *le Westmarshe* 1549 *LindDep 67*, *the west marshe* 1593 *ib*, *Lee Westmarsh* 1604 *ib*, *Goxell West marshe* 1615 *Dudd*, *Goxhill west Marsh* 1638 *Terrier* (Thornton Curtis), *the West marsh* 1648 *LindDep 67*, *the west marsh* 1648 *Foster*, - *of Goxhill* 1660 *LindDep 78*, (*the*) *West Marsh* (*of Goxhill*) 1655 *MiscDon 14*, 1662 *Terrier* (Thornton Curtis), 1693 *Foster*, 1703 *BPD et passim*, *yᵉ West Marsh* 1685 *LindDep 67*, self-explanatory, *v.* **west**, **mersc** and cf. East Marsh *supra*.

ALLENS WOOD (lost), *Allens Wᵈ* 1828 Bry, named from the *Allen*

family cf. John *Allen* 1818 *BT*. The wood is still marked on the 6"
map, but is not named. It is situated on the south-west boundary
with Barrow upon Humber and Thornton Curtis. BROOK HILL,
Brook hill 1842 White. BUTTERS WOOD is *Tunnard's Plantation*
1824 O, *Tunnards* - 1830 Gre, presumably from a family called
Tunnard, though none has been noted in the parish. It is also
Bottom W^d 1828 Bry. For *Butter* cf. *a place called butters* 1648
LindDep 67, *a certain place Called Butters* 1753 *ib*, *- called Butters*
1771 *ib*, *Butters gate* 1728 *BPD*, *Butters Well Drain* 1775 *EnclA*, no
doubt named from an ancestor of William *Butter* 1728 *BT*, 1746 *Inv*.
CARR GUTTER, cf. *(le) Kerdik'* 1260, lHy3 (114) *Gox, the Carr
Dike* 1693 *Foster* (*v.* **dīc, dīk**), *Kerdaile* 1268 Ch (*v.* **deill**), *keer* (sic)
(114) *Gox, le carr* m16 *Cragg, the Carre* 1631 *Dudd*, 1648 *LindDep*
67, 1660 *ib* 78, 1678, 1709 *Dudd, the Carr* 1648 *Foster*, 1775 *EnclA*,
y^e *Carr* 1685 *LindDep* 67, *the Carr heads* 1678 *BPD*, *- Bank* 1775
EnclA, from **kjarr** 'brushwood' in ME 'a bog, a marsh, especially
one where brushwood grows'. CHAPEL FM, 1830 Gre, *Chapel
F.*^{m} 1824 O, cf. *chappell gate* 1601 *Terrier, Chappell* - 1638 *ib*, 1648
LindDep 67, 1697, 1700 *Terrier, - Gate* 1668 *ib*, (*the*) *Chappel gate*
1679 *ib*, *- Gate* 1718, 1724 *ib*, *Chapel gate* 1671 *ib*, *Chapel-Gate* 1745
ib (*v.* **gata** 'a road'), *Chappell stigh* 1631 *Dudd* (*v.* **stīg, stīgr** 'a path,
a narrow road'), *Chappel marfer* 1648 *LindDep* 67 (*v.* **marfur** 'a
boundary furrow'), for Chapel *v.* Chapel Field Rd *supra*. EAST
MARSH RD, *- Lane* 1817 *Map* and it is *East Marsh Bank* 1828
Bry, *v.* East Marsh *supra*. FERRY FM, cf. *Gowsle Ferry* 1628
Dudd, the fferry or passage over Humber from Gouxhill 1633 *AOMB*
390, *the hamlet of Goxhill ferry* 1842 White. FERRY RD, 1775
EnclA, 1775 *BPD*, 1822 *Terrier*. FIELD HO, cf. *campis de Gousel*
lHy3 (114) *Gox, - guxshulle* (sic) m16 *Cragg, Goxhill Field* 1669
LindDep 67, *v.* **feld**. GOXHILL HAVEN, 1828 Bry and is *Goxhill
Ferry* 1824 O, 1830 Gre, cf. *Haven Close* 1817 *Map*. HOWE
LANE, *How Lane* 1693 *Foster*, 1775 *EnclA, the Howle laine* (sic)
1648 *LindDep* 67, *How-laine* 1688 *MiscDon* 14, and cf. *le houe* lHy3
(114) *Gox, del Howe* 113 (114) *ib, atte Howe* 1332 *SR*, 1389 Pat all
(p), 'the hill', *v.* **haugr**, topographically appropriate, close to the
village. LITTLEWORTH, 1775 *EnclA*, 1824 O, 1830 Gre,
presumably an uncomplimentary nickname. LOW RISBY HO.
MANOR HO. MILL FM, cf. *molendini de Golse* 1155-60 Dane, *-
de Goussa* c.1155 *ib, ad viam molendini* lHy3 (114) *Gox, the old Mill
hill* 1631 *Dudd, the millgate* 1648 *LindDep* 67, *the Mill gate* 1679

Terrier, ye Millgate, the mill hill gate 1648 *LindDep 67, Millhillgate* 1693 *Foster, Millcroft* 1685 *LindDep 67, Milcroft* 1749 *Dudd, the Millfield* 1775 *BPD, Mill Field* 1775 *EnclA, v.* **myln**, with **hyll, gata, croft** and **feld**. NORTH END, *Northend* 1652 WillsPCC, *Goxhill North End* 1828 Bry, self-explanatory. PRIORY, 1842 White. SALT MARSH, *the* - 1775 *BPD*, - *Saltmarsh* 1775 *EnclA*, cf. *the saltmarsh dike* 1648 *LindDep 67, v.* **salt, mersc**. SANDHAM PLANTATION, cf. *Sandholm* lHy3 (l14) *Gox, Sandholmes* 1648 *LindDep 67, Sandholme* 1678 *BPD,* 1693 *Foster,* 1749 *Dudd, Sandom* 1728 *BPD, (the) Sandam, Sandham,* - *Drain* 1775 *EnclA,* 'the sandy island of land, water-meadow', *v.* **sand, holmr**. SKITTER NESS, 1824 O, 1830 Gre, *the Nesse* 1604 *Cragg,* cf. *the Nesse end* 1678, 1709, 1710 *Dudd*; the Ness (*v.* **næss, nes**^{2}) is situated on the north-east coast of the parish, nearly two miles north of East Halton Skitter and East Halton Beck, the continuation of Skitter Beck (in Ulceby parish), so unless the Beck has radically altered its course, and note the name Skitter Ness is unrecorded before the 19th century and earlier seems to have been simply called *The Ness*, it can hardly have been named directly from Skitter Beck, and presumably was a name transferred from the Skitter for some reason, now apparently obscure. SOFT LANE is *Soff Lane* 1775 *EnclA, Sough Lane* 1678, 1684 *BH,* cf. *Sough Leazes* 1678, 1684 *ib,* from OE **sōg, sōh** 'a bog, a marsh', and **læs** 'pasture, meadow land'; it forms in part the boundary between Goxhill and Thornton Curtis. SOUTH END, *the southend of Goxhill* 1653 WillsPCC, *South Goxhill* 1828 Bry, cf. North End *supra.* SYKES' LANE, cf. *Sikes* lHy3, 1312 (l14) *Gox, the sikes* 1648 *LindDep 67, (the) Sikes* 1685 *BPD,* 1693 *Foster,* 1775 *EnclA, le Sykes* e14 (l14) *Gox,* m16 *Cragg,* 'the small streams or ditches', *v.* **sīc, sīk**; in ME f.ns. this word came to mean 'a piece of meadow along a stream'. TOTNEY HILL FM, *Tottney heads* 1662 *Terrier, Totney heads* 1668 *ib* (*v.* **hēafod**), *totney dike* 1697 *ib, Totney* - 1709 *ib,* - *Dike* 1712, 1724, 1822 *ib, Totney-Dike* 1745 *ib* (all *Terrier* references are from Thornton Curtis terriers) (*v.* **dīc, dīk**), *Totney Close* 1648 *Foster,* 1683 *BPD,* 1775 *EnclA, Totney* 1775 *ib*; though the name is not recorded before the mid 17th century, it is likely that it is old, in which case it probably means 'Totta's island of land, piece of dry ground in a fen or marsh', from the OE pers.n. *Totta,* found also in Tottenham PN Mx 78, and **ēg** 'an island', but also used in p.ns. of a piece of dry, higher land in a fen, a sense topographically appropriate here. VICARAGE, *the Vicaridge of goushill* 1601, *- of Goxhill* 1611, *Goxhill Viccaridg* 1606, *the vicaridge* 1638, *- Vicarage* 1679, cf. *Vicaridge Close* 1724 and note *y[e] Viccar Lane* 1606 all *Terrier, ... abutts upon Vicar Lane over against the Vicarage* 1648 *LindDep 67.*

Field-Names

Principal forms in (a) are 1775[1] *EnclA.* Spellings dated 1549[1] are *LindDep* 78, 1549[2], 1550, and 1566 are *Pat,* 1589-91 and 1605-7 are *MinAcct,* 1601, 1606, 1611, 1638, 1662, 1668, 1671, 1679, 1690, 1691[1], 1700[2], 1707[2], 1718, 1724[1], 1745[1]. 1765, 1788 are *Terrier,* 1674, 1697[2], 1709[1], 1712, 1724[2], 1745[2] and 1872 are *Terrier* (Thornton Curtis), 1607 are *Rental,* 1615, 1631, 1678[1], 1682[1], 1702, 1707[1], 1709[2], and 1749[2] are *Dudd,* 1633 are *AOMB 390,* 1648[1], 1649[1], 1685[1], 1687, 1700[1], 1713, 1714, 1723, 1749[1], 1753, 1771, 1772, 1775[2], 1777, and 1803 are *LindDep 67,* 1649[2], 1655, 1667, and 1676 are *MiscDon 14,* 1649[3] are *ParlSurv,* 1672, 1678[2], 1682[2], 1683, 1685[2], 1703, 1728, 1741, and 1775[3] are *BPD,* 1648, 1693, 1706, 1730, 1750, 1770, and 1774 are *Foster,* unless otherwise marked. The forms for 1309 (e14) *Bridl* have all been checked from the MS.

(a) Barnards Farm 1771, *that Messuage ... called Barnards Farme* 1775[2] (1723, 1749[1], *that Mesuage or Tenement in Goxhill ... sometymes called Barnards Farme* 1648[1], *one messuage ... sometimes called Barnards Farme, now in the occupation of John Neelson sometimes (called Barnard) John Neelson* (sic) 1653 WillsPCC, *Bernards* - 1723, from the surn. of John *Barnard* 1648[1], who occupied land in Goxhill in that document, cf. George *Barnard* 1593 *Inv*); Barrow Rd; Beans Farm 1765, 1788 (*- farm* 1745, *Beane Farme* 1707[2], *Bean farme* 1724, from the surn. of John *Beane* 1707[2], named in the *Terrier,* cf. also Philip *Beane* 1587 *BT* and John *Beane* 1672); Blacksmith('s) Shop Rd; a place called Bramores 1772 (*Brademere* 1Hy3 (114) *Gox,* great *Braymeres* 1667, 'broad pool', *v.* **brād, breiðr, mere,** the first el. in the 1667 spelling being in a Scandinavianised form and the second el. later confused with **mōr**[1]); Brewster Lane (*Brewster* Lane 1685[2], *- lane* 1693, from the surn. or occupational name *Brewster*); Burmar Drain (perhaps to be identified with *Brendmar* 1Hy3 (114) *Gox,* Burmoorgate 1693, possibly 'the burnt boundary', *v.* **brende**[2], **(ge)mǣre,** *mar(e)* being a common ME reflex of **(ge)mǣre** in north L); Calf Croft (*calfe croft side* 1631, *Calf Croft Leas* 1730, *v.* **calf, croft**); Chappel Cl 1775[1], Chapel - 1777, 1803 (*the Chappel close in Chappell Quarter* 1648[1], cf. *the chappell stigh* 1638, *Chappell Steigh* 1697[1], *Chappell Snabb* 1649[1], *v.* Chapel Field Rd *supra,* **stig, stigr** and **snabbe,** here and elsewhere in this par. probably 'a piece of dry ground projecting into a bog', cf. Ch 5, i 343); Church Lane, the Church Rd; the College Rd, the Colledge Lane, Thornton College Rd (leading to Thornton Abbey, Thornton Curtis); the Counter Nook 1822 (1724[2], - alias *Colt-hold Nook* 1745[2], *Colthold* 1682[1], *Counter nooke* 1709[1], *the* - 1712, *Counter* seemingly a corrupt form of *colt-hold* 'the colt shelter', v. colt, hold[1]); the East End (cf. North End and South End *supra*); the East Sikes 1775[1], East Sykes 1775[3] (v. Sykes' Lane *supra*); the Eeel Hole (sic) 1822 (1724, y^e *eele hole* 1697[2], y^e *Eele whole* 1709[1], *the Eel-Hole* 1745[2], 'an eel pond', v. ēl[2], hol[1]; for the same name, no doubt referring to the same place, v. y^e *eele-hole* in Thornton Curtis f.ns. (b)); Fox Holes Gate 1822 (*inter magnum Foxoles et paruum foxoles* lHy3 (l14) *Gox, foxholes, foxholegate* 1648[1], *foxhole gate* 1662, 1668, 1674, *Foxhole, Foxholegate* 1693, *fox hole gate* 1697[2], 1730, *fox holes* - 1709[1], *foxholes* - 1712, *Fox-Hole's Gate* 1724[2], *Foxholes* 1728, *Foxhole's Gate* 1745[2], evidently a location characterised by fox-holes, rather than merely the burrows themselves, v. fox-hol); Garth 1817 *Map* (cf. *the Garth Sides* 1749[2], v. garðr); Hobtrust Lane 1775[3] (clearly Hobtrust is for *Hobthrust* (v. EDD s.v.) 'a hobgoblin, etc.', also a name for Robin Goodfellow); Hogcoat Cl 1775[1], Hobcoat Cl (in Goxhill Marsh) 1822 (the later form probably arose from dissimilation of the -*gc*- cluster, v. hogg, cot 'a shed'); the Hooks (v. hōc); Humber Flg 1750 (1648[1], 1693, *Humberforlonge* 1589-91, *Humberfurlonge* 1605-7, 1607, *Humberfurland* (sic) 1631, *Humber Furlonge* 1648[2], *humber furlong* 1714, *Humber furlong* 1730, v. the R. Humber and furlang, and cf. *Humber Field* 1667); Inside Dike (*the inside dike* 1649[1], self-explanatory); Leys 1770 (v. Teathering Ground *infra*); Lopham Cl 1775[1], 1775[3] (*loppen* m16 *Cragg, Lopham* 1663, *Lopham Nooke* 1685[2], *Lophams Close* 1703, *Lepham* (sic) 1730, *a Close ... called or known by the name Lopholms* 1741), Lopham Lane (an ancient Lane called -) 1775[3] (from details in *EnclA* Lopham Lane seems to have run north from the village main street; the meaning is uncertain and early forms are needed to suggest a convincing etymology); Mill Firth Drain (*Mill Frith* 1693); Moor 1775[3], the Moors 1753, 1771, - of Goxhill 1775[1], Moors Drain 1775[1] (*la More* 1309 (e14) *Bridl,* y^e *mores* 1601, 1671, *the moores* 1638, *the moores* 1648[1], *the Moores* 1649[2], 1702, 1707[1], y^e *moors* 1685[1], *the Forther Mores* (sic) 1679, *the Moor* 1693, 1697[1], y^e *Marrs* 1668, *the mare, the Moors forth* 1700[2], *the Moors* 1700[2], 1718, 1745[1], y^e - 1724[1], *the Moorgate* 1693, v. mōr[1], y^e *Marrs* is clearly an error in the *Terrier*); Netherhams 1775[1], 1775[3], Nitherhams 1775[3] (*Netheram Nooke in the Eastmarsh* 1648[2], y^e *Netherholme Close, Netherholmes* 1685[1], *Netheram Dike* 1693, 'the lower water meadows', v. neoðera, holmr, the latter frequently occurs as *ham(m)* in L); New Close(s) (*New Close heads* 1685[2]); New Pasture; the Nooking; Norwells Drain (*Norwells* 1685[2], presumably 'the north springs', v. norð, wella); the Outgates 1750, 1775[1] (v. ūt, gata); Pismire Hill(s) 1772 (*Pismire Hills* 1713, 'ant hills'; *pismire* here is recorded more than a century before the earliest NED reference (1821)); Porch Farm 1765, 1788 (- *Farme* 1707[2], - *farme* 1724, - *farm* 1745); Skitter Cl (- *close* m16 *Cragg*, it was near to East Halton Beck (in East Halton) *infra*, formerly Skitter Beck); Skitter Marsh 1817 *Map* (cf. prec.); Smithy Green 1770, 1774; (pasture called) Leys or Teathering Grd 1770, 1774, Teathering grd 1753, - Grd 1771, teathering grd 1775[2] (*Tethering ground* 1648[1], *pasture called tetheringe ground* m16 *Cragg*, - *called Tethering ground* 1649[2], *a halfe acres of pasture called tetheringe grounde* 1653 WillsPCC, *Tethering Ground* 1693, *Tetheringe grounde* 1655, *Tethering ground* 1676, *teathering* - 1749[1], *five Stong* (sic) *of pasture called Teathering Ground* 1749[2], cf. *in pratis de Gousel* 1268 RRGr, 'pasture on which cattle were tethered'); the Town Side rd, the Town Street 1775[1], 1775[3], 1822 (1718, 1745[1], *y^e* - 1724[1], *the Common Townes street* 1678 *BH*, 1684 *ib*); antient Homestead of the Corporation of the Trinity House (Trinity House held land in Goxhill 1790 *LTR*); Walkrophow 1753, 1771 (*Walgriphau* Hy3 (l14) *Gox*, *Wagriphwe* (sic) m13 *HarlCh*, *wrawgrippe Howe* 1631, *Waggrey* (sic) 1693, *Walkery Pow* (sic) 1703. Dr John Insley notes that ODan *Wilgrip* is on record and actually occurs in L in the lost Wilgriphaven in Saltfleetby, but *Walgripr* is apparently unrecorded. Such a pers.n. seems to be the first el. of this name, compounded with **haugr** 'a (burial) mound, a hill'. He suggests that *Walgrip (Valgripr)* is perhaps "an AScand formation formed by analogy with such names as ON Valbrandr, Valgarðr, Valþjófr etc."); the Warlots 1775[1], Warlets, The Warletts 1777 (*Le Warlotes* lHy3 (l14) *Gox*, *Warlots*, *Warlott* 1685[2], *v.* **warlot**, and for similar 13th century forms of this word, and a discussion, *v.* Waterhill Wood in Brocklesby parish *supra*); the West Rd (2x); the West Sikes 1750, 1775[1], - Sykes 1775[1], 1775[3] (*the West Sikes* 1678[2], *west sike*, *West sikes* 1682[1], *v.* **sīc, sīk**); Gt Wood Cl 1750 (*Wood daile* 1648[1], *Wood-dale* 1713, *v.* **wudu, deill**).

(b) *a ripa q' voc' A* lHy3 (l14) *Gox*, *the River called the Eah* 1648[1] (the earlier form is from ON **á** 'a river, a stream', the later from the cognate OE **ēa**); *the Abbey Garth* Eliz ChancP, *the queens ma^s manor called the Abbot garthe* m16 *Cragg*, *the site of the Manor of Gouxhill called Abbottes Garth* 1566 (*v.* **abbaye, abbat, garðr** and *the Queen land infra*); *ye acre dickes* 1685[1], *the Acredike* 1728 (identical with *ye acredikes* in Barnetby le Wold f.ns. (b)); *Adlingsaltes* 1649[1], *Addlesall* 1693; *unius clausȝ vocat Agney holm* m16 *Cragg*, *baghaghdike* lHy3 (l14) *Gox* (obscure); *Baidail* e13 (e14) *Bridl* (the same first el. seems to occur in *Baiberge* in Immingham f.ns. (a) *infra*, the second is **deill** 'a share of land'); *the Ballclose* m16 *Cragg* (perhaps *v.* **ball** 'boundary mark', but the first el. may well be the surn. *Ball*); *Barrow bank* (*west of worth hills*) 1649[1], *Barrow Banks* 1693 ('river banks of Barrow upon Humber' (*v.* **banke**, it was probably in Barrow upon Humber parish); *Barrow hedg* 1601, - *hedge* 1638, 1671, *barrow* -

1700, *Barrowhedge* 1693 (the hedge marking the boundary with Barrow upon Humber, *v.* **hecg**); *super divisionem de Barw* e14 (114) *Gox, - diuisionem de Barw* 1312 (114) *ib, Barrow meare* 1648[1], *Barrow meer* 1679, 1697[1], *- mear* 1682[1], *- Meer* 1693, 1718, 1724[1], 1749[2] ('boundary with Barrow upon Humber', *v.* **(ge)mære**; there is also a Barrow Mere on the boundary of Barrow and Barton upon Humber *supra*); *Barrow Rayles* 1693 ('railed boundary of Barrow upon Humber', *v.* **reille**); *Bayarsyke* e14 (114) *Gox, Bayarsic* 1312 (114) *ib* (probably from the surn. *Bayard* (*v.* Reaney s.n.) and **sīc, sīk**); *Beggar Lane* 1685[2]; *Bell daile* 1648[1], *Bell-dale* 1690, *bell dale* 1700[2], *Bell Sinks* 1685[1] (dial. *sink* is recorded from north L in EDD s.v. 13 as 'a gutter, drain, sewer' and for a discussion of this word *v.* Sinks Covert in South Killingholme *infra*) (from the surn. *Bell* and **deill**; George *Bell* is named in 1648[1]); *Billings Croft* 1678[1], *Billing Croft* 1709[2] (probably from the surn. *Billing* and **croft**, though the family has not been noted in the sources searched); *Bragge Garth* (sic) 1682[2], *Gagge Garth* 1683 (it is impossible to know which form is correct, but the *Gagg* family is recorded from the adjacent parish of East Halton, cf. Richard *Gagge* 1641 LPR); *super viam de bremhil?* (sic) Hy3 (114) *Gox, Bremhil, bremhil', - hill', Bromhil* lHy3 *Gox, Brymmell heads* 1648[1], *Brimell* 1685[2], 1728 (the early forms in *Gox* appear to refer to the same place, but it is difficult sometimes to differentiate between *e* and *o* in this MS); *the Bromford* 1601, *the Common Brumford* 1679, y^e *Brumforth* 1690, *the Brunforth* (sic) 1697[1], *bromforth* 1700 (*v.* **brōm** 'broom', **ford**); *Caldwelles* lHy3 (114) *Gox* ('cold springs or wells', *v.* **cald, wella**); *Catthehagh* lHy3 (114) *Gox* ('(wild) cat enclosure', *v.* **cat(t), haga**[1]); *Chapmans ffarme* 1633 (named from the *Chapman* family, cf. William *Chapmande* 1607 *Inv*, John *Chapman* 1639 *ib*); *a Certain Place there called Chancery Furlong* 1749[2] (perhaps alluding to some past litigation); *cocheueland* (sic) lHy3 (114) *Gox* (*v.* **cocc**[2], **hēafod-land**); *Cock croft* 1693; *the Commons* 1648[1], y^e *Comon* 1697[1], *the common* 1700, *Common* 1718, y^e *- 1724*[1], *the - 1745*[1]; *Cotes* 1312 (114) *Gox* (p), *terra Johannis de Cotes* e14 (114) *ib, unum toft' Cotes* 1313-14 Inqaqd, *Cotes* 1375 Peace (p) (these forms are no doubt from a family *de Cotes*, which held land here as in the e14 reference); *Cotte Garth* 1550 (*v.* **cot, garðr**); *Covehouse* 1589-91, 1605-7, *Cowehouse* 1607 (*v.* **couhous**); *le Crossegate* 1309 (e14) *Bridl* ('road by or to a cross', *v.* **cros, gata**); *lez Dales* 1549[1], *les dale* 1549[1], *Daile Gripps* 1702, 1707[1] (*v.* **deill, grype** 'a ditch, a drain'); *Cotag' ... voc' Darbye* 1605-7, *Cot' ... voc' darbye* 1607 (presumably from the surn. *Darby*, though it has not been noted in the sources searched); *dodhagh, dodhaghdike, Dodhaedic'* (sic) lHy3 (114) *Gox* (the first el. is probably the OE pers.n. *Dodd*, with **haga**[1] 'enclosure', though, as Dr John Insley suggests, **dodde** 'the rounded summit of a hill' might also be thought of); *Drimelsyk'. Drymelsyk'* lHy3 (114) *Gox* (the readings are not absolutely certain, but if they are correct Mr J. Field suggests that they perhaps allude to a stream through land as dry as meal, *v.* drȳge, meolu, sīc, sīk); *in orientall' campo* lHy3 (114) *Gox, in campo oriental'* e14 (114) *ib, in campo oriental' de Gousel* lHy3 (114) *ib* ('the east field of Goxhill'); *Elbrough bottome* 1648[1], - *Slack* 1693 (*v.* botm 'a valley bottom', and slakki 'a shallow valley', an OWScand word, rare in the East Midlands, but cf. *Potteredale slacke* in Barrow upon Humber f.ns. (b) *supra* and PN Nt 290 s.v.; *Elbrough* is presumably a family name, though it has not been noted in the sources searched); *Estcrofte* m16 *Cragg* (*v.* ēast, croft); *Fawemar* lHy3 (114) *Gox, Faulkmarre, faukmarre* 1648[1], *Faukmorehill, Faulkmore hill, Faulknerhill* 1693; *Flete, le Flet* lHy3 (114) *Gox* (*v.* flēot 'stream'); *the frith* 1638, *the Furth* 1668, *y^e* - 1671 (*v.* fyhrð(e) 'a wood, woodland'); *Fulscoat Nook* 1749[2]; *the furre close gate* 1648[1], *the Furr Close* 1685[2]. ('the far, distant close', *v.* furr (feor), clos(e)); *le Gayres* 1309 (e14) *Bridl* (*v.* geiri); *Gilbyes headland* 1687, *Gilbys* - 1700[1] (named from the *Gilby* family, cf. Richard *Gilby* 1649[1]); *Gildecroft,* lHy3 (114) *Gox, Gildegarth* 1309 (e14) *Bridl* (*v.* gild 'a guild', croft, garðr); *Godney Pitts* 1693 (presumably from a surn. and pytt); *Goslingmarre* lHy3 (114) *Gox* (alluding either to young geese or to the surn. *Gosling*); *le Grayninges, Greininges* lHy3 (114) *Gox* (perhaps 'meadows in a stream-fork', *v.* grein, eng); *gretlandes* m13 *HarlCh* ('gravelly strips', *v.* grēot, land); *le Hages* lHy3 (114) *Gox* (*v.* haga[1] 'an enclosure'); *the Hanging Lea butts* 1730 (*v.* hanging, lēah, butte); *ye Headland* 1601, *the headland* 1678[1], 1709[2] (*v.* hēafod-land); *Herbord Houodeland* 1312 (114) *Gox* (*v.* hēafod-land, and if the MS reading is correct hēafod has been replaced by the cognate Scand hofuð, the first el. *Herbord,* as Dr John Insley suggests, is from the Low German pers.n. *Herebord*); *hertesgate* 1309 (e14) *Bridl,* 1312 (114) *Gox, Hertesgat'* e14 (114) *ib* ('deer's track', *v.* heort, -es[2], gata); *Hestecroft* 1273 (114) *Gox* (perhaps the same as *Estcrofte supra,* with intrusive *H-,* but if the form is correct then it may be 'the horse croft', *v.* hestr, croft); *the Holmes Close* 1648[2] (*v.* holmr); *Horchardhowedland* e14 (114) *Gox* (certainly a mistake for *Herbord-supra,* the two relevant charters in *Gox* contain the same list of names); *bercar' q' vocat' Huchuncotestede* 1273 (114) *Gox* ('Huchon's cottage-site', from the ME pers.n. *Huchon* from OFr *Huchon,* a double diminutive of *Hue,* i.e. *Hugh,* and cot-stede, for which *v.* Sandred 99); *Inge* 1649[1] (*v.* eng); *Kaheuedelande* lHy3 (114) *Gox* (probably a compound of ME *cā* (OE *cā, ON *ká* 'a jackdaw', and hēafod-land); *Kiluingstigh* lHy3 (114) *Gox* (probably for *Kiluingholmstigh* 'the path to Killingholme', *v.* stīg, stīgr); *Kokermat* 1309 (e14) *Bridl* (probably an error for *-mar*), *Cockermarr* 1601, *Cokermare* 1671, *Cocker Meer* 1718, 1724[1], *Cocker-Meer* 1745[1], *Cocker Moor* 1693 (perhaps from the ME surn. *Coker* and (ge)mǣre 'a boundary, land on a boundary'); *layrhille, layrhilles* lHy3 (114) *Gox* ('muddy, clayey hill(s)' *v.* leirr, hyll); *limekill leazes* 1648[1] (i.e. limekiln, *v.* also lǣs); *threstonge next a land called Lyard* 1653 *WillsPCC, one land called Lyards* 1693 (probably from a surn., the naming of a single land being noteworthy); *Marfer* 1693 *v.* **marfur**); *the Marsh dike* 1709[2] (cf. *midmerskdik' infra*); *Mawmdam Crike* 1682[1], *Manndam* - 1702, 1707[1], *Mandome* - 1706 (*v.* **crike** (**kriki**) 'a creak'); *merskwra in Gouxsil'* 1273 (114) *Gox* (the first el. is a Scandinavianised form of **mersc** 'a marsh', the second ON **vrá**); *Mikelhil, mykelhill', mykelhilgat'* lHy3 (114), *Gox*, cf. *de Monte de Gouxl'* lHy3 (114) *ib* (p), *del Hil'* lHy3 (114) *ib* (p) (*v.* **mikill, hyll**); *midmerskdik', middmerskekik'* (sic) lHy3 (114) *Gox* ('(dike in) the middle marsh', *v.* **mid, mersc, dík**; the *-merske-* spelling is a Scandinavianised form, cf. *merskwra supra*); *mykeldayles, mykeldaylegate* lHy3 (114) *Gox, Mikeldayle* 1309 (e14) *Bridl, Mickledailes* 1685[2], *Mickle Dale* 1671, *-dales* 1697[1], *Michaeldales* 1638, *Michael dales* 1668 ('the big, large allotments', *v.* **mikill, deill**, a Scand compound); *Middales* 1693 (*v.* **mid, deill**); *the middfurlong* 1648[1], *the middle furlong* 1649[1], *Middle Furlong* 1685[2] (*v.* **mid, middel, furlang**); *Mill Mastall butts* 1730 (*v.* Mill Fm *supra*; *Mastall* probably has the same origin as *le Marstal* in Killingholme f.ns. (b)); *Neudik'* lHy3 (114) *Gox* (self-explanatory, *v.* **níwe, dík**); *le Neuil Croft* lHy3 (114) *Gox* (from the surn. *Nevill*, cf. Hugh *de Neuill'* e13 *HarlCh*, with **croft**); *in campo borial'* lHy3 (114) *Gox, in north campo de Gousil'* lHy3 (114) *ib* ('the north field of Goxhill'); *Northcoate garth* (*v. Worthcote garth infra*); *Northsnab* lHy3 (114) *Gox* (*v.* **snabbe**, cf. *Chapel Snab* under Chappel Cl in (a) *supra*); *Nunthorn headland* 1693 (cf. *the Nunhouse* 1672); *the olde yawde hill* 1631; *the Oatgates* 1693 (presumably for *Out-* and so the same as the Outgates in (a) *supra*); *the oxdaills, - Oxdalls* m16 *Cragg, Oxedales* 1587-8 (1650) *ParlSurv, Oxdales* 1589-91, 1605-7, 1607, 1649, *the Oxdaleends* 1633, *Oxdale heads* 1693 (*v.* **oxa, deill**); *a place ... sometimes called Page Lea, which I lately purchased of George Page* 1653 WillsPCC; *the Parsonage land* 1649[1], *parsonage* - 1682[1], cf. Vicarage *supra*); *paynott Nook* 1601, *- nooke* 1638, *Pennat Nook* 1697[1], *Pannott* - 1718, *Panott* - 1724[1], *Pannet Nooke, Pannett Nook* 1730, *Panott-Nook* 1745[1], *Pennant nook gate* 1693 (named after the family of Thomas *Paynet* 1592 *Inv*, Richard *Paynott* 1609 *ib*, and Richard *Pannott* 1626 *ib*, *v.* **noke**); *Pesedale, Pesedalemar* 1309 (e14) *Bridl* (*v.* **pise** 'pease', **deill** with (**ge**)**mǽre**); *pindermarr* 1601, 1638, *pindermar* 1631, *Pinder mare* 1679, *- meer* 1697[1], *Pinder-mar* 1690, *pindar Moor, great Pinder Meer* 1693 (from the surn. *Pinder* and probably (**ge**)**mǽre** 'a boundary, land on a boundary', cf. Edward *Pinder* 1629 *Inv*); *Potterdayle heads* 1667 (named from the surn. *Potter* and **deill** 'a portion of land', with the plural of **hēafod**); *Pow Wharlett Dike* 1693 (*v.* **warlot, dík**, the meaning of *Pow* is obscure); *Le Prestmar* 1309 (e14) *Bridl, preistmair* 1601, *preistmarr* 1638, *Priest Marr* 1668, *preistmare* 1671, *Prestmare* 1679, *Priest-mar* 1690, *Priest Meir headland* 1693 (*v.* **hēafod-land**), *Priestmeer* 1697[1], *preistmarr* 1700, *Priest Meer* 1718, 1724[1], 1745[1], *Priestmar* 1730 (*v.* **prēost**, (**ge**)**mǽre** 'a boundary, land on a boundary'); *priorcrofts* 1638, *Prior Crofts* 1679, *- Croft* 1724[1], *Prior-Croft* 1745[1],

Pryor Crofts 1667, *ye Pryar-crofte* 1690 (*v.* **prior, croft**, the reference probably being to the Prior of Bridlington Priory); *Pytonthinge* 1589-91, *Pytenthinge* 1607 (no doubt from an unidentified family and **þing** 'a possession, property'); *the Queen land, the queens land, the queenesland* 1638 (it is described in 1601 as *the land of the Soveraigne Ladie the Queen,* cf. *the Abbey Garth supra*); *Radewaygate, Rudewayhil, Rodweye* lHy3 (114) *Gox* ('the way, road suitable for riding', *v.* **rād, weg**); *Rayninghagh hoce* (sic) lHy3 (114) *Gox; Redcoathill* 1693; *Rye Dale* 1749² (*v.* **ryge, deill**); *Sand Leyes* 1693; *Barcarie vocat Shepecote* 1589-91, *Barcarrye voc'* - 1605-7, *un' Barcario voc' Shepcote* 1607, *Meadow ground where upon formerly a house hath stood cald ... Sheepecoate* 1649³ (*v.* **scep-cote**); *Shepherd Steigh* 1730 (probably from the *Shepherd* family and **stīg, stigr** 'a path', cf. Robert *Shepherd* 1566 *BT*); *Cl' i vocat Shrewthes* 1589-91, - *voc' Shrewes* 1605-7, *un' Cl'i voc' Shrewthes* 1607; *Smalcharnnnarpes* (doubtful reading) lHy3 (114) *Gox; Smaldemars* 1631, *Smaldemarrs* 1649¹, *small Demare* 1693; *Smothescroft* 1273 (114) *Gox* (the reading is not certain, but if it is correct, Dr John Insley suggests that the first el. may be a byname from OE *smōð* 'serene, calm', the second being **croft**); *in austral' marisco de Gouxl* lHy3 (114) *Gox* ('Goxhill south marsh'); *le Soutergarth* 1309 (e14) *Bridl* (*v.* **sūtere**, ME *soutere* 'shoe-maker', or the derived surn., and **garðr**); *in Speldhalkes and Adly Sikes* 1633; *the stake homes* (sic) m16 *Cragg, Stockhooke* 1648¹; *the stoope* 1648¹ (*v.* **stolpi** 'a stake, a post'); *Swardledale* 1648²; *the Swarth* 1730 (*v.* **swæð**); *swinesroote leas* (sic) 1631, *Swinecutt Leas* 1728 ('pig shelter', *v.* **swīn, cot**, the earlier form possibly either from **wrōt** 'snout of a pig' or from OE *wrōtan* 'to grub up with the snout, in the manner of swine', cf. *swine-wroting* NED s.v. *swine* 5, i.e. 'a place in which swine root'); *Sybsfordesikes* lHy3 (114) *Gox* (the first el. is probably the ME pers.n. *Sibbe,* a pet-form of *Sibyl,* compounded with **ford** and with **sīc, sīk** added); *the Tenn Stongs* 1693 ('ten roods of land', *v.* **stong**); *terram ospital' de Thornton'* lHy3 (114) *Gox* (i.e. of Thornton Abbey, Thornton Curtis); *Thornton maire balke* 1601, *Thornton meere* 1638, - *meare* 1648¹, - *Meare* 1667, - *Mare* 1671, - *Meer* 1697¹, 1718, 1745‘, *Thornton-Meer* 1724¹, *Thorneton Moore* 1653 WillsPCC ('the boundary with Thornton Curtis', *v.* **(ge)mǣre**); *tofte* lHy3 (114) *Gox, Toft gate* 1685¹ (*v.* **toft, gata**); *Trolleheudland'* 1309 (e14) *Bridl* ('headland haunted by a troll', *v.* **troll, hēafod-land**); *in locum qui vocatur Tubhaes* m13 *HarlCh* (*v.* **haga**¹ 'enclosure' in the pl., the first el. being probably the ODan pers.n. *Tubbi* or the derived surn.); *Turfker, turfker* lHy3 (114) *Gox Turfscarre* 1589-91, *Turfecarre* 1605-7, 1607, *Turfe Carre* 1633, *Turfe Carre* 1653 WillsPCC ('the marsh in which turf was cut', *v.* **turf, kjarr**); *in Turfemoore* 1633 (*v.* **turf, mōr**¹); *Twygrayn* 1273 (114) *Gox* ('two-fold fork', *v.* **twegen, grein** and, further, for the same name in Barton upon Humber f.ns. (b) *supra*); *vtfurlanges* lHy3 (114) *Gox* ('outer furlongs', *v.* **ūt, furlang**); *Verecotis* m16 *Cragg, le shepegate ... vocat Veercote* 1549¹, *shepegates* *called Veercote* 1549[1], *the vere Cote* 1648[2], *verecoat daile* 1648[1] ('near the Humber is Verecourt, which belonged to the ancient family of that name' 1724 Stukeley, cf. Walter *de Ver* 1212 Fees and note Simon *de Veer de Gousil* held land here Hy3 (114) *Gox*); *Walehagh* lHy3 (114) *Gox, Walesham* (*head*) 1648[1], *Walsham* (sic) 1648[2] (with only a single 13th century form it is impossible to suggest a firm etymology, but *formally* it might be 'the enclosure of the Welshmen', *v.* **walh** (gen.pl. **wala**), **haga**[1]; the 1648 references may not be related to it); *Walkington Barne, one land called Walkington* 1693 (named from the *Walkington* family, cf. John *Walkinton* 1590 *BT*); *Le Wathegate* 1309 (e14) *Bridl* ('the road to the ford', *v.* **vað, gata**, a further Scand. compound in Goxhill f.ns.); *Wayn Gapp* 1693 ('the gap for a cart or waggon', *v.* **wægn, gap**); *the west close* 1682[1], - *Close* 1687, 1700[1]; *in campo occidental'* e14 (114) *Gox, in campo occidental'* 1312 (114) *ib, the west Feild* 1631 (one of the open fields of Goxhill); *a place called Whidhills* 1649[1]; *Widdales* 1693 (*v.* **wīd, deill**); *Wilingdam* lHy3 (114) *Gox* (perhaps 'the dam or pond growing with willows', *v.* **wiligen, dammr**); *Worthcote garth alias Northcoate garth* 1615, *North coatclose dicke* 1685 (for *Worthcote garth v. Worth supra* in the adjoining parish of Barrow upon Humber; for the alternative name, *v.* **norð, cot, garðr**); *worth hills* 1649[1], *Worthill* 1693 (no doubt also named from *Worth* in the adjacent parish of Barrow upon Humber *supra*); *Wrangland* lHy3 (114) *Gox* ('crooked strip', *v.* **vrangr, land**); *Wyrdhe* lHy3 (114) *Gox* (this is also from the lost *Worth* in Barrow upon Humber parish, with **ēa** 'a stream, river', unless it is merely a scribal variant for *Wyrde*, which is certainly possible).

Grasby

GRASBY

> *Grosebi* (2x) 1086 DB
>
> *Grosbi* 1086 DB
>
> *Grossebi* c.1115 LS, 1160 Dugd vi, 1160-62 (1287) YCh iii, 1166, 1167, 1168, 1169 P *et freq* in P, 1204 Cur, 1219 Ass, -*biam* 1190 (1301) Dugd vi, -*by* 1208 FF
>
> *Gressebi* 1165, 1177, 1185 P (p), 1187 ib (p), lHy2 Dane (p), 1201 P (p), 1202 Ass, 1202 P (p), 1204 ib, -*by* 1209-35 LAHW, 1125 FineR *et freq* to 1384 Pat, -*b'* c.1220 Welles, 1235 IB, *Greseby* 1212 Fees, 1428 FA
>
> *Gresby* 1238-43 Fees. 1347 Pat, 1382 Cl (p), 1519 DV i, 1554 Pat, 1606 *Terrier et freq* to 1762 *ib*, -*bye* 1556 CA, 1542-3 Dugd vi, 1576 Saxton, 1610 Speed, -*bie* 1649 *Foster*, 1671 *Terrier*, 1685 *Red*

Griseby 1343 Pat, *Grisseby* 1364 Cl, 1387, 1397, 1400 Pat,
    Grysseby "next" *Sereby* 1421 WillsPCC
Grisby 1387 Peace, 1550 Pat, 1607 *BT*, 1612 *Terrier*, 1621
    Foster, 1625 *Terrier*, *Grysby* 1431 FA, 1469 Pat, 1526 Sub,
    1535 VE iv, 1556 LNQ xiv, 1562 *BT et passim* to 1587 *BT*,
    Gyrsseby 1472 WillsPCC, *Gyrsbe* 1539 LP xiv, *Girsbie*
    1576 LER, 1597 SC, *-bye* 1590 ib, *-by* 1601 *Terrier*
Grassebi 1202 Ass, *Grasby* 1697 *Terrier et passim, Grassby*
    1781, 1822 *Terrier*, 1833 *MiscDep 74*

Ekwall (DEPN s.n.) explains Grasby as 'the bȳ in a stony
district', the first el. being ON **grjót** 'gravel, stones', and he thinks
this name is identical with Grössby in Sweden. This is topographically appropriate, as Mr Ifor Barton has indicated to me, but
Fellows-Jensen (SSNEM 50-1) points out that it is difficult to
explain the spellings in *Gro-* "on the basis of *grjót*', unless they are
"mistakes" for *-e-*. As she says, this is difficult name and it is really
impossible to determine what the first el. actually is, so that it is
safer to leave the name unexplained. It is possible that the forms
in *Gresse-*, etc., and later *Gras-*, "represent substitution for the
original first el., whatever that may have been, of the appellative
"grass" (OE *gærs, græs, gres* n., OIcel *gras, gres* n.)", *v.* further
SSNEM 51.

AUDLEBY LOW COVERT, - *Cover* 1824 O, named from Audleby
in Caistor *supra*. BENTLEY HO, presumably named from *Bentley*
family, cf. *Mr Bentley* 1783 *LTR*. CROSS KEYS (P.H.), 1842
White. GRASBY BOTTOM, 1824 O, 1828 Bry, 1830 Gre.
GRASBY TOP, cf. *super les Wolds versus culmen eorum anglice*
topp 1650 *MiscDon 275*. GRASBY WOLD LANE, *yᵉ woldgate* 1697
Terrier, (*the*) *Woldgate* 1703, 1707 *ib*, cf. *les Wolds* 1650 *MiscDon*
275, the Wold 1864 *Terrier*, *v.* **wald**, **gata** 'a road'. GREAT DRIFT
(lost), 1828 Bry, *Drift* 1707, 1724 *Terrier, yᵉ Great Drift* 1745 *Terrier,*
the great drift 1762, 1781 *ib*, cf. *the North drift* 1699 *MiscDon 275*,
from *drift* 'a cattle-road'. LOW FM (lost), 1824 O, the farm is
marked but not named on the 6" map. VICARAGE, *yᵉ Vicarighe*
of Grysby 1577, *the vicarage of Grisby* 1612, *The Vicarage house* 1707
all *Terrier*, cf. *Vicarage land* 1606, *vicarage land* 1612 both *ib*, *the*
Vicarage ground, - land, - Lathe garth 1643 *MiscDon 275* (*v.* **hlaða**

'a barn', garðr 'an enclosure'), *Vicarage thirteene acre Close* 1643 *ib*, the *Vicarage Close* 1697 *Terrier*.

Field-Names

Undated forms in (a) are 1781 *Terrier*. Spellings dated 1621 are *Foster*, 1636, 1643, 1649, 1650, 1690, and 1699 are *MiscDon 275*, 1728 are *Td'E*, 1833 are *MiscDep 74*, and the remainder are *Terrier*, unless otherwise marked.

(a) Babb lane (*babe gatt* 1577, *the Babb gate, babb laine* 1606, *bab lane* 1671, 1674, *Bab-lane* 1679, v. **gata, lane**); Barnetby gate 1781 (*barnayby gatt, barnabye gath* 1577, *Barnaby gate* 1606, *Barnetbie gate* 1697, *Barnetby Gate* 1745, 'the road to Barnetby', v. **gata**); the Beck 1762, 1781 (1643, 1679, y^e *beck* 1674, 1745, *the comon beck* 1606, *the Common Becke* 1664, *Common beck* 1674, v. **bekkr**); Bracken Dale 1762, 1781 (1745, presumably self-explanatory, v. **brakni, deill**); Braygate 1762 (1703), Bray-gate 1781 (*bray(e) gatt* 1577, *braygate, bray gate* 1606, 1724, - *Gate* 1745, *Bray gate* 1697, 1707, probably 'the broad road', v. **breiðr, gata**, a Scand. compound); the long Chalks 1762, 1781 (*les Cawkes* 1650, *the Long Chalks* 1724, y^e - 1745, v. **c(e)alc** 'chalk', referring to chalky places); Churchgate 1762, Church gate 1781 (- *Gate* 1745, y^e *Church gate* 1724, 'road to the church', v. **gata**, the same as Kirkgate q.v., *infra*); Collinson's Cl (*Dallison Close* 1606 (sic), *Collisons close* 1671, *Collison-* 1674, *Collison-Close* 1679, no doubt from the *Colli(n)son* family, represented, as Mr Ifor Barton points out, in the neighbouring parish of Searby, cf. e.g. Agnes *Collinsone* 1601 *PR* (Searby)); Cuthbert's Farm 1864 (named from the *Cuthbert* family, cf. Richard *Cuthbert* 1773 *Inv*); The East Fd 1762, 1781 (*the* - 1697, y^e - 1745, *The est fyeld* 1577, *the East feild* 1601, 1612, 1625, *the east feild* 1606, *the Eastfeild* 1636, - *East field* 1679, *Eastfield* 1724, v. **čast, feld** and cf. The West Fd *infra*); the Eight Acres Cl 1762, the eight acre cl 1781, the eight Acres 1822 (*the eight acrees Cloase* (sic) 1664 (the spelling *acrees* occurs several times in 17c. terriers of this parish), *eight Acre Close* 1674, *Eight-Acre close* 1697, *One close called 8 Acre* 1703, *a close calld Eight Acre* 1707, *A Close called the Eight Acres* 1724, *One Close called* y^e *Eight Acres* 1745, v. **æcer**); Ferrygate 1762, Ferry gate 1781 (*fery gatt* 1577, *ferrye -, ferrie gate* 1606, *Ferrie gate* 1697, *Ferry gate* 1703, *Ferry Gate* 1707, *Ferry-Gate* 1745, 'the road to the ferry', v. **ferja, gata**); the Field 1762, 1781, the Field Cl 1762, The field cl 1781 (*Girsbie feild* 1577 *Terrier* (Searby), y^e *Field* 1724, 1745); the Field Pce 1833 (v. **pece**); the First Cl 1833 (cf. Second Cl *infra*); the Furze gate 1762, the furze 1781 (*the furrs* 1606, *the furs* 1697, 1703, y^e *Furrs* 1707, v. **fyrs**); Headland 1762 (1745, y^e *Headland* 1707, y^e *h(y)edland* 1577, *the headland*

1606, 1697, 1703, and cf. ye heads 1697, 1707, v. hĕafod-land, hĕafod); the Holmes Cl 1762, The - 1781 (the homes (sic) 1577, the holmes 1606, 1664, 1668, - Holmes 1679, the Holms 1707, ye Holm 1703, the Holmes 1668, 1679, 1724, y^e - 1745, the Holme Close 1728, ye East Holmes 1724, the little Holms 1697, v. holmr 'an island of land, raised land in marsh, a water-meadow'); Home Cl 1864, the - 1833; Kirkgate 1762, Kirk gate 1781 (kyrke gatt 1577, the kirk gate 1606, - kirke gate 1621, kirkgate 1664, Kirkgate 1697, 1703, 1707, Kirk-Gate 1745, 'road to the church', v. kirkja, gata, cf. Church gate supra); Kirk's Acre dikes 1762, - Dykes 1781 (Mr Kirks - 1745, named from the family of Robert Kirk 1745, formerly Rhodes - and Ticklatts Acre Dykes in (b) infra, v. æcer, dīc); the Long Cl 1833; the lower hills 1762, - hill 1781 (1621, 1703, ye Lower hills 1697, - Hills 1724, 1745, - lower Hill 1707, cf. the upper hills, infra); the Moor 1762, 1781, the Moors 1833 (The Moor 1707, 1724, y^e - 1745, v. mōr[1]); Mounceys lane 1864 (Mr Ifor Barton points out the presence of the Mouncey family here, cf. James Mounsey 1829 PR); Occupation Lane Cl 1864; Second Cl 1833 (cf. First Cl supra); the Street (the Town Street 1643); One Close ab^t 13 Acres 1762 (One close called commonly by the name of 13 Acres 1697, One close called 13 Acre 1703, - thirteen Acre 1707, - Acres 1745, One Close called Thirteen Acres 1724); Town end cl 1762, 1781 (1703, - Close 1707, Townend - 1724, 1745, 'close at the end of the village', v. tūn, ende[1]); the Vicar's Townsend(s) Cl 1762; the upper hills 1762, 1781 (1606, y^e - 1724, - Hills 1707, 1724, 1745, the Upper hills 1697, Vpper Hill, ye Vpper Hills 1703); the Watson Yd 1822 (named from the Watson family, cf. Christopher Watson 1594 BT); The West Fd 1762, 1781, (y^e - 1745, The West fyeld 1577, the West feild 1601, 1612, 1625, the Westfeild 1621, the west field 1668, (the) west feild 1606, 1664, 1674, the West field 1679, Westfield 1697, 1724, the West Feield (sic) 1703, West Field 1707, Westfield 1724, v. west, feld and cf. The East Fd supra).

(b) ye est acardycke 1577, the East Acre dykes 1697, the west Akerdikes 1606, Gregsons Acredike Close 1636, (John Gregson is named in the document), the Acree Dike Cloase 1664, the acreedike Cloase (sic) 1668 (v. æcer, dīc, dīk, and for the same name v. Barnetby le Wold f.ns. (b)); Andrewe Platt (close of pasture) 1699 (John Andrewe is named in the same document); Bairdhouse m16 Cragg (presumably from a surn. not noted in the documents searched); Barnetby Bottome 1650 (named from Barnetby le Wold supra and botm); Bend Lane 1643; Bra(c)klans 1606; burt land dall (sic) 1577, Burkland dayll' (sic) 1606; Caster Poor Close 1728 (a charitable endowment for the poor of Caistor); ye Commons 1674, the - 1679; the Corne fieldes 1668; Croft de Grisby 1387 Peace (p) (v. croft); lez demeane landes 1550 Pat (self-explanatory, v. demeine 'demesne'); dowcott gatt 1577 ('the road to the dovecote', v. douve-cote, gata); Dowryhouse 1550 Pat; Five

Acre Field 1707; *in campo de Goldcroft* 1208 FF (*Goldcroft* probably denotes 'a small enclosed field' characterised by its gold colour, perhaps from the colour of plants growing there, *v.* **gold, croft**); *how gatt* 1577, *the howgate, how-gate* 1606 ('the road to the hill or mound', *v.* **haugr, gata**); *the Kings street* 1671, 1674, *the Kingstreet* 1679; *the little close* 1697; *Robert Marris clos* 1577, *marris Close* 1606 (the *Marris* family is well evidenced in the parish); *the Meers* 1697 (*v.* **(ge)mære** in the pl.); *ye mylcroft* 1577 (*v.* **myln, croft**); *nortlanges* e13 HarlCh, *-langis* John ib (*v.* **norð, lang** 'a long strip of land'); *Parcershaft* 1707, *Parcers shaft* 1724 (probably from the family name *Parcer,* cf. Edward *Parcar* 1600 *BT,* with an uncertain second el.); *the ploote* 1668, *the Plat* 1697 (*v.* **plot, plat**[2]); *Rhodes Acre dykes* 1724 (named from the family of *Mr Rhodes* 1724, *v.* Kirk's Acre dikes *supra* and *Ticklats Acre dykes infra*); *ye shortt buttes* 1577, *the short -* 1606 (*v.* **butte**); *6 leas of meadow* (*three acre dike lease one long lea and two stinting leas*) 1636 *Ticklat Acre dykes* 1697, *Ticklats -* 1703, 1707, *Ticklats Plat* 1707 (named from the family of William *Ticklatt alias Tickler* 1621, William *Ticklat* 1697, *v.* Kirk's Acre dikes and *Rhodes Acre dykes supra*); *atte Wayur* 1296 *Ass* (p), *Atte Waiur* 1327 *SR* (p), *atte Wayour* 1332 *ib* (p) (*v.* **weyour** 'a pond'); *The West low field* 1649; *the Windinges* 1621 (cf. *the wyndinges* in Great Limber f.ns. (b) *infra*); *Wood Crofts* 1690 (*v.* **wudu, croft**); *ye ynges* 1577, *ye est ynges, ye west ynges* 1577, *the West Ynges* 1643 (*v.* **ēast, west, eng**).

Habrough

HABROUGH

   Aburne 1086 DB

   Haburne (6x) 1086 DB, *Haburn'* 1196 ChancR, *Haburn* 1218 FF

   Haburc c.1115 LS, c.1150, 1150-60, eHy3 Dane, 1159-81 (e13)
      NCot, c.1160 Dane, 1165, 1166, 1167, 1168, 1169 P *et freq* to
      Hy3 HarlCh, 1252 Cl, *Aburc'* 1219 Fees, *Haburk* Hy3 HarlCh,
      -burch 1143-47 Dane, c.1150 (e13) *NCot,* c.1150, a1155 Dane,
      eHy2 (e13) *NCot,* 1157-63, 1160-66 Dane *et passim* to RI
      (1318) Ch

   Haburg(') eHy2, a1180, 1180 (e13) *NCot,* 1187 P, 1190, l12
      (e13) *NCot,* 1202 Ass, 1205 ChR, 1219 Fees *et passim* to
      1300 *NCot, -burga* 1190-95 Dane, *-burge* 1235 Dugd vi,
      Aburg' 1242-43 Fees, 1280 RSu

   Haburh Hy2 Dane

   Haburgh(') 1259 RRGr, 1281 QW, 1281 Tax, 1298 Ass, 1303
      Orig, 1303 FA, 1303 Pat, 1305 ib *et freq* to 1817 *Yarb*

Habur 1159-81 (e13) *NCot*, 1271-2 *Ass*, 1536-7 Dugd vi, *-ber*
   1554 *Anc*, 1690 *Terrier*, 1729 *BT*
Hauburc 1197 P
Hauburg(') 1255 Cl, 1268 Pat, *-burgh* 1298 ib, 1316 FA, 1399 Cl
Alta Bargta (sic) 1303 FA
Haltbaroc 1338 Pat
Heyburgh 1409 Pat, 1409 Fine, 1429 Cl, 1507 Pat, 1536 *AOMB*
   209, 1539 LP xiv, 1539 *AOMB 212*, 1639 *Foster*, *-brughe* 1551
   Pat, 1599 *Yarb*, 1634 *Foster*, *Hayburgh* 1535 VE iv, 1536-7
   Dugd vi, *-burghe* 1539 LP xiv, Hy8 *Rental*, 1552 Pat, *-bur*
   1539 LP xiv, 1569 Pat, (*alias Haybrugh*) 1570 ib,
   Haeboroughe 1596-7 *MinAcct*
Harburgh 1548 Pat, *-brough* 1587 *Yarb*
Habrough 1569 Pat, 1602 *Terrier*, 1610 Speed, 1697, 1703, 1706
   Terrier et passim, *-broughe* 1586 *Yarb*, *-browgh* 1573 *Anc*
Aborough 1554 Pat

This name is discussed by Kristensson (SMETT 30), who ad-
duces an ON *hár in some such sense as 'a slope, a slight elevation'
as first el. This is, however, based on a misinterpretation of the
form *del Ha* (p) in the Subsidy Rolls of 1327 and 1332 for
Somercotes. The actual source of *Ha* here is ON á 'a river, a
stream', as numerous forms in the Lincolnshire collection clearly
show. He is right, however, in considering Ekwall's suggestion
(DEPN) that the name is derived from **hēah** 'high' in the sense
'chief' and **burh** 'a fortification, a fortified place' "not un-
objectionable". OE **hēah** would normally give ME spellings in *He-*
and none is found for Habrough. Kristensson also finds Lindkvist's
suggestion (Lindkvist 180) that the first el. is ON **há(r)** 'high'
similarly open to question, since he claims that this word is Old
West Scandinavian in origin, whereas Scandinavian borrowings in
Lincolnshire are generally OEScand in character. It may be pointed
out that Gillian Fellows-Jensen notes the occurrence of ON **ærgi** 'a
lower lying shieling here JEPN x, 20), while examples of Old West
Scandinavian **slakki** 'a small shallow valley' and **skáli** 'a temporary
hut or shed' are also found in north Lincolnshire, as in e.g.
Elbrough Slack in Goxhill f.ns. (b) and *Walgerscales* in Immingham
f.ns. (b) and *Aldescales* in Brocklesby f.ns. (b). Mr Stanley Ellis
draws my attention to the fact that a local pronunciation [ɛ əbrə]
or [heibrə] presupposes a ME *a* or *ai* in this area, and he believes

we should look to ON **há(r)** as the source of the vast majority of the ME spellings for Harbrough in *Ha-*, as does also Professor Raymond Page. It is at least possible that the original name was **Hēahburh* 'the high fortified place', as suggested by Ekwall, and that the first el. **hēah** has been replaced by its cognate ON **há(r)**, a possibility already noted by Smith (EPNE i, 234). The spellings in *Alta-* and *Halt-* suggest that twice the first el. was in fact interpreted as meaning 'high'. The DB form in *-burne*, though supported by the 1196 and 1218 spellings, is presumably an error or just possibly a weakened form.

So far as the topography of Habrough is concerned, through the good offices of Dr Rod Ambler, Mrs Bettie Watkinson has prepared a map of the immediate environs of the village from which it is clear that Habrough stands on an island of relatively high ground marked by the 15 metre contour, rising to greater heights within it, with the church lying on a northern spur. A meaning 'the high fortified place' would, therefore, seem topographically appropriate.

GLEBE FM. HARBROUGH GRANGE, *Haber grawnge* 1554 *Anc*, *Harbrough graunge* 1569 *Yarb*, *haburgh graunge* 1571 *ib*, *graunge* 1587 *ib*, *Grang' de Hayburgh* 1609 *Foster*, *Grange F.^{m}* 1828 Bry; according to 1609 *Foster* it was a grange of Newsham Abbey, *v.* **grange**. HABROUGH MARSH, *in marisco de haburch* c.1150 (e13) *NCot*, *in marascalo de haburg* c.1160 (e13) *ib*, *in marescis de Haburch* 1160-66 Dane, *in marasco de haburg* eHy2, a1180 (e13) *NCot*, *in marisco de Habur'* 1159-81 (e13) *ib*, *in marisco salso de haburc* eHy2, l12 (e13) *ib*, *in marisco de Haburg* l12 (Ed1) *Newh*, *marescum de haburc* e13 *HarlCh et freq* in Dane, *Newh* and *NCot*, *in salso marisco* m14 *HarlCh*, *Hayburm'she* Hy8 *Rental*, *Heyburgh' Mershe* 1536 *AOMB* 209, *Hayburmershe* 1539 LP xiv, *the marshe* 1577-80 *Terrier*, *Harbrowgh marsh* 1587 *Yarb*, *the marshe of habrough* 1602 *Terrier*, *Hayburmarsh* 1609 *Foster*, *Haborow Marsh* 1670 *Inv*, *Habor Marsh* 1690 *Terrier*, *ye Marsh* 1697 *ib*, *Habrough Marsh* 1828 Bry, a detached part of Habrough parish, now in Immingham parish, *v.* **mersc**. MANOR FM (lost) 1828 Bry. NEW FM. NEWSHAM BOOTH (lost), 1824 O, *White or Newsham Booth* 1828 Bry, cf. *Newsam Coate garth* 1613 *MinAcct*, no doubt commemorating the holdings of Newsham Abbey; it was in

Habrough Marsh, now in Immingham parish, *v.* **bōth** 'a booth, a temporary shelter'; cf. *neusom dale* in f.ns. (b) *infra.* NUN'S CREEK (lost), 1824 O, *Nun Creek* 1828 Bry, *portum qui vocatur le Nunnecryke 1250-60 HarlCh,* the *Nune cryke* 1500 *ib,* *Nuneryk* (sic) 1536 LP xi, *none Creke* 1587 *Yarb, v.* **nunne, crike**; the nuns were those of Coatham Nunnery. It was in Habrough Marsh and its outfall was at TA 208158.

Field-Names

Undated forms in (a) are 1817 *Yarb.* Spellings dated 1545 are LP xxi; 1576-77, 1596-97, 1612-14 and 1613 are *MinAcct,* 1577-80, 1602, 1690, 1697, 1700, 1703, 1706, 1709 and 1822 are *Terrier,* 1587, 1718, 1772 and 1787 are *Yarb,* 1654 are WillsPCC, and 1732 *Foster.*

(a) Cherry Garth (*v.* **garðr**); Church Cl (cf. *semita que tendit versus oriente ad ecclesiam de Haburg* eEd1 *HarlCh, ad Ecclesiam de Haburg'* m13 *HarlCh* (p), *ad ecc'am* Ed2 *ib* (p), *ad ecclesiam* 1327 *SR* (p), *atte Kirke* 1332 *ib* (p), *Atte Kirk* 1343 NI (p), *Atthekirk' de Haburgh* m14 *HarlCh* (p), *Attekirk de Haburgh'* 1379 *ib* (p), *attekirk' de Haburgh* 1381-2 *AddR* (p), *ye Churche* 1587, the frequent forms from ON **kirkja** are noteworthy); Cottagers Pasture; dove-cote pce; Fitties ('outer marshes', *v.* further Fitties in East Halton f.ns. (a)); Furze Cl (*v.* **fyrs**); Green Cl; Hill Cl; Home Cl; Long Cl; Low Btm; Low Cl; Meadow Marsh (cf. Haborough Marsh *supra*); Middle Garths (*v.* **garðr**); Ming Lane (dial. *ming* denotes land of different owners lying mixed, *v.* EDD s.v. 4); Mount Cl; North Field (Plat) (*in aquilon' campo de Haburg* l12 (Ed1) *Newh,* 1244 (Ed1) *ib, in campo aquilonali, In aquilonali campo de Haburg'* Hy3 *HarlCh, - Campo de Haburc* Hy3 *ib, - campo de Haburk* Hy3 *ib, in campo boriali de Haburg', in camp' borial'* Ed2 *HarlCh, in boriali campo de Haburgh'* 1325 *ib,* one of the two great fields of Habrough, cf. *the north and South feilde* 1587); Nuns Cl (*Nuneclosses* 1545, *Nunclose* (...*in Haeboroughe*) 1576-77, 1596-97, 1612-14, named from the nuns of Nun Coatham Priory cf. *Nun's Creek supra*); Pingle (*v.* **pingel**); Portes Cl (probably named from the family of William *Portas* (sic) 1666 *BT*); Seed Cl; South Carr (cf. *ad Ker* l12 (Ed1) *Newh, Ker* Hy3 *HarlCh, v.* **kjarr**; South Fd (*in australi campo* l12 (Ed1) *Newh,* e13 (Ed1) *ib,* 1244 (Ed1) *ib,* m13 *HarlCh,* Hy3 *ib, in campo austral'* Hy3 *ib, the south feild* 1577-80, *the north and South feilde* 1587, *the South Feild* 1690, *ye South field* 1697, *Southfield* 1700, *the south feild* 1709, *the southsyde feild* 1706, one of the great fields of Habrough); Summer-eaten Marsh, (*ye Summer eaten Marsh* 1697, 'marsh used as summer pasture', *v.* **summer-eat**, EDD s.v. 'to use land as summer pasture', cf. Kirk Summereater Carr in Bonby f.ns. (a)); Haborough Summergate Marsh 1772 (*Habrough* - 1718, - *Somergate Marsh* 1732, alluding to a road used only in summer, *v.* **sumor, gata**); Swine Garth (*v.* **swīn, garðr**, cf. *Swinstig'* e13 (Ed1) *Newh*, *v.* **stīg, stigr**); Thorn Cl (*Thorn Cloase* 1587, cf. *ad Spinam* c.1190 Dane, *þornecroft* 112 (e13) *NCot, thorncroft* e13 *ib, v.* **þorn**); Wells Cl.

(b) *Abbemare* p1186, c.1190 Dane (the first el. seems to be the OE pers.n. *Abba*, the second being **(ge)mǣre** 'a boundary, land on a boundary' as elsewhere in this parish); *the vii ac', the ix ac', the vi acr'dalle, the viii acre dalle* 1587 (*v.* **æcer, deill**); *adhelmundcroft, Ahelmundcroft* (sic) eHy2 *NCot, Adelmundecroft* p1186 Dane, *Edmundecroft* c.1190 *ib* (Dr John Insley suggests that the first el. is a Continental pers.n. and compares it with OSaxon *Athalmund* which is uncommon, as he points out; the c.1190 form shows confusion with the common OE *Ēadmund*); *appleton medow* 1602 (in Habrough Marsh, cf. *appleton on the northe* in the description of bounds 1577-80, from a holding of Nun Appleton Priory YW, cf. PN YW 4 220); *ab aqu^e ductum de broclousby* 112 (Ed1) *Newh*, *Austen cryke* 1500 *HarlCh, Austene Creeke* 1587 (presumably from the pers.n. or surn. *Austen* and **crike** (ON **kriki**); it was in Habrough Marsh); *austcroftdic* 112 (Ed1) *Newh, Haustcroftdich'* Hy3 *HarlCh* ('eastern croft', *v.* **austr, croft**, with **dīc**); *Austerwelles* c.1190 Dane, *austerwelles* Hy3 *HarlCh, Ouster well* 1697, *ye Oyster Wells* 1700, *oyster wels* 1602, *the* - 1703, *the oyster weeles* (sic) 1706, - *weels* 1709 (apparently from ON **austarr** 'more easterly' and **wella** 'a spring'); *Austlang furlanges* c.1190 Dane, *Austlanghefurlanges* lHy2 *ib, haustlanges* e13 (Ed1) *Newh* ('(the eastern part of) the long furlongs', *v.* **austr, lang, furlang**, cf. *Croslangfurlanges infra*); *le Baddepypes* Ed2 *HarlCh* (the second el. is the pl. of OE *pīpe* 'a pipe, a conduit', the first may be the OE pers.n. *Badda* or the ME derived surn. *Badde*); *bec, Le Bec* 112 (Ed1) *Newh, ad uiam in Bec, extendentes del bec, (le) Bech* Hy3 *HarlCh, bekes* 1226-38 (Ed1) *Newh, del Bec* 1244 (Ed1) *ib, Haburgbeke* lHy3 *HarlCh, in Beckes in campo australi* Ed2 *ib* (*v.* **bekkr**); *ad belleswella* c.1150, a1180 (e13) *NCot, Bellewelle* Hy3 (Ed1) *Newh, belleswell* 1239 *NCot* (from **wella** and the surn. *Belle*, cf. *terra Thome belle* 1241 (Ed1) *Newh*); *benaker* 112 (Ed1) *Newh, benakers* e13 (Ed1) *ib, Benhaker* Hy3 *HarlCh, bouneaker* 112 (Ed1) *Newh*, ('strip(s) on which beans were grown', *v.* **bēan, æcer**, the last form being probably a Scand. compound, *v.* **baun, akr**, as is also *Bouneakergate* Hy3 *HarlCh*, with **gata** 'a road' added); *ab charia philippi de Kyma* eHy2 (e13) *NCot, super berc' p'dcorum canonic'* 112 (Ed1) *Newh, unam sedem bercharie* lHy2 (e13) *NCot, bercariam ... canonicorum* Hy3 *HarlCh, cum situ ... vnius Bercarie in marisco de Haburg* 1269 *ib, Parcarium meam* (i.e. *Hugo filius Symonis Berner de Haburc*) Hy3 *ib* ('the sheepfold'); *in Bodem, Bodhem* Hy3 *HarlCh, Boymare* Hy3

HarlCh, *boymar'* 1244 (Ed1) *Newh* (*v.* **(ge)mǣre**); *Boitoft* l12 Dane (*v.* **toft**); *Boiwelle* prob. e13 (e13) *NCot*, e13 (Ed1) *Newh*, Hy3 *HarlCh* (- *in marisco de Haburc*), *boiwelledaile* e13 *NCot*, *-daila* 1256 *ib*, *boywelle* l12 (Ed1) *Newh*, *Boywelle* e13 *ib*, Hy3 *HarlCh* (for Boi- *v. Boyouedlande* in Brocklesby f.ns. (b); *v.* also **wella**, and **deill**); *bramberg'* l12 (Ed1) *Newh*, *bramberg* e13 *ib*, *Bramberg* Hy3 *HarlCh* ('broom hill', *v.* **brōm, beorg**); *Brunebroc* 1229 Cl (Dr John Insley agrees that this is perhaps 'the dark-coloured brook', *v.* **brūn**[1], **brōc**, but it should be noted that there is no indication in the text of its location); *bulldalle* 1587 (*v.* **bula, deill**); *caldewelle* c.1160 (e13) *NCot*, *caldwelle* e13 (e13) *ib*, *iuxta caldewellam* lHy2 (e13) *ib*, *Caldwelle* l12 (Ed1) *Newh* ('cold spring', *v.* **cald, wella**); *Castergatemare* Hy3 *HarlCh* ('the road to Caistor', *v.* **gata**, with **(ge)mǣre**); *le Cotedule* (sic) l12 (Ed1) *Newh*, *-daile* Hy3 *HarlCh* (*v.* **cot** 'a cottage', **deill** 'a share, a portion of land'); *cotunedaile* eHy2, c.1180 (e13) *NCot* ('the share or portion of land belonging to Nun Coatham Priory (in Brocklesby parish *supra*)', *v.* **deill**; cf. *Nun's Creek* and Nuns Cl *supra*); *the Cowe pastures* 1709; *crakemare* eHy3 (e13) *NCot* (probably the same as *Crakemar'* in Immingham f.ns. (b)); *Crispinland* Ed2 *NCot* (from the ME surn. *Crispin* and **land**; note, Walter son of Roger *Crespin de Keleby* held land in Habrough John *HarlCh* 49A8); *Croslangfurlanges* c.1190 Dane, *Crosfurlanges* m13 *HarlCh* ('long furlongs (by or with a cross)', *v.* **cros, lang, furlang**, cf. *Austlangfurlanges supra*); *iuxta dunemarc* eHy3 (e13) *NCot*, *feryngdail* (with y for þ) e13 (Ed1) *Newh*, *Ferthingdaile* 1327 *HarlCh* ('portion of a fourth part or paying a farthing rent', *v.* **feorðung, deill**); *Fileker* 1155-60 (e13) *NCot*, l12 (e13) *ib* (probably, as suggested by Dr John Insley, from the OE byname *Fīla* and **kjarr** 'a marsh'); *la gaire* p1186 Dane, *la gair'* lHy2 (Ed1) *Newh*, *la Gaire* c.1190 Dane, (*ad*) *la Gele* l12 (Ed1) *Newh*, Hy3 *HarlCh* (possibly an error for *Gaire*), *super Gairam* l12 (Ed1) *Newh*, - *Gayram* Hy3 *HarlCh* (*v.* **geiri** 'a triangular plot of ground'); *Grimestoft* l12 *Newh*, c.1190 Dane (from the pers.n. *Grim* (ON *Grīmr*, ODan *Grīm*) and **toft** 'a curtilage'); *Grisewell* 1205 ChR (perhaps 'spring visited by pigs', *v.* **grīss, wella**); *Gunwathou* e13, *-hau* eHy3 both *HarlCh* ('Gunnhvat's mound, hill', from the AScand pers.n. *Gunnewate*, ON **Gunnhvati* (SPNLY 116, Insley 324 ff.) and **haugr**, and cf. *le toft Gun(n)ewate* in Kirmington f.ns. (b)); *Haburgh'nesse* (... *iuxta portam de Stalyngburgh*) 1347 *HarlCh*, *Haybrough Nesse(s)* 1613 (a 15th century endorsement on the 1347 charter reads *Southnesse de Hab*. This is *Sudnesse* 1150-60, eHy2 Dane, *Suhnesse* c.1160 (e13) *NCot*, *sudnesse* Hy2 (e13) *ib*, *Suthnesse* c.1190 Dane, *the South Nesses* 1613, and cf. *Northnesse* eHy2 (Ed1) *Newh*, c.1190 Dane, *Nordnesse* 1150-60 *ib*, *Norhnesse* c.1160 (e13) *NCot*, *Nortnesse* p1186 Dane, *the Northnesse* 1500 *HarlCh*, *the North Nesses* 1630. *Habrough Ness* (*v.* **nǣss, nes**[2] 'a headland') was situated in a detached portion of the parish, now included in Immingham, *v.* also Habrough Marsh. There were clearly two "headlands" here until at least the early 17th century, distinguished as *north* and *south*); *ad hofddail, ouetdaile, hofdland* eHy2 (e13) *NCot, heueddesdal* 1155-60 (e13) *ib*, John *HarlCh, in horved deila, ouedaile* c.1180 (e13) *NCot, Ouedlandes* 112 (Ed1) *Newh*, John *HarlCh, houedlandeile* e13 (e13) *NCot, the headland dalle* 1587 *Yarb* (*v.* **hēafod-land, dãl, deill**, many forms being influenced by ON **hofuð**); *Hokehendes* e13, eHy3 *HarlCh* (*v.* **ende**[1]), *le Hokes* Ed2 *ib* (*v.* **hōc**); *hordberg'* 112 (Ed1) *Newh, yorthbrighe* 112 (Ed1) *ib, portdbrighe* (sic) Hy3 *HarlCh, le yoryebrigge de haburg'* Hy3 (Ed1) *Newh, ad Hordbrighe* Hy3 *HarlCh* (the spellings, which all seem to refer to the same place, are too varied to suggest a plausible etymology); *horwelles* e13 (Ed1) *Newh* ('filthy wells or springs', *v.* **horu, wella**); *Humber bank* 1690, - *Banks* 1697 (presumably this was in the detached portion of the parish, cf. Habrough Marsh *supra*); *Hwaitacres* p1186 Dane, *Hwate-* c.1190 ib, *Hwaitakres* e13 (Ed1) *Newh* ('strips on which wheat was cultivated', *v.* **hveiti, æcer, akr**, the forms in *Hwait-* certainly reflecting Scand. **hveiti**); *innames* 1241 *NCot* ('land newly taken into cultivation', *v.* **innōm**); *ab orient' parte vie uersus Kelingholm'* lHy2 (Ed1) *Newh* (the road to Killingholme (the adjacent parish)); *Kylingdales, Kilingdale* 112 (Ed1) *ib, Kyluingdale* eHy3 (14) *HarlCh, Kylingdale* (sic) Hy3 *ib* (presumably these are shortened forms of *Kylingholmdale(s)* etc. 'the portions of land next to or belonging to Killingholme', *v.* **deill**); *langeberg'* lHy2 (Ed1) *Newh, Langeberghe* lHy2 Dane, *Langeberge* c.1190 ib, *Langberg'* Hy3 *HarlCh, langeberg'* 1244 (Ed1) *Newh, Langbergláche* eHy3 (14) *HarlCh* (*v.* **læc(c)** 'a stream') ('the long hill', *v.* **lang, beorg**); *Lang(e)mare* eHy2 (e13) *NCot, langemar'* 112 (Ed1) *Newh, Langemere* Hy3 *HarlCh, Langmar* Ed2 *ib* ('the long boundary', *v.* **lang, (ge)mǣre**); *Leptoft* lHy2 (e13) *NCot* (the etymology of the name is given in *toftum quod fuit Leppe* 112 (e13) *NCot, Leppe* perhaps from the rare OE pers.n. *Leppa*; the same pers.n. occurs in Saltfleetby LSR 112 Dane); *ye low gate* 1700; *maluetoft* c.1160, Hy2 (e13) *NCot* (probably 'the toft where mallow grows', from ME *malwe* and **toft**); *le meregate* Hy3 *HarlCh* ('the boundary road', *v.* **(ge)mǣre, gata**; probably identical with this is *del merygate* 112 (Ed1) *Newh*); *Micelgate* Hy3 *HarlCh, micelgate* 1244 (Ed1) *Newh* ('the high road', *v.* **mycel, mikill, gata**); *middefurlange* Hy3 *HarlCh* ('the middle furlong', *v.* **mid, furlang**); *midmerscdik* Hy3 (Ed1) *Newh, de medio fossato* Hy3 *HarlCh,* 1244 (Ed1) *Newh* (presumably 'the middle marsh (dyke)', *v.* **mid, mersc, dīc, dík**); *le Moldfanch(e)* e13 *HarlCh, le Moldefang* e13 (Ed1) *Newh* (this f.n. has apparently not been noted previously in the Survey and its etymology is uncertain. It is recorded in MED s.v. *mold(e)* 1c, where the compound appears under *-fong* and its meaning is ? 'a piece of land held in someone's keeping'. MED quotes an appellative use of the word from Skidbrook LSR -- *vnum toftum ... cum meo moldfang' quod est inter moldfang' Radulfi fratris meo & moldfang' predicti Willelmi* 1220-30 RA v, 188. A further appellative example is recorded from

Habrough itself in *Stayn Mour cum le Moldfang adiecente* 1250-60 *HarlCh* 50D41. It may be suggested that it is a compound of ME *mold(e)* (OE **molde**) 'earth, soil' and ME *fang* (OE *fang* 'what is taken, booty') 'that which is taken into (a person's) possession' (*v.* MED s.v.). It is tempting to connect this word with dial. *mudfang*, recorded in EDD only from north L and defined as "When two properties are divided from each other by a hedge only, without a ditch, the hedge has usually been planted at the extreme limit of one of the properties; and in that case the owner of the hedge has a right to a mudfang, if it be an old enclosure; that is, a certain portion of land, usually two feet wide, in which the roots of the hedge grow .... The earth in which a hedge grows, and about two feet on each side, ... is sometimes called a mud-fang". ME *molde* might well have developed to [moud], comparable to the dial. development of *moud(e)warp, mowdwarp* of mouldwarp 'a mole', *v.* EDD s.v. *mouldywarp.* The further development to *mud,* in *mudfang,* would then, presumably, be the result of popular etymology. So far, the only examples of the appellative *moldefang* and its occurrence as a f.n., are from L, just as is *mudfang,* too, recorded in EDD only from north L. Whether the word has the precise sense of *mudfang* in the 13th century is, of course, impossible to say. The place was in Habrough Marsh); *ad moram* l12 (Ed1) *Newh, in mora* lHy3 *HarlCh* (*v.* **mōr**[1]); *neudic* l12 (e13) *NCot,* e13 (e13) *ib* ('new ditch or dike', *v.* **nīwe, dīc,** cf. *inter vetus fossatum & nouum* eHy2 (e13) *NCot,* references to the corresponding 'old dike' being only in Latin forms, e.g. *inter vetus fossatum* l12 (e13) *NCot, de veteri fossato* e13 (e13) *NCot, inter vetus fossatum & nouum* m13 *HarlCh*); *neuelandes* c.1160 (e13) *NCot, nevelandes* Hy2 (e13) *ib, Newe-, newelandes* e13 (e13) *ib, neweland* 1587 *ib, Newelandes* 1602, *the newlands* 1703, 1709, *the new Lands* 1706 ib (newly drained land in Harbrough Marsh, *v.* **nīwe, land**); *neusom dale* 1602, *dale of meadow ground called Newsham Dale* 1728 *PT* (in Habrough Marsh, a portion of land belonging to Newsham Abbey, *v.* **deill**); *Newsham Sheep Walk* 1700; *stagni nort molendini* p1186 *Dane, stagni north molendini supra toft* (sic) c.1190 *Dane, Northmolendin'* lHy2 (Ed1) *Newh, stagnum North molendini* lHy2 (Ed1) *Newh,* l12 (Ed1) *ib,* John *HarlCh, super stagnum ... abbatis* (i.e. of Newsham Abbey) Hy3 *HarlCh* (*v.* **norð, myln**); *Northwra* Ed1 *HarlCh* (*v.* **norð, vrá** 'a nook, a corner'); *ouergank* 1256 *NCot* (probably 'the upper track, road', *v.* **uferra, gang**); *Parsonage* 1587; *iuxta pontem* 1155-60 (e13) *NCot, inter pontem de Haburc et pontem Haldani* John *HarlCh, pontem de Haburg'* e13 (Ed1) *Newh, pontis de Haburc* e13 *HarlCh, pontem ... vltra fossatum inter Mariscum de Stalingburg & mariscum de Haburg'* Ed1 *HarlCh* ('Habrough bridge'); *Redmarehil'* l12 (Ed1) *Newh, Redmarhil* e13 (Ed1) *ib, Redmarehyl* Hy3 *HarlCh* (probably 'the boundary, land on a boundary, where reeds grow', *v.* **hrēod, (ge)mǣre** with **hyll**); *risewella* 1155-60 (e13) *NCot* (*v.* **hrīs, wella**); *Riskemersc* l12, e13 (e13) *NCot* ('rushy marsh', the first el. showing Scand. influence, v. **risc, mersc**); *Rockestone way* 1709; *Rofhowcott* 1379 *HarlCh*, *Rudeflet* 112 (Ed1) *Newh*, *Ruddeflet, Rudefleth* 112 Dane, *ruddeflet* e13 *HarlCh* (perhaps 'the reedy stream', v. **hrēod, flēot**); *Saltheim* c.1160, Hy2 (e13) *NCot* (apparently a unique example of this compound, OE **salt**[1] 'salt' and ON **heimr** 'a home, homestead, estate', though the second el. may originally have been OE **hām**, replaced by the cognate ON form; it may perhaps denote a salt-pan, - *una salina* is recorded in the same *NCot* charter and several are mentioned in Dane 199, 207-9); *Samberlaghe* (sic), *sandberglache* m13 *HarlCh*, ('the sandy hill', v. **sand, beorg**, with **læc(c)** 'a stream'); *Sarnesse* lHy2 Dane, *Sarenesse* c.1190 *ib* (v. the same name in Killingholme f.ns. (b) *infra*); *Scopemere* lHy3 *HarlCh*, *Scothow* 112 (Ed1) *Newh* (v. **haugr** and for the first el. the discussion under *Scotgate* in Croxton f.ns. (b)); *sedich* e13 (e13) *NCot*, *the See dicke* 1587, *Sedickebincke* (sic) 1577-80 ('the sea-dyke (bank)', v. **sǣ, dīc, dīk**, with **banke**); *ad Seldes* m13 *HarlCh* (probably from ME *selde* 'a shop, a booth, etc.'); *the skrubb cloase* 1587; *Stableland* Ed2 *NCot* (self-explanatory); *Stayn Moure* 1250-60 *HarlCh* (perhaps 'stony marshland', from ON **steinn** 'a stone' and **mor**[1]; it was in Habrough Marsh); *ab australi fossato* e13 *HarlCh*, *Suddik* 1256 *NCot* (v. **sūð, dīc, dīk**); *Thigdaile, le tygydaile* Hy3 (Ed1) *Newh*, *Tygye dayle* Ed1 *HarlCh* (v. **deill**, the first el. being obscure, but all the forms are variants of the same name); *le Thigstac* (2x) Hy3 *HarlCh*, *le thigstac* 1244 (Ed1) *Newh* (no suggestion can be made for the first el., the second is ON **stakkr** 'a (hay)stack'); *Tigelpittes* 112 *Newh*, Hy3 *HarlCh*, *Tygelpitgate* lHy3 *ib* (v. **gata**) ('tile pit(s)', where clay was dug for their manufacture, v. **tigel, pytt**); *the tithe dalle* 1587 (v. **tēoða, deill**); (*in loco qui dicitur*) *Toftes* John *HarlCh*, (*locum qui uocatur*) *Toft* eHy3, m13, Ed2 *ib*, 1244 *Newh* (v. **toft** 'a messuage, a curtilage'); *tolletoft* eHy2, e13 (e13) *NCot*, (the first el. is probably, as suggested by Dr John Insley, a ME pers.n. *Tolle*, a hypocoristic form of ON *Þorleikr* of *Þorleifr*, the second is **toft**); *campum de Haburc* 1205 ChR, *Campum de Haburg* 13 *HarlCh*, *in campis de haburg'*, - *de haburc* 112 (e13) *NCot*, *in Campis de Haburc* eHy3, Hy3 *HarlCh*, *the Town Fields* 1654 Wills PCC (cf. North Field (Plat), South Fd in (a) *supra*); *ad vadum inter Neuh' & Haburg'* 112 (Ed1) *Newh*, *ad uadum inter nehus et haburc* Hy3 *HarlCh* ('the ford'); *les Hutlandes* 112 (Ed1) *Newh*, m13 *HarlCh*, *vthlanges* (sic) a1233 *NCot*, *vtlandes* 1237 *Newh*, *vtlangis* 1256 *NCot* ('lands on the outskirts of the parish', v. **ūt, land**, forms in *-langes* and *-langis* are presumably errors); *Walwrt* Hy2 (e13) *NCot*, eHy3 *HarlCh*, *Walewudthe* (sic) p1186 Dane, *Walewrt* 112 (Ed1) *Newh*, c.1190 Dane, Hy3 *HarlCh*, *Waluurt* 1226-38 (Ed1) *Newh* (this may well be 'the enclosure of the Welshmen', v. **walh** (gen.pl. **wala**), **worð**, and cf. *Walehagh* in Goxhill f.ns. (b)); *the waste medowe without the See dicke* 1587 (cf. *Sedich supra*); *le Wendinge* m13 *HarlCh*, *le Wending'* lHy3 *ib* ('(land in the) bend in a road or stream', *v.* **wending**); *le westdaile* 112 Dane, *le Westdaile* 112 (Ed1) *Newh,* e13 *HarlCh* (*v.* **west**, **deill**); *Westiby* m14 *HarlCh* (p) (*v.* **vestr, í, bý**); *Westlangtoft* eHy3 (14), m13 *HarlCh* (*v.* **west, lang, toft**); *ad Wilkeflet* eHy2 (e13) *NCot* (Dr John Insley suggests that this is derived from the ON pers.n. *Vígleikr* (also found in Wilksby L) and **flēot** 'an inlet, a stream'); *le Windemilnedayle* 112 (Ed1) *Newh, Le Wyndmilnedayle* Hy3 *HarlCh* (*v.* **wind-mylne, deill**); *yadrichheuedland'* 112 (Ed1) *Newh, yadericheudland* 1237 (Ed1) *ib, yedericstand* (sic) m13 *HarlCh* (*v.* **hēafod-land**, the first el. probably being the OE pers.n. *Ēadrīc*; note an *Edric* held land in Habrough Hy2 Dane).

East Halton

EAST HALTON

> *Haltune* 1086 DB, *-tun* c.1115 LS, 1143-47 Dane (p), c.1155 ib, eHy2 ib (p), 1178-81 PapDec, Hy2 Dane, R1 (1318) Ch (p), 1338 Pat, *-tuna* a1147, c.1155 Dane, *-tunia* 1150-60 ib , *-tona* 1143-47, a1150, 1155-60, 1177, lHy2, 1195-6, R1, 112, (*super Humbram*) 112 all Dane, *-ton*(') 1190 (1301) Dugd vi, 1202 Ass, c.1221 Welles, 1224 FF, c.1240 (Ed1) *Newh,* 1241 Cl *et freq* to 1576 LER, ("by" *Killingholm*) 1289 Pat, ("by" *Kilvingholm*) 1292 Ch, (*sur Humbre*) 1291 *DuLaCh,* (*super Humber*) 1334 Abbr, (*super Humbre*) 1401-2 FA, (*super Humbr'*) 1414 *AddCh,* (*super Humbre*) 1431 FA, (*super Humbre*) 1535 VE iv, ("by Humber") 1291 Ipm, ("on" Humbre) 1312 Cl, ("on Humber") 1314 Ipm, ("upon" *Humbre*) 1386 Cl, *-thon* 1286 Ipm, *-tonne* 1562-67 LNQ v
>
> *Altunia* 1155-60 Dane, *Alton* 1472 Pap
>
> *Hautona* 1177 Dane, *-tone* 1190-95 Dane, (*super le Hombre*) 1281-82 *AD,* *-ton*(') 1202 Ass, 1240 Cl, 1250 FF, ("near" *Grimesby*) 1331 Cl, ("by" *Grimesby*) 1331 Ipm, ("on the" Humbre) 1282 Cl, *Hawton* 1475-85 ECP xvi, ("upon" *Humbre*) 1532 LP i, *Haweton iuxta Humber* 1568-70 *MinAcct*
>
> *Houton'* 1242-43 Fees, *-ton* 1303 FA, *Howton* ("on Humber") 1487 Ipm
>
> *Haulton* 1325 Ipm, *Hawlton* 1572 Pat
>
> *Esthouton* 1331 Ch, *Est Houton* 1354 *Cor*
>
> *Esthalton* ("on Humber") 1415 WillsPCC, 1429 Pat, 1557 *Inv,* 1557 InstBen, 1601 *Terrier, Est Halton* 1535 VE iv
>
> *Easthalton* 1612, 1626, 1634 *Terrier,* 1671 *Inv,* 1693 PR

(Brocklesby), *East Halton* 1662 *Inv,* 1670 *Td'E,* 1671, 1703, 1707 *Terrier et passim, East Halton alias Haughton* 1727 *TLE East Hawton* 1667 FMB, *East Haughton* c.1740 *Yarb*

This is derived from **halh** 'a nook, a corner of land' and **tūn** 'a farmstead, a village'. OE **halh** has been studied in depth by Margaret Gelling (PNITL 100-11), where she suggests that in some areas it is used to denote land between rivers or in a river-bend, and "perhaps for slightly raised ground isolated by marsh". A sense of 'dry ground in marsh' is topographically appropriate for the site of East Halton, with Halton Marshes to the east and the lower lying ground sloping to East Halton Beck to the north and west. The spellings in *Hau-, Haw-* are due to AN influence with the vocalisation of *-l-*. It is *East* to distinguish it from *West* Halton LWR and it is described as "upon Humber", "near Killingholme" and "near Grimsby". DB lxi points out that the present boundaries between East Halton and Killingholme were not established before the latter part of the twelfth century. The editors go on to say "In the charters of the period, South Killinghome included both North and South Killingholme; and the church of St. Denis of South Killingholme was the church which is now known as the church of that dedication at North Killingholme; while North Killingholme then meant East Halton". Note the references *ecclesiam sancti Petri de Haltuna que uocatur Nordkiluingholm* c.1155 *Dane, ecclesia sancti Petri de Nortkiluingholm que alio nomine uocatur Haltuna* c.1155 ib. No similar later forms have been noted.

LOPINGHAM (lost), *Lobingeham* (5x) 1086 DB, *Lopingheham* c.1115 LS, probably 'the homestead of the *Loppingas*' *v.* **hām**, *Loppingas* denoting 'the people of *Loppa*', as suggested by Ekwall, PN -ing 145. Although the form in *Lob-* occurs five times in DB, it seems more likely that the LS spellings is to be preferred, for the OE pers.n. *Loppa* appears to be the first el. in Lopham Sf and is found in *Loppan cumb* 947 (14) BCS 828 (S 524) and *Loppandyne* 1000-02 (11) BCS 1289 (S 1486). The site is not known but was presumably in East Halton or Killingholme, *v.* further DB lx-lxi.

EAST HALTON SKITTER, *Skyter* lHy3 (l14) *Gox,* *Halton Skitter* 1824 O, 1842 White, cf. *Skytterferre* 1542 LP xvii, *skitterferrye* m16 *Cragg, Ferrey voc' Skytter Ferrey* 1568-70 *MinAcct, le Ferrey vocat'*

Skitterffery 1589-91 *ib, Skitterferrye* 1605-7 *ib, passag' aque de Humber vocat' Skitter Ferrie* 1618-20 *ib, the Skitter Ferry* 1804 *EnclA, the Skitter ferry house* 1817 *Map, the Ferry over the River Humber at Skitter in the Parish of East Halton* 1827 *Brad, Skitter Ferry House* 1828 Bry, *Ferry* 1833 *Yarb,* and cf. *molendini de Scitra* c.1155, - *Scihere* (sic), - *Schitere* 1155-60, - *Scithre* 1160-66 all Dane, *molendinum de Scittra super Humbram* 1190 (1301) Dugd vi, *molendino de Skiter* 1219 Ass, *del molin de Skyttre en Vlseby* e14 *HarlCh, Skitermilne* 1312 Cl, *Skytermylne* 1440 Visit, *molendi* (sic) *de Skytter* 1540 *Cragg,* "the hamlets of *Skittermilne* and *Skitterferye*" 1541-43 LDRH, *Skyttermylle* 1542 LP xvii, *skylter Mylnes* (sic) Hy8 ib xxi, *skytter mylne* 1557 *Inv, mol'i aquatici voc' Skittermille* 1568-70 *MinAcct, Skittermylne* 1589-91 *ib,* - *milne* 1605-7, 1618-20 *ib,* - *Milles* 1609 *Inv,* - *Mills* 1652 *ib,* - *milles* 1671 *ib* and *Skitter milne haven* 1613 *MinAcct,* named from Skitter Beck, under Ulceby parish *infra.* The lower reaches of Skitter Beck are called East Halton Beck and East Halton Skitter is the outfall into the R. Humber.

BAYSGARTH FM, BASS GARTH (2½"), *Bassegarth* 1587 *Yarb, Bays Garth* 1804 *EnclA,* the same name as Baysgarth in Barton upon Humber and a f.n. in Brocklesby f.ns. (a). BLACK BULL (PH), 1842 White. BRICK LANE, cf. *Brick Holes Yard* 1824 *Yarb,* presumably alluding to clay-digging for bricks. EAST HALTON BECK, *the Beck* 1804 *EnclA, v.* East Halton Skitter *supra.* EAST HALTON GRANGE, *terram Joh' de Grangia* 1260 (l14) *Gox, Grangia de Halton* 1533-37 LDRH, *Halton grange* 1543 LP xviii, *the Grange house of Halton* 1612 *Terrier, East Halton Grainge* 1679 *ib, Halton Grange* 1824 O, *Court Hills or Halton Grange* 1828 Bry; it was a **grange** of Newsham Abbey (in Brocklesby). For *Court Hills, v.* Cote Hill in f.ns. (a) *infra.* HALTON MARSHES, 1824 O, *iuxta mariscum* 1260 (Hy4) GCB, *in marisco de haltun* Hy3 *HarlCh,* - *de Halton'* lHy3 (l14) *Gox,* "the marsh of East Halton" 1538-44 ECP, *Halton Marshe* 1587 *Yarb, the mershes of Halton* 1612 *MinAcct, the Marshes of East Halton* 1641 *BRA 833, the marsh of Easthalton* 1670 *Cragg, the Marshes of East Halton* 1739 *Yarb, the Marshes* 1761, 1781, 1788 *ib, the Marsh* 1768, 1786, 1800 *ib,* 1804 *EnclA,* - *of East Halton* 1777, 1801 *Yarb,* self-explanatory, *v.* **mersc.** LANGMERE COVERT, *Lang more furze* 1819 *Yarb, Langmeer Furze* 1824 O, *Lang-mere Furze Cover & Plant.*[t]*, Langmore Furze Cover* 1833 *Yarb,* cf. *langmergat'* lHy3 (l14) *Gox, Long Meergate* 1693 *Foster* (both in

Goxhill, *v.* **gata** 'a road'), *Langmare* 1670 *Cragg, Langmeer* 1710 *Elm,* *Langmore* 1733 *Yarb,* -*moor* 1786 *ib, High* -, *low langmore* 1819 *ib,* *Langmere* 1781, 1801 *ib,* 1804 *EnclA,* c.1825 *Yarb, Longmere* 1800 *ib*; the forms are varied, but this may well be 'the long mere or pool', *v.* **lang, mere**[1], with the second el. influenced by **mor**[1]. In the Covert, today, there is a very narrow long strip of water, some 280 yards in length, which may well be the remains of the long pool suggested by the etymology. MANOR HO, *the Mannor house ... in East Halton* 1681 *Yarb, the Manner house of Ellerkers Manner* 1708 *ib, the Mannor house* 1720 *ib.* MEERGATE HEDGE (lost), 1824 O, cf. *maregathe* 1260 (Hy4) *GCB,* (*le*) *maregate* Hy3 (Ed1) *Newh, Mere Gate* 1786, 1800 *Yarb*; this must be 'the boundary road', *v.* **(ge)mære, gata**; on 1824 O it forms in part the boundary between East Halton and North Killingholme. SCRUB LANE, *Scrub Close Lane Road* 1804 *EnclA* and cf. *Scrub Close 1804 ib.* SKITTER RD, *the Skitter Road* 1804 *ib, v.* East Halton Skitter *supra.* VICARAGE FM is *Micklemeer Hill F.* 1824 O, -*moor Hill* 1828 *Bry,* -*mere hill* 1842 White, -*mare Hill* 1670 *Cragg,* -*more hill* 1781 *Yarb*; as with Langmere Covert *supra,* the original second el. has been confused with **mōr**[1]; the forms are also late and the earliest is in -*mare.* One possibility is that the name means 'the big pool', *v.* **micel, mikill, mere**[1] and though there is a pool near the farm it can hardly be described as 'big'. An alternative is that the second el. may be **(ge)mære** 'a boundary, land on a boundary, etc' in f.ns. 'the balk of a ploughland', dial. *meare* 'a strip of grassland forming a boundary', a word which seems to occur frequently in north L with ME and ModE spellings *mare.* The same development has been noted in C, *v.* PN C 338 s.v. The farm is situated on a hill about 40 ft. contour sloping sharply to the west, one of the highest points in the parish. WEST FIELD, 1824 *Yarb, the* - 1761, 1780, 1786, 1800 *ib,* 1804 *EnclA,* 1820 *Yarb, in occident'* -, *in occidentali campo de halton'* 1230-40 (Ed1) *Newh, in campo occident' de Halton'* 1260 (l14) *Gox, in campo occidental' de Halton'* lHy3 (l14) *ib, the west field* (sic) 1587 *Yarb, the West feild* 1670 *Cragg,* - *Feild* c.1740 *Yarb,* - *field* 1731 *ib, the west field* 1781 *ib,* - *Westfield* 1733 *ib, the East and West Fields of East Halton* 1751 *ib, the late West field* 1806 *ib,* - *Field* 1810 *ib,* self-explanatory, *v.* **west, feld**, one of the open fields of the village, cf. The East Field in f.ns. (a) *infra.*

Field-Names

Principal forms in (a) are 1804 *EnclA*; spellings dated 1260 are 1260 (Hy4) *GCB*; 1568-70, 1589-91, 1605-7, 1613, and 1618-20 are *MinAcct*; 1634, 1662, 1664, 1668, 1671, 1674, and 1822 are *Terrier*; the remainder are *Yarb*, unless otherwise noted.

(a) Four - (4x) 1833, Seven - (8x), Long Sixteen Acres 1833 (*v.* **æcer**); Ash Holt 1824, 1833 (*v.* **æsc, holt**); Barton Street Rd (leading to Barton upon Humber); Beck Bank 1833 (from East Halton Beck *supra* and **banke**); The Blacksmith's Shop 1763, 1780, 1788, 1791; Boggy Btm 1833; Bonny Carr Leys 1761 (*Boane carr Leays, Bonne carr Hill* c.1740); Brodmore Dale 1761, 1781, 1788, 1791, 1801 (*Bradmare* Hy3 (Ed1) *Newh*, *Bradmer* lHy3 (l14) *Gox*, *Broodmore Deall* c.1740, 'the broad boundary, land on a boundary', *v.* **brād, (ge)mǣre** (replaced by *moor*) with **deill**); Butcroft Dale (*v.* **butte, croft, deill**); Calf Close stile 1781 (*Calfe Close Nuke* c.1740, *v.* **nōk**); First -, Second -, Third -, Fourth Car 1833, Carr 1851, Car Drain 1804 (cf. *mikylkeres* lHy3 (l14) *Gox*, *v.* **mikill, kjarr**, *mikylkeres* is probably a Scand. compound); the Church Cl 1806, 1810, 1812, The - 1818, Church Leaze 1804 (*v.* **cirice, lǣs**, cf. *Kirchil, Kirkehil* Hy3 (Ed1) *Newh, kirkehil* 1260, *Kyrkehil'* lHy3 (l14) *Gox* (*v.* **kirkja, hyll**, perhaps the same as *Kirkehil* (s.n. Church Paddock) in Killingholme f.ns. (a) *infra*), *the Church Lane* 1731 BRA 333); the College Rd 1804, 1820 (the road to Thornton College, Thornton Curtis); the Cornfields 1781, the Corne fds 1801 (*the Corne-feilde* 1670 *Cragg*, - *Cornefield* 1731, - *Corn fields* 1733); Cote Hill 1833 (*Courte Hill* c.1740, *v.* **cot** and East Halton Grange *supra*); Cottage Cl 1833; Cover Cl 1833 (*v.* **cover(t)**); Far -, Nr Crook Mill Furz 1833, Crook Mill Lane 1804 (*super calcetam* (sic), for *calcetum* 'causeway') *de Crocmilne, crokyde milne* c.1230-40 (Ed1) *Newh, Crokemylne* 1387 Peace, *Crokemyllnepingle* 1589-91, (*the*) *Crooked Mills* 1681, 1708, 1720 (the two references in *Newh* are to the same mill and a similar variation between Crook and Crooked occurs in the 16th-19th centuries. Perhaps the original name meant 'the mill in the bend of a stream', *v.* **krókr, myln**, with the first el. interpreted as 'crooked'; cf. also *Crokepingle* 1568-70, 1589-91 (*v.* **pingel**), also in this parish. From references in *EnclA*, the Lane led from Barton Street Rd, *supra*, to a ford crossing East Halton Beck, TA 119193, apparently now the site of College Bridge in Thornton Curtis and presumably where the mill stood. It probably gave its name to Crook'd Mill Pingle in Thornton Curtis f.ns. (a)); the East Fd 1761, 1780, 1786, 1800, 1804, The - c.1825, the North or East Fd 1781, East Fd 1824 (*in orientali campo* Hy3 (Ed1) *Newh, in orient' campo* -, *in oriental' campo de Halton'* lHy3 (l14) *Gox*, *theast Feild* 1662 BRA 833, *the East feild* 1670 *Cragg*, *the Eastfields* 1731, *the East* *and Westfeilds of East Hatton, the Eastfield* 1733, *the East Feilde* c.1740, cf. West Field *supra*); Eastham 1781, Eastrom 1833 (cf. *Heastom Leays* c.1740); Ferry gate 1819, R^d to Ferry & haven 1824, the Ferry Rd 1863 *BM* (*le Ferigate* lHy3 (114) *Gox*, *v.* **ferja**, **gata** 'a road' and East Halton Skitter *supra*); Fisher Cl; Fitties adjoining the Humber 1824, Fitties c.1825, - next the Humber 1833, Fitty Paddock 1824, 1833 (a common name in north L coastal parishes meaning 'outer marsh', dial. *fitty*, *fitties* 'the outermarsh or land lying between the sea or Humber and the bank, generally intersected by numerous reticulating creeks', *v.* E, Peacock, *A glossary of words used in ... Manley and Corringham* (EDS) 1899, 206; this must be ultimately of Scand. origin, cf. **fit** 'meadowland on the bank of a river'); the ford over the Beck or River drain (towards Thornton); Garth 1824, 1833 (*v.* **garðr**); the Goat 1781, Gote drain 1804 (*v.* **gotu** 'drainage channel'); (the) Gravel Pit 1804, 1824, - Cl 1833, - Way 1804; Hacksted hill 1781 (*Hackstead* is not recorded in Sandred); the half hundred Stongs 1781 (*Halfhundred Stangs* c.1740, *v.* **stong** 'a rood'); Harbour Headland 1786, 1800 (*headland* here being a coastal feature, and not the head of a furlong); ye haws 1783 *LTR*, Lt Haw, the Hawes (perhaps to be identified with *usque ad paruum Howe* Hy3 (Ed1) *Newh*, *Littelhow*, *littilhou*, *lutilhou* lHy3 (114) *Gox*, *v.* **haugr** 'a mound, a hill'); Hob Lane (probably a lane haunted by a hobgoblin, *v.* **hob**); Hollam Lane (Road); Home Cl 1824, 1833; Ioffin Drain (*Jofen* lHy3 (114) *Gox*; the reading of the initial letter is uncertain but it is probably correct; the second el. is **fenn**); Kealbarr hill 1761, Keal barr Hill 1780 (*barr* here may be dial. *barr* (OE **beorg**) 'a hill'; *Keal* is probably a surn., cf. Thomas *Keal* (1833 *BT*) who died aged 83); Kettle Brigg -, Kettlebridge Lane (*Ketelbrige* c.1260 (114) *Gox*, from the Scand. pers.n. *Ketill* and **brycg**); Killingholme Mere Gate (probably '(the road to) the boundary with Killingholme (the adjacent parish)', *v.* **(ge)mære**, **gata**); Kilnhouse Gate 1786, 1800; King Street; Landmere Car 1804 (probably an error for Langmere, *v.* Langmere Covert *supra*); Lastham Hill 1819; Lawsons Pingle (named from the *Lawson* family, cf. Thomas *Lawson* 1682 *BT* and **pingel**); Little Cl 1751, 1777 (c.1740); Marris Cl 1780, 1788, 1791, 1801 (named from the *Marris* family, cf. Thomas *Marris* 1627 *BT*, and Thomas *Marris* of Barton upon Humber 1780, who held land here); Marsh Cote Hill 1819, Marsh drain, - Rd 1804, the Marsh Gate 1761, 1780, - Rd 1863 *BM* (all named from Halton Marshes *supra*); ye Mill 1790 *LTR*, The Mill, Mill Grd (cf. *milnehil* 1260, *milnhille* Hy3 *HarlCh*, *Milnehill'* Hy3 (Ed1) *Newh*, *milnehill* lHy3 (114) *Gox* and perhaps *Hylnehil* lHy3 (Ed1) *ib* (with *H-* for *M-*), and *milneclif* 1230-40 (Ed1) *Newh*, *v.* **myln**, **hyll**, **clif**); the New Outlet of the Haven; North Carr (*le Northkerre*, *Northker* lHy3 (114) *Gox*, North Carr Side c.1740, *v.* **norð**, **kjarr**, and cf. *le Westker* lHy3 (114) *Gox*); The North-Field 1822 (*in campo borial'* lHy3 (114) *Gox*, *the North Feild* 1662 *BRA 833*, one of the open fields of the village);

North Hill 1828 Bry; Obkirkforlong 1781 (*Noblurke* (probably for *Nobkirke*) lHy3
(114) *Gox, apud subkirke* (sic) lHy3 (114) *ib, Hobkirk* c.1740; the early forms are
inconsistent and some almost certainly corrupt); Paddock 1824, East -, West
Paddock, Paddocks 1833; Far -, Nr Palmer 1833 (named from the *Palmer* family,
cf. Francis *Palmer* named in the document); Pointers Lane (named from the
Pointer family, cf. Brian *Poynter* 1622 *BT*); Potters Lane; Queen's Cl 1830 *BRA
833* (cf. *the Queene's land* 1587, and note in the same document Edward *Quene*
1587); Rea furze 1781, that stong of Lea or furze Ground called Rear Furze
1801 (*Ray Furrs* c.1740, *v.* fyrs, *Rea(r)*, *Ray* possibly representing *atter ee* 'at the
stream'); Red Car (*v.* hrēod, kjarr, cf. *Redlaghe* (b) *infra*); Road Drain; Round
Carr (*v.* kjarr); Sandmoor, Sandmoor flg 1781 (*Sandmore, Sandmore furrs* c.1740,
v. sand, mōr[1], while *furrs* is probably the pl. of furh 'a furrow'); Sandpit Dale
1777, Sandpitdale 1781, sand pit dale 1801 (cf. *Sandputtes, sandpittes* 1260, Hy3
HarlCh, Hy3 (Ed1) *Newh, Sandpitt Nooke* 1731, *Sandpitt Deall, Sand pitt nuke*
c.1740, *v.* sand, pytt, with deill, nōk); Scott gate 1786, - Gate 1800 (the same
name occurs in Clixby f.ns. (b) and Croxton f.ns. (b), recorded in the latter
from the 13th century, and leading towards Wootton, where the name is in fact
discussed in some detail. At present it is impossible to say whether this is the
same road, but it should be noted, that the *Scott* family is found in East
Halton, cf. John *Scott* 1761, and this name may well be from that family); Seed
Cl 1833; Slack Steads (sic) 1833 (*Stack Steads* c.1740, 'site of a stack or rick', *v.*
the discussion under *Stakstede* in Nettletom f.ns. (b) *infra*); the Slaves 1781
(*slaues, slauegate* Hy3 (Ed1) *Newh, Slaues, Slauegat'* lHy3 (114) *Gox, Sleaves*
c.1740, *v.* slæf 'mud' and gata, no doubt the same as Slaves botm in
Killingholme f.ns. (a) *infra*); Sleightings btm 1819, Far -, Nr Sleightings 1833 (*v.*
slēttr 'smooth, level', eng, cf. *slectfen* 1230-40, Hy3 (Ed1) *Newh, slechfen, Slectfen,
slecthfen* 1230-40 (Ed1) *ib, sclegfen, Slectfen, Slehctefen* lHy3 (114) *Gox, v.* slēttr,
fenn); The South-Field 1822; Stack Yard Pce 1833 (cf. Slack Steads *supra*);
Stand Lands 1761, Standlands 1780, Standillons (sic) 1781 (*stainlandes* Hy3 (Ed1)
Newh, Steinlandes, stenlandes 1260, *Stainland Dale* 1260 (114) *Gox, staynland,
staynlandes, staynlandgate* lHy3 (114) *ib, v.* steinn, land, the 18th cent. forms
having intrusive -d-); Stone Carr (*v.* stān, kjarr); Suttoft Hill 1819 (*Stustoftes*
(sic) lHy3 (114) *Gox, Suthetoftes, Suthetoft* 1260, *v.* sūð, toft 'a building site, a
curtilage, a messuage', the first form in *Stus-* presumably being an error);
Swinster(s) Lane; Sykeheadlands 1781, the Sykes 1804 (*The Sike* 1731, *Sikemouth*
c.1740, *v.* sīc, sīk, hēafod-land); Tewitt Carr 1804, 1812, 1818, Tewitt Car 1806, -
Cl 1810 (presumably the first el. is a term for the common lapwing or pewit, *v.*
NED s.v. *thewit, tewit*; the second is kjarr); the west Three Stongs 1781 (*v.*
stong); Tom Bee Cl 1833; First -, Second -, Third Top 1833; the Town Street
or Lane 1804 (*The Town Lane* c.1740), the Townside Rd 1804, Townside - 1810,

1812, 1818; Traneham 1781 (for the same name *v.* Traynam in Cadney f.ns. (a) *supra* and **trani, holmr**); Tutty Lane (Road); Up Close End 1761; the Wet Carr 1804, Wet Car 1806, 1820, - Carr 1810, 1812, 1818, Wet Carr Land Drain (*v.* **kjarr**); Willow Tree Plot 1833.

(b) *Akerheuedes* lHy3 (114) *Gox* (*v.* **æcer, hēafod**); *Arneberg, Arnesberg'* 1260 (114) *Gox, Harnesberig'* lHy3 (114) *ib* ('Arni's mound', from the ON pers.n. *Arni* and **beorg, berg**); *Barne grave* c.1740; *Bartonehil* 1260 (it is unclear to what *Bartone* refers); *Blackmare* 1670 *Cragg* (*v.* **(ge)mǣre**); *Blindsykes, blindesikes* 1670 *Cragg* (*v.* **blind, sīc** probably a small stream or ditch partly hidden by the vegetation); *Boothes Lande* 1587 (from the surn. *Booth,* cf. William *Booth* named in the same document); *bounacres, Bounacr'* lHy3 (114) *Gox* (from ON **baun** 'bean' and **æcer, akr** 'a plot of land'); *Brigesti* 1260 ('the path to the bridge', *v.* **brycg, stīg, stigr**); *brodland, bradelandes, Brodelandes, brodlangat'* lHy3 (114) *Gox* (*v.* **brād, land**, with **gata**); *brotland* Hy3 (Ed1) *Newh, Brotelandes, Brotlantes* lHy3 (114) *Gox, Bratt lands* c.1740 (*v.* **brot** 'a small piece (of land)', **land**); *Caldewellehil* 1260 ('the hill by *Caldwell,* i.e. cold spring or well', *v.* **cald, wella** with **hyll**); *Caleberg* 1260, *Kalberig'* lHy3 (114) *Gox* (perhaps 'the hill where rape or cole grows', *v.* **cāl, beorg**); *caselacres, Caslalurs* (sic) lHy3 (114) *Gox* (*v.* **æcer,** the first el. perhaps being from the family name of Robert *de Casteill,* witness to charters lHy3 (114) *Gox*); *Codmore* c.1740; *Coleswell* 1260, *Colleswelles* Ed1 (Hy4) *GCB* (probably named from the family of Roger *Colle* lHy3 (114) *Gox* and **wella**); *le dale* Hy3 (Ed1) *Newh, le Dale, places q' vocat' le dale* lHy3 (114) *Gox* (cf. perhaps *de valle infra*); *Atte Dykende* 1327 *SR* (p) (*v.* **dīk, ende**[1], cf. *le Humbredik' infra*); *the East Closes* 1720; *The fallow feild* 1634; *Feldetoftes* 1260 (*v.* **toft** 'a curtilage, a messuage, and cf. foll.), *in campis de Haltona* l12 Dane, *in campo de Haltona* 1234 (Ed1) *Newh, - de Halton'* lHy3 (114) *Gox, in campis de Halton'* 1260 (114) *ib, in campis de Halton' super Humbr'* Ed1 (Hy4) *GCB, The Field* c.1740 (self-explanatory, *v.* **feld**); *Folcerhehy* (sic) Hy3 (Ed1) *Newh, Folkerikehil* (sic) lHy3 (114) *Gox, Folcrikehil* 1260 (*v.* **crike, (kriki)** with **hyll,** the first el. being doubtful); *le Ganges* lHy3 (114) *Gox, Houerganges, houergange* lHy3 (114) *ib* ('the paths, the tracks', 'the upper paths, tracks', *v.* **uferra, gang**); *Goat Trough* c.1740; *Godemare* 1260 (the first el. is probably to be compared with that of *godestig* in Keelby f.ns. (b) *infra, v.* also **(ge)mǣre**); *Gayre* 1260 (*v.* **geiri**); *Atter graues, Attergraue Carre* 1670 *Cragg, marsh called the Groves or Greaves* 1613 ('at the diggings (probably for turf)', cf. *Haldturfegraues* 1260, *v.* **ald, turf,** *grove* being the dial. term for such sites throughout the Fenland); *Gummesthripenes* 1260 ('Gumme's threepence', possibly alluding to a rent, *v.* **þrēo, peni**; Dr John Insley comments that the first el. is an unrecorded ME pers.n. **Gumme,* a hypocoristic form of ON *Guðmarr*); *halecotemar* Hy3 (Ed1)

Newh, Hallecotomar' (sic) lHy3 (l14) *Gox; hardelandes* 1260, *Hard Lands* c.1740 (*v.* **heard** probably in the sense 'hard to till', **land**); ... *called or knoown by the name of a Halfe penny common* 1731 *BRA 333* (referring to the rent paid by users of the common); *hareberc* Hy3 *HarlCh, harebergh* Hy3 (Ed1) *Newh, hareberga* 1260, *Hauerbergh, harberc, Harreberghe* lHy3 (l14) *Gox* (if the form *Hauerbergh* belongs here it is 'oat hill', *v.* **hafri, beorg**; if not the name probably means 'the hill abounding with hare', *v.* **hara, beorg** and would then be the same as *harberg* in Killingholme f.ns. (b) *infra*); *Healboare* c.1740; *Holm'* (2x) lHy3 (l14) *Gox* (*v.* **holmr**); *Hestholm, vna placea q̄ vocat Hestholm* lHy3 (l14) *Gox* (this is no doubt the same name as *Hestholm* in Killingholme f.ns. (b); since all the forms are in *Hest-*, this is 'the island of land, water-meadow, where horses or stallions are found', *v.* **hestr, holmr**, a Scand. compound and cf. *Hestholm* PN YE 325); *holmarehill* lHy3 (l14) *Gox; horsegate in the Corne-feild* 1670 *Cragg* (*v.* **hors-gate** 'right of pasturage for a horse, a horse pasture'); *super Humberg'* Hy3 (Ed1) *Newh,* lHy3 (l14) *Gox* (for the same name *v.* Lt Humber Flg in Killingholme f.ns. (a) *infra*); *Humberdik', le Humbredik'* lHy3 (l14) *Gox* (a ditch flowing into the R. Humber, *v.* **dīc, dīk**); *Jerry goe Nuke* c.1740 (prob. for *Jericho*, often used for land on which sick animals were isolated, *v.* **nōk**); *Ketelbernwarlotes* Hy3 (Ed1) *Newh, -berghwarlottes* (sic) lHy3 (l14) *Gox* (from the Scand. pers.n. *Ketilbjorn* and **warlot** discussed under Waterhill Wood in Brocklesby parish *supra*; the form *Ketelbergh* is no doubt an error; cf. *Warlotes infra); Kideshale* 1260 (perhaps *v.* **kide** 'a kid' or the derived surn. *Kidd and* **halh***); lachlandes, laghelandes* 1260, *lagland gate* Hy3 (Ed1) *Newh, laghelandheuedland, lagheuelandes* (sic) lHy3 (l14) *Gox* (possibly 'swampy or boggy land', from **læc(c)** 'a stream, a bog', dial. *lache* and **land, hēafod-land** and **gata**; spellings in *-ch-* and *-gh-* are found side by side particularly in *Gox,* cf. *Redlaghe infra); le Landesik'* lHy3 (l14) *Gox* (*v.* **land, sīc, sīk**); *langfurlanges* 1260, *langfurlang, langfurland* lHy3 (l14) *Gox* ('long furlong', *v.* **lang, furlang**; *furland* is found elsewhere in north L as a variant of *furlang); Langelandgate* lHy3 (l14) *Gox* (*v.* **lang, land** and **gata**); *Littelhow, littilhou, lutilhou* lHy3 (l14) *Gox* ('the little hill or mound', *v.* **lȳtel, haugr**); *longbergh* l13 (l14) *Gox* ('the long hill', *v.* **lang, beorg**); *the lordes House* 1589-91; *Manimares* Hy3 (Ed1) *Newh, manimaris, Hanimares* (sic) lHy3 (l14) *Gox, manimares* 1260 (apparently a compound of **manig** 'many' and the pl. of **(ge)mǣre** 'a boundary', presumably a multiple boundary, cf. *thremares infra); mikelberc* lHy3 (l14) *Gox* ('the great hill', *v.* **mycel, mikill, b(e)org***); mydell (soyll) marsh* 1587; *Nortbutes* lHy3 (l14) *Gox* (*v.* **norð, butte**); *northgate* c.1260 (l14) *Gox* (*v.* **norð, gata**); *pastura de Haltona* 1234 (Ed1) *Newh, picles, Pycelede* (*v.* **hēafod**) lHy3 (l14) *Gox, le Pyngle* 1587 (the reading of the lHy3 spellings are doubtful, but probably correct and they might well represent **pichtel** 'a small enclosure', replaced by **pingel**); *Poorfolk Stile* c.1740;

Redlaghe, Ridlaghe, Ridlache, Ryhelhagh (sic), *Redlaghoc, Ridlaghoc* lHy3 (114) *Gox* ('reedy boggy land', *v.* **hrēod** 'a reed, a rush', **læc(c)**, cf. *lachlands supra*); *Sandalurs* (probably for *-akurs*) lHy3 (114) *Gox, Sandacre gate* 1670 *Cragg* ('sandy strips, *v.* **sand, æcer** with **gata**); *Sandberg* 1260 ('sand-hill', *v.* **sand, b(e)org**); *Sande Carr gate* 1670 *Cragg* (*v.* **sand, kjarr** with **gata**); *Scalawe* lHy3 (114) *Gox* (probably identical with The Scallows Hall in Binbrook, Walshcroft Wapentake LNR, and comparable with Scallow PN Cu 407 'the bare hill' from ON **skalli** 'a bald head', used of 'a bare hill' and **haugr** 'a hill'); *Sclechfurlanges* 1260 (for the first el. cf. the comparative forms for Sleighting btm in (a) *supra*); *scortbuttes* Hy3 (Ed1) *Newh* (*v.* **sc(e)ort, butte**); *lez Sedyke* 1559 *Anc* ('the sea dike', *v.* **sǣ, dīc, dīk**); *le Shepcote* 1572 *Pat* ('sheep house'. *v.* **scep-cote**); *Shipton Closes* 1662, 1664, 1668, 1671, 1674 (probably from a surn. *Shipton*, though none has been noted in the parish in the material searched; it is no doubt the same as Shipton Acre, Shiptons cl in Killingholme f.ns. (a) *infra*); *Molend' in Halton voc' Skerne milne* 1618-20 (the form is late but the mill may take its name from the stream on which it presumably stood. *Skerne* is perhaps to be compared with Skerne Beck and the derived village-name Skern (PN YE 11 and 155), which Ekwall (RN 367-68) takes to be an OE name *Scīranēa* 'the bright, clear river, stream', *v.* **scīr**[2], **ēa**, with initial *sk-* due to Scand. influence. The 17th century form here is found in the 16th century spellings for Skerne. The situation of the mill is not known, so that no certainty is possible, but this explanation seems reasonable enough); *Skypedales, -dayles, Skipdayles* lHy3 (114) *Gox* (*v.* **scēap. deill**, the first el. in a Scandinavianised form); *the South -, the southe marshe* 1587 (*v.* Halton Marshes); *stagnum molendini dm Abbīs de Thornton'* 1260 (114) *Gox, streces* (sic) lHy3 (114) *Gox, strenges* 1260 (perhaps from the pl. of ON **strengr** 'a watercourse'); *Sronghwelle* (sic) lHy3 (114) *Gox* (probably 'the strongly-flowing spring', *v.* **strang, wella**); *Struxwelle* 1260 (114) *Gox, a Crike called Summeris ganges Crike* 1613, *sumergangs* 1634 ('paths usable in summer', *v.* **sumor, gang** with **crike (kriki)** and cf. the same name in Killingholme f.ns. (b)); *Sunday Crike* c.1740; *Sutton garth* 1641 *BRA 333, - Garth* 1731 (presumably from the surn. *Sutton* and **garðr**); *lez Swynstye* 1559 *Anc* ('the path for swine', *v.* **swīn**[1], **stīg, stīgr**); *Tanner Town end* c.1740 (the craft of the tanner was normally practised on the edge of the inhabited area); *Taveles* 1260; *Tewforth Carr* 1731; *Thiressenabbe* (sic) lHy3 (114) *Gox* (*v.* **nabbi**); *a sheep-pasture called Thorneton Course* 1552 *Pat* (the same name, referring to the same place, occurs in Thornton Curtis f.ns. (b)); *thremares* Hy3 *HarlCh, Thremares* 1260, *thurmares* (sic) Hy3 (Ed1) *Newh* ('the three boundaries', *v.* **þrēo, (ge)mǣre;** the same name occurs as *thremares* in Killingholme f.ns. (b), and cf. *Manimares supra*); *thuaynthorn'* Hy3 (Ed1) *Newh, Twaynthorn, thuaynthorn* lHy3 (114) *Gox, Waynthorn* (sic) 1260, *Thvaynthoren* Ed1 *HarlCh* ('twin or forked thorn-tree', initial *T*- evidently being mistaken for the definite article at some stage and so giving rise to the *th*- and *W*- forms, *v.* **twēgen, þorn**); *de valle* ('valley') *usque ad northgate* c.1260 (114) *Gox* (and cf. *le dale supra*); *pratum quod vocatur Warlotes* 1190 (1301) Dugd vi, *suth warlotis* Hy3 (Ed1) *Newh, Warletts* c.1740 (*v.* **warlot**, and *Ketelbernwarlotes supra*); *Waterdales* lHy3 (114) *Gox* (apparently 'the wet shares of land', *v.* **wæter, deill**); *Watrelandes* lHy3 (114) *Gox, Watlandes* (sic) 1260, *a certain place there called Waterlands* 1662 *BRA 833* (*v.* **wæter, land**); *Suth Wendes usque ad North Wending* c.1260 (114) *Gox, le Wendings* Hy3 (Ed1) *Newh, del Wendinges, Wendingges* lHy3 (114) *Gox* ('the bend(s), in a road or stream' probably develops in meaning to denote places where there is a bend or bends, *v.* **wende, wending**; for the same name, presumably referring to the same place, *v.* Killingholme f.ns. (b) *infra*); *Whittmore* 1662 *BRA 833, Willebycroft* Hy3 (Ed1) *Newh, Wilby Croft* lHy3 (114) *Gox, Willeby croft* 1260 (114) *ib*, 1260, *Wilbysike* lHy3 (114) *Gox, Willebysich* 1260 (*v.* **sīc, sik, croft**, the first el. being probably the family name of William *de Wilxby* lHy3 (114) *Gox*); *Wilg dayle* c.1260 (114) *Gox* (*v.* **wilig** 'a willow', **deill**); *Winnemare* 1260; *apud Wra* lHy3 (114) *Gox, Wra* 1260 (*v.* **vrá** 'a nook, a corner'); *wokmiln' clos, wokmiln' pingle* 1587 (*v.* **walke-milne** 'fulling mill'); *Wrandik'* (sic), *Wrangdik'* lHy3 (114) *Gox* (*v.* **vrangr** 'crooked', **dík**); *Wrangbonelandes* 1260 (perhaps '(crooked) bean strips', *v.* **vrangr, baun, land**); *Ygelmare* Hy3 (Ed1) *Newh, hihelmare* 1260 (apparently 'the boundary land where leeches are found', *v.* **igil, (ge)mære**).

Horkstow

HORKSTOW

> *Horchetou* (sic) 1086 DB
>
> *Horchestou* c.1115 LS
>
> *Horkestowe* 1115 (14) *Bard*, 1155-58 (p1240) YCh iii, 1175 (14) *ib* xi, Hy2 (1230) Ch, 1192-1218 (114) YCh xii, 1233 FF, 1242-43 Fees, 1254 ValNor, 1271 Ch *et freq* to 1570, 1595, 1614 *BT, -stow(')* 1202 Ass (p), *-stow* 1298 Ipm, 1535 VE iv *et passim* to 1640, 1661 *BT, -stou* 1125 (p1269) *Bard*, Hy2, l12 (l13) *Stix, -stoue* c.1140 Dane, 1147-67, c.1150 (m13) Pontefract, 1178 (p1269) *Bard, -stouwe* 1338 Hosp,
>
> *Horkkestowe* 1564 *Foster*
>
> *Horkeston'* (with *-n-* for *-u-*) 1188, 1190, 1191, 1193, 1194 all P (p)
>
> *Horkestau* l12 (l13) *Stix*, 1238-43 Fees
>
> *Orkestowe* 1248 Cl, 1278 RRGr

Horkstowe 1278 RRGr, 1293 RSu, 1380 Pat, 1383 Peace, 1464
    Pat, 1526 Sub *et passim* to 1644, 1663 *BT,* -*stow* 1566, 1593,
    1600 *BT et passim*
Hourcustowe 1351 *Cor*
Horestowe 1352 Pat, *Horstowe* 1392 Cl, 1401, 1414, 1415 Fine,
    1559 Pat, 1576 Saxton, 1685 *Yarb, - alias Horkstowe* 1566
    Pat, - *alias Horkesowe* (sic) 1572 ib, *Horstow* 1428 FA, 1577
    Harrison, 1610 Speed, - *al's Horkstow* 1618 *Yarb*
Horkystow 1395 Works
Horxstow 1539 LP xiv
Horckstoo (*alias Horkstowe*) 1565 Pat, -*stow* 1604, 1625 *BT*
Horkestowe alias Horstowe 1620, 1622, 1680 *Yarb,* -*stow al's*
    Horstow 1688 *ib, Horkstowe al's Horstowe* 1640, 1684, 1715
    ib, -*stow als Horstow* 1722 *ib*

Ekwall is probably correct (DEPN s.n. Horkesley) in suggesting
that the first el. of Horkstow is an unrecorded OE **horc**, a word
related to dial. *hurk* 'a temporary shelter for young lambs, made of
hurdles wattled with straw' and to *hurk* 'to crouch, to cower'. Smith
(EPNE s.v.) takes the meaning as "possibly 'a shelter'" and suggests
that Horkstow means "a place where people squatted together, a
shelter for the gathering of people". If the meaning is indeed 'a
shelter', then the sense might well be 'the place of shelter', *v.*
stōw.

CARR LANE, 1812 *BT, Carr-Lane-End* 1680, *Carr lane end* 1685, -
Lane End 1715, - *end* 1722 all *Yarb,* leading to Horkstow Carrs
infra. CLAY PIT, situated near "Brick Works". Clay Cl in f.ns. (a)
infra, is not associated with Clay Pit, being itself situated on the
boundary with Saxby All Saints, next to the road from Saxby to
Horkstow. HORKSTOW BRIDGE, 1824 O. HORKSTOW
CARRS, *the Carrs* 1762 *Yarb,* cf. *South Care dich* 1606 *Terrier, the*
South carre 1635 *Yarb,* - *Carr* 1680 *ib, South carre* 1685 *ib,* - *Carr*
1715, 1722 *ib, the common Carre* 1638 *Terrier, West Carre* 1635
(c.1900) *LindDep 78, Far Car* 1832 *Yarb,* - *Carr* 1840 *TA.* On both
sides of the R. Ancholme are a series of *Carrs* named from the
parish in which they are situated, as here. In the list of f.ns. *infra*
are a number of names in *Carr,* those of individual fields in
Horkstow Carrs. The meaning is 'the marshes', *v.* **kjarr.**
HORKSTOW GRANGE, 1824 O, 1830 Gre, *South Grange* 1828

Bry, cf. *Grange West Carr* 1715, 1722 *Yarb*, apparently a late occurrence of the term **grange**, for which cf. Croxton Grange in Croxton *supra*. HORKSTOW HALL, 1824 O, 1830 Gre, *North Grange* 1828 Bry. HORKSTOW WOLD, *Wold* 1832 *Yarb*, 1840 *TA*, *Horkstow Wold F*. 1824 O, cf. *Wold Lane* 1792 *Yarb* and f.ns. (a) *infra*. Most parishes, here, situated below the scarp slope have their *Wold(s)*, stretches of higher open land upon the scarp, *v.* **wald** (3) and (4). MIDDLEGATE LANE, *Middle Gate Road* 1840 *TA*; *v.* the same name in Bigby *supra*. OSTLER'S LANE 1822 *Terrier*, presumably from a family name. SWALLOWS LOW WOOD is *Thorn Close Plantation* 1824 O, 1830 Gre, cf. *Thorn Close* 1762 *Yarb*, earlier *Thorne tree Close* 1685, *Thorn tree Close* 1685, *Thorn tree close* 1715, *Thorntree Close* 1722, *Thorn Tree Close* 1832 all *ib*. The modern name is no doubt from the family of Joseph Bramley *Swallow* 1872 White. TURTON'S COVERT is *Plantation & Cover* 1840 *TA*, the modern name being from the family of Edward John *Turton* 1882 White. VICARAGE, *the viccaridge* 1601, - *Vicaridge* 1606, (*the*) *vicarage house* 1638, 1718, y^e *Vicarage House* 1715, *the Vicarage* 1664, 1668, 1679, 1706, 1724, y^e - 1690, *the vicarage* 1671, 1674, y^e - 1697, 1703, *the Vicarage* 1822 all *Terrier*. WEIR DIKE, *Wear Dike* 1768 (1791) *LindDep Plans*.

Field-Names

Principal forms in (a) are 1840 *TA* (ex Rex C. Russell); forms dated 1601, 1606, 1638, 1664, 1668, 1671, 1674, 1679, 1690, 1697, 1700, 1703, 1706, 1715, 1718, 1724, 1822, 1855 are *Terrier*; other dated forms are *Yarb*, unless otherwise noted.

(a) Ancholme Bank 1832, 1840, Ancholme Carr 1840 (*v.* **banke**, **kjarr**, cf. *the Inges lyeing between the old River of Ancolne and the new River of Ancolne* 1684); Bain Cl; Betsy Garden 1832, Betsey's - 1840; Bottoms, Far bottoms 1762 (*v.* **botm**); Brick Yard (unconnected with two foll. f.ns.); Brickyard Pce, Brick Yard Cl (cf. Clay Pit *supra* and *Bricklaith Close* (b) *infra*); Causey Carr 1762, 1840 (1715, 1722), - Car 1832 (- *Carre* 1685, *the Caucey Carr* 1680, *v.* **caucie** 'causeway', **kjarr**. Car(r) is *freq* in f.ns. here and each is part of Horkstow Carrs *supra*); the Church lane 1855; Clay Cl 1832, 1840 (cf. Clay Lane *supra*); Cottage Carr; Cottagers Car 1832, - Carr 1840, - Cl 1840, - Pce 1792, - Mdw 1792 (cf. *Cotchers Common* (*cotcher* is common in L for *cottager*), *the Cottagers Platt* 1635 (c.1900) *LindDep 78*, *v.* **plat**[2] 'a plot of ground', as elsewhere in the parish);

Cottager(s) Sheep Carr 1762 (*v.* Sheep carr Nooking *infra*); Cottager(s) wrays 1762 (- *South Wray* 1685, *v.* Low wrays *infra*); Far Cottom Intack 1762 (*v.* **inntak** 'a piece of land taken in', freq. in the parish); High -, Low Cow Cl 1762, Cow Cl 1832 (1722), (Btm -, Top) Cow Cl 1832, 1840 (*Cow close* 1685, 1715); Cow Gates 1792 (*v.* **cow-gate**); (Btm) Croft (*v.* **croft**); Crow Garth 1832, Btm -, Top - 1840 (*v.* **cräwe, garðr**); Crow Holt 1832, 1840 (*v.* **cräwe, holt**); Cryke Carr (*v.* **crike, (kriki), kjarr**); Dogkennell Cl 1762; Dove Coat Cl 1762, Dove Cote Lares 1832 (cf. Far -, South Lairs *infra*), Dovecote Cl 1840 (*v.* **douve-cote**); Drain Car 1832, - Carr 1840 (*Land-draine carre* 1685, *Land-drain Carr* 1715, *Land Drain* - 1722, self-explanatory and *v.* **kjarr**); Drinkings 1762 (*close called great Incrofts and drinkings* 1715, *Great Incrofts and Drinkings* 1722, *v.* **in, croft** and Incrofts *infra*, drinkings being perhaps 'drinking places for animals', but this explanation is unsupported by dictionaries); Eighteen Acres 1832, 1840 (2x); Eleven Acres 1832, 1840, 11 Acres 1840 (*sic*, 4x); Feeding Pasture 1762, - Cl 1832, 1840; Fifteen Acres 1832, 1840 (7x); Four Acres 1832, 1840; Fourteen Acres 1832, 1840 (2x), 14 Acres 1840 (*fourteene acres* 1685); Fox Cover 1832; Fur Trees and Stone Pit 1832 (cf. Stone Pit Cl *infra*); Garth (*v.* **garðr**); Gateland Cl 1762 (1722), Far gate Lands 1762 (*Gateland* 1685, 1715, *v.* **gata** 'a road', **land**); Green Cl (*v.* **grēne**[1]); Harbour Cl 1762 (*Arbor Close* 1680, *arbor Close* 1685, *Arbour* - 1715, 1722 perhaps from **erber** 'a grass-covered piece of ground, a garden, an orchard'); Heads, Little heads 1762 (*Heads* 1685, cf. *the low heads* 1606, *the Three Hades*, - *Heads* 1680, *Middle & north heads* 1685, *Middle Heades, North-heads, Southheads* 1715, *Middle heads, Northheads, South heads* 1722, *v.* **hēafod** in the pl.); Hill Cl 1762, 1840 (- *close* 1685, 1715, 1722); Hillside 1762, Hill Side Cl 1832, 1840; Home Cl; Far -, Nr home Lairs 1762 (*v.* Far -, South Lairs *infra*); Horse Cl 1762, 1832, 1840; Horse Intack 1762 (*v.* **inntak**); Horse Pasture; Incrofts 1762, Btm In -, Top In Croft 1832 (*the North Incrofts* 1680, (*little*) *Incrofts* 1685, *little Incrofts* 1715, *Little* - 1722, *v.* Drinkings *supra*); Kirk Flatt 1762, - Plat 1832, 1840 (- *plat* 1715, - *platt* 1685, 1722, - *Plott* 1680, (*a place called*) *the Church plate* 1601, 1606, *v.* **kirkja, plat**[2]); (Grass) Laces, The Laces (perhaps an error for The Lares *infra*); Far -, South Lairs 1762, New Lair Intake 1762, (The) Lares 1832 (*the great* -, *the little Layers* 1680, *Laires, North* -, *Middle* -, *South Lairs* 1685, *Middle* -, *South Laires* 1715, 1722, *Lairs and dovedales* 1715, *Close called Laires and Dovedales* 1722, probably from ON **leira** 'a clayey place' in the pl., cf. Clay Lane and Clay Cl *supra*); Lamb House Intack 1762 (*v.* **inntak**); The Lames (a field east of the lane around Horkstow Grange); Leys (cf. Low Leys *infra*); Little Cl 1832; Long Intack 1762 (*v.* **inntak**); Low (end) Carr 1762; Low Ings (*the Inges* 1622, 1684, - *ings* 1641, *y*[e] *Inges* 1640, *the West Ingge* 1635 (c.1900) *LindDep 78*, *v.* **eng**, cf. Ancholme Bank (a) *supra*); Low Leys 1830, 1840, - Leyes 1832 (probably from the pl. of **lēah** in the later sense 'the meadows'); Low wrays 1762 (cf. *Cowgates in the Wrays* 1685, probably from **vrá** 'a nook, a corner of land', in the pl. The form *wray* seems to have been a northern development, being found in Cu, La and Y. It appears likely that *Wray* is an old name in the parish, giving rise to a surn. frequently recorded early in *BTs*, from John *Wray* 1565. A *cowgate*, a common term in L, was the right of pasturage for a single animal, in p.ns. and f.ns. being usually found in the pl.); Markham Car 1762, 1832, Markhams Carr 1840 (named from the *Markham* family and **kjarr**, cf. John *Markham* 1685); Meadow Carr (*v.* **mǣd** (dat.sg. **mǣdwe**), **kjarr**); Bottom -, Top Mill Cl 1832, 1840 (named from Saxby Windmill *infra*); Moor Cl 1762, 1832, 1840 (1715, 1722, *Moore Close* 1685); Nineteen Acres 1832, 1840; Nooke 1762, Nook 1832, 1840 (*v.* **nōk**); Nursery 1762; Great Oat Carr (*v.* **āt**, **kjarr**); Paddock 1832, 1840; Pale Intack 1832, 1840 ('intake fenced with a paling', *v.* **pale, inntak**); Parson Cl 1762, Parsons Cl 1832, 1840, (*v.* **persone**); Pingle 1762 (*v.* **pingel**); Plantation Cl, - Fd; Old Plough Cl; High -, Low Powels 1762 (*Close of pasture Comonly Called or knowne by the name of Powells* 1685, *close called powels* 1715, *Close called Powells* 1722, presumably from the surn. *Powell*); Road bottoms 1762; Rush Ings (*v.* **risc, eng**, cf. Low Ings *supra*); Rye Grass Intake 1762 (v. **rye-grass, inntak**); Saint Foin Intack 1762 (*v.* **sainfoin, inntak**); Seed Cl; Seven Acres 1832, 1840 (2x); Seventeen Acres 1832, 1840 (3x); Sheep carr Nooking 1762 (cf. *Sheepe Carre* 1635 (c.1900) *LindDep 78, Sheep carre, the two sheep carres* 1685, *Sheep & west carre nook* 1685, *Sheep and West Carr Nooks* 1715, 1722, *v.* **scēap**, **kjarr, nōk**); Shirt Butts; Sixteen Acres 1832, 1840 (6x); Snab Cl (*v.* **snabbe** and for an earlier example under Chapel Cl in Goxhill f.ns. (a)); Stone Intack 1762; Stone Pit Cl 1832, 1840, - Plat 1840 (*v.* **plat²**); Summer Cl 1762 (*Summer-Close and Pingle* 1680, 1715, 1722, apparently unconnected with the foll. n., **sumor, clos(e), pingel**); Bt -, Lt summer Gums (sic) 1762, Summers Gums 1832, Summer Gams 1840 (*Close of pasture comonly called or knowne by the name of Summergames* 1685, 1715, - *Summer Games* 1722, 'field in which midsummer festivities were celebrated', alluding to the entertainments which took place on St John the Baptist's Day, Midsummer Day, 24th June); Therse Tree Cl (perhaps for *Fir Tree*, confused with *furze*, cf. Fur Trees *supra*); Thirteen Acres 1832; Thompson's Hills 1762, 1832, Thompsons Hill 1840 (*Tomson* - 1685, *Thompsons Hill* 1715, *Thompson* - 1722, named from the *Thompson* family, cf. Robert *Thompson* 1640); Thompsons Holt 1768 (1791) *LindDep Plans* (*v.* **holt** and prec.); Thorpe Cl including Fishpond 1762 (*Thorpe Close* 1680, 1685, 1715, *Thorp Close* 1722, from the *Thorpe* family, frequently found in *BT* from Robert *Thorpe* 1563); Tray foyn Intack 1762 (undoubtedly referring to the fodder crop, clover or trefoil (*Trifolium* spp.), the form here is the converse of the occasional *-foil* spellings of *Sainfoin* f.ns.); Twelve Acres 1832, 1840 (4x); Twenty Acres; Twentytwo Acres; New -, Old Warren Garth 1762; Wellhouse Intack 1762 (*v.* **wella**, cf. *Atte Well'* 1327 *SR, atte*

Welle 1332 *ib, Atte Well* 1343 NI all (p)); Willow Head 1832, - Heads 1840; Cottagers Wold Cl Winney, Nr -, Farr Wold Cl (whinney) (sic) 1762, Wo(u)ld Cl (for Wold, *v.* Horkstow Wold *supra; whinney* 'thicket of furze bushes', imitating the form of *spinney,* is noted as "rare" in NED, which cites an 1892 reference; note that *whinny* occurs in ME as an adj. and is found in *Whinnylandes,* PN Nt 287, and in We in such a name as Whinnyrigg, PN We 2 188, in the sense 'overgrown with whin or gorse', *v.* EPNE 1 270-71 s.v. **hvin**); Wood Cl.

(b) *atte Beek* (sic) 1327 *SR* (p), *atte Bek* 1332 *ib* (p) (*v.* **bekkr**); *in The Boure* 1327 *SR* (p), *de Camera* 1332 *ib* (p) (the reference is to the same lady in both, *v.* **būr**); *Brick-layth Close* 1680, *Bricklaith close* 1715, - *Close* 1722 (from an unrecorded ME **brike-lathe, v.* **hlaða** 'a barn, a store-house', and cf. Brickyard Pce (a) *supra*); *the Corne-Close* 1680, *Corne close* 1685, *Corn* - 1715, - *Close* 1722; *the Two Crow Closes* 1680, *lower Crowe close* 1685, *(little) Crow close* 1715, *(Little) Crow Close* 1722; *Crowther close Pingle* 1715, - *Close Pingle* 1722 (from the surn. *Crowther,* commonly found in the parish, cf. Hugh *Crowder* 1608 *BT,* and **pingel**); *Downes his Farme* 1680; *Judith Gautby's little close* 1715, - *Little Close* 1722 (*Judith Gautby* is named in the 1715 document); *close ... called ... Homestead* 1685, *close called the Homestead* 1715, 1722; *camp' de horkestau* Hy2 (l13) *Stix* ('Horkstow field'); *House Orchard* 1685 (a close); *the hye waye to Barton* 1606 (i.e. Barton upon Humber); *Ingdales* 1685 (*v.* **eng, deill,** cf. Low Ings in (a) *supra*); *The kinges streate* 1606; *Kirton Garth* 1680 (presumably named from an untraced family and **garðr**); *the Manor Garth Close* 1680; *molendinum in territorio de horkestou* Hy2 (l13) *Stix* (*v.* **myln**); *the North-feild* 1680; *Parsonage of Horkestowe* 1620, *Close ... called ... the Parsonage* 1685 (cf. Vicaridge *supra*); *the Rectory whereof was Impropriate to ye prior & his brethren of ye Hospitall of St John of Jerusalem* 1664; *Saxby Close and Pingle* 1685, 1715, 1722 (from Saxby All Saints, the neighbouring parish, and **pingel**); *the South feild* 1680 (cf. *the North-feild supra*); *Close of pasture Commonly Called or knowne by the name of three hemp yards* 1685 (an enclosure evidently consolidating three small patches; the terms *hempyard* or *hempland* were aplied to pieces of land held by small tenants, irrespective of the produce of the soil); *the vicaridge hempland* 1606 (*v.* prec. and cf. Vicarage *supra*).

Immingham

IMMINGHAM

Imungeham (sic) 1086 DB

In Mingeham (sic) 1086 DB

Immungheham c.1115 LS, *Immingeham* c.1115 ib, 1205 ChR,
   Ymmingeham 1205 ib
Imingeham 1220 FineR, *-yngeham* 1305 Ch, *Ymingeham* 1209-35
   LAHW, c.1221 Welles
Immingham Hy1, 1100-15 (c.1240) YCh ii, 1233 Welles, 1249
   Ch, 1276 Cl, 1281 QW, 1315 Ipm, 1610 Speed *et passim*,
   -yngham 1281 Tax, 1286, 1291, 1294 Ipm, 1316 *Yarb*, 1323
   Ipm, 1327 *SR et passim* to 1428 FA, 1576 Saxton,
   Ymmingham 1157-80 YCh iii, 1203 P, Hy3 (13-14) Selby,
   -yngham 1545 LP xx
Iminghaim c.1190 Dane (p), 1242-3 Fees, 1254 ValNor, 1290
   RSu, 1559 InstBen, 1576 LER, *-yngham* 1259 Cl, 1276 RH,
   1303 FA, 1308 Inqaqd, 1316 FA, 1332 *SR*, 1338 Cl *et passim*
   to 1565 Pat, *Ymingham* 1202 Ass (p), 1265 RRGr, *-yngham*
   1535 VE iv
Himmingehaim c.1163 *CottCh*
Himmingham 1163-70 YCh i, 1212 Fees
Himingham lHy2 (m13) *NCot*, 1212 Fees, 1237 Pap, *Hymingham*
   1238-43 Fees, 1539-40 Dugd iv, *-yngham* 1256 FF, 1543 LP
   xviii, 1545 ib xx
Emmingeham a1135 (c.1240) Whit, 1216 OblR
Emmingham c.1078 (c.1240) Whit, 1090-96 (c.1240), 1145-48
   (c.1240) YCh ii, *Emmigham* (sic) c.1148 YD vii, 1166-80
   YCh xi, *-yngham* 1136 (c.1240) ib ii, 1539 LP xiv
Emyngham 1389 Cl, 1424 *Yarb*
Iningham (sic) 1276 RH, 1351 Ipm, *-yngham* 1501 ib, 1566 Pat
Imingham alias Innyngham alias Iningham 1566 Pat

'The homestead of the Immingas', *v.* -**ingahām**, the first el.
being the gen.pl. *Imminga* of the group-name *Immingas* 'the
followers, the people of *Imma'*, as suggested by Ekwall (PN -ing
145). The DB spellings are clearly errors, while the c.1163 form in
-haim shows the influence of ON **heimr**, cognate with OE **hām**.
Immingham is one of four such group-names in north-east L, north
of Grimsby, the others being Healing in Bradley Wapentake, the
lost *Lopingham* in East Halton parish *supra*, Killingholme and
Stallingborough *infra*. These names are confidently believed to
belong to an early period of Anglo-Saxon settlement in the areas in
which they occur.

ROXTON FM

 Rocastun (sic) 1159-81 (e13) *NCot*

 Roxtun eHy2, a1170, 1170, Hy2 (e13), 1241 all *NCot*, 1238-43
  Fees, *-tuna* e13 *EgCh*, *-ton* 1212, 1242-43 Fees, 1258 Ch,
  1272 *Ass*, ("near" *Newus*) 1274 Ipm, 1276 RH, 1286 *Ass*,
  1298 Ass, 1303 FA *et freq*, *Roxton F.^{m}* 1828 Bry, - *Fm* 1830
  Gre

 Roxthon 1286 Ipm

 Rokeston 1291, 1294 Ipm

 Roxston 1415 Pat, 1428 FA, 1538-39 *AD*

'Hrōc's farmstead or village', *v.* **tūn**, the first el. being the OE
pers.n. *Hrōc*, found in Roxeth (PN Mx 53-54), (*et*) (sic) *Hroces
seaðum* 845 (m9) BCS 448 (S 1194), and adduced for several p.ns.
including Roxholm, earlier Roxham, L Kest. It is once described as
"near Newsham". Spellings in *-x-* represent *-ks-*.

BACK LANE (lost), 1828 Bry. BROAD PIECE (lost), 1828 ib.
CHURCH LANE, *the Church way* 1697, *ye church way* 1703, -
Church way 1708 all *Terrier*. THE CLOUGH (lost), 1828 Bry, *v.*
clōh; it formed part of the boundary with South Killingholme.
FOXHOLE WOOD, *Fox Hole Wood* 1841 *TA*, and is *Foxhole Close*
1824 O, 1828 Bry, 1830 Gre, *Foxhole Close Plantation* 1824 *Yarb*.
GATEHOUSE FM. IMMINGHAM DOCK is on the site of
Immingham Haven 1824 O, *the hauen* 1674, 1690, *the haven* 1697, *y^e
haven* 1703, *ye Haven* 1708, *the Haven* 1822 all *Terrier* and cf.
portum de Iningham (sic) 1276 RH. IMMINGHAM GRANGE,
"grange" 1545 LP xx, a grange of Nun Appleton. IMMINGHAM
LOUGH (lost), 1828 Bry, the name of the stream leading to
Immingham Haven. INGS LANE, cf. *the Ings* 1715, 1772, 1821 all
Yarb, *the Ings of Immingham* 1732 *Foster*, *The Ings* 1842 White, 1841
TA, *Ings* 1824 *Yarb*, *Immingham Ings* 1828 Bry, *the Common Ings*
1756 *Yarb*, *v.* **eng**. LONG STRIP. LUXMORE FM. MANBY
RD. MARSH COTTAGES, cf. *in Marisco de Imyngham* 1241
HarlCh, "the salt marsh of" *Immyngham* 1286 Ipm, *in marisco de
Ymyngham* c.1300 *Yarb*, "the marsh of" *Imyngeham* 1305 Ch, *in
marisco de ymyngham* c.1295 *Yarb*, *in maresco de Imyngham* 1317 *ib*,
in maresc' 1339 *ib*, *ye Marsh* 1708 *Terrier*, *the Marsh Lane* 1772
Yarb, *the Marsh Close* 1810 *ib*, *the Marsh* 1822 *Terrier*, *Marsh* 1841

TA, self-explanatory, *v.* **mersc.** MILL HILL HO (lost), 1828 Bry, cf. *Mill Hill* 1841 *TA, Imingham Milne* 1674 *Terrier, the Milne* 1690 *ib, ye windmill* 1708 *ib.* NORTH BECK DRAIN, part of the boundary with Stallingborough is *Stallingbrough beck* 1674 *Terrier, Stallingburgh beck* 1690, 1697 *ib,* - *Beck* 1702, 1708 *ib, Stallingborough Beck* 1822 *ib* (Immingham). PELHAM RD, named from the *Pelhams,* Earls of Yarborough, who held land here certainly from the 18th century. POPLAR HOLT (lost), 1828 Bry. REEDS MEER (lost), 1824 O, 1830 Gre, *Reed Meer Bank,* - *Carr,* - *Close,* - *Holt* 1824 *Yarb, Reed Mare Holt* 1828 Bry, *Reed Meer Close,* - *Holt* 1841 TA; there does not seem to have been a pool here. ROXTON WOOD, 1824 O, 1838 Bry, 1830 Gre. STALLINGBOROUGH RD, cf. *Stallingboro' Lane Close* 1824 *Yarb.* WASHDYKE LANE, *Wash Dyke Lane* 1828 Bry, self-explanatory.

Field-Names

Principal forms in (a) are 1841 *TA* (forms and map supplied by Mr Rex C. Russell); Spellings occurring in both *TA* and 1824 *Yarb* are marked with an asterisk; forms dated 1343 are ChancCert (checked from MS); those dated 1579, 1601, 1606, 1611, 1626, 1664, 1671, 1674, 1690, 1697, 1703, 1708, and 1822[2] are *Terrier,* those dated 1678, 1743, 1746, 1758, 1779, 1789, 1792, 1796, 1821, 1824 are *PT*; and those dated 1712 are *Inv.* Other dated forms without source references are *Yarb.*

(a) Alcock Cl (named from the family of John *Alcocke* 1709 *BT* and **clos(e)**); Appleby Cl (named from the family of George *Appleby* 1841 *TA* and **clos(e)**); Ashes 1819, The - 1824, Ashes West, Far Ashes East (*v.* **æsc**); Audland Fd 1796 (*aldlandes, holdelands* lHy3/Ed1 (114) *Gox, v.* **ald, land,** the two spellings are forms of the same f.n., cf. the same name in Stallingborough f.ns. (a)); Barbarah Garth (perhaps to be identified with *Baiberge* l12 *Yarb, Baiberg', Baibergmar'* c.1240 (Ed1) *Newh, baybersmare* lHy3 (114) *Gox, baibermar', baybremer'* (sic) lHy3/Ed1 (114) *ib, bayberg* c.1295, c.1330, *baiberg* c.1330, the first el. is doubtful. Dr John Insley suggests that it is AN *bai* (ME *bai(e)* MED s.n.) 'bay, laurel', but this would be recorded here two hundred years earlier than in MED; the second is **beorg, berg,** with **garðr** and **(ge)mære,** the modern form then being possibly a folk-etymological development, influenced by the Christian name *Barbara*); Beck Cl* (*v.* **bekkr,** cf. Immingham Beck Carr *infra*); (Low) Bottom Cl (SW of Immingham); Bromhead Cl 1810 ("some long time since in the Tenure of William Bromhead" 1810, v. the Shift Cls *infra*); Byron's Marsh (named from the family of Samuel *Byron* 1841 *TA* and **mersc**); Calf Cl* (2x); Carr (Cl), Far Carr 1841, Upr Carr 1824, Lt Carr Cl*, Btm -, Top Carr Cl 1824 (*le ker* 1256 FF, 1307 *NCot, kerfurlanges* a1170 (e13) *ib, kerfurlanges* l12 (e13), c.1240 *ib, Kerfurlandes* (sic) 1241 *ib, kerfurlanghes* e14, *le ker furlanges* c.1330, *Carr-close* 1664, *carr-close* 1671, v. **kjarr, furlang**); Clarke Plat (named from the family of Thomas *Clarke* 1562 *BT*, Anne *Clarke* 1661 *ib*, and **plat**^{2} 'a plot of ground', as elsewhere in the parish); (Lt) Coney Greens (*ye great* -, *ye little Cunny Greens* 1712, 'the rabbit warrens', v. **coninger**); Coomb Briggs; Cover Pce; Cow Cl* (2x, one being between roads in the village); great cornfield 1819, Crackhill 1772, Craikhill 1821, Crake Hill, Craken Hill (*Crackhill* 1715; the two fields so called in *TA* are next to each other; presumably this is 'crow, raven hill', v. **kráka, craca, hyll**); Croft Cl (*Croft* 1241 *HarlCh*, 1343, *Crofth* c.1295, *Croftes* 1339, v. **croft**); Day Cl (named from the family of Elizabeth and Robert *Day* 1761 *Inv* and **clos(e)**); Dove Cote Cl*; Draught Horse Cl*; Eight Acres* (2x); Eighteen Acres (2x); Far Cl; Faulding Plat ('a plot for folding animals', v. **falding, plat**^{2} and perhaps cf. *ad Faldam* 1332 *SR*, and *ad ouile* (sic) 1327 *ib* both (p)); Fitty Marsh* ('outer marsh', dial. *fitty, fitties*, on which v. Fitties in East Halton f.ns. (a) *supra*); Franky Cl; the Freeholds Carr 1822^2 (*ye freeholds Carr* 1708, *the South Carr* 1674, *the South Carr Commonly known by the Name of freeholders Carr* 1690, *the South Carre Commonly know* (sic) *by the Name of the freeholders Carr* 1697, *ye South Carr commonly known by ye name of free holds* (sic) *Carr* 1703, a marsh (v. **kjarr**) held by *freeholders*); Freers Marsh; Fresh North Cow Hills 1796; Furze Close Wd 1824, Furze Cl 1841; Garden Cl; Glebe Pce; Grantham Plat (- *Platts*, named from the family of Thomas *Grantam* 1595 *BT*, Brian *Grantham* 1598 and **plat**^{2}); Great Close Plantation 1824; Ground Hill (Btm); Habrough cl 1819, - Cl* (from the neighbouring parish of Habrough); Gt Hardy Plot 1819 (named from the family of Sarah *hardye* 1603 *BT* and **plot**); Hawks Moor 1819, Hawksmoor Btm 1824, - Cl 1841 (probably to be identified with *houkesmare* l13, perhaps to be derived from the ON pers.n. *Haukr* and **(ge)mǣre** 'a boundary, land on or forming a boundary', with a similar interchange of *mare* and *moor*, as occurs elsewhere in north L); Hepworths Marsh (presumably from the family name *Hepworth*); High fd 1819, - Fd* (of Roxton); Hill Cl; Hockett Wells (1712); Holt & Moat 1819, 1824, Moat & Island 1841 (this is north-west of Mauxhall in Stallingborough and is unconnected with the Moat next to Roxton Fm); Home Cl(s)* (8x); Home Cl (adjoins foll.); Homestead; Horse Cl 1819, 1824; Horwells (NW of Immingham, by Haborough and Soujth Killingholme bdy); House Cl 1824 (*y^e* - 1712); Humber Croft* (one field west of Fitty Marsh *supra*); Hundred Acres 1819, The Hundred Acres* (the naming is approximate, rather than ironic, as the area is just over 76 acres);

Immingham Beck Car, Immingham Carr both 1796 (*v.* **kjarr**); Immingham Fd
1796 (*in campis de Imyngham* 1499); Kersey Garths 1796, - Garth 1822[2] (1708, -
garths 1690, 1697, *Kersy Garths* 1703, *Cersey Garth* 1674, no doubt the same f.n.
as Kersey Garth in Stallingborough f.ns. (a) where the etymology is suggested);
Laming cl 1819, Lamming Cl* (no doubt named from the family of Richard
Laminge 1593 *BT* and **clos(e)**); Limehill (*sic*) 1772, 1821, Line Hills 1822[2], 1826
(- *Lane*), 1834, 1827, 1841 (*Linehill* 1715); Long Cl* (4x) (named from their
shape, some being of abnormal length); Long Cl West (at some distance from
Long Cl); the Long Meer 1758, the long Meer 1779, Long Meer 1792, the long
Meer Cl 1824, - Long Mere Cl 1821, High -, Low langmore 1819, - Longmear
1824, Far High Lang Mere, Low Lang Mere (*langemare* c.1240 (Ed1) *Newh,
Langmare* 1241 *NCot, langmare* 1Hy3 (l14) *Gox, southend hof lang mar, langemar*
c.1330, y[e] *Farr Lang Moor* 1712, *the Long Mere* 1743, - *Moore* 1746 *ib*, probably
'the long boundary', *v.* **lang, (ge)mære**, with the same interchange with *mere* and
moor as occurs in Hawks Moor *supra*. There are many springs in Immingham
parish, but no real pools as such. It is unlikely that the second el. is ODan
marr[1] 'fen, a marsh', though this is formally possible in f.ns. in *-mar-*); Long
Plott; Lords Marsh (cf. *the Lordes closses* 1601 (b) *infra*); Gt Low Fields 1824;
Low Bottom (*v.* **botm**); Little Low Fd (adjoins Gt Row Fd *infra*); (Far -, Fore
-, Gt* -, Lt -, Long* -, Low) Marsh, Marsh Cl, Marsh or Lt Middle Plat 1841
(y[e] *lowmarsh Closes* 1703, *the Low Marsh* 1715, *v.* Marsh Cottages *supra*);
Marshall Cl* (on the Habrough boundary; named from the family of Simon
Marshall 1623 *BT* and **clos(e)**); Mauvison Cl (prob. from a surn.); Meadow Cl;
Meer green 1819, Mear Green 1824, Meer - 1841 (y[e] *Mare Greens* 1712, the
field abuts the road from Immingham to Roxton Fm and there does not appear
to be a pool here, so perhaps it is from **(ge)mære** 'boundary', **grēne**[2] 'a green,
a grassy spot'); Mundy Cony Greens 1810, 1811, - Coney Green 1812, 1818,
Munday - 1826 (named from the family of William *Mundy* 1684 *BT* and
coninger, cf. Coney Greens *supra*); Near Cl; New Cl; Nine Acres; Oak Tree Plat;
Ogle Marsh (*Mr Ogles Marsh Close* 1674 and cf. John *Ogle* 1665 *BT*); Gt -, Lt
Old Nook Marsh 1824, - Cl 1841; Pan Moor (*pannemar* c.1295, *panmar, pane
mare* c.1330, perhaps a compound of **panne** 'a pan', used in a transferred
topographical sense, and **(ge)mære** 'a boundary'); parsons croft 1822[2] (*toftum
quod vocatur P'sonescroft* 1209-35 *LAHW, parsons crofte* 1606, *the parsons Croft*
1611, - *Crofte* 1626, self-explanatory, *v.* **persone, croft**); Pea Cl; Pear tree Cl
1819, 1841; Pim Cl (probably from the surn. *Pim(m)*); Pingle (*v.* **pingel** 'a small
field')' Priest Hill; Primrose Holt (*v.* **holt**); Pyes Marsh 1824, 1841 (probably
from the surn. *Pye*, which has been noted as early as John *Pye* 1332 *SR*);
Robinson Cl (named from the family of Thomas *Robinson* 1841 *TA* and **clos(e)**);
Rough Close Wd, - Pln 1824 (*v.* **rūh**); Gt Row Cl (cf. Lt Low Cl *supra*);

Roxton marsh 1819, - Marsh 1841 (presumably a piece of marsh belonging to Roxton; it is situated some distance from the farm); Ryegrass Cl 1819, Rye Grass Cl*; Seed Cl; Seven Acre(s); Sheep Cl (*y^e* *Sheep Closes* 1712); Shift closes formerly in one close and called Bromehead Cl 1810, the Shift Cls - 1811, - formerly one Close and then called Bromehead Cl 1818, - formerly in one Close and then called - 1826 (doubtless referring to *shifts* in crop rotation, *v.* Bromehead Cl *supra*); Six Acres; Slaves Btm, - Marsh, Far Slaves Cl (*Sclaues* 1256 FF, cf. *Shauedailes* (sic) 1305 Ch (*v.* **deill**; this is probably to be connected with **slæf** 'mud', perhaps in the sense of 'the muddy places' or the like, cf. the same name in East Halton f.ns. (a) *supra* and Killingholme f.ns. (a) *infra*); Smith's Marsh (named from the family of William *Smith* 1841 *TA*, William *Smith* 1597 *BT*, James *Smith* 1607 *Inv* and **mersc**, and cf. *tofte Walteri fabri in* f.ns. (b) *infra*); South end Cl, South-end Garths 1824, South End Garth (*v.* **garðr** 'an ecnlosure'; they are at the south end of the village); First & Second Stallinboro' Cl, Stallingboro' Cl* (3x, the first two being separated from the other three by Stallingborough Rd), Stalingboro' Plat* (*v.* **plat²**, all being named from the neighbouring parish of Stallingborough); Steads Plat 1824, Stead Plat 1841 (by a house, *v.* **stede, plat²**); Stone Gate Cl (adjoins the road to Habrough, which presumably was once called Stone Gate, *v.* **stān, gata**); Tackhill Cl 1824 (probably from a surn.); Tares Cl; Twelve Acres; Twenty Acres; Urhills 1824; Vicars Cl (cf. parsons croft *supra*); Washing Stools 1819, 1824, 1841; Wheat Cl (*v.* **hwǣte**).

(b) *aceragke* (sic) c.1330; *aldfeld, aldfeld heuedland* c.1330 (*v.* **hēafod-land**), *Auldfeld* 1339 (*v.* **ald, feld**); *le Berhes'* c.1295, *berg* c.1300, *le berg* c.1330 (*v.* **beorg, berg**); *bifurlanges* e13 ('(the place) by, beside the furlong', *v.* **bī, furlang**, cf. *Bicroft* in Keelby f.ns. (b)); *b^amehilhoueland* (sic) c.1240, *bramhilhouedland* 1241 *NCot, bramhilheuedland, forera q' vocat' bramhilheuedland'* lHy3 (l14) *Gox* ('the headland (*v.* **hēafod-land**) by *Bramhill*, i.e. broom hill', *v.* **brōm, hyll**; in the first two references, *-houed-* is a Scandinavianised form); *le braythebecke* c.1295 ('the broad stream', *v.* **breiðr, bekkr**, a Scand. compound); *buledaile* c.1240 (Ed1) *Newh* ('the bull plot', *v.* **bula, deill**); *burge heuedland, le burgeland, le burge dail* c.1330 (from the surn. of the Roxton family *de Burgh* cf. William *de Burge* lHy3 (l14) *Gox*, William *de burg'* c.1300, with **hēafod-land, land** and **deill**); *ye church way* 1664, *ye church-way* 1671, *the Church way* 1674, 1697, *ye Church way* 1708; *the commond feld* 1579 (i.e. 'common'); *coppe mare* c.1330 (*v.* **copp** 'summit, peak', **(ge)mǣre**); *Cotedayl* 1343 (*v.* **cot(e), deill**); *Cotescroft* 1256 FF (*v.* **cot, -es²**, **croft**, or from the surn. *Cote*); *Crakemar', -mare* lHy3/Ed1 (l14) *Gox* (no doubt the same place as *crakemare* in Habrough f.ns. (b); Dr John Insley suggests that this is 'the boundary marked by a pole', from ON **kraki** and **(ge)mǣre**, rather than 'the boundary where crows or ravens are found', from ON **kráka** and **(ge)mǣre**, though either interpretation is formally possible); *Crosdayl* 1343 (*v.* **cros, deill**); *Crosholm'* lHy3 (114) *Gox, crossholme* c.1330 (*v.* **cros, holmr,** identical with Crossholme in Bishop Norton parish LWR); *dallemare* 1241 *NCot, dalmar', -mare* lHy3/Ed1 (114) *Gox* (*v.* **(ge)mære**); *Darnellande* 1314, *darnel heuedlands* c.1330 (no doubt from the surn. *Darnel,* cf. *Galfrid Darnel* c.1295, with **land** and **hēafod-land**); *doucy dail(e)* c.1330 (*v.* **deill,** the first el. being the surn. derived from ME *douce* 'sweet, pleasant'); *ductum aque* c.1240 *NCot* ('a conduit'); *in orientali campo de Roxton'* 1299 *HarlCh, in campo orient' de Roxton* lHy3 (114) *Gox, in oriental' campo de Roxetun* c.1300, 1339, *in campo orientali de -* c.1300, *in campo orient' de Roxton* 1301, *in campo orientali de Roxton* 1314, 1343, *the East feilde* 1601, y^e *East fealde* 1606 (cf. *in campo de Roxtun* eHy2 (e13) *NCot, in campo de Roxtun* 1159-81 (e13) *ib, in campis de Roxtun* Hy2 *HarlCh, de campis de Roxton* 112 (e13) *ib, ad campum de Roxtun* Hy3 *HarlCh, in campo de - 1381, inter campum de Roxtu'* m13 *HarlCh* and cf. High field in (a) *supra*); *le Estdike* 1314 (*v.* **ēast, dīk,** cf. *ad fossum* (sic) *de Hymmigham, fossatum de Imingham* Hy3 *HarlCh*); y^e *Ewe Groves* 1712 (for *Groves, v.* the growes in South Ferriby f.ns. (b) *supra*); y^e *fiev and thirty acres* 1712; *foremare* 1241 *NCot* (*v.* **fore** 'in front', **(ge)mære**); *scorte fot aceres* c.1220 ('(short) strips at the foot (of a slope)', *v.* **sceort, fōt, æcer**); *John Foxes marsh-close* 1664, *John Foxs-marsh close* 1671 (later Ogle Marsh in (a) *supra*); *le gat land, le gat mar* c.1330, *Gattmarhyll* 1450 (*v.* **land, (ge)mære,** with **hyll,** the first el. being uncertain); *butant sur gerarde lane* c.1330 (Fr document) (from the OGerm pers.n. *Gerard* or the derived surn.); *godefrai daile* c.1330 ('Godfrey's allotment' from the OFr pers.n. *Godefroi,* or its derived surn., and **deill**); *le Gothe* c.1295 (*v.* **gotu**), *gotwelle* c.1330 ('the spring giving rise to a water-channel', *v.* **gotu** (found elsewhere in the parish), **wella**); *a le gardin mils le grais* c.1330 (Fr document); *le grengat* c.1330 (plerhaps 'the road to the green', or 'the green, grassy road', *v.* **grēne**[1], **grēne**[2], **gata**); *Haburgate* 1327 *SR* (p), 1332 *ib* (p) ('the road to Habrough (an adjacent parish)', *v.* **gata,** as also in Killingholme f.ns. (a) *infra*); *hacmar', hakemere* lHy3 (114) *Gox* (the first el. is probably **haca** (ME *hake*) 'a hook', used in p.ns. of a topographical feature resembling a hook, the second is **(ge)mære** 'a boundary'); *Hakerhac(c)it* c.1300 (this name appears as *Hakeinyesike* 1314 in a charter containing the same names as those in that dated c.1300; it is impossible to suggest which is correct); *le Hald* 1256 FF (sheep to be numbered in) (probably **hald**[1] 'a refuge, a place of safety'); *Le Hall Place* 1565 Pat (*v.* **hall, place**); *iuxta paruum haustmare* eHy2 (e13) *NCot, - haustemare* Hy2 (e13) *ib* (probably 'the eastern boundary', *v.* **austr, (ge)mære**); *himinghamgate* c.1330 ('the road (from Roxton) to Immingham', *v.* **gata**); *le Hirne* 1332 *SR* (p) (*v.* **hyrne,** cf. *in Angulo* 1327 *SR* (p), the reference is to the same person); *Holm'* 1343 (*v.* **holmr**); *Holmar'* 1339 (perhaps 'the boundary in a hollow', *v.* **hol**[2], **(ge)mære**); *ungeril*

1159-81 (e13) *NCot, hungerhil* eHy2 (e13) *ib*, 1241 *ib, hungeril* Hy2 (e13) *ib, hungerhilhouedland* 112, e14, *hongerhil, hongerille* c.1330 ('the hungry, unproductive hill', a frequent name for an infertile slope, *v.* **hungor, hyll**, with **hēafod-land** in a Scandinavianised form); *houdaile* c.1240 *Newh* (perhaps 'the allotment by the mound', *v.* **haugr, deill**); *houesmar', housemar'* c.1240 (Ed1) *Newh* (perhaps *v.* **haugr, (ge)mǣre**; if so the name is in genitival composition); *hutlanges* lHy3 (114) *Gox* ('outer long strips', **ūt, lang**); "common called" *Comen Ingroose* 1545 LP xxi (possibly alluding to enclosure by *engrossing*); *Kelbi Warlotes* c.1330 (probably named from the family of Walter *de Keleby* e14 and **warlot**, for which *v.* Waterhill Wood in Brocklesby *supra*); y^e *Kings Street* 1606, - *street* 1671, *the* - 1674, 1690, 1697; *the high Laith Feild* 1671 (*v.* **hlaða** 'barn'); *langberg'* c.1240 (Ed1) *Newh* (*v.* **lang, beorg, berg**); *ledebetereberg* 1241 *HarlCh* ('leadbeater's hill', from the occupational name *Ledebeter*, or its derived surn. and **berg, beorg**); *vna placea que vocat' lolkes* 1343 (this is perhaps from a pers.n. or surn. *Lolke*, found in *pratum fuit lolke* p1170 (e13) *NCot*, in the adjacent parish of Stallingborough); *the lordes closses* 1601, - *ground* 1606, y^e *lordes* - 1664, y^e *Lords* - 1671, - *Ground* 1703, 1708, *the lords ground* 1674 (cf. Lords Marsh (a) *supra*); *Middelbeckes* 1343 (*v.* **middel, bekkr**); y^e *first Middle platt,* y^e *Sec^d Middle Platt* (*v.* **platt^2**); *Milneflat* 1305 Ch (*v.* **myln, flatt**, cf. *Milo molendinari de Roxtun* a1170 (e13) *NCot*); *mirhals* (sic) lHy3 (114) *Gox; mireswelle* lHy3 (114) *Gox, miresuuel* lHy3/Ed1 (114) *ib* (Dr John Insley agrees that this is probably 'the spring by a swamp', *v.* **mýrr, es^2, wella**, if so the name is a genitival composition); *Nahahefars* c.1295 (obscure); *le North furlanges* lHy3 (114) *Gox, Northfurlangs* c.1295, 1339, *le norde* -, *le north furlanges* c.1330, (*v.* **norð, furlang**); *northewelleberg'* c.1240 (Ed1) *Newh* (named from *Welberg infra* and cf. *suthwellebergh infra*); *Ogotwelle forlanges, ovgotWell hille* c.1330 (this is derived from the ON pers.n. *Asgautr*, anglicised to *Oȝgot, Ongot*, and **wella**, with **furlang** and **hyll**); *ad Pontem* 1327, 1332 *SR* both (p) (*v.* **brycg**); *ad pontem maresdaile* lHy3 (114) *Gox, punthoumarisdayl, ponthawemaresdayl* lHy3/Ed1 (114) *Gox, punhaumare* lHy3 (114) *ib* (*v.* **(ge)mǣre, -es^2, deill**, the etymology of *punthou-* etc. is obscure, but cf. *Punhage* 13 (Ed1) *Newh* in Ulceby f.ns. (b) which probably refers to the same feature); *potkin mar* lHy3 (114) *Gox, potkin mar', pottekin mar'* c.1330 (*v.* **(ge)mǣre**, the first el. being the pers.n. or surn. *Potkin, v.* Reaney s.n. but for an alternative etymology of *Potkin v.* Insley JEPN **10** 45); y^e *Queen Street* 1703, y^e *Queens hygh way* 1708 (the same as y^e *Kings Street supra*); *reske mar, riskemar* c.1330 ('rushy boundary' *v.* **risc, (ge)mǣre**, the first el. being Scandinavianised); *Rumar, rumarmarfur* lHy3 (114) *Gox* (*v.* **rūh** 'rough', **(ge)mǣre**, with **marfur**; *en rougemar* c.1330 (Fr document) is probably identical, the result of scribal unfamiliarity with *Rumar*, as Dr John Insley suggests); *roxsten Welle, le welle* c.1330, *apud fontem de Roxt'* lHy3 (114) *Gox, ex parte* *borial' fontis de Roxetvn* c.1300 (*v.* **wella**); *Sandeberec* e13 *EgCh*, e13 *HarlCh*, *Sandeberg* c.1241 (Ed1) *Newh*, *Sandberghevedeland* c.1300 (*v.* **hēafod-land**), *Sandberges* 1301, *sandberg(e)* c.1330 ('the sand hill', *v.* **sand, beorg, berg**); *Sandgote* lHy3 (l14) *Gox*, *le sand got(e)* c.1330 (*v.* **sand, gotu**); *Scandmar'* (sic) lHy3 (l14) *Gox* (*v.* **(ge)mǣre**); *scirmare* c.1330, *Scirmarhil* lHy3 (l14) *Gox*, c.1330, *Skyrmarhill'* 1339 (*v.* **scīr²** ' 'bright', in a Scandinavianised form **skirr**, **(ge)mǣre**, with **hyll**); *Scotel mar* c.1330 (the first el. may be the OE pers.n. *Scottel*, but no certainty is possible; the second is **(ge)mǣre** 'a boundary, boundary land'); *Shortfurlangs* 1339 (*v.* **sc(e)ort, furlang**); *le Sikedayl* lHy3 (l14) *Gox* (*v.* **sīk, deill**); *Sledefurlanges* 1241 *HarlCh* (perhaps 'the furlongs in a valley', *v.* **slæd, furlang**); *Soumsdayl* 1343 (if the reading is correct, and *-um-* is an interpretation of five minims, Dr John Insley suggests that the first el. is the ON byname *Saumr*, the second is **deill** 'a share, a portion of land', hence a Scand. compound); *South Carr* 1674 (*v.* the Freeholds Carr (a) *supra*); *South Farme* 1678; *Southyby* 1339 (p) (*v.* **sūð, ī, bý**); *Staynwellebekfurlanges* 1241 *HarlCh*, *Staynwelle* c.1300, *Stainwelle bek* c.1330 ('the stony spring', *v.* **steinn, wella**, with **bekkr, furlang**, the first el. being Scand. as well as **bekkr**); *en stonge daile* c.1330 (Fr document) (*v.* **stong, deill**); *Stuarcotested* 1339 (*v.* **cot-stede** 'the site of a cottage or shed'; the first el. is probably a pers.n. or surn.); *suthwellebergh* c.1300, 1314 (named from *Welberg infra* and cf. *northwelleberg supra*); *Suyerwelleberge* (sic) c.1330 (perhaps for *Sutherwelle-*, with *y = þ*, cf. *suthwellebergh supra*, but the document is badly stained and the reading is doubtful); *suty* (sic) *enges de Himingham* lHy3 (l14) *Gox*, *suhtenges de Immynghham* 1314 ('the south meadows of Immingham', *v.* **sūð, eng**; it is also *in suthe pratis* c.1295, *Suthepratis de Ymmyngham*, *in suthepratis de Imyngham* c.1300); *þeuelwadhe* 112, e14 ('the ford by a thorn-bush', *v.* **þefel, vað**); *Thornchort* a1170, Hy2 (e13) *NCot* (additional forms are needed to be certain of the origin of the second el.); *thorncroft* e13 (*v.* **þorn, croft**); *Thorndaill* 1381, *Thornsdall* 1450 (*v.* **þorn, deill**); *Thornholmdaile* 1170 (e13) *NCot* (*v.* **þorn, holmr** with **deill**); *þiornotehille, piornothil* c.1330 (obscure); *thurgmar', thurg' mar'* c.1240 (Ed1) *Newh* (Dr John Insley suggests that this is 'Þorgeirr's or Þorgrím's boundary, land on a boundary', *v.* **(ge)mǣre**, both pers.ns. being ON in origin); *tofte Walteri fabri* e13 *EgCh* ('Walter Smith's toft', *v.* **toft** and cf. *foreram fabri* 1241 *HarlCh* 'the headland of the smith, or of Smith'); *le tounefurlanges, le townefurlanges* c.1330, *Townforlong* 1450 (*v.* **tūn, furlang**); *tounges* 1339 (*v.* **tunga** 'a tongue of land'); *tunmanneswelle* c.1240 (Ed1) *Newh*, *le gote de tunmawell'* (sic) lHy3 (l14) *Gox*, *tunmanwele* c.1295, *iuxta fontem que vocatur tounmanwelle* c.1300, *Tonmanwelle* 1314 ('the villager's well or spring', *v.* **tūn-mann, wella**); *uiam de Rocastun* (sic) 1159-81 (e13) *NCot*, *viam de Roxtun* a1170 (e13), Hy2 (e13) *ib*, *uia de Roxton* e13 (cf. *himinghamgate supra*); *the Vicaridge of Immyngam* 1597, *the Viccaridge of Imingham* 1606, *the Vicarage house* 1611, 1690,

1697, y^e *viccaridge* 1664; *Wadacres* c.1240 (Ed1) *Newh, vadacres* c.1241 (Ed1) *ib,*
Wadeacres lHy3 (l14) *Gox,* c.1295, *Wadaccres* e13 *HarlCh, Wadaker(s), Wadlacras*
(sic) lHy3 l14) *Gox* (perhaps 'selion(s) on which woad was grown', *v.* **wǎd,**
æcer); *Walgerscales* c.1300 ('Walger's temporary hut or shed', *v.* **skáli,** the first el.
being the pers.n. or surn. derived from OGerm *Waldger, Walger* (Forssner 242).
The second is a distinctively OWScand. word found only rarely outside areas
settled by Norwegians. Ocasional examples have been noted in L (cf. *Aldescales*
in Brocklesby f.ns. (b) *supra*) as well as Nf and Nth); *Warlotes* 1256 FF (*v.*
warlot, for which *v.* Waterhill Wood in Brocklesby *supra*); y^e *Weather Groves*
1712 (cf. y^e *Ewe Groves supra,* and *v.* **weðer** 'a castrated ram'); *Welberglag* (sic)
c.1300 (*v.* **læc(c)**), *Welberge* c.1330 (this is presumably 'the hill with a spring', *v.*
wella, be(o)rg, and cf. *northewelleberg* and *suthwellebergh supra*); *le wellebeckesse*
(sic) 1334 (*v.* **wella, bekkr**); *le wellegrene* 1334 (*v.* **grēne^2**), *Wellesik* 1241 *HarlCh*
(*v.* **wella, sík**); *le Welmar'four'* 1339 (*v.* **wella, marfur**); *extendentem del Wend*
usque ad campum de haburg' l13 (*v.* **wend** 'a turning, a bend in a road'); *le*
Westdike 1314 (*v.* **west, dík,** cf. *le Estdike supra*); *in campo occidentali de*
ymyngham c.1295, *in campo occidental' de Imyngham* 1339, *in occidentali campo*
de Roxtun l12, *in occident' campo* c.1240 (Ed1) *Newh, in campo occident' de*
Roxton lHy3 (l14) *Gox, in campo occid'* 1301, *in campo occidentali (de Roxton)*
1328, 1343 ('the west field', of both Immingham and Roxton, cf. *the East Feilde*
supra); *Wiligholm'* lHy3 (l14) *Gox* ('the willow water-meadow', *v.* **wilign, holmr,**
note that it is not clear from the MS whether this is actually in Immingham);
wynedyngs c.1295 (this is recorded as an appellative in the same parish in *ab*
uno wyndyng c.1295, perhaps a compound of **(ge)wind^2** 'something winding' and
ing^1, literally 'a winding place' in some topographical sense, apparently
unrecorded in dictionaries. It is found as *the wyndinges* in Great Limber f.ns.
(b) *infra*, where an appellative use has also been noted. Its exact sense has yet
to be determined); y^e *Far Wray,* y^e *wett Ray* 1712 (probably from **vrá** 'a nook, a
corner of land' and for an earlier example *v.* Low wrays in Horkstow f.ns. (a));
yerlesdaile l12, *perllesdayle* Hy3 *EgCh, yerlesdailes, Yerledil* (sic) lHy3 (l14) *Gox*),
herlesdaile (sic) 1241 *NCot, hyernesdayl* c.1295, *yernes dayle* 1301, *-dayles* 1328,
yiernesdaile, -dailes forlanges c.1330 (the forms appear to refer to the same **deill**
'share or portion of land' and Dr John Insley suggests that, since the *y* forms
seem to represent *þ* i.e. *th,* the first el is ME *erl* 'an earl', perhaps here used
as a byname, preceded by the definite article. Spellings with *-n-* instead of *-l-*
presumably suggest confusion with **hyrne** 'an angle, a corner', though certainty is
impossible, with such variant forms).

Keelby

KEELBY

> *Chelebi* (9x) 1086 DB, (7x) c.1115 LS, 1157-81, Hy2 (e13) *NCot*
> *Chilebi* 1086 DB, 1171-75 Dane
> *Kelebi* 1143-47, a1147, p1182 Dane all (p), 1190 (e13) *NCot,*
>   c.1190, l12, c.1200 Dane all (p), 1203 Cur (p), 1208 ib, 1212,
>   1213, 1238-43 Fees, *-by* c.1150, c.1155, eHy2, 1160, a1166
>   (e13) *NCot,* 1166-75 Fulstow, a1167, a1180, l12 (e13) *NCot,*
>   1210-12 RBE, 1218 (e13) *NCot,* a1219 Welles, 1226 FineR,
>   1226 ClR, 1226 FF, 1233 (Ed1) *Newh et freq* to 1634-42
>   Holles, *-bya* 1200 ChR, *-bye* 1576 Saxton, 1610 Speed, *Kelaby*
>   1364 *Cor*
> *Kelesby* 1181-85, l12 (e13) *NCot*
> *Kileby* 1208 FF, 1292 Orig, *Kyleby* 1268 Cl, 1303 FA
> *Keileby* c.1215 RA ii, 1576-77 *MinAcct*
> *Keylby* 1500 LouthCA, 1530 Wills ii, 1539 *AOMB 212,* 1539 LP
>   xiv, 1550 Pat, *-bye* 1545 LP xx, 1550-52 *MinAcct,* 1551 Pat,
>   *Keilbye* 1553 ib, *-bie* 1562-67 LNQ v, *-by* 1639 *Foster,* 1666
>   VL
> *Kyeleby* 1218 Ass
> *Kelby* 1376 Cl, 1463 Fine
> *Kilby* 1635 *Foster*
> *Keelby* 1380, 1381, 1387 Peace, 1536-37 Dugd vi *et passim,*
>   *Kielby* 1634 VisitN, *Keeleby* 1629 *Yarb*

Both Ekwall (DEPN s.n.) and Fellows-Jensen (SSNEM 55)
agree that Keelby is a compound of kjǫlr 'a keel, a ridge (of hills)
and bȳ 'a farmstead, a village'. Ekwall translates this as 'the bȳ at
a ridge', while Fellows-Jensen comments that kjǫlr refers "to the
spur on whose slope Keelby stands". Spellings in *Ch-* are due to
AN influence. This etymology, a Scand. compound, is philologically
unexceptionable, but the topography calls for some comment.
Through the good offices of Dr Rod Ambler, Mrs Bettie Watkinson
has drawn a detailed map of the village, which shows that Keelby is
situated on a rising piece of ground between the 15 and 20 metre
contours (with one small patch above 20 metres). This forms a
distinct elongated "ridge" running roughly south-east-north-west. Mr
D.H. Appleby of Keelby comments that all the roads out of the old
village have a sharpish dip in them mainly to what was carr land.

He notes that approaching from the east along the Stallingborough road the old line of buildings from the church and farm does dominate the sky line.

CADDLE BECK, CADDLE HEAD, cf. *Catewell'* 1233 (Ed1) *Newh, -welle* 1333 *Ipm, Catwellstrem, Catewellestrem* (checked from MS) 1344 (14) Selby, *Caddle* 1844 *LindDep 29*, 'the spring frequented by cats', v. **cat(t), wella**, with the 1344 forms referring to the beck. CISSPLATT LANE. DODD'S LANE is perhaps named from the family of William *Dodds* 1856 White. HIGHFIELD WOOD (lost), 1828 Bry, situated in the extreme southern corner of the parish, cf. *campum de Keleby* eHy2, Hy2 (e13) *NCot, camp' de Keleby* 1230 (Ed1) *Newh, Kelebye felde* 1577, *Keilbie feild* 1601, 1611, 1625, 1634, 1637, *Keilby feild* 1664, *Keelby feild* 1674, *Keilby Feild* 1690 all *Terrier* (Great Limber), *campis communibus de Keelby* 1664, 1668 *ib* (Keelby), self-explanatory. KEELBY GRANGE, 1795 *BT* (Bigby), 1824 O, 1828 Bry, *the Grange House* 1824 *Yarb*, apparently a late example of **grange**, for which cf. Croxton Grange in Croxton *supra*. KING'S HEAD, 1842 White. MANOR FM is *Mawkes Hall* 1828 Bry, *Maux Hall* 1830 Gre. There are two further examples of this name in Yarborough Wapentake, Maux Hall in Great Limber and Mauxhall in Stallingborough, and it may be tentatively suggested that it is a derogatory nickname for a delapidated building 'Maggots Hall', the first el. then being dial. *mawk* 'a maggot', v. EDD s.v. The name does not seem to have been noted previously in the Survey and so far occurs only in a restricted corner of north-east L. MILL LANE, cf. *Mill Plot* 1824 *Yarb*. MOUNT PLEASANT. NEW BECK DRAIN, apparently the upper reaches of Skitter Beck in Ulceby *supra*. NORTH END. SAND PIT. SOUTH END. STEPNEY. SUDDLE SPRING is *Keelby Springs* 1824 O, but note *Suddles* 1844 *LindDep 29*; unfortunately the form is too late to suggest a certain etymology. TOPPER LANE, presumably named from the *Topper* family, cf. George *Topper* 1777 *BT*. VICARAGE, cf. *a vicaridge house* 1671 *Terrier*. WALNUT HO. WEST LANE.

Field-Names

Principal forms in (a) are 1845 *TA* 193. Spellings dated 1333 are *Ipm*; Hy3 and 1344 (14) are Selby; the 1344 spellings have been checked from the MS; 1671, 1707, 1709, 1724, 1745, 1762, 1822, and 1864 are *Terrier*; 1810 and 1824 are *Yarb*; and 1844 are *LindDep 29*.

(a) Baptist Pce (through the good offices of Dr Rod Ambler, Mrs Dinah Tyszka of Keelby has provided the following notes on Baptist connections with Keelby. "A note at the beginning of the General Register of the General Baptist Church, Killingholme, says that, in 1686, there were Meetings at Elsham, Melton, Keelby, Killingholme and Winterton. Keelby Baptists are mentioned in the parish church registers in the late 17c and in the Killingholme Baptist register throughout the 18c." Further, a licence was given in 1787 for meetings in the "House of George Taylor in the parish of Keelby"); Burnt House Cl; Chapel (Cl); Church Cl, Church and Church Yd (cf. *atte Kirke de Keleby* 1292, 1293 *NCot, atte Kirke of Keleby* 1293 *Pat*, 1299 *NCot, atte kirke de* - 1329 *Ass*, all (p), *v.* **kirkja**); Cote Garth 1824 (*v.* **cot, garðr** 'an enclosure', as elsewhere in the parish); Cottom Lane 1822, Cottam - 1864 (cf. *Cotumsike* 1333, named from Coatham in Brocklesby and **sík**); the East Fd 1822 (*in orientali campo de Kelebi* Hy3 *HarlCh, in Campo Orientali de Keleby* 1333, one of the great fields of Keelby); Epworths Warlots 1810, (*v.* **warlot**, on which *v.* Waterhill Wood in Brocklesby *supra*), Epworth's Cl 1844 (named from the *Epworth* family and **clos(e)**, cf. Christopher *Epworth* 1683 *BT*); Gale's Cl 1844 (named from the *Gale* family and **clos(e)**, cf. Joseph *Gale* 1729 *BT*); Garth 1824 (*v.* **garðr**); ye Holmes 1762, Holmes 1822 (*ye Holmes* 1707, 1745, *the* - 1709, *ye Holms* 1724, *v.* **holmr**); Home Cl 1824, (3x) 1845; House, Mill and Paddocks; Inn, Yard, Garden & Buildings; Keelby Car 1844 (*v.* **kjarr**); Keelby plot warlots 1810 (*Kelbi Warlotes* 14 *Yarb, Keleby Warlottes* ?1459 *ib* (both from decayed documents in LAO), *v.* **warlot**); Lr -, Upr Long Meer 1824; Part of Mill Cl; Old Inclosed Pce; Old Pinfold Cl; Orchard; Paddock; Parson's Yd 1824; Pond cl 1810; Publick House and Paddock; School House; Suscar 1762 (probably to be identified with *Suthker* c.1230 and *Sutheker* 1233 (Ed1) *Newh*, 'southern marsh', *v.* **sūð, kjarr**); Three Corner Pce; 3 Houses, Maltkiln etc.; Whom Cls 1762.

(b) *ackerdicke* c.1233 (Ed1) *Newh* (*v.* **æcer, díc**, and for the same name, *v.* Barnetby le Wold f.ns. (b)); *Aggehou* c.1233 (Ed1) *Newh* (from the ON pers.n. *Aggi* and **haugr** 'a mound, a hill'); *Andrewbarnland* 1344 (*v. Andreubarnland'* in Stallingborough f.ns. (b); it was on the boundary between Keelby and Stallingborough); *in aquilon'li campo* Hy2 (e13) *NCot, in campis aquilon'libus de Keleby* 112 *ib, in aquilonali campo* e13 *HarlCh*, Hy3 (Ed1) *Newh* ('in the north field(s) of Keelby'); *in australi campo* (*de Kelebi*) 1233 (Ed1), c.1233 (Ed1) *Newh, - de Keleby* Hy3 (Ed1) *ib* ('in the south field of Keelby'); *Baddocwelle* 13 *HarlCh* (this must be the same feature as *Baddocwelle* in Brocklesby f.ns. (b), where the name is discussed); *barlandes* 112 (e13) *NCot* (perhaps from ON *barr* 'barley' and *land*); *Becke* 1607 *Rental* (*v.* **bekkr**); *Bellowes Lande* 1587 *Yarb* (no doubt from the surn. *Bellow(e)s* and cf. Bellows Pipe in the adjacent parish of Great Limber *infra*); *Bicroft* 112 (e13) *NCot*, John *HarlCh*, *Bycroft* 1333 (probably '(place) by, near the croft', *v.* **bī**, **croft**, cf. *bifurlanges* in Immingham f.ns. (b) *supra*); *le Billand'* 1233 (Ed1) *Newh* (perhaps, as Dr John Insley suggests, the first el. is OE **bile**, used topographically of 'a headland'); *Buckishowe* 1333 (*v.* **haugr**, the reading of the first el. doubtful as the MS is faded); *Castregate* Hy3 (Ed1) *Newh* ('the road to Caistor', *v.* **gata**); *domus vocat'* a *Churchehouse* 1550-52 *MinAcct*, y^e *Corn-fields* 1707, *Cornefeild* 1709, y^e *Corne field* 1724, - *Corne Fields* 1745; *Cotedailes* 112 (e13) *NCot*, *-dailes* John *HarlCh*, *Coddayles* (sic) 1333 (*v.* **cot**, **deill** and cf. Cote Garth in f.ns. (a)); (*de*) *Dene* 1332 *SR* (p) (*v.* **denu**); *Depdaleheuedland'* 1344 (*v.* **hēafod-land** and Deepdale in Stallingborough f.ns. (a); it was on the boundary with Stallingborough); *a Cloase Called draper* 1587 *Yarb* (no doubt from the surn. *Draper*); *super viam q' vocat' estgate* c.1230 (Ed1) *Newh* (*v.* **ēast**, **gata**); *del England* c.1233 (Ed1) *Newh* (*v.* **eng**, **land**); *le Fletgate* 1344 (*v.* Fletgat in Stallingborough f.ns. (b); it was on the boundary with Stallingborough); *Fouketoft* 1333 ('Fouke's curtilage', *v.* **toft**, the first el. being the ME pers.n. *Fouke*, ultimately OGerm *Fulco*); *Fridailache* John *HarlCh* (from *Frigedæg* 'Friday' and **læc(c)** 'a stream (flowing through boggy land)', comparable with *Fridaieslake*, *-lache*, PN Ch 2, 215, where it is suggested that it was so-named because the Friday diet was caught there); *Fugelhau* Hy3 (Ed1) *Newh* (perhaps from the OE pers.n. *Fugel* and **haugr** 'a mound, a hill'); *Gayrsick* Hy3 (Ed1) *Newh* (*v.* **geiri**, **sīc**, **sík**); *godestig* Hy3 (Ed1) *Newh* (Dr John Insley suggests this is derived from the OE pers.n. *God* or *Gōd* and **stīg**, **stīgr** 'a path'); *Grymesbygate* 1333 ('the road to Grimsby', *v.* **gata**); *Guyldhallgarth* 1555 *Pat*, *Guildhall garth* 1607 *Rental* (*v.* **gild-hall**, **garðr**); (*atte*) *Halle* 1343 *NI*, 1364 *Cor*, 1373 *Peace*, *at* - 1381 ib, *atte hall de Keleby* 1352 *AASR* xxiii all (p) (self-explanatory); *Hampton thyng* 1472 *Wills PCC* (*v.* **þing** 'possession, property', the first el. being a surn.); *Hillertre* John *HarlCh* (from ME **hildertre** 'an elder-tree'); y^e *Ings* 1707, 1724, *the Ing* 1709, y^e *Field Ings* 1745, (*v.* **eng**); *Krachewell'* 1233 (Ed1) *Newh* ('the spring frequented by crows', *v.* **krāka**, **wella**); *Langberche* 112 (Ed1) *Newh*, John *HarlCh* (*v.* **lang**, **be(o)rg**); *Langwath* n.d. (e13) *NCot* ('the long ford', *v.* **lang**, **vað**); *Launheuedland* 1344 (*v.* **hēafod-land**; the first el. is presumably **land**; it was on the boundary with Stallingborough, cf. the foll.); *Laundmare* 1344 (for *Landmare* from **land-gemǣre** 'a boundary'; it was on the boundary with Stallingborough); *Lefquengarht* Hy2 (e13) *NCot*, *lefquengarth* e13 *HarlCh*, *Lefquengarth*, *Lefquengaryè* (with *y* for *þ*) c.1233 (Ed1) *Newh* (from the OE fem. pers.n. *Lēofcwēn* and **garðr**); *Le Lilieland, Liliedʲand* (sic) Hy2 (e13) *NCot*, *le lililand* e13 *HarlCh*,

Lililand 1233 (Ed1), *le* - c.1233 (Ed1) *Newh* (the first el. is probably ME *lilie* 'a lily' (*Lilium candidum*), the second being **land**); *a via parue Limbergie* l12 (e13) *NCot* (the road to Little Limber in Brocklesby parish); *Littelwathe* John *HarlCh* (*v.* **lytel, vað**, 'a ford'); *terr* ... *voc' le Loes* 1607 *Rental* (obscure); *Lowegarth'* 1333 (*v.* **lágr** 'low', **garðr**); *ex occidentali parte vie de Luda* l12 (Ed1) *Newh* ('from the west side of the way from Louth'); *Muswelles* 1344 (*v.* **mûs, wella**); *le park'* 1333 (*v.* **park**); *Peslandes* 1233 (Ed1) *Newh, peselandes* Hy3 *HarlCh, Peselandes* 1333 ('strips on which pease were grown', *v.* **pise, land**); (*de*) *pissale* 1327 *SR*, (*de*) *Pishale* 1332 *ib*, both (p) (*v.* **pise, halh**); (*ad*) *Pontem* 1332 *SR* (p); *Scothil* Hy3 (Ed1) *Newh* (for the first el. *v.* the discussion s.n. *Scotgate* in Croxton f.ns. (b)); *Siche* 1233 (Ed1) *Newh* (*v.* **sīc**); *Staynhill* 1344 (*v.* Stanel Pasture in Stallingborough f.ns. (a)); *Stretegate* 1333 (*v.* **strǣt, gata**); *Sunnindail* John *HarlCh, Sunningdale* l12 (Ed1) *Newh* (the readings are not certain); *Swaluegate* Hy2 (e13) *NCot, de Swaluegate usque ad filum aque* e13 *HarlCh, Swaluegate* c.1233 (Ed1) *Newh* ('the road to Swallow', *v.* **gata**); *S.alhull* 1333 (*v.* **hyll**, the second letter is illegible owing to a hole in the document); *in aquilonali parte del Wathe* 1233 (Ed1) *Newh* ('on the north side of the ford', *v.* **vað**); *Watredales* Hy3 *HarlCh* (*v.* **wæter, deill**); *Wende* 1233 (Ed1) *Newh* ('(land in) a bend', *v.* **wende**); *Westholm* lHy3 *NCot* (p), 1271 FF (p), *Westholme* 1327 *SR* (p) (*v.* **west, holmr**, though this may not be a local surn.); *Westmare* Hy3 (Ed1) *Newh* (*v.* **west, (ge)mǣre**, but the initial letter is not certain); *west'toftes* 1333 (*v.* **west, toft**); *Worlyn Butts* 1695 *Holywell*; (*de*) *Wra de Keleby* lHy3 *NCot* (p) (*v.* **vrá**).

North Kelsey

NORTH KELSEY

  Colesi (2x) 1086 DB
  Chelsi 1086 DB
  Calisei 1094 France
  Chaleseia c.1115 LS, 1146, 1163 RA i, 1166, 1194, 1195 P, *-iam*
    1191, 1192, 1193, 1194 ib, *-ea* 1170 ib
  Keleseye 1123-47 RA iv, *-ey* c.1150 (1409) Gilb, *-eie* 1157-63
    Dane, a1199 ib (p), 1200, 1203 Cur (p), 1206 P (p), *-eia*
    1166 ib (p), RA ix (p), lHy2 Dane (p), 1200, 1201, 1205,
    1206 P, 1206 Ass *et passim* to 1214 P
  Kelesega (sic) 1188 P (p), *-eye* 1247 Ch, 1275 Ipm, 1275 Cl,
    1292, 1295 Ch, 1335 Pat, *-eya* 1229 RA iii, *-ey* 1254 ValNor,
    1265 Pat, 1281 QW, 1303 FA, 1394 Pat

Kelesia 1190, 1191, 1199 P all (p), *-ee* 1203 Cur

Kelesay 1275 RH, *Kelsay* 1380, 1383 Pat, 1383 Fine, 1387
Peace, 1395, 1397 Pat, 1407 Fine, *-aie* 1554 PrState

Kelseye 1362 BPR, 1367 Ipm, 1369 Fine, *-ey* 1384 ib, 1401-02
FA, 1426 Cl, 1461, 1552, 1553 Pat *et passim*

Keleshai e13 RA iv, *-heiam* 1206 Ass

Kaleseye 1210-12 RBE

Kelcheye (sic) 1276 RH

Kellesh' 1150-80 (Ed3) *ChorCart, -hey* 1187 (1409) Gilb, 1294
RSu, 1384 Fine, *-heie* 1201 OblR, *-haye* 1361 Cl, *-hay* 1373
Peace

Kelleseia c.1200 RA viii, *-ie* 1202 Ass

Kellesay 1242-43 Fees, *-aye* 1330 FA

Kelleseye 1264 Pat, 1281 Ipm, 1306, 1322 Pat, 1322, 1327 Ipm,
1348 Pat *et passim* to 1422 ib, *-ey* 1286 Pap, 1303 Ipm, 1316
FA

Norchelsei 1086 DB, *-cheleseia* 1146 RA i, *-keleseie* 1163 ib i,
-keleseia 1238-43 Fees

Nortchelesei 1086 DB, *-keleseye* 1244 Orig, *-kelleseye* 1244
FineR, 1272 FF, 1344 *FF, -kellesheye* 1276 Ipm, *-kelsey* 1323
Cl

Nordchelesia c.1115 LS, *-chelesi* 1136-47 RA i, - *Kelisia* 1177
ChancR, *-chuleseia* 1177 P, *-keleseie* 1196 ChancR, *-keleseia*
1204 P, *-kelesey* Hy3 (1409) Gilb

Norhtchelesia c.1141 RA i

Northcheleseia c.1141 (1329) Ch

Northkeleseye 1190 (1301) Dugd vi, a1218 RA iv, 1292 Orig,
1346 Pat, *North Keleseye* 1272 FF, 1316 Misc, - *Kelesey* 1316
FA, *-kelesey* 1375 Peace, 1557 Pat

Northkelleseie e13 *HarlCh, -eye* 1262 Ipm, 1322 Cl, 1323 Ipm,
1331, 1363 Cl, *-ey* 1291 Tax, 1340 *Monson,* 1343 NI, 1396
Cl, 1504 Ipm, *North Kellesey* eHy3 (1409) Gilb, 1303 Cl,
1428 FA, *-eya* 1276 RRGr, *-eye* 1276, 1322 Cl, 1328 Banco,
1380 Pat, - *Kellesay* 1285 Ipm, 1332 *SR,* 1465 LNQ xvii,
-kellesay 1295 *Ass,* 1477 Cl, *-kelliseya* 1277 RRGr

Northkelseye 1276 RH, 1323 Pat, *-kelsey* 1318 ib, 1329 *Ass,*
1353 Inqaqd *et passim* to 1623 *Monson, Northekelsey* 1427
HarlCh, 1550 Pat, *North Kelsey* 1324 Inqaqd, 1400 Pat,
1415 Cl *et passim*

North Kelsay 1322 Misc, 1327 *SR,* 1373 Peace, 1408 Fine,

1416 Pat *et passim* to 1535 VE iv, *Northkelsay* 1549
MiscDon 554, 1595 *Monson, North Kelsaie* 1554 InstBen
Kelsey borialis 1526 Sub

The forms without the affix *North* refer to either North or
South Kelsey, but are included together here for convenience, since
it is not always possible to decide to which each form relates.

Ekwall (DEPN s.n. Kelsale) has associated the first el. of
Kelsey with that of Kelsale (Sf), Kelshall (Ch) and Kelshall (Hrt).
It is, however, highly likely that Kelshall can now be removed from
this series for Dodgson (PN Ch **3** 277-78) has proposed a separate
etymology for that particular name. Ekwall's suggestions are that
the first el. may be an OE pers.n. *Cĕll(i)*, though no such name is
known, an OE pers.n. *Cĕol*, with Scand. *K-* for *Ch-*, or an OE
pers.n. *Cĕnel* (gen.sg. *Cĕnles*), which he claims would give *Kĕles-*.
Even with the full lists of early forms collected here (and for South
Kelsey in Walshcroft Wapentake), it is hardly possible to say more
than that the first el. appears to be a strong OE pers.n. with a
gen.sg. in *-es*. So, Margaret Gelling's inclusion of Kelsey in her list
of "names which are ambiguous or too obscure to be classified"
(*Place-Names in the Landscape*, London 1984, 39) seems most
sensible. The second el. is OE ēg probably in the sense of dry or
higher ground in marsh and it is noteworthy that to the west of the
village is a whole series of minor names and f.ns. in Carr (from ON
kjarr, ME *ker*), including North Kelsey Carrs *infra*. If the original
OE pers.n. had initial [k] then the spellings in *Ch-* would be due to
AN influence. On the other hand, if the source is in fact OE *Cĕol*,
then *K-* would be due to Scand. influence. It is worth noting that
an apparently identical name has been noted as that of a meadow
(parish unknown) in *Keleseye* 1279 (c.1350) Rams ii, 343. It is
North to distinguish the village from *South* Kelsey in Walshcroft
Wapentake.

SMITHFIELD FM, cf. *Smethefeld* lHy2 Dane, e13 *HarlCh*, 1250-70,
1337 *Foster, -felde* a1200 *ib, -feud* 1276 RH, *Smeyefeld* Hy3 (1409)
Gilb, 1275 RH (*y=þ*, i.e. *th*), *Smetfeud'* John *HarlCh, Smedesfeld'*
a1218 RA iv, *Semedhefeld* 1220-40 *Foster, Smethfeld* c.1289 *ib,
Smetfeld* 1378 *ib, Smithefeud'* 1226-28 Fees, *Smythfeld'* c.1370 *Extent,*
1541 (1658) HollesM, *-feild(e)* 1598 *Nelthorpe*, 1646 *Monson*, 1656

Nelthorpe, -field 1658 HollesM, 1728 *MiscDon 509*, *Smithfeild* 1649 *Dixon*, 1691 *MiscDon 509*, *-field* 1685, 1764 *Nelthorpe*, 1781, 1800 *Terrier* (Barnetby le Wold), *Smithfield House* 1830 Gre, 'the level open land', *v.* **smēðe, feld**, the first el. already by the early 13th century being influenced by *smith*.

BARFF VALE, cf. (*a furlong cauled*) *Barfe* 1662, 1663, 1669 *Terrier*, *barffe* 1673 *ib*, (*the*) *Barg* 1763 *Nelthorpe*, 1812 *Dixon*, *the Sowre barth* 1615 *Nelthorpe*, *Soure Barfe* 1776 *ib* (*v.* **sūr** 'sour, damp, coarse (of land)'), *the little barfe* 1625 *ib*, dial *barf* (OE **beorg**) 'a low ridge or hill'. BARROW LING, *Barwell Inggs* 1635 (c.1900) *LindDep 78*, *- Ing* 1657 *Nelthorpe*, *a place comonly called Barwell Ings* 1685 *ib*, *Barril Ings* 1764, 1776, 1780 *ib*, *Barrel Inge* 1767 *Stubbs*, *- Ings* 1790 *Monson*, *Barrow or Barrell Ings* 1768 *Nelthorpe*, *Barrow Lings* 1739, 1748 *Dixon*; the forms are too late to suggest an etymology for *Barwell* and it is impossible to know whether it is an old p.n. or a surn., *v.* **eng** 'meadow, pasture', probably in the pl. in the sense of 'outlying pastures'. BELT PLANTATION. BROW HILL, *Browhill* 1662, 1663, 1669 *Terrier*, 1733 *Nelthorpe*, *browhill* 1666, 1673 *Terrier*, *Brow-hill* 1706 *ib*, 1722 *Nelthorpe*, *Browell* 1686 *Dixon*, *a place called Brewell* 1763 *Nelthorpe*, 1793 *Dixon*, *East Browhill* 1793 *MiscDep 118*, from **brū** 'the brow of a hill, etc.' with **hyll** added. BRUFF FM, *Brough* 1842 White, it is uncertain whether this has any archaeological significance. CAPHAM HALL. CARR FM is *Square Ho.* 1828 Bry. COLD HARBOUR. CREEK DRAIN, 1840 *Map*, cf. *the Comon Creake* 1615, *the Creake* 1693, *Creeks* 1705, 1710, 1720, *great -, little Creek* 1708, *Great -, Little Creeks, Creek* 1819 all *Nelthorpe*, from **kriki**, ME **crike** 'an inlet'. CROSS LANE, 1828 Bry, *Crosse laine* 1700 *Nelthorpe*, *the Cross Lane* 1703 *ib*, presumably self-explanatory. CUTLEY BECK, 1828 Bry. CUTLEY BRIDGE, cf. *Cutler brigge layne alias the Morelayne* 1622 *Nelthorpe*; if the form *Cutler* is original, then presumably this is from the occupational name or the derived surn., though none has been noted in the sources searched. DECOY HO, 1824 O, 1830 Gre, *Old Decoy Ho.* 1828 Bry, cf. *the Duck Coy Closes* (sic) 1762 *Terrier*, *the Decoy* 1767 *Nelthorpe*, 1767 *Stubbs*, 1790 *Monson*, *Decoy House Closes* 1812 *Dixon*, self-explanatory. DOVECOTE FM, cf. *The Dovecoate Close* 1673 *Dixon*, *dovecoate close* 1673 *Nelthorpe*, *the Dove coat Close* 1684 *ib*, *Dovecoat close* 1685 *ib*,

Dove Cott^e 1828 Bry. DRABBLES HILL, cf. *Drables Plat* 1762
Terrier, -plat 1793 *MiscDep 118* (*v.* plat²), *Drabald's Furlong* c.1776
Nelthorpe, from the surn. *Drabble.* EASTHALL FM, *manerio de
Esthall'* 1344 *FF,* "manor called" *Esthall* 1477 Cl, *Easthall* 1615
Nelthorpe, East hall 1661 *ib,* - *Hall* 1663 *ib,* 1687, 1710, 1733 *Dixon,
that Scite ... where a Messuage or Tenement heretofore Called or
known by the Name of East Hall formerly stood but is now
demolished* 1738 *ib, East Hall Gate* c.1776 *Nelthorpe, East Hall
Road* 1812 *Dixon,* 1840 *Map,* 1864 *Terrier,* self-explanatory, *v.* east,
hall, and cf. *Northehall'* in f.ns. (b) *infra.* EAST MOOR FM.
ELLMORE FM, perhaps to be identified with *Ailmer* eHy3 (1409)
Gilb; more early forms are needed to suggest a plausible
etymology. FIR LANE. FOLLY LANE. GRAVELPIT FM.
GUILICAR LANE, cf. *Gaigelker* Hy3 (1409) Gilb, *Guile Carre* 1635
(c.1900) *LindDep 78, -car* 1673 *Nelthorpe,* - *Carr* 1684 *ib,* 1686
Dixon, 1728 *MiscDon 509,* - *Car* 1776 *Nelthorpe, the guile-Carr* 1708
ib, ghile Car 1662, 1669 *Terrier, ghilecar* 1673 *ib, the gile Car* 1666
ib, the Gile-Carr 1691 *MiscDon 509, Gile Carr, great Gile Carr* 1767
Stubbs, Great - 1790 *Monson, Guyle Carr* 1673 *Dixon,* 1684, 1685
Nelthorpe; if the 13th century form *Gaigelker* belongs here, then it
is perhaps 'the marsh where bog-myrtle grows', *v.* gagel, kjarr. but
the subsequent development is as "somewhat obscure" as the editors
of NED find modern *gale* from OE gagel. HIGHFIELD
PLANTATION, HIGHFIELDS, *the hie field* 1662, 1666 *Terrier,*
1733 *Nelthorpe, West High Field* 1776 *ib,* cf. *campo de Northkeleseye*
a1218 RA iv, *campum de Northkellesay* 1491 *Nelthorpe,*
self-explanatory. INGS FM, *Ings House* 1824 O, 1830 Gre, *Ings F^m*
1828 Bry, cf. *the South Ings* 1595 *Monson, le Southinges* 1616 *ib,
Northkelsey southinges* 1611 *Terrier* (South Kelsey), *the South Ings*
1635 (c.1900) *LindDep 78,* 1673 *Dixon,* 1684, 1685 *Nelthorpe, the
south ings* 1673 *ib, South Ings close* 1683 *ib, the Ings* 1710, 1720,
1735, 1767 *ib,* 1802 *Red, Ings* 1776 *Nelthorpe,* 1790 *Monson, v.* eng.
INGS LOCK is marked *Lock* 1824 O and *Ings House* is shown just
to the north. They are close to the boundary with South Kelsey.
LAND DRAIN, c.1776 *Nelthorpe,* 1768 (1815) *LRA 6.* LITTLE
LONDON FM, *Little London* 1824 O, 1830 Gre, cf. Little London
in Stallingborough parish *infra.* MANOR HO, *Mannor house* 1684
Nelthorpe, that capitall Messuage or Manour house 1685 *ib.* MILL
HILL is named from *North Kelsey Old Mill* 1824 O, 1830 Gre,
North Kelsey Mill 1828 Bry, and is probably to be identified with

Lady Mill Hill 1684 *Nelthorpe*, - *mill hill* 1685 *ib*, - *Milne-Hill* 1710 *ib*, cf. *the Lady Mill Hill Close* 1673 *Dixon, Lady Mill Hill Close* 1673 *Nelthorpe*, - *miln hill Close* 1720 *ib*, and note also *the two Mill Hills* 1748 *Dixon, one of the Mill Hills being that on which the Wind Corn Mill does not stand* 1798 *ib*, the other being perhaps North Kelsey Mills *infra*. MINNITT'S FM is *Cream Poke* 1824 O, 1830 Gre, *the Creame poke* 1652 *Nelthorpe, Cream poake* 1663 *ib, one litle Carr commonly called or knowne by the name of Cream poke* 1685 *ib, Cream Poke* 1711, 1733, 1739, 1796 *Dixon*, - *poak* 1767 *Stubbs*, - *poke* 1790 *Monson, Cream Poke als Thornholme pingle* 1716 *Nelthorpe, Cream Poke Bridge* 1828 Bry; the same name is found in Bigby f.ns. (b), where it is suggested that this is a complimentary nickname. *Minnitt* is a local surn, cf. *Mr Minnitt* 1790 *LTR*. NORTH KELSEY BECK, 1768 (1791) *LindDep Plans*, 1824 O, 1830 Gre, *N Kelsey Beck* 1834 *Dixon, Kelsey Becke* 1629 *Yarb*, - *Beck* 1844 *TAMap*, cf. *Atte Bek* 1327, 1332 *SR* both (p), 1344 *FF* (p), *atte Bekke de North'kelsey* 1329 *Ass, v.* **bekkr**. It is *Cadney Beck* 1828 Bry, 1840 *Map, Kadney Beck* 1762 *Terrier*, which is earlier *Cadney dike* 1677, 1690, 1697, 1700, 1702, - *Dike* 1706, 1707 all *Terrier*, it forms in part the boundary with the adjacent parish of Cadney. NORTH KELSEY CARRS, 1824 O, 1830 Gre, *North Kelsey Carr* 1734 *Terrier, ye carrs of Northkelsey* 1598 *Nelthorpe, the Carr of North Kelsey* 1694 *MiscDep 118, the Carr of Kelsey* 1726 *Nelthorpe, the Car(r)s of North Kelsey* 1761, 1778 *ib, the Carre* 1635 (c.1900) *LindDep 78, the Carr* 1694 *MiscDep 118*, 1807 *Dixon, the Carrs* 1762 *Terrier*, 1767 *Nelthorpe*, 1802 *Red*, cf. *north carre* 1466 LNQ xvii, *North karr* 1467 *ib, North Carr common* 1559 SP, *the great & litle North Carr* 1685 *Nelthorpe* (cf. South Carr *infra*), *the Carr Close* 1653 *Monson*, 1710 *Nelthorpe, v.* **kjarr**, ME **ker** 'a marsh, especially one overgrown with brushwood', and numerous f.ns. in (a) and (b) *infra*. NORTH KELSEY GRANGE, 1693, 1705 *Nelthorpe, Atte Graunge* 1327 *SR* (p), *atte graunge de North'kelsay* 1329 *Ass* (p), *atte Graunge* 1344 *FF* (p), "grange in" *North Kelsey* 1537-9 LDRH, *North Kelsey, firma grang'* 1538-39 Dugd vi, *Grangie de Norkelsaye* 1543-45 *MinAcct, Grange* 1545 LP xxi, *the grange house* 1615 *Nelthorpe, the Grange Farm* 1707 *Terrier* and cf. *grange lane* 1739 *Dixon, Grange Lane Close* 1796, 1798 *ib*; it was a **grange** of North (or Nun) Ormsby Priory. NORTH KELSEY MILLS (disused) is *Kelsey New Mill* 1824 O, 1830 Gre, and is perhaps *Windmill* 1685 *Nelthorpe, North Kelsey Wind-Mill* 1724 *Terrier*.

NORTH KELSEY MOOR, *le Comon Moore* 1598 *Nelthorpe, the Moore* 1656 *ib,* 1687 *Dixon, (the) Moor* 1733 *ib,* 1776 *Nelthorpe, Kelsey Moor* 1774 *Red,* - *Moors* 1828 Bry, *the Moors* 1828 *Terrier,* cf. *the moore close* 1607 *Yarb, Upper Moor Close* 1684 *Nelthorpe, Moor-close* 1828 *Terrier* and *the Moor Laine* 1700 *Nelthorpe, the Moore Lane* 1703 *ib, the Moor lane* 1796 *Dixon,* self-explanatory, *v.* mōr[1]. OWMBY LANE, - *lane* 1828 *Terrier,* leading to Owmby in Searby cum Owmby parish *infra.* RED HO, 1824 O, 1828 Bry, 1830 Gre. SADNEY, HIGH SADNEY, SADNEY PLANTATION, *Sadney* 1638, 1677 *Terrier,* 1686 *Dixon,* 1690, 1697, 1700 *Terrier et passim, old Sadney* 1702 *Nelthorpe;* it is *Gadney* 1824 O, 1830 Gre, and it is possible that *Sabaneia* eHy3 (1409) Gilb belongs here too. The forms are too late for a certain etymology, though the first el. may be an OE weak pers.n. with gen.sg. in -*an,* the second el. being ēg as in the parish name. SETCOPS, cf. *the great setcops, little -, vpp settcops* 1673 *Nelthorpe, Greate -, Little -, Upper Settcops* 1684 *ib, great settcopps, litle settcops, upper Sett Copps* 1685 *ib, Lower Sett copps* 1687 *Dixon,* from set-copp probably in the sense 'a flat-topped hill'. SHEEPCOTE HILL, cf. *Shipcoots Car* 1662 *Terrier,* - *Close* 1663 *ib, Shipcootes Close* 1669 *ib, Shipcoate yarde* 1673 *ib, the Sheep Coate-hill Close* 1673 *Dixon, Sheep Coat Hill close* 1685, *Sheep Coat Hill* 1710, *Sheepcoott Hill* 1716, *Sheepcoat Hill* 1720, *Sheep Coat Hill* 1735, *Sheepcote Hill* 1819 all *Nelthorpe,* self-explanatory. SMALLTHORNE FM, cf. *in the Thornes* 1343 NI (p) and Long Thorn Cl in f.ns. (a) *infra.* SOUTH CARR, 1685 *Nelthorpe,* 1726 *Monson,* 1767 *Stubbs,* 1790 *LTR,* 1824 O, - *carre* 1635 (c.1900) *LindDep* 78, *the South carr* 1687 *Dixon,* cf. *South Car(r) Lane* 1739, 1789, 1798 *ib, v.* sūð, kjarr and cf. *north carre* under North Kelsey Carrs *supra.* SOUTHFIELD RD, 1840 *Map,* cf. *Westfield Rd infra* and the East Fd in f.ns. (a) *infra.* STARHAM, 1607, 1622 *Nelthorpe,* 1635 (c.1900) *LindDep* 78, 1661, 1733, 1762, 1767, 1778, 1783 *Nelthorpe, Starrham* 1659 *ib, Starrome* 1606 *Terrier, Starholme* 1606, 1638 *ib,* 1652 *Nelthorpe,* 1679 *Monson,* 1699, 1701, 1720 *Nelthorpe,* 1812 *Dixon, Starreholme* 1626 *Nelthorpe, Star Holme* 1710 *ib, Starholm* 1778 *ib, Starram* 1677, 1690, 1697 *Terrier,* 1708 *Nelthorpe, Starrum* 1693, 1698 *ib,* 1700, 1703, 1706 *Terrier et freq* to 1775 *MiscDon* 509, 'the higher ground amidst the marsh where sedge, bent grass grows', from ODan star and holmr, with a common development of -*holme* to -*ham,* -*am,* -*um.* STINGRAVES HO, *Stevengraves* 1633 *MiscDon* 554, - *Graves* 1700,

1703, 1733, 1736, (*the*) *Lower* - 1761, 1778, *Stephen-Grave* 1703, *Steengraves* 1710, - *close* 1720, *Steen Graves* 1819 all *Nelthorpe*, *Stiengraves* 1828 *Terrier*, *Stinggraves* 1762 *ib*, from the pers.n. or derived surn. *Steven* and perhaps **græf** 'a pit, a trench'. STREET LANE, *ye Street* 1706 *Terrier*, *the Street* 1762 *ib*, *Streetlane* 1733 *Nelthorpe*, *Street Lane* 1761 *ib*, 1828 Bry, cf. *Street Close* 1673 *Dixon*, *Street Close* 1673 *Nelthorpe*, *Street close* 1683, 1685 *ib*, 1687 *Dixon*, *Street Close Plat* c.1776 *Nelthorpe*, *Street-Close otherwise Street-land-Close* 1796 *Dixon*, *Street Platt* 1772 *Nelthorpe*, *Streets Plat* 1793 *MiscDep 118* (*v.* **plat²**); this is the name of a short stretch of road running south from the Roman road from Caistor to North Kelsey, Margary no. 271, and it may be part of an ancient trackway, *v.* **strǣt**. TWELVE MONTH FM, TWELVE MONTH HILL WOOD. VICARAGE, *the vicarage* 1606 *Terrier*. WASHDYKE HO, 1830 Gre, *Washdike House* 1824 O, 'the ditch for washing (sheep)', *v.* **(ge)wæsce, dīc, dīk**. WESTFIELD RD (lost), 1840 *Map*, cf. *in occident' campo de Nordkelsey* 1376 *Monson*, *in campo occiden' de North kelsey* 1557 *MiscDon 554*, *in occident campo de North Kelsey* 1597 *Monson*, *the west feild* 1598 *ib*, *in occident campo de Northe Kelsey* 1598 *Nelthorpe*, *the West feild* 1618 *ib*, *the Westfeild of Northkelsey* 1626 *Monson*, *the west feild*(*e*) 1663, 1669 *Terrier*, *the West feild* 1683 *Nelthorpe*, *the west Feild* 1684 *ib*, - *field* 1666 *Terrier*, 1710, 1736 *Nelthorpe*, *the West Field* 1673 *Dixon et freq* to 1798 *ib*, No: *Kelsey Westfield* 1715 *Yarb*, one of the open fields of North Kelsey, *v.* **west, feld** and cf. Southfield Rd *supra* and East Fd in f.ns. (a) *infra*. WEST HOLMES, 1635 (c.1900) *LindDep 78*, 1828 Bry, *Westholm'* a1218 RA iv, *-holme* 1597, 1598, 1623, 1646, 1676, 1686, 1790 *Monson*, *-Holme* 1718 *MiscDon 108*, 1767 *Stubbs*, 1812 *Dixon*, cf. *west holme cloose* c.1600 *Monson*, *West homes great close* 1673, *Great West Holmes close* 1683, *great west Holmes close* 1685, *Westholme Closes* 1693, - *Holme Close* 1720 all *Nelthorpe*, *v.* **west, holmr**; it is *west* of South Kelsey, and on Bry it is actually in South Kelsey parish. WESTLAND LANE, *West Land Road* 1840 *Map*, cf. *West land* 1687 *Dixon*, *Westland* 1710 *ib*, *West-lands* 1776 *Westland*(*s*) 1819 and *Westlands close* 1708, *West Lands Close* c.1776 all *Nelthorpe*, *v.* **west, land**. WHITE HOUSE FM. WOODBINE COTTAGE, - HO, the two being quite separate, the cottage being west of the village, the house to the north.

Field-Names

Forms dated 1340, 1376, 1551, 1554, 1556, 1595, c.1600, 1616, 1623, 1626 and 1790 are *Monson*; 1579, 1606, 1638, 1662, 1663 T, 1666, 1669, 1673 T, 1677, 1690, 1697, 1700 T, 1703, 1706, 1707, 1762, 1828 and 1864 are *Terrier*; 1607 and 1715 are *Yarb*; 1673 D, 1676 D, 1686, 1687, 1710 D, 1733 D, 1734, 1726 D, 1736, 1738, 1739, 1748, 1776 D, 1787, 1789, 1792, 1796, 1798, 1801, 1807, 1812, 1813 and 1839 are *Dixon*; 1690, 1714, 1720 R, 1726, 1745, 1774 and 1838 are *Red*; 1694 and 1793 are *MiscDep 118*; 1767 S are *Stubbs*; and 1771 are *MiscDep 149*. Other dated forms, marked N where necessary, are *Nelthorpe*, unless otherwise noted.

(a) Back House Carr 1767, Backhouse - 1790 (*Back House* is probably for *Bake House*, v. also **kjarr**; the f.ns. in Carr(s) are almost all parts of North Kelsey Carrs *supra*); (Lt) Barlams 1838; Beck Bryar 1774, East -, West Beck Cl c.1776 N, Beck Cls 1776 N, 1812 (*Becke bryer* (*closes*) 1673 D, 1687, - *Bryer* 1683, Beck Bryar 1673 N, (- *in the tenure or occupation of ... Beck widdow*) 1690, (- *formerly in the occupacon of ... Beck widdow*) 1684, *Beck Brier in the occupacon of Widdow Beck* 1685, *Beckbryer* 1714, 1720, 1745, evidently 'scrubland occupied by the *Beck* family', v. **brēr** and cf. the forms for North Kelsey Beck *supra*, from which the surn. may have been derived); Blake Hows flg 1772 (*Blackoe Furlong* 1623), Blacow 1796, 1798, Blacow or Housedale Cl 1787, 1792, 1798, - or Housdale Cl 1801, (- *or Housedall* 1735 D), Blackhow 1810 (*Blachou* 1276 Ipm, *a Close ... Called Blaco* 1595, *Blacow close, Blacoe Close* 1673 N, *Blackcow Close* 1676 D, - *close* 1683, *Black Cow Close* 1684, *Blacowe Close* 1685, *one close called Blacow* 1715, 'the black mound', v. **blæc, haugr** (cf. Blacko PN La 67), the second el. being taken to be *cow* or *house* in some later spellings; the alternative name is the Housedale Close *infra* and earlier *Hausedal* a1218 RA iv, *Housdaile* 1666, *Housdale* 1671 *Terrier* (South Kelsey), *House Dal* 1703, *house dail* 1706, *Housedale* 1710 D, - *sike* 1611 *Terrier* (South Kelsey), *Housdale Sike* 1623, *Hows*(*e*)*daile sike* 1663 T, 1666, *howsedaile sicke* 1669, - *sike* 1673 T, *house dail sike* 1706, *housdale close* 1625 *Terrier* (South Kelsey), *Housedale close* 1703 *ib*, *housedaile field* 1669, *Housdall Stile* 1703, the first el. possibly being altered from *Hause, Hows*, the pl. of **haugr**, to which **deill** was added, with the further additions of **sīc, sik, feld** and **stigel**. It is noteworthy that **deill** is not found with *Blacow* etc. forms); Bourdon Briggs 1771, Bordanbriggs, Bordenbriggs flg 1772, Boarden Bridge Flg, Booarden Bridge Gate (sic) c.1776, Boarden Bridge (Rd) 1812 (*broodden bridge end* 1662, *boorden* - 1663 T, *Brrden bridge End* (sic) 1666, *bording bridge End* 1669, *bordding bridge* 1673, *Borden Brig end* 1703, *Boarding bridge end* 1706, *Boarden briggs* 1733 N, alluding to a wooden bridge, *v.* **bord**, -**en**[2], **brycg**, the same name being found in Cadney f.ns. (b) *supra* and may well refer to the same bridge); bragg Carr 1767, Bragg - 1790 (named from the surn. *Bragg* and **kjarr**, cf. Richard *Bragg* 1662 *BT*); Brakes flg c.1776 N, Bracks - 1772, Breakes Flg 1793 (*Brakes* eHy3 (1409) Gilb, *v.* **bræc**[1], 'underwood, thicket'); Brigg-lane 1828, Brigg Rd 1864 ('road to Brigg', *v.* Glanford Brigg *supra*); the church-lane 1828, the Church Lane 1864; Codales 1812 (*Cotedaile* eHy3 (1409) Gilb, (*great*) *Cowedaile Close* (sic) 1662, 1663, 1666, 1669, -*Cowe daile Close* 1673 T, *Coate Dale* 1692, -*dale* 1705, *Codayle* - 1710, *Coodaile* 1703, *Coedaile* 1706, *v.* **cot, deill**; if these all refer to the same piece of land, the first el. has been confused with *cow*); Common Bottom 1767 N, 1767 S, 1790 (cf. *Lower common* 1687); Common Cls 1776, (The) Common Cl c.1776 N, 1798 (*the* -) 1607, 1693, *the Upper* - 1683 N, *the upper comon* - 1684, - *Common close* 1685, *the common close* 1708; Cow-cl 1828, Cow Cl 1838; Creckbeck flg 1772, Creek Beck 1812 (*Crack beck* 1579, - *becke* 1637, *the Creck beck* 1611 *Terrier* (South Kelsey), *the Creck* - 1675 *ib*, *Creckbeecke furlong* 1669, *Creecke beecke furlong* 1673 T, *Crackbecke furlong* 1703, *Crachbeck Furlong* 1706, the forms being too late to suggest an etymology for the first el., which seems to have been later associated with *creek*, cf. Creek Drain *supra*; the second is **bekkr**); Crook acre 1776 N, Crook'd Acers 1772, Crookacre Cl c.1776 N, Crook Acres Dale 1793 (*Crokyacre* a1218 RA iv, *Crookes Acres* 1693, *Crook Acre* 1708, 1710, 1720); the Cross-lanes 1828 (*cross lane* often signifies a passage connecting two other thoroughfares, *v.* **cros**); Cross Middle Dikes 1762, 1774, Cross mid: dikes 1767 S (*Cross middle Dikes* 1635 (c.1900) *LindDep* 78, *Crossmiddledykes* 1733 N, - *Middle Dykes* 1736, *v.* **cros** and the Middle Dikes *infra*); Dale Pits 1812; Dirthills 1793, Dirt-hill Gate, Dirt Hill Flg c.1776 N (*v.* **drit, hyll**); The Second East cl 1839; East Fd 1758 *MiscDon 509*, the Eastfield 1763, c.1776 N, the East Fd 1813 (1673 D and *passim* to 1793, y^e *east feild* 1598, *the East* - 1615, 1618, - *Feild* 1683 N, 1684, 1735 N, *the east feilde* 1673 T, *the east Field* 1685, *the* -, y^e *East field* 1685, 1703, 1729, *the eastfield* 1710 N, *the Eastfield* 1708, 1733 N, *in campo orientali de Kell'* l13 *LindDep 88*, - *orient' de Kellesey* 1340, - *orien' de Northkelsey* 1557 *MiscDon 554*, cf. *Westfield Rd supra*); High -, Low -, Short 5 Gad c.1776 N (*the Four and the Five gadds* 1702 *v.* **gadd**[2], 'division of an open pasture, in L usually 6½ feet wide' NED s.v. *gad* sb. 6b, but also a measure of arable land, equivalent to a square perch, *v.* EDD s.v. sb[1] 9 with a quotation from L, and note the appellative use in *10 gads of meadowe* 1606); Foal Race 1767 S, 1790 (cf. *Foal Carr* 1733 N); (dowry Leas) Fowlings 1819 (1630, 1685, 1710, 1720, *Fuleng* eHy3 (1409) Gilb, *Close of pasture ground ... called or knowne by the name of Fowlinges* 1684, *Fowle Ings* 1705, *Fowlings* 1710, 1720, *the great Fouldings* 1673 D, - *Foldings* 1685, *Fowld Engs* 1693, the forms seem to refer to the same place, so the meaning must be, as indicated by the eHy3 spelling 'the dirty meadow(s)', *v.* **fūl, eng**); Fox Cover 1819; Glascow 1767 S, 1790; Grange Carr 1762, 1767 S (*the* - 1693, 1705, 1710 N, 1720 N, *Grange Turfe Car* 1686, *Marris grange Carr, the graunge house ... of John Marris* 1615, *v.* **grange, kjarr**, from North Kelsey Grange *supra*); the Grange-lane 1828, the Grange lane 1864 (cf. prec.); the Great Carrs 1828 (*Marris great Carr* 1615, *v.* **kjarr**, cf. Grange Carr *supra*); Greatland flg 1772, greatland hill c.1776 N; High -, Low Greets 1772, Low Greets 1812 (cf. *a furlonge called gretes* 1579, *Greete* 1611, *greets* 1625, *Little Greets* 1703 all *Terrier* (South Kelsey), *the Greets* 1652 *Rad, the Greets* 1671 *Terrier* (South Kelsey), *les Upper Greeth alias Touthill* 1623, probably 'the gravelly places', *v.* **grēot, grēote**. For *Touthill* 'look-out hill', *v.* **tōt-hyll**); new -, old Hasham 1774, (*Old Hasham Close* 1598, *Old* -, *new Hasham* 1673 N, 1684, *old* -, *new Halsham* (sic) 1685, *New* -, *Old Hasham* 1690, *Little* -, *Old Hassam* 1714, *little Hasshams* 1720 R, *Little Hasshams, Old Hassham* 1745); Haverdale Leys c.1776 N, 1776 N (*the Haverdale leazes Closes* 1708, *v.* **hafri** 'oats', **deill** with **lǣs** and **clos(e)**); the Heads 1762 (*v.* **hēafod**); Headland c.1776 N (*the* - 1707, y^e *headland* 1700 T, 1706, *v.* **hēafod-land**); Hell flg 1772; Hill Cl 1819 (1710, *the* - 1607, *great hill* - 1693, *Great Hill close* 1705, *v.* **hyll**), Hill Gate c.1776 (*v.* **hyll, gata**); Hippmoor 1776 N, c.1776 N (*Hippmoor or Upper Moor Close* 1684, *Hipp moor or upper moor* 1685, *Hupmoor Leas* 1693, *Hipmore Lease* 1705, *Hip-more Close* 1708, *Hipmore als Upper Moor* 1710, - *alias upper moor* 1720 N, *the upper Moore Close* 1673 D, *Vppmoor close, the Upper Moor Close* 1673 N, *v.* **mōr**^{1}); Holms, Holms flg 1772 (*les Holmes* 1623, *the Hoolmes* 1662, *a furlong cauled the hollmes* 1663, *the Holmes* 1666, 1669, *the holmes* 1673, y^e *Holmes* 1703, 1706, *the Holmes furlong, Holmes hedge* 1735 D (*v.* **holmr**); (the) Home Cl 1762, 1819, the Whome Cl 1772 (the Whome Platt 1772, *infra*, seems to be a different piece of land); Homehold Cl 1776 D; Horse Common 1767 S, 1790 (*the Horse Comon* 1739, cf. Snape Carr *infra*); the Housedale Cl 1771 (*v.* under Blake Hows flg *supra*); Howsel Btm c.1776 N, Housel - 1812, Housel Rd 1812; Howl Ing 1767 S, 1767 N, - Ings 1790, Howling Carr 1790 *LTR* (*Upper Howleings* 1673 D, 1684, *Lower* -, *Upper Howlinges* 1684, 1685, *uper howlings* 1685, *Upper and lower Howlings* 1720; the forms are too late to suggest an etymology for the first el.; the second is **eng**); Jolland Carr 1790 *LTR* (the first el. is no doubt a surn.); Kelsey Bottom 1762, c.1776, - bottam 1772 (*Kelsey bottom* 1733 N, *v.* **botm**); Kelsey dale furlong 1772, Kelsey Dale c.1776 N, 1793, 1812 (1703, *le dale* 1376, *Kelsey dale* 1623, 1733 N, - (*sike or*) *daile* 1662, 1663 T, 1666, 1669, 1673 T; it is *Kelsey South-dail* 1706, *v.* **sīc, deill**); Gt -, Lt Lair Sikes 1774 (*Laresikes Close* 1598, *new* -, *old lar sikes* 1673 N, *Old Laresikes, new Larsikes* 1673 D, *New* -, *old Lare Sikes* 1684, *new* - *old Larsikes* 1685, *great Layer Sikes* 1714, *Great* - 1720 R, 1745, *Little* - 1714, *little* - 1720, *Little Layer Sykes* 1745, 'the muddy ditches', *v.* **leirr, sík**, probably a Scand. compound);

Lamb Coates Btm 1767 S, Low Lamb Coates 1767 S, Lamb Cotes Btm 1790 (*Lambecotes* a1218 RA iv, *Lamcotes* 1276 Ipm, 1376, *lamcoots* 1663 T, *East* - 1666, 1669, *east* - 1673, *East lamcootes or Tythedaile* 1662 (*v.* tēoða, deill), *East Lamcots* 1703, - *lamcoat* 1706, *v.* lamb, cot, and botm); Laundry Gate 1771, Laundry Gate 1772, Landtree Gate c.1776 N (*Langedicate* eHy3 (1409) Gilb, *Langdikgat* 1376, *Landiegate* 1626, *Landeygate* 1733 N, '(the road by or to) the long dike', *v.* lang, dīk, with gata); Leg Carr 1767 S (probably named from its shape, *v.* kjarr); Lingdales 1819 (*Lyndale close* 1611, *Lindale Close* 1626, *great lindale close* 1625 all *Terrier* (South Kelsey), *great Lyndale close* 1673 D, *Great Lindall Close* 1684, *Lower* -, *Upper Lindall* 1687, *Lynn Dale* 1710, *Lyndale* 1720 N, *the Lyndale close* 1735 N, probably 'the share of land where flax was grown', *v.* līn, deill); Longbar 1819 (perhaps for Long Car q.v.); Long Bottom Carr 1767 S, 1790 (*v.* botm, kjarr, cf. Kelsey Bottom *supra*); Long Carr 1767 S (*v.* kjarr); long cl 1767 N, Long Cl 1772, 1790, 1838 (1673 D, 1673 N, 1684, 1710, - *close* 1684, 1685, *long Close* 1720); long middle dike(s) 1767 N, 1767 S (- *Middledikes* 1694, - *middledikes* 1708, *v.* the Middle Dikes *infra*); Long Pce c.1776 N; Long Thorn Cl 1762, Long Thorn Rd 1812, Longthorns 1819 (*Langethorn* eHy3 (1409) Gilb, *Long Thorne al' Lindale close* 1673 N (*v.* Lingdailes *supra*), *Long Thorne Close* 1673 D, - *close* 1685, *longthorne Close* 1720, *Long-thorngate* 1733 N, *Longthorne close* 1735 N, *v.* 'the tall thorn-tree', *v.* lang, þorn and cf. (*le*) *Longethorn* PN Ch **3** 256); Love Leys 1819 (*lovell leazes close* 1673 N, *the Lovell Leaze Close* 1673 D, 1684, *Lovell Leys* 1716, - *Leys Close* 1720, *v.* læs 'pasture, meadow-land', the first el. being probably the surn. *Lovel*, cf. *Osberto Luuel*, who witnessed a North Kelsey charter eHy3 RA iv, the 1819 form arising from misdivision of *Love*(*ll*) *Leys*); Malton's Plat 1793 (from the surn. *Malton*, cf. perhaps John *Malton of Southkelsey* 1665 *Inv* and plat² 'a plot of ground' as elsewhere in the parish); Meadow Cl 1819; (the) Middle Dikes 1761, c.1776 N, 1776 N, 1790, 1796, 1798, Middledikes 1778 (1633 *MiscDon 554*), Middle Dykes 1853 *MiscDon 140*, Middle Dyke(s) Carr 1769, 1828 (*v.* kjarr), (*myddledikes* 1598, *Middledike* 1655, *middledikes* 1687, *Midledike* 1691 *MiscDon 509*, *Middledykes* 1728 *ib*, *great middle dikes* 1635 (c.1900) *LindDep 78*, *Summer-eaten Middle Dikes* 1708, *v.* middel, dīk, with hēafod and for *summer-eaten v.* Summer-eaten Marsh in Habrough f.ns. (a)); Mill Gate c.1776, Mill Rd 1812 (*via vocat' hye gayt vell' old mylne gayt* 1557 *MiscDon 554*, *the Millgate* 1733 N, *v.* myln, gata, and *Hauerocthorn' infra*); North Carrs 1798 (*Northkarr* 1556, *Northkerre* m17 *Monson*, *Lower* -, *Upper North Carrs* 1687 *v.* kjarr); Nordale, North-dale Furlong 1771, North Dale Btm 1812 (*the North Dale farme* 1607); North -, South Middle Dikes Heads 1790 (*v.* hēafod and (the) Middle Dikes *supra*); North Plat c.1776 N *v.* plat² 'a small piece of ground'); the Occupation Lane 1828 ('a green lane allowing access to strips in the open field'); Odling Cl 1812 (named from the

surn. *Odling*, cf. Jackson *Odling* 1832 *BT*); Open Gad meadow (at Starham) 1813
(*v.* **gadd**^{2}); oxland dale 1772 (*v.* **oxa, land**, with **deill**); (the) Pease Cl c.1776 N,
1776 D, 1776 N, 1790 *LTR* (*the great -, the little pease Close* 1708, *v.* **pise**);
Lands called Peter in Moor 1812; Pettecoat Dale 1793 (the name of a small
triangular plot or portion of land, *v.* **deill**); Pimperknowl 1767 S, 1790; Pingle
1819, 1828 (*the little pingle* 1716, *- Pingle* 1720, 'the enclosure', *v.* **pingel**); the
Platt(s) 1772, 1796 (*v.* **platt**^{2}); Puge Carr (*sic*) 1762; Ridge 1767 S; Rouel Cl
1776 N; Round Cl c.1776 N (*the round close* 1708); Rush Carr 1767 S, 1790 (*v.*
risc, kjarr); Salters Pinfold c.1776 N (*Salter pind fould* 1606, from the
occupational name or derived surn. and **pynd-fald**); Sand Cl 1761, c.1776 N,
1793, 1796, 1798, 1819 (1710 D, *the -* 1685), Sand Cl Plat c.1776 N (*v.* **sand,
clos(e), plat**^{2}); Sand Land flg 1772, (cf. *Sandlandes* 1623, *v.* **sand, land**, with
furlang); Sann(d)by Gate (*sic*) 1812 (from the surn. *Saun(d)by* and **gata**, cf.
Nathaniel *Saunby* 1767 S); Seg Carr 1790, 1790 *LTR* ('the marsh where sedge
grows', *v.* **secg, kjarr**, *seg* being a Scandinavianised form); The Seven Acres 1838;
Shortbutt Flg c.1776 N (*short buts* 1669, *shortbutts Close* 1673 T, *Shorte butts*
1693, *Short Butts* 1698, *shorbuts close* 1662, *short butts Close* 1666, *ye Short Butts
Close* 1706, *Short Butt close* 1710, *short butts* 1720, *v.* **sc(e)ort, butte**); Snape
c.1776 (1607, 1708), Snape Carr 1767 S, 1790 (cf. *Snape close* 1673 N, 1673 D,
1683 N, 1687, *-Close* 1684, 1685, 1733 D, *- or Snape Common* 1734, *Snape
Common otherwise Horse Common* 1748, 'the bog with a patch of scanty grass',
the first el. being probably **snap**, rather than **snæp**, with **kjarr**); the Middle
South Cl 1839; South Dike c.1776; the South east cl 1839; Long Spellah 1772,
1793, Short *-* 1772, 1793, Spellar Flg, Long Spella (*sic*) c.1776 N (probably
'speech mound', a community assembly place, *v.* **spell, haugr**); Square Cl 1838
(named from its shape); Stack Yard Cl 1838; Standwells 1772, Sandwells (*sic*)
c.1776, Stanwells 1812 (1733, *Steyn Well, Staynwell*' a1218 RA iv, *Stanewell*' 1557
MiscDon 554, v. **stān, wella**, the a1218 forms being from the cognate Scand.
steinn; some forms develop to *Stand-*, influenced by the intrusive *-d-* in the 1772
spellings); One Stinting ... North of the Stinter 1772 (note the appellative use
of **stinting**, presumably in the dial. sense 'a portion of common meadow set
apart for one man's use', *Stinter* is probably used with a similar sense, but the
word is not recorded in dictionaries); Stone Bridge cl 1822, 1840 *Dixon* (*the
stone brige* 1579, *stonebridge close* 1662, 1663, *stone bridge -* 1666, 1669,
Stonebridge Close 1673 T, *Stone Brigg:-* 1703, *Stone Brigg -* 1706, self-explanatory,
but the Scandinavianised forms in *-brigg* are worthy of note); a place known by
the Name of Strowm, Strown (*sic*) flg 1772, Stroum Furlong 1771, Strown 1812
(*Strome* 1653 *Monson, Strome Walk* 1703); Stub Firs Flg c.1776 N ('a cleared
area on which gorse grew', *v.* **stubb, fyrs**, cf. *stoubelandes* (*sic*) l13 *LindDep
88*); Swinsty Gate 1771, Swin(e)sty Gate 1772, Swinstead *-* (*sic*) c.1776 N,

Swinstee Butts 1812 (*Swynesstigd'* c.1218 RA iv, *le swyn stye* 1551, *Swine stie gate* 1662, *Swinestie gate* 1663 T, 1666, *swinestie* - 1673 T, *swine stie* - 1669, *Swinsty Gate* 1703, *Swinstygate* 1733 N 'the path, narrow road for swine', *v.* swin[1], stigr, with gata); Syke Flg 1793, the Sykes 1812 (*lee sik* 1598, *lee* = *le*, *v.* sik); Teanby Mills 1828; Ten Acre Carr 1767 S, 1790; The Ten Acres 1838; Ten Gad Coche, Thirteen Gad c.1776 (*the 9 gadds*, *the Thirteen Gadds* 1635 (c.1900) *LindDep 78*, *the thirteen gadds* 1702, *v.* gadd[2]); Tesh's Homestead 1776 N, Mr John Tesh's Farm c.1776 (named from the surn. *Tesh*, cf. also John *Tesh* 1676 *BT*); The Thorn-Tree Cl 1838 (cf. *Thornes gate* 1618, *Thorn Pingle* 1733 D, *v.* þorn, gata, pingel, cf. *in Spinis* 1327 *SR*, *en le Thornes de North'kelsey* 1329 *Ass* both (p)); Toft Hill flg 1772 (*a furlong cauled Toft* 1666, *Tooft* 1669, *v.* toft 'a curtilage', hyll, furlang); Turf Carr 1767 N, 1767 S, c.1776 N, 1776 N, 1790 (1703, *turffe carr* 1598, *Turfe Carr* 1615, *Turffe Carre* 1629, *Turffe Carres* 1635 (c.1900) *LindDep 78*, *Turfe Care* 1663 T, 1669, *- Car* (*Close*) 1666, 1673 T, *Marris Turfe Carr* 1615 (cf. Grange Carr *supra*), *Turfe Carr* 1691 *MiscDon 509*, 1728 *ib*, *Turff-carr* 1706, *the turf-carr* 1708, *turfe Carr* 1720 *TLE*, 'the carr from which peat was got', *v.* turf, kjarr); Twelve Acre Carr 1767 S, 1790 (*v.* kjarr); twelve Acre Cl 1807; South East Twenty Acres Car 1789, North West twenty -, South East Twenty acre Car 1796, the South East -, the North West Twenty Acres Car 1798 (*the South West twenty Acres Carr* 1748, *v.* kjarr); the Vicarage Carr 1762 (cf. Vicarage *supra*); the Vicars Rd 1864; The Second west cl 1839; West low Fd c.1776 N; West Plat c.1776 N (*v.* plat[2]); the Willows, Willows flg 1772, Willows Dale 1812 (cf. *the west willowes* 1579, *y*[e] *West Willowes* 1612 *Terrier* (South Kelsey), *West willowes furlong* 1623, and *Brices Willows* in (b) *infra*); the Whome Platt 1772 ('the home plot', in West Field, and so presumably distinct from Whome Close, *v.* the Home Cl *supra*, which was in East Field); Withlands 1819 (*v.* land).

(b) *the Ash Close* 1693, 1705 (self-explanatory); *a Close ... called Bards* 1595 (named from the surn. *Bard*, cf. *Raphe Bard* 1595); *furlong called Little Barwith* 1629; *lez baylhouselandes* 1558 (this would appear to be from unrecorded ME *baille-hous* 'a house with a pallisade' and land); *bayslandes* 1554; *birke pound* 1706; *a Furlong called Brawyn* 1618, *a furlong called Browing* 1655; *Brice Willows* 1715 *Yarb*, 1743 *LindDep 82* (presumably from the surn. *Brice*); *bundale Close* 1720 (perhaps *v.* bune 'reed' and deill); *the Butts* 1629, 1710, *the Buttclose* 1657, *the Butt Close* 1673 D, 1673 N, 1684, *- close* 1685, *But(t)close* 1710, 1720 (these forms may not belong together, but *the Butts* probably refer to archery buts, *v.* butt[2]); *Cadney Close* 1623 (near Starham); *Cattam hill* 1693, 1705; *the Coney-garth Close* 1623 D, *the Conny garth close* 1673 N, *Coney garth Close* 1684, *- close* 1685, *Coney Green* 1710, *Cunny Green* 1720 ('rabbit warren', *v.* coni, garðr,

coninger 'a rabbit warren'); *the Corne field* 1693, - *Field* 1698; *Crow Garth* 1710, *Crowgarth* 1720 (*v.* **garðr**); *Dodeker* 1276 Ipm (from the OE per.n. *Dod(d)a* or perhaps the surn. *Dodd* and **kjarr**, as suggested by Dr J. Insley); *donyby* 1340 (p) ('down, lower in the village', *v.* **dūne, í, bȳ**, and cf. *Vpiby infra*); *dothercarre-Close* 1633 *MiscDon 554, dother Carr* (*close*) 1676 N, 1688, *Dotter Car close* 1715 (perhaps 'reedy or rush-covered carr', from **kjarr** with *dodder* MnE dial. 'coarse reeds or rushes in swampy land', cf. *Rutland Gloss.* quotation, NED s.v.); *Dove close* 1710, *Doveclose* 1720; *Elsham More Close or Elsham Becke Close* 1622 (sold by George *Elsham of Serebie,* but the family is found in the parish from at least Lawrence *elsam* 1562 BT); *estholmes* 1376 Monson (*v.* **ēast, holmr**, and cf. West Holmes *supra*); *Estyton'* 1340, *Estiton'* 1344 FF both (p) (*v.* **ēast, í, tūn**); *the fleat dicke* 1606, *fleet-dike* 1623 N, *Fleet dike* 1638, *fleet -* 1677, *Flette -* 1690, *fleete -* 1706, *Fleetdike* 1697, 1702, *Fleete dike* 1700 T, *Fleet-dike* 1707 (*v.* **flēot, dík**); *Forskes Holes* (sic) 1340, *frostall close* (sic) 1708 ('frog holes', *v.* **frosc, forsc, hol**[1], the earliest form is Scandinavianised); *the Freehold' Carre* 1629, *the freehold Carre* 1635 (c.1900) *LindDep 78, the freehoulders Carr* 1662, *freehouldes Car* 1663, 1669, *freehoulds Carr* 1666, 1673 T, *Freeholds Carr* 1706 ('carr cultivated in common by the freeholders', *v.* **freehold, kjarr**); *Graideng* eHy3 (1409) Gilb (Dr J. Insley suggests that the first el. is ON *greiðr* 'ready, useful', cf. dial. *gradely* from ON *greiðligr,* the second el. is **eng**); *Grasse becke Furlong* 1618 (*v.* **bekkr**); *Greens Meadow* 1738 (probably from the surn. *Green,* cf. John *Greene* 1623, William *Greene* 1673 D); *a place comonly called Halker alias Helker* 1685; *Hardynwell' syke* 1557 *MiscDon 554* (from the surn. *Harding* (OE *Harding*) and **wella** 'a spring', with **sík**); *Hauerocthorm'* a1218 RA iv, *Haueracthorne gayt alt' nuncupat' hye gayt* 1557 *MiscDon 554, le high gate* 1623, *the hie gate* 1666 (*v.* **þorn, hēah, gata**, cf. *regie strate Linc'* a1218 RA iv, and Mill Gate (a) *supra; Haueroc-* is obscure); *Hopp Garth* 1710, *Hopgarth* 1720 ('hop yard', *v.* **hoppe, garðr**); *ye houllney* 1703 (obscure); *Kellokeswath* 1190 (1301) Dugd vi (Dr John Insley suggests that the first el. is the Irish pers.n. *Cellach* (cf. D. ÓCorráin and F. Maguire, *Gaelic Personal Names,* Dublin, 1981, pp. 48-49). *Kellok* has been noted in LNR as a surn. in Walter *Kelloc* Hy3 *HarlCh* 49A23, a Killingholme charter. The second el. is ON **vað** 'a ford'); *the Kilnhouse Close* 1693, 1705, *little and great Kilnhouse closes* 1720 (self-explanatory); *Kirk Choome* 1662, - *Coombe* 1666, *the kirke Choombe* 1663 T, *Kirke Chome* 1669, *kirkecoombe* 1673 T, *cerkome* 1703 (perhaps 'church hollow', *v.* **kirkja, cumb**, though the rarity of **cumb** in L is to be noted); *theland syke* 1595 (*v.* **land, sík**); *les Langeswers* (sic) 1340 (obscure); *locketts pingle* 1710 N, *Lockett pingle* 1716 (*v.* **pingel**, the first el. is from the surn. *Lockett*); *Long swarth* (sic) 1656, *long Swath* 1693, *Long Swath* 1705, *Long Swaith close* 1710, - *Close* 1720 ('long strip of grassland', *v.* **lang, swæð**); *Lynams* (*Close*) 1629, 1630; *one broode land ... called -, - cauled by the name of the mare and* *foale* 1662, 1663 T, 1673 ('a foaling strip of land', *v.* **land**); *marisco de Northkeleseye* 1190 (1301) Dugd vi (North Kelsey marsh); *Mawdsons platt* 1733 N (from the surn. *Mawdson*, cf. Roger *Mawdson* 1623, John *Mawdson* 1646 *BT*, and plat², and cf. *Roger Mawdsons cloose* c.1600); *Netker* 1276 Ipm (perhaps *v.* **nēat** 'cattle' and **kjarr**, for the first el. cf. Neatgangs Fm in Goxhill *supra*); *the North End Farme* 1710; *Lower -, Upper north Garth* 1736; *Northehall'* 1427 *HarlCh* (self-explanatory, cf. Easthall Fm *supra*); *Northiby* 1327, 1332 *SR*, 1340, 1344 *FF* all (p) (*v.* **norð, í, bȳ**, cf. *Vpiby infra*); *Northlanges* lHy2 Dane, *Nordlanges* eHy3 (1409) Gilb (*v.* **norð, lang²** 'a long strip of land'); *selionem prioris & monialiu' de Ormesby* 1491, *Nunn Dale* 1693, 1705, *Nundale Close* 1710 (*v.* **nunne, deill**, from the nuns of North Ormsby L); yᵉ *out dicke* 1606, *the outdike* 1623, *a river called the Outdike* 1638, *the out dike* 16697, yᵉ *outdike* 1690, 1700 T, 1703, 1706, *the Out Dike* 1707 ('outer drainage ditch', or 'outflow ditch', *v.* **ūt, dík**); *(the) Pid Close* 1673 N, *Pidd -* 1673 D, 1684, 1685, 1710 N, 1720 (from the surn. *Pidd*, cf. John *Pidd* of South Kelsey 1666 *Inv*, George *Pidd* 1687 *Dixon*); *Scrub(b) Pingle* 1739, 1748 ('enclosure overgrown with brushwood', *v.* **scrubb, pingel**); *le Sike* 1616 (*v.* **sīc, sík**); *Stokes Brigges* 1340 (the sense of *Stokes* is not clear here); *Stokynges* 1376 ('land cleared of stumps', *v.* **stoccing**); *Sworthkerthorn'* a1218 RA iv (Dr John Insley points out that the first el. is probably ON *svartr* 'black' and for the *-o-* spelling, cf. SPNLY 274, s.n. Svartr; it is, of course, possible that the first el. is the pers.n. *Svartr* itself. In any case, this would be a Scand. compound, the second el. being **kjarr** 'a marsh', with **þorn** 'a thornbush'); *Tatam hill Close* 1720 (the first part is presumably a surn.); *the thirteene rigges* 1623 (*v.* **hryggr** in the sense 'a measure of land'); *the Town gadds* 1702 (*v.* **gadd²**); *(the) Tranam close* 1598, *John Marrys More Close ... heretofore two Closes one part whereof was heretofore knowne and called by the name of Tranam* 1622, *Traneham* 1678 (it is impossible in this area to be certain of the second el. of *Tranam*, but *-am*, *-ham* is often a later reflex of ON **holmr** 'an island (of land), a water-meadow'; the first el. is ON **trani** 'a crane' or the derived pers.n. For the surn. *Marris*, cf. also John *Marris* 1615); *Tythedaile* 1662, 1673 T, *(the) Tithe daile* 1663 ib, 1666, *tithe -* 1669, *Tythe Daile* 1703, 'the tithe portion of land', possibly for the tithe of lambs, cf. Lamb Coates Bottom (a) *supra*, *v.* **tēoða, deill**); *Vpiby* 1327 *SR* (p) ('higher up in the village', *v.* **upp, í, bȳ**); *Wenlergitefeudland* eHy3 (1409) Gilb (*Wenlergite-* is obscure; for *-feudland v.* **feld, land**).

Killingholme

KILLINGHOLME
Chelvingehou (sic) 1086 DB

Cheluingeholm (2x) 1086 DB, 1180, 1181, 1182, 1183 O
Chiluingheholm (4x) c.1115 LS
Kiluingeholm c.1141 BMFacs, c.1155, c.1185, 1190-95 Dane,
    1194 ChancR, 1205 OblR, 1205 ChR, 1218, 1219 Ass
Chilmingeholme (sic) 1155-60 Dane
Killingeholm 1194, 1195 P, 1196 ChancR, 1202 Ass, 1205 Cur
    (p), 1218 Ass, 1235-36 Fees (p), -*helm'* (sic) 1205 P, -*hum'*
    (sic) 1216 OblR (p)
Kiluingeham 1176 P (p), -*hom'* 1206 FF, *Kylvengeham* 1225 Cur
Cheluingholme 1086 DB
Kiluingholm 1143-47 Dane, c.1153 (e14) Bridl, c.1155, eHy2
    Dane, 1160-66 ib, 1166-75 Fulstow (p), a1180 (e13) *NCot et*
    freq to 1264 RRGr, -*holme* c.1150 Dane, *Kilvingholm* 1152
    (e14) YCh iii, eHy2 (e13) *NCot*, 1166-81 YCh v, c.1180
    Bly, *et passim* to 1319 Pat, *Kilwingholm* Hy2 (e13) *NCot*,
    c.1185 Dane, p1186 ib (p), 1195-96, R1 ib, l12 ib (p),
    1238-43 Fees, 1303 FA, *Kilwyngholme* 1346 ib, *Kyluingholm*
    1245 FF, 1269 *HarlCh*, 1301 *FF*, 1317 *HarlCh*, *Kylvingholm*
    1254 ValNor, 1281 QW, 1292 Ch, 1386 Fine, - *alias*
    Killingholm 1305 Ipm
Chiluingholm 1150-60 Dane, lHy2 (e13) *NCot*, *chiluinholm*,
    chilvinholm 1159-81 (e13) *ib*
Killvingholm l12 RA iv
Kilingholm 1148-56 BS (p), 1198, 1204 Cur (p), 1212 Fees,
    1240 FF, 1242-43 Fees *et passim* to 1353 Ipm, -*yngholm*
    1336 *HarlCh*, 1350 Ipm, 1407 Cl, *Kylingholm(e)* 1350 FF,
    1266 Misc, 1291 RSu, 1303 FA, 1316 Orig, 1316 Fine,
    -*yngholm(e)* 1317 Pat, 1327 *SR*, 1331 Ipm, 1331 Cl *et*
    passim to 1428 FA
Killingholm(e) 1190 (1301) Dugd vi, 1197, 1198 P, 1207 ib
    (p), 1208, 1231, 1256 FF, 1268 Ch, 1275 *NCot et freq* to
    1373 Peace, 1507 Ipm, 1556 InstBen *et passim*, -*yngholm(e)*
    1323 Pat, 1327 Banco, 1336 Cl, 1345 Ipm *et passim* to 1402
    Fine, *Kyllyngholm(e)* 1228-32 (1409) Gilb, 1291 Tax, 1316,
    1365 Pat, 1383 Cl, 1461, 1549, 1564 Pat, -*whome* 1486-93
    ECP xx
Kelyngholm(e) e13 *NCot*, 1294 *Ass*, 1298 Ass, 1332 *SR*, 1335
    HarlCh et passim to 1458 Pat, 1502 Ipm, 1530 Wills iii,
    1546 LP xxi, -*ingholm(e)* 1301 Pat, 1315 Ipm, 1335 Pat, 1495
    IBL, 1535-46 *MinAcct*, 1549 Pat, *Kelwyngholm* 1303 FA

Kellingholm 1213 OblR, 1327 Banco, *-ynghollme* (sic) 1494 Ipm
Kylvingham 1292 RSu
Killyngham 1305 Ass, 1404 Fine, 1405 Cl, *-ingham* 1542-43
    Dugd vi, 1552 Pat, *Kyllyngham* 1473 ib, 1538-39 *AD*, 1541
    Dugd v, 1553 Pat, *-ingham* 1551 ib
Kelingham 1519 DV i, *-yngham* 1549 Pat

NORTH KILLINGHOLME is recorded in *ecclesia sancti Petri de Nortkiluingholm que alio nomine uocatur Haltune* 1149-62 Dane, *-Haltuna* c.1155 ib, *north Kiluingholme* John HarlCh, *North Kiluingholm* 1160-66 Dane, *Northkilvingh'* R1 (1318) Ch, *Killingholme Northend* e17 Nelthorpe, *- north end* 1711 *Foster, - North* 1749 *ib*, 1830 Gre.

This is a very difficult name. Ekwall, DEPN s.n., suggests that the original name may have been an OE **Cylfingas* (from *Cynwulfingas*) to which was added OScand **holmr**. "Or it may simply be 'the HOLM of the *Cynwulfingas*'". This is extremely unlikely since the gen.pl. of a group-name like *Cynwulfingas* 'the people, the followers of Cynwulf' as the first el. of a p.n. is confidently believed to belong to an early stratum of name-giving in this country. Gillian Fellows-Jensen (SSNEM 218) supposes that "it might rather be an inhabitants' name in *-ingas* derived from OE (Anglian) *celf* "calf". The second el. is the Scand appellative *holmr* m. in the sense "island of higher ground in a low-lying marshy area" and this would be topographically appropriate. She goes on to argue that spellings in *Kil-* would be the result of the raising of *e* to *i* before a dental consonant and compares this with Kilpin YE from OE **celf-penn*. She does not note that the *c-* in *celf* was pronounced [ʧ], so that initial *K-* in Killingholme in this case would be due to Scand. influence.

A likely explanation is that Killingholme was originally a p.n. derived from the gen.pl. of a group name compounded with OE **hām** 'a homestead', but the source of the group name is uncertain. The most plausible solution has been proposed by Dr John Insley, who takes it to be the pers.n. *Cēolwulf*, giving a form **Cēolwulfingahām*, later **Cēolfingahām*, 'the homestead of the followers of Cēolwulf', accepting that this name originally had OE **hām** as second el. He points out that the DB form in *-hou* and the DB and ME forms in *-holm(e)* show confusion with Scand.

haugr 'a mound, a hill' and **holmr** 'an island, a piece of raised ground in a low-lying marshy area, etc', the latter completely replacing *-ham*. He argues that "the initial consonant, Germanic /k/, is palatalised to [c] before primary front vowels in Primitive OE. The phonetic development leads to the fully assibilated late OE /ʧ/ by way of an intermediate stage [tç]." He further points out that the fact that the Scand. settlers could associate the initial consonant of such p.ns. as Keswick Cu, Nf, YWR from OE *Cēsewīc*, etc. with North Germanic /k/ shows that this process was still incomplete in the Danelaw at the time of the Scand. invasions. Thus, there is no difficulty in taking the initial consonant of Killingholme to be the original Primitive OE [c] contained in the reflexes of the OE pers.n. *Cēolwulf*, on the palatalisation and assibilation discussed above, *v.* further Brunner paragraph 207, Anm. 9. The OE pers.n. *Cēolwulf* occurs as *Cēolulf* already in the 8th century (*v.* Feilitzen 76), and the reduced form *Cēolf* occurs as the first el. of Chelston So (DEPN s.n.) and Chelveston (PN Nth 190). Finally, Dr Insley "comments that the ME forms in *-i-* reflect late OE shortening of /ēo/, followed by mononthongisation to /ø/ and subsequent unrounding to /e/, which was raised to /i/, *v.* further Jordan paragraph 34". So, it is likely that Killingholme means 'the homestead of the *Cēolwulfingas* ('the followers of Cēolwulf')', *v.* **hām**, in which **hām** was replaced by OScand **holmr** in the sense 'island of higher ground in a low-lying marshy area'.

INGOLD TOFT (lost), *Hyngeltoftes* e13 *HarlCh*, *hingeltoftes* Hy3 *ib*, *Ingeltoft*(*es*), *Engeltoftes* lHy3 (Ed1) *Newh*, *Engeltoftes* l13 *HarlCh*, *Ingold Toft* 1824 O, *Engletoft* 1828 Bry, probably 'Ingeld's curtilage(s), messuage(s)', *v.* **toft**, the first el. then being the ON pers.n. *Ingialdr*, ODan *Ingiald*, *Ingœld*, rather than the rare OE *Ingeld*. In this case, *Ingold Toft* would be a Scand. compound. It was situated on the boundary with East Halton, due west of Chase Hill Fm at approx. TA 152197.

BURKINSHAW'S COVERT, - *Cover* 1824 O, *Brikinshaws Cover* (sic) 1828 Bry, *Burkinshaws Cover* 1830 Gre, from the *Burkinshaw* family, cf. Thomas *Burkinshaw* 1824 *Yarb*. BYGOTT'S COVERT, 1824 O, 1833 *Yarb*, *Bygotts Cover* 1830 Gre, *Bygott's Plantation* 1869

Yarb, from the *Bygott* family, cf. John *Bygott* 1779 *Yarb*. CHASE HILL FM, *Chase Hill Farm House* 1833 *Yarb* and it is *New England* 1828 Bry, no doubt a nickname of remoteness, since the farm is situated close to the boundary with East Halton. CHASE HILL WOOD is *Chase Hill* 1824 O, 1828 Bry, 1830 Gre, *Chase Hill Cover* 1833 *Yarb*, *Chase hill Plantation* 1869 *ib*. CHURCH SIDE is named from East Halton Church, *Halton Church* 1824 O. EAST FIELD RD, 1833 *Stubbs*, *East Lane* 1828 Bry, cf. *In Orientali Campo* John *HarlCh*, *in orientali campo* l12, eHy3 (Ed1) *Newh*, m13, Hy3 *HarlCh*, c.1311 *Anc*, - *de Kiluingh'* Hy3 *HarlCh*, - *de Kiluingh'* Hy3 *HarlCh*, - *de Kilwingholm* Hy3 *ib*, *in orientali Campo* 1278 *ib*, *orient' campo* 1581 *Nelthorpe*, *theast and west fieildes* (sic) 1587 *Yarb*, *the est felde* 1601, *the Easte feild* 1606, *the east feeld* 1626, *the East feild* 1664, *the east field* 1822 all *Terrier*, *the East Field of North Killingholme* 1779 *Encl4*, self-explanatory, *v.* ēast, feld, one of the open fields of Killingholme. FOX COVERT, - *Cover* 1828 Bry. KILLINGHOLME MARSHES, 1824 O, cf. *in marisco de Kilwingholm* lHy2 (e13) *NCot*, *in marisco* l12 (Ed1) *Newh*, - *de Kilwingh'* eHy3 (Ed1) *ib*, *ad Mariscum* 1230-50, Hy3 *HarlCh*, *super Mariscum*, *in Marisco de Kilingholm'* Hy3 *ib*, *in Marisco de Kiluingholm* c.1270 *ib*, *Marisco* l13 *ib* (p), *Kelyngholme marsh* 1546 LP xxi, *the marshes* 1581 *Yarb*, *Killingholme marshe* 1582 *ib*, *the mayrche* c.1584 *Nelthorpe*, *the marshe* 1585 *ib*, *the marsh* 1601, 1626 *Terrier*, *the Marsh* 1690 *ib*, *Killingholme marsh* 1733 *Nelthorpe*, *in Australi Marisco de Kyluingh'* 1263 *HarlCh*, *in australi Marisco in Kyluing'* Hy3 *ib*, *Killingholme St marshe* 1587 *Yarb*, *the southend Marsh* 1713 *ib* ('the south marsh'), *the north marshe* 1587 *Yarb*, *the northend marsh of Killingholme* 1612 *Terrier*, *the Northend Marsh* 1634 *ib*, 1650 *Nelthorpe*, *the northend marsh* 1664, 1671 *Terrier*, *the Northend Marsh of Killingholme* 1711 *Foster*, *the North end Marsh of Killingholme* 1713 *Yarb*, *ye northeren marsh* 1708 *Terrier*, *the Northern marsh* 1745 *ib*, ('North Killingholme marsh'), self-explanatory, *v.* mersc. LOW FARM is *Long Looks* 1824 O, 1828 Bry, 1830 Gre, presumably a derogatory nickname. MANOR HO. MEERGATE HEDGE (lost), 1824 O, cf. *maregate* lHy2 (Ed1) *Newh*, John *HarlCh*, eHy3, m13, Hy3 (Ed1) *Newh*, *le* - Hy3 *HarlCh*, *uiam que uocatur le Maregate* Hy3 *ib*, *viam que vocat' maregate* lHy3 (Ed1) *Newh*, *Margate* l13 *HarlCh*, (*le*) *Margate* Hy3 *ib*, lHy3 (1301) Ch, l13 *HarlCh*, *margatte* c.1311 *Anc*, *margat*, *mare gaat* (sic) 1585 *Nelthorpe*, *the mare gate* 1601, *maregate* 1664, *Margate*

1671, *Maregate* 1679, *mare Gate* 1708 all *Terrier, Marrgates* 1733
Nelthorpe, Meargate 1777 *Yarb,* and *Nordmargate* John *HarlCh,*
nordmaregate Hy3 *ib, suhtmaregate* m13 (Ed1) *Newh, South mar gayt*
1585 *Nelthorpe, the South maregate* 1634 *Terrier, South margate* 1638
ib, Grangmargate lHy3 (Ed1) *Newh,* 'the boundary road', *v.*
(ge)mǣre, gata, distinguished also as 'north', 'south' and 'grange'. It
formed in part the boundary between North Killingholme and East
Halton; for the forms found in East Halton documents, *v. Meergate
Hedge* in East Halton *supra.* MIDDLE GATE LANE (lost), 1828
Bry, *v.* **middel, gata,** forming in part the boundary with East Halton.
EAST & WEST MIDDLE MERE RD, *Middle Mere Road, West
Middle Mere Road* 1779 *EnclA,* 1833 *Stubbs,* cf. *mittillmar* 1585
Nelthorpe, 'the middle boundary', *v.* **middel, (ge)mǣre.** West
Middle Mere Rd is called *South Mere Gate Lane* 1828 Bry. It
forms in part the boundary between North and South Killingholme.
NORTH KILLINGHOLME HAVEN is *Killingholme Haven* 1779,
1780 *Yarb,* 1824 O, 1830 Gre, and cf. perhaps *a Crike called North
Crike* 1613 *MinAcct.* NORTH GARTHS, *north garths* 1585
Nelthorpe, Nor Garths 1833 *Yarb,* 'the north enclosure, small plots
of ground', *v.* **norð, garðr.** ROSPER RD, cf. *Rosseberghe* John
HarlCh, -berg Hy3, 13 *ib, -bergh* Hy3 *ib,* lHy3 (1301) Ch, l13
HarlCh, 1311 *Anc, -berghe* Hy3 *HarlCh, -berc* Hy3 *ib, Rosberg* Hy3
ib, Rosbar hadland 1634 *Terrier, Rosber hedland* 1638 *ib* (*v.*
hēafod-land), *Rosper* e17 *Nelthorpe,* 1833 *Yarb, Raspar* 1779, 1833,
1869 *ib, Rasperbank* 1733 *Nelthorpe,* probably 'the horses' hill,
mound', from **hross** and **berg** (or possibly OE **beorg**) and very likely
a Scand. compound, cf. *Rossebergh* PN YW 7 209, s.v. **hross.**
WOODLANDS.

SOUTH KILLINGHOLME is *Sud Kiluingholm* 1160-66 Dane,
Suthkilvingh' R1 (1318) Ch, *Sutd Kiluingholm* Hy3 *HarlCh, Suth
Kilwingh'* lHy3 (Ed1) *Newh, the Southend of Killingholme* 1665 *Inv,*
1713 *Yarb, the South End of Killingholme* 1692 *ib, Killingholme
South End* 1697 *Inv, Killingholm Southend* 1723 *ib, Killingholme
South end* 1757 *Yarb, Killingholme South* 1824 O, 1830 Gre, *South
Killingholme* 1828 Bry.

INGTON (lost), *toft de Enchetun* Hy2 Dane, *Enketoft* (sic) Hy2

(Ed1) *Newh, Bercarie de Enketun* Hy3 *HarlCh, enketun* m13, Hy3 *ib, Enketun* Hy3 (Ed1) *Newh* (p), *toft' de Enketon* m13 (Ed1) *ib, clausum de Enketon'* Hy3 *HarlCh, campo de Enketon'* Hy3 *ib, Enketon'* 1272 *ib,* l13 (l14) *Gox, Enketon Marfur* lHy3 (1301) Ch (*v.* **marfur**), *Bercariam de Enketon'* 1279 *HarlCh, Henketun, Hynketona* Hy3 *ib, Hincketon* c.1311 *Anc, Inckston close* 1709 *Terrier,* - *Close* 1745 *ib, Ington Close dike* 1779 *Yarb, Ington Close,* 1824, 1833, 1869 *ib,* - *Hill* 1833, 1869 *ib,* - *Bottom* 1869 *ib,* 'Ennica's farmstead', *v.* **tūn**, alternating once with **toft**. The first el. is an unrecorded OE pers.n. **Ennica,* probably a diminutive of OE *Enna* adduced for Enston (PN O 347), Eney (PN Berks 456) and *æt ennanbeorgum* (PN Berks 727, 729) in the bounds of Wootton and Sunningwell. Dr Insley compares this pers.n. with OHG *Enno* and "such Old Saxon formations as *Enike, Enikin, Ennelin*". The site of this lost settlement is indicated by the f.ns. on the 1833 and 1869 plans in the Earl of Yarborough's Estate Office, Brocklesby Park, at approx. TA 175164.

CAWBER FM, *Calueberg* Hy3 *HarlCh, calfbergmare* lHy3 (Ed1) *Newh* (*v.* **(ge)mære**), *Caleberc, Calberg* Hy3 *HarlCh, Calbergmare* 13 *ib,* 'the calves' hill', *v.* **calf, beorg, berg,** cf. Rosper Rd in North Killingholme *supra.* It is *Byrons F.^{m}* 1828 Bry. COW FM, cf. perhaps *Cow Close* 1833 *Yarb.* GREENGATE RD, cf. *Grenegate* l12 (Ed1) *Newh, le Grengate* Hy3 *HarlCh, Green Gate* 1777 *Yarb, viridum iter quod extendit usque ad Mariscum* 1230-50 *HarlCh,* 'the green, grassy road', *v.* **grēne^1, gata.** HOULTON FM. HOULTON'S COVERT, - *Cover* 1824 O, *Houltons Cover* 1828 Bry, 1830 Gre, named from the *Houlton* family, cf. George and Thomas *Houlton* 1824 *Yarb.* MARSH FM, cf. Killingholme Marshes *supra,* from which it was no doubt named. MILL HILL, cf. *Mill Hill Furlong* 1777 *Yarb,* and *de via molendini* e13 (Ed1) *Newh, the mill furlong* 1612, 1634, *the old milne* 1626 all *Terrier.* RYE HILL FM, *Ryehill farm* 1779 *Yarb, Rye Hill* 1824 O, 1830 Gre, *Rye Hill F.^{m}* 1828 Bry, cf. *Ryhill* Hy3, Ed1 *HarlCh, Ryhille* l13 (l14) *Gox, the Rye Hill* 1614 *Deeds, Rye hill* 1777, 1779 *Yarb,* 'the hill where rye grows', *v.* **ryge, hyll.** RYE HILL PLANTATIONS is *Fox Cover* 1828 Bry. SINKS COVERT, *Sinks Cover* 1833 *Yarb, Sink Wood* 1869 *ib,* cf. *Sencmare, Sencchermare, Senkemare* Hy3 *HarlCh* (*v.* **(ge)mære**), *Sinks* 1777, 1833 *Yarb.* It is *Fox's Cover* 1824, *Fox*

Cover 1830 Gre. This must be the same as dial. *sink* (EDD s.v. 13) 'a gutter, drain, sewer' recorded from North L and found in *Bell Sinks* in Goxhill f.ns. (b). The word is also recorded (as ME *sinke*) in NED s.v. from c.1440 as 'a pool or pit formed in the ground for the receipt of waste water' and from 1499 as 'a conduit, drain ... a sewer', *v.* also PN YW 7 243. Etymologically NED takes the noun *sink* to be from OE *sincan* 'to sink', but the early spellings here suggest that this is ME *senk* from OE *sencan* of similar meaning. The forms would then show the raising of *-e-* to *-i-* before a covered nasal (Jordan 34.2). The Covert lies low beside Skitter Beck and a small stream flows through it. It should be noted that Smith, PN YW 5 189, interprets the f.n. *Cramuill Sengk* 1278 as being from a surn. and ON **senk* 'a hollow where water collects'. SOUTH KILLINGHOLME GRANGE, *Grangia ... Abbatis ... de Neuhus ... que vocatur Suthus* ('south house') *in Killingholm* Ed1 *HarlCh*, *Kyllingholme graunge* 1569 *Yarb*, *Killingholme graunge* 1571 *ib*; if the earliest form refers to South Killingholme Grange, then it was a **grange** of Newsham Abbey in Brocklesby parish. SOUTH KILLINGHOLME HAVEN, 1830 Gre, cf. *a Crike called the South haven* 1613 *MinAcct* and North Killingholme Haven *supra*. WALMER HO is *Manor F.^{m}* 1828 Bry and *Houltons Ho* 1830 Gre, for which cf. Houlton's Covert *supra*. Cf. *Wallmoor Mear Furlong* 1777 *Yarb*, *Wallmere Plot* 1833 *ib*, *Wallmeer Plot* 1869 *ib*.

Field-Names

Forms dated c.1150, Hy2, lHy2, l12, eHy3, c.1245, m13², 1253, Hy3², lHy3², 1272² are (Ed1) *Newh*; John, e13, 1224, 1230-50, 1250, m13¹, 1263, Hy3¹, lHy3¹, c.1270, 1272¹, 1278, 1279, l13, 13, Ed1 are *HarlCh*; lHy3 (1301) are Ch; 1311, c.1311, 1521, 1530, 1531, 1533, 1584 are *Anc*; 1339, 1422, 1581¹, 1587, 1590, 1757, 1777, 1779¹, 1824, 1833 and 1869 are *Yarb*; 1581², 1583, c.1584, 1585, e17 and 1733 are *Nelthorpe*; 1779² are *EnclA*; 1601, 1606, 1612, 1626, 1634, 1638, 1664, 1671, 1679, 1690, 1700, c.1705, 1708, 1745 and 1822 are Terrier.

(a) Avenue (SK) 1833; Balemoor gate Cl 18 *Measure*; Barton Rd 1779² (to Barton upon Humber); Beck Bank 1833, 1869; Blaid Plot cl 1869; Bland Cl 1833, - cl 1869 (no doubt from the surn. *Bland*); Far -, First -, Gt Bottom 1833, 1869 (*v.* **botm**); Brameere 1833, -meeres 1869 (*Bramars, Bramar forland* 1585 (*v.*

furlang), perhaps 'the broad boundary, land on a boundary', v. brād, (ge)mǣre); Braysgate 1777; Gt -, Lt Brick Plat 1824 (v. plat^2 'a plot of land', as elsewhere in the parish), - Plot (SK) 1833, 1869, Brick Kiln Plat (SK) 1833, - Plot 1869; Bull Cl (SK) 1833, 1869 (1664, self-explanatory); Far -, First Cant Meere 1833, Cantmeer 1869 (*cantemare* 112, m13^2, the first el. may be the OE pers.n. *Canta*, a shortened form of *Cantwine*, probably found in *Cantan leah* 681 (10) (BCS 61 (S 236)) and suggested by Ekwall (DEPN s.n.) for Cantley Nf; the second el. is (ge)mǣre 'a boundary, etc.', with a similar development to *meer*(e) as occurs elsewhere in LNR); Carr Cl 1824, 1869, Carrhead 1779^1, Car (Cl) 1833, 1869, Far -, First Car Flg 1833, 1869 (cf. *le Ker* m13^2, 1253, Hy3^1, 1311, *del* - Hy3^1, *le ker* lHy3^2, *les kers* m13^2, *Kersic* eHy3, Hy3^1, *-sik* eHy3, lHy3^2, *-sike* m13^2, *-sick* lHy3 (1301), *Nordkersich* Hy3^1 (v. norð, sīc, sík), *the Carr* e17, *the great Carr* 1733, *Carr Close* 1664, *carr close* 1671, *ye Carr close* c.1705, *Kar forland* 1585, *Carre furlong* e17, *Carrffurlong* 1733 (v. furlang) ('the marsh', v. kjarr); Castor gate Marfur 1777 (cf. *Castergate* lHy2, lHy3^2, *-kate* (sic) e13, *Kastergate* lHy3^1, *castar gaat*, *Caster gat* 1601, *Caster gate* 1634, *great* - 1638, *Caistergate* 1733, *Caister road* 1708, *Caster Road* 1745, 'the road to Caistor', v. gata and marfur 'a boundary furrow', as freq. in this parish; note too the common use of *marfur* as an appellative in 1777 *Yarb*); Chappel Dale Marfurr 1777 (cf. *terre capele* Hy3^1, self-explanatory and v. marfur); Church Paddock 1833 (cf. *ad ecclesiam* 1327, 1332 SR (p), *Kirkehil* 112, Hy3^2, Hy3^1, *-hille* lHy3^2, Ed1, *Kirkhyl* lHy3^2, *nortekirchille*, *Sutkirckhille* m13^2, *le Kyrkeland* Hy3^1, - *Kirkland* lHy3^2 (v. hyll, land and the Church Cl in East Halton f.ns. (a) *supra*; it is noteworthy that all the early spellings are from ON kirkja 'a church'); Clay Hill (SK) 1833, Far -, First Clay Hill 1869; North Clough Rd 1779^2; Constable Marfur 1777 (cf. Castor gate Marfur *supra*); Long -, Nr Court Meer 1833, 1869 (no doubt *Court* is for *Cote*, v. cot 'a cottage, a shed'); Cover Btm, - Plot 1869; Covert Flg, - Pce, - Plot 1869; Dannets plat, - Garth 1779 (named from the family of John *Dannet* 1721 BT with plat^2 and garðr 'an enclosure, a small plot of ground'); The Dingwell 1869 (cf. *culture que vocatur ding* lHy2 (e13) NCot, *Dinge* 1205 ChR, Hy3^1, *ding, dyng, ad dinghe* all Hy3^1, *Ding'* lHy3 (1301), *Dynge* 1272^1, *Dingedale* R1 (1318) Ch (v. deill), probably from OE dynge 'a dung-heap'); Eleven Acres 1833, 1869; Fallmoor Marfur 1777 (v. marfur); Far Plot 1833, 1869; Far -, First -, Middle 15 Acres 1833, - Fifteen Acres 1869, Top -, Cover Fifteen Acres 1869; The Fitties (v. the same name in East Halton f.ns. (a)); Folly Bank, - Marfur 1777 (v. marfur) (Folly is here the name of pieces of land); Fore Steight 1777 (*the fore steigh* 1700, from fore 'in front of' and steigh(t), a variant of *sty*, from stīg, stīgr 'a path, a narrow road'); Four Acres (SK) 1833; Garth 1824, 1833 (v. garðr 'an enclosure'); Habrough Carr, - Round Cl 1869 (cf. *Haburgland* m13^2, 1253, Hy3^1, from the neighbouring parish of

Habrough); Habro Road Plot (SK) (cf. *Haburg(g)ate* John, Ed1 (p), *Haburygate*
(sic) Hy3[1] (p), *uiam que uadit ad Haburc* Hy3[1], 'the road to Habrough', *v.*
gata); Hall gate 1777 (*Hallegate* John, Hy3[1], 13, lHy3[2], *Halgate* m13[1], Hy3[1],
Hallesgate 13, *hallegatte* c.1311, *Suthallgate* eHy3, *-hallegate* Hy3[1] (*v.* **sūð** 'south'),
'the road to the hall', *v.* **hall, gata**); Haverholme (SK) 1833, Far -, First
Haverholme Bottom 1869 (cf. *hauerholmedaile* lHy2 (e13) *NCot* (*v.* **deill**),
hauerholmhil Hy3[1], *haverholm hyll* 1509 *Foster* (*v.* **hyll**), 'the higher ground amidst
marsh, the water-meadow where oats grow', *v.* **hafri, holmr**, a Scand. compound,
identical with Haverholme L Kest); Hell Holes 1777 (perhaps a derogatory
nickname); Home Cl 1824, 1833, 1869, (SK) 1833, (North -, South) Home Cl
1869; Horse Pasture 1833, - pasture 1869; Huddlestons platt 1779[1] (*v.* **plat** 'a
small piece of land', as elsewhere in this parish; Thomas *Huddleston* is named in
the same document); Lt Humber Flg 1777, Humber Plat 1824, Lt Humber,
Humber Plot (SK) 1833, (Nr -, Far) Lt Humber 1869 (cf. *Humber banke* 1585,
littelhumberdayle lHy3[2] (*v.* **deill**) and perhaps *littelhumberge* c.1311 (but note
Humberg' in East Halton f.ns. (b), no doubt the same feature), named from the
R. Humber); Long Lands (SK) 1833, 1869 (*v.* **lang, land**); Melbourne Lane 1779[2]
(*melborne Laine* 1585, *a place called Melborne* e17; if this is indeed an old p.n.
then it is probably 'the mill stream', *v.* **myln, burna**, though *burna* is uncommon
in north L, but cf. *Walleburne* in f.ns. (b) *infra*); Micklemeer, -meere (Btm)
1833, Micklemere btm 1869 (*mikelmare* m13[2], lHy3[2], *Mikelmare* Hy3[1],
mikelmar(e)sik m13[2] (*v.* **sīc, sík**), 'the big boundary', *v.* **micel, mikill, (ge)mǣre**);
Mutton Pce 1833; Muzmore Rd 1779[2] (cf. *musmare* m13[2], lHy3[2], *Musmare* Hy3[1],
Musemare Hy3[1], *mussemare* c.1311 ('the boundary (land) infested by mice', *v.*
mūs, (ge)mǣre, though the first el. could formally be the OE pers.n. *Mūsa* or
ON *Músi*); new Cl 1777 (*New Close* 1664, *new close* 1671, *the new close* c.1705,
self-explanatory); Osier Bed 1869; Far Peat Stone Pit 1869; Pinder Marfur 1777
(probably a boundary furrow belonging to the village pinder, *v.* **marfur**, and cf.
foll.); Pinfold Marfur 1777 (self-explanatory, cf. prec.); Far -, Middle, Nr Plat
(SK) 1833, 1869, (*v.* **plat**[2], **plot**); Long Puddocks 1777 (probably to be identified
with *putdic* lHy2 (e13) *NCot*, *puddedik* eHy3, *pudedik* m13[1], *Puddich* Hy3[1], and
pudikeheuedland Hy3[1] (*v.* **hēafod-land**; the etymology of Puddocks is uncertain,
but Dr John Insley suggests that it might be a tautological compound of OE
pudd 'a ditch' and **dīc, dīk**); Rampart end 1779[1] (cf. *The Rampart*, PN L 1, 92,
where it is pointed out that *rampart* is a variant of L dial. *ramper* 'a raised way
or road, the highway'); Old Road Pce 1869; Lt Rosmere 1833, - Rossmere 1869
(the first el. is perhaps the same as in Rosper Rd *supra*, the second being
(ge)mǣre); Sandhole Cl 1833, 1869 (cf. *sandhakers* m13[2] (*v.* **æcer**), *sandhil* lHy2
(e13) *NCot*, *sandehil* m13[2], *sandhille* Hy3[1], self-explanatory); Seed Pce 1824; Btm
-, Top 17 Acres (SK) 1833, The 17 Acres (SK) 1833, (Btm -, Top) Seventeen

acres 1869; Shipton Acre 1833, Shiptons cl 1869 (from the surn. *Shipton*, no doubt the same family as gave their name to Shipton Cls in East Halton f.ns. (b) *supra*); Far -, Nr Short Cross 1833, - cross 1869 (cf. *super Cros, apud crucem Roberti Martel* Hy3[1], *Cros* l13, *v.* **cros**; the latter was in the Westfield); Short Lands 1777; Shoulder of Mutton Pce 1833, 1869 (named from its shape); Slaves Btm (SK) 1833, 1869, Slaves dike 1779[1] (*Slauedick* lHy3 (1301), c.1311 (*v.* **dīk**), cf. *Slaue* Hy3[1], lHy3[2], *Slaues* Hy3[1], 1272[1], *Slawes* Hy3[1], *the slaues* 1581, 1587, *- slaves* 1581, *- Slaues* 1587, *Nortslaue* Hy3[1], *Suthslaues* m13[2], *Slaueland* m13[2], *-greues* 1311 (this form is uncertain), *-hende* c.1311 (*v.* **ende**[1] 'the end of something'); this is the same as the Slaves in East Halton f.ns. (a) *supra* and is presumably from **slæf** 'mud', in the sense 'the muddy place(s)'); South gate 1777 (*v.* **gata**); Far -, Long Square Paddock (SK) 1833 (cf. Paddock *supra*); Stack Yard Cl 1833, Stack Yd (SK) 1833; Stone dale 1777; Far -, Nr Stone pit Plat (SK) 1833; Summergates 1779[1], The Summergate 1779[2], Far -, First Summer Gate 1833, 1869, - gate 1869 (cf. *a salt marsh called Sumergates, Somergates* e17, *the sumer gates* 1671, 'the road(s) usable only in summer', *v.* **sumor**, **gata**); Tackle Mear Flg 1777 (from the surn. *Tackle* and **(ge)mǣre**; *Wm Tackle* is named in the same document); Thorn Tree Cl 1833, Thorntree cl 1869 (*Thorne tree close* 1671, cf. *Thorn* e13, *Thorn'*, *Thoren* lHy3[1], *ad spinam* Hy3[1], self-explanatory, *v.* **þorn**); Town end fd 1869; Town Plot 1833, - plot 1869; Townside Flg 1777; Turmer Hole 1777 (cf. *Turfhmar, Turhmar, Turmare* Hy3[1], *turfhmar* lHy3[2], *Turfmar* lHy3 (1301), the exact sense is unclear, but the first el. is **turf** 'turf, greensward', the second **(ge)mǣre** 'a boundary, boundary land', perhaps the meaning is 'the turf-covered boundary', or 'the boundary where turves are got'); the 12 Acres (SK) 1833; Far -, Nr 20 Acres (SK) 1833, 1869; Twenty Eight Acres 1869; 22 Acres (SK) 1833; Ulceby Rd 1779[2] (the road to Ulceby); Wades Cl 1777 (named from the surn. *Wade*); Water Mill Houses Pce (SK) 1833, - plot 1869; The West Fd 1777, - of North Killingholmes 1779[2], the West fd 1822, West Fd 1824, 1833, - fd 1869 (*in occidentali campo* l12, eHy3, m13[1], Hy3[1], lHy3[2], 1272[2], 1311, c.1311, - *Campo* Hy3[1], *in Occidentali Campo* Hy3[1], *in campo occident* 1533, 1581[2], *the west feild* 1587, 1614 *Deeds, the west feild* e17, *The West felde* 1601, - *west feild* 1612, - *feeld* 1626, - *field* 1664, 1671, 1679, 1745, - *Feild* 1690, - *West field* 1700, - *Westfield* 1733, one of the open fields of Killingholme, *v.* **west**, **feld** and cf. East Field Rd *supra*); Lt Whitemoor Marfur 1777 (probably to be identified with *Witemare* m13[1], Hy3[1], 'the white boundary (land)', *v.* **hwīt**, **(ge)mǣre**, with the same interchange between *mear* and *moor* as occurs frequently in north L; the sense of 'white' here is uncertain; *v.* also **marfur**).

(b) *akar dike* 1585 (for the same name *v.* Barnetby le Wold f.ns. (b) *supra*);

alnestoueland m13², *terram que uocatur Alnestoue* Hy3¹ (the readings are not absolutely certain, but they are probably to be associated with *Elnestowstange* 1272¹, the latter clearly named from the Abbey of Elstow (Beds), which held land in the neighbouring parish of East Halton, *v.* VE iv, 188, and **stong** 'a pole', in ME a measure of length); *ad Pomarium* 1294 *Ass,* - *de Kelyngholm* 1298 *Ass, atte Appelgarth* 1340 *FF, atte Appilgarth' de Kylyngholm'* 1388 Peace, *atte Appulgarth' de Kylyngholm'* 1395 *ib* all (p), *appulyarth thyng* 1531, 'the apple orchard', *v.* **apaldr(s)-garðr**, the 1531 form being from the derived surn. with **þing** 'a possession, property', cf. Robert *Appullyard* 1521); *arnaldholm* lHy2 (e13) *NCot, Arnaldholm, Harnaldholm* Hy3¹ (from the OGerm pers.n. *Arnald* and **holmr** 'higher ground amidst the marshes, a water-meadow'); *haustorppegate* lHy2 (e13) *NCot, Haustorpgate* Hy3¹, *houstorpgate* eHy3, *Houstthorpgate* Hy3¹, *housthorpgatte* c.1311, *Austorpgate* m13¹, Hy3¹, 1272¹ *austorpgate* 1272², *Austrorpe gate* (sic) Hy3¹, *Oustþorpgate* m13¹, Hy3¹, *Ousthorpgate* Hy3¹, *Oustthorpegate* lHy3 (1301), *Oustorpgate* m13², 13, 'the road to *Austthorpe*', *v.* **gata**, *Austthorpe* being 'the outlying settlement lying to the east', *v.* **austr, þorp**, a Scand. compound. It is odd that no reference has been found to *Austthorpe* itself); *aver closse* 1585 (probably from **hafri** 'oats' and **clos(e)**); *bechtoftmare* m13² (more spellings are needed to determine the etymology of *bech-* v. **toft, (ge)mǣre**); *Benacrehil* l12, lHy3², *-hille* lHy3¹, *Bounakerhil'* m13², lHy3², *-acrehil, -hille* lHy3² (*v.* **hyll**), *Bounacremare* Hy3¹ (*v.* **(ge)mǣre**) ('the plot of cultivated land where beans are grown', *v.* **æcer, akr**, with an interchange in the first el. between OE **bēan** and ON **baun** 'a bean'); *benemar'* eHy3, *Bennemare* Hy3¹ (presumably 'the boundary land where beans grow', *v.* **bēan, (ge)mǣre**; *berg'* eHy3, Hy3¹, *Berg* Hy3¹ (this is probably from ON **berg** 'a hill, a mound;)); (*le*) *Biridale* Hy3¹, *Byridayl(e)* Hy3¹, 13, *le Northebiridale* Hy3¹, *Suthbyridayle* Ed1 (the first el. is perhaps the ME surn. *Biri, Byri* (from OE **byrig,** dat.sg. of **burh**) or even **byrig** itself with **deill** 'a share of land'); *Blindwelles* 1311 ('the hidden springs', *v.* **blind, wella**); *bodoms arforth land* 1585 (*bodoms* is probably *bottoms, v.* **botm,** while *arforth* may well be a surn.); *Bounlandmare* lHy3² (probably identical with *Bowlamar Runnles* (sic) 1733 (*v.* **rynel** 'a small stream, a runnel') ('the strip of arable land where beans grow', *v.* **baun, land** with **(ge)mǣre**); *braddewater* m13², *Bradewatre* Hy3¹ (*v.* **brād, wæter**, though the exact sense of the latter is uncertain; it may denote 'a pool' or 'a stream'); *bradewad* m13² ('the broad ford', *v.* **brād, vað**); *le Brademarfure* 1311 ('the broad boundary-furrow', *v.* **brād, marfur**); *Bramaker* lHy3 (1301) ('the plot of arable land where broom grows', *v.* **brōm, æcer, akr**); *Branzthoft* c.1150 Dane, *-toft* c.1150, Hy2, lHy2 Dane, lHy2, e13, *Brandestoft* Hy3¹, *brancetoft mar* eHy3 (*v.* **(ge)mǣre**) (a Scand. compound of the pers.n. *Brandr* and **toft** 'a building site, a curtilage', with a distinctive Scand. gen.sg. form in *-s.* The same name occurs in Dunholme LWR as *Branztoft* Hy2, lHy2, l12 (13)

Kirkst); *braydberhg'* m13^2 ('the broad mound, hill', probably a Scand. compound of **breiðr** and **berg**); *Briniglandes* lHy3^1 ('Brýning's land, estate', from the OE pers.n. *Br ning* and **land**. Dr John Insley draws attention to a Nf example of this pers.n., spelt *Brinig*, v. *Studia Anthroponymica Scandinavica* 3, 1985, p. 25 and n. 17); *Broclosgate* lHy3^1, lHy3^2 (probably a reduced form of *Broclosbygate* 'the road to Brocklesby', v. **gata**); *Bruntoft* Hy3^1 (no doubt the same as *toftum Ri'cus Brun tenuit* c.1230 *HarlCh*, from the surn. *Brun*); *burghil* eHy3 (probably 'the hill with a fortification', v. **burh**, **hyll**, but the exact significance of 'fortification' is unknown); *bercar'* ... *de caldham* m13^2, *caldham*, *Caldeham* lHy3^2, *Bercarie que vocatur Caldhame* Ed1, *Kaldham* Hy3^1, Ed1 ('the cold, cheerless, exposed homestead', v. **cald**, **hām**; there are no spellings in *-hamme* (from **hamm**), so it is almost certain that the second el. is in fact OE **hām**; the name may well, therefore, belong to an early period in the AS settlement of the area); *Cannelandes* 1568-70 *MinAcct* (the first el. is perhaps **canne** 'a can, a cup' used in p.ns. in the transferred topographical sense 'a depression, a hollow', or perhaps more likely it is the derived surn. *Canne* (Reaney s.n. *Cann*); the second el. is **land** 'a selion, a strip of land'); *pratum quod dicitur Catstal* Hy3^1 (although the reading has been checked and is correct, there do not appear to be any parallels to this name, i.e. of birds or animals compounded with **stall**, and it may be an error for *Cotstal* 'the site of a cottage', v. **cot**, **stall**); *chapehoues* e13, Hy3^1, *-howes* lHy3^1, Hy3^2 (the first el. is uncertain, but it may be the ME surn. *Chape* (Reaney s.n. *Chapp*) with the pl. of **haugr** (ME *howe*) 'a mound, a hill'); (*Le*) *Clote* 1279 (this is a further example of ME **clote**, first noted in PN C 115-16. It is a fenland term apparently having to do with draining and barring waters, but its history is obscure and its meaning uncertain); *Coale close* 1671; *Colswaingate* Hy3^1, *colsuuayngate* lHy3^1 (from the AScand pers.n. *Colswein* (ON *Kol(l)sveinn*) and **gata** 'a road'. On this pers.n. v. Insley 554-56. Perhaps with the same pers.n. is *colsūmargate* lHy3^1, *Kols'margate* l13, probably 'Colswein's boundary road', v. **(ge)mǣre**, **gata**); *ye common* 1671, *the Comon* 1690, *ye Comons* 1700, *the Commons* 1708, 1745 (self-explanatory); *common mirfer* 1585, *the Common Marfar* 1614 (v. **marfur**); *Corneland* Hy3^1, *Cornland* lHy3 (1301) (probably 'the strips of land where grain is grown', v. **corn**^{1}, **land**, though **corn** is rare in p.ns. and f.ns.); *cotedaila* lHy2 (e13) *NCot*, *Cotedeile*, *Le Cotedaile* Hy3^1, *del cotedayl* lHy3^2 ('the share of land with, by, or belonging to a cottage or shed', v. **cot**, **deill**); *Cracheberg*, *Crakeberg* Hy3^1, *Crokeberg hille* lHy3^1 (probably 'crow hill', v. **kráka**, **berg**, a Scand. compound, with **hyll** added); *le dale* 13, *ad vallem* m13^1, eHy3, Hy3^1 (v. **dæl**, **dair**; it is perhaps the same as *le dale* in East Halton f.ns. (b) *supra*); *Damesdic* e13, lHy3^2, *Dameshil* l12, m13^2, *dammesgate* Hy3^1, *damesgate* lHy3^2, *damesclaue* m13^2 (the first el. is probably ME **damme** (ON **dammr**) 'a dam, a body of water, e.g.

a pond or stream' in the gen.sg. with dīc, dīk, gata, hyll, slæf 'mud, a muddy place'); *la dayl* Hy3[1] (*v.* deill 'a share of land') *Dowty howsse* c.1584 (named from the family of William *Doughty* 1584); *A River called the Ea* 1614 *Deeds* (from OE ēa 'a river, a stream'); *Elvy garths* 1711 *Foster* (named from the surn. *Elvy* and garðr 'an enclosure'); *Enendemare, Henendemare* Hy3[1], *henandemare* 1311, *enedmare, Enedemar, enedemare, Henedmare* Hy3[1] (this is very likely to be from ME *ened, end(e)* (OE ened) 'a duck' and (ge)mǣre 'a boundary, boundary land'); *engeberyg* m13, *Engeberge, Enge-, Eng-, Hengberg* Hy3[1], *Engbergmare* 13, *hengeberghdale* c.1311 (apparently 'the mound, hill by the meadow', *v.* eng, berg (a Scand. compound) with (ge)mǣre, and deill; forms with *H-* are fairly frequent in names derived from eng); *engedik* m13[2], *del engedike* Hy3[1] (*v.* eng, dīk, probably a Scand. compound); *estlangcros* (sic) lHy2, *austlangcros* (sic) lHy3[2] ('the (east) long cross', *v.* lang, cros; it is noteworthy that the affix shows a variation between OE ēast and ON austr 'east'); *Farmanaker* l12, *-akeres* m13[1], *farmanacres* e13, *Faremanmacres* e13, lHy3[2], *Farmanacres, -aceres* lHy3[2] (from the ON pers.n. *Farmann* and the pl. of æcer or akr, and so perhaps another Scand. compound); *Filiholm'* e13, lHy3[2], l13 (perhaps a Scand. compound from filja (ME *filli* (MED)) 'a filly' and holmr 'an island of higher ground in a marsh, etc.'); *folisland* lHy3[2] (perhaps the first el. is the byname or surn. *Fol* (Reaney s.n. *Foll*) with land); *Folkingmare* eHy3, Hy3[1] (Dr John Insley suggests that this is from the ON pers.n. *Fólkungr* (*v.* Lind 279) and (ge)mǣre 'a boundary, land on or forming a boundary'); *Forstalcroft* 1205 ChR (from fore-stall 'a place in front of a house', as in The Forstall PN Sx 378, with croft); *foster thyng* 1531 (from the surn. *Foster* and þing 'a possession'); *la Frauncheray* eHy3 (from OFr or AN *fraunicherie 'a freehold', and cf. *le -, la francherei* in Nettleton f.ns. (b) *infra*); *Furlang dayl* eHy3 (*v.* furlang, deill); *furlangrighes* Hy3[1] (*v.* furlang, hryggr 'a cultivated strip of land'); (*le*) *Gayre* l12, Hy3[1], lHy3[2], (*le*) *Gaire* lHy2, e13, eHy3, *Geyre* m13[2], Hy3[1], *le Gayres* lHy3[2] ('the triangular plot(s) of ground', *v.* geiri); *Galgtrewath, Galgthetrewath, Galketrewathe* Hy3[1], *Galghetrewath* lHy3 (1301) 'the ford by the gallows', *v.* galga-trēow, vað); *Gategraynes* c.1311 (*v.* gata, grein 'a small valley forking from another', a Scand. compound and note that grein is rare in north L f.ns.); *Gawbers lands* m16 *Cragg* (no doubt from the surn. *Gawber* and land); *Gebbescales* Hy2 *Dane* (the first el. may be *Gebb*, a voiced form of *Gepp*, itself a hypocoristic form of *Geoffrey*, *v.* Reaney s.n. *Jebb*, with OWScand skáli 'a temporary hut or shed' in the pl., for which cf. Old Scales in Brocklesby f.ns. (a) *supra*); *Gilberdbuttes* lHy2 (from the OFr pers.n. *Gilbert* (OGer *Gisilbert*) and butt 'a strip of land abutting on a boundary, etc.' in the pl.); *goot* 1585, *goate close* 1664, y[e] *Goat close* c.1705, *the got forlong* 1601, *- goat furlonge* 1606, *- goate furlong* 1634, 1638, *- Goat Hill* 1612 (*goot, goat, etc.* are from OE gotu 'a watercourse, a channel, a stream', with clos(e), furlang, hyll); *Gosetun(e)* Hy3[1], *Gosetunedaile* R1 (1318) Ch, *Goseton Daylle* lHy3 (1301), *Gosetunmare* Hy3[1] ('the farmstead where geese are raised', *v.* gōs, tūn, with deill and (ge)mǣre; another lost settlement site in Killingholme); *Gossecroft* m13[2] (probably from the ME pers.n. *Gosse and croft* and cf. *mansuram ... Gossi* 112 Dane, e13; for this pers.n. and surn. *v.* Reaney s.n. *Goss*); *the greaves of Killingholme* 1613 *MinAcct*, *a peece of medowe called Groves* e17 (for *greaves, v. Atter Greaves* in East Halton f.ns. (b) *supra*); *La Gren* e13, *le Grene* lHy3[2], *- grene* c.1270 (p), *atte Grene* lHy3 (1301), 1305 Ass, 1316 Pat, 1327, 1332 *SR, ad le Grene* 1279, *Attegrene* 113, 1339, *attegrene* c.1311 all (p) (*v.* grēne[2] 'a village green, a grassy spot'); *Hadersich* John, Hy3[1], *Hadhersich* Hy3[1] (*v.* sīc, the first el. being uncertain); *Harberg* 112, *hareberg', Hareberg'* lHy3[1], 113, *Westhareberþe* (sic) Hy3, *-berg* lHy3[1] (perhaps 'the hill abounding in hares', *v.* hara, berg, the same name as *hareberc* in East Halton f.ns. (b) *supra*); *Harnesey Cloase* 1587 (perhaps the same as *Harnes close* 1640 *Foster*, no doubt from a surn. or surns.); *le Hendickes* 1311 (presumably 'the dikes frequented by water-hen', *v.* henn, dīk); *Hest-, Hesteholm* Hy3[1] (the same name as *Hestholm* in East Halton f.ns. (b) *supra*); *heuedlande* Hy3[1], *(del) Heuedland* 113, *the Headland* 1614 *Deeds* (*v.* hēafod-land 'the head of a strip of land left for turning the plough', as frequently elsewhere); *hilgate* eHy3 (presumably 'the road to the hill', *v.* hyll, gata); *Hillebusche* eHy3, Hy3[1], *hyllebuche* (sic) eHy3, *Hillebuske* m13[1] ('the bush on the hill' *v.* hyll, busc, with *-buske* in a Scand. form, *v.* buskr); *Hofdland deile, -dayle* Hy3[1], *Hofdlandayl* 13 (this is from the Scand. cognate of OE hēafod-land, *v. heuedlande supra*, from hofuð and land, with deill; it is noteworthy that both the English and the Scand. forms occur in the same parish); *holmacres* lHy3[2] (*v.* holmr, æcer, akr); *holmesdikes* Hy2 (e13) *NCot, holm' dyke* 1585 (*v.* holmr, dīk, but the earlier form is in the gen.sg.); *Hoppertoft* lHy3[1], *hopperetoft* lHy3[2] (from the ME surn. *Hoppere* 'dancer' and toft 'a curtilage'); *super hou* m13[2], *houeland* Hy3[1] (*hou(e)* is probably from ON haugr 'a mound, a hill', with land); *Houflet* e13, lHy3[2], 113, *howflet* lHy3[2], *a place called holefleet* 1634 (this is identical with *Houhflete* (PN YER 323), where the first el. is taken to be hōh, though haugr is likely here as in the prec.; the second el. is flēot probably in the sense 'a stream'); *Hupmerske* Hy3[1] ('the upper marsh', *v.* upp, mersc, the second el. in a Scandinavianised form); *hwelteseuedland* lHy2 (the reading is uncertain, as is the etymology of the first el.; the second is hēafod-land); *le hirne, del Hirne* eHy3, *le Hyrne* m13[1], *del Hyrne* Hy3[1], *in Angulo* eHy3, *in Angl'o* 113 (114) *Gox* all (p) ('the angle, the corner of land, etc.', hyrne); *le Inne Ground* 1546 LP xxi, *Ingrownde* 1588 *Ipm* (it was in the marsh); *Iocemhil* m13[2] (the MS is torn and the etymology of *Iocem'* is uncertain, but Dr John Insley wonders whether it may be an adaptation of the Gaelic pers.n. *Eogan* suggested for Yockenthwaite

PN YW 6 117-18); *Ketelbarnland* m13 (*Ketelberne* is in fact mentioned as having held land here in a charter dated 1253 (Ed1) *Newh*); *in campis de Kiluingholm* Hy2 *Dane*, 113, Hy3[1], lHy3[2], - *de Kiluingeholm* 1205 ChR, - *de Kilwingh'* m13[2], - *de Kilwingholm* Hy3[1], - *de Killingholm'* 1305 Ass, *in ... Campis de Kelingholme* 1535-46 *MinAcct, Killinghom feildes* (sic) 1587 (self-explanatory); *krike* m13[2] (from ON *kriki*, ME *crike* 'a creek'); *Lachesik* m13[2] (from *læc(c)* 'a stream, a bog' and *sīc, sík* 'a small stream, a ditch', also 'a field, a piece of meadow along a stream'; the exact sense here is not clear, since its site cannot be identified); *ladhesik* 112, *ladsik* m13[2] (the first el. is perhaps **hlaða** 'a barn' with **sīc, sík**, as in the prec., and spellings in *Ladhe-* from **hlaða** have been noted in PN YE 323, s.v. **garðr**, OE **(ge)lād** 'a water-course' is formally possible); *Lambecotes* John, m13[2], *lambcotis* 112, m13[2], *-kates* (sic) m13[2], *-cotes* lHy3[2], *lambecotis* lHy3[2], *Lambkotemare* m13[1] (*v.* **(ge)mǣre**) ('the sheds for lambs', *v.* **lamb, cot**); *landhoukes* (sic) m13[2]; *Landsich* Hy3[1], *-sik* m13[2], *-sic* l13 (*v.* **land, sīc, sík**, though the sense is not clear; perhaps it denoted a small stream or ditch in a strip of arable land in the common field); *le lanende* lHy3[1], lHy3[2] (self-explanatory, *v.* **lane, ende**[1]); *Langefurlanges* lHy3[1], lHy3[2] (*v.* **lang, furlang**); *langemare* Hy3[1] ('the long boundary', *v.* **lang, (ge)mǣre**); *langhaues* 112 ('the long mounds', *v.* **lang, haugr**); *langware* 112, *-war* lHy3[2], *Vuerlangwar'* lHy3[1] (*v.* **uferra** 'upper') (formally this could be 'the long weir, dam', *v.* **lang, wer, wær**); *larkehil* lHy2 (self-explanatory, *v.* **lāwerce, hyll**); *lerkemare* eHy3[2], m13[1], *Lerkmare* Hy3[1], *lerke mar'* lHy3 (114) *Gox, Ler(c)kesmare* Hy3[1], 13 (the first el. is uncertain); *Leuericcrike* Hy3[1] (from the OE pers.n. *Lēofric* and **kriki**, ME **crike** 'a creek'); *Ligolfe Wra, Ligholwra, Lyolwra, Ligheholmwra* (sic), *Lingholfwra* (sic) Hy3[1] (from a pers.n. *Ligulf, Liulf*, thought to be an AScand formation, though its exact source is uncertain. It is in fact found in this parish in *toftum Petri filii Lioff* (sic) e13, perhaps the man who gave his name to the f.n., and in Keelby 112 (e13) *NCot* in ... *quod fuit Ligulphi*. The pers.n. is discussed by Fellows-Jensen, SPNLY 189 s.n., and by *Insley* 573-75 s.n. **Liulf*. The latter believes that *Hllfólfr* "is the only one of the explanations proposed for the English forms *Ligulf, Liulf, Liolf* etc. which has been actually noted in Scandinavian records and, on the whole, it would seem to be the most plausible explanation as the evidence stands at present". The second el. is *vrá* 'a nook, a corner of land', and so we have another Scand. compound in Killingholme); *litteltoftes* 112, *liteltoftes* m13[2], *Lytill toftes* 1585, *Littletoftemare* e13, m13[2], *liteltoftmare* lHy3[2] ('the little curtilages', *v.* **lȳtel, toft**, with **(ge)mǣre**); *tofto Hospitalis de Malteby* Hy3[1] (i.e. Maltby by Raithby LSR, a Commandery of the Knights Hospitallers); *terram que dicitur Manesloth* Hy2 *Dane, unam terram ... que uocatur manneslot* lHy2 (e13) *NCot, mannesloth* Hy3 *ib, Mannesloth* 1230-50 (this is OE *manslot* (*v.* BTSuppl s.v.), more correctly **manneshlot*, of which BTSuppl's meaning 'a man's lot or share' is a literal translation; it goes on to define it as "the amount of land allowed to the head of a family when the hundred was divided up". The word is discussed by Stenton, Dane xx-xxi n. 9, who draws attention to one other example, in Wrangle L Holland, in addition to the examples quoted above from Dane and *NCot.* He defines the word as "the portion of land which falls to a man, which a man should have" and claims that there is in the Wrangle text an "explicit equation between the manslot and the bovate". The Killingholme name is apparently the first example of **manneshlot**, as a p.n. or f.n., noted by the Survey. It should be added that all the examples of the word so far found are from L and Nf. The quotation in BTSuppl refers to *Elsingtunhundred*, now part of Freebridge-Marshland Hundred (*v.* Anderson 63-64), *Elsingtun* itself being identified with Islington Nf (*v.* DEPN s.n. and EHR 43, pp. 376-83). With our present state of knowledge of the distribution of the word, it is, therefore, *possible* that late OE **manneshlot** is a loan-word from ON **mannshlutr*); *Manihawes, -hauues* e13, *-hous* m13^2, *-howes* lHy3^2, *-houdaill'* e13, *-howdayles* lHy3^2 (*v.* **deill**) ('the many mounds', *v.* **manig, haugr**); *Maredich, -dic* Hy3^1, *-dik* lHy3^2, *le Maredic* 1272^1, *le maredik* 1272^2, *Mardyk* lHy3 (1301), *-dick* 1279 ('the boundary ditch', *v.* **(ge)mære, dīc, dīk**); *marfures* l12 (a very early reference to a name now noted in many north L parishes, *v.* **marfur** (OE **mœrfurh*) 'a boundary furrow', as also elsewhere in this parish); *le marstal', - Marstal* lHy3^1 (this name has been discussed by R. Forsberg, *Studia Neophilologica*, 56, 13-14, who suggests that it is derived from an OE **mær(e)stall*, with some such meaning as 'a pool of stagnant water, a pool', a sense perhaps supported by the name *Mill Mastal butts* in Goxhill f.ns. (b) *supra*); *Maunce Hedland* 1634, *Maunse hedland* 1638, *Monsheadland* c.1705; *medelfurlang'* lHy3 (l14) *Gox* (the first el. is ON **meðal** 'middle', the second being **furlang**); *the medowe Marsh(es)* e17; *meltongate* eHy3 ('the road to Melton Ross', *v.* **gata**); *mensethil* m13^2, *Mensathil* lHy3^2, l13, *mengethil* (sic) m13^2 (*men-* is perhaps from **(ge)mæne** 'common', cf. *Sathil infra*); *in medio campo de Kilwingh'* m13^2, *- de Kiluingholm* lHy3^2, Ed1, *- de Kilingholm* lHy3^1, *medius Campus de Kilyingholm* Hy3^1 ("the middle field of Killingholme"); *midelmersk* m13^2, *-merske dike* 1250 (*v.* **dīc, dīk**) ('the middle marsh', *v.* **midel, mersc**, with the second el. in a Standinavianised form); *ye middle close* c.1705; *the mill furlong* 1612; *milnestikg* (sic) l12 (*v.* **myln, stīg, stīgr** 'a path'); *Mylnerclose* 1573 *Anc* (from the occupational name or derived surn. and **clos(e)**); *Nabberg'* lHy3^1 (apparently 'the hill with a nab', a compound of **nabbi** 'a point, a peak' and **berg** 'a hill, a mound'; if this is correct it is another Scand. compound); *namannesmare* lHy3^2 (literally 'no man's boundary', *v.* **nān-mann, (ge)mære**, probably a disputed boundary); *Neucroft* Hy3^1 (*v.* **nīwe, croft**); *Neuhusumdaile* Hy3^1 (a share of land (*v.* **deill**) belonging to or named after Newsham Abbey in Brocklesby parish *supra*); *Neuilleland* 1272^2, *Nevilleland*

1272¹ (from the *Neville* family, members of which witness Killingholme charters, cf. Peter *de Neuilla* 112 Dane, e13 and **land**); *Niccallmill Closes* 1664, *Nycamill close* 1671, *Nickamill close* c.1705 (the forms are too late to suggest a certain etymology); *Northdaile* Hy2 (e13) *NCot*, *-deile* Hy3¹, *-dayl* 13, *Norddayle* Hy3¹, *-daile* m13¹ (v. **norð**, **deill**); *Northelane* eHy3 (self-explanatory, v. **norð**, **lane**); *Northerdayle* eHy3, *-deyle*, *northerdayle* (sic) Hy3¹ ('the more northerly share of land', from ON **norðor** and ON **deill**); *Nunnemandeyl* lHy3 (1301) (Michael *Nuneman* is mentioned in the same document and the family is found in Killingholme from at least Walter *le Nunneman* e13, v. **deill** 'a share of land'); *Otinghamland* 1250-60 *CottCh*, *Oleringham Houthland* (sic) lHy3 (1301) (the latter described in the text as 'a headland', v. **hofuð**, **land**; *Otingham* is no doubt for *Oteringham*, as is *Oleringham*; note that Anric and Stephen *de Otringham* and Richard *de Otringham* witness Killingholme charters c.1160 and 112 Dane); *parker thyng* 1531 (from the surn. *Parker* and **þing** 'a possession'; the earliest reference to a member of this family so far noted is Mathew *Parker* 1606 *BT*); *Parsonage Garth* 1533, *the Parsonag* (sic) 1587, *the Rectorie and parsonage of Killingholme* 1590, *the vicarage house* 1626 (v. **garðr** 'an enclosure, especially close to a house'); *pott crike* 1585 (probably 'the creek in a depression' from **potte** and **kriki**, ME **crike**); *Presthil* lHy2, 112, m13², 113, *-hille* eHy3, *presthilbopem* lHy3² (v. **botm**, **boðm**) (self-explanatory, v. **preost**, **hyll**); *Ratholfwell'*, *Raþelwell'*, *Raþeuuelle* (sic) Hy3¹ (the first el. is probably the ON pers.n. *Ráðúlfr*; the second is **wella** 'a spring'); *Rawcroft close* 1573, 1574 *Anc*; *Rawe Cloase* 1587; *le Rededaile* 1311 (the first el. may well be **hreod** 'a reed', ME **red**, in the sense 'a reed-bed', the second being **deill** 'a share of land'); *Redewindland*, *terra Redewyne* m13² (the first charter states *terra qua Redewind quondam tenuit & vocata Redewindland*); *redmargate* m13², *Redmaregate* lHy3¹, *redmar gait* 1585, *redmar heuedland* m13², *Redmoreland* 1733 (it is impossible to decide whether the first el. is **hreod** 'a reed' or **read** 'red', but it is perhaps the former, hence 'the boundary (land) where reeds grow', v. **(ge)mære**, with **gata**, **heafod-land** and **land**; the 18th century form shows typical confusion of *mare* and *moor*, (*more*)); *Rieholm* Hy2 Dane, lHy3 (1301), *Riholm* Hy3¹ ('the island of land, raised land in marsh where rye grows', v. **ryge**, **holmr**); *fossatum salc'* ... *que appellatur paruum Rudigwrd* (sic) lHy2 (e13) *NCot*, *Rodingword* m13², *-wrd'* c.1270 (the first el. is uncertain, the second being **worð** 'an enclosure'); yᵉ *Rush close* c.1705; *in salso marisco* Hy3¹, *in Salso Marisco de Kiluinghol'* Ed1, *the salte marshe* 1606 (self-explanatory, v. **salt²**, **mersc**); *clausum voc' Sarnesse* eHy3, *Sarnescroft* ... *quod Walt' Sarnes aliquando tenuit* Hy3¹, *clauso quod vocat' Sarnesse* 1272², *Sarnesse marefore* 1272² (v. **marfur**) (the explanation is given in the form dated Hy3¹ and *Simon Sarenesse fil' Walt' de Sarenesse* is mentioned eHy3); *Sathil* lHy2, 112,, Hy3¹, m13², lHy3², *-hill'* e13, lHy², *-hille* eHy3, lHy3², *shathill'* e13, *Northende de*

Sathil 113 (Dr John Insley suggests that this is 'the hill with a lair', *v.* **sǣt, hyll**, but no certainty is possible); *Sauitteberguele* e13 (the reading is uncertain); *Scellemare* m13[1], Hy3[1], *Skellemare* Hy3[1], lHy3[2], *Schellemare* Hy3[1], *Scelmare versus Humbriam* Ed1, *Skelmaredayl* 13 (*v.* **deill**) (this is a difficult name, but it may be 'the boundary where shells are found', from ON **skel** 'a shell' and **(ge)mǣre**); *scortbuttes* e13, m13[2], Hy3[1], lHy3[2], *schorthebuttes* Hy3[1], *Scortebuttes* lHy3[1]. *scortbutte mare* Hy3[1] (*v.* **(ge)mǣre**) (from **sc(e)ort** 'short' and **butte** 'a strip of land abutting a boundary, a short strip or ridge at right angles to others, etc.'); *scorttoftes* lHy2 (the reading of the first el. is uncertain, but if it is correct it is 'the short curtilages', *v.* **sc(e)ort, toft**); *le Shepgate House* 1535-37 LDRH, - *Howse* 1535-46 *MinAcct, Le Shipgate House* 1546 LP xxi, *Sheepgate* 1588 *Ipm* (from ME **shep-gate**, dial. *sheepgate* 'the right of pasturage for sheep (or a sheep)'); *le siket* Hy3[1], *-sikette* lHy3[2] (from ME **siket** 'a small watercourse or sike' and cf. *Sichet* PN Wa 324 s.v. **et**); *del slade* 1509 *Foster* (*v.* **slæd** 'a valley', also 'low flat marshy ground'); *slemare* m13[2]; *Snaudberg, Snoutheberg'* Hy3[1], *Snoutheberhemare* lHy3[1] (*v.* **(ge)mǣre**) (the MS is faint, but the reading is probably correct; if so it is perhaps 'Snauð's mound, hill', *v.* **berg**, the first el. being an unrecorded byname from *snauðr* 'poor', though Dr John Insley suggests that it is rather the ON adj. itself, the sense being 'the bare mound or hill', *v.* **berg**); "south field of" *Kylingholm* lHy3 (1301), *per medium Australis Campi de Kilvingholm* 1279, *in australibus campis de Killingholm* 1311, c.1311 (self-explanatory, the south of the great fields of Killingholme); *spilledeyle* m13[1] (from the ON pers.n. **Spillir* and **deill** 'a share of land', a Scand. compound; the same pers.n. is the first el. of Spilsby LSR); *a Cottag Called Springes thing* 1587 (from the surn. *Spring* and **þing** 'a possession'); *Stainacres, Stayn acers* Hy3[1], *stayneacres* 1311 (from ON **steinn** 'stone' and **æcer, akr** 'a plot of arable land'); *Staingrunt* Hy3[1], *Steyngrund* lHy3 (1301), *staingrundheuedland* Hy3[1] (*v.* **hēafod-land**) ('the stony stretch or piece of land', *v.* **steinn, grund**; the second el. could be either OE or ON, perhaps the latter here); *Stanedick'* c.1311 (*v.* **stān, dīk**); *Staynbergdayle* Hy3[1] ('the stony hill or mound', *v.* **steinn, berg**, with **deill**; a Scand. compound); *Steuendaile, -dayle* Hy3[1], *-dayl* 1250-60 CottCh, *Nordsteuendayle* Hy3[1] (*v.* **norð**) ('Steven' share of land', from the ME pers.n. *Steven* and **deill**); *Stodfoldes, -faldes* m13[2], lHy3[1], *Stodefalde* lHy3[2] ('the studfold(s), the horse enclosure(s)', *v.* **stōd-fald**); *ye sowth(e) forlang* 1601, *the south furlong* 1606, 1634, 1638, 1671 (*v.* **sūð, furlang**); *suhfurlangdaile* lHy2 (e13) *NCot, suthfurlangdaile* Hy3[1] (*v.* **deill**); *Suthdayles* m13[2], *suhtdayles* 1253, *del Suthdeile, sudailes, suddayle, -daile, -dayles* Hy3[1] (*v.* **sūð, deill**); *Suttoftes* 112 (probably 'the south curtilages', *v.* **sūð, toft**); *Syricmare* Hy3[1], *Sighrichmar* lHy3 (1301) (probably from the OE pers.n. *Sigerīc* and **(ge)mǣre** 'a boundary, land on or forming a boundary', though the corresponding ON pers.n. *Sigríkr*, ODan *Sigrik* is alternatively possible);

Tedmerstoft Hy3[1] (Dr John Insley rightly points out that this is 'Theudmer's curtilage', from the Continental Germanic pers.n. *Theudmēr* and **toft**); *le tempelland* m13[2], *Templecroft* Hy3[1] (references to **tempel** in p.ns. and f.ns. usually allude to property of the Knights Templar, though none has so far been found in the parish, but note that the Knights Hospitallers of Maltby by Raithby held at least a toft here, *v. supra*); *tetheringe lees* 1583 (self-explanatory; *lees, leas* are common as appellatives in north L for meadow or pasture land); *thornberg* m13[1], *porneberc* Hy3[1], *thornebergh* c.1311, *thornbergate, thornberghille* lHy3[2], *Thornbersich* John, *pornebergsike* m13[2], *thornebersich* Hy3[1], *thornbergsik* 13 ('the hill where thorn-trees grow', *v.* **þorn, berg**, with **gata, hyll** and **sīc, sík**); *Thorngate* m13[2] (*v.* **þorn, gata**); *Thorwardehil* 112 (the first el. is a partially anglicised form of the ON pers.n. *porvarðr* (on which *v.* Namn och Bygd 70, p. 89); the second el. is **hyll**); *thralholm* 112, *pralleholm* e13, *thrallholm* lHy3[2], *thraholmdayle* (sic) lHy3[1] (from ON **þræll** 'a thrall, a serf' and **holmr** 'raised land in marsh, etc.', a Scand. compound); *threfurlang(e)s* 112, m13[2], *-furlonges* Hy3[1] (self-explanatory, *v.* **þrēo, furlang**); *thremares* lHy2, Hy3[1], lHy3[2] ('the three boundaries', *v.* **þrēo, (ge)mǣre**, presumably where three boundaries met; the same name occurs in East Halton f.ns. (b) *supra*); *le pweresty, Thuerstig, del twersti, therstig* (sic) Hy3[1], *Schwerstiges* (sic) 1311 ('the transverse path', *v.* **þverr, stīg, stígr**, perhaps a Scand. compound; the meaning is explained in *ad semitam transuersam* Hy3[1]); *Tofte* m13[1], *Tofto quod Hug' de Hol quondam tenuit* Hy3[1] ('the curtilage, the building site', *v.* **toft**; the two references probably refer to different curtilages); *Toftegate* m13[1], Hy3[1], m13[2], lHy3[2], lHy3 (1301), *Toftesgate* m12[2], Hy3[1], 13, *-gatte* 1311, c.1311, *tuftesgate* (sic) m13[1] (*v.* **toft, gata** 'a road'); *le tofterdayl Walt'i de Wellewyk* eHy3, *Thofteredeile* Hy3[1] (this is apparently an unrecorded ME **toftere* 'one who lives at a toft' and **deill** 'a share of land'); *Toftheshyl* Hy3[2], *Tofteshil* 13 (literally 'the hill of the toft', *v.* **toft, -es², hyll**, unless of course the first el. is a surn. *Toft* from **toft** itself); *toftmare* 112 (*v.* **toft, (ge)mǣre**); *tungate* m13[2] ('the road to the village', *v.* **tūn, gata**); *land called xx osganges* (sic) 1587 (i.e. 'twenty oxgangs', *v.* **oxgang**); *le twyneling'* lHy2, *twynling'* m13[2], *Twyneling'* lHy3[1], lHy3[2] (obscure); *Tynghille* lHy3 (l14) *Gox* ('the hill where the assembly, the meeting is held', *v.* **þing, hyll**); *Waddelandes* e13, lHy3[2] (this does not seem to be a variant of *wat(e)landes infra*, so it is perhaps, as Dr John Insley agrees, 'land where woad is grown', *v.* **wād, land** (OE **wād-land*), with late OE shortening of the vowel before two consonants, *v.* Jordan paragraph 23); *Waithberg, Vateberg* (sic) Hy3[1], *waitberghil, Waitebergmare* Hy3[1] (probably 'the hill where wheat grows', *v.* **hveiti, berg**, if so a Scand. compound, with **hyll** and **(ge)mǣre**); *Walleburne* e13, lHy3[2], *Walburnsike* lHy3[2], *Walleburnewelle* 113 (apparently a compound of **wall** 'a wall' and **burna** 'a stream', but the significance is not clear; *v.* also **sīc, sík** and **wella** 'a spring'); *Wardike* 1509

Foster (the form is too late to suggest an etymology); *acras .. que appellatur Warlot* lHy2, *prato que dicitur le Warlot* John, *prato quod dicitur le Warlot in Hestholm* Hy3[1], *Warlotegade* (sic) lHy3[2] (*v.* **warlot**, under Waterhill Wood in Brocklesby *supra*, and note the appellative use of the word in *vnum Warlot* and *en graunt Warlotes* (sic) both Hy3[1]; the form *Birlotegarthe* e13 is an error for *Warlotegarthe* lHy3[2], as a comparison of the names in comparable charters shows, and *Warlotegade* lHy3[1] itself is no doubt for *Warlotegarthe*, *v.* **garðr**); *Watergate* lHy2 (presumably 'the road to the water', *v.* **wæter, gata**); *Watheacres* m13, *Watacres* Hy3[1], *-akres* lHy3[1] (it is uncertain, though likely, that these forms belong together; if so, this is 'the plots of arable land by the ford', *v.* **vað, æcer, akr**); *Watlandes* l12, lHy3[1], lHy3[2], *Watelandes* m13, *Watlandgate* lHy3[1] (*v.* **gata**), *Wathlandes* m13, *Weatlandes* 1585 (again it is difficult to know whether all these forms belong together, but the earlier occurrence and preponderance of those in *Wat(e)-* suggest that the form in *Wath-* is simply a scribal error; *Wat(e)landes* is probably 'the wet lands, selions', *v.* **vátr, land**, but it could perhaps alternatively be 'the selions where wheat grows', *v.* **hwǣte, land** and cf. *Wateland* PN BedsHu 295); *Watmare* Hy3[1] (the reading is uncertain); *ad Fontem* lHy3[1], *ad fontem* lHy3 (14) *Gox*, Ed1, 1327, 1332 *SR*, *Atte welle de Kyluingholm* 1300 *FF*, *- Welle -* 1301 *ib*, *atte Well' de Killyngholm* 1375 Peace, *at Welle de Kelyngholm* 1383 *ib et freq* to *atte Well' de Kylingholm'* 1422 all (p) (*v.* **wella** 'a spring'); *Wendinges, Vendinges* m13, *le vending* lHy3[1] (*v.* **wending** 'the turn(s), bend(s) in a road or stream', no doubt developing the sense of place(s) where there is a bend or bends; the same name occurs in East Halton f.ns. (b) *supra*, presumably with reference to the same place; note also the appellative use of the word in *vna Wendinge, alia vendinge* m13); *Wervelmare* 1205 ChR, *Wheruelmare* 13, *ywruelmare* eHy3, *ywrulmar* (sic) Hy3[1] (if the forms in *W-* are original the first el. is OE **hwefel** 'a circle' compounded with **(ge)mǣre** 'a boundary, land on or forming a boundary', but the significance of 'circle' is not clear; it could refer to a stone circle or a round-topped hill or even a circular boundary; forms in *yw-* are almost certainly for *þw-* (i.e. *thw-*) and may simply be errors in a name no longer understood); *Westland schaphous* m13[1], *Westlangscaphous* m13[2] (the first part of the name means 'the west long strip of land', *v.* **west, lang**[2]; the second part is uncertain, but it may well be 'the mounds where sheep are found' from **sceap** and the pl. of **haugr**, with the first el. in a Scandinavianised form, for which cf. Scopwick L Kest, which has spellings in *Scap(e)-* from 1086 DB); *terra Ric' Westiby* eHy3[2] ('west in the village', *v.* **vestr, í, bý**); *a Crike called White Booth Crike which divideth the greaves of Killingholme ... & the marshes of Halton* (i.e. East Halton) 1613 *MinAcct* (*White Booth* is 'the white temporary shelter', *v.* **hwīt, bōth**, presumably from the colour of the building, with **kriki**, ME **crike** 'a crike, an inlet', and for *greaves, v. the greaves of Killingholme supra*); *Wilegbysic* c.1245, *Wylegbisic* Ed1 (no doubt from the family of William *de Willegby* 1243, 1245 and sīc, sīk, and cf. *Willebycroft* in East Halton f.ns. (b) *supra*). *Withe-, Withmare* Hy3[1], *Wymare* Hy3[1] (*Wymare* is the same as *Withmare*, as the details of the charters show; perhaps this is from the ME pers.n. *With* and **(ge)mǣre** 'a boundary, land on or forming a boundary', and cf. *toftum Johannis filii With* e13); *Wlgerland* Hy3[1] (from the OE pers.n. *Wulfgār and* land); *Northwrangmares* 112, *Wrangmare* 1634, 1638, *-gate* lHy3[1], *Wrangmar gayt, wrang mar gat* 1585 ('the crooked boundary', *v.* **wrang, (ge)mǣre** with **gata** 'a road'); *yaldehaudale* eHy3[2], Hy3[1] (the same name occurs in Croxton f.ns. (a) s.n. Yellow Dales).

Kirmington

KIRMINGTON
  Chernitone (4x) 1086 DB
  Chirnigtuna c.1115 LS, *Chirningtun* c.1160 Dane
  Cherligtuna c.1115 LS, *Cherlingtuna* c.1115 ib
  Chirringtune 1155-60 Dane, *Chiringtona* Hy2 (1409) Gilb
  Kirningtun (3x) 1143-47 Dane, a1150, 1160-66, 1175-79 ib, *-tuna*
     c.1155 ib, 1318 Ch, *-tune* c.1160 Dane, *-tona* 1153-54 (Ed1)
     Newh, -ton(') 1233 Welles, lHy3 *NCot*, 1275 Cl, 1287 RSu (p),
     1314 Ipm, 1569 InstBen, 1585, 1587, 1590 *et freq* to 1696 *BT*,
     - alias Kirrington Eliz ChancP, *-yngton*(') 1294 Ass, 1315 Cl,
     1316 FA, 1319 Pat *et passim* to 1402, 1428 FA, 1461 Pat, 1576
     Saxton, *Kyrningthon* 1278 Ipm, *-ington* 1281 ib, 1301 FF, 1331
     Ipm, *-yngton* 1303 FA, 1327 *SR*, 1343 NI, 1351 Pat, 1356 Ipm,
     1385 Pat *et passim* to 1570, 1582, 1583 *BT*, *-igt'* Hy2 (1318)
     Ch, 1237-8 RRG, c.1290 *HarlCh, -ygton* 1428 FA, *Kirnigtona*
     1195-96 Dane, 1212 Fees, 1250-51 RRG, 1267 RRGr
  Kirningetune 1155-60 Dane, *-ton* 1285 Cl, *-igetun* c.1160 Dane,
     -ighetun c.1160 ib
  Kirnintune 1155-60 Dane, *-ton'* 1176 P (p), *-tona* 1190-95 Dane,
     -ton c.1221 Welles, 1698, 1699 *BT, Kyrnynton* 1539 LP xiv
  Kiringtun 1143-47 Dane, 1147-73 (l13) Bodl, 1238-43 Fees, *-ton*
     1270 Ipm, 1275 RH, 1281 QW, 1309 Ipm, 1323 Inqaqd,
     -yngton 1303 FA, *Kyrington'* 1242-43 Fees, 1346 FA, *-yngton*
     1287 Ipm, 1291 Tax, 1331 Cl, *Kirinton'* 1203 P
  Kerniton' 1193, 1194 P (p), 1196 ChancR (p), *Kernyton'* 1260 Cl
  Kerinton' 1195, 1197 P (p), 1252, 1255 Cl, *-yngton* 1428 FA

Kerninton' 1168 P (p), *-ington* 1219 FF, 1278, 1301 Cl, 1608,
   1703, 1713, 1719, 1721 *BT*, 1774 *Yarb*, *-tonne* 1577 *ib*, *-yngton'*
   1373 Peace, *-ton* 1461 Pat, 1463 Fine, 1480-3 ECP xvi, 1504
   Ipm
Kermintton 1200 ChR, *-iton'* 1202 Ass (p), *-ington* 1548 Pat, 1664,
   1703 *Terrier*, 1704, 1705 *BT*, 1779, 1810 *Yarb*, *-igton* 1700
   Terrier, *Kirmton'* 1203 ChR
Kirmington(') 113 *NCot*, 1219 Fees, 1225 Welles, 1270 Ipm, 1576
   LER, 1603 *Terrier*, 1606, 1629, 1630, 1635 *BT et passim*,
   -yngton 1610 Speed, *Kyrmington* 1190 (e13) *NCot*, *-yngton*
   1343 Cl, 1347 Pat, 1383 Cl, 1491, 1498 Ipm, 1513 LP i, 1535
   VE iv, 1538-39 *AD*, 1547 Pat, *Kyrminton* 1281 Ipm

The from *æt Coringatune* 1066-68 (12) ASWills has been identified with Kirmington by Stenton (DB xlii), followed by Whitelock
(ASWills 211), who states that the identification is "very probable".
She comments that in this case the form "must be corrupt with
omission of the nasal, which may have been represented by a stroke
over the *r*, and probably with *o* for *e*, a common error".   Ekwall
(Studies[3] 25) considers this identification "in itself probable, but
Coringatūn cannot be an early form of Kirmington, which probably
goes back to OE *Cynemæringatun*". He goes on to make the
impossible suggestion that it is a form for Carrington LSR, since
Carrington was not so-named till 1812 after Robert Smith, Lord
Carrington. The *Coringatun* of the AS will may well be intended to
denote Kirmington, as has been claimed, but it certainly does not fit
in with the variant spellings now collected above.
   Nor do these spellings support Ekwall's interpretation of the
name as 'the tūn of *Cynemær's* people', from the gen.pl.
*Cynemæringa of **Cynemæringas*, the base of which is the OE
pers.n. *Cynemær*, and tūn 'a farmstead, village', if these forms are
compared with those, for example, for Kempsford (PN Gl 1 38),
Kilmersdon (So, DEPN s.n.), Kimberley (PN Nt 148), Kimmerston
Nb (PN NbDu 127-28), and Kimsbury (PN Gl 1 133), the first el.
in each case being certainly *Cynemær*. Furthermore, there are only
four spellings in the whole collection for Kirmington with medial *-e-*,
so that it is extremely doubtful that this is indeed from the gen.pl.
-inga of a group name in *-ingas* as Ekwall proposes. On the whole
the evidence suggests an *-ingtūn* formation based on a pers.n., i.e.
'the farmstead, village associated with or called after X'. What that

pers.n. was it is impossible to say and the full interpretation of
Kirmington remains obscure.

BETTY HOLMES WOOD, cf. *Holmes Fox Cover* 1832 *Yarb*; the
name may well have been taken from the Elizabeth *Holmes*, who is
recorded from 1794 to 1803 *BT*. HORNS WOOD, cf. *The Thorns
infra*. HUDSONS GORSE COVER (lost, it was on the site of the
present airport), 1824 O, *Hudsons Fox Cover* 1828 Bry, *Hudsons
Cover* 1830 Bry, *Hudson's Fox Cover* 1832 *Yarb*, named from the
Hudson family, cf. John *Hudson* 1779 *Yarb*, Francis *Hudson* 1793 *ib*.
KIRMINGTON HALL (lost), *Hall* 1828 Bry, cf. *the Hallcroft* 1709
Terrier, y^e *Hall Land* 1724 *ib*, *Hall Close*, - *Yard* 1793 *Yarb*.
KIRMINGTON VALE, 1820 *MiscDep 204*, 1824 O, 1828 Bry, 1830
Gre. MICKLE HOW HILL (lost, it was on the site of the present
airport), 1824 O, *Micklow Hill* 1832 *Yarb*. The forms are late, but
it may be tentatively suggested that it is 'the big (burial) mound or
hill', *v.* **micel, mikill, haugr**. THE MOORS (lost), 1828 Bry, (*the*)
Moor 1779, 1792, 1810 *Yarb*. NORTH FIELD WOOD (lost), *North
Field* W^d 1828 Bry, cf. *Northfield* 1779 *Yarb* and East Field and
Westfield in f.ns. (a) *infra*. THE THORNS (lost), 1828 Bry; it was
situated close to the modern Horns Wood *supra*, whose form may
have been influenced by it.

Field-Names

Principal forms in (a) are 1832 *Yarb*; those dated 1779, 1793, and 1810 are
Yarb; the remainder are *Terrier* (some Barnetby le Wold, Croxton and Great
Limber as indicated), unless otherwise noted.

(a) Ash Cl 1810; Barn Walk (from ModE **walk** 'a range of pasture, a
sheep-walk', cf. EDD s.v. 13 'unenclosed land', as in other modern f.ns. in this
parish); Bean Cl 1793, 1810; Bottoms (*v.* **botm**); Bownham cl 1793, Bownhams -
1810, Bowlands 1832 (perhaps to be identified with *Bounlandes, Bounelanddale*
1312 *DC, Bowland or Bowlam Closes* 1611 (1779) *Nelthorpe, v.* **baun** 'a bean',
land); Brandy Hill; Breeches Pce; Brick Yard; Brigg Rd 1779, 1810, Brigg Road
Cl (self-explanatory); Brocklesby Road Walk 1793 (*v.* **walk** and Brocklesby *supra*,
cf. Barn Walk *supra*); Butt Cl 1793, 1832, But - 1810, Butt Hill 1832; Castorgate
Cl 1779, 1810, Caister-, Castor Gate - 1793, Castor Rd 1793, Caister Lane Cl

1832 (*Cast'gate* 1312 *DC*, 'the road to Caistor', *v.* **gata**); Clay Cl; Clay Pit Cl 1793, Claypit - 1810; Cooks Cl 1793 (named from the *Cook* family, cf. John *Cook* 1699, 1712, 1752 *BT*); Cottagers Pasture (held by the cottagers, freq in LNR); Cow Cl; Cowpasture 1810; Dog House Cl, Dog Horse - (*sic*); Dove Cote Cl 1793, 1832, Dovecote garth 1779 (*v.* **garðr**); the Eastfield 1779, East Fd 1810 (*In Orientali campo* Hy3 *HarlCh, in orient'* - Hy3 (Ed1) *Newh, in orientali* - c.1290 *HarlCh* (*de Kyrnigton'*), 1312 *DC, the East Feild* 1709, *East field* 1724, one of the great fields of Kirmington, cf. North Field Wood *supra*, Westfield *infra*); Enham platt 1779 (perhaps to be identified with *le West Innames* 1312 *DC*, y^e *Innoms* 1664, *the inome plat* 1700, *the innam* - 1703, *Innam* - 1709, *Ingham* - 1724, *v.* **innōm** 'a piece of land taken in or enclosed' and **plat**^{2} 'a plot, a small piece of ground', as freq. elsewhere in this parish); Far Pit Plat; Fir Cl; Little firth 1779, Forth 1832; Fourteen Acres; Fox cover 1793, Fox Cover Plat 1832; Garth 1793, 1810, the Garth Pond 1810 (*v.* **garðr** 'an enclosure, a small plot of ground', as elsewhere in this parish); the gravel pitt 1779, Gravel Pit Cl 1793, 1832); Haburgh Road 1779, Habrough Road Walk 1793 (*v.* **walk**, cf. Barn Walk *supra*), Harborough Lane Plat 1810, Habro Lane Wd (i.e. Habrough *supra*); highfield 1779; Holme Garths 1822 (- *garths* 1709, *v.* **garðr**), Holme Hill 1779, 1810, 1832 (*Holm* c.1290 *HarlCh, Holme hill* 1664, *v.* **holmr, hyll**); Home plot 1810, - Cl 1832; Kennington Fd 1762, Kenington feild 1769 (both Croxton) (*campus de kirnington'* 112 (e13) *NCot, campis de Kirming'* e13 (Ed1) *Newh, kirlinton felde* 1601 (Croxton), *Kirmington feild* 1634 (Great Limber), *Kirmington field* 1638, 1700 (Barnetby le Wold), *Kirmington feild* 1662 (Croxton), *Kirlington field* 1664 (Croxton), *Kernington Feild* 1690 (Croxton), - *field* 1707 (Croxton), *Kirmington Field* 1724, 1733 (Barnetby le Wold), *Kennington Field* 1748 (Barnetby le Wold), self-explanatory; the variant spellings for Kirmington in the 17th and 18th centuries are noteworthy); Kiln House Orchard 1793, - house Orchard 1810 (*v.* **kiln-hous**); Laith Cl 1793, 1810 (*v.* **hlaða** 'a barn'); Lane End Cl; Lie Lands; Limber Lane Cl; Little Cl; Long Cl; (Farr) Middle Plot 1810, Middle Plat 1832 (*v.* **plat**^{2}); Mill Cl 1793 (cf. *kermington-mill* 1601 (Barnetby le Wold), *the milne of Kirmington* 1662 (Croxton), *the milne stigh* 1662, *v.* **myln** with **stīg, stigr**)); Moon Croft 1793 (presumably named from the surn. *Moon*, not noted in the sources searched); Paradise 1793 (probably a complimentary nickname, but ME **paradis(e)** also denoted 'a garden, an orchard, a pleasure-garden', *v.* MED s.v. 3); the Pond 1793; Pudding Poke Cl (a common fanciful name for soft, sticky land); Sainfoin next Hendale Wd 1810 (*v.* **sainfoin** and Hendale Wood in Great Limber *infra*); Sand Pit Cl; Schoolhouse Sykes 1810 (*v.* **sík**); Scots Cl (named from the *Scot*(*t*) family, cf. John *Scott* 1672, 1755 *BT*, William *Scot* 1688); Seed Walk 1793; Sodwall 1779; Southwell pond 1779 (cf. *Soutwelhill* 1312 *DC, v.* **sūð, wella**); Spinning Garth 1793; Steensons Plat (probably from the surn. *Stevenson*, cf.

Thomas Stevenson 1596, 1664 *BT,* Richard *Stiuenson* 1672 *ib*); the Stone pitt in the Eastfield 1779, Stone Pit Plat, Stone Pit Walk 1832 (*v.* **walk**, cf. Barn Walk *supra*); Stripe Sand Streams; Summer Pasture; (Far) Syke 1832, Great -, Little Sykes 1793, Long -, Narrow - 1793, 1810, Sykes Inclosure 1810, (First -, Second) Sykes 1832 (cf. *le sike, sikedayle* e13 (e13) *NCot* (*v.* **deill**), *the Sykes* 1574 (1779) *Nelthorpe, the Sykes Closes* 1611 (1779) *ib, the Syke Closes* 1625 (1779), 1657 (1779) *ib, the sikes closes, ye sikes* 1709, *v.* **sik**); Thirty Acres; Thornhill Cl 1793, 1810, Thorn Hill 1832 (*Thornhill* 1709); Trinity Cl 1783 *LTR,* Trinity House Cl 1841 *TA* (self-explanatory); Twenty three Acres; Gt Walk (*v.* **walk**, cf. Barn Walk *supra*); Well Cl 1810, Well Plat 1832; Westfield 1779, West Fd 1793 (*in Occidentali campo* Hy3 *HarlCh, in occidentali -* 1312 *DC, the -, ye west feylde* 1634, *- feild* 1662, *- field* 1664, 1674, 1724, *the West Field* 1679, *the west Feild* 1709, *v.* **west, feld**, cf. Eastfield *supra*); White House platt 1779, - Peice, - Plot 1793, Whitehouse 1810 (*v.* **pece, plat^2, plot,** in 1810 associated with Cowpasture *supra*); Wold 1793 (*v.* **wald**); Wong Btm (*v.* **vangr** 'a garden, an in-field', **botm**).

(b) *abbotesbrige* c.1290 *HarlCh, abbotisbrig* c.1290 (Ed1) *Newh, abbotbriges* 1312 *DC* (*v.* **brycg**; presumably named from the abbot of Newsham Abbey in Brocklesby, the abbey having holdings in the parish); *Bek* 1281 Cl, *atte Bek* 1285 ib, *atebek'* (sic) c.1290 *HarlCh,* Atte Bek' 1294 *Ass, Attebek* 113 *HarlCh* all (p) (*v.* **bekkr**); *Bekebygate* 1312 *DC* ('the road to Bigby', *v.* **gata**); *Berg* c.1290 *HarlCh* (probably from ON **berg** 'a mound, a hill'); *in le Birne* (sic) *of Kirnington* 1275 Cl (p) (probably for *Hirne, v.* **hyrne** 'an angle, a corner of land, etc.'); *Calkedik* 1312 *DC* (*v.* **calc, dik**); *de campo equitando* 1357 *Cor, Clyffurlangges* 1312 *DC* (*v.* **clif, furlang**); *la Cotedaile* e13 (Ed1) *Newh* (*v.* **cot** 'a cottage', **deill** 'a share of land'); *creame poake close* 1709 (probably a complimentary name for pasture producing good cream, cf. Cream poke in the f.ns. (a) of Cadney *supra,* and *Creame Poake Nooke* in the f.ns. (b) of Bigby *supra,* as well as Pudding Poke Cl in (a) *supra*); *ad Crucem* 1327 *SR, ad crucem* 1332 *ib* both (p) (*v.* **cros**); *Dimigdale* c.1290 *HarlCh,* 1312 *DC, dimingdale* c.1290 (Ed1) *Newh* (a recurring name of uncertain meaning, found as a minor n. or f.n. in Brk, Db, Lei, St, and YW; it is discussed in PN Db 169, PN YW 6 108, and PN Berks 282. The most likely explanation seems to be 'a dull place', from ME **dimming**, 'the action of growing dim', though Mr John Field points out that this is not borne out from an inspection of examples in Frisby on the Wreak Lei and elsewhere); *grang' de Kyrnyngton* 1535 VE iv, "grange of" *Kyrmyngton* 1547 Pat (these are apparently two distinct granges, the first reference being to Thornholme Priory, the second to Newsham Abbey, *v.* **grange**); *le toft Gun(n)ewate* c.1160 *Dane, Gunewate toft* 1160-66 ib (from **toft** with the AScand pers.n. *Gunnewate* from ON **Gunnhvati,* on which *v.* SPNLY 116 and *Insley* 324ff.); *Ioppittes* 1312 *DC* (the first el. is obscure); *Kirnington Cowdyke* 1607 LH ii (self-explanatory); *iuxta viam que tendit de Meleton* (Melton Ross) *ad paruam limbergiam* e13 (Ed1) *Newh*, *Lymberggate* 1312 *DC* (presumably 'the road to Little Limber (in Brocklesby parish)', *v.* **gata**); *Linland* c.1290 *HarlCh* ('a strip on which flax was grown', *v.* **lin, land**); *Melton Stigh* 1674, *Melton's gate* 1679, *Melton - * 1700 ('path or road to Melton Ross', *v.* **stig, gata**); *Northiby* 1327, 1332 *SR* both (p), ('north in the village', *v.* **norð, i, by**, cf. *Southiby* and *Westiby infra*); *Nusam pitts* 1724 (commemorating the holdings of Newsham Abbey here); *ye parsonage* 1664; *Paul's Lands* Eliz ChancP; *othe Roche* 1373 Peace (p) (*v.* **roche**[1] 'a rock, a cliff'); *Ruholm* 1150, 1157-63, *Rugholm* 1160-66 all Dane (apparently 'the rough island of ground', *v.* **ruh, holmr**; its site is unknown but is said by Stenton, Dane index, to be in or near Kirmington); *Steynhill'* c.1290 *HarlCh*, *staynhill'* c.1290 (Ed1) *Newh* (*v.* **steinn, hyll**); *Suthiby* Hy3 (Ed1) *Newh*, *Southiby* 1312 *DC*, 1327 *SR* all (p) (*v.* **suð, i, by**); *Westiby* e13 *HarlCh*, 1312 *DC*, 1327, 1332 *SR*, *Westeby* 1357 *Cor* all (p) ('west in the village', *v.* **vestr, i, by**, cf. *Northiby supra*).

Great Limber

GREAT LIMBER

Lindbeorhge 1066-68 (c.1200) ASWills xxxix, *-berge* 1200 ChR, *-bergh* 1200 CartAnt, *Lindeberg'* 1296 *NCot*, *Lyndeberg* 1259 RRGr

Lindberge (5x) 1086 DB, 1171-75 Dane, 1223 Cur, 1246 Ipm, *-berga* c.1115 LS, 1130 P, *-berg'* 1212 Fees, 1222 Cur, *-bergia* 1294 *Ass*, *Lynberge* 1210-12 RBE, *-bergh* 1332, 1333 Ipm

Linbergham 1086 DB

Limberge 1086 DB, 1193 P (p), 1210-12 RBE, 1212 Cur (p), 1225 FF, *-berga* 1157, c.1178 France, 1194 P (p), a1219 Welles, *-berg'* 1159-81 (e13) *NCot*, 1195 P (p), 1212 Fees, 1256 FF, 1291 Tax, *-bergia* c.1185 Dane, 1159-81 (e13) *NCot*, 1276 RH, *-berghe* 1230 Welles, *Lymberge* 1263 FF, *-bergh* 1314 Fine, 1334 *FF*, 1338 Ipm, 1338 Hosp *et freq* to 1488 Ipm, *-beregh* 1385 Cl

Linburgia 1190 (1301) Dugd vi

Linnebergh 1305 Ipm

Lingeberch 1185 Templar, *Lingberge* R1 Dane (p), *Lyngeberc'* 1361 *Cor*

Lymber 1430 Pat, 1450 LDD, 1526 Sub, 1568 InstBen, *Limber* 1576 LER

Magna Linberga c.1115 LS, *magne Linberge* 1155-60 Dane,
magnam Linbergiam c.1160 ib, *magna Linbergia* Hy2 (e13)
NCot, Magna Linbergh' 1281 QW, - *Lynberg* 1250-1 RRG,
- *Lynbergia* 1327 *SR*

Magna Limbergia 1143-47 Dane, *magna Limbergia* 1150-60 ib,
magna - c.1155 (e13) *NCot*, c.1155, 1160-66 Dane, a1166,
a1167 (e13) *NCot, mangna* (sic) *Limberga* 1202 Ass, *Magna
Limberg'* R1 (1318) Ch, 1238-43 Fees, 1258 Cl, 1275 RH,
1275 RH, 1291 RSu, *magnam limberg'* 1263 *HarlCh, magna
Limberg'* Ed1 *ib,* "Great" *Lymberge* 1250 FF, - *Limberg'* 1257
Ch, *Magna Limberge* 1264 Abbr (p), *magna* - 1270 *HarlCh,
magna Limbergia* lHy3 *NCot, Magna* - 1330 *CottCh,* "Great"
Lymberg 1234 FF, 1391 Pat, *Magna Lymberg'* 1260 Cl, 1294
Pat, 1395 Peace, - *Lymberge* 1287 (1317) Pat, - *Lymbergia*
1343 Cl, - *Limbergh* 1258 ib, 1431 FA, *magna limbergh'* 1300
FF, "Great" *Limbergh* 1395 Fine, *Magna Lymbergh* 1316 ib,
1316 Pat, 1316 Ipm, 1316 FA *et passim* to 1357 Pat,
Lymbergh Magna 1317 Inqaqd, 1317 Pat, 1342 Fine *et passim*
to - *magna* 1425 IBL, *Lymberghe Magna* 1576 Saxton,
"Great" *Lymbergh* 1259 Ch, 1328 Banco, 1329 Pat, 1332 Ipm,
1364, 1378 Pat, 1383 Fine, 1383 Misc, 1390 Fine, *Great
Lymbergh* 1604 LNQ x, - *Lymberghe* 1610 Speed

magna Lingbergie 1155-60 Dane

magne Lindberge 1202 Ass, *Magna Lyndeberg'* 1304-5 RA ix
Mikellymbergh' 1329 *Ass*

Moche Lymbergh 1493-1500 ECP xx, *Much Lymber* 1537 LP xii

Magna Lymber 1509-10 LP i, *Lymber Magna* 1528 Wills ii,
1535 VE iv, 1552 AD, - *magna* 1554 InstBen, *Lymbergh
Magna* 1529 Wills ii, 1530 ib iii, 1536-37 Dugd vi

Gret Lymber 1529 Wills ii, *Great* - 1551, 1552, 1553 Pat, 1611
Terrier, *Lymberch alias Lymber alias Great Lymber* 1545 LP
xx, *great Limber* 1577, 1634, 1637, 1664 *Terrier, Great* -
1671, 1674, 1690 ib *et passim, Limber Magna* 1708 *Foster,*
- *alias Limburgh Magna* 1741 *PT*

All simplex forms are included here for convenience and cf.
Little Limber in Brocklesby parish *supra* for comparable spellings.

'The hill where lime-trees grow', *v.* **lind, beorg**. It is *Great* to
distinguish it from Little Limber. The affix is recorded once as
Mickell, v. **mikill,** and twice as *Much.*

HENDALE LODGE, 1830 Gre, 1833 PR (Brocklesby), HENDALE WOOD, 1793 *Yarb*, *Hendale New Wood*, - *Old Wood* 1832 *ib*, cf. *Hennedale* 1143-47, 1150-60, 1155-60 Dane, c.1160 (Ed1) *Newh*, 1160-66 Dane, R1 (1318) Ch, *-dala* c.1155 Dane, *-dele* 1155-60 ib, *Hendall* 1587 *Yarb*, 1637 *Foster*, 1637, 1644 *Yarb*, 1671 *Terrier* (Barnetby le Wold), 1676 *ib* (Searby), *hendall* 1611, 1637 *ib*, 1661, 1665 *ib* (Searby), *Limber Hendale* 1638 *ib* (Barnetby le Wold), 1700, 1709, 1733, 1748 *ib* (Barnetby le Wold), 1765, 1769, 1779, c.1812 *Yarb*, *Hendalls* 1676 *ib*. This appears to be 'the valley where (wild) hens are found', *v*. **henn, dæl, dalr**, but hardly fits the situations of the modern Lodge and Wood, which are situated on the side of a fairly steeply sloping hill. There is, however, a valley running eastwards some half mile from the Lodge where Cottagers Dale Wood in Brocklesby parish *supra* is marked on the map and it is perhaps this which gave rise to the name.

ANTHONY CORNER (lost), c.1812, c.1832 *Yarb*, *Anthonys Corner* 1828 Bry. ANTHONY'S CLUMP (lost), *Anthonys Clump* 1828 *ib*, *Anthony's Clump Plat* c.1832 *Yarb*, *v*. **plat²** 'a plot of ground'. BELLOWS PIPE, - *Pipes* c.1832 *ib* and it is *Highfield Wood* 1828 Bry. Dr Rod Ambler points out that *Bellows* is from the surn. *Bellows* and draws attention to the fact that John *Bellows* was granted the Rectory of Great Limber in 1544-45, *v*. *Yarb* 3/3/2/2/1, p. 129. BLACK MILLS (lost), 1793 *Dixon*, 1828 Bry, *Blackmills* 1706 *Terrier*, *East* -, *North Black Mills* c.1832 *Yarb* and is probably to be identified with *Blakemildes* a1167 (later hand) *NCot*, *blackmales* 1611, *black meales* 1625, *blackmeals* 1634, *Blackmeales* 1637, *blackmels* 1674, *Black-mells* 1690, 1697, *Blackmells* 1724 all *Terrier*, *Blackmauls* 1779 *Yarb*, 'the black, dark-coloured soil, earth', *v*. **blæc, mylde**, found as a f.n. in PN Nt 288, PN Nth 268, PN Wa 331 and PN YE 327. There may have been later confusion with **melr** 'a sand-hill'. Bry shows it to have been the name of the open space between New Close Wood and Swallow Wold Wood. BLACKNALL COVER (lost) 1824 O, 1830 Gre, presumably from the surn. *Blacknall*. BROMPTON DALE, cf. *brumton furz* 1611, *Brumton furs* 1664, *Burnton furrs* (sic) 1625, *Brunton furz* 1637, *brunton Furs* 1671, *brumpton furs* 1674, *Brumpton Furs* 1697 all *Terrier*, - *Furze* c.1812 *Yarb*, *Brompton-Firres* 1690, *Brompton furrs* 1706 both *Terrier*, - *Furze* 1824 O, 1832 Gre, - *Firs* 1828 Bry, named from the *Brompton* family and **fyrs** 'furze', cf. Jane *Bromptonne* 1565 *Inv*, John *Brumton* 1570 *Yarb*, 1571 *Inv*, John *a brompton* (sic) 1576 *Inv*. CAEN HILL, *apud Cane* 1333 *Ipm, cane hyll* 1577, *Cane hill* 1611, 1625, 1634, 1637, 1671, 1724, *Cane-hill* 1697 all *Terrier*; in spite of the regularity of the forms the etymology of *cane* is obscure. CHALK HOUSE BOTTOM (lost), 1828 Bry, and cf. *New -, Old Caulkus, Caulkus Lane* c.1832 *Yarb*; it was the name of the open space south of the modern New Close Wood on the parish boundary. CONEYGREEN WOOD, *Coney green plant^n* 1779 *Yarb*, - *Green Wood* c.1812, c.1832 *ib*, a typical variant development of **coninger**, **coningre** 'a rabbit-warren', cf. *warennam in Magna Limberg'* 1275 RH, *the warren* 1577 *Terrier*, *Limber warren* 1637, *Warran* (sic) 1676, *Warren lodge* 1637, *Warren Walk* c.1812 all *Yarb*, v. **wareine**. FOX DALE, 1824 O, 1830 Gre, - *Dales* 1828 Bry, partly in Caistor parish *supra*, for which see an early form. GRASBY BOTTOMS, *Girsby bottome* 1625, *girsbie bottam* 1634, *Grasbie bottome* 1671, 1674, *Gresby bottome* 1690, - *bottom* 1706, - *Bottom* 1745, *Grasby bottom* 1697, - *Botom* 1724 all *Terrier*, - *Bottom* 1824 O, 1828 Bry, 1830 Gre, c.1832 *Yarb*, named from Grasby (the neighbouring parish) and **botm** 'a bottom, a valley bottom' and cf. Grasby Top in Grasby parish *supra*. GREAT LIMBER COVERS (lost), 1824 O, 1830 Gre; it is now Sparrow Clump and Limber Hill Wood. GREAT LIMBER GRANGE, *Limber Grange or Davis Streights F^m* 1828 Bry, *Davis Straits* 1830 Gre. Dr Rod Ambler draws attention to Greenland Fm *infra* and suggests that there could well have been a clear link between the names Greenland and Davis Straits. He points out that Edward Gillet, *A History of Grimsby*, Oxford 1970, pp. 178-79, has shown that whaling voyages were made to Greenland and the Davis Straits by two Grimsby-based ships between 1803 and 1821. Dr Ambler comments "the two farm names suggest some sort of link with activity in Grimsby". It certainly seems most likely that Davis Straits Fm and Greenland Fm do reflect Grimsby whaling activities in the early 19th century, though the historical connections between the Great Limber names and Grimsby has not so far been discovered. For the late occurrence of **grange**, cf. Croxton Grange in Croxton *supra*. GREENLAND FM, 1824 O, 1830 Gre, *Richardsons or Greenland F^m* 1828 Bry, on which v. prec. The *Richardson* family has long association with Great Limber, cf. Thomas *Rycherdson* 1540 Inv, Robert *Richardson* 1637 *ib*.

HALFWAY HO. Dr Rod Ambler points out that this seems to be referred to in *cottages in Great Limber between Keelby and Limber lordships* 1796 *Yarb*. HALLIDAY HILL, *Holliday Hill* 1828 Bry, c.1832 *Yarb*. HEAD LANE (lost), 1828 Bry; it led s. from *Walk Lane* w. of the village. LIMBER FOLLY (lost), 1828 Bry, *Folley* c.1832 *Yarb*; this is not the name of a building, and lay on the edge of a wood n. of Swallow Wold Wood. The exact sense of **folie** here is uncertain. LIMBER HILL, *super Montem* 1327, 1332 *SR* both (p), *atte hill'* 1361 *Cor* (p), *othe Hill* 1369, 1370 Fine both (p), *atte Hill' de Lymbergh* 1374 Peace (p) and cf. *Hill Plat* c.1832 *Yarb* (*v.* **plat**²), self-explanatory. LIMBER HO is *Old Inn Fm* 1828 Bry. MAUSOLEUM WOODS, named from Mausoleum in Brocklesby parish *supra*. MAUX HALL, on which *v.* Manor Fm, in Keelby *supra*, earlier *Mawkes Hall*; the same name occurs as Mauxhall in Stallingborough parish *infra*. NELSONS FM (lost), 1828 Bry, named from the *Nelson* family, cf. John *Nelson, a Farmer* 1760 *BT*. NEW CLOSE WOOD, c.1812 *Yarb*, 1824 O, 1828 Bry, 1830 Gre, cf. (*the*) *new close* 1577, 1611, 1637, 1664 *Terrier*, 1644 *Yarb*, *yᵉ* - 1706, 1724 *Terrier*, (*the*) *New close* 1625, 1671 *ib*, *New Close* 1637 *Yarb*, 1637 *Foster*, 1676, 1774 *Yarb*, *yᵉ* - 1697 *Terrier*, *yᵉ New-close* 1690 *ib*, self-explanatory, *v.* **nīwe**, **clos(e)**; it is on the parish boundary. NEW INN, according to P&H 257 "1840s, but still Georgian". OLD INN FM, now Limber Ho *supra* and is *New Inn* 1778 *Yarb*, (*the*) - c.1812 *ib*, c.1832 *ib*. It is *New-Inn* 1779 *Yarb* in a document containing the accounts for its building in 1779-80. I am indebted to Mr and Mrs Anderson of Great Limber, through Dr Rod Ambler, for disentangling the problems of New Inn and Old Inn. PIMLICO, a transferred name from Pimlico (PN Mx 171), the farm being situated well out of the village and close to the parish boundary and so may well be a nickname of remoteness. SEVENTY ACRE LANE, cf. *Seventy Acres* c.1832 *Yarb*, self-explanatory. SPARROW CLUMP is *Butters Plant.*[n] 1828 Bry, named from the *Butter* family, cf. John and Martin *Butter* 1822 *Terrier*, and is *Great Limber Cover* 1830 Gre. The modern name is presumably from the *Sparrow* family, cf. George *Sparrow* 1851 *Census*. SWISS COTTAGE. WALK LANE (lost), 1828 Bry, cf. *Walk* 1792 *Dixon*; it led from Grasby Bottom to the village. WEST HILLS (lost), c.1812 *Yarb*, 1828 Bry, *west hyll* 1577, - *hill* 1611, 1625, 1637, 1664, *West hill* 1634, 1671, 1724 all *Terrier*, - *Hill* 1676 *Yarb*, *West-hill* 1690, 1697, *Westhill* 1706 all *Terrier*, *v.* **west**, **hyll**; it is difficult to say exactly what it was *west* of.

Field-Names

Undated forms in (a) are c.1832 *Yarb*. Forms dated 112, c.1260, Hy3, Ed1, e14 are *HarlCh*; those dated 1333 are *Ipm*; 1577, 1601, 1611, 1625, 1634, 1637[1], 1664, 1671, 1674, 1690, 1697, 1706, 1724, 1745, 1762[1] are *Terrier*; 1587, 1637[2], 1644, 1676, 1779, c.1812 are *Yarb*; 1637[3] are *Foster*; 1762[2] are *Monson*.

(a) Ammley Cl c.1812 (cf. perhaps *armeclyffe* 1333; if the 1333 form belongs here, the first el. may be the unrecorded OE pers.n. **Earma*, adduced for Armley (PN YW 3 210-11)); Barton-Lane Cl 1762[1] (cf. *in clauso quod vocatur Bartoncroft* m13 *EgCh, unum toftum ... in croft quod vocatur Barton'croft, Bartuntoft, Barton' toft', terra vocatur terra de Barton', Campum Bartunland, Bartunland* all Ed1 (*Barton croft* 16 endorsement), *Barton land ende* 1577, *barton lane* 1577, 1671, 1674, *Barton lanes* 1611, *Barton close adjoining on Barton lane* 1625, *Barton lane* 1634, - *laine* 1664, *Barton-Lane Close* 1745, *Barton close* 1637, 1674, 1724, *Barton Close* 1690, 1697, 1706, from Barton upon Humber *supra*); Low Black Hills; Old Bone Plat; Bowles Cl c.1812 (Dr Rod Ambler draws my attention to John *Bolles* 1662 *Hearth Tax* (PRO E179/140/800) from whose family this name is no doubt derived); Brakenburgh 1762[2], First Brackenbury c.1832 (*Brakenberch* c.1210 *CottCh, Brakenbergh'* 1333, *brokinborow, brokynborow* 1577, *Brackenbrough* 1601, *brackenborrow* 1611, *brakenborow* 1625, *Brackenbarrow* 1634, 1637, *brakon barrow* 1664, *braconbarrow* 1671, *Brakonborow* 1674, *Brackenborrow* 1676, *Braken-borow* 1690, *Brackenbrough* 1697, *brakenbar(r)ow* 1706, *Brakenborough* 1724, 'the hill where bracken grows', *v.* **brakni, be(o)rg**); Brickhills; Brigg Gate, Brigg Rd (*brige gate* 1664, *brigg* - 1671, *Brigg-gatte* 1690, *Brigg gate* 1697, 1706, 1724 'the road to Brigg', *v.* **gata**); But Lane Cl c.1812 (*the butt Cloase* 1587, cf. *but thorne* 1611, *the but-thorne* 1625, *the but thorne* 1634, *the butt* - 1637, the significance of *But* here is uncertain); Buxhow c.1812, Buckstow c.1832 (*Bux How* 1676, *v.* **haugr**); Cliff hill 1779; Clump Plat; Cotcherfer Pit plat (from dial. *cotcher* 'cottager', with **furh, pytt, plat**[2]); the Cornefield 1762[2]; Cover Pce; Cow Pasture c.1812; Crake How c.1812 (1676, - *how* 1637, - *Howe* 1664, *Cracow* 1634, *crakehow* 1671, *Crakehow* 1674, *v.* **kráka** 'a crow, a raven', **haugr**); Cross Garth c.1812; Dove-cote Cl 1779, Dove Cote Cl c.1812, - cl c.1832 (*v.* ME **douve-cote**); ye East Fd 1762[1] (*in Campo orientali* 1333, *East feild* 1601, *the East feild* 1611, 1625, 1634, one of the open fields of Great Limber, *v.* **east, feld**); Eighty Acres; Fanney's Hole; Gt Fiddow 1779, Fiddow Seeds 1792 *Dixon*, Gt Piddow (sic) c.1812 (*viam de fidhow* c.1260, *fido, fido gate, fido head lande, fido lande* 1577,

Fiddow 1664, 1690, 1697, 1706, 1724, *Fidow* 1674, *Fidhowe, Fiddhow* 1671, *Fedow* 1601, *feddow* 1611, *Feddow* 1634, *fedow* 1637, *fewdow* 1625, 1634, the second el. is probably ON **haugr** 'a (burial) mound, a hill', but the first is obscure); Fifty Acres; Forty Acres; Fox Cover (Plat); Furze Cover c.1812; Goosehills c.1812 (*gosheil, goshuyl* a1167 (later hand) *NCot, Gosehull* 1333, *goosehill* 1601, 1674, *Goose hill* 1611, 1634, *Goxse-hill* (sic) 1625, *Goxsehill* 1637, *gousehill* 1671, *Gouse Hill* 1676, *Gooshil* 1690, *Goos hill* 1706, *v.* **gōs**, **hyll**, but the a1167 form *-huyl* is apparently from OE **hygel** 'a hillock', while that in *-heil* defies explanation); Gravely Pit Pce (sic); Upr Green c.1812; Green Eppa 1793 *Dixon* (*greneaper* 1577, *grinaper* 1601, *greenaper* 1611, *Greeneapper* 1625, *Greenaper* 1634, 1637, *grene Hoper* (sic), *greencloper* (sic) 1664, *greeneaper* (2x) 1671, *greeniper* 1674, *Green Upper* (sic) 1676, *Greeniper* 1690, *Greenvpper* 1697, *greeniper* 1706, *Green upper* 1724, obscure); Hall Cl c.1812 (cf. *ad aulam* 1327 *SR* (p), *v.* **hall**); Harecliff -, Haudliff hill 1779, Haracliff Hill c.1812 (perhaps earlier *Harye Headlande* 1577, *Harrie headland* 1601, *Harry* - 1625, 1634, 1637, *Herry* - 1674, *Herry-head-land* 1690, *Henry headland* 1697, 1706); Hare Hills (y^e *Hare-hill* 1690, y^e *Hare Hill* 1697, 1724, *Hare hill* 1706, probably self-explanatory); Heads Plat (*the heades* 1664, 1671, y^e *heads* 1674, 1706, y^e *Heads* 1724, y^e *heades or lynges* 1611 'headlands', *v.* **hēafod** and cf. Ling Mear btm *infra*); Home Cl; Hornsey Grave c.1812 (*Hornesey Graue* 1676, probably from a surn.); How Flg c.1812, Middle Howess (sic) c.1832 (*le howes* c.1260, *the Howes* 1577, 1664, y^e *Howes* 1601, 1690, *Howes* 1634, *the howes* 1611, 1625, 1634, 1637, y^e - 1674, *ye Hows* 1706, *the howe heades* 1577, *how heads* 1674, y^e *howes-heads* 1690, y^e *hows head* 1724, y^e *Hows headland* 1697, y^e *Hows side* 1697, y^e *hows* - 1706, *How Furlonge* 1676, *v.* **haugr** 'a mound, a hill' in the pl., **hēafod(-land)**, **furlang**); Keelby Rd Platt 1793 *Dixon* (cf. *viam de Keleby* a1167 (late hand) *NCot, Kelebye gate, Kelebye east gate* 1577, *Kellbie gate* 1611, 1624, 1625, 1637, *Keelby gate* 1671, 1674, *Kielby gate* 1690, *Keilby-gate* 1697, *Kiellby gate* 1706, *Keelby gate* 1724, 'the road to Keelby' (the adjacent parish), *v.* **gata** and *Kelebye Caster Gate* 1577, *low Keilbie cayster gate* 1611, *Keilby Castor gate* 1625, *Keilbie caister gate* 1634, - *Cayster gate* 1637, *Keelby Caster gate* 1671, 1674, *Keilby-Caister-gate* 1690, *Keilby Castergate* 1697, *Keilby Caister-gate* 1706, *Keilby Caster Gate* 1724, 'the road from Keelby to Caistor' (both adjacent parishes), *v.* **gata**); Keelby Plat c.1832 (*v.* **plat**^{2} 'a plot', as elsewhere in the parish, and cf. prec.); Kirk Hill Side c.1812 (*Kirke hill* 1611, *Kerke hill* 1625, 1671, *Kirkehill* 1634, *kirkhill* 1637, *Kirk Hill* 1664, *Kirke Hill* (*Side*) 1676, *Kirk-hill* 1690, *kirk hill* 1706, *Kirkhill* 1724, *v.* **kirkja**, **hyll**, cf. *ad ecclesiam* 1327 *SR* (p)); Laborers Cl; lane end 1779; Langmere (*the long mere* 1577, *the long mare* 1577, 1625, *long mare* 1664, - *meire* 1637, y^e *Long-Meere* 1690, y^e *longe mare* 1671, 1674, y^e *long* - 1674, y^e *Long-Meere* 1690, y^e *long meer* 1706, *longemare hyll* 1577, y^e *long mair hill* 1601, *long mare hill* 1625, *long maire* -

1634, *Long mayre* - 1637, 'the long boundary', *v.* lang, (ge)mǣre (as elsewhere in this parish) with hyll); Leighton's Home cl (named from the *Leighton* family; Joseph *Leighton* was a tenant c.1832); Limber Lane 1779; Limber Wind Mill 1774 (cf. y^e *Milln* 1671); Ling Mear btm, Lings (Moor) c.1812 (*Ling Moore* 1676, cf. *the lynges* 1577, *the lings* 1634, 1637^3, *the Lynges* 1644, y^e *heades or lynges* 1611, y^e *ling heads* 1674, y^e *Ling-heads* 1690, y^e *Ling heads* 1697, y^e *ling* - 1706, y^e *Lingheads* 1724, *the south linges* 1634 (from lyng 'heather', with (ge)mǣre, botm, hēafod and cf. Heads Plat *infra*); Little Cl; Lock Beds (*Lockbedes* 1611, 1634, *Lockbeds* 1697, 1706, *Lock-beds head-land* 1690, - *headland* 1724); Lodge Plot (*v.* loge, plot); (the Short) Longdales 1762^2 (*langedayles* c.1260, *langdailes* c.1260 (Ed1) *Newh, Long Lang Dayles, Short Lang Dayle* 1676, *lang dale head land* 1577, *Langdale head-land* 1697, *langdale headland* 1706, *Langdale* - 1724 (*v.* hēafod-land), *v.* lang, deill 'a share of land'); Lord's Cl, Lord's Plot c.1812, Lords Cl (Plat) c.1832 (*Richard Lordes landes* 1568-70, 1589-91, 1605-7 *MinAcct,* ter' ... *voc Richard Lordes landes* 1612 *Rental, the Lords Cloase* 1587, from the surn. *Lord,* Richard *Lorde* is also mentioned in 1577 *Terrier*); Old Mare plat (cf. *mayre hill, the mayre stone* 1634, from (ge)mǣre 'a boundary' with hyll, stān, plat^2); Mill btms 1779, -btm 1793 *Dixon,* Mill Cl, Old Mill Hill plot, Old Milne Plot c.1812, Mill Pce, Mill Plat c.1832 (cf. *the milne gate* 1664, *Milne Bottam, Old Milne Hill* 1676, y^e *Mill-hill* 1690, y^e *Mill hill* 1706, 1724, y^e *miln bottome* 1674, *v.* myln, botm, plat^2, cf. *Milnerheuedland* in (b) *infra* and Limber Wind Mill in f.ns. (a) *supra*); Padock Platt 1793 *Dixon* (perhaps from the surn. *Pad(d)ock*); Premium Plat; Riby forty acres (from the adjacent parish of Riby); Richardson's Walk c.1812 (William *Richardson* is named in the document, cf. Greenland Fm *supra*); Sand Plot c.1812, First -, Second Sands Plat c.1832 (cf. *apud Sablones* a1167 (later hand) *NCot, Sands furlong* 1676); Sargeants Cl c.1812, Sergeant Cl c.1832 (from the surn. *Sergeant,* cf. John *Sergeant* 1571 *Inv,* Agneta *Seargent* 1576 *BT*); Shepherd's Cl; Sixty five Acres; Southwell Plot c.1812, South well Cl c.1832 (*Suuduelle* a1167 (later hand) *NCot, v.* sūð, wella); Stephenson's Plat (from the *Stephenson* family, cf. William *Stevenson* 1679 *BT* and plat^2); Stone Pit Plot c.1812, Stone Pit (Cl) c.1832 (*the Stone pitt* 1664, *Stone pitt hill* 1671, *stone pitt hill* 1674, *Stonepit-hill* 1690, *Stonepit hill* 1697, *Stone Pit Furlonge* 1676, cf. *depedale* in (b) *infra*); Syke platt 1779, Sykes Plot c.1812, Sykes c.1832 (*le Sike* c.1260, *the syke, the sykes* 1577, y^e *Sykes* 1601, 1690, 1706, 1724, *the Sykes* 1611, 1634, 1637, - *sikes* 1625, *the sicke, the sike* 1664, y^e *sikes* 1671, y^e *Sikes* 1674, *v.* sīk); Tatham's Cl c.1812 (from the *Tatham* family, cf. Edward *Tateham* 1685 *BT*); Three Corner Platt 1793 *Dixon;* Tomison's Cl c.1812 (probably from the *Thompson* family, cf. John *Tomson* 1567 *BT* and *freq* in the parish); Townend Plot c.1812, Town End Plat c.1832 (cf. *Towne -, towne end* 1577); Triangle; West Dale; West End c.1812 (cf. y^e *west-End gate* 1690, y^e *West end* - 1697; Wood

End Plat.

(b) *ad viam de Apmardale* c.1260; *the arnett Cloase* 1587 (from the surn. *Arnott* (Reaney, s.n. *Arnold*)); *terram Arnewi* a1167 (later hand) *NCot* (from the OE pers.n. *(E)arnwīg*); *viam de Asfardale* c.1260 (*Asfar* is the reflex of the ON pers.n. *Asfrǫðr*, with **dalr** or **deill**); *Ash garth* 1587 (*v.* **æsc, garðr** 'an enclosure, etc.', as elsewhere in this parish); *Audlesbie Bank* 1676, *Audleby-bank* 1690, *Audleby-Bank* 1697, *Audleby bank* 1706, 1724 (named from Audleby in the neighbouring parish of Caistor); *the foote of the banck* 1611, *- of ye banck* 1634, *the banke* 1625, *the banck* 1627; *apud Berge* a1167 (later hand) *NCot* (*v.* **berg**); *berneuang* a1167 (later hand) *NCot*, *bar...wing* 1611 (blot in MS), *Barmeswing* 1625. *Barmswang* 1634, *-wong* 1637, *Barneswong* (*stigh*) 1664, *Barnsing furlong* 1676, *Barnesdale* 1577, *barmdale* 1674, *Barmesdale* 1690, *Barmsdale-heads* 1697, *barmesdale* 1706, *Barmsdale heads* 1724, *Barmswell* 1601, *barmwell* 1671 (from **vangr** and, later, **deill** and **wella** with the ME pers.n. *Beorn* (ON *Biorn*); all the forms appear to be variants of the same name); *Basterd thing* 1568-70 *MinAcct*, *terr ... voc' Bagster* 1589-91 *ib*, *un' pec' ... voc' Bagster* 1605-7 *ib* (from **þing** and presumably the surn. *Bastard*, seemingly modified to *Bagster* in later forms); *beacon hill* 1601 (*v.* **bēacon, hyll**); *atte Beck' de lymbergh* 1334 *FF* (p) (*v.* **bekkr**); *John Bennetes Dale* 1611 (*v.* **deill** 'allotment'); *Bilchemare, Bilgemarewel* a1167 (later hand) *NCot* (the first el. is obscure, *v.* also **(ge)mǣre** and **wella**); *Brocklesby gate* 1625, 1724, *Brocklesbie -* 1634, *Brocklesbiegate* 1637, *Brocklesby gate* 1690, 1697, 1706 ('the road to Brocklesby', *v.* **gata**); *Bullard Cloase* 1587 (from the surn. *Bullard* (Reaney s.n.)); *burnt house dale* 1611, *- howse dale* 1625, 1634 (self-explanatory, and *v.* **deill**); *viam de Caster* c.1260, *low Caster gate* 1577, (*low*) *Castor -* 1625, *low caister gate* 1634, *Cayster -* 1637, *Low Casterr Gate* 1664, *lowe Caster gate* 1671, *Caister gate* 1690, *Castor gate* 1697, *Caistor low Gate* 1745 ('the (low) road to Caistor', *v.* **gata** and cf. *the strete infra*); *Calcotts* 1637[2] (probably *v.* **cald** 'cold, cheerless', **cot**); *Catheadland* 1634, *Cattheadland* 1674, *Cat-head-land* 1690, 1706 (perhaps from **cat(t)** 'a (wild) cat' and **hēafod-land** 'a strip of land at the head of a furlong, for turning the plough', but the first el. may be a surn. cf. *terram quondam Matilda Catte* c.1260); *caudell stigh* 1601, *Cawdell stigh*, *Cawdells* 1611, 1634, *Caudale Steigh*, *Caudales* 1625, *Caudale* 1664, *Cawdales*, *Coudall-*, *Cowdale stigh* 1671, *Caudals stigh* 1674, *Cawdles-Stigh* 1690, *Cawdals* 1674, *Caudles* 1690, 1724, *Cawdles Stigh*, *Caudwell-Stigh* 1697, *Caudles stigh* 1706, 1724, *Coodells Furlong* 1676 (uncertain); *uiam eccle'* a1167 (later hand) *NCot*, *Church heades* 1634, *y^e -* 1637 (*v.* **hēafod** in the pl.); *Claxhou* a1167 (later hand) *NCot* (probably a Scand. compound 'Clac's mound', *v.* **haugr**, the first el. being the ON pers.n. *Klakkr*, ODan *Klak* found in Claxby LNR, Claxby Pluckacre LSR etc.); (*del*) *clay* e14 (p), *clay hyll*, *clay pitt gate* 1577, *the Clay* *pites* 1611, - *pitts* 1625, *the clay pittes* 1634, - *claypittes* 1637, *the Clay pits* 1664, *the clay pit hill* 1601, *clay pitt* -, - *bottome* 1674, *Clay-pit hill*, *Clay-pitt bottome* 1690, y^e *Clay-pitt-hill* 1697, *Clay Pit hill* 1706, y^e *Clay pit hill* 1724, y^e *Clay pitt bottom* 1697, y^e *Clay pitt-Bottom* 1724 (*v.* **clæg, pytt, hyll, botm**); *in campis de limb'ge* l12, *the commonfeld* 1577, *Lymber feild* 1587 (self-explanatory); *Conye stye(s)* 1577, *Connie Stigh* 1601, *conny stigh* 1611, *Cony-stigh* 1625, *Conney stigh* 1637, *Coney stighes* 1664, *Connie stigh* 1671, y^e *Short Cony-stighs* 1690, *Short Coney-stighs* 1697, *short Conney stighs* 1706, y^e *Short Coney Stighs* 1724, *Cunnystigh headland* 1674 (*v.* **hēafod-land**), *the Conny garthe cloases* 1587 (*v.* **coni**, **stīg** 'a path', **garðr**, and cf. Coneygreen Wood *supra*); *viam de Cotum* c.1260, *Cottam gate* 1577, 1601, 1634, *the waie to Cotham* 1611, *Cotham gate* 1625, 1664, 1674, 1724, *Cotham-Gate* 1690, *Cotham-gate* 1706, *Cotham gate* 1724 ('the road to Coatham (in Brocklesby parish)', *v.* **gata**); *cowe stygh gate* 1577, *Cow stigh* 1611, 1634, 1637, - *steigh* 1625, *Cow stigh gate* 1664, 1671, 1674, 1706, y^e *Cow-stigh* - 1690, *Cowstigh* - 1697, 1724, *Cowsteigh Gate* 1745 ('the path for cows', *v.* **cū, stīg, stigr**, with **gata**); *the dam* 1634; *Dautons loue* (sic) 1577 (from the surn. *Dauton*, *Dawton*, cf. Robert *Dawton* 1558 *Inv*); *Daw pitt* 1601, *the Daw-pit* 1625, *the dow pit* 1637, *Daw Pitt Furlong* 1676 (the forms are late but the first el. may be ME *dawe* 'a jackdaw', the second being **pytt**); *depedale in qua fossorium lapidum est* l12 *HarlCh* (*v.* **dēop, dæl, dalr**); *atte Dike* 1294 Ass (p), *dycke forlandes* 1577, *Dike furlongs* 1637[3], *dik furlonges* 1644, *dike furlong* 1664, y^e *dike furlonge* 1674, *Dike Furlong* 1676 (*v.* **dík, furlang**, note the form *forlandes* for *forlanges*, not uncommon in LNR); *donnegarthe cloase* 1587 (the first el. is obscure, but may well be a surn. in a compound with **garðr**, *v.* also **clos(e)**); *upper low east gate* 1577 (*v.* **ēast, gata**); *Est outlandes* c.1260, *Esthoutlandes* c.1260 (Ed1) *Newh, Esthowtlande* 1333 (cf. *the outelandes, West outlandes infra*); *Farding greene* 1676 (*v.* **feorðung** in ME 'a fourth part', 'a farthing', the latter with reference to rent, **grēne**[2]); *finhou* a1167 (later hand) *NCot* (probably, as Dr John Insley suggests, from the ON pers.n. *Finnr* and **haugr** 'a (burial) mound, a hill', a Scand. compound); *Foxholdyle* a1167 (later hand) *NCot* (*v.* **fox-hol, deill**); *Byhyndethegarth* 1341 RIL (p), *Bihynd the Garth* 1342 Fine (p), *garthe furlonges* 1577 (*v.* **garðr, furlang**); *gibb Lane* 1634, - *laine* 1637 (the sense of *gibb* here is uncertain; it may be *Gibb*, the hypocoristic form of the pers.n. *Gilbert*, and it may be noted that ME **gib(be)** is recorded in MED s.v. 1b as a popular name for a cat); *terram ... Conuentus de gracia dei* Ed1 (i.e. Gracedieu Lei); *greene gate marpher* 1611, 1634, *greene gate* 1625, *Greenegate* 1637, *Green-gate Meere-furre* 1690, *Greengate Meerefurre* 1697, *green gate meerefurre* 1706, *greengate meere* 1724 (probably 'a green lane or access road' *v.* **grēne**[1], **gata**, with **marfur** 'a boundary furrow'); *Grenehowbergh* 1333 (*v.* **grēne**[1], **haugr**, with **beorg**); *viam de Gressebi* c.1260, *Gresbye gate* 1577, *Grisbie* - 1611, *girsbie* - 1634, 1637, *grisby* - 1664,

Gresby-gate 1690, *Grasby gate* 1697, 1724, *Gresby* - 1690 ('the road to Grasby', *v.* **gata**; it is the same as *Grisby stygh way* 1625, *v.* **stīg, stīgr** 'a path, a narrow road'); *Grymsbie gate* 1611 ('the road to Grimsby', *v.* **gata**); *the headland* 1611, 1625, 1634, *the Head Land, (the)* head land dale 1634, *the Headland dale* 1637, (*v.* **deill**), *ye head land* 1706, *ye Headland* 1724 (*v.* **hēafod-land**); *Hedesti* a1167 (later hand) *NCot, Ede styg* c.1260, *Edestyg'* c.1260 (Ed1) *Newh* (as Dr John Insley points out this is probably from the ME pers.n. *Ede*, a short form of *Edward*, and **stīg, stīgr**; perhaps identical with this are the later forms *edge styghe* 1577, *edg stigh* 1611, *Edg-* 1634, *Edge-* 1637, *ege-* 1664, *Edge steigh* 1625, *ege stigh* 1664, *Edgstigh* 1671; if so the original first el. has been associated with *edge*); *Holeyn* 1314 Fine (p) (*v.* **holegn**); *Hop welles* 1333 (perhaps 'springs by an enclosure', the el. **hop** having that sense in fenland, *v.* **wella**); *le Hundrth'* 1333, *Hundreds* 1577, 1676, *the* - 1664, *y^e* - 1690, 1697, *the hunderethes* 1587, *ye hundreds* 1601, 1671, 1674, 1706, 1724, *the* - 1611, 1625, 1634, *the Hundredes* 1637 (from **hundred**, but in what sense is uncertain); *the Kilnhous garth* 1664 (*v.* **kiln-hous, garðr**); *Kynges Crofte* 1551 Pat (named from the *King* family, cf. William *King* 1599 *PR*, and **croft**); *the Lady close* 1634, (*v.* **hlǣfdige** 'a lady, a nun, our Lady'); *langberg'* c.1260, *langeberg'* c.1260 (Ed1) *Newh*, *Langebergh'* 1333, *shorte longe borow* 1577, *long -, short Longbrough* 1601, *long -, short Langbrough* 1611, 1625, *long -, Short* - 1634, 1637, *Short* - 1697, *Short Langbrough* 1690, *short langbrough* 1706, *short Langbroug* (sic) 1724 (*v.* **lang, be(o)rg**, the second el. here possibly having the sense 'a barrow, an artificial mound'); *lavoracke Hall* 1577, *leverock Hall* 1587, *Lauerocke Hall* 1601, 1625, *Lauerock hall* 1611, 1634, *Laverocke Hall* 1637, *Laverick Hall* 1676 (possibly 'lark hall' (*v.* **lāwerce, hall**) in some figurative sense, perhaps ironically of a small piece of land as in the f.n. Lark's Lease, found elsewhere; the same name occurs in Searby f.ns. (b), *v.* the discussion PN YW 2 102-3 s.n. Gawthorpe Hall, where it is suggested that bird-names frequently used in the names of houses may possibly have much the same significance as the numerous Folly Halls); *Limber gate* 1634 (*v.* **gata**); *the long furlong* 1664, *ye longe furland* 1671, *ye long furlonge* 1674, *Long Furlong* 1676, *ye long-Furlong* 1690, *long furlong* 1697, *ye long furlong* 1706 (*v.* **lang, furlang**, cf. *shorte forlande infra*); *Longhuil* (sic) a1167 (later hand) *NCot, Longe hyll* 1577, *long hill* 1601, 1611, 1625, 1634, 1637 (*v.* **lang, hygel** 'a hillock', later associated with *hill*, as in Goosehills *supra*); *the Lowe Cloase* 1587; *the Low garth farme dale* 1625 (*v.* **garðr, deill**); *the Low gate* 1611, 1664, *ye low* - 1625, *the Lowe waye* 1637, *Low stigh gate* 1671 (*v.* **stīg, gata**; the references are to the same road); *Lymber feild* 1587 (self-explanatory, *v.* **feld**); *One messuage ... Commonly called the manner howse* 1587; *de Marisco* Hy3, e14 (p) ('the marsh'); *forum in Magna Limberg'* 1276 RH, *the markett place* 1587; *marlepit* a1167 (later hand) *NCot* (self-explanatory, *v.* **marle, pytt**); *the meane grounde* 1625, 1634, 1637,

Meane Grounde 1676, y^e *Meane-ground* 1690, - *meane Ground* 1697, - *ground* 1706, y^e *mean* - 1724 (v. **(ge)mǣne** 'common'; it was on the parish boundary); *apud attemerdale* 1333 (v. **atter** 'at the', **(ge)mǣre, deill**); *Milnerheuedland* c.1260 (from the occupational name or surn. *Milner* and **hēafod-land**); *tofto ... quod vocatur Mometoft* 1333 (v. **toft**, perhaps there is a minim confusion in the first el. for *Moine* from OFr *moine* 'a monk', as Dr John Insley points out); *the monke headland* 1611, 1634, y^e *Monke* - 1625, *monk headland* 1637 (v. **munuc, hēafod-land**); *the myle pit* 1611, 1634, 1637, *the mile pitt* 1664, y^e - 1671, y^e *Mile-pit* 1690, y^e *mile pit* 1674, 1706 (perhaps from OE **milde** 'loam' (confused with *mile* by popular etymology) and **pytt**); *Morlie thing* 1587 (presumably from the surn. *Morley* and **þing** 'a possession'); y^e *Nettle-buske land* 1690, y^e *Netle buske land* 1706, 1725 ('land infested with nettle-beds', v. **netle-bush, land**, and for an early example v. *Nettelbustmar* (sic) in Stallingborough f.ns. (b) *infra*); *Newsam land* 1577 (presumably land held by Newsham Abbey); *no gate* 1611, *noe* - 1625, *no waye* 1634 ('a dead-end way'); *the north feild* 1634, 1637, y^e *North Field* 1745 (one of the four open fields of Great Limber); *the north pit* 1634; *the outelandes* 1577, 1611 (self-explanatory, v. **ūt, land**); *Padgetes dale* 1611 (from the surn. *Padget*, cf. John *Padget* 1607 and **deill** 'a share, an allotment'); *the parsonage head land* 1577 (v. **hēafod-land**); *Peselandes* 1333, *pease landes* 1577, 1664, *Pease landes* 1611, 1634, *pease-landes* 1625, *peaselands* 1637, *Peaslands* 1671, *peaslands* 1674, *Pease Lands* 1676, *Peas-lands* 1690, *Pease-lands* 1697, *pease-lands* 1706, *the pease Cloase* 1587, *pease Close* 1611, - *close* 1634 (v. **pise, land** and **clos(e)**); *the pit* 1625, *a pit* 1637 (v. **pytt**); *the preist dicke* 1587 (v. **dīc, dīk**), *the priest-pit* 1690, y^e *preist pit* 1697, y^e *priest* - 1706, y^e *Priest Pitt* 1724 (v. **prēost, pytt**); *Riby-hedg* 1690, *Riby-hedge* 1697, *Ryby hedge* 1706 (from the neighbouring parish of Riby); *Rosemare* a1167 (later hand) *NCot* (perhaps from ON **hross** 'a horse' and **(ge)mǣre** 'a boundary, land on a boundary'); *Salter gate* 1611 (v. **saltere** 'a salt-worker, a salt-merchant', **gata**; a common name for a salt-way); *Scardhou* a1167 (later hand) *NCot, Scharthou* c.1260, *Scar'howe* c.1260 (Ed1) *Newh* (probably 'a notched or mutilated mound', v. **sceard, haugr**); *Scayhull'* 1333 (v. **hyll**); *Schothoudale* c.1260, *Scohthowdale* (sic) c.1260 (Ed1) *Newh*, *Skottesdeale* 1577, *Scoshey* (sic) 1601, - *dale* 1637, *Scotchy Dale* 1625, *Scotch dale* 2664, *Scoch* - 1671, *Skosher dale* 1611, *Scotcher-dale* 1690, 1697, *Scosbe daile* (sic) 1634, *Scots Furlong* 1676, *Scotts furlong* 1724 (this is probably from **Scot(t)** 'a Scot, a Gael' and **haugr** 'a mound', with **deill** 'a share of land', later modified to '(the) Scot's share of land'; for a discussion of the first el. v. Scotgate in Croxton f.n. (b) and cf. *Scothil* in Keelby f.ns. (b) and *Scosteholm* in Stallingborough f.ns. (b)); *viam de Seuerby* a1167 (later hand) *NCot, Searbye styghe* 1577 ('the path, narrow road to Searby (the adjacent parish)', v. **stīg**); *the Shoples* 1587; *shorte forlande, shorte forelong heades* 1577 (v. **hēafod**), *the short furlong* 1611, - *furlonge* 1625,

Short furlonges 1634, *the Short* - 1637, y^e *short furlong* 1674 (*v.* **sc(e)ort, furlang**, cf. *the long furlong supra*); *the showes* 1587 (perhaps from **sceaga** 'a small wood'); *the Shubbes* 1577, 1634, y^e *Shubes* (sic) 1601, *the shubes* 1611, *Shubbes* 1637, *the Shubes* 1664, y^e *Shube* 1671, - *shubs* 1674, - *Shubbs* 1690, y^e *Shubbs* 1697, *ye Shubs* 1724, *the Shubb Close* 1637, *the Shrubes* (sic) 1625 (the persistent forms without -*r*- before and after 1625 seem to rule out a derivation from **scrubb** 'a shrub, brushwood, a place overgrown with brushwood', so that the name must be left unexplained); *the Smakeroles* 1625, *Smackrells* (sic) 1634, 1676, 1724. *the Smakerels* 1637, *Mackerills* 1690, *Mackrills* 1697, 1706 (obscure); *the Souter well Cloase* 1587 (probably the ME occupational name or derived surn. *Sutere* and **wella** 'a spring'); *in Australi campo* c.1260, *the south feild* 1634, 1637, *the South Field* 1697, y^e - 1745 (one of the four open fields of Great Limber); *staning stigh* 1611, 1634, 1637, *Stanninges steigh* 1625 (probably from **stænen** 'stony' and **stig** 'a path'); *Staynhill'* 1333 (*v.* **steinn, hyll**, the first el. is Scand.); *Stainberg, Steyneberg* a1167 (later hand) *NCot*, *Stenebarow hyll* 1577, *stonbrough hill* 1601, *Stonebrook hill* (sic) 1611, - *Hill* 1637, *Stone brough hill* 1625, *stonebrough* - 1634 (*v.* **steinn, berg**, probably a Scand. compound, with **hyll** added in the later forms); *The stray Cloase* 1587 (from ME **stray** 'piece of unenclosed common pasture', evidently enclosed here by the late 16th cent. and cf. Stray Pce in Riby f.ns. (a) *infra*); *the strete* 1577, *the stright* 1664, y^e *streete* 1674, *Caister Street* 1690, *Caister street* 1706, *Caister street* 1724 (*v.* **stræt**); *Stubdal'* a1167 (later hand) *NCot* (*v.* **stubb, deill**, though the first el. may be the ME nickname or surn. *Stubb* (Reaney s.n.   Stubbe)); *terram quondam Ade Suthinby* c.1260 ('land formerly belonging to Adam South-in-the-Village', *v.* **sūð, in, bý**; the English form from **in** is noteworthy; cf. *Westiby infra*); *Swallow gate* 1577, 1664, 1674, 1706, 1724, *Swallow-gate* 1690, 1697 ('the road to Swallow (an adjacent parish)', *v.* **gata**); *Swallow marpher* 1611, 1634, 1637, - *marfer* 1625, *swallow Marfer side* 1671, *Swallow marfar* - 1674 (*v.* **marfur** 'a boundary furrow' and prec.); y^e *Swarth, the Swarth headings* 1625, *the swarth* 1637 (from dial *swarth* 'a piece of grassland'); *t'ram mag'ri Milicie templi* c.1260 ('land of the master of the Knights Templar', *v.* **tempel**); *vie de Thorp* c.1260, *thorpe gate* 1634, *thorp* - 1637, *Thorpe* - 1674 ('the road to Thorpe', *v.* **gata**; this is presumably Kettleby Thorpe in Bigby parish); *Threhowes* c.1260 ('the three mounds', *v.* **þrēo, haugr**); *toftes* c.1260, 1333, *the toftes* 1577, 1611, 1634, 1637, *The Toftes* 1625 (*v.* **toft** 'a building site, a curtilage'); *Ulceby gate* 1664 ('the road to Ulceby', *v.* **gata**); *upwell gate* 1577, *Upwell* - 1664, *Vpwell* - 1690, 1706, *Upwell* - 1724 ('the spring higher up', *v.* **upp, wella**); *Vestmare* a1167 (in a later hand) *NCot* ('the west boundary', *v.* **west, (ge)mǣre**); *warleye pittes* 1577; *Warmspittes* 1601, 1634, 1637, *Warmes-pittes* 1625, *Warmspites* 1664, *Warmespits* 1674, y^e *warmes-pit* 1690, y^e *Warmspit* 1697, y^e *Warmspit* 1706, y^e *Warmspitt* 1724 (the forms are late, but it may be a compound of the OE pers.n. *Wærmund* and **pytt**; if it is a comparatively late name, then the first el. may well be the surn. *Warme* (v. Reaney s.n.); *water close* 1634, *watclose* (sic) 1637; *Atte Welle de magna Limbergh'* 1300 *FF* (p), *the Well farme* 1631 *PR* (v. **wella**); *Westiby* 1287 (1317) Pat (p), *Westyby* e14 (p) (v. **vestr, í, by**); *In occidentali campo, in campo occidentali* c.1260, Ed1, *in Occidental' campo de Lynbergh'* 1333, *west feild* 1601, *the West feild* 1611, 1625, *West -* 1634, *the west feild* 1637, y^e *West Field* 1745 (v. **west, feld**, one of the four open fields of Great Limber, cf. ye East Fd *supra*); y^e *west gate* 1706 (v. **gata**); *Westhill* 1333; *West outlandes* c.1260, *Westhowtlande* 1333, *the west ought landes* 1577 (cf. *the outlandes supra*); "the West soke of" *Magna Lymberge* 1287 (1317) Pat (v. **west, sōcn**); *wollmar rigge* 1577, *Woolman rigg* 1601, 1671, - *Rigg* 1664, - *rige* 1674, *Woollmer-rigge* 1690, *Woolmer Rigs* 1697, - *rigg* 1706, - *Rigge* 1724 (probably from the surn. *Woolmer*, ultimately OE *Wulfmær*, and **hryggr** 'a ridge, a cultivated strip of ground'); y^e *Wraigh* 1601 (v. **vrá**); *the wyndinges* 1577 (*windinges* has been found as an appellative in Nettleton Terriers of the 16th century, though it is not noted in dictionaries. An earlier example has been noted in *wynedyngs* in Immingham f.ns. (b), where an appellative use has also been found, and where the name is briefly discussed).

Melton Ross

MELTON ROSS

> *Medeltone* 1086 DB
>
> *Meltuna* c.1115 LS, *-tona* 1146 RA i, l12 ib ii, 1238-43 Fees, *Melton('*) 1187-93 (e14) YCh x, 1200, 1201 Cur, 1212 Fees, 1230-39 RA ix, 1242-43 Fees, 1265 Misc, 1269 *HarlCh*, 1271-2 *Ass*, 1276 RH, 1280 RA ii *et freq* to 1428 FA, 1526 Sub, - *in Lyndeseye* 1342 Orig, 1342 Pat
>
> *Mealtun* c.1160 Dane (p), *-tona* 1176-90 (e14) YCh x, *-ton('*) 1191-95 RA ii, 1207 P (p), *Mealtona in Lyndeseya* l12 RA ii
>
> *Miauton'* 1200 CurR, *Meauton'* 1201 Cur
>
> *Meleton('*) 1189 (1332), 1227 Ch, 1242-43 Fees, 1346 FA, 1415 Cl
>
> *Meuton'* 1204 Cur, 1243-43 Fees
>
> *Melton Roos* 1375 *MiD*, 1381 Peace, 1386 Cl, 1386 *FF*, 1402 FA *et passim* to 1608 *Yarb*, - *otherwise Melton Ross* 1752 *ib*, *Meltonroos* 1382 Cl, 1397 Pat, - *Roose* 1539 LP xiv
>
> *Milton Roos* 1394 Pat
>
> *Meelton Roos* 1424 NCWills ii

prebendarius de ... *Melton Rose* 1437 LCStatutes, *Meltonrose*
1562-67 LNQ v, 1576 Saxton, - *Rose* 1703 *Terrier*
Melton Rosse 1535 VE iv, 1653 WillsPCC, 1664 *Terrier,*
Meltonrosse 1610 Speed, *Melton Ros* 1542 NCWills, *Melton
Ross* 1677, 1709, 1724 *Terrier et passim*

This is a partial Scandinavianisation of *Middleton* 'the middle
farmstead, village', *v.* **middel, tūn**, with **meðal** replacing the cognate
OE **middel**. The same name occurs in Lei, Nf and YER. Forms
in *Mealtun*, etc. represent the AN loss of ð between vowels (ANInfl
90ff, Feilitzen 102), while those in *Meuton'* similarly represent AN
influence with the vocalisation of pre-consonantal *l* (ANInfl 146ff,
Feilitzen 78). It is not clear to which places *middle* refers. The *de
Ros* family held one fee in Melton in 1303 FA, but they have been
noted there first in 1265 Misc.

CAMP COVERT, - *Cover* 1832 *Yarb*, 1848 *TA*, named from
Yarborough Camp in Croxton *supra*. CATTA FURZE (lost), 1824
O, 1830 Gre, cf. *Farre Catta Mar-fur* 1664, *Long Catta* 1666, - *Cattoe*
p1671, *catta marfer* 1703, *Cattamarfer* 1706, *Catta marfar* 1724, 1822
all *Terrier* (*v.* **marfur**), *Catta* 1832 *Yarb*, 1848 *TA*; the forms are late,
but it may be suggested that this is 'the spur of land where (wild)
cats are found', *v.* **cat(t), hōh**; the development to -*a* would be
paralleled by Clougha (PN La 169) and to -*oe* by a series of names
like Cranoe Lei (DEPN s.n.), Keysoe and Putnoe Bd (PN BdHu
14-15 and 60) and Moulsoe (PN Bk 36-37). GALLOWS COVERT,
- *Cover* 1824 O, 1830 Gre, 1832 *Yarb*, named from Melton Gallows
infra and now in Barnetby le Wold parish. It is *West Field Cover*
1828 Bry, cf. *Melton West field* 1838 *Terrier, the west Feild* 1649
Survey, - *West Field* 1664, *yᵉ west Field* 1668, *the Westfield* 1709, *ye
West field* 1724, *Melton west-field* 1722 (Barnetby le Wold), *yᵉ west
field* 1822, *melton west field gate* 1662 (Barnetby le Wold), *Melton
West fiel Gate* (sic) 1690 (Barnetby le Wold), - *West field Gate* 1697
(Barnetby le Wold), - *west-field Gate* 1700 (Barnetby le Wold) all
Terrier (*v.* **gata** 'a road'), *Lower -, Upper West Field* 1832 *Yarb*, 1848
TA, self-explanatory, *v.* **west, feld;** one of the open fields of Melton
Ross. KNAB'S CROSSING, cf. *the nab close* 1677, *nab Close* 1709
both *Terrier*, named from Knab's Hill in Barnetby le Wold *supra.*
MELTON GALLOWS, 1828 Bry, *Gallows* 1824 O, 1830 Gre and

Melton furc' 1276 RH. MELTON HALL, *Hall* 1828 Bry, cf. *Melton Hallgarth, ye Hall garth* 1666, - *Hallgarth* 1668, *the hallgarth* 1677, *halgarth* 1709, *ye Hall garth* 1724, 1822, *Hall Garth* 1832 all *Terrier*, 1848 *TA*, 'the enclosure, the small plot of ground by or belonging to the hall', *v.* **hall, gar͞or**. MELTON HIGH WOOD, 1830 Gre, - *High W.^{d}* 1828 Bry, *High Wood* 1792 Yarb, 1824 O, 1832 Yarb, named from its situation and cf. Low Wood in Barnetby le Wold *supra.* MIDDLEGATE RD, *Middle Gate Lane* 1824 O, 1828 Bry, the name of the ridgeway from Caistor to South Ferriby, *v.* Middlegate Lane in Bigby *supra.* RACE LANE, 1828 Bry, also in Wootton *infra.* WELBECK SPRING, *a spring of Water ... called Wellbeck* 1638 (Barnetby le Wold), *Well Becke* 1666, *Welbeck marfarr* 1662 (Bigby), - *Marfare* 1668 (Bigby), *Wellbecke Marfurr* 1671 (Barnetby le Wold), - *marforrow* 1690 (Bigby) all *Terrier* (*v.* **marfur** 'a boundary furrow'), *Wellbecks* 1820 *MiscDep* 204, *Welbeck* 1828 Bry; this is identical with Welbeck (PN Nt 103-4) meaning 'the stream rising from a spring', *v.* **wella, bekkr**, an AScand compound.

Field-Names

Principal forms in (a) are 1848 *TA* 230; spellings dated 1649 are *Survey*, 1832 are *Yarb*; other dated forms are *Terrier* unless otherwise noted.

(a) Barnetby le Wold pce (named from the adjacent parish); Bird House Cl 1832; Brough Hill 1832, 1848 (*v.* **burh**, referring to Yarborough Camp in Croxton *supra*); Bull Cl 1832 (cf. *ye Bull-Marfurre* 1666, *the Bull marfurr* 1671, *the bull meadow* 1677, *Bullpeece* 1706, *bullpeece* 1709, *ye bull peece* 1724, *v.* **bula, marfur** 'a boundary furrow', as elsewhere in this parish, **pece**); ye bush pce 1822 (*v.* **busc, pece**); y^e by Marfar 1822 (*By-mar-fur* 1664, *by marfure* 1668, *y^e by marfer* p1671, *the by marfar* 1677, *ye bymarfer* 1703, *Bymarfra, Bymorfray* (sic) 1709, *ye by Marfar* 17, formally this could be an elliptical formation '(the place) by the boundary furrow', *v.* **bī, marfur**); Church and Church Yd, Church Cl 1832, 1848, - Plat 1832, 1848 (*ad ecclesiam* 1327 *SR*, *atte Kirk'* 1332 *ib* both (p)); Clay Pits 1832, 1848 (*Clay:pitts* 1664, *Claypitts* 1668, *Clay pitts* 1671); Cottagers Mdw 1832, 1848 (2x), Cottages - (sic) 1848, Cottagers Pasture 1848; ye Cow cl 1822, Cow Cl 1832, 1848 (1709, *ye cowcloses* 1703, *Cow close* 1724, (*the*) *Little cow close* p1671, 1677); dunnes Hedge 1822, The Dunnace, Low -, Top Dunnace 1832, The

Dunnace, Top Dunnace 1848 (cf. *in Dunnis* 1664, *Dunnies* 1668, *Dunnis James wood* 1671, *donas hedge* 1709, *dunnes hedge* 1724, *dunnis hedge* 1724); 18 Acres 1832, Eighteen Acres 1848; New -, Old 50 Acres 1832, - Fifty Acres 1848; ye fool pit 1822 (*foolpit* 1703, *fool pitt* 1709, *ye fool pitt* 1724, *fowlpitdich* 1706, 'the dirty pool', the 1706 form evidently alluding to a drainage ditch feeding the pool, v. **fūl, pytt, dīc**); Forty five Acres 1832, 1848; Fryer Bob (2x) 1832, 1848, Fryer Bole (sic) 1832, 1848 (obscure); Holliwells 1832, Halliwells 1848; Hammers Hall Cl 1832; Harbour Cl 1832; Hill Cl 1832, Pt of Hill Cl and Plantn (2x) 1848 (ye hill 1703, hill 1709, cf. *del Hill'* 1327 *SR*, *de monte* 1332 *ib* both (p)); Holme Cls, ye Holmes hedge, ye Holmes and Leas 1822, Gt Holmes. Lt Holmes (2x) 1832, 1848 (cf. *Holme meadowe* 1649, y^e *Holmes* 1668, *the* - 1671, *holmes* 1703, 1709, *the holmes and Leas* 1709, y^e *Holmes and Leas* 1724, *the Holme(s)gate* 1664, *the holmes yeat* 1677 (v. **geat**), *the Holmes hedge* 1664, *the holmes hedge* 1671, y^e - 1703, *Holmes hedge* 1724, *the east holmes hedge* 1709, y^e *Lower Holmes* 1668, *the Low Holmes* 1677, *the upper Holmes* 1664, 1668, y^e *high holme* p1671, *Westholme farmeland* 1666, y^e *west holme closes* p1671, y^e *west holmes* 1703, *west holmes Closes* 1709, *west holme closes* 1724, v. **holmr** 'an island of land, raised land amidst marshes' as frequently in north L, cf. ye leas *infra*); Home Cl 1832, 1848; ye Ings cl 1822, Ings Cl 1832 (*the Ing Close, Ing Close nooke* 1664, y^e *Inges,* y^e *Inge-close* 1668, *the ingclose, the far ingclose marfarr* 1677, y^e *Ings Close* 1703, 1724, v. **eng**, 'meadow, pasture' (as elsewhere in this parish), **clos(e)**, **marfur**); Kirmington Pasture 1832, - Plat 1848 (from the adjacent parish and **plat**^{2} 'a plot of ground'); ye leas 1822, The Leys 1832 (*the Leas (hedge)* 1677, y^e *Leas* 1703, *Leas* 1709, v. **lea**, a later development of **lēah** in the sense 'meadow', and note the use of *leas* as an appellative for meadow in 1822, cf. Holme Cls *supra*); Low Fd 1832 (3x), 1848; Low Paddock 1832, 1848; Melton Fd 1762, - feild 1769 both *Terrier* (Croxton) (*Melton field* 1671 *Terrier* (Barnetby le Wold), 1707 *ib* (Croxton)); Middle Fd 1832, 1848 (y^e *midle feild* p1671); Narrow Walk 1832, 1848; North Fd 1832, 1848; Ozier -, Oziers Holt; Paddock (- and Plantn, - and Moat); ye Parsonage Ings 1822 (*the parsons Ings* 1664, *the parson Inges* 1668, *- ings* p1671, *the parson Ings which ings belongs the parsonage* 1677, *ye personageings* 1703, *personage ings* 1709, *ye Personage* - 1724, v. **eng**); Plantation (3x), Plantation Ride; Priest (sic) 1832, Prieste 1848; Pudding Poke Fd 1832, Pudding Poke 1848 (a fanciful name for land with sticky soil); Line of Railway (and Garden); Roads Cl; Screed; (Lt) Stone Pit Walk 1832, 1848 (cf. *Stone pitt hill* p1671, *the* - 1677); Thirty Acres 1832, Pt of Thirty acres; Tommy Thornham 1832, 1848; Town end Cl 1832; Willow Holt 1832 (v. **wilig, holt**); Wold Hill 1832, 1848; Wood Cl, - Plot 1832, (Low) Wood Cl, - Plat (2x), - Plot 1848; Woodside;

(b) *Barnards house of Melton* 1634 *Terrier* (Barnetby le Wold) (from the
surn. *Barnard*, cf. Thomas *Barnard of Melton Rosse* 1638 *Inv*); *Bateman close* 1668
(from the surn. *Bateman*); *Croxton mare, Croxton gate End* 1664, *Croxton gate*
(*end*) 1668, p1671 ('the boundary with Croxton', '(the end of, or part of the
parish near) the road to Croxton', *v.* (ge)mǣrc, ende[1], gata); *ad crucem* 1354
Ipm (p) (*v.* cros); *the East Feild* 1649, 1664, *y*^e - 1668, - *field* 1724 (1822), *y*^e
easte field 1703, *y*^e *east feild* 1709 (*v.* ēast, feld, cf. West Field Cover under
Gallows Covert *supra*); *Elsham Mare* 1664, *elsham mare* 1677 ('the boundary with
Elsham', *v.* (ge)mǣre); *Foot-bridge* 1664, *y*^e *Foott-Bridge* 1668, *the foote bridge*
1677; *the gareing marffar* 1677 (*v.* geiri, eng, marfur); *Limbergate end* 1677 ('the
road to Great Limber', *v.* gata, with ende[1]); *la mare de Melton'* 1271-72, 1297
Ass, La Mare de Melton, la mare 1317-18 *FF*, 1327, 1332 *SR, del Mar de Melton*
1346 FA all (p), *the mare* 1677 (*v.* (ge)mǣre 'a boundary'); *Melton Acre-dikes*
1662 *Terrier* (Barnetby le Wold) (cf. *y*^e *acredikes* in Barnetby le Wold f.ns. (b));
Melton bottoms 1626, - *bottome* 1634, 1638 all *Terrier* (Barnetby le Wold) (*v.*
botm); *Melton oatclose-nooke* 1662, - *oat close nooke* 1664, - *Oat close* 1668 all
Terrier (Barnetby le Wold) (*v.* nōk); *Melton Shop* 1664, 1671, - *Shopp* 1668, 1671
all *Terrier* (Barnetby le Wold) (*v.* sc(e)oppa, ME *shop(pe)* 'a shop, a shed' but
the reference is not clear); *the Oxe pasture* 1649; *penny greene* 1664 (*v.* pening,
grēne[2], perhaps alluding to a rent for pasturage); *watry Furrs* 1671 (*v.* furh in
the pl.; *furrs* is a frequent variant of *furrows* in north L).

Nettleton

NETTLETON

> *Neteltone* (4x) 1086 DB, -*tune* c.1115 LS, 1150-60, l12 Dane
> both (p), -*tun(')* 1150-60 ib, 1218 Ass, 1226 Cur, 1238-43
> Fees, 1245 *HarlCh*, -*tune* Hy3 *ib*, -*tona* 1187 (1409) Gilb,
> 1219-26 RA ix (p), 1225-30, 1230-40 ib iv, -*ton* John Abbr,
> 1210 Cur, 1212 Fees, 1220 FF, c.1220 *DC* (p) *et passim* to
> 1428, 1431 FA, 1664 *Terrier, Neteleton'* 1225 Cur
> *Nettiltona* c.1150, 1187, e13, 1276 (1409) Gilb, -*ton(')* 1242-43
> Fees, 1344 Cl, 1346 FA, 1359 Ipm *et passim* to 1526 Sub,
> 1548 Pat, 1577 *Terrier*
> *Netheltun* 1150-60 Dane
> *Netleton(')* 1175 ChancR (p), 1176 P (p), 1224 FF, 1224 Cur,
> 1231 Cl, 1235 Dugd vi, 1271-72 *Ass*, 1274 RRGr, 1298 Abbr,
> 1636, 1657 *Foster*, 1648, 1709 *Yarb*, -*tun'* 1218 Ass
> *Netteltona* a1219 Welles, -*tun* 1242 *HarlCh*, -*ton* (') 1252 Ch,

1254 ValNor, 1263 FF, 1281 QW, 1282 Ipm, 1291 Tax *et passim* to 1492 Fine, 1552, 1555 Pat, - "by" *Thwangcastre* 1349 ib

Netiltona 1230-40 RA iv, c.1250, 1276 (1409) Gilb, *-ton*(') 1325 Cl, 1332 *SR*, 1336 RA iv, 1340 Cl, 1343 NI *et passim* to 1393 Cl, 1472 WillsPCC, *-tun* 1346 Cl, *-tone* 1389 Dugd vi, 1540 Whit, 1547 *MinAcct, Netylton* 1428 FA, 1529, 1530, 1531 Wills iii

Nettleton(') 1242-43 Fees, 1271 *Ass*, 1303 Ipm, 1305, 1342 Pat, 1576 LER, 1576 Saxton, 1610 Speed *et passim, Nettylton* 1535 VE iv, 1550, 1561 Pat

'The farmstead or village where nettles grow', *v.* **netel(e), tūn.** For *Thwangcastre v.* Caistor *supra.* Before the widespread use of fertilisers, the presence of nettles indicated a phosphate content in the soil, suggesting that the ground where they grew had been previously settled.

DRAYCOTES (lost), 1212 Ass, *Dreycotes* 1281 ib (LNQ ix), *Draycote* 1298 ib (p), 1316 FA, *-cotis* 1327 *SR* (p), *-cotes* 1327, 1333 *ib* both (p), *Dracottes* 1634 *Lamb*, probably 'the shed(s) where drays are kept', *v.* **dræg, cot**; the site is not known, *v.* DB liv.

HARDWICK (lost)
  Herdwic Hy2 (1409) Gilb, 1200 Cur, 1202 Ass, 1206 FF, 1208-9 Ass, 1209 P (p), 1242-43 Fees, *-wyk* e13 (1409) Gilb, 1242 *HarlCh*, 1350 Cl, 1428 FA, *-wyck* 1237 FF, 1242-32 Fees, *-wik* 1250 FF
  Herdewych Hy2 (1319) Dugd vi, *-wic* 1202 P, 1202 Ass, 1203 FF, 1218 Ass, *-wych* 1245 FF, *-wyk* 1330 Orig, 1359, 1367 Ipm, *-wyke* 1388, 1393 Cl, *-wik* 1346 FA, *-wike* 1388 Cl
  Hertwich' 1200 Cur, *-wik* 1303 FA
  Herthwic 1202 FF, *-wike* c.1275 LNQ vi, *Herthewyk* 1284 Ipm, *-wic* Ed1 *HarlCh*
  Hardewic 1218 Ass
  Herwic 1230-40 RA iv (p), *-wik* 1346 FA, *-wyk* 1316 ib, 1327 *SR* (p), 1387 Peace
  harwick 1587 *Yarb*

Hardwick Close 1794 *EnclA* (Plan), 1825 *BC*
'The herd farm', *v.* **heorde-wīc**. The site of the lost settlement
is shown on the Plan of the Enclosure Award and is marked on the
6" O.S. map, and *v.* DB lvii for details.

WYKEHAM (lost)
    Wiham 1086 DB
    Uicheim c.1115 LS
    Wycham l12, e13 (13) *Alv*, e13 (1409) Gilb, 1230-40 RA iv (p),
        1242-43 Fees, 1428 FA, 1535 VE iv, *Northywycham* 1271-72
        Ass, Wicham 1200 Cur, e13 *HarlCh* (p), e13, a1205, a1218
        RA iv, m13 *HarlCh* (p), 1346 FA, *Wykam* 1242-43 Fees,
        -ham 1263 FF, 1327, 1332 *SR* both (p), 1343 NI (p), 1367
        Ipm, Hy8 Lanc, *Wikam* Hy3 *HarlCh*, *-ham* c.1275 LNQ vi,
        1316 FA, - *iuxta Nettiltona* 1276 (1409) Gilb
    Wikeham 1236 Fees, 1336 RA iv, - *de Netelton'* 1330 *CottCh*
        (p), *Wykeham* 1282 Ipm, 1303 FA, 1557 Pat, 1832, 1833,
        1852, 1875, 1889 *Yarb*, *-hame* 1365 Bodl
    Wycholm 1521 *Anc*
    wicame 1577, *Wicame* c.1580, *Wicam* 1662 all *Terrier*
    wickham Cloase 1587 *Yarb*

This is derived from OE **wīc-hām**, discussed at length by
Margaret Gelling, 'English Place-Names derived from the
Compound *wichām*', *Medieval Archaeology*, xi, 1967, pp. 87-104,
reprinted in *Place-Name Evidence for the Anglo-Saxon Invasion and
Scandinavian Settlements*, EPNS 1987, pp. 8-26, and also *Signposts to
the Past*, Chichester 1988, pp. 67-84 and 245-48. The exact meaning
and significance is uncertain, but from an analysis of a group of
p.ns. derived from **wīc-hām** it has been suggested that it was an OE
term for a small Roman settlement which "survived without being
swamped by neighbouring Germanic settlers, and was given this
name by neighbouring Germanic communities in recognition of its
non-Germanic characteristics" (*Signposts to the Past*, pp. 70-71). It
should be noted that a significant number of these names occur
near smaller Roman settlements, rarely near the larger. The
nearest Roman town in Caistor, two and a half miles away. In
Nettleton parish itself, Romano-British pottery has been found at, at
least, seven sites, and similar finds are recorded from the adjacent

parish of Claxby, where a "substantial building" is marked on the *Map of Roman Britain*, O.S. 1956, about one and a half miles from *Wykeham*, v. also B.N. Eagles, *The Anglo-Saxon Settlement of Humberside*, BAR British Series 68 1979, pp. 383 and 362-63. In addition, the f.n. *Chesterfelde*, in f.ns. (b) *infra*, has been noted three times in 16th century Nettleton documents, and frequently p.ns. containing *Chester-* (v. **ceaster**) have Roman associations. Unfortunately, it does not seem possible to identify the site of this f.n. It should also be noted that an AS inhumation cemetery has been identified between Nettleton and Caistor. *Wykeham* is an example of one group of **wīc-hām** names, which are now depopulated and which lie near the boundary of a large parish. Its situation is shown on the 6" O.S. map and is indicated by the f.n. *Whicum Close* 1794 *EnclA* (Plan). Its land extended to the south to the boundary with Normanby le Wold, as is indicated in a charter dated l12 (13) *Alv*, f. 145 and in two similar documents, e13 RA iv, 201 and a1205 ib, 191, and to the east it is bounded by High Street, on which v. Margary no 270, p. 240. The name survives in WYKEHAM WELL, 1824 O.

ASH HOLT is *Hill Holt* 1828 Bry. BIG WOOD. BLACK BULL (lost), *the blackbull* 1636 *Foster*, - *Black Bull* 1657 *ib*. GLEBE FM. HIGH STREET, *ye high street* 1707 *Terrier*, *the high street* 1762 *ib*, the name of the ridgeway from Horncastle to Caistor, known as Middlegate Lane northwards from Caistor to South Ferriby. HOME FM. HOWE HILL (lost), 1828 Bry, *How Hill Close* 1825 *BC*, cf. *the howe* 1577, *ye how* c.1580, *the how* 1662, y^e *great howe* 1577, *Great howe* c.1580, *great how* 1602, 1662, - *houghe* 1644, *Great how* 1671, y^e *Great How* 1690, - *great How* 1703, - *great How* 1707, *the Great How* 1762 all *Terrier*, probably 'the mound, hill', v. **haugr**. LONG WOOD. NETTLETON BECK, BECKLANDS, BECK PLANTATION, cf. *atte Begke* (sic) 1346 Cl (p), *beckedaile* Hy3 *HarlCh* (v. **deill**), *le* -, *the Beck* 1639 *Foster*, - *Becke* 1652 *ib*, y^e *beck running to Nettleton* 1677 *Terrier*, *Beck* c.1689 *BRA 866*, *the Beck* 1822 *Terrier*, *The* - 1825 *BC*, 'the stream', v. **bekkr**; it is referred to as *the common water course* in 1652. NETTLETON BLEAK HO, *Prospect Farm or Bleak Top or Bleak House* 1860 *Dixon*, so-named from its situation. NETTLETON BOTTOM is *Nettleton Lodge* 1824 O, 1830 Gre, *Lodge F.^{m}* 1828 Bry, *Nettleton Lodge Farm* 1836

Dixon. NETTLETON GAP. NETTLETON GRANGE, "granges in
..." *Nettilton* ... 1537-39 LDRH, *Nettilton, firma grang'* 1538-39 Dugd
vi, *Grangia* m16 *MiscDep 43, Grange* 1707 *Terrier, the Grange Farm*
1734 *Foster, The Grange* 1842 O, 1830 Gre; it was a **grange** of
Sixhills Priory. Cf. *Grange Wood* 1825 *BC.* NETTLETON HILL,
1828 Bry, cf. *le Hilles* Ed1 *HarlCh, ye hyll* 1577, *- hill* c.1580, *ye Hill
side* 1690, *ye hillside,* 1703, *the Hill side* 1707, *- Side* 1762 all *Terrier,
Nettleton Hillside* 1724, 1734 *Foster,* self-explanatory. NETTLETON
HO is *The Rectory Ho* 1830 Gre, *Rectory Farm* 1838 *Dixon.*
NETTLETON LODGE. Note that Nettleton Bottom, *supra,* was
earlier called *Nettleton Lodge.* NETTLETON MANOR, MANOR
FM, MANOR WOOD, *the Mannor House* 1734 *Foster.*
NETTLETON MOOR, 1824 O, *- Moore* 1677 *MiD.* NETTLETON
TOP, TOP BARN, *Top F.^{m}* 1828 Bry. NETTLETON WOLD FM,
cf. *Far Wold* 1832, 1852, 1875, 1889 *Yarb, v.* **wald.** NETTLETON
WOOD. NEW FM. OXGANGS. SAND PIT. SOUTH MOOR,
South Moor F.^{m} 1828 Bry, cf. *South Moor Common* 1794 *EnclA*
(Plan). STOPE HILL FM, *-* GRANGE, cf. *Stoop Hill* 1690, *Stope
hill* 1703, *- Hill* 1707, 1762 all *Terrier,* 1801 *Dixon,* 1828 Bry and
probably *Stupdayle* 1242 *HarlCh.* TUGDALE WOOD, cf. *Tugedale*
e13, *Tughedale* eHy3, *Tugdale* eHy3, 1242, *togdaylheueddallyth* 1245
all *HarlCh* (*v.* **hēafod, deill, hliđ^1** or **hliđ^2** 'a slope'), *Tugg Dale*
1825 *BC,* perhaps, as Dr John Insley suggests, the first el. is an
unrecorded OE pers.n. **Tugga,* adduced for Tughall (PN NbDu
201), the second being **deill** 'a share of land'. WARREN HILL
(lost) 1828 Bry. WOOD FM. WYKEHAM WELL, *v. Wykeham
supra.*

Field-Names

Principal forms in (a) are 1825 *BC.* Spellings dated l12, e13, 1205, eHy3,
1242, 1245, Hy3, lHy3, l13, Ed1, Ed2 are *HarlCh;* those dated 1577, c.1580, 1602,
1644, 1662, 1671, 1690, 1703, 1707, 1762, and 1822 are *Terrier;* 1638, 1801, 1802,
1838, 1843, 1845, 1860, and 1878 are *Dixon;* 1754, 1770, 1794-9, 1832, 1833, 1852,
1875, and 1889 are *Yarb;* 1794 are *EnclA.* Other sources are noted.

(a) First -, Second Able Banks 1843, 1845, 1860 (cf. *Able* c.1580, 1602, 1644,
1662, *Able side* 1644, 1662, *Able -, able well(e)* 1577, 1602, 1644, 1662, 1671),
Able btm 1762 (*able bowdam* 1577, *- boddom, - bottom* c.1580, *Abel bottom* 1602,

1703, 1707, *Able bottom* 1644, 1662, *able bottom* 1671, *Abel-Bottom* 1690 (*v.* **botm**)), Abel Wrinkle 1762, (1707, *able wrinkells* 1577, *Able wrinckles* c.1580, 1644, 1662, - *wrincles* 1602, - *wrinckle* 1703, *Abel wrincke* (sic) 1671, *v.* **wrengel** 'a twisted place or stream'; since *Able* occurs four times as a name in itself, it is possible that it is 'Abba's glade', *v.* **lēah**, the first el. being the OE pers.n. *Abba*, but because the forms are late, this is speculative); Ash Hill (*v.* **æsc, hyll** and cf. Ash Holt *supra*); Azary 1832, 1852, 1875, 1889; Barland 1762 (*Berland* 1230-40 RA iv, Hy3, *hyebarlandes fur'* 1577, *Hyghebarlandes* c.1580, *High Barlands* 1644, - *barlands* 1661, *Higby barlands* (sic) 1602, *Barlands* 1690, 1703, 1707, perhaps 'the (high) strips on which barley was grown', *v.* **bere, land**); Bartle Ings (*v.* **eng**, the first el. perhaps being the diminutive form of the pers.n. *Bartholomew* or a surn. derived from it); Barton Cl; Blackmells 1762 (1707), Blackmel Cl 1825 (*high blacmels* 1577, *law blak mels* 1577, *High blackmells, Lawblackmels* c.1580, *High -, Low blackmells* 1602, 1662, *high -, low -* 1671, *High -, Low Blackmells* 1644, perhaps 'the dark coloured sand hills', *v.* **blæc, melr**, the forms do not seem to be directly comparable with those for *Black Mills* in Great Limber parish *supra*, which appears to have a different etymology); Bratts 1762 (1602, 1707, *brattes* 1577, *Brattes* c.1580, *ye bratts* 1644, *the -* 1671, *Brats* 1690, 1703, *v.* **brot** 'a small parcel of land'); Bull Garth 1794, 1825 (*v.* **garðr**); Buncroft mdw 1794, 1822 (*boncrofte* 1577, *Buncroft* c.1580, 1671, *Bouncroft* 1644, perhaps 'the bean croft', from ON **baun** 'a bean' and **croft**); Cawd How 1762, Cawder Cl 1825 (*Kalde Hou* 1230-40 RA iv, *Caldehoudaile* Hy3 (*v.* **deill**), *Cawd-How* 1690, *Cawd how* 1707, *Cawdhou* 1703, 'the cold mound or hill', *v.* **cald, haugr**); Cawdwell(side) 1762 (*Cawdwell* 1577, 1690, 1703, 1707, - *Sydd* 1577, - *side* c.1580, 1662, 1671, *caudwell* c.1580, *Caudwell, Caudewell side* 1602, *Cadwell* (sic) 1644, 1662, 1671 ('(the side of) the cold spring', *v.* **cald, wella, sīde**); Chalk Pit cl 1825, 1833, 1875, 1889, - pit Cl 1852 (*Calkepittes* 1242, self-explanatory, *v.* **calc, pytt** and cf. *Chalcholes, Kalkeholes* eHy3, *v.* **hol**[1]); Church Mdw 1794 (cf. Kirk Hill *infra*); Coat Hill Cl; Cockermouth 1762 (1644, 1671, 1703, 1707, *Coker mowth* 1577, *cokermothe* c.1580, *Cokermouth* 1602; the situation of Cockermouth is not certainly known, but the name has at least a superficial similarity to Cockermouth (PN Cu 361-2), the first el. of which is a pre-English r.n. found also in Du and La and in Cocker Beck (PN Nt 3). According to Ekwall (RN 84), it is a PrW name meaning 'the crooked stream', though Jackson (LHEB 578) appears to consider the etymology of this stream-name to be uncertain. Early spellings are clearly needed before it can be firmly proposed that the first el. of Cockermouth is indeed a pre-English r.n., but this possibility should be left open); the Common 1762 (*y^e* - 1707 and cf. *West Common* 1707); Common Hall 1801 (cf. *Halledayle* Ed1, *v.* **hall, deill**); Common Moor 1794; coney Green 1762 (*Coneygreen* 1703, *Coneygreen* 1707, *v.* **coninger** 'a rabbit warren;, and cf.

conigarthe close c.1580, *Cunny garth* 1664, *Connygarth* 1671, 'the enclosure for rabbits', *v.* **coni, garðr**); Cottage Pingle (*v.* **pingel**); Cow cl (*v.* the Marsh or Cow Cl *infra*); Cow Fold Cl; Crank Mire (*sic*), Crank Mere Pce; Cuckold Plat 1762 (*Cuckeld Plet* (sic) 1690, - *platt* 1707, *cuchold plat* (sic) 1703, *v.* **plat²** 'a small piece of land', a common name for a secluded place, a place of illicit love-making); cut Lane 1762 (*Cuttlan* (sic) 1577, *venellam vocat le Cutt lane, a lane called Cuttlane* 1639 *Foster, ye Cut laine* 1644, *Cuttlaine* 1651 *Foster, cutt laine* 1671, *Cut Lane* 1690, - *laine* 1703, *Cutlane* 1707, perhaps 'a lane beside or leading to a channel or drain', *v.* **cut**); Dales Sands 1802 (cf. The Sands *infra*); Drakers Cl 1794, Draker's - 1825 (from the surn. *Draker*); Duck Hole Ings (*v.* **eng** 'meadow, pasture', as elsewhere in this parish); the East Fd 1762, 1845, 1860, East Fd 1794 (*in campo orientali* Hy3 (Ed1) *Newh, in orientali campo* 1245, Ed1, - *de Nettleton* 1638, *the Est fyld* 1577, *ye east filde* c.1580, *the east field* 1602, - *East Field* 1690, 1707, *the East Feild* 1702, one of the great fields of Nettleton, cf. South Field, West Field *infra*); The Far Moor; The Far Valley; Farthing Well 1762 (- *well* 1707, *farthing Well* 1690, *v.* **feorðung** (though in what sense is uncertain), **wella**, cf. *farding* -, *Farding fures* 1577, c.1580, - *furres* 1664, *farding furres* 1662, *Farthings furrs* 1671, *v.* **furh** 'a furrow' in the pl., cf. *shooteing furrs* in Barton f.ns. (b) *supra*); A Folly 1794, The Folly 1825 (*v.* **folie**; this is not the name of a building); Frankish Bank 1762 (1690, 1707, - *bank* 1703, named from the family of Hugh *Franckishe* 1596 *Inv*); The Freehold; The Furze Cl (*v.* **fyrs**); Grass Garth 1794, 1825 (*v.* **garðr** 'an enclosure'); Gravel Pit 1794; Great Cl 1794, 1825; The Green, Green Cl; Grimeshill 1762 (*Grimse hil* 1577, *Grimshill'* c.1580, *Grimshill* 1602, *Grimeshill* 1644, 1671, *Grims Hill* 1662, *Grimes-Hill* 1690, *Grimes hill* 1703, - *Hill* 1707; the forms are late and it is impossible to know whether *Grim* is a pers.n., a surn. or even a by-name of Woden); Hargat 1762 (the form is late, but this is perhaps a compound of **here** 'an army' and **gata** 'a way, a road', ME **heregate,* in the sense 'a highway', cf. OE **here-weg**); Harston 1762 (1690, 1703, *Harstone* 1707, *v.* **hār** 'a boundary', **stān**); the Head Lands 1762 (*the common headland* 1644, 1662, *Headland* 1690, *headlands* 1703, *ye Commonheadland* 1707, *v.* **hēafod-land**); Houghton Thorn 1762 (- *thorn* 1707, *one furlong callyd Howdinge* 1572, *one furlonge callid howdinge* c.1580, - *called houdinge* 1602, *one furlong called Hooding* 1662, *Hooding* 1638, 1644, *hooding* 1671, *Hooding headland, - plaine* 1638 (*v.* **hēafod-land, plain**), *Howdinge thorne* c.1580, *howron thorn* 1577, *Hooding Thorne* 1644, *hooding thorne* 1662, *Holton thorne* 1671, *Howton-thorn* 1690, *Howton thorn* 1703, *v.* **þorn**; the forms are too varied to suggest an etymology for *Houghton, Howding, hooding* etc.); Hubbles Croft (from the surn. *Hubble*); Kiln Cl 1794, 1825; Kirk Hill 1762 (*ye furlonge called Dunstan hyll* 1577, - *callid dunston hill* c.1580, *Dunston hill* 1602, 1644, *Dunstan Hill now called Kirke Hill* 1662, *Kirke hill* 1671, *Kyrk Hill*

1690, *kirk hiil* 1703, *Kirkhill Pill* (sic) 1707, *v.* **kirkja, hyll,** *Dunstan, -ston* is presumably a family name, but none has been noted in the sources examined); Lamphead Land 1762 (y^e *Lampe head Land* 1577, (y^e -, *the* -) *lampheadland* c.1580, 1602, 1671, y^e *lamp headland* 1644, *the* - 1662, *Lamp-Headland* 1690, *Lamp headland* 1703 (probably endowed land, the rent of which was used for a church lamp, *v.* **lampe, hēafod-land**)); The Lane End Cl; Lime Kiln Cl; Longham Leas 1762 (*v.* **lea,** cf. the appellative *leas,* common in north L); Low Cl 1794, 1825; Low Fd 1794; The low -, - Low Ings (y^e *Lawe ynges* 1577, y^e *Law inges* c.1580, *v.* **lágr** 'low', **eng**); The low Moor (cf. Nettleton Moor *supra*); Lyal (Mouth) 1762 (probably an error for Ryal (Mouth), cf. *Ryall mouth* 1690, 1693, - *Mouth* 1707, *v. Rhill tope* in (b) *infra*); Mansgate 1762 (*Mengattes, Menegattes* 1577, *Northend Mengates* c.1580, *Mengate* 1602, *Mens gate* 1662, *mens gate* 1644, *mansgate, Mensgate* 1671, *Mens Gate foot* 1690, *Mans gate foot* 1703, *Mansgate* - 1707, in view of the variant spelling the first el. is doubtful, the second being **gata**); Manton Cross 1762 (1671, 1702, 1707, - *Cros*(*s*)*e* 1577, c.1580, - *Crosse* 1602, 1644, 1662, *Manton-cross* 1690, presumably from the surn. *Manton* and **cros**); Two lands called Mare and Foal 1762 (*Meare & fole* 1577, - *and folle* c.1580, *ii lands called mare and foale* 1602, *2 lands called Mare & foale* 1644, *two lands called the* - 1662, *2 lands Called the mare & the fole* 1671, *2 lands called Mare Foal* (sic) 1690, *Two lands called Mare and foal* 1703, - *Mar & foal* 1707, possibly two adjoining strips of unequal sizes, but cf. the f.ns. of North Kelsey (b) *supra*, where it refers to *one broode* (i.e. broad) *land* and it is suggested that the name refers to a foaling strip of land); The Marsh or Cow Cl ("the" *Merse* 1226 FF, *pratum quod uocatur Marays iacens inter Rachaw et Neteltun'* 1245 (*v.* **mareis** 'a marsh' later replaced by *marsh* itself), *marisci ... Abb'is (de Neuhus)* Hy3 (i.e. of Newsham Abbey in Brocklesby)); Middle Cl 1794, 1825; our own Moore 1762, Moor head Hills 1825 (*v.* **mōr**[1], **hēafod, hyll**); Nettleton Ings (*Nettleton-Inggs* 1707 *Monson, Nettleton-Ings* 1708 *Terrier* (South Kelsey), *v.* **eng**); Btm Nine Acres 1843, 1860; Normanby Gate 1762 (- *gate* 1703, 1707, *Normanbie Gate* 1690, 'the road to Normanby le Wold', *v.* **gata**); Normanby Meer Bank 1762, Normanby Hedge 1794 (*Normanbie Meare* 1577, - *meer bank* 1690, *Normanby meare* c.1580, - *meere* 1644, 1662, - *Meere* 1671, - *Meer bank* 1703, 1707, *v.* **(ge)mǣre** 'a boundary', **banke**); Old Dam Cl 1794, 1825 (*old Damm* 1690, *a Close called Old Dam* 1734 *Foster*); Oldgate 1762 (*old Gate* 1690, - *gate* 1703, *Oldgate* 1707, 'the old road', *v.* **ald, gata**); Osmondale 1762 (1690, 1703, 1707), Osmond Dale 1825 (*Osmundalesich* 1226 FF, *Osmandall wrynkell* 1577, - *wrinkles* c.1580, *Osmondal wrincles* 1602, - *wrinckeles* 1644, *Osmandale wrinkles* 1662, *osmandal wrinckle* 1671, 'Osmund's allotment', from the OE pers.n. *Ōsmund* and **deill** 'a share, a portion of land' with **wrengel** 'a twisted place or stream', perhaps replacing **sík** 'a small stream'); The Out Coat Plain

('(level land by) the outer cottage', *v.* **ūt, cot**, with **plain**); Ox Pasture 1762 (-
Pastures 1690, - *pastures* 1707, *Oxpastures, ye Southings Oxpasture* 1703,
self-explanatory and *v.* South Ings *infra*); Ozier Holt (*v.* **holt**); Low pill, Pill rush
1762 (*hye pyll, Lawpyll furlonge* 1577, *Hyghe Pill, Lawpill'* c.1580, *High* -, *Low pill*
1602, 1644, *High pill, low* - 1662, *Hyghe Pyll, high pill, low hill* (sic) 1671, (*Low*)
Pill 1690, 1702, 1707, *pyll rushe* 1577, *Pilrishe* c.1580, *Pilrish* 1602, *Pilrush* 1638,
1707, *Pill rush* 1644, - *rushe* 1662. *Pill-Rush* 1690, *Pillrush* 1703, *v.* **risc**; *Pill* is
probably ON **pill** 'a willow'; Dr John Insley points out that OE **pīl** 'a spike etc.'
is ruled out on philological grounds. *High* and *Low* (*Law*) are self-explanatory);
The Rasen Rd 1822; Red Hill 1843, 1845, 1860; Rise Dale (*v.* **hrís** 'brushwood',
deill); Round Hill Cl; North -, South Salter Gate (*v.* **saltere, gata**); The Sands
1762 (*Sandes* 1577, c.1580, *Sands* 1602, 1644, 1662, *y^e* - 1690, *Nettleton Sands*
c.1689 *BRA 866*, cf. *sandhil* e13, Hy3, *Sandhill'* 1327 *SR* (p)); Scald's Cl 1794,
1825 (probably from the surn. *Scald*); Sedder Meadow cl; Sedway 1762 (1690,
1703, *Sedevay* 1226 FF, perhaps, as Dr John Insley suggests, a compound of OE
sǣd, sēd, ME *sed(e)* 'seed, corn' and **weg**, a road on which seed or corn was
carried); Selve Acres 1762 (*Selveacre* 1577, *Selveacres* c.1580, *Sealveacres* 1602,
Selue acres 1662, *Selueacres* 1671, *Selve-Acres* 1690, *Selve Acres* 1703, obscure);
Btm -, Top seven Acres 1843, - Seven Acres 1845; Sheep Gates (*syepgates* 1239
CottCh, 'pasturage, or the right of pasturage, for sheep', *v.* **shep-gate**, a very
early reference to this compound (not recorded in MED), common in L); Shog
Dale; Short Butts 1762 (1703, - *Butt* 1707, *Scorbuttes* 1239 *CottCh*, *v.* **sc(e)ort,
butte** 'a strip of land abutting on a boundary'); Shot Furze (*v.* **fyrs**); South'ard
Bank; the South Fd 1754, 1770 (one of the great fields of Nettleton); South
Ings 1762, 1794, 1825 (*Sowth ynges* 1577, *South Ings* 1644, *the South Ing(e)s* 1657,
1659 *Foster, Southings* 1690, *the South Ings* 1703, *the South Inge* 1707, *ye Southings
Oxpasture* 1703, *v.* **sūð, eng** and Ox Pasture in (a) *supra*); Span Mouth spring
Cl; the old Stone Pit 1762, Stone Pit 1794 (*ye Old Stone Pit* 1690, *ye Old Stone
pit* 1703, *the Old* - 1707); Stony Holms 1762 (*Stone holme* 1577, 1602, 1638, *stone*
- c.1580, *Stone holms* 1644, *stouny holme* 1671, *Stony-Holme* 1690, *Stony holm*
1703, *v.* **stān, holmr**, cf. *Stane* 1226 FF); the Streets 1762; Swindale side 1762
(1707), Swine Dale 1825 (*Swyndalelith* c.1240 *CottCh* (*v.* **hlið^1, hlið^2** 'a slope'),
swyndall hedland 1578, - *head land* 1644, *swindall headland* c.1580, *Swindall* -
1602, *Swinedale* - 1671, *Swindale* - 1662, *Swindale Side* 1690, - *side* 1703, 1707, *v.*
swīn^1 'a swine, a pig', **dalr** (the c.1240 form suggesting it is named from a
valley) with **hēafod-land** and **sīde**); Thoro'fare Ings ('meadows by a road', *v.*
thurgh-fare, eng); Three cornered Cl (so called from its shape); Thurstle 1762
(*trusdall* 1577, *Thrusdale* 1644, *thrusdale* 1662, *Trusdale* 1671, *Thrustalls* 1690,
Thrustall 1703, 1707, the forms are late, but perhaps we have a metathesised
form of ON **þurs** 'a giant' and **deill** 'a share of land' the significance of which

is open to speculation, but archaeological sites and ruins were not uncommonly regarded as haunted places, the dwellings of giants and demons); Tinker lane 1822, First -, Second -, Third -, Fourth -, Fifth Tinker Lane Cl 1843 (probably 'a lane frequented by gypsies or tinkers'); Toft 1762, High -, Low Toft Cl 1847 (*toft* (2x) eHy3, 1242, *Thoft* 1245, *Toft* 1707, *Tofte furlonge* 1577, c.1580, 1644, *Toft furlong* 1602, 1662, *toft furland* 1671, *v.* **toft** 'a building site, a curtilage', **furlang**); Top Plat 1843, 1845, 1860 (*v.* **plat**^{2}); Turpets 1762 (1707, *Turpites* c.1580, *Turpitts* 1602, *turpitts* (*otherwise farre Sands*) 1644, 1662, *turpits* 1671, 1703, *Turpits* 1690, 'peat diggings', *v.* **turf, pytt**, cf. *Turpettes* PN BedsHu 295 s.n. **turf**); Waid How (*sic*) 1762 (*wardhowe* 1577, *Ward how* c.1580, *Ward Hough* 1644, *ward how* 1662, 1671, *Ward-How* 1690 (probably from OE **weard** 'watch, ward, protection' or ON **varða** 'a cairn, heap of stones' and **haugr**, so probably a look-out mound or hill); Wen Wood Cl (sic) (*Welwood nabbe* 1577, *weluode* - c.1580, *Well wood nabb* 1644. *Wellwood nabb, well wood* 1662, *Wellwood nadd* (sic) 1671, *Wellwood* 1690, *Welwood* 1703, 1707, 'the wood with a spring', *v.* **wella, wudu**, with **nabbi** 'a knoll, a hill'); West Common 1762 (1707); West Fd 1762, 1794, (*the* - 1707, *in occidentali campo* Hy3 (Ed1) *Newh, in campo occidentali* 1245, 1276 (1409) Gilb, - *de Netelton'* 113, *in occidental campo de Nettelton'* Ed1 *ib, in campo occident* 1521 Anc, *in occidentali campo de Nettleton* 1638, *West fylde* 1577, *westfylde* c.1580, *West feild* 1644, *the West field* 1602, 1671, *West Field* 1662, *y*^{e} *West Field* 1690, - *Feild* 1703, one of the great fields of Nettleton, cf. the East Fd and the South Fd *supra*); the West Ings 1762, 1794, 1822 (*Westenges* Hy3, *the West Ings* 1636, 1657, 1659 all *Foster, West Ings* 1703, *v.* **west, eng** 'a meadow'); West Land 1762 (*west Land* 1577, *Westlandes* c.1580, *westlands* 1602, 1671, *West lands* 1644, 1690, *Westlands* 1703, 1707, *v.* **west, land**); Wheat Lane 1762 (*Wateland, Watheland'* (sic) 1230-40 RA iv, *wheatland gate* 1644, 1662, *Wheatland* - 1671, *Weatland* 1690, 1703, *v.* **hwǣte, land**, cf. *Watetorft* (for *-croft* ?) 1226 FF); White Pit 1843, 1845, 1860 (*v.* **hwīt, pytt**); The Willow Ings (*v.* **eng**); Wind Croft 1762 (*wincrofte* 1577, *winthcroft* c.1580, *Wincroft* 1644, 1662, *wincroft* 1671, *Wind croft* 1690, *windcroft* 1703, 1707, the first el. is uncertain); Yoke Gate 1762 (*yoke Gate* 1690, - *gate* 1703, 1707, the sense of *yoke* here is uncertain); Zachary Hill.

(b) *Argulhill* 1638; *Bachehagh* 1226 FF (perhaps 'the enclosure by the stream' *v.* **bæcce**^{1}, **haga**^{1}); *Beckedaile* Hy3 (*v.* **bekkr, deill**); *Benecroft* 112, *Benecroftewelle* 1205, *benecroftewelle* Hy3 (Ed1) *Newh,* one peece of meddow called *Bancroft* 1602 (*v.* **bēan, croft** with **wella** and cf. Buncroft mdw in (a) *supra*); *berhille* 112 (perhaps 'the hill where barley grows', *v.* **bere, hyll**); *Berneholes* 1242 (apparently referring to the same hollows is *Bernesholes* eHy3, lHy3, so it is impossible to determine the etymology of the first el.); *blay bryges* 1577, - *briges* c.1580, - *briggs* 1602, 1644, - *bridge* 1671; *boston pytt*, - *pyttes* 1577, *Boston Pitte* c.1580, - *pitt* 1602, 1644, *Bawston* -, *bauston pitt* 1662 (presumably from a surn. and **pytt**); *broken land* 1521 *Anc* (*broken* here meaning 'ploughed' or especially 'newly ploughed'); *Butt Meadow* 1690; *Caster Crosse furlonge* 1638 (a furlong adjacent to *Caistor Cross*, which has not been noted in Caistor documents); *caster gate* c.1580, *Castor* - 1602, *Caster* - 1644, 1662 ('the road to Caistor (an adjoining parish)', *v.* **gata**); *Chesterfelde* m16 *MiscDep 43*, *Chester fyld* 1577, - *feld* c.1580 (*v.* **ceaster, feld** and *Wykeham supra*); *Claigates* 1230-40 *RA* iv, *Claygates* 1242, *Claigatesfurlonges* Hy3 (*v.* **clæg, gata**); *Dunstan Hill* (*v.* Kirk Hill in (a) *supra*); *Elsimare* 113 (from the surn. *Elsi* (itself derived from the OE pers.n. *Ælfsige*) and **(ge)mǣre** 'a boundary, boundary land', the earliest reference to the family so far noted is to Walter *Elsy* 1332 *SR*); *estdale* 112, *in Estdale Vuerhende* 1205, *estdale* < ... > *hende* Hy3 (Ed1) *Newh* (the second word is partly illegible owing to a tear in the MS) (probably 'the east valley', *v.* **ēast, dæl, dalr** with **uferra** 'upper' and **ende**[1] 'the end of something'); *v acre dalle* 1577, c.1580, *5 acre dale* 1644, *five acredale* 1671, *5 Acre Dale* 1690, *meadows called 5 acre* 1703; *folbecsike* 113 (*v.* **bekkr, sík**; the first el. may be **fūl** 'foul, dirty, filthy' or perhaps **fola, foli** 'a foal'); *Foxdalelid* 1225 *FF*, *Foxdale, Foxedale* eHy3, *Foxdal'* 1242, *Foxdaleslede* Ed1 (probably 'the valley where foxes are found', *v.* **fox, dæl, dalr** with **hlið**[1] or **hlið**[2] 'a slope', cf. *Suddale infra*); *vnum essartum Bosci ad frith Wude* 1205, *essartum bosci ad Fridhwode* Hy3 (Ed1) *Newh* (*v.* **fyhrð** 'a wood, woodland'); *the fore how* 1671 (*v.* **fore** 'in front', **haugr**); *le* -, *la francherei* Hy3, *le Francheray* Hy3 (Ed1) *Newh* (presumably this is ME (from AN) **frauncherie*, unrecorded in MED, in the sense 'a freehold' and cf. an appellative use in *inter duas Franchereie* lHy3. The same name has been found in Brocklesby f.ns. (b) and Killingholme f.ns. (b) *supra*); *ad Gairam* 1205, *super Gayram* Hy3 (Ed1) *Newh* (*v.* **geiri** 'a gore, a triangular plot of land in the open field'); *gate Shakells* 1577, *Gatte shakles* c.1580, *gate shakells* 1602, *Gate shakles* 1664, - *shackles* 1662, *shacklegate* 1671 (perhaps, like Gate Shackles, PN YWR 2, 112, from ME **gate-shadel** 'cross-roads'); *geuedayle* Hy3 (possibly 'Geva's allotment', from the ME fem. pers.n. *Geva* and **deill**); *Gresbeckes* 1638 (probably a Scandinavian compound, *v.* **gres** 'grass', **bekkr**); *Gyldenwellelith'* 1245 ('the slope near *Goldenwell*, i.e. a spring or well with golden flowers, *v.* **gylden, wella** with **hlið**[1] or **hlið**[2]); *haggengates* 112, *Hagenegate* 1205, *hagenegate* Hy3 (Ed1) *Newh*, *Hakengates* Hy3 (probably from the ON pers.n. *Haghni* and **gata** 'a road'); *molendinum de Haker* ... Hy3 (Ed1) *Newh* (the reading is uncertain); *uno selio vocat an hempland* 1638 (*v.* **hemp-land** 'land on which hemp is grown' (MED)); *ad crucem de Herdwyk* 1242, *in campo de Herdewic'* 1203 *FF*, *in campis de Herthewike* Ed1 (the cross and open fields of the lost settlement of *Hardwick supra*); *Holme* 1644, 1662, *y*[e] *Holms* 1707 (*v.* **holmr**); *horsker garthe, horsekergate* 1577, *Horskergarthe* c.1580,

Horsgargarth (*thorne*) 1602, *Horse Kerke garth* 1644, *Horse Kirkegarth* (*thorne headland*) 1662, *the horse kirkegath thorne* 1671 (*v.* **hors, kjarr** and **garðr**, with **kjarr** (ME *ker*) confused with or replaced by *kirk*); *Kelsdail* 1226 FF (*v.* **deill;** the first el. is perhaps an ON pers.n. **Kel*, a later syncopated form of *Ketil*, assumed by Reaney to be the source of the surn. *Kell*, *v.* also *Insley* 576); *Kynholdal'* 1245 (perhaps 'Cynewald's allotment', from the OE pers.n. *Cynewald* with **deill**); *Kysekhauerfurlang'* 1245, *Kithaver lands* 1703 (the two forms may be only superficially similar, the first being 'the furlong on which oats were grown', *v.* **hafri, furlang**, the second 'the strips on which oats were grown', *v.* **land**; the first els. *Kysel-* and *Kit-* are uncertain); *Ladthecroft* (2x), *Ladhecroft* Hy3, *ladhecroft* Hy3 (Ed1) *Newh* ('the croft with or near a barn', *v.* **hlaða, croft**); *Langheng* e13 (1409) *Gilb* (*v.* **lang, eng**); *Lencdiholmes* 1298 Abbr (probably a mistake for *Leuediholmes*, 'the water-meadows dedicated to our Lady', *v.* **hlæfdige, holmr**); *Lewindailes* (*Le Windales*, variant spelling in *R* c.1330), 1230-40 RA iv, Hy3 (from the OE pers.n. *Lēofwine* and **deill** 'a share of land'); *licdail* Hy3 (Ed1) *Newh* (Dr John Insley makes the interesting suggestion that this is a Scand compound, ON **lika-deill* 'the parcel of land set aside for burials'); *Linhylles* c.1240 *CottCh* (it is impossible to determine the first el.); *Lokermeteng'* Ed2 *HarlCh* (Dr John Insley suggests that this is a compound of ME *lockere* 'a locksmith' and OE **mǣte** 'mean, poor', **eng** 'a meadow, pasture', hence 'the poor-quality meadow (belonging to the locksmith)'); *quoddam pratum vocat Longdale* 1638 (*v.* **lang, deill**); *lorthille* 1242, lHy3 (perhaps from **lort** 'mud, dirt' and **hyll**); *Merwen welle sik* 1245 (from the OE fem. pers.n. *Mærwynn* and **wella** with **sik**); *Milnecroft* 1245 (*v.* **myln, croft**); *Mudinghamsik* 1245, *Medigam* 1577, *Modicam* c.1580, *Moddingham dale* 1644, *Modding ham dale* 1662 (*v.* **sik** more early forms are needed to determine the etymology of *Mudingham*); *in campis de Neteltona* 1230-40 RA iv, - *de Netelton;* Ed1, *in campis villae de Nettilton* 1469 Dugd vi (*v.* **feld**); *the furlong at Nevilgarth endes* 1638, *Nevil Garth* 1707 (from the *Nevil* family, cf. *Hernisus de Neuill'* 1238-41 Fees, John *de Nevil* 1282 Ipm, and **garðr** with **ende**[1], and cf. *terram Gilberti de Neuill'* Ed1); *Newcrosse well* 1638 (self-explanatory); *Northdale* Ed1 (*v.* **norð, dæl, dalr**, cf. *suddale infra); persons platte* 1577, *Person platte* c.1580, *p'son platt* 1602 (cf. *y*ᵉ *parsonage meadow* 1577, *parsonage land* 1644, *v.* **persone, plat**[2] 'a small piece of land'); *Pinkenhov* c.1240 *CottCh, Pinkenhou, pinkenhowe* Hy3, *Pinkenhoucroftes, Pinkinghoucroftes* 1230-40 RA iv, *pinkenhoucroftes* Ed2 (the same name occurs as *Pinkenhou* 1150-60 Dane in Claxby and was on the boundary of Nettleton and Claxby. Formally this could be 'Pinca's mound, hill', *v.* **haugr**, and for the pers.n. *Pinca, v.* Redin 106, but Dr John Insley, no doubt correctly, prefers 'the mound, hill where finches, chaffinches are found', *v.* **pinca**); *Pratbusches* 1239 *CottCh* (apparently from the ME nickname or surn. *Prat* and the pl. of **busc** 'a bush'); *Rachow* 1245 (obscure); *Ramondall fur'* 1577, *Rammondalle* c.1580, *Ramondall* 1602 (the forms are late, but this is probably 'Rámund's share of land', *v.* **deill**, the first el. being the ON pers.n. *Rámundr*, hence a Scand. compound); *Ryehilholes* c.1240 CottCh (*v.* **hol**[1]), *Rhill tope* 1577, *Ryall Toppe* c.1580, *Riall Topp* 1602, *Riall-Topp* 1644, *Ryall Top* 1662, *the top of ryell* 1671, y^e *Top of Ryall* 1690, *top of Ryal* 1703, *Ryall* 1707, *Riall Slake* 1577, 1602, *Ryall - * c.1580, *Ryall slacks* 1644, *Ryall Slacke, ryell Slacke* 1671 (*v.* **slakki** and *Elbrough Slack* in Goxhill f.ns. (b) *supra*), *Ryall* 1690 (*v.* **ryge** 'rye', **hill**); y^e *Ryshes* 1577, *- Rishes* c.1580 (*v.* **risc** 'a rush'); *de Sayntmariland* 1332 SR (p) ('land dedicated to the Blessed Virgin', *v.* **land**, the same name occurring in the adjoining parish of Caistor, *v.* f.ns. (b) s.n.); *Schauhacres* 1245, *Sheveacres* 1577, *Shaueacres* c.1580, *Sheauacres* 1602, *sheaue Acres* 1662, *Sheaveacres* 1644 (obscure, but cf. Selve Acres in (a) *supra*); (y^e) *Scroles* (sic) 1577, 1662, *Scorles* (sic), *Skorles* c.1580, 1602, *Scrolles* 1644 (obscure); *Shepeng* Ed1, Ed2 (*v.* **scēap, eng**); *Southyby* 1327 SR, *Southiby* 1332 ib, *Southeby* 1343 NI all (p) ('south in the village', *v.* **sūð, ī, bȳ**); *Spelhou* eHy3, *-how* 1242 ('speech hill', used of assembly meeting-places, *v.* **spell, haugr**); *Staggarthe, stakgarthe* c.1580 ('the stack-yard', on which *v.* NED s.v. *stack-garth*, where forms in -gg- are noted. It is from ME **stak-garth** (ON **stakkr, garðr**)); *Stakstede* 1577, *-stedes* c.1580, *Stacksteads* 1602, 1662, *Stack steades* 1644, *short stacksteeds* 1671 (*stackstead* is not recorded in dictionaries and is not noted in Sandred. It must mean 'the site of a stack or rick', from ME ***stak-stede** (from ON **stakkr** and **stede**), but the earliest form of it so far noted is in 1577, here and in Croxton f.ns. (b); a further, but later example has been found in East Halton f.ns. (a) s.n. Slack Steads (sic). It is worthy of note that in the pl. in two instances, 'The Stacksteads' were presumably not identical with *Staggarthe*, for whereas the latter was evidently an enclosure, a *stackstead* could be found in the open field); *Strathorne Leas* 1638; *suddale* 112, e13, Hy3, 113, *vnum Lyd quod uocatur suddalelyd* Hy3, *suddalelyd* 113, *suddale* Hy3 (Ed1) Newh ('the southern valley', *v.* **sūð, dæl, dalr**, with **hlið**[1] or **hlið**[2] 'a slope'); *subtus le supoping* Hy3 (this is no doubt for *le suphoping*, cf. (*del*) *hoping* e13 HarlCh in the adjoining parish of Claxby in Walshcroft Wapentake; it is from ME **hopping** (OE ***hopping**) 'a hop-garden'; *v.* also **sūð** 'south'); *Thorkellith* c.1240 CottCh (from the ON pers.n. *þorkell*, ODan *Thorkil* and **hlið**[1] or **hlið**[2] 'a slope'); *Thunestalle* 1242, *Tunstal* eHy3 (*v.* **tūn-stall** 'the site of a farm, farmstead'); *thwerdayle* Hy3 (Ed1) Newh, *Thwerdeil* 1226 FF ('an allotment lying across another or others', *v.* **þverr, deill**); *Todsyke* 1577, *Toodsike* c.1580, *Tood sick, - sike* 1602, *Toad sickes, Toadsicke* 1644, *Toad sicke* 1662, *toad sike* 1671 (probably self-explanatory, *v.* **tāde** 'a toad', **sīk**); *Tomcrofte* 1577, c.1580, *Tomcroft* 1602, 1644, 1662, *Tomcroft* 1703, *Tom Croft* 1707 (perhaps 'the village croft', *v.* **tūn** and PN Ch 5 ii 369, s.v. **toun, croft**); y^e *towne bottes* 1577 (*v.* **butte**[2] 'an archery butt'); y^e *towneshend* c.1580, *Toonsend*

1602, *Townesend* 1644, *Townend* 1662, *Townes end* 1671 (self-explanatory); *Treshouhes* 1230-40 RA iv; *Trigtoft* 1242 (in *Hardwick*) (the name is explained in *quoddam toftum ... quod Willelmus trig quandocumque tenuit* 'a certain toft ... which William trig at one time held' eHy3); *Tunegatebrig* 1245 ('(the bridge by) the village street', *v.* **tūn, gata, brycg**); *le Tunge* Ed1 (*v.* **tunge** 'a tongue of land'); *Uppam ende* 1577, *Upham townes* 1662, *Vppon towneshead* c.1580; *Warlotes* e13 (*v.* **warlot**, and for a discussion Waterhill Wood in Brocklesby *supra*); *Westclif* eHy3, 1242, *-cliue* lHy3 (self-explanatory); *West Wendinges* 1230-40 RA iv, *Westwendinges* Hy3 (*v.* **west, wending**); *White house Fm* 1707; *Whytstra* (sic) 1239, *Whetstraw* c.1580, *Whitstraw* 1662 (obscure); *crucem de Wicham* eHy3 ('Wykeham cross'); *Wirmodewellesich* 1205, *Wrmodewelle* Hy3 (d1) *Newh* (Dr John Insley comments that, at first sight, the first el. could be the OE unrecorded pers.n. **Wyrmmōd*, but he notes that compounds in *Wyrm-* are not usual in OE. He inclines to the view that it is OE (Angl) *Wærmōd*, with shortening of the first vowel and raising to [i]. Hence, perhaps 'Wærmōd's spring', *v.* **wella** with **sīc** 'a small stream'); *Wlhoucroft* 1245 (*v.* **wulf** 'a wolf', **haugr** 'a mound, a hill', with **croft**).

Riby

RIBY

> *Ribi* 1086 DB (2x), c.1115 LS, 1177 P (p), 1199 CurR, 1200 Cur, c.1200 Dane, 1200 FF, 1202 Ass, 1205, 1206 P both (p), c.1300 RA iii
>
> *Riby* c.1150, 1159-81, a1180 (e13) *NCot*, 1210 Abbr, Hy3 (e14) Selby, 1218 Ass, 1247-8 RRG, 1290 RSu, 1316 FA *et passim*, *-bie* 1556 InstBen, 1576 LER, 1589, 1592, 1605 *BT*, 1606, 1693, 1700, 1703 all *Terrier*, *-be* 1650 WillsPCC, *-bye* 1596, 1606 *BT*, 1733 *PT*
>
> *Riebi* 1155-58 (1334) Ch, 1159, 1160, 1163 P, 1177-82 RA ix (p), 1198 Cur, 1202, 1203 P both (p), 1205 ChancR (p), 1207 P, 1461 Pat, *-b'* 1163 RA i, *-bia* 1212 Fees, *-by* 1201 P, 1202 FF, 1202 Ass, 1207 OblR
>
> *Ryby* 1200 OblR, 1226 FF, eHy3 *And*, 1251 FF, 1254 ValNor, 1276 RH, 1281 QW, 1291 Tax, 1310 Cl *et freq* to 1530 Wills ii, 1602 *Terrier*, 1713 *PT*, - als *Rybye* 1664, 1680 *ib*, *-be* 1535 VE iv, *-bye* 1538 LP xiiii, 1544 *PT*, 1576 Saxton, 1578, 1580 *PT*, 1604 *BT*, 1610 Speed, 1608, 1674 *PT*, *Rybie* 1570, 1587, 1597 *et passim* to 1706 all *BT*

Ryebi 1201 ChancR, c.1275 LNQ vi, 1759 *PT*
Rybi 1211-12 RBE

The most likely explanation of this name is, as Ekwall (DEPN
s.n.) suggests, that it was originally OE **Rygetūn* 'the farmstead or
village where rye grows', *v.* **ryge, tūn** and that OE **tūn** was replaced
by ODan **by** 'a farmstead, a village'.

ALMSHOUSES. BLACK WOOD. BRATLANDS, *Riby Bratlands*
1824 O, 1830 Gre, cf. *Bratlings Wood* 1803 *LindDep 29,* - *Plot* 1820
ib, Bratlands Plot 1844 *ib,* - *Cover* 1828 Bry, - *Wood* 1844 *LindDep
29,* probably 'a small piece of land', *v.* **brot, land.** GRANGE
WOLD FM is *Lower Wold F.^{m}* 1828 *Bry.* GREEN PIT, 1828 ib.
HANGING DALES, cf. *Hanging Dale Plot* 1803, 1848 *LindDep 19,
v.* **hangende** 'hanging, steeply sloping', **deill.** HERMITAGE
WOOD, cf. *In a sequestered part of the park, is an hermitage
appropriately fitted up* 1842 White, *Hermitage* 1824 O, 1828 Bry, 1830
Gre, *Hermitage Plantation* 1844 *LindDep 29.* HORSE PASTURE
(lost), 1828 Bry, *horse pasture* 1700 *Terrier, the Horse Pasture* 1803
LindDep 29, self-explanatory. HUNGER HILL WOOD, *Hunger
Hill Plantation* 1803, 1844 *LindDep 29, Hunger Hill* 1824 O, 1830
Gre, *Hunger Hill W^d* 1828 Bry, *Hungry Hill Plantation* 1839 *TA,* a
common term of reproach for poor or barren land, *v.* **hungor, hyll.**
OAK HOLT, 1803, 1844 *LindDep 29,* self-explanatory, *v.* **āc, holt.**
THE OLD KNOT (lost), 1828 Bry, *Old Knott Plot,* - *Plantation*
1803 *LindDep 29, Old Knot Plot* 1844 *ib,* probably from ME **knot**
(ON **knottr**) 'a hillock or the like'. It was situated at Riby Bottom
(i.e. Riby Grove Fm) *infra.* OLD PARK HILL (lost), 1828 Bry; it
was situated south of Hermitage Wood. RIBY GAP, 1828 Bry,
1830 Gre, *Ryeby Gapp* 1645 LNQ xxii, self-explanatory, *v.* **gap.**
RIBY GRANGE, for the late occurrence of **grange** cf. Croxton
Grange in Croxton *supra.* RIBY GROVE, 1824 O, 1830 Gre, 1837
PT, 1842 White, *Grove* 1828 Bry and note *Riby Hall ... sometimes
called Riby Grove* 1842 White. RIBY GROVE FM is *Riby Bottom*
1828 Bry, 1830 Gre. RIBY PARK, *Park* 1829, 1844 *LindDep 29,
Park Plantation* 1803 *ib,* self-explanatory, *v.* **park.** RIBY SLINGS
MEER (lost), 1824 O, *Slingmore* 1713 *PT,* cf. *Slingsmoor (Bottom)*
1703, 1844 *LindDep 29, Great* -, *Little Slingsmoor, Slingsmoor Wood*
1839 *TA,* - *Plantation* 1844 *LindDep 29,* on the boundary with

Aylesby, so *Meer* is no doubt from OE **(ge)mære** 'a boundary', with the common confusion with *moor*. The first el. is probably to be connected with *Slenggesberg* c.1200 Dane, *Slengesberg* Ed1 (Hy4) *DuLaGCB*, the first el. of which is an ON byname **Slengr*, on which v. SPNLY 255, where the first of the two forms is quoted and Reaney s.n. *Sling*, the second el. is probably ON **berg** 'a hill', perhaps 'a mound', hence a Scand. compound. RIBY WOLDS is *Upper Wold F.ᵐ* 1828 Bry, cf. *Far -, Near Wold Plot* 1803, 1844 *LindDep 29, Far -, Near Wold Walk* 1820 *ib, v.* **wald**. SYKES POND (lost), 1803, 1820, 1844 *LindDep 19*, 1828 Bry, probably named from the surn. *Sykes*, though the earliest reference to the family so far noted is to William *Sykes* 1851 *Census*. It was situated just south-west of Riby Grange.

Field-Names

Principal forms in (a) are 1844 *LindDep 29*; those dated c.1200 are Dane; Ed1 (Hy4) are *DuLaGCB*; 1713 are *PT*; 1756, 1758, 1759, 1761, 1762, 1763, 1804 are *Dixon*; 1803, 1820, 1829 are *LindDep 29*; 1839 are *TA 263*; other dated forms are *Terrier*, unless otherwise marked.

(a) Ash Holt 1803, 1844 (*v.* **æsc, holt**); Barn Plot 1803, 1820, 1844; Beast House Pce 1803, - Plot 1844; Becks Cl 1839; (Lr -, Upr) Blengmoor 1803, (Upr) Blingmoor (sic) 1839, Lr -, Upr -, 1844; Brackon Hills 1763 (*v.* **brakni**, cf. *Brakenhougate* in (b) *infra*); Brames Cl 1803, 1844; Brather Plot 1803, (Lr) Brather Plot 1803, - plot 1829, Low - 1844, North -, South High Brather 1829, N. -, S. (*sic*) High Brather 1844 (earlier forms are needed to suggest an etymology for Brather; *v.* **plot** 'a small piece of ground', *freq* in this parish); Brickiln Cl 1758, Brickkiln Plot 1803, Brick Kiln Plot 1804, 1844, Brick Kiln (Cl) 1829 (cf. *Kilne Close* 1713); Brick Pit Cl 1839; the Broome Cl 1761, Brooms - 1803, 1844 (*v.* **brōm**); Burton's Cl 1803, Burtons - 1839 (named from the family of John *Burton* 1694 *Inv*); Caister Road Plantn, - Plot 1803 (*ad uiam Castrie* c.1200, *ad viam de Castre* Ed1 (Hy4), 'the road from Caistor'); Canty's Cl 1803, 1839, 1844 (named from the family of Andrew *Cantie* 1641 LPR); Car Cl (Plantn) 1803, Far Car Cl 1803, 1844, Near - 1803, Far -, Nr Carr Cl 1804 (*the Carr Close* 1713, *v.* **kjarr**); Chapman's Cl 1803, 1844 (from the family of Joseph *Chapman* 1741 *BT*); Childs Cl 1761 (from the family of John *Child* 1699 *BT*); Clay Plot 1803 (2x), 1820, 1844; Far -, Nr Clover Cl 1803, 1844; Collier Cl 1839; Cottagers Wold 1803, 1844 (*v.* **wald**); the Cratch Yd 1778 LNQ xix (*v.* **cracche** 'a hurdle, a framework, a rack for fodder', evidently the last as the source alludes to the keeping of pigs in the yard); Dam's - 1803, Dam - 1839, Dams Cl 1844; ye Dike Hedge 1758, Dike Hedge 1763, Far Dyke Hedge 1844, Dike Hedge Walk 1759, Far -, Nr Dike Hedge Plot 1803, Nr Dyke Hedge Plot 1820, New Dyke - 1844 (*Dyke Hedge Close* 1713, *v.* **dīk, hecg**); Lr -, Upr 15 P^d Cl 1763, - Fifteen Pound Cl 1803, Low fifteen - 1804 (*the fifteen pound Close* 1713, possibly alluding to the purchase price (or rent) of the land, cf. Seven P^d Cl, *fourpound closes* (b) *infra*); Fugglemoor 1803, 1839, 1844, Gt -, Lt Fuggle moor 1829; Gallinborough 1758, Gallingbro 1778 LNQ xix, Gallimbers 1803, Gallimbus 1844 (*v.* **beorg** the first el. is uncertain); Giles Cl 1759, North -, South Giles Cl 1803 (from the surn. *Giles*); Hall Fd 1803, 1844, Hall Paddock 1803 (*v.* **hall**); Halls Walk 1762, Far -, Nr Tom Hall's Walk 1803, - Halls Walk 1804, 1844, - Thorn Halls Walk (sic) 1820 (probably a sheep-walk, cf. Keelby Walk *infra*; Thorn 1820 is perhaps for *Thom* (i.e. Tom), with the surn. *Hall*); Healing Well Cl 1803, 1844, - Wells Cl 1839 (named from Healing Wells in the adjacent parish of Healing); Healing Road Cl 1839 ('(close adjoining) the road to Healing'); the Hills 1763; Hole Mare 1803, Hole mare 1820, - Mare 1844 (*v.* hol^2, (ge)mǣre); Lt Holm Btm 1803, ye Holmes 1758, Holmes 1803, 1804, 1820, 1844, The - 1839, Lt -, Middle -, West Holmes 1839, Holmes Cl 1803, 1839, Far - 1839 (*Holmes, the Holmes Close* 1713, *v.* **holmr** with **clos(e)** and **botm**); Holmes Rd 1804; Home Cl 1803, 1844; the Homestead 1829; the Great Hows 1756 (probably from **haugr** 'a hill, mound'); the Ings 1756 (*v.* **eng** 'a meadow'); Keelby Cl 1803, 1844; Keelby Mdw (Cl) 1803, 1804, - mdw Cl 1820; Keelby Walk 1762, 1803, 1804, 1820, 1844 (a sheep-walk, said to be 'Grass' in the 1844 document, leading to the parish of Keelby); Lidget Orchard 1803, - Yd 1803, 1804 (*v.* **hlid-geat** 'a swing-gate, esp. one to prevent cattle straying from pasture across a road or on to arable land'); Linedikes Cl, - Hill 1803, Line Dykes (Hill) 1844 (*v.* perhaps **līn** 'flax', **dīk**); East Lings 1803, North - 1803, 1820, West - 1803, N. Lings (sic) 1844 (*Risby Norlings* (sic) 1676 *Yarb* (Map), *v.* **norð, lyng,** cf. *the Lings* 1634, y^e - 1674, 1693, presumably the meaning is 'the places where heather grows'); Low Cl 1803, 1839, 1844 (*the Low Close, the low-close* 1713); Low Pingle 1803 (*v.* **pingel**); Melon Grd 1803 (possibly 'mill ground', *v.* **myln**); Gt -, Lt Mussles 1803, - Mussels 1844, Mussles North -, South Plantn 1803 (cf. perhaps *Mushowe* 1332 *SR* (p), 'the mouse-infested mound', *v.* **mūs, haugr**); Osier Holt 1803, Ozier - 1844 (*v.* **holt**); Pinder Cl 1803, Pindar - 1804 ('close assigned to the pinder', *v.* **pyndere**); Plantation 1839 (2x); Rattan Garth 1803, 1820, 1829, Ratton - 1844 ('the enclosure infested by rats', *v.* **raton, garðr**); Round Plantation in Park; First -, Second Rye Grass Cl 1803, 1844; Saintfoin Plot 1803, 1829, St Foin Plot 1844 *v.* **sainfoin**); Sallow Holt 1803 (*v.* **salh, holt**); Sand Hole 1844, - Plot 1803, Sand hole Plot 1829; Saxby Cl 1756; Seven P^d Cl 1759, Seven

Pound Cl 1763, 1803 (*the Seaven pound Close* 1713, cf. Lr -, Upr 15 P^d Cl *supra*); Shooting Pit Plantn 1803, 1844 (probably alluding to a 'pit dug by a sportsman for purposes of concealment', cf. NED *shooting-hole* s.v. *shooting* vbl.sb. 8 (b)); the Little Slows 1756; Stanna Green Btm 1803, Stannergreen - 1829, Stanza Green Btm 1844; Stewards Cl 1839 (from the occupational name or surn. *Steward*); Stone Pit Plot 1803, 1804, 1820, 1844; Stray Pce 1763, 1803, 1844 (perhaps 'a piece of unenclosed common pasture' from ME **stray** (*v*. The Stray PN YWR 5 109) and **þece**, and cf. *The stray Cloase* in Great Limber f.ns. (b) *supra*); Swallow Holt, Plantn adjoining Swallow 1803; Tinkers Grave 1829; Far -, Middle -, Near Top Wold Plot 1844 (cf. Riby Wolds *supra*); Town End Plot 1803, 1844, Townend - 1804, 1820 ('(the piece of land at) the end of the village', *v*. **tūn, ende**^1, **plot**); Tuplin's Cl 1803, Tuplins - 1804, 1820, Tupling - 1844 (from the family of Henry *Tuplin* 1615 *BT*, John *Tupling* 1624 *ib*); Twelve Acre 1803, - Acres 1820, 1844; Warren Hill 1829, - Side 1844, - Side Plot 1803 (*v*. **wareine, hyll**); Whitcar 1803, 1820, 1844, Whits Car 1839 (*v*. **kjarr**); Winters Cl 1839 (probably from the surn. *Winter*).

(b) *the backe side* 1693 (*v*. **bak-side**); *Brakenhougate, Brakenhouwelle* c.1200, Ed1 (Hy4) ('bracken hill', *v*. **brakni, haugr**, with **gata** 'a road' and **wella** 'a spring, well'); *Brameberg* c.1200 (probably 'the broom hill', *v*. **brōm, berg**); *the Braymors* 1713; *Brown Close* 1703, 1709, 1715, 1724, *brown close* 1706 (perhaps named from the *Brown* family, well-evidenced in the parish, cf. Mark *Browne* 1635 *BT*); ye *Commons* 1693, y^e - 1700, *the Common* 1703; *the Corn Close* 1713; y^e *Cow pasture* 1709, 1715, *the* - 1724; *atte Crosse* 1327, 1332 *SR* both (p) (*v*. **cros**); *Filecher* c.1150, a1180 (e13) *NCot*, *Filaker* 1159-91 (e13) *ib* (this must be the same name and feature as Filcar in Stallingborough f.ns. (a) *infra*); *four Pound Closes* 1703, *fourpound closes* 1706, y^e *four pound Close* 1709, 1715, *the four pound Close* 1713, 1724 (probably a rent or purchase price, cf. Upr 15 P^d Cl (a) *supra*); *Fulwel* c.1200, *furwel* (sic) Ed1 (Hy4) ('the foul spring', *v*. **fūl, wella**); *grisewel'* c.1150 (e13) *NCot*, *-welle* a1180 (e13) *ib* (perhaps 'the spring or well used by or for young pigs', *v*. **griss, wella**); *Holmberg* c.1200, Ed1 (Hy4) (*v*. **holmr, berg**); *ad houedesdeil* c.1150, a1180 (e13) *NCot* ('the share of land on the headland', *v*. **hofuð, deill**, a Scand. compound); *Little plat* 1713 (*v*. **plat**^2); *manerij de Rybi vocati loutham maner* 1417 *FF*, "the manor of Ryby called Loudeham" 1432 Cl, *Loudeham manere* 1437 Fine (named from a family, John *Loudeham* had died by 1433 Cl); *del More* 1327 *SR*, *de la More*, *atte More* 1332 *ib* all (p) (*v*. **mōr**^1); *the new Close* 1713; *Nine Pound closes* 1703, 1706, y^e *nine pound Close* 1709, *the* - 1713, *the Nine pound Close* 1724 (cf. *four Pound closes supra*); ye *Oxe pasture* 1693, y^e *Ox* - 1700; *campum de Riebi* Hy3 *HarlCh*, - *de Ryby* 1344 Selby, *Rybe feld* 1577 Terrier (Great Limber) (*v*. **feld**); *Ribi toft* c.1200, *Ribitoft* Ed1

(Hy4) (*v.* **toft** 'a curtilage'); *viam de Riby* Hy3 Selby; *Riskes* c.1200, Ed1 (Hy4) 'the rushes', with Scandinavianisation of OE **risc**, in the pl.); *propinque sal'tina* (i.e., 'a saltern') c.1150 (e13) *NCot*, *Scalehil* c.1200, Ed1 (Hy4) (*v.* **skáli** 'a temporary hut or shed', **hyll**, an early reference to an OWScand word, uncommon in the East Midlands); *Smithou* c.1200, *Smtherr* (sic) Ed1 (Hy4) (probably 'the smooth mound or hill', *v.* **směðe**, **haugr**); *Steinhil* c.1200, *Staynhil* Ed1 (Hy4) (*v.* **steinn**, **hyll**); *Tungacre* c..1200, *Tungate* Ed1 (Hy4) (*v.* **æcer**, apparently confused with **gata**, though several forms in *DuLaGCB* are clearly erratic; the first el. is probably **tunga** 'a tongue of land'); *the Tyth Barn Yard & Brumetts Yard* 1713; *attewell* 1327 *SR*, *atte Well'* 1332 *ib*, *Atte Well* 1343 NI, all (p) (*v.* **wella**); *the West field* 1713; *Whinship's Farme* 1713 ("*in the possession of Thomas Whinship*" 1713); *Close … known by the name of Whittiker* 1713 (presumably from a family name).

Saxby All Saints

SAXBY ALL SAINTS
> *Saxebi* 1086 DB, 1166, 1167, 1171, 1172, 1173, 1174 P, 1175
> ChancR *et freq* to Hy3 *HarlCh*, *-by* 1179 P, 1202 FF, (*in
> Lindissai*) c.1212 (m13) Pontefract, 1221 *AD*, 1212 Welles,
> 1242-43 Fees, 1250 FF, (*iuxta Bondeby*) m13 *HarlCh*, 1254
> ValNor *et passim* to 1441 Cl, 1664 *Monson*, (*iuxta Ouneby*)
> 1288 *Ass*
> *Saxbi* 1238-43 Fees, *-by* 1327 *SR*, 1338 Misc, 1343 NI, 1353
> Ipm, 1365 Pat, 1372 Misc, 1372 Pat, 1373 Peace, (*iuxta
> Ouneby*) 1396 ib, 1397 *LindDep* 88 *et freq*, (*iuxta Bondeby*)
> 1408, 1438 ib, (*iuxta Horkestow super Ankcoln*) 1459 *ib*,
> *-bye* 1563 *BT*, 1576 Saxon, 1610 Speed, *-bie* 1576 LER,
> 1580, 1582 *Yarb*

'Saxi's famstead or village', *v.* **bý**, the first el. being the ON, ODan pers.n. *Saxi*, as in Saxby LWR and Lei (*PN LeiR* 166). This name is so common in L and Nf that there is no point in looking for an alternative etymology. Fellows-Jensen SSNEM 66 seems to prefer the gen.pl. of the folk-name OE *S(e)axe*, Scand *Saksar* 'Saxon' but in view of the frequency of *Saxi* in the county her suggestion seems less likely. It is described as near Bonby, Owmby and Horkstow, as well as in Lindsey. All Saints is from the dedication of the church.

BENNETT'S NEW COVERT is named from the family of Thomas *Bennett* 1842 White. CROW WOOD PLANTATION. ELEVEN ACRE PLANTATION. FIELD HOUSE FM is *Saxby Wold F.* 1824 O, - *Farm* 1830 Gre, and cf. *campo de Saxby* Hy3 (Ed1) *Newh.* FORTH CARR PLANTATION, cf. *Forth Carr* 1819 *Monson,* - *Car* 1837 *TA;* the same name occurs in the adjacent parish of Bonby f.ns. (a) s.n. Firth Carr, where it is stated that the first el. is uncertain. FOUR ACRE CLUMP. FOX COVERT PLANTATION, cf. *Fox Cover* 1837 *TA;* it is *Bartons Cover* 1828 Bry; *Barton* is a family name, cf. John and Richard *Barton* 1819 *Monson,* Henry *Barton* 1821 *BT.* GORSE COVERT. GRANGE FM, for the late use of **grange,** cf. Croxton Grange in Croxton *supra.* HILL SIDE PLANTATION, cf. *Hillside* 1819 *Monson, Hill side* 1837 *TA* and *the top(p) of the hill* 1664 *Monson,* 1668 *Terrier,* y^e *top of* y^e *hill* 1690, 1724, y^e *Top of* y^e *Hill* 1697, 1700, 1788, *the Top of the Hill* 1748, 1762 all *ib.* LAND DRAIN, cf. *(the) old Land dike* 1662, 1668, 1674, - *Land-dike* 1762, y^e *old land dike* 1690, - *Dyke* 1697, - *Old Landike* 1700, - *old Land-dike* 1724, 1788 all *Terrier,* self-explanatory, *v.* **land, dīc, dīk.** MIDDLEGATE LANE, *v.* the same name in Bigby *supra;* this is the name of the ridgeway northwards from Caistor to South Ferriby. MANOR HO. MOUNT PLEASANT (lost), 1828 Bry. NORTH CARR LANE, cf. the South Carr in f.ns. (a) *infra.* OLD BELT PLANTATION. PIKENDALE PLANTATION. ROUND CLUMP. SAXBY ALL SAINTS BRIDGE, *Saxby Br.* 1824 O, 1830 Gre. SAXBY ALL SAINTS CARRS, *Saxby Carres* 1635 (c.1900) *LindDep 78,* - *Carrs* 1767 *Stubbs,* 1824 O, - *Carr* 1830 Gre, *Saxby Carr Plantation* 1828 Bry, *the Carrs* 1662, 1674, 1762 all *Terrier, v.* **kjarr,** the name of the low-lying land by the R. Ancholme. SAXBY HALL. SAXBY WINDMILL, y^e *Miln* 1724 *Terrier, Windmill* 1819 *Monson, Saxby Mill* 1824 O, 1828 Bry, 1830 Gre. SAXBY WOLDS, cf. *the Wold, High -, Low Wold* 1819 *Monson, Wolds,* - *Bottom,* - *End* 1837 *TA, v.* **wald.** SOUTH PLANTATION. WEAR DYKE, 1824 O, *Were Dyke Drain* 1819 *Monson, Were Dyke* 1837 *TA,* cf. *the Way dyke Carr or Were Dyke Carr* 1819 *Monson,* the local name of the New River Ancholme. WILLOW PLANTATION.

Field-Names

Principal forms in (a) are 1837 *TA 276*. Forms dated m13, Ed1 are *HarlCh*, 1606, 1662, 1668, 1674, 1690, 1697, 1700, 1706, 1724, 1748, 1762, and 1788 are *Terrier*; m17 are *MiscDep 115* (Map); 1667 are *LCL*; those dated 1664 and 1819 are *Monson*.

(a) Back Land's (sic); Bank (2x); Barton-Mear 1762, Barton Meer 1788 (*Barton meere* 1606, - *meare* 1662, 1668, - *Meare* 1674, 1697, 1700, *barton mear* 1690, - *meare* 1706, *Barton-meare* 1724, *Barton-Mear* 1748, 'the boundary with Barton upon Humber', *v.* (ge)mǣre); Bottom, Bottoms Cl (2x) 1819, East -, North -, South -, West - 1819, Bottom Cl, Bottoms (3x), Bottom's Cl 1837 (*v.* botm); Broom or Brown Cl 1819 (the alternative name is perhaps from the *Brown* family, cf. William *Brown* 1782 *LTR*); Bull platt 1819, - Plat (2x) 1837 (*v.* plat^2 'a plot of land', as elsewhere in this parish); the Butt Stone 1762 (1748), ye Butt-Stone 1788 (*the* -, y^e *Bull Stone* (sic) 1668, - *stone* 1690, 1697, 1700, *the bull stone* 1674, y^e *but-stone* (sic) 1724); Upr Carr 1819, Car (*freq*), Car Lane, Low Cars, Upr Car (6x) 1837 (*the Carr Lanes* 1667, *v.* kjarr, named from Saxby All Saints Carrs *supra*); Chequie Cl or Chequer Cl 1819, Chequer 1837 (*Chequer Close* m17, *v.* cheker); Church Yard Cl 1819, Church Cl, Church Yd 1837 (cf. *Attekircke* (sic) 1209 FF (p), *v.* kirkja); Corn Cl but now called Common Cl 1819, Common Cl 1837; Cottager's Car (2x) 1837 (*the Cotagers Car,* a '*somer pasture*' 1667, held by the cottagers, as commonly in north L); Cow Carr 1819, - Car 1837; Cow Pasture; the Croft 1819, Croft 1837; adjoining upon the Cross road 1819 (from Saxby to South Ferriby); Dimkin Garth (*v.* Mutton Cl *infra*); Dog Garth (*v.* the Paddock *infra*); the Drain Bank 1819, Drain Bank 1837 (2x); the Earth Swarths 1819; the eaten Carrs 1762, ye Eaten Carrs 1788 (1697, 1700, 1724, *the eaten Carrs* 1668, y^e *eaten Carrs* 1690, *v.* kjarr 'a marsh, marshy ground'; the explanation is given in 1662 *Terrier*, before the first recorded form of the name - *Free Common of pasture without stint for all kind of goods throughout all the Carrs commonly eaten from old Land dike unto old Ancolne* - and it is repeated in 1664 *Terrier*); the fallow-Field 1762, ye fallow-field 1788 (*the Fallow Feild* 1662, *the fallow field* 1668, *the Fallow feild* 1674, y^e *fallow field* 1690, 1697, y^e *Fallow field* 1700, y^e *fallow-field* 1724, *the Fallow-Field* 1748); Folly Cl ('a parcel of Arable land') 1819, (2x) 1837, Folly (6x) 1837 (these are pieces of land); the Platt of Ground called the Frather 1762, ye Ground called ye Frather 1788, Frater Cl 1819, Frater 1837 (*a parcell of medow called the frater* 1606, *parcel of ground ... called the Fraters* 1635 (c.1900) *LindDep 78*, *a platt of ground called the Frather* 1662, 1668, *the platt of ground called the Frater* 1674, y^e *plat of ground called* y^e *Frather* 1690, - *the Frather* 1700, *i plat of ground called* y^e

Freather 1697, *a Plat of Ground called the Frather* 1706, 1748, perhaps alluding to a monastic *frater*, ME *freitour*, or refectory, the transfer to field-name use being emphasised by the repetition of the formula *plat(t) of ground called, parcel(l) of ground called*, etc., cf. *the Froyter* in Thornton Curtis f.ns. (b)); Gal(l)way -, Gallways Platt 1819 (from the surn. *Galloway*, cf. Joseph *Galloway* 1740 *BT*, and plat², Garths (*v.* gar[ð]r 'an enclosure'); the Gateland Cl 1819, Gateland, Gatelands (3x), Gate lands, Gateland Cl (2x) 1837 (cf. *Atte Gate* 1327 *SR*, *atte Gatehend* 1332 *ib* both (p), *v.* gata, ende¹, the two references are almost certainly to the same man); Goose Hill Carr 1819, - Car 1837; the hard-ings 1762, ye Hard-Ings 1788, Hard Ings 1819, 1837 (3x) (*ye great hard ings* 1606, *ye hard Ings* 1662, *the Hardings* 1664, 1674, *y^e* - 1690, 1697, 1700, *ye hard-Ings* 1724, *the Hard-Ings* 1748, *v.* h(e)ard 'hard to till', eng 'meadow' as elsewhere in this parish); the High Fm 1819 (cf. Low Fm *infra*); the Hill Cl 1819; Home Cl; the Horse Cl 1819; Horse Carr 1819, - Car (5x) 1837 (*v.* kjarr); the Ings 1819, Ings 1837 (4x) (cf. perhaps *in prato de Saxebi* 1191 P, *v.* eng); Intack(s) otherwise Intake 1819, Intake (5x), Btm -, Far -, Top Intake 1837 (*v.* inntak); the Lares Cl 1819, Lares (4x), Lares Bottom, Lares S. Side, Lare's Cl 1837 (probably 'the muddy or clayey places', *v.* leira); Lings 1762, 1788 (1668, 1674, 1690, 1697, 1700, 1724, 1748, *the Lings* 1662, - *lings* 1706, 'the places where ling grows', *v.* lyng); Little Cl 1819; the Little Ings 1819 (*Little-Ings* m17, *v.* eng); Long Cl 1819; the Low Carr(s) 1819, Low Cars 1837 (W. of R. Ancholme, *v.* kjarr); Low Fm 1819 (cf. the High Fm *supra*); Mill Garth (cf. Saxby Windmill *supra*); (the) Moor Cl 1819, 1837 (4x), Moors 1837; Mutton Cl and now Dimkin Garth 1819, Dimkin Garth 1837 (the form on a plan a1819 *Monson* 17/4 is *Dunkin Garth*, from the *Dunkin* family, cf. Michael *Dunkin* 1687 *BT* and gar[ð]r); Narrow Cl 1819, 1837; the Nooking 1819, Nooking 1837; the North Fd 1762, ye North Fd 1788 (1700, *the* - 1748, *in aquilonali campo de saxeby* Hy3 (Ed1) *Newh, in campo aquilonali* m13, *ye north feild* 1606, *the North* - 1664, *the Northfeild* 1662, 1668, 1674, *ye north field* 1690, *ye Northfield* 1697, *the* - 1706, *ye North-field* 1724, one of the open fields of Saxby, *v.* nor[ð], feld); Nursery; Old Oval; Old Square; open Eatage 1762 (1662, 1668, 1674, *y^e* - 1697, 1700, 1724, 1748; *ye corn eatage* 1690 refers to the same piece of land; for *eatage*, *v.* NED s.v. 'grass available only for grazing'; *eatage* usually refers to grass on roadside verges, but here clearly denotes pasture in the open fields); Paddock, ... heretofore called Paddock but now called Dog Garth 1819, Paddock (2x); Pasture; Penny Carrs 1819, - Car 1837 (2x) (*v.* pening, kjarr); Penny Platt 1819, - Plat 1837 (*v.* plat²); the Pindle or Pingle 1819 (*v.* pingel, the first form being a rarely recorded variant); Platt 1819, Plats 1837 (3x) (*v.* plat²); Red Ings 1819, 1837 (2x) (*Reddings* 1635 (c.1900) *LindDep* 78, probably from the pl. of ryding 'clearing', local conditions perhaps accounting for the later form); Seven Acre Cl 1819; the Shift Carr, Shift Ings 1819, Shift Car

(2x), Shift Ings 1837 (*v.* **kjarr, eng** *shift,* as in other parishes, probably alluding to a course in crop-rotation); ye Short four-sweaths 1762 (1724), ye short Swathes 1788 (*the short Fower Swathes* 1662, *the short foure swathes* 1668, - *Foure swathes* 1674, y^e *short four swaths* 1690, y^e *Short* - 1700, *the short four swaths* 1706, - *four-sweathes* 1748, *v.* **swæð**, used as a unit of measurement of grassland); Shoulder of Mutton 1819 (no doubt a reference to shape); ye Slaughts 1788, Slought(s), Far Sloughts 1837 ((*the*) *Slaught(e)s* 1635 (c.1900) *LindDep 78, the Slaughts* 1662, 1668, 1748, *the slaughts* 1674, 1704, 1706, y^e *Slaughts* 1697, 1700, *Slaughts* 1724; this is presumably the same as dial. *slought* 'a sewer, a drain', *v.* EDD s.v., where it is recorded only from north L and is apparently a derivative of OE **slōh**, *v.* also NED s.v. *slough* sb[1] 3 'a ditch, dike, or drain'); the South Carr 1819, South Car 1837 (*v.* **kjarr**); the South-Fd 1762, ye South Fd 1788 (*in australi campo* Hy3, m13, c.1260, *the Southfeild* 1662, *the South feild* 1664, 1668, - *Feild* 1674, y^e -, *the Southfield* 1690, 1697, 1706, y^e *southfield* 1700, y^e *South field* 1724, *the South-Field* 1748, one of the great fields of Saxby, cf. ye North Fd *supra*); North -, South Stones 1819, Stones 1837 (5x), (S.) Stones Cl 1819, Stone's Cl 1837 (perhaps from the surn. *Stone*); Waddingham Plat (from the *Waddingham* family, cf. Richard *Waddingham* 1736 *BT,* Thomas *Waddingham* 1833 *ib,* and **plat²**); Wheatcroft or Wheatclose, Wheat Cl 1819 (*le Whetecroft 1459 LindDep 88, v.* **hwǣte, croft**),

(b) *Dayle* Hy3 (Ed1) *Newh* (*v.* **deill**); *The Dove-Coat-Close* m17; *the Football-Close* m17; *the Gleeb land* 1635 (c.1900) *LindDep 98, A Hemp-garth* m17 ('the hemp garden or yard', *v.* **hænep, garðr**, usually a small plot near a dwelling); *ye Kyngs streete* 1606, *the Towne Streete* 1667 (probably referring to Middlegate Lane *supra*); *The Mannor-garth* m17 ('the yard beside the manor house', *v.* **manere, garðr**); *super mariscum* m13, *de marisco* Hy3 (Ed1) *Newh* (p), (*de*) *Marisco* Ed1 *ib* (p.n.) ('the marsh'); *The North-Close* m17; *Northiby* 1332 *SR* (p) ('north in the village', *v.* **norð, í, bý,** cf. *clausum Hugon' Suthyby infra*); *the north tetherings* 1606 (perhaps to be identified with pasture *ex prato boriali, prato sancti Johis Jerusal'* 1397 *LindDep 88, tethering* being a means of limiting grazing, practised before general enclosure, cf. Adams 163); *toftum persone* m13 ('the parson's toft', *v.* **perso(u)n,** toft); *the pinfold* 1667 (*v.* **pynd-fald**); *the Stone-pitt Commons* 1667; *clausum Hugon' Suthyby* Hy3, *pratum Wateri Suthiby cleric de Saxeby* Ed1, cf. *Suthiby* m13, *Southiby* 1327, 1332 *SR, Sutheby* 1352 *Cor, Sutheby de Saxby* 1397 *LindDep 88* all (p) ('south in the village', *v.* **sūð, í, bý,** cf. *Northiby supra*); *viam Thedgate* Hy3 (Ed1) *Newh* (*v.* **gata**); *a place called* y^e *town fould* 1606, *The Towne-Fold* m17 (*v.* **fald** 'a fold').

Searby cum Owmby

SEARBY CUM OWMBY, 1824 O, 1828 Bry.

SEARBY
> *Sourebi* 1086 DB, 1196 ChancR (p), 1214 P (p), *Sowerbi* 1202
> Ass
> *Sauerbi* 1155-58 RA i, Hy2 Dane (p)
> *Seurebi* (4x) 1086 DB, c.1115 LS, c.1190 RA iv (p), 1197, 1198,
> 1199, 1209, 1210, 1211, 1212 P all (p), 1212 Cur (p)
> *Safrebi* c.1115 LS
> *Seuerbia* 1148-52 LAAS vii, 1190 (e13) *NCot,* 1198-1205 RA ix
> (p), 1212 Fees, *-bie* c.1150 *TYR,* 1563 InstBen, *-bi* c.1155
> Dane, 1155-58 RA i, 1155-60 Dane, 1158-63, c.1160 ib both
> (p), 1185, 1186 P (p) *et passim* to 1238-43 Fees, *-by* c.1155,
> a1167 (e13) *NCot,* Hy2 (1409) Gilb, 1200-5 RA i, e13,
> 1210-18, c.1215, a1219 ib iv, 1219 Ass, 1223-24 RA iv *et*
> *freq* to 1443 *DCAcct,* 1463 *LCCA,* 1550 Pat, *-bye* 1577
> *Terrier, Seuyrby* 1380 Pat, *Severbya* 1200 ChR, *-by* 1205 Cur
> (p), 1279, 1280 RSut, 1281 QW, 1291 Tax *et passim* to
> 1437-38 Inqaqd, 1535 VE iv, 1563 *BT et passim* to 1723
> SDL, *-bye* 1550-52 *MinAcct,* *-bie* 1599 *LCCA,* - als Sarby
> 1616 *Foster*
> *Seuerebi* 1155-60 Dane, 1177-82 RA ix (p), 1191-95 ib i, 1202
> Ass (p), 1202 SelectPleas, 1202 P (p), *-by* 1202 FF, 1275
> RH, *Severebi* 1204 Cur (p)
> *Seuredebi* 1195 P, 1196 ChancR, 1197 P all (p)
> *Seueresbi* 1199 P (p), 1202 Ass (p), 1202, 1203 P (p), 1206
> Ass (p)
> *Sereby* 1394 Fine, 1399 Pat, 1414 Fine, 1535 VE iv, 1543
> WillsA *et passim* to 1671 *Terrier, Serbee* 1539 LP xiv, *-by*
> 1542-43 Dugd vi, 1621 *Foster,* 1666 VL
> *Sewerby* 1488 Ipm, 1525 CA
> *Seerby* 1526 Sub, *Seirebye* 1604 LNQ x, *Searby* 1661 *DCLeases,*
> 1665 *Terrier,* 1688 *DCLeases et passim, Seareby* 1675 *ib*
> *Saverby alias Sereby alias Sowerby* Eliz ChancP

Both Ekwall (DEPN s.n.) and Fellows-Jensen (SPNLY 284)
agree that this is 'the farmstead or village of *Sæfari',* v. **by**, the first
el. being an ON byname 'seafarer'. However, in SSNEM 68 the

latter seems to prefer the gen.pl. of the appellative *sæfari*, from
which the pers.n. is derived. This hardly seems plausible
considering that so many of the Scand. settlers in the area might
well have been described as 'seafarers'. On the whole, the pers.n.
is to be preferred and Searby certainly appears to mean 'Sæfari's
farmstead or village'.

OWMBY

    Odenebi (3x) 1086 DB, c.1155 Dane, 1207 Cur (p)

    Autneby 1100-5, a1135 (14) Whitby

    Authneby 1100-15 (14) Whitby

    Andeneby 1190 (1301) Dugd vi, i (*An-* = *Au-*)

    Oudenbi 1155-58 RA i, *-by* 1240-50 ib iii, *Oudeneby* 1212 Cur
        (p), *Audenbi* 1238-43 Fees

    Outhenebi 1155-60 Dane, *-by* 1220-30 RA iv, *-b'* c.1230 ib iii,
        Oupeneby m13 *HarlCh*, *Outhenbi* 1155-60 Dane, *-by*
        1196-1203 RA iv, c.1215 (c.1330) *R* (p), a1219, 1239-45 RA
        iv, 1274 Ipm, (*iuxta Seuerby*) 1282 *FF*, 1299 *ib*, 1301 Ch *et*
        passim to 1368 Ipm, *Ouyenby* 1275, 1276 RH (*y*=*þ*),
        Outhenneby iuxta Seuerby 1308 *LCCA*, *Outenby* 1268 Ch

    Ounebi c.1115 LS, l12 (e13) *NCot* (p), 1202 SelectPleas (p),
        1218 Ass, *-by* e13 RA iv (p), 1220-30 ib, 1288 *Ass*, 1298
        ib (p), 1301 *FF*, 1309, 1315 Ipm, 1309 Fine, 1373 Pat,
        Owneby 1221-29 RA iv, *Ouenby* 1236 ib iv

    Oumesby (sic) 1206 Cur, *Ounesbi* 1219 Ass

    Ougnebi (sic) 1218 Ass (p), 1311 Ipm

    Owneby 1477 WillsPCC, 1504 Ipm, 1535 VE iv, 1550 Pat,
        1641 *DCLeases*, *Ownby* (*by Saxby*) 1551 Pat, 1732 *DCLeases*,
        (*next Searby*) 1745 *ib*

    Owmbye next Serebye 1598 *Nelthorpe*, *Owmbie* 1615 *Foster*, *-by*
        1621 *ib*, 1662 *Terrier*, 1710 *DCLeases et passim*, *Owmeby*
        1681 *DCLeases*

Owmby has usually been taken with Owmby by Spital LWR,
Aunby in Careby and Aunsby Kest, though the forms for each do
not show exactly the same patterns. Owmby by Spital has many
ME spellings in *Ounebi, -by*, but only three in *-th-* and one in *-d-*
(and these not until the 14th century) and four with gen.sg. *-es-*.
Aunby, first recorded in 1219, again has a number of spellings in

Ounebi, -by, none in *-th-* or *-d-,* but four with *-es-.* Aunsby, on the other hand, has a preponderance of spellings in *-es-,* but only one in *-th-* and one in *-d-,* both from the 13th century. The characteristic forms they share, with the exception of Aunsby, are *Ounebi, -by.*

Both Ekwall (DEPN s.n. Aunby and Owmby) and Fellows-Jensen (SPNLY 41-42) take the first el. of all four to be the Scand pers.n. *Auðunn* (gen.sg. *Auðunar, Auðuna*), according to the former, some perhaps in a shortened form *Aun.* The gen.sg. forms in *-es-* would represent what is now being called "a secondary OE gen.sg. in *-es-*". The developments of the first el. are discussed by Fellows-Jensen (SPNLY 42). It should be noted that *Auðunn* is recorded independently in L in DB as *Oudon* and *Houden,* and in 12th century charters (Dane) as *Oudhen,* in Killingholme, and *Oupein,* in Faldingworth. So, the meaning of Owmby may well be 'Auðunn's farmstead or village', *v.* bȳ.

However, Fellows-Jensen (SSNEM 33-34) looks for an alternative explanation and proposes an OScand appellative *auðn* 'an uninhabited tract of land', 'a deserted farm', a word found in p.ns. in Norway and Sweden. These latter seem in the main to belong to the period after 1400, so that they cannot be used to support the proposal that *auðn* is to be found in this country. Nonetheless, Fellows-Jensen claims "there seems no reason why the el. *auðn* should not have been used with the meanings in question in the Viking period", though this seems to be special pleading, and, though *auðn* remains formally a possible first el. of this group of names, a pers.n. *Auðunn (Aun)* certainly cannot be ruled out.

BULL HOUSE FM. HARDING'S WOOD, *Hardings Plant.*[n] 1828 Bry, cf. *the Tethering Hardinges* 1662 *Terrier, tethering hardings, harddings* 1665 *ib,* 'the meadows hard to till', *v.* heard, eng; *tethering* is self-explanatory. IVY HO. MANOR HO, cf. "the manor of *Sereby* called *Le Northall*' 1394 Fine. MIDDLEGATE LANE, *Middle gate* 1661, *the Middell gate* 1665, *yᵉ midle gate* 1671, *- Middle Gate* 1676 all *Terrier;* the name of the ancient ridgeway from Caistor to South Ferriby, found in many parishes in the west of this Wapentake, cf. the same name in Bigby *supra.* OWMBY LANE, *Oumby Lane* 1765 *Terrier.* OWMBY MILL (lost), 1824 O, 1830 Gre, cf. *Milncroft* 1662, *yᵉ Milcrofts* 1665 both *Terrier.* OWMBY MOUNT, 1828 Bry. OWMBY TOP is *Top or Wold Barn* 1828

Bry. OWMBY VALE. OWMBY WOLD LANE, 1828 Bry, cf. *a high way called the would gate, the wouldes* 1662, *the Woulds* 1661, *the Would* 1665 all *Terrier*, v. **wald, gata**. SEARBY HILL. SEARBY MOOR FM. SEARBY TOP. SEARBY WOLD LANE, 1828 Bry, *the Wold Road* 1765 *Terrier, the New Wold Road* 1765 *ib*, cf. *ye Wowld* 1671 *ib*, - *Would* 1676 *ib* (cf. Owmby Wold Lane *supra*), *Searby Wold* 1820 *MiscDep 204*.

Field-Names

Forms dated 1577, 1606 (Grasby), 1661, 1662, 1665, 1671, 1676, 1690 (Great Limber), 1697 (Grasby and Great Limber), 1724 (Grasby), 1764, 1765 are *Terrier*, unless otherwise marked; those dated 1873 are *DCLeases*.

(a) The Acre Dikes 1764, 1765 (*the Acredikes* 1661, *the North* -, *the South* - 1662, *north* -, *south Accerdikes* 1665, *ye Ackerdikes* 1671, *ye Acre dikes* 1676, *North acre* -, *South Acre dykes furlonge* 1661, and *v.* the same name in Barnetby le Wold f.ns. (b) *supra*); Barton High Rd 1765 (to Barton upon Humber); chalk lands 1766 *TLE* (cf. *short Calkes, Short Cawkes, Long Caulks* 1661, *the short Calkes* 1662, - *Caukes* 1665, *ye long Caulks* 1671, *ye Long-Calkes* 1676, *v.* **calc**, in the 17th century forms in the pl.); Ferry Gate 1764, 1765 (*sub Ferigate* 1240-50 RA iv, 'the road to the ferry', *v.* **ferja, gata**, and cf. Middlegate Lane *supra*); First Cl 1873; Fourth Cl 1873; The Furze 1764 (*v.* **fyrs**); Golden Hill 1873 (cf. Silver Hill *infra*); the High Fd 1764; the Hill 1765 (*ye hill* 1665, 1671, - *Hill* 1676, cf. *atte Hull' de Seuerby* 1357 *FF* (p)); Hill Side 1764, the Hill side 1765, Hill Side (Cl) 1873 (*the Hillside* 1662, *the hill side* 1665, *ye hill side* 1671, - *Hill-Side* 1676); the North -, the South Hill side Rd 1765; Howsam Cls, Howsam Lane 1765 (from Howsham in Cadney parish *supra*); the Ings 1764, 1765 (*v.* **eng** 'meadow, pasture'); the Low Fd 1764, - of Searby 1765, North low Fd 1764, 1765, the North Low Fd of Searby 1765, South low Fd 1764, 1765, the South Low Fd of Searby 1765 (*the low field* 1661, *the Lowfeildes* 1662, *ye Low feild* 1665, *ye Low field* 1671, presumably one of the fields of the parish); the Moor Heads 1764, the Moorheads 1765, Moorheads 1873 (*the more heades* 1665, *ye Moor heads* 1671, *ye Moor-heads* 1676, *v.* **mōr**[1], **hēafod**); the North -, The South High Fd (of Searby) 1765, the South Wold or South High Fd 1765; Oumby Fd 1764 (*in campis de Oudenby* 1240-50 RA iv, *Owmby feild* 1606, *Owmeby Field* 1690, *Ombie field* 1697, *Owmby Field* 1697, *Omby Field* 1724, *v.* **feld**); Red House Cl 1873 (named from the Red Ho in North Kelsey); Ringroses Cl 1873 (probably from the surn. *Ringrose*); the Sands 1764, 1765 (1661, 1665, 1671, *y^e* -

1676, cf. *Sand close* 1661, 1665); Searby Mill 1765; Second Cl 1873; Silver Hill 1873 (*v.* **scolfor**, cf. Golden Hill *supra*); Somerby Walk 1765 (cf. *Somerby hedges* 1665, *Somerbye hedge* 1661, - *Hedges* 1671, - *Hedg* 1676, from the neighbouring parish of Somerby, *v.* **walk, hecg**); (the) Stone Pitts 1764, 1765; Third Cl 1873; Townend Cl 1873; The Water Furrows 1764; a windmill 1766 *TLE* (*molendinum ad ventum* 1223-4, 1236-8 RA iv); Wold Furze 1764 (*v.* **wald, fyrs**);

(b) *ye bra gates* 1665, *Bra gattes* 1671, *ye Bragates* 1676 (*v.* **breiðr** 'broad', **gata** 'a road', a Scand. compound); *brokebrydge* 1545-9 *MinAcct* (presumably 'the bridge over the brook', *v.* **brōc, brycg**, unless it is an error for *brokenbrydge*); *Buckehouse* 1550-52 *MinAcct*, *Calfe close* 1661, - *Close* 1662, *Caulfe Close* 1665; *Caster gates* 1665. - *Gates* 1676, *Cayster gate* 1671 ('the road to Caistor', *v.* **gata**); *the chappell of Owmbie* 1577; *church gate* 1661, *the Church gate* 1665, *ye Church gate* 1671, - *Church-Gate* 1676 (*v.* **gata**); *the Closes* 1662; *le Dale* 1239-45 RA iv (self-explanatory); *damper thing* m16 *Cragg* ('property or premises belonging to Damp(i)er', *v.* **þing**, though no reference to the family has been noted in the sources searched); *Dicfurlanges* c.1215 (c.1330) *R*, a1219 RA iv (*v.* **dík, furlang**); *ye dog garth* 1665, *Doggarth* 1671, *Dog-garth* 1676 (*v.* **garðr**); *Drithylles, Drithilles* 1239-45 RA iv, *Brichill* 1239-45 ib (*recte Drichill*, i.e. *Drithill*), commons called *Dirthhill* 1661, *Durthills* 1662, *durt hills* 1665 ('dirt hills or heaps of dirt', *v.* **drit, hyll**); *Fewekener lande* 1550-52 *MinAcct* (*v.* **land**, with a surn., perhaps a variant of *Fauconer*, though it has not been noted in the sources searched); *Gildegath* (sic) e13 RA iv, c.1215 (c.1330) *R*, *Gildecroft* 1236-9 RA iv, c.1240 (c.1330) *R* ('the enclosure held by a guild', *v.* **gildi, garðr, croft**); *illam grangeam que situat' ex parte borial' eiusdem Rectorie* 1463 *LCCA* (*v.* **grange**); *Grenefeld Thinge* 1550 Pat ('Greenfield's property or premises', *v.* **þing**, but, again, no reference to a family of that name has been noted in the sources searched); *y^e heades* 1665, - *Heads* 1676 ('the headlands', *v.* **hēafod**); *the hill foote* 1665, *y^e* - 1671, *y^e Hill-Foot* 1676 (cf. the Hill *supra* in (a)); *Honedland* 1190 (1301) Dugd vi, i (*n* = *u*), *y^e Headland* 1676 (*v.* **hofuð, land**, the later form apparently anglicised (*v.* **hēafod-land**), if the two refer to the same feature); *Howebecke lande* 1550-52 *MinAcct*, *Howgates* 1661, *the how gate* 1665, *y^e Howgate* 1676, *y^e Low gate* (sic) 1671; *Le Hyrne* 1327 *SR* (p), *la Hirne* 1332 ib (p) (2x) (*v.* **hyrne** 'an angle, a corner'); *Infurlainde* 1661, 1671, *Infurlaine* 1676, *the Ing furlaine* 1665 (*v.* **furlang**, the first el. is uncertain, but may well be **eng** 'meadow, pasture', or in denoting a piece of meadow taken in, as in **infeld, inland** etc.); *kysyng thinge* m16 *Cragg* (from **þing** with a surn., not noted in the parish independently); *Lavericke Hall* 1662, *Laverrick hall* 1665 (*v.* **lāwerce, hall** and the same name in Great Limber f.ns. (b)); *the long furlonge, Long furlongs* 1661, *the Long furlandes* 1662, *Longfurland, the Longfurlong* 1665, *ye long Furlongs* 1671, - *Long Furlong* 1676 (*v.*

lang, furlang; note that *furland* is frequent as a variant of *furlang*); *the long lands* 1661, y^e - 1665, - *Lands* 1671 (*v.* lang, land); *the Lordship Close* 1661, *the Lordshipe close* 1665, y^e *Lordshippe Close* 1671, y^e *Lordship-Close* 1676 ('the enclosure of demesne land', *v.* lordeship(e), clos(e)); *the Lowest Furlong* 1662, - *furlong* 1665; *towe Marfers* 1577 (i.e. *two*; *v.* marfur 'a boundary furrow'); *the meares* 1665 (*v.* (ge)mǣre 'a boundary'); *the middle furlonge* 1661, *the Middle Furlong* 1662, *the middle furlong* 1665; *the Moar* (sic) 1662, *the More* 1665 (*v.* mōr[1]); *Northeby* 1220-30 RA iv, *Northiby* 1239 *ib* both (p) ('north in the village', *v.* norð, i, bȳ); *the Northe feild* 1662, y^e *North-field* 1671, *the upper North Field* 1661, y^e *lower North Field next unto Somerby* 1676 (one of the great fields of the village); *the Northe feilde of Owmbie* 1577; *vie de Ouenby* 1236 RA iv; *a messuage & garden called Parcisfe* 1550 Pat (from ME *fe* 'an estate'; William *de Perci* held Owmby in 1086 DB and the fee was held by Richard *de Perci* 1238-41 Fees); *petter greene garth* 1665 (cf. perhaps *Attegrene* 1288 *Ass*, *atte Grene* 1332 *SR* both (p), *v.* grēne[1], or grēne[2], garðr; *Petter* is presumably a surn.); *Riskedam* 1220-30, 1239-45 RA iv (apparently 'the dam or pool where rushes grow', *v.* risc, dammr (ME damme), with *Riske-* a Scandinavianised form); *Searby drift* 1661, - *dryft* 1665, *Sereby Drift* 1662 ('Searby cattle road', *v.* drift); *Severbie feild* 1577, - *Fielde* 1650 ParlSurv, *Sereby feild* 1662, *Searby* - 1665 (self-explanatory and cf. the High Fd in (a) *supra*); *Le Sike*, *Le sich* 1239-45 RA iv, *the Sikes* 1662, 1665, *Sike close* 1661, - *Close* 1662 (*v.* sīc, sīk 'a small stream, a ditch' later 'a piece of meadow along a stream'); *Smalling Close* 1662, *Smallinges* - 1665 (perhaps 'the narrow meadows', *v.* smæl, eng); *the Sowthe feilde* 1557, y^e *South field* 1671, *Upper South field* 1661, *the low* -, *the upper Southfeild* 1662, y^e *upper South feild* 1665, y^e *Upper South-Feild, ye Lower-South Feild* 1676 (one of the great fields of the village); *stintinge* 1577 (*v.* stinting 'a baulk, an end-to-end meeting place of lands', cf. Adams 87, in ModE dial. also 'a portion of common land set apart for one man's use', cf. y^e *stintings* in Barnetby le Wold f.ns. (b)); *bosc' voc' Talland* 1545-47 MinAcct (the first el. is uncertain, *v.* land); *the upper feild* 1662, *the Upper fielde* 1665; *the upper furlonge* 1661, - *Furlong* 1662, *the Upper furlong* 1665; *Warlotas* 1190 (1301) Dugd vi, i, *Meadow called Warlets, Warlet close* 1661, *Warlettes, Warlett close* 1662, *Warllets* (*Close*) 1665 (*v.* warlot, discussed under Waterhill Wood in Brocklesby *supra*).

Somerby

SOMERBY

Sumerledeby 1190-96 (c.1240), 1100-15 (14), a1135 (15), 1174-79 (c.1240), *Summerledeby* 1100-15 (Ed3) all Whitby

Sumertebi, Summertebi 1086 DB, *Sumeretebi* 1219 Ass, *-by* 1254
ValNor, *Someretteby* 1291 Tax, *Sumeretbi* 1238-43 Fees, *-by*
1242-43 ib, 1245 FF, 1338 Pat, (*North*) *Someretby* 1274 Ipm,
1303 FA, 1308 Ipm, 1316 FA *et passim* to 1450 LDD, *-bi*
l13 (14) Percy, *Somertby besydes Bekeby* 1557 VisitN, - *Iuxta
bekby* 1562 *BT*
Sumerdebi (2x) c.1115 LS, 1212 Fees, *-b'* 1204 Cur, *Summerdeby*
1242-43 Fees, *Somerdeby* 1287 Abbr, 1335 Pat, *Sumeredeby*
a1221, 1234 Welles, 1315 Ipm, *Sumeredby* 1279 RRGr,
Sumerdby 1240-45 RA iv
Somerebi 1194 CurP (p), *Sumereby* c.1234 BS, *Somerby* 1332
SR, 1343 NI, 1346 FA, 1368 Ipm, 1375 Works, 1428, 1431
FA *et freq*, (*next Bigby*) 1664, 1668, 1671 *Terrier*, *-bye* 1552
Pat, 1556 ASSR xxxvii, 1576 Saxton, 1610 Speed, *-bie* 1576
LER, 1593 BT, 1635 *Terrier*, *Sumerbie* 1638 *ib*, *Summerby*
1697, 1700, 1707, (*juxta Bigby*) 1712 *ib*
Someresby 1428 FA, *Somersby* 1548 ChantCert

'Sumarliði's farmstead or village', *v.* **by**. The first el. is the
Scand pers.n. *Sumarliði*, an original byname, probably meaning 'the
summer traveller', which is recorded six times in L (all in Lindsey)
in DB. The spellings in DB, *Summerled* (2x), *Summerlede*,
Sumerled, *Summerd* and *Summerde* are paralleled by forms found in
the p.n. Somerby. Identical in origin are probably Somerby LWR,
Somerby Kest, Somersby LSR and Somerby in Lei.

CARTWRIGHT MOOR (lost), 1828 Bry, named from the surn.
Cartwright, cf. perhaps Robert *Cartwright* (*retired farmer*) of the
neighbouring plarish of Searby 1851 *Census*. CATHOLIC MOOR
SCREED, cf. *Catholic Moor,* - *Wood* 1847 *TA*. *Screed* is EModE
screed 'a strip of land, a parcel of ground', cf. PN Nt 289 s.v. The
explanation of *Catholic* has not been discovered. DAWSON'S
COVERT, *Dawsons Cover* 1847 *TA*, cf. - *Carr,* - *Field* 1847 *ib*,
named from the family of George *Dawsonne* 1609 *Inv*. FERRY
GATE BOTTOM (lost), 1828 Bry; this is close to High Street, the
name of the ridgeway from Horncastle to Caistor, which becomes
Middlegate Lane from Caistor to South Ferriby, so presumably *Ferry
Gate* is 'the road to the ferry (at South Ferriby)', *v.* **gata**. JOHN
JAMES' SCREED, cf. *James' Close* 1847 *TA*. It is named from

the *James* family, perhaps from the *John James*, who was a tenant farmer in 1783 *LTR*. LONG PLANTATION (lost), 1828 Bry. MONUMENT, *Obelisk* 1828 Bry, *Monument Hill* 1847 *TA*. Mr Ifor Barton draws my attention to *Lincolnshire Life* 7, 7, p. 53, "In the middle of a field below the woods, is a tall column erected in 1770, with a Latin inscription expressing the gratitude of Edward and Ann Watson "in the 29th year of happy conjugal union"." SOMERBY DOLTER, 1824 O, cf. *Dolter Bottom*, - *Top* 1847 *TA*, *Delta Fox Cover* 1828 Bry, *Delta Cover* 1830 Gre; the Covert is situated in the triangular extreme north-east corner of the parish, being shaped like the Greek letter *delta*; *Dolter* itself is obscure, and if this is the original name, the *Delta* of Bry and Gre may be an attempt by the map-makers to interpret a name the meaning of which was not understood. SOMERBY HALL, 1776 *Foster*, 1842 White, 1847 *TA*, (*the*) *Hall* 1822 *Terrier*, 1824 O, 1830 Gre; it is *the old house* 1662 *Terrier* and note also *the highway from the Old Hall to the new* 1690, *the way from the old hall to the new Hall* 1700, *the way betwixt the old and new Hall* 1707, - *ye Old and new Hall* 1712, - *yᵉ old & new Hall* 1715, 1724 all *Terrier* and cf. *the Hall garth* 1697 *ib* (*v.* garðr), *yᵉ Old Hall yard* 1712 *ib*. SOMERBY LOW FM, *Low Somerby* 1824 O, 1828 Bry. SOMERBY TOP, *Top Somerby* 1866 *PR*, cf. prec. SOMERBY WOLD LANE, 1828 Bry, cf. *Wold* 1776 *MiscDep 118*, *v.* **wald**. TUP CLOSE PLANTATION (lost), 1847 *TA*, - *Plantⁿ* 1828 Bry, from **tup** 'a tup, a ram' and **clos(e)**.

Field-Names

Principal forms in (a) are 1847 *TA*; spellings dated 1602, 1626, 1635, 1638, 1644, 1662, 1668, 1671, 1690, 1697, 1700, 1707, 1712, 1715, 1724, 1762, 1822, 1853 are *Terrier*; those dated 1776 are *MiscDep 118*.

(a) Allisons Cl, - Wd (presumably named from an ancestor of Charles *Allison* 1865 *PR*); Ash Holt Wd; Barn Plat, South Barn Fd; Basin (a small patch of ground (no. 29 on *TAMap*) in Belvedere *infra*); Beech Plantn (Plat) (*v.* **plat**² 'a plot of ground', as elsewhere in this parish); Belvedere (wd) (it is, in fact, the name of a strip of woodland immediately north-east of the church, and there does not seem to have been a building there); (Lt) Bottoms; First -, Second -, Third Chalks; Church and Church Yd; Churchwood; Colliers-Cl, the Collier-cl

1776, Colliers Fd, South Colliers 1847 (from the occupational n. or derived surn. *Collier*, though this has not been noted in the parish); Corner Wd; Lt Cow Cl; Days Great Cl (from the family of Isabel *Day* 1586 *BT*); Dean Plantn, Deans Cl (probably named from the family of John *Dean* 1847 *TA*); Denzell Fd, North Denzell Plantn, North Denzells (perhaps from the surn. *Denzell*); Drying Grd; the eighteen-acres cl 1776; Engine Carr (*v.* **kjarr**); Ferriby's cl (probably named from the family of John *Ferraby* 1752 *BT*); Folly (there is no building here; the field (no. 64 on *TAMap*) is on the western boundary of the parish and Folly is perhaps a reference to a poor piece of ground here); the furze cl 1776, Furze Cl 1847 (*v.* **fyrs**); Garden Paddock; Glebe Fd; Goodgarth 1822 (1697, 1700), Good Garth 1847 (1724, *Good garth* 1690, 1712, *Good-garth* 1707, *Good-Garth* 1715, from a family well represented in the parish, cf. Richard *Good* 1587 *BT* and **garðr**); grass cl 1855; Gravel Pit Fd; Great Plat; Hardgraves (perhaps from a surn., cf. *W. Hargraves* 1783 *LTR*); Hill side; Home Fd; Gt -, Lt Homestead; House and Chicken Yd; Lawn, Pleasure Grds etc. (pasture); Little Gilden Cl 1762, little Guilders - (sic) 1822, Little Guilden - 1855, (*one close callyd Gyldhowse* 1602, *the guild-howse* 1626, *the litle gildhouse* 1638, *litle Gildhouse* 1664, *little -* 1662, 1668, 1671, *little Guild house close* 1690, *little Guild House Close* 1724, *little Gill close* (sic) 1697, *Little Gill -* 1700, *little Guilden close* 1707, *little Guilden-Close* 1715, *Little Gildens close* 1712, *v.* **gild-hūs**, **gildi-hús**, **clos(e)**, presumably a close belonging to a guild-house); New lands; Greet Norby (sic) 1762, Gt - 1822, 1855 (1724), Gt -, Lt Norleys (sic) 1847 (*one close ... commonly callyd Norby* 1602, *the greate-wood and norbye* 1626, *Great Norby* 1690, 1700, *Great - 1697, great -* 1707, 1712, *a Close call'd Great -* 1715; this is perhaps to be compared with Midby, in Barrow upon Humber *supra*, and may then be a shortened form of *norð ī bȳ* '(place) north in the village', a Scand. form; on *TAMap* the fields lay north-west of the village); Oak Tree Fd; Orchard Cl; Btm -, Top Paddock; Plantation (2x); Pond, Pond Screed; Quarry Fd and Stone Pit; (South) Rampart Fd (probably from *rampart*, a variant of dial. *ramper* 'a raised road or way', cf. *The Rampart* PN L 1 92); Sanfoin Fd (*v.* **sainfoin**); The Sheep-walks 1776 (*v.* **shepe-walk**); Shepherd Fd North, - South (probably from the surn. *Shepherd*, cf. Jane *Shepherd* 1770 *BT*); Shrub Cl; the twenty-acres cl 1776; Warren; the closes late Watson's 1776, Watsons Cl 1847 (from the *Watson* family, cf. Margery *Watson* 1591 *Inv*, John *Watson* 1682 *BT*, Joshua *Watson* 1776); the Wheat-Cl 1776, Wheat Cl 1847; Wilderness (Fd, - Paddock); Willmore Cl, Willmore Old yard (named from the family of Joseph *Willmore* 1847); the North Walk or Wold 1776 (cf. Somerby Wold Lane *supra* and The Sheep-walks *supra*); Wood (Cl) (cf. *the greate-wood and Norbye* 1626 (cf. Greet Norby *supra*), *a Close called the great Wood* 1662, 1664, *- yᵉ Great Wood* 1671, *the Great Wood* 1668, cf. *wood end* 1635, *the Wood end* 1638).

(b) *Bigbie feild* 1635; *Bigby hills* 1690, - *hils* 1712 (from the neighbouring parish of Bigby); *Carters landes* 1607 *Rental* (presumably from the surn. *Carter*, cf. *Jacobo carter* 1332 *SR*); *in domo vocat' chauntr'house* 1439 *Foster* (recorded in the foundation charter of St Mary's Chantry *in ecclesia de Someretby*); *the conye-hilles* 1626 (*v.* **coni, hyll**); *Atte Grene* 1327 *SR* (p), *atte Grene* 1332 *ib* (p) (*v.* **grēne²**); *milnehouse yathous* 1439 *Foster* (*v.* **milne-hous, gate-hous** 'a gate-house'); *Skolehowse* 1439 *Foster* (*v.* **scole-hous** 'a school-house'); *Sumerby Hills* 1638, - *hils* 1712.

Stallingborough

STALLINGBOROUGH
> *Stalingeburg* (2x) 1086 DB, 1204 ChR, *-burc* 1200 CartAnt,
> *-burgh'* 1288 *FF*, *-yngeburgh* 1303 Pat, *Stalingaburg* 1155
> (c.1200) CartAnt
> *Stallingeburc'* 1200 Cur, *-burg* 1202 FF, 1203 P, 1263 FF
> *Stalinburg* (5x) DB, c.1150, eHy2 (e13) *NCot*, *-burc* (5x) c.1115
> LS, *-burgh'* 1453 Pap, *-ynburgh* 1299 Ch, 1371 Ipm, 1383
> Peace, 1428 FA
> *Stalingburg* 1109-19, 1120-33, 1154-62 (13-14) Selby, 1155-61
> (13-14) YCh i, Hy2, a1180 (e13) *NCot*, l12, John, c.1206,
> 1230 (13-14) Selby, 1235, 1239, 1240 *NCot*, 1254 ValNor,
> 1264 Pat *et passim* to 1344 Selby, *-burch* 1185 Templar,
> *-bur'* 1159-81 (e13) *NCot*, 1263 RA ii, *-burc* 1186, 1190 P,
> 1206 Ass, 1238-43 Fees, 1239 *NCot*, *-burgh* 1154 (13-14)
> YCh i, 1155-62, 1189 (13-14) Selby, 1190 (1301) Dugd vi,
> 1199-1213 (13-14) Selby, 1263 FF *et freq* to 1553 Pat,
> *-burght* 1508 Cl, *-borough* 1557 Pat, *-yngburg* 1291 Tax, 1295
> (l13) Bodl, 1303, 1308, 1320 Pat, 1323 Ipm, 1324 Pat, 1325
> Orig, 1328 Banco *et freq* to 1564 Pat, *-bourgh* 1468 ib,
> *-borowe* 1472 WillsPCC, *-borough* 1303 FA
> *Stallingburg* eHy2 (e13) *NCot*, eHy3 (13-14) Selby, 1242-43
> Fees, 1245 RRG, *-burghe* 1576 Saxton, *-burgh* 1601 *Terrier*,
> 1610 Speed, 1611, 1690, 1697, 1822 *Terrier*, *-brughe* 1591
> *TYR*, *-brugh* 1634 VisitN, *-borough* 1557 WillsL, 1592
> *Holywell et passim*, *-yngburgh* 1339 Pat, 1374 Peace, 1393
> Cl, 1457 Pat, 1527 Wills ii, 1548 CA, *-burght* 1508 Cl
> *Stauuingburg* (sic) 1109-12 (13-14) YCh i
> *Staliburg'* 1185 RotDom, *Staligburc* 1212 Fees

Stalingburn (sic) 1200 ChR, *Stallingburne* 1577 Harrison
Staningeburg' (sic) 1225 Cur, *-burgh* 1267 Abbr, *Stanyngburg*
  1295 Cl, *-burgh* 1490 ib
Stanyngbroke (sic) 1540 *AOMB 402*
Stallinbur' 1664, *-burgh* 1700, 1706, 1724, *-burg* 1709 all *Terrier*

Ekwall (DEPN s.n.) is probably right in arguing that the persistent single *-l-* suggests that this is 'the fortified place of the
Stælingas' from the gen.pl. *Stælinga*, of the group-name *Stælingas*,
and **burh** 'a fortified place'. However, the problem is in suggesting
the etymology of the group-name itself, and no definitive answer
can be found, so that *Stælingas* must be left unexplained at the
moment.

OLDFLEET DRAIN, *holflet* Hy2 (e13) *NCot, Holflet'* 13 (13-14)
Selby, *portu de Holeflet* 1276 RH, cf. *Holfletwra* Hy3 (13-14) Selby
(*v.* **vrá** 'a corner of land'), and probably to be identified with *portu*
.. *de Houflet* 1155-58 (1334) Ch and perhaps *Huffeld', Hufflot* (sic)
1200 Cur (p). It is tentatively identified with *Wenflet* 1086 DB by
the editors. The meaning is 'the stream, creek flowing in a hollow',
v. **hol²**, **flēot**. If *Wenflet* does belong here then it is clearly an
error. *v.* also *rivulum de Hegeling'* in f.ns. (b) *infra*.

BECK'S PATCH (lost), 1824 O, *Becks Patch* 1830 Gre, cf. *Beck's
North Moss* 1844 *LindDep 29*, probably named from the family of
John *Beck* 1796 *ib 40*, which may have taken its name from "the
Beck" Hy3 (1301) Ch; cf. also Beck North Cl in f.ns. (a) *infra*.
BUTT LANE (lost), 1828 Bry. CARR LANE, 1828 ib, cf. *Northker*
Hy3 (1301) Ch, *Kerdales* 1680 *PT, v.* **kjarr** 'brushwood', 'marsh',
deill 'a share of land'. CHURCH ST, *the Church-way* 1690, - *Way*
1697, *yᵉ Church way* 1706, 1709 all *Terrier*. EPHAM'S LANE, 1828
Bry, cf. *Epham* 1796 *PT*, 1822 *Terrier*, 1826 *PT*, 1844 *LindDep 29*,
1842 *TA*, the forms being too late to suggest an etymology.
FREEHOLD LANE (lost), 1828 Bry. GREENLAND TOP is
Lawyers Plat or Bonners F.ᵐ 1828 Bry. GREEN MAN, 1842
White. GURNELS BARN (lost), 1828 Bry, named from the family
of William and Barbara *Gurnell* 1768 *BT*; it is shown on the
modern map, but is not named. HEALING COVERT, 1842 *TA*

and is *Stallingborough Cover* 1824 O, 1830 Gre, *Healing Well Cover* 1828 Bry, from the adjoining parish of Healing. KILN LANE, cf. *Kiln house cloase* 1734 *PT*, *Kiln & Ferry Ho* 1828 Bry, *Kiln House Close* 1844 *LindDep 19*, self-explanatory. LITTLE LONDON, 1824 O, 1828 Bry, 1830 Gre, the same name being found in North Kelsey parish *supra*, presumably a nickname of remoteness, though it is not on the parish boundary. LONG LANE (lost), 1828 Bry. MANOR HO, *the mannor house* 1592 *Holywell*, *ye Manor house* 1664 *Terrier*, *the Mannor house of Stallingborough* 1675 *Holywell*, cf. *manner holme* 1601, *Mannerholm* 1634 both *Terrier*, and cf. *le manoir de Stalyngburgh* 1340 Percy. MAUXHALL, the same name occurs as Maux Hall in Great Limber *supra* and *v.* also Manor Fm in Keelby *supra*, earlier *Mawkes Hall*. MIDDLE DRAIN, 1881 *LindDep 19*, which leads to *Middle Clough* on the coast. NORTH MOSS LANE, *Normoss Lane* 1828 Bry, cf. (*the*) *North Moss* 1690, 1700, 1706, 1724 all *Terrier*, (*the*) *North-Moss* 1697, 1709 both *ib*, *North Moss* 1737 (1828) *PT*, 1822 *Terrier*, 1822, 1828 *PT*, 1842 *TA*, 1844 *LindDep 29*, and *le Mosse* Hy3 (13-14) Selby, *v.* norð, mos 'moss', 'a bog, a swamp'. THE OAKS (lost), 1824 O, 1828 Bry, 1830 Gre, *Oaks* 1842 *TA*, cf. perhaps *the Oake Parke* 1592 *Holywell*. SCRUB WOOD, *Scrub Close* 1824 O, 1830 Gre, 1842 *TA*, *Scrub Close W.^d* 1828 Bry. THE SHIP, 1828 Bry, *Ship Inn* 1881 *LindDep 19*. SKIPWORTHS FM (lost), 1828 Bry, 1830 Gre, named from the family of *Phillip Skipworth* 1842 *TA*; it is marked on the OS map but is not named. SOUTH MARSH RD, *Marsh Lane* 1828 Bry, cf. *in Suythmarisco* (checked from MS) eHy3 (13-14) Selby, *suthmerse de Stallingburg'*, *sudmersc de Stalingburg'*, *suthmersc* eHy3 (e13) *NCot*, *Suthmers, in Suthmarisco* 13 (13-14) Selby, *the South Marsh* 1645 *Holywell*, 1728 *PT*, 1796 *LindDep 40*, 1828 *PT*, *South Marsh* 1822 *Terrier*, 1842 *TA*, self-explanatory, *v.* suð, mersc, and note also *in marisco salso de Stalingburg* eHy2 ('salt marsh'), *in marisco de Stalinburg'* c.1150, *- de Stalingburg'* a1180, 1235 all (e13) *NCot*, 1236 (13-14) *Selby*, *in mariscis de Stallingburg'* lHy3 (Ed1) *Newh*, *mariscum de Stalingbur'* 1278 *NCot*, *ye M'she of Stalyngburgh* 1518 *Monson*, *Stalling:brough marsh* 1587 *Yarb*, *Stallingburgh Marsh* 1680 *PT*, *the -, ye Marshes* 1690, 1697, 1700, 1706, 1709, 1724 *Terrier*, *Marsh* 1822 *PT*, 1842 *TA*; the references from 1690-1724 *Terrier* appear to refer to the same as *South Marsh* 1822 *ib*; cf. North Marsh in f.ns. (a) *infra*. THE SPROTHORNS, 1824 O, 1830 Gre, *Sprothern Wood* 1828 Bry, *Sprouthorn* 1333 *Ipm*; the first el. is uncertain, the second being þorn 'a thorn-tree', probably a reference to a prominent thorn-tree as a boundary marker, since it is on the boundary with Keelby. STALLINGBOROUGH GRANGE, *la Graunge* 1352 AASR xxiii, Newsham Priory, Nun Coatham Priory, Selby Abbey and Thornton Abbey, at least, each held land in Stallingborough, but this reference is to the grange of the heirs of Walter of Stallingborough. STALLINGBOROUGH HALL (lost), 1824 O, *Hall* 1830 Gre. STALLINGBOROUGH KILN FERRY (lost), 1824 O, cf. Kiln Lane *supra*. STALL-INGBOROUGH WINDMILL, *the Mill* 1671 *Terrier, Mill* 1824 O, *Mill Ho* 1828 Bry, *Windmill* 1842 *TA*, cf. *the Wind Mill Close* 1790 *PT, the milln close* 1592 *Holywell, the (Great) Milne Close* 1675 *ib, Mill Close* 1796 *LindDep 40*, 1842 *TA, (the) Mill Field* 1796 *ib*, 1822 *Terrier*, 1828 *PT*, 1842 *TA*. WENTWORTH'S COTTAGE, named from the family of John *Wentworth* 1822 *PT*. WEST FIELD (lost), 1742 *PT*, 1822 *Terrier*, 1828 Bry, 1828 *PT*, 1844 *LindDep 29, in parvo -, in magno occident' campo* 1591 *TYR, the Westfield Pasture* 1796 *LindDep 40*, one of the great fields of Stallingborough, *v.* west, feld.

Field-Names

The principal names in (a) are 1842 *TA* 305. Forms dated eHy3, Hy3, 1236, 1263, 13, and 1344 are (13-14) Selby; doubtful readings have been checked from the MS and are marked (c); Hy3 (1301) are Ch; 1352 are AASR xxiii, 1518 are *Monson*, 1591 are *TYR*; those dated 1592, 1645, and 1675 are *Holywell*; 1728, 1734, 1737, 1737 (1828), 1742, 1790, 1796[1], 1822[1], and 1828 are *PT*; 1796[2] are *LindDep 40*, 1664, 1671, 1690, 1697, 1700, 1706, 1709, 1724 and 1822[2] are *Terrier*; c.1823 and c.1832 are *Yarb*; 1844 are *LindDep 29*.

(a) Acre Cl (*the Acre Close* 1734); Andersons House and Homestead (named from the *Anderson* family, cf. Thomas *Anderson* 1566 *BT*); Ashton's Cl 1844 (named from the family of Anna *Ayshton* 1683 *BT*, Joel *Ashton* 1735 *ib*, and Joseph *Ashton* 1842 *TA*); Audland Fd 1790, 1796[1], 1822[2], - fd 1842, (the) Audland Fd 1822[2] (1737 (1828), 1742), Audland Fd (Marshalls) (sic) 1842 (*v.* Marshall Fd *infra*), Audland Fd (late Morvinson) (from the surn. *Morvinson*, cf. Robert *Morvinson* 1842), Audland Fd (Vesseys) 1842 (*v.* Vessey's Cowdam *infra*), Audland 1844 (*Aldeland, Audeland* 13, *Aldelandes* Hy3, *Aldlandes* Hy3, *auldlande* 1591, *Aldlandik'* 13, *Audland Field* 1737 (1828), *Audland Field Lane* 1742, *v.* ald,

in the sense 'long used' or even 'formerly used', **land**, and cf. the same name in
Immingham f.ns. (a)); Ayscough seeds (from the *Ayscough* family, cf. Edward
Aiscoughe 1591); Back North Moss (perhaps an error for Beck North Moss
infra); Back Orchard (2x) (cf. Front Orchard *infra*); Bank Side; Beck North Cl, -
North Moss 1842 (*v.* North Moss Lane *supra*), Beck Cl 1844 ((*the*) *Beck close*
1675, cf. *Stallingbrough becke* 1613 *MinAcct, v.* **bekkr**, and cf. Beck's Patch *supra*);
Beck House Yd; Bicar 1796^1, 1796^2, Knott -, Low -, Top Bicar 1842 (*Biker*
eHy3, Hy3, 13, *Biker* 1352, *By Carrs* 1671, *Byker* 1690, 1697, 1700, *Bicar* 1706,
1709, 1724, *Birker* (sic) 1734; this is identical with Bicker, Holland L, and
apparently also with *Bycarrs Dike*, the name of a canal between the R. Idle and
the Trent, *v.* PN Nt 1-2, where it is acknowledged "This is a very difficult
name". Ekwall, DEPN s.n., interprets Bicker as 'the village marsh', *v.* **bȳ, kjarr**
and while this is formally possible, it should be noted that p.ns. with forms with
bȳ as first element are normally in the gen.pl. *bȳjar*, giving forms like *bier*, and
it is difficult to find a parallel to **Bȳkjarr*. It is highly unlikely that it is
derived from ME **biker** 'a fight, quarrel, dispute' in the sense 'the place where a
fight or dispute took place'. A more likely explanation is that it is an elliptical
formation from OE **bī** 'by, near' and **kjarr** '(the place) near or by a marsh',
though no certainty is possible); Blow well fd (self-explanatory); Brewhouse
Paddock; Brickyard Cl; Brooks yd (presumably from the surn. *Brooks*, cf. Thomas
Brooks 1842); Buckles Cottage (probably named from the family of Roger
Buckells 1737 *BT*); Bull & Pinder Mdw in South Marsh; Burbanks Cottage
(named from the family of Alexander *Borebank* 1734 *BT*); Cabbage Gdn;
Challens Garth 1796, 1842 (*v.* **garðr** 'an enclosure', as elsewhere in this parish);
Church Yd; Clark Hill West Fd (from the *Clark(e)* family, cf. John *Clerke*
1558-59 *Inv*, Thomas *Clarke* 1612 *ib*); Clifton Seeds (named from the family of
William *Clifton* 1842 White); Clover Cl; Club Garth; Coney Garth (*the*
connygarthe 1518, (*the*) *Cony garth* 1571, 1675, and note *the Conygree* 1592, *v.*
coni, garðr, coninger); Corner Cl 1844; Cottagers Cl; Cowdam 1790, 1796^1, 1822^2,
1842 (4x), 1844 (on the *TAMap* Cowdam is the name of a group of fields in
what was carr and marshy ground; the name is presumably self-explanatory, 'the
cow pond', the second el. being ME **damme** (ON **dammr**), though no pond is in
fact shown on the map); Cow house and Hermond (sic); Cow house &
stackyard; Cross Cl (cf. *Crosacris* 13, *v.* **cros, æcer, clos(e)**); Deepdale 1796^1,
Deepdales or Mill Fd 1842 (*Depedal* e13, *Depedale* eHy3, Hy3 (1301), *depedaile*
1591, 'the deep valley', *v.* **dēop, dalr, dæl**; it was on the boundary with Keelby);
Dovecote cl; the Drain next Habrough Marsh 1790; Epworths Homestead 1796^1
(named from the family of *Margarie epworthe* 1590 *BT*, Edward *Epworth* 1630
Inv); Top far Cl; Far fd; Feeding Cl; Filcar 1796^1, 1842 (*Fileker* 1235, 1240
NCot, lHy3 (l14) *Gox, fileker* Hy3, c.1240 (13) *Alv, Filker* 1352, *filkars* 1592; the

first el. may well be the OE byname *Fila* or ON **Fyla*, for the latter *v. Insley* 143-45, the second el. being **kjarr** 'a marsh, etc.'); Fish Pond; the Fitties 1796[1], Fitties 1842 (for a discussion of this name, *v.* East Halton f.ns. (a) s.n. Fitties); Fox Cover 1822[2]; Fresh North Carr Hills 1796[1], 1796[2] (cf. *the Fresh Meadow* 1645); Frith North Car Hills; Front Orchard; Fussey North Moss (named from the *Fussey* family, cf. John *Fussey* 1783 *LTR* and *v.* North Moss Lane *supra*); Garden Wd; Gares, Mill Fd 1822[2], the Gares 1828, The - 1844, Gares Lane cl 1842 (*v.* **geiri** 'a triangular plot of land'); Garness seeds (named from the *Garness* family, cf. William *Garnes* 1651 *BT*, Thomas *Garness* 1795 *ib*); Garth (freq) (*v.* **garðr** 'an enclosure'); Grass Yard; Great Car Immingham Field (sic) (*v.* **kjarr**); Great Hills 1796[1], 1842; Hall Yard(s) (cf. *Stallingborough Hall supra*); (the) Haws 1796[1], Hawes 1842 (*in ... Loco vocat' ... Hawes, Hawedyke* 1591, *the Hawes* 1592, 1675, *v.* **haga**[1] 'an enclosure'); Healing Carr 1822[2], 1842, - Car 1844, Healing Fd 1842 (from the adjacent parish of Healing); Het Cl; Hills 1796[1], 1842, The - 1844, Hills marsh 1842; Home Cl 1842 (several), 1844; (House and) Home Garth 1842 (*v.* **garðr**); Home Paddock; Home Walk (*v.* **walk**); Horse Bottom (*v.* **botm**); Horse Cowdam (cf. Cowdam *supra*); Horse Pasture; How Croft (*v.* **haugr**); Hudsons Yd (named from the *Hudson* family, cf. John & Frances *Hudson* 1776 *BT*); Humber Marsh; Jockey Plot 1796[1], 1796[2], Jockey Plot West Fd 1842; Keelby Fd; Keelby Lane (*Kelebigate, Kelebygat'* Hy3, *viam qui ducet ad Keilbye* (sic) 1591 (*v.* **gata**) and *Kelebyhille* 13, *Kelebyhill'* Hy3, from the neighbouring parish of Keelby); Kersey Garths 1796[1], - Garth 1842 (*Cressy garth* 1352, *Kersey Garth* 1685 (*v.* **garðr**), and cf. *Cressik* Hy3 (1301), 'the stream where cress grows', *v.* **cærs, sík**; it is no doubt the same f.n. as Kersey Garths in Immingham f.ns. (a) *supra*); Kirks Garth (possibly named from the *Kirk* family, cf. William & Mary *Kirk* 1770 *BT*, but cf. *Kyrkedailes* (b) *infra*); Kirmond Cl 1796 (named from the family, earlier *Kirman*, cf. John *Kyrman* 1562 *BT*, John *Kirman* 1602 *ib*, William *Kirman* 1641 *LPR*); Knott 1796[1], Knot Ricar (sic) 1842 (*ground called Knot* 1664, cf. *Sidknote* 1352, *v.* **sīd** 'broad', **knǫttr** 'a hillock etc.'); Lane from Immingham Fd; Meadow or Pasture Ground called Long Bridge 1896[2], Longbridge 1822[2], 1844, Long Briggs 1822, - Bridge 1842 (5x) (1737 (1828)) (cf. *iuxta pontem* c.1150, 1159-81 (e13) *NCot, Briggedik* eHy2, Hy2 (e13) *ib, v.* **brycg, dík**, but note the Scandinavianised forms in Brigg-); Long Cl 1842, 1844; Low Cl; Low gdn; Maltbys Yd (named from the *Maltby* family, cf. William *Maltby* 1663 *BT*, William *Maltby* 1842 *TA*); Marshall Fd 1844 (named from the *Marshall* family, cf. John *Marshall* 1562 *BT*); Lt Mill Carr (*v.* **kjarr**); Mumby's Gdn (from the surn. *Mumby*, common locally, cf. Thomas *Mombye* 1591 *TYR*); Gt -, Lt Mussles (*Musewelles* 13, probably 'the mice-infested springs', *v.* **mūs, wella**); Nak[d] Beggars Hill (perhaps a derogatory nickname for poor land); Newton Mill Fd (named from the *Newton* family, cf. Robert *Newton* 1783 *LTR*);

Nine Acres, 1842, The Nine - 1844; Noddy Cock Cl, Nudy cock (it is possible that Noddy Cock is to be compared with dial. *nodcock* 'a simpleton', recorded only from So in EDD s.v.; *noddy* itself is recorded from L in EDD with a similar meaning); (the) North Marsh 1796[1], 1842, North Marsh West End, - East End (*in boriali marisco de Stalingburg'* Hy3, *in Northmarisco* 13, *in boriali marisco* 1591, *the North Marsh* 1728, cf. *longnorth marshe* 1518, and cf. South Marsh Rd *supra*); North Mdw; Orchard (Cl) (*the Orchard* 1734); Paddock (Lane), Paddock in exchange from Mr Boucherett; Park; Parsons Marsh; Pear Tree Cl 1842, - Garth 1842, 1844 (*v.* **garðr**); Plantation (Garth); Plough[d] Cowdam 1842 (cf. Cowdam *supra*); Plough[d] Hills; Pond and Plantn; Public House and Gdn, Public House & Homestead; Pudding Poke (no doubt, as elsewhere, a fanciful name for soft or sticky land); Riby Lane Cl (2x) (cf. *via de riby* Hy3, from the adjacent parish of Riby); Roxton Cl, Lt Roxton, Roxton plot, Roxton Wood Cl 1844 (from Roxton Fm in the neighbouring parish of Immingham *supra*); Rush Cl; Ryegrass Cl c.1823, Rye Grass - c.1832; Sand Hills; Scarman (from the *Sca(r)man* family, well represented in the parish, cf. William *Skayman* 1527 Wills i, Robert *Scamon* 1536-37 *Inv*, Thomas *Scamone* 1547-49 *ib*); Gt -, Lt Scroggs (*v.* **scrogge** 'a bush, brushwood', cf. PN Nt 289 s.v. **schrogge**); Sea Bank and Foreshore; Seven Acre Cl 1844; Shepherds House & Gdn (2x) (perhaps from the *Shepherd* family, cf. Adam *Shepherd* 1352); The Sounds 1796[1], Sounds Cl, - Plot 1842; Square Bridge; Lt Square Cl 1844; Stable & pig yd; Stack Yard Fd 1844; Stanel Pasture 1796[1], Stanhills plot (probably to be identified with *Stainhill'* (c) Hy3, 13, *-hille* (c) Hy3, *Staynhill'* 1344, *standhill'* 1591, *Stainhilleheuedland'* (c) 13; it was on the boundary with Keelby, *v.* **steinn** 'stone', **hyll** with **hēafod-land**); Street Cl; Swan Hill; Taylors Yd (named from the *Taylor* family, cf. William *Taylor* 1842, but the family is recorded in the parish from at least *edwerd tayler* 1540 *Wills*); Thornton platt (from the *Thornton* family, cf. Gilbert *Thorneton* 1641 LPR and **plat**[2] 'a plot of ground', as elsewhere in this parish); Tinker Cl, - Fd, - Lane 1842, - Marsh 1796[2]; Low top Cl; Top Platt 1844 (*v.* **plat**[2]); Town end Plot 1796[2]; Triangle (self-explanatory); Twelve Acres; Vessey's Cowdam 1842 (cf. Cowdam *supra*), Vesseys Fd 1844 (named from the family of Nicholas *Vessey* 1603 *BT*); Vicar Yd (cf. *a close called Vicarcroft* 1444 Cl); Wards Cottage 1796[1] (named from the family of John *Warde* 1665 *BT*); Warlots c.1823, Warlotts c.1832 ((*le*) *Warlotes* 13, *in Warlothes de Kyrkedailes* eHy3, *v.* **warlot** and the discussion under Waterhill Wood in Brocklesby *supra*); Water mdw; Well Garth (*v.* **garðr**); Wet Cl 1796[1] (*le* -, *the great* -, *the little weete close* 1592, *the wett close* 1675, *Greate* -, *the Little wett close* 1675); Wickentree plot 1842, Wilkentree Plat (sic) 1796[1], 1796[2] (from dial. *wickentree* 'a mountain ash', *v.* EDD s.v. quicken 1 (2) and **plat**[2]); Wilson Yd (named from the family of John *Wilson* 1590 *BT*); Little -, Old Wray (*the little* *wraye otherwyse called Bagshawes wraye* 1592 (from the *Bagshaw* family, cf. Edward *Bawgshaw* 1558-59 *Inv*, Edward *Bagshawe* 1579 *ib*), *the Little Wray* 1675, *the old Wray* 1645, cf. *le Wrascroft, Northwra* lHy3 (Ed1) *Newh, the Wray* 1675, *the fore -, the Middle Wraye* 1645, *v.* vrá 'a nook, a corner of land').

(b) *Abby Garth Closes* 1664 (presumably commemorating the former holdings in the parish of Selby Abbey, *v.* also garðr and clos(e)); *Aldwelleker* 13 ('the old (i.e. long-used or even formerly used) spring', *v.* ald, wella, with kjarr 'a marsh' as freq in this parish); *Alesbigat'* Hy3 ('the road to Aylesby', *v.* gata); *Aluineland* Hy3, Hy3 (1301) (from the OE pers.n. *Alwine* (on which *v.* Feilitzen 158-60) and land; Dr Mark Bateson suggests that from the construction of the charters it is likely that *Aumeland* is a mistake for *Aluineland*); *terram filii Andreæ* Hy3 (c), *Andreubarnland'* (c) Hy3, *Andrewbarnland* 1344 (the Latin form confirms that this is 'Andrewbarn's land', *v.* land (it was on the boundary with Keelby). *Andrewbarn* is formed from the ME pers.n. *Andrew* and the ON byname *barn*, equivalent therefore to *Andrewson* 'the son of Andrew'. On this formation, which so far does not seem to have been noted in L, *v.* Feilitzen 257-8, Tengvik 237 and SPNLY 239-40); *Appleholme, Apelholmeker* 13 (*v.* æppel, holmr, with kjarr); *arneswelle* p1170 (e13) *NCot, (fons) arneswell'* lHy3 (l14) *Gox* (*v.* wella: the first el. is the ON pers.n. *Arni*, cf. *Arneberg, Arnesberg'* in the f.ns. of East Halton (b) *supra*); *the Ash pingle* 1645 (*v.* pingel and *the Pingle infra*); *Aumeland* 13 (c) (*v. Aluineland supra*); *Barhill', Barhille, BareHille* (c) 13 (probably *v.* bere 'barley', hyll); *le Belke* (c) 13; *Belwelgote* Hy3 (1301) (*v.* wella 'a spring', gotu 'a watercourse, a channel', the etymology of *Bel* is uncertain); *bercar' de Stalinburg'* 1278 *NCot, Bluntes landes* 1592, *Blunts lands* 1645 (from the surn. *Blunt*); *Bordlande* 1278 *NCot* (the first el. is perhaps a ME surn. *Bord(e)* with land); *Briggedik* eHy2 (e13) *NCot* (*v.* brycg (in a Scandinavianised form) and dík); *BungberMar'* (sic) (c)) Hy3 (*v.* (ge)mære; *Bungber-* is obscure); *Burdunmcln* (sic) Hy3 (1301) (from myln and the surn. *Burdun*); *Bybrigge 1352* ('(the place) by the bridge', *v.* bi, brycg, the latter in a Scandinavianised form); *Caldholme* 1675 (*v.* cald, holmr); *Catters Close or Chaters Close* 1645 (named from the family of John *Chatters* 1591); *Celrermar'* (c) Hy3 (*v.* (ge)mære 'a boundary, boundary land'; the first el. is celerer 'a cellarer, a monastic official in charge of provisions'); *Charnell Garth* 1645 (cf. *Arcy als darcy Mannor Selby Mannor Charnell Mannor and Terwhitt Mannor* 1645; *Charnell* is from the family which held ¼ of a fee in Stallingborough, cf. Robert *de Charneles* 1241-43 *Fees*; for *Arcy*, cf. *Arsy Maner in Stalyngborgh* 1463 *Pat*, *Darcye mannor Selby mannor* 1592, *Manner of Darsie* 1611 *Terrier*, the *de Arci* family held land here in DB, while Norman *Derci* held ½ fee 1238-41 *Fees*; for *Selby*, Selby Abbey was assigned the manor of Stallingborough 1264 *Fees*; and for *Tirwhitt*, cf. *Manor of Stallingborough called Tirwhite Garthe*

1557 WillsL, *Tirwhitt mannor* 1737 (*v.* **garðr**); no indication has so far been found of the acquisition or holding of this manor by the *Tirwhitts*, but the family is commemorated in the village church, *v.* Holles 77); *Clay Close* 1645; *Clintdic'* Hy3, *Clintesdik'* 1236 (the latter is an error of transcription for *Clintessik* (c)); *ad coldem* (sic) Hy2 (e13) NCot; *Cookes garden* 1592, - *garden close* 1675 (named from the family of William *Cooke* 1590 BT and Katherine *Cooke* 1639 *Inv*); y^e *Cow Pasture*, 1700, - *Cowpaster* 1709, *Cow pasture* 1724; *Crikewelle* 13 ('the spring by an inlet or creek', *v.* **crike (kriki), wella**); *deadlaine close* 1592, *deadlands close* (sic) 1675 (referring to a cul-de-sac); *foreram quae dicitur Dreuland, Dreuheuedlond'* 13 (from the ME pers.n. and surn. *Dreu* (note *Willelmus filius Druganis* and *Willelmus filius Willelmi Dreu* 13, who gave land to Thornton Abbey, in Stallingborough) and **land, hēafod-land**); *duckett Leyes* 1645 (named from the family of Jennett *Duckett* 1592 BT and Thomas *Docket* 1622 *ib*); *Dumping dykes* 1592, *Dunken dyke* 1675; *the Ewe-Sheepe-walke* 1645 (*v.* **shepe-walk**); *Fanbund land* 1352 (the first el. is obscure); *Fletgat* Hy3, (*le*) *Fletgate* 1344 ('the road to the stream', *v.* **flēot, gata;** it formed part of the boundary with Keelby); *the Fresh Meadow* 1645; *Frisecroft* lHy3 (Ed1) *Newh* (perhaps 'the Frisians' croft', *v.* **Frīsa, croft**); *Frostlande* 1352 (perhaps from the ME nickname or surn. *Frost* and **land**); *in Fuythmarisco'* eHy3 (an error of transcription for *S-*, *v.* South Marsh Rd *supra*); *Gillecroft* 13 (from the ME pers.n. or surn. *Gille* and **croft**); *a place called the greenes* 1638 *Inv*; *Hardecunt, Hardcunt* (c) Hy3 (e14) (the second el. is apparently ME **c(o)unte** 'the female private parts', used topographically of a cleft or a spring, the first el. being **heard** 'hard', perhaps in the sense 'hard to till' or even 'cheerless'); *a dall callyd hedlanddall* 1518 (*v.* **hēafod-land** and **dāl** or **deill**); *rivulum de Hegeling'* 13, *Helingbeck'* Hy3, *Heghlingbek* Hy3 (1301), *Heilingebek'* lHy3 (l14) *Gox*, *Heilingbeckes* 1591 (*v.* **bekkr**), *Heilingdyke* 1591 (*v.* **dīk**) ('Healing stream and dike', named from the adjoining parish; the waterway was possibly part of Oldfleet Drain *supra*); *Heilingate* 13, *viam de Heling'* Hy3, *via que tendit versus Helling* Hy3 ('the road towards Healing (the adjoining parish)', *v.* **gata**); *Hegterdic* 13 (c) (*v.* **dīk**); *Herdhill* (c) Hy3; *Hethenesse* 13 (2x), *Heyenes, -nesse* (c) (with y = þ) Hy3, 13, *Hathenesse* 1351 AD, *Hathenes, Haythenes* 1352 (probably 'the heather-covered headland', *v.* **hǣð, nesu, nes**^{2}); *the High close* 1675; *Houcroft* 13, *Howle croft* 1592, *Hough croft* 1675 (the last two forms seem to refer to the same croft); *Houwardmar* (c) Hy3 (*v.* **(ge)mǣre** 'a boundary, boundary-land'; the first el. is the ME pers.n. or surn. *Houward*); *ex orientali parte viae de Ymmingham* Hy3, *hymhynhaygate* (sic) lHy3 (l14) *Gox* ('the road to Immingham' *v.* **gata;** the lHy3 MS spelling is corrupt); *Imingham crosse* 1591; *Imnghamgale* (sic) 1591 (cf. *la gale* 1352 (p); the 1591 form means 'the way to Immingham (a neighbouring parish)', the second el. being ME *gale* 'a way, a course', *v.* MED s.v. *gale* n. (2)); *Jakelindeile* 1240 (m13) *NCot* (from the ME pers.n. or surn. *Jakelin* and **deill** 'a portion of land'); *Ketelholme* 13 (a Scand. compound from the ON pers.n. *Ketill*, ODan *Ketil* and **holmr** 'an island, a water-meadow, a raised piece of land in marsh'); *pratum Knolri* (c) 13 ('*Knolri's* meadow' from an obscure pers.n. or surn., which occurs in the parish in the name of William *Knolry* 1332 *SR*); *Kyrkedailes* 13, eHy3, *-deyles* 1287 *Ass*, *Kirkedailes* 13, 1239 *NCot*, *Kirkedeiles* 1240 *ib*, *Kirk-dales* 1664 (*v.* **kirkja, deill**); *Langmar'* Hy3 (1301), *Langmarrs* 1591 (probably 'the long boundary, land on a boundary' *v.* **lang, (ge)mǣre**); *Langetoftes* 1236 (*v.* **lang, toft** 'a curtilage'); *the Laye closes* 1592 (*Laye* is probably OE **lǣge** 'fallow, untilled'); *Layth Close or Dovecoat Close* 1734 (*v.* **hlaða** 'a barn'); *the long garth* 1675 (*v.* **garðr**); *the Low Close* 1734; *lylflet* eHy2 (e13) *NCot* (*v.* **fleot** 'an estuary, a stream'; the first el. is uncertain); *medelfurlanges* 13 (l14) *Gox*, *Middelfurlangmar'* Hy3 (1301) (*v.* **middel, furlang**, with **(ge)mǣre**, the first form having as first el. Scand. **meðal** for the cognate OE **middel**); *miledaile* 1240 (e13) *NCot* (the first two letters are uncertain); *minswells* 1591 (the first three letters are a guess, interpreting six minims); *Munsons Close* 1707, 1724 *Terrier* (Keelby), *Munstone closes* 1709 *ib*, *Munstones Close* 1745 *ib* (from the surn. *Monson* or *Munstone*); *Nesebigate* 13 (this is an error for *Alesbigate* (c) *supra*); *Nettelbustmar* (*t* = *c*) Hy3 (1301) (from ME **netle-bush** and **(ge)mǣre** 'a boundary, boundary land'. MED s.v. **netle** n.1 (c) gives only two examples of the compound, both from glosses; *A Netyl buske* : *vrticetum* ?c.1475 and *Urticetum : a netyl buske* a1500.   Mr John Field draws attention to the fact that the second example quoted in MED is from T. Wright and R.P. Wülcker "A Nominale" in *Anglo-Saxon and English Vocabularies*, 2nd ed., Darmstadt 1968, columns 673-744, where the text actually reads *urticetum, a netylbuske* (column 711), while another term in *-buske* is *felicetum, a brakynbuske* (column 712). Two further examples of *-etum, caricetum* (column 712) and *floretum* (column 711) are not translated, but each is glossed as *locus ubi crescunt* 'the place where they grow'. Professor Peter Dronke suggests that *urticetum* may well denote a nettle-patch, a nettle-bed and this seems eminently reasonable, especially taking into consideration the glosses for *caricetum* and *floretum*. It is worth noting, further, that in both MED's examples, as in the present f.n. recorded over 200 years earlier, *bush* is in a Scand. form, as is a *brakynbuske* and *ye Nettle-buske land* in Croxhill f.ns. (b) *supra*. It is, therefore, likely that the compound should be given in the form ME *netle-busk* (from ON **buskr**), and not as *netle-bush*); *Nettle-Garth* 1664 (*v.* **garðr** and prec.); *the new closes* 1592, *the new Close, the little new Close* 1645; *Nordhiby* Hy3, *Norhiby* (sic) 1271-2 *Ass*, 13, *Northeby* 13 all (p) ('north in the village', *v.* **norð, í, bý**); *norloft, northeloft* 1591 (this appears to be a compound of **norð** and ON **lopt** (ME *loft*) 'a loft', presumably referring to a building with an upper chamber); *Northcroft* 13,

Hy3 (self-explanatory, v. norð, croft); *the north dyke furlong* 1592; *in boriali campo* 1591 (i.e. north field); *Northtoft* lHy3 (l14) *Gox, Northoft* (sic) Hy3, *in longo -, - parvo Northtoft* 13 (v. norð, toft 'a curtilage'); *Osgottoftes* 13, *Osgartoft* 1728 ('Osgot's building site, curtilage', from the pers.n. *Osgot*, an AScand form of ON *Asgautr*, and toft); *the Pingle* 1645 (v. pingel); *Pustayn* (sic) 13 (l14) *Gox* (obscure, though the second el. appears to be ON steinn 'a stone'); *Pyttmares* 1591 (v. pytt, (ge)mǣre in the pl.); *Rendeles* (c) Hy3 (obscure); *Ribye ffeld* 1591 (from the adjacent parish of Riby); *Ridal* 13 (v. ryge 'rye' and perhaps dalr); *riswelle* p1170 (e13) *NCot, riskewell'* lHy3 (l14) *Gox* (the references are to the same feature; probably 'the spring where rushes grow', v. risc, wella, the first el. in the lHy3 spelling being in a Scandinavianised form); *Rivilan'* 1591; *Roxton Dymple* 1591 (from dympel (ME *dimple*) 'a pit, a dip in the surface of the land' and Roxton Fm in the neighbouring parish of Immingham); *Salterwar'* (c) (an error for *-wra*), *Salterwra* (2x) 13 ('the salter's nook of land', v. saltere, vrá or from the derived surn. *Salter*); *le Sceeld'* (c) 13; *Schauedailes, -dayles* (c) 13 (v. deill); *the Schoolhouse Close* 1645; *scortebuttes* Hy2 (e13) *NCot* (v. sc(e)ort, butte 'a strip of land abutting on a boundary, etc.'); *Scosteholm* (sic) Hy3 (1301), *Scotholme* Hy3, *Scozholme* (c) (*z = ts*) Hy3, 13 (v. holmr and for the first el. v. the discussion s.n. *Scotgate* in Croxton f.ns. (b))); *Scouelmar'* Hy3 (1301) ('the shovel-shaped boundary, boundary-land', v. scofl, (ge)mǣre); ... *in eodem marisco inter Sedick -, - Sedyk et aquam de Humbr* 13, *ad sedige* (sic) 13 ('the sea-dike', v. sǣ, dīk); *seuenstang* eHy3 (e13) *NCot* ('seven poles', v. seofon, stong here 'a pole', a measure of land); *Shawe* 1352 (v. sceaga 'a small wood, a copse'); "beyond" *sikam* Hy3 (1301) (v. sīk); *Silkholme* 13, Hy3 (1301), *Silkeholme* 13 (this may be from the Scand. byname *Silki* (perhaps found in *Silkby*, Kest L, now Silk Willoughby) and holmr 'an island (of land), a water-meadow', v. SSNEM 82, s.n. Silkby); *super Sitebihau* (c), *Sitbihau* (c) 13, *Sybyhowe* (3x) 1591 (v. haugr, *Sitebi-* is obscure); *Southolme dayle, Southolmedale* 1352 (v. sūð, holmr, with deill); *in campo de Stalingbur* 1159-81 (e13) *NCot, in campis ... de Stalinburg'* Hy3, *in campis de Stalingb*^{ro} lHy3 (l14) *Gox, in Campo de Stalingburgh'* 1305 Ass, *Stallingborough field* 1707 Terrier (Keelby), *- feild* 1724 *ib* (Keelby) (v. feld); *ultra portum que est inter mariscum de Haburg' & Stalingburg* lHy3 (Ed1) Newh, *iuxta portum de Stalyngburgh'* 1345 HarlCh (Stallingborough harbour); *in prato de Stalinburc* Hy3 (13) Alv, *in pratis de Stalingburg* lHy3 (l14) *Gox* ('in the meadows(s) of Stallingborough'); *in australi campo de Stalingburgh'* 13 (l14) *Gox* (the south field); *suddich* eHy3 (e13) *NCot* (probably 'the southern ditch', v. sūð, dīc); *suthesik'* eHy3 (e13) *NCot* (v. sūð, sīk 'a ditch', 'a piece of meadow along a stream'); *Suthtoft 1263, 13* (v. sūð, toft, cf. *Northtoft supra*); *Suthwelker, Thuswelker* (c) Hy3 (v. sūð, wella, kjarr); *Thorndyk' de Stalyngburgh'* 1367 FF (p) (v. þorn, dīc, dīk, though it may not be a local name); *thornholm* 1278 *NCot* (v.

þorn, holmr); *the Thornes* 1645; *tofors* (c) Hy3 (obscure); *Utlandes* 13 (self-explanatory, *v.* ūt, land); *le Utlanges* 13 (*v.* ūt, lang² 'a long strip of land', if it is not an error for the prec.); *Watermilncroft* Hy3 (1301) (self-explanatory); *Westgard* eHy3, *Westgard'* (*d* = *th*) 1236 ('the west enclosure', *v.* west, garðr); *Willkemerke ffurlonge* 1591; *Withmar', Wytmar'* (both (c)) Hy3 (the same name ocurrs in Killingholme and Brocklesby f.ns. (b) *supra*; for a possible explanation, *v. Withemare* in Killingholme f.ns. (b) *supra*); *Wyteker, campum de Wyteker* (both (c)) Hy3 (*v.* kjarr, the first el. perhaps being hwīt 'white, etc.').

Thornton Curtis

THORNTON CURTIS
> *Torentune, -tone* 1086 DB, *-tuna* c.1115 LS, *-tun'* 1157, 1158 P, *-ton*(') 1167, 1177 ib, 1189 (c.1200) CartAnt *et passim* to *Torentone* 1222 FF, *Torrenton'* 1152-55 RA i
>
> *Torntune* 1155-60 Dane, *-ton* 1246 RRG
>
> *Torintun* 1158 P, *-tona* 1163 RA i, *-ton'* 1190, 1191 P, 1194 CurR, 1202 Ass, 1203 Cur, 1204, 1205 P, 1205 Cur, 1209, 1210 P, 1234 FF
>
> *Tornenton* 1160 Dugd vi
>
> *Torneton* 1159-78 PapDec, 1163-76 (e14) YCh x, (*in Lindesaye*) 1226 (l13-e14) Guis, *-tun* a1180 (e13) *NCot*
>
> *Thorentone* 1139-47 (1301) YCh ii, *-tona* 1148-52 LAAS vii, c.1150 *TYR*, 1165-85 YCh ii, *-tune* 1155-60 Dane, *-ton* a1219 Welles, 1221 Cur, 1228 Pat, 1230 Cur *et passim* to 1548 *Yarb, Thorrenton'* c.1221 Welles
>
> *Thorneton*(') 1154-70 (Ed3) YCh i, 1203, 1263 FF, 1264 Pat, (*super Humbr'*) 1272, 1273 Cl, 1275 Fine *et freq* to 1576 LER, *-tone* 1440 Visit, 1541 LP xvi, *Thornaton* (sic) 1354 Ipm
>
> *Thorinton'* 1222 Cur, 1248 RRG, 1248 Cl, *-tun'* 1242-43 Fees
>
> *Thornton*(') 1115 (14) *Bard*, 1190 (1301) Dugd vi, R1 (1301) Ch, 1213, 1229 Cur, 1245, 1254 Cl, 1256 Pat, 1268 RA iii, 1271 Pat, 1276 RH, 1291 Tax, 1292 Pat *et freq*, ("on Humber") 1305 Pat, ("upon Humber") 1313 ib, (super Humbr') 1325 *ExchAMisc*, (*super Humbre*) 1332 Orig, (*super Humber*) 1373 Peace, (*in Lindesey*) 1383 Gaunt, (*super Humbre*) 1395 Peace
>
> *Thorniton* (sic) 1235, 1236 Cl

Thornton Curteys 1430, 1452 Pap, 1455 WillsPCC, - *Curteis* Eliz
ChancP, - *Curtase* 1466 Pap, - *Curtesey* (sic) 1546 LP xxi,
- *Curtoys* 1555 CA, - *Curtes* 1601 *Terrier,* - *Curtess* 1681
Yarb, - *Curtis* 1662, 1674, 1697 *Terrier et passim, Thornnton'*
curtasse 1517 ECB, *Thorneton Curtes* 1521 LP iii, - *Curtis*
VE iv, *Thaurnton Curtis* 1712 *Terrier*

'The farmstead, village where thorn-trees grow', *v.* þorn, tūn.
Forms in *T-* for *Th-* are due to AN influence, *v.* Feilitzen 100. It
may be noted that the wealth of documentation for this name is in
large measure due to the fact that it was the site of an important
abbey. The origin of *Curtis* is unknown.

BODEBI (lost), 1086 DB. This may be an error for Bonby *supra,*
as first suggested in DB 155 and then retracted in DB lxxxvi as
being improbable. It is mentioned between Thornton and Wootton
and the editors of DB tentatively refer to it as "probably an extinct
hamlet in or near the parish of Thornton Curtis". They point out
that "Bodebi is elsewhere the equivalent of Boothby". It is found
with the identical form *Bodebi* in *DB Abbreviatio* (PRO, Treasury of
Receipts, E 36/284) a MS dated to the first half of the 13th
century. Accepting the form, then, at face value, the meaning is
literally 'the village of the booths, temporary shelters', from the
gen.pl. of bōth and bȳ, identical with Boothby (Welton le Marsh)
LSR, Boothby Graffoe and Boothby Pagnell Kest.

BURNHAM
   Brune (2x) 1086 DB, *Brunne* 1190 (1301) Dugd vi
   Brunum c.1115 LS, 13 Dugd iii, 1327 *SR, Brunnum* 1156-57
      (Ed2) YCh i, R1 (1308) Ch, 1268 FF, 1301 Ch, 1343 Ipm,
      Brunhum l12 Dane, 1242-43 Fees, c.1275 LNQ vii
   Brounhum 1115 (14) *Bard*
   Brunham 1242-43 Fees, 1286, 1288 Ipm, 1303, 1316 FA, 1343
      Cl, 1346 FA, 1350, 1354 Ipm, 1415 Cl, 1428, 1431 FA
   Bronnum 1329 *Ass, Bronhom* 1332 *SR*
   Bornome 1398 Cl
   Burneham 1381-82 *AddR 37683,* 1462 Pat, 1535 VE iv, 1547,
      1550, Pat, *Burnham* 1428 FA, 1465 Pat *et passim, -hame*

1589-91 *MinAcct, Burnam* 1576 *BPD*

Gillian Fellows-Jensen is no doubt correct in taking this to be from the dat.pl. of ON **brunnr** 'a well, a stream', hence 'at the wells, springs', topographically appropriate. For similar dat.pl. formations, cf. Coatham and Newsham in Brocklesby parish *supra*, in each case a similar development to *-ham* taking place.

ABBOT'S LODGE, self-explanatory, being named from the abbot of Thornton Abbey. BURNHAM BEECHES is *Burnham Wold* 1824 O, 1830 Gre, 1850 *TA, v.* **wald.** BURNHAM GRANGE *Burneham Graunge* 1541-43 LDRH, *- grange* 1542 LP xvii, *Burneham - Grangia* 1542-43 Dugd vi, "the granges of ..." *Burneham* 1547 Pat, *Burneham Grange* 1604 LNQ xi, *that Farme or Grainge of Burnham* 1670 *Yarb, the Mannor farme or Grainge of Burnham* 1683 *ib, - Farme or Grange of Burnham* 1696 *ib, the Mannor Farm or Grange of Burnham* 1728 *ib*; it was a **grange** of Thornton Abbey. BURNHAM LODGE. BURNHAM MANOR, cf. Burnham Grange *supra.* BURNHAM PARK. BURNHAM PLANTATION, 1824 O. BURNHAM WARREN, c.1817 *Yarb, Warren house* 1810 *ib, Warren Ho.* 1828 Bry. THE CANCH (lost), *the Canche* 1578 *DChB, one Water called the Canche* 1587, *vnam aquam vocat the Canche* 1588, *the Canche* 1602, *the Caunche* 1625, *the Canch* 1653, (*that Water called) -* 1681, 1720 all *Yarb, The Canch* 1824 O, 1830 Gre, cf. *the Canche garthe* 1578 *DChB, - Garth* 1587, *- garthe* 1588 *et passim* to the *Canch Garth* 1720 all *Yarb, Canch Close* c.1792 *MiscDon 242*; this is an early example of dial. *canch* (EDD s.v. 1) 'a sloping trench, a water-channel cut on a road', cf. the forms for 1587, 1588, 1681 and 1720. COLLEGE BRIDGE, COLLEGE FM (2x), cf. *the Colledge Close* 1687 *Yarb, College Close* 1850 *TA*, named after Thornton College, described in VCH ii, 237 as "one of the short-lived foundations of King Henry VIII", which was supressed at the beginning of the reign of Edward VI, *v.* further ChantCert no. 124. Note the references: *the Colleige Churche of thornton* 1545 LNQ *v, situm .. nuper Collegii de Thorenton* 1548 *Yarb, nuper Collegio de Thorneton* 1549 *LindDep 78, the Site of the late Colledge of Thornton* 1553 *Yarb, the Colledge of Thorneton* 1558 CA, *Thornton nuper Collegium* 1569 PrState, *the late dissolued Colledge of Thorneton* 1575 *Yarb, ye Colledge* 1601 *Terrier, the Colledg* c.1612

ib, Thornton Coledge 1648 WillsPCC. DAM LANE, cf. *atte Dame*
1327 *SR* (p), - *Damme* 1332 *ib* (p), *damholms slack* c.1612 *Terrier,*
damholme 1626 ib, *Dammon* (sic) 1638 *ib, Dam Close* c.1817 *Yarb,*
self-explanatory, *v.* ME **damme** (**dammr**) 'a dam, a pool' with
holmr and **slakki** 'a small shallow valley', an OWScand word, rare
in L. FOX COVERT, *Fox Cover* 1833 *Yarb,* 1850 *TA,* and is
Gorse Cover 1824 O, cf. *Fox Cover Close* 1850 *TA.* FROGMORE
FM, cf. *Frognoor Close* 1850 *ib.* THE GRANGE (Thornton
Curtis), apparently a late use of **grange**, for which cf. Croxton
Grange in Croxton *supra.* GRAVEL PIT. LOW FM. MANOR
FM. NORTHFIELD LANE, cf. *in Boriali Campo de Thorneton*
1545, *the North .... feildes* 1575, *le borial' .... campis de Thornton'*
1577, *the North feild* 1649 all *Yarb, the North side or feild, northfeild*
1674, *ye North field* 1679 both *Terrier, Thornton Northfield* 1687
Yarb, - *north feild* 1697, - *north field* 1709, - *North Field* 1724, 1745,
1825 all *Terrier, North field* 1850 *TA, Thaurnton North feld* (sic)
1712 *Terrier,* one of the great fields of Thornton, *v.* **norð, feld**.
RACE LANE, 1824 O, cf. *Raze lane Platt* c.1817 *Yarb, Race Lane*
Close 1833 *ib,* also in Wootton parish *infra.* SOUTH CLOISTER
COVERT is *Colledge W.^d* 1828 Bry, no doubt commemorating
Thornton Abbey or College. THORNTON HALL, *atte Halle* "of"
Thorneton 1325 Pat (p), *Hall* 1824 O, 1830 Gre, *The Hall* 1828 Bry,
perhaps *domus mansional' de Thorneton* 1559 *BP,* cf. *the hall garthe*
1601, *ye Hall garth* c.1612, 1626, *the Hall garth* 1638, *ye hall garth*
1674 *et freq* in *Terrier* (*v.* **garðr** 'an enclosure'), *ye Hall lane* c.1612,
- *hall lane* 1626 *ib.* THORNTON MOOR (lost) 1625, 1708, 1720
Yarb, 1824 O, 1830 Gre, *Thorneton Moore* 1602, 1653, 1681 *Yarb,*
1653 WillsPCC, *the more of Thornton Curtys* 1649 *Yarb;* it lay low
by East Halton Beck, and so was presumably 'the marshy land', *v.*
mōr[1]. TUNNARDS (lost), 1830 Gre, cf. Butters Wood, earlier
Tunnard's Plantation, in Goxhill parish *supra.* VICARAGE, cf. *y^e*
vicaregh close 1601, - *vicaridge closes* c.1612, - *vicaridge closes* 1638,
The lesser vicarage close 1664, *The greater -, The lesser vicaridge*
closse 1671, *The vicaridge closse* 1674, *Two Closes calld Vicaridge*
Close 1679 all *Terrier.* WALK HO, 1824 O, 1830 Gre, - *Ho.* 1828
Bry, cf. *Walk Close, - Intake, - Plat* 1850 *TA, v.* **walk** denoting land
used for the pasture of animals, especially sheep, hence the
common *Sheepwalk; v.* also **inntak** 'land taken in' and **plat**[2] 'a plot
of ground', as elsewhere in the f.ns. of this parish.

Field-Names

The principal forms in (a) are 1850 *TA 338*. Forms dated 1549[1] and 1552 are Pat; m16 are *Cragg*, 1601, c.1612, 1626, 1638, 1662, 1664, 1668, 1671, 1672, 1674, 1679, 1697, 1703, 1707, 1709, 1712, 1724, 1745, and 1825 are *Terrier*, 1549[2], 1550, 1575, 1577, 1587, 1588, 1602, 1624, 1625, 1649, 1653, 1670, 1681, 1683, 1687, 1696, 1708, 1720, 1728, 1810, c.1817, 1824, and 1833 are *Yarb*, c.1792 are *MiscDon 242*.

(a) the Ashgarth Side 1825 (*the Ashe garth side* 1662, *Ash garth* - 1697, y^e *ash garth Side* 1709, *The Ash garth side* 1712, y^e *Ash Garth side* 1724, *the Ash-Garth side* 1745, referring perhaps to 'an ash-yard, a refuse-tip', but it may simply be 'the enclosure where ash-trees grow or marked by an ash-tree', *v.* æsc, garðr); the Bank 1810, Bank c.1817, 1850 (*atte Bank'* 1327, *de Bannk'* 1332 *SR*, *del Banks* 1343 NI, *del Bank* 1340 Pat all (p), self-explanatory, *v.* banke); Bare Pce 1833; Barley Cl; Barn Platt c.1817 (*v.* plat^2); Barrow Fd, Barrow Intake (*v.* inntak 'a piece of land taken in or enclosed', as elsewhere in this parish), Barrow Meer 1825 (*barrow mear* 1601, *Barrow meare* 1662, 1674, 1697, - *Meare* 1668, *Barrow-meer* 1709, *Barrow Meere* 1712, 1745, - *Meer* 1724, 'the boundary with Barrow upon Humber', *v.* (ge)mære); Barrow Wold (*v.* wald and cf. prec.); Barton Road Cl; Barton Walk (from Barton upon Humber parish); Bas bowl Cl c.1792, Bush Bowl Cl 1850; Bayards Cl (perhaps from ME bayard 'a bay horse' or the surn. *Bayard*); Far Beech Tree Cl 1833; Bonby dale; Bonby Hollow Cl 1833 (from the neighbouring parish of Bonby); Lt Bottoms (*v.* botm); Brackin Cl c.1792, Bracken Cl Cover 1824, 1833, Bracken Hill 1825 (*brackenhills* 1664, *Brackinhill* 1671, *Brackinhills* 1674, *brakan hill* 1697, *brockon* - 1709, *Brackon hill* 1712, *Brackon-Hill* 1724, 1745, *v.* brakni, hyll); Brick Kiln Plot c.1817, Brick Kiln Cl 1850; Brigg Rd Cover c.1817, Brigg lane Cl 1850 (by the road to Glanford Brigg); Burnham Fd 1825 (*burholm feeld* (sic), *burnholm field* 1601, *Burneholme feild* c.1612, - *feeld* 1626, *Burnham feild* 1638, *burnholm field*, - *feild* 1662), Burnham dale (*Burneham Dale* 1546 LP xxii, 1635 (c.1900) *LindDep 78*), - Green, - Walk 1850 (all named from Burnham *supra*); Gt Carr (Hill), Lt Carr (*v.* kjarr); Chapel Fd (Burnham) (cf. *the Chapplegarth* 1625, *the Chappell-garth* 1670, *the Chapple Garth* 1683, 1728, *the Chappell* - 1696, *v.* garðr); Church Cl c.1792, 1824, 1833; the Church Lane 1825 (1745, y^e *Church lane* (*dale*) c.1612, y^e *church lane* 1626, *the church lane* 1662, y^e *church lane* 1697, y^e *Church lane* 1709, *the Church* - 1712, y^e *Church Lane* 1724, *churchlane dale* 1601, *churchlane daile* 1671, *the Kirklane dale marfur* 1664, *Church lane dale Marfer* 1668, *the churchlane dale Marfurr* 1674, *Church lane marfur* 1638, and cf. *ad ecclesiam* 1327 SR (p), *atte Kirk'* 1332 *ib* (p), *v.* deill, marfur 'a boundary furrow'; it is noteworthy that *Kirk* from Scand. kirkja, found in the 1332 form, appears once in 1664 as an alternative to *Church*); College (Lane) Cl, College Pingle (*v.* **pingel** and cf. College Bridge & Fm *supra*); Coney Garth c.1792, - garth 1850 (*Cony Garthe* 1549[1], 1577, *the Conny garth* m16, *Cony garthe* 1575, - *garth* 1681, *Conygarth* 1550, 1625, 1653, *Conygarthe* 1602, *the Coney Garth* 1708, *the Cony* - 1720, *v.* **coni, garðr** 'an enclosure', as elsewhere in this parish); Corn Cl 1810, c.1817 (cf. *the corngarthe* 1601, *v.* **garðr**); Cottagers Moor; Couch hill; Cover Cl 1833 (*v.* **cover(t)**)); Cow Cl 1833, 1850; Cow Croft; Cow Intake; Croft; Crook'd Mill Pingle c.1792 (in all probability from the mill giving name to Far -, Nr Crook Mill Furz in East Halton f.ns. (a)); Dale Btm c.1817; Darnon Cl, Far -, Nr Darnon (*A Dale called Darnell Dale* 1649, from ME *darnel*, the plant name, or the derived surn. and **deill**); Dove Cote Cl (cf. *the dovecote* 1576 *BPD*); Drury Intake (named from the family of Thomas *Drury* 1646 *BT* and **inntak**); East End Plot c.1817 (cf. *West end Lane* in (b) *infra*); East Fd (*inter orientales campos de Thorneton* 1549[2], *the east field* 1601, one of the open fields of Thornton, cf. Thornton South Fd in (a) *infra*); Elsham corner 1833 (in Burnham; the parishes are not actually contiguous, so this must refer to the corner *nearest* Elsham); the Fallow Fd 1825 (*the fallow field* 1709, *the fallafeld* (sic) 1712, y[e] *Fallow Field* 1724, cf. *the fallow heades* 1638, y[e] *fallow heads* 1697, *v.* **hēafod** in the pl.); Far Intake (cf. Intake *infra*); Fifty Acres 1833; Foal Cl; Foot ball Cl; Fore or College Yd 1824, 1833 (*the foreyard* 1649, *v.* **fore** 'in front', **geard** 'an enclosure, a yard'); Forty Acres 1833; Forty five Acres 1833; the fours 1825 (*the fower* 1601, c.1612, 1745, y[e] - 1638, 1697, *the foare* 1662, *the foure* 1674, y[e] *foower* 1697, y[e] *four* 1709, 1724, *The fouer* 1712; the explanation of this f.n. may well be given in *the new field now divided into four Closes* 1681, and *v.* Newfield Cl *infra* in (a)); Far -, Grass -, Middle furrows; East Furze Cl c.1792, East furze 1850 (*le Est furres* 1549[2], *Este furrs* m16, *le Estefurres* 1552, *East furres* 1625, *the Eastfurres otherwise Sheepe-cote Close* 1653, *the East Furrs otherwise Sheepecoote Close* 1681, *the East Furz otherwise Sheep Coate Close* 1708, - *Furze otherwise Sheepecoate Close* 1720, 'the east furrows', from **ēast** and **furh** in the pl., commonly found written *furres* in north L, here later confused with *furze*, cf. *Gouxhill Furres* in Barrow upon Humber f.ns. (b) *supra* and *Sheepcoate Close* in (b) *infra*); South -, West Furze Cl c.1792, Middle -, Top furze, West furze Cl, Furze Cl 1850 (all are adjacent to East furze and are, therefore, comparable); Furze Cover 1810, - Plantation & Wd 1824 (in Burnham, and they are probably from **fyrs** 'furze'); Garth c.1817 (*v.* **garðr**); Golden Plain; Goxhill Intake c.1792, 1850 (named from the adjoining parish of Goxhill and **inntak** 'a piece of land taken in or enclosed', probably belonging to Goxhill); Grass Bottom ("grass" in 1850); Great Cl (*great close* 1601, *the great Close* c.1612, - *close* 1626); Hawes Cl c.1792 (cf. *le Hawes* 1552, from the pl. of **haga**[1] 'an enclosure'); the Headland Dale 1825 (y[e] *headland* 1626, *the* - 1638, - *Headland* 1668, *the headland dale* 1662, y[e] *headland dale*

1697, - *head land dale* 1709, *the Headland* - 1712, *ye Head Land Dale* 1724, *the Head-land Dale* 1745, v. **hēafod-land** with **deill**); Herne Cl; Home Cl c.1817, 1833, 1850 (*the West home Close* 1576 *BPD*); Homestead Cl c.1817; Horse Intake (*v.* **inntak**); Hudson Nook 1825, Hudsons Cl, - nook 1850 (*Hudsons nooke* 1638, *Hudson nooke* 1662, 1671, 1674, - *Nooke* 1664, *hudson* - 1697, *Hudson nooke* 1709, - *Nook* 1724, *Hudson-Nook* 1745, *Hidson noke* (sic) 1712, named from the *Hudson* family, cf. John *Hudson* 1585 *BT*, Richard *Hudson* 1674 *Terrier*); Hutchinsons Cl (named from the *Hutchinson* family, cf. Edward *Hutchinson* 1602 *BT*); Intake (*ye intack* 1638, v. **inntak**); Jericho Cl c.1792, 1850, - cl 1824, Jericho (Cl) 1833 (cf. *the Two Jerricoes* 1649; on the eastern boundary with East Halton. This remoteness name was sometimes used for land to which sick animals were sent); Kings Head plat (v. **plat**^{2}); Lane Pingle c.1792, 1824, 1833, (New) Lane Cl, Lane Intake 1850 (v. **inntak**); Lawn; Lodge Cl (named from Bonby Lodge in Bonby parish *supra*); Long Cl c.1792, 1850; Long Pingle c.1792, 1824, 1833 - Cl c.1792, 1850 (v. **pingel**); Low Gate 1825 (*the low gate* 1601, *y^e* - c.1612, *ye Low gate* 1697, *low gate* 1709, *Low* - 1712, - *Gate* 1724, *Low-Gate* 1745, *Burnham gate* 1638, *Burnham lowgate* 1662, 1668, - *low gate* 1674, v. **lágr** 'low', **gata**); Marcow plain; Maries -, Marris's Cl (named from the *Maries*, *Marris* family, cf. John *Maries* 1850); Marsh Intake; Maws Cl (named from the family of Richard *Mawe* 1628 *Inv*); Meadow Cl c.1792, 1850; Meadow Intake; Middle fd; Middle Intake; Mill Hill Platt c.1817, Mill Hill 1850 (cf. *sextam partem molendini in Brunna* 1190 (1301) Dugd vi, i, *the millne, the millners house* c.1612); Mire bottom (v. **mýrr**, **botm**); Moor bottom (v. **botm**, cf. *Thornton Moor supra*); Far -, Nr narrow Intake (its narrowness is accurately described); Nr Intake; New Cl (*the new close* 1638, *the Newclose* 1649, *the New Close* 1687); Newfield Cl c.1792, 1850 (cf. *the Newe feild* m16, *Newfelde* 1549^2, *the New field or the Bigger new field* 1602, *the Newfeild or the bigger Newfeild* 1625, *the Newfeild* 1653, *the new field now divided into four Closes* 1681, *the new Feild divided into* - 1708, *the Newfield* - 1720, on the boundary of the College lands, cf. the fours *supra*); Ninety Acres 1833; Norcroft Cl c.1792, 1824, 1833 (*North Crofte* m16, *Le Northe crofte* 1549^2, *Northecroft* 1549^1, 1550, 1625, *Northe Crofte* 1575, *Northecrofte* 1577, *North croft* 1602, *the Norcroftes* 1649, *Northcroft* 1653, 1708, *North Croft* 1681, *the* - 1720, *North Croft Shawe* 1681, - *Shaw* 1708, 1720 (v. **norð**, **croft**, with **sceaga** 'a copse'); North Fd (Burnham) (*the North and Eastfield of Burnham* 1670, *ye North and est feilds* - 1683, *the North and Eastfields* - 1696, 1728, cf. *the South Feild of Burnham* (b) *infra*); North Lings (sic) 1810, North Ings c.1817 (*the Northynge* 1670, *ye North Ings* 1683, *the* - 1696, 1728, v. **norð**, **eng** 'meadow, pasture'; the 1810 form seems to be an error); Nursery Cl c.1792, 1850, - cl 1824, 1833, Little Nursery 1850 (*the Nursery Close* 1649); Nutwood Cl c.1792, Nut Wood Cl 1824, 1833; Oler Carr Cl c.1792, Alder carr 1824, - Car 1833 ('the marsh where alders grow', *v.* **alor, kjarr**); Ozier Holt; Paddock; Peartree Cl c.1792, Pear-tree cl 1824, Pear tree Cl 1833, 1850 (cf. *peer garth nook* c.1612, *peere garth nowke* 1626, *v.* **garðr, nök**); Pingle (cf. *the Pinghill* 1602, - *at the Wall end* 1625, *the Pingle under the wall* 1649, *the Pingle at the wall end* 1708, - *Wall end* 1720, *v.* **pingel** 'a small enclosure', (as elsewhere in this parish), and *the wall end* in f.ns. (b), *infra*); Plantation & Wood (Burnham) 1833; Plantation Cl 1850; Plat (2x) (*v.* **plat**^{2}); Pond Cl; Potter Steigh 1825 (*Potter stigh* 1668, y^e *potter Steigh* 1709, *poter steigh* 1712, *the Potter Steigh* 1724, *Potter's Steigh* 1745, named from the *Potter* family, cf. Agnes *Potter* 1593 *BT* and **stig** or **stigr** 'a path, a narrow road'); Railway Intake; Richardson Cl c.1792, Richardsons - 1850 (named from the *Richardson* family, cf. Richard *Richardson* 1591 *BT* and Thomas *Richardson* 1850); Richmond Gardens 1833 (presumably from the surn. *Richmond*; it may be noted that a Roger *de Richemund* was assessed in Thornton Curtis 1332 *SR*, though this may be purely coincidental); Road Intake; Ross lands (named from the family of Thomas *Ross* 1850); Sainfoin Cl 1833, 1850, Saint Foin pce 1850 (*v.* **sainfoin**); Sand pit Cl; Scary Dale 1825, Scarra Dale 1850 (*scavy dale* (sic) 1697, *Scary dale* 1703, 1707, 1709, 1712, *Scary-Dale* 1745, *starry Dale* (sic) 1724; the forms are too late to suggest an etymology); Screeving Cl; Second Intake; Gt -, Lt Seed Platt c.1817 (*v.* **plat**^{2}); Seventy Acres 1833; Sheep fold Cl; Sheep Walk 1810, c.1817, (Btm -, Lower -, Middle -, Top -, Upr) Walk 1850 (cf. *the Sheepwalks* 1670, 1728, y^e *Sheepe walkes* 1683, *the Sheepe Walkes* 1696, *the great Sheep Walk* 1745, *v.* **shepe-walk** 'a range of pasture for sheep'); Sink dale (for *sink, v.* Sinks Covert in South Killingholme *supra*); Slack Cl; Smooth Hill 1825, Sneath hill (sic) 1850 (*the Snoothill* (sic) 1662, *the snothill* 1674, *Snooth hill* 1697, *Smouth Hill* 1703, *smouth hill* 1712, *Smooth hill* 1709, - *Hill* 1724, 1745; earlier forms are needed to suggest an etymology); Spring Cl; Stack Yard -, Stack yard Cl 1833, 1850; Stone Pit Cl (cf. *stone pitts* 1601, 1638, - *pittes* c.1612, *Stone* - 1626, self-explanatory); Street Lane Cl, - Plat (two fields on opposite sides of the road leading from Croxton to Barton upon Humber, cf. *the streete* 1601, 1638, y^e *Street* c.1612, y^e *street* 1626, *the* - 1674, *the Streete* 1668, *v.* **strǣt**); Thirty Acres 1833; Thornes 1810, Far -, Nr Thorns 1850, Thornes Cl c.1817 (*the Thorneclose* 1625, *the Thorne-close* 1670, y^e *Thorne close* 1683, *the Thorne Close* 1696, - *Thorn close* 1728, and cf. *Westthorne Close* 1576, *v.* **þorn**); Thorn Tree Cl 1833; Thornton Common c.1792; Thornton Intake (*v.* **inntak**); Thornton South Fd 1825 (*in australi campo* 1549^2, *le ... australi campis de Thorneton* 1577, *the ... Southfieldes of Thornton* 1575, *the ... South fieldes* 1602, - *feildes* 1625, *the ... South feildes of Thornton* 1653, *Thornton south feild* 1697, - *field* 1709, *the south feild* 1649, *the South field* 1662, - *feild* 1668, *the southfield* 1674, y^e *South field* 1679, *the ... South Fields* 1720, *Thournton south feld* (sic) 1712, *Thornton South Field* 1724, 1745, cf. *in campis Thornton* 1190 (1301) Dugd vi, i, *In campis de Torenton'* 1202

Ass; one of the open fields of Thornton); Thornton Top Walk (*v.* **walk**); Thornton Wold (*the Would* 1664, *the Woald* 1668, *cf. the northe* -, *the south Would* 1601, *v.* **wald**); Top Intake (*v.* **inntak**); Town end intake, - plat; Far -, Middle -, Nr Turnip Plat (*v.* **plat**^{2}); Two dales (*v.* **deill** 'a portion of land'); Two Pit Cl 1833; Far Ulceby Intake c.1792, 1850, Ulceby Gt Intake 1850 (they are on the boundary with Ulceby, *v.* **inntak**); Vicars Cl; Walk Cl, - Intake, - Plat (*v.* **walk**, **inntak**, **plat**^{2}); Btm Warren (*v.* **wareine**); Wash dike Cl, Lane & Pingle c.1792; Water Intake (*v.* **inntak**); Werlaby lane Cl (sic) (next to Brigg lane Cl *supra*); (South) West Side Lane c.1817; Wheat lands (cf. *Wheat close* 1625, *the Wheat close* 1670, *y*^{e} - 1683, *the Wheate* - 1696, - *Wheatclose* 1729, *v.* **hwǣte, land, clos(e)**)); Whin Cl (*v.* **hvin**, ME **whin** 'whin, gorse'); White Stable Cl c.1792, 1833, 1850, - cl 1824 (*the whit-stable close* 1649); Long -, Middle Wold (*v.* Thornton Wold *supra*); Wood Cl c.1817; Wootton Meer 1825 (1724, 1745, *Wytton meare* 1576 BPD, *Wotton meare* 1662, 1674, - *Meare* 1668, *Wotton meere* 1697, *Wootton meer* 1709, *Woton meere* 1712, 'the boundary with Wootton', *v.* **(ge)mǣre** 'a boundary'); Wootton Wold (*v.* **wald**); Worlaby Wold (from the adjoining parish of Worlaby and **wald**).

(b) *le Abbottescourse* 1549^1, 1550, 1557, *illam pasturam ovium vocat le Abbot course* 1549^2, *the Abbotes Course* 1575, *Abbottescourse* 1602 (*course* is used as an appellative in this document), *the Abbottes Course* 1625, *the Abbottescourse* 1653, *the Abbots Course* 1681, *the Abbotts* - 1708, - *course* 1720 (*v.* **course**, here presumably used to mean 'fold-course, the area allotted to each manor for its flocks to graze over the open fields', a meaning not recorded in MED. This land did not coincide with the arable holdings of the owners of the sheep (cf. Adams 81)); *Almeshowse Garth* 1602, *Almeshowse Garth* 1625, 1653, *Almes house garth* 1681, *Almeshouse Garth* 1720 (self-explanatory, and *v.* **garðr**); *Ashdale Hill* 1601, 1638, - *hill'* c.1612, *ashdale* - 1626; *backhouse garthe* 1649 (perhaps for *bakehouse*, as in EDD s.v. *backhouse* sb^2, ME *bake-hous*, with **garðr**); *Barker garthe* 1602, - *garth* 1625, *Barkers garth* 1653, 1681, - *Garth* 1708, 1720, *Barkers Hawes* 1602, 1653, - *hawes* 1625, - *house* (sic) 1681, 1708, 1720, - *shaw(e)* 1602, 1625, - *shaws* 1653, - *Shawe* 1681, - *Shaw* 1708, - *shaw* 1720 (from the surn. *Barker*, cf. Mrs Ann *Barker* 1664 *Inv*, with **garðr**, **haga**^{1} 'an enclosure', sometimes in the pl., later confused with *house* and **sceaga** 'a copse, a little wood'); *y*^{e} *bloody crosse* 1601, *ye bloodie cross* c.1612, *bloody cross* 1626, - *Crosse* 1638 (cf. *ad Crucem* 1327, - *crucem* 1332 *SR* both (p), *Thornton Cros* 1375 *Works*, *v.* **cros**); *bradley land, bradley house* (*land*) 1601 (named from the *Bradley* family, cf. William *Bradley* m16, John *Bradley* 1619 *BT*, *Marriall Bradley* 1623 *ib*); *Tofti vocat' Brickhouse* 1589-01 *MinAcct* (a compound form not found in dictionaries); *del Brigge* 1294 Ass (p) (*v.* **brycg**, in a Scandinavianised form); *ye bucklane* 1601,

Bucklane end c.1612, 1638; *the Catclose* 1625; *Clacknolde gate* 1549^2 (*v.* **gata**); *the clark mastall* 1601, *clark* - c.1612, *Clerk Mastall* 1626, *Clarke mastal* 1638 (for *mastal, v. le marstal* in Killingholme f.ns. (b) and cf. *Mill Mastall butts* in Goxhill f.ns. (b) *supra*; the first el. is perhaps the surn. *Clarke,* cf. William *Clerke* 1549^2); *Cl'i vocat' le Couen'* 1589-91 *MinAcct,* - *voc' le Coven* 1606-7 *ib,* *Covent howse* m16, *the covent land* 1601 (*v.* **covent** 'a convent, a religious house (for either sex)'; the forms agree with the NED account of the orthographic history of the word, that the spelling *convent* replaced the earlier *couent* only between c.1550 and c.1650, cf. Covent Garden PN Mx 167); *Le Cowhouse* 1549^2, "a cowhouse" 1549^1 (a messuage), *messuagium et tenementum meum vocat a Cowhouse* 1550, *the Cowehowse* 1575 (a messuage), *a Cowhouse (messuagium)* 1577, *messuage and tenement called a Cowhouse* 1602, *a Cowhouse* 1625, 1708, *a Cow howse* 1653, *that Messuage or Tenement called a Cowhouse* 1681, *Cowhouse garth* 1549^1, *Cowehousegarth* 1549^2, *Cowhouse garth* 1550, *Cowe howse garthe* 1575, *Cowhousegarthe* 1577, *Cowhowse garth* 1602, *Cowhousegarth* 1625, *Cowhowse Garth* 1653, *Messuage or tenement called Cowhouse Garth* 1720 (*v.* **couhous, garðr**); *the Crooke of ye mear* 1601, *the crook of ye meare* c.1612, *ye crook of y^e* - 1626, *ye Crooke* - 1638 ('the angle in the boundary', *v.* **crōc, (ge)mǣre**); *ye eele hole* 1697 (the same name occurs in the neighbouring parish of Goxhill, as the Eel Hole in f.ns. (a) and no doubt refers to the same place); *le Farmerye Yarde* 1549^1 (a garden), *the farmery yarde* 1549^2, *one garden called the Fermarie* 1575, *the Farmery* 1602, *the farmery yard* 1653, *the Farmery yard* 1681, 1708, *One garden called the Farmary yard* 1720, (*the) Farmery Garth* 1625, 1653 (alluding to the infirmary (ME *fermeri(e)*) of Thornton Abbey, with **geard** 'an enclosure, a yard', alternating twice with Scand. **garðr** 'an enclosure'); *the house commonly called le Froyter* (sic) 1547 *Pat* (probably from ME *freitour* 'a refectory', i.e. of Thornton Abbey, cf. the Frather in Saxby All Saints f.ns. (a)); *the furbushe dale marfurr* 1601, *furbush-dale marford* (sic) c.1612 (*v.* **fyrs** 'furze', **busc,** with **deill** 'a portion of land', and **marfur** 'a boundary furrow'); *le furley end* 1601; *le garner* 1549^1 (a barn), 1550, 1577, *le Garner* 1549^2 (from ME *gerner* 'a granary', no doubt of Thornton Abbey); *Garton shaw* 1602, - *Shaw* 1708, *that peece or close of woodland ... called Garton Shaw* 1653 (from **sceaga** 'a small wood', probably with the surn. *Garton,* for which, however, there has, as yet, been no independent evidence noted in the parish); *le great gardeine* 1575, *greatgarden* 1602 (*v.* **gardin**); *atte Gatende* 1327 *SR* (p) (*v.* **gata, ende**^{1}); *Goodhands fearm* 1601 (the home of the *Goodhand* family, cf. Robert *Goodhand* m16, Cecily *goodhand* 1587 *BT, v.* **ferme**); *atte Haghous* 1327 *SR,* *de Haghouses* 1332 *ib* both (p) (this compound is discussed by M.T. Löfvenberg, *Contributions to Middle English Lexicography and Etymology,* Lund 1946, 93-4, who quotes an example dated 1400 and the definition 'a house for chopping and storing firewood' given by NED s.v. *hag* sb³, 4. He comments, however, that the first el. is the stem of the verb *hag* 'cut', 'hew', 'chop' from ON *hoggva*. The present example is the earliest so far noted and predates the instance given in NED by 400 years; *v.* also MED *hag-hous*, s.v. *haggen* (c)); *hamon' howse, hamondhouse* m16 (from the surn. *Hamond*); *Hawton Lane* 1602, 1625, *Halton Lane* 1649, 1653, 1681, 1708, *a parcel of Ground called* - 1720, *Houghton* - 1681 (the lane to East Halton); *the Haze-garth* 1670, - *Haze Garth* 1683, 1696, 1728 (*v.* garðr); *the heads* 1601, yᵉ *heads* c.1612, - *heades* 1626, (*v.* hēafod in the pl.); *Holmes* 1601, 1638, *holmes* c.1612, 1626 (*v.* holmr in the pl.); *Hode & lippil* (sic) 1601, *hood & typpett* c.1612, *hood & tippit* 1626, *Hood & Tippit* 1638 (probably, like most field-names referring to garments, an allusion to the shape of the piece of land; *a tippet* was a scarf-like attachment to a hood, suggesting that this land had such an elongated extension); *the hop yard* 1649 (self-explanatory, an enclosure where hops are grown, *v.* hop-yard); *kilnehouse, unum domum vocat a Kylnehouse* 1549², 1550, *a Kylne house* 1577, *one howse called a kyllnhowse* 1602, *one howse called a Kilne howse* 1653, *one house called a Kilne House* 1681, *the Kiln house* 1708, *the Kilne* - 1720 (*v.* kiln-hous); *the Knole* 1601 (*v.* cnoll); yᵉ *lady(e) land* 1601, *Lady lande* 1605-7 *MinAcct, ladie land* c.1612, 1626, yᵉ *lady land* c.1612, - *ladye land* 1626 (*v.* hlæfdige, probably a reference to 'our Lady'); *atte Lathe* 1327, *ofthe* - 1332 SR both (p) (*v.* hlaða 'a barn'); *Lathropes Lodging* 1625, *Lathrops lodgeing* 1681, *Lathorps lodging* 1720 (from the surn. *Lathrope, Lathorp*, but the name has not so far been noted independently in the parish); *le Launderhouse* 1549¹ (a cottage) 1550, *launder house (illud cottagium)* 1549², *vnum cottagium ... vocat le launderhouse* 1577, *one cottage called the Launder* 1602, *the Launder house* 1653, - *Launders house* 1681, 1708, 1720 (presumably from ME *launder(e)* 'a laundress, a washerwoman'); *Lockman pitts* 1601, 1671, - *pittes* c.1612, *lockman pittes* 1626, *lockman great pitt* 1674 (*v.* pytt), *lockman hill* 1626 (*v.* hyll, the first el. is doubtless the surn. *Lockman*); *Lylbornes Lodging* 1625, *Libbornes Lodgein* (sic) 1653, *Lilbornes lodgeing* 1681, *Lilburnes lodging* 1720 (from the surn. *Lilborn, Lilburn*, but so far there is no independent local evidence of the name); *Martyne Closes* 1625, *Martins Close* 1708, 1720 (no doubt from the surn. *Martin*); *the mear* 1601, yᵉ - c.1612, yᵉ *meare* 1626, *the* - 1638, *the Meare* 1668, - *meare* 1674 ('the boundary', *v.* (ge)mære); *michelmar* 1601, *micklemar* c.1612, *Miglemore* (sic) 1626, *Miclemer* 1662, *Miclemarr* 1664, *Micklemar* 1668, *Micklemarr* 1671, *Mickle marr* 1674 (probably 'the great boundary', *v.* mikill, (ge)mære); yᵉ *midfurlong* 1638, *Mydylclose* 1549¹, *le Myddleclose* 1549², *Myddelclose* 1550, *myddel Close* 1575, *mydylclose* 1577, *Middleclose* 1602, 1625, *Middle close* 1653, 1720, - *Close* 1681, 1708, *midlecrofte* m16 (each self-explanatory); *Nanpye nest* 1649 (from *nantpie*, an obsolete form of dial. *nantipie* 'a magpie', *v.* EDD s.v.); *de Nedderdale* 1327 SR, *de Nedirdale* 1332 ib both (p) (perhaps *v.* neoðera 'lower', dalr or deill, though this may not be a local surn.); *ten' vocat' Nedelarplace* 1381-2 *AddR* (from the ME occupational name or surn. *Nedler(e)* and **place**); *north dale hill* 1601; *the Oakclose* 1625 (perhaps for *Oatclose*, cf. foll.); *the oate Close* 1649, *the Oat-close* 1670, *ye Oate close* 1683, *the Oate Close* 1696, *the Oat* - 1728; *the orchard Close* 1649; *le Park* m16, *the park of Thorneton* 1558 CA, *the little Parke* 1578 *DChB*, 1587, 1653, 1681, 1708, *Litle* - 1588, *le Lytle Parke* 1602, *the litle* - 1625, *the Little* - 1720 (*v.* **park**); *le pinfold* 1605-7 *MinAcct* (*v.* **pynd-fald**); *the pitt* 1601, c.1612, *the pittes* 1626, *a pit* 1638 (*v.* **pytt**); *Plummer howse* 1625, *Plumer Howse* 1653, - *house* 1681, *Plummers house* 1720 (from the surn. *Plummer*, which, so far, has not been noted independently in the parish); *Robinsons house* 1649 (the home of the *Robinson* family, cf. William *Robinson* 1619 *BT*); *Sheepcoat Close* 1625 (this is not identical with the foll., *v.* East Furze Cl in (a) *supra*); *le Shepehowse close* m16, 1549[2], *Shepehouse Close* 1549[1], - *close* 1550, 1602, *Shepehowse Close* 1575, *Shepehouse close* 1577, *Sheepehouse close* 1625, *Sheephowse Close* 1653, *Sheephouse close* 1681, *Sheep house Close* 1708, 1720 (*v.* **shep-hous**); *Shoregate pitts* 1601, 1638, *shoregate pittes* c.1612; *Snore Hill* 1601, *ye Snoore hill* c.1612 (it is possible that these are earlier forms of Smooth Hill in (a) *supra*); *South close* m16, *le South Close* 1549[2], *le Southclose* 1552, *South Close* 1681, 1708, *the* - 1720; *the South Feild of Burnham* 1670, *ye South fields* 1683, *the Southfeilds of Burnham* 1696, *the Southfields* - 1728 (cf. North Fd in (a) *supra*); *ye South lane* 1709; *Spencer lane* 1601, *Spenser lane* c.1612, - *end* 1628 (named from the *Spencer* or *Spenser* family, cf. Robert *Spooncer* 1647 *BT*, Robert *Spoonser* 1664 *ib*); *the Stone horse Close* 1625, *the Stonehorse close* 1670, - *Close* 1696, *the Stone horse close* 1683, *the Stonehouse Close* (sic) 1728 (from *stone horse* 'a stallion', *v.* EDD s.v. *stone* II and NED s.v. *stonehorse* and *stone* 11); *le Thornton Course* 1549[2] (*v.* **course** and *le Abbottescourse supra*; the same name, referring to the same feature, occurs in East Halton f.ns. *supra*); *trewman house* m16, *Cl'icum Crofto vocat' Trewmanhowse* 1589-91 *MinAcct*, *Trewmans House* 1605-7 *ib* (from the surn. *Trewman, Trueman*, not so far noted independently in the parish); *Vlceby meare* 1649, *Ulseby* - 1687 ('the boundary with Ulceby', *v.* **(ge)mǣre**); *le Uttercourte* 1549[1] (a precinct), *le Vtter Courte* 1549[2], *the utter Course & Inner course* 1575, *le Utter Course* 1577, *the Utter court* 1602 (note that *course* is used as an appellative in this document), *the Uttercourt* 1625, *the utter Court* 1653, 1708, *the Utter Court* 1720, *the Vtter Court* 1681 (*v.* **court, course**; it is difficult to see whether there are two names here (in - *course* and in - *court*), or one, in which *court* has replaced *course* because of a scribal or other error; the reference dated 1575 makes it clear that *Vtter*, etc. is *Outer*); *the Wall end* 1625, *the Wall* 1649, *the wall end* 1653, 1681, *the Wall end* 1720 (presumably this is self-explanatory, *v.* also Pingle in f.ns. (a) *supra*); *waterskales* 1601, *waterscales* c.1612, *Water Scales gate* 1638 (from **wæter** 'water' also 'wet' and **skáli** 'a temporary hut or shed', on which *v.* Old Scales in

Brocklesby f.ns. (a) and *Walgerscales* in Immingham f.ns. (b)); *one water milne* 1575; *the Wellclose* 1670, 1728, *the Well Close* 1683, - *well close* 1696; *Wellwick shawe* 1625, - *Shaw* 1720, *Wellwicks shawe* 1681, - *shaw* 1708 (the first el. is presumably the surn. *Wellwick*, the second is sceaga 'a small wood'); *West end Lane* 1724, *the West End Lane* 1745; *White house garth* 1681, *White house Garth* 1708, *White House garth* 1720 (*v.* the following); *Wryghthowse Garth* 1625, *Wrighthowse Garth* 1653 (presumably from the surn. *Wright*, cf. Roger and Nicholas *Wright* 1641 LPR, with garðr. The *White house* names begin in 1681, suggesting that they are altered from *Wrighthouse*, the forms for which cease in 1653).

Ulceby

ULCEBY

> *Ulvesbi* (3x), *Uluesbi, Vluesbi* 1086 DB
> *Ulesbi* c.1115 LS, a1147, c.1150, 1150-60, 112 Dane, -*by* 1190
>   (1301) Dugd vi, 1202 Ass, 1219 FF, 1343 NI, *Uleseby* c.1155
>   Dane (p)
> *Hulesbi* c.1160 Dane, 1212 Fees
> *Ulseby* 1163-76, 1175-78, 1187-93 (e14) YCh x, 1190 (1301)
>   Dugd vi, 112 (e13) *NCot*, 1228 Cur, 1231 Cl (p), 1242-43
>   Fees, 1254 ValNor *et freq* to 1431 FA, -*bye* 1276 RH, -*bi*
>   112 Dane, 1277 Pap, *Vlseby* 1178, a1178, 1189-95 (1285) RA
>   ii, 1272 *Ass*, 1303 *HarlCh et passim* to - *iuxta Claxby* 1391
>   FF, -*bia* 1236-47 *HarlCh*, *Vlsseby* 1383 Peace
> *Wlsebi* 1238-43 Fees, -*by* 1268 Ch, 1383 Peace, 1428 FA
> *Hulseby* 1209-35 LAHW, -*b'* c.1221 Welles, *Hulsbe* 1539 LP
>   xiv
> *Olesbi* 1202 Ass, -*by* 1504 Ipm, *Olseby* c.1220 (e13) *NCot*, 1277
>   Cl, 1383 Peace, *Olsby* 1294 *Ass*
> *Ulceby* 1270 RRGr, 1281 Tax, 1325 FA, 1343 Ipm, 1428 FA,
>   1464 WillsPCC, 1465 Pat, 1495 IBL, 1552 Pat *et passim*,
>   - *alias Wolceby* 1539 LP xiv, 1571 Pat, -*bye* 1552 ib, 1601,
>   1606, 1612 *Terrier*, -*bie* 1554 Pat, 1576 LER, *Vlceby* 1327
>   SR, 1375 Peace, -*bie* 1587 *Yarb*
> *Vlsby* 1294 *Ass*, *Ulsby* 1346 FA, 1398 Cl, -*bye* 1576 Saxton,
>   1610 Speed
> *Usseby* 1283 Ipm
> *Hwlceby iuxta Newsom* (sic) 1381 Peace

Wolsby 1515-18 ECP
Howsby 1519 DV, *Housby* 1690 *Terrier* (Croxton)
Usselby alias Ulceby 1571 Pat
Owlsebye 1581 *Yarb*

'Ulf's farmstead or village', from the Scand. pers.n. *Ulfr* and **bý**.
It is noteworthy that the first el. has the Scand. gen.sg. [s], as in the
identical name Ulceby LSR and other p.ns. in L, like Braceby,
Haceby, Laceby, Rauceby and Winceby, and this survives today.
One can only presume that this group was given by Scand. speakers,
otherwise the pronunciation would have been [z].

SKITTER BECK, *uadum de Scithere* 1150-60 Dane, *aque de schitre*
a1170 (e13) *NCot*, *super Schitaram* (sic) p1170 (e13) *ib*, *in filum
aque de Scitre*, - *Schiter* p1186 Dane, *aqua de Scytre* Hy2 (e13)
NCot, *aquœ de Scittra* 1190 (1301) Dugd vi, *in filum aque de
Schytere* c.1190 Dane, *scitter* John *HarlCh*, *aque de Schitre* e13 *Yarb*,
aque q' uocat' Scitter e13 *HarlCh*, "the water of" *Skitere* 1219 FF,
skitre eHy3 (e13) *NCot*, *aquam de Skittre* Hy3 *HarlCh*, *aque de
Skiter* 1260 (l14) *Gox*, *ad filum de Scitter* Ed1 *HarlCh*, *aque de
Skittre* 1307 *NCot*, "the bailiffs of ..." *Skyter* 1342 Cl, *aque de Skyttere*
1381 *Yarb*, *Skytter* 1536 LP xi, derived from OE **scitere** 'a sewer, a
stream used as an open sewer', with OE initial *sh-* replaced by
Scand. *sk-*. It is today the name of the stream forming the
boundary between Ulceby and Killingholme, called New Beck Drain
in Keelby upstream and downstream East Halton Beck, whose
outfall is at East Halton Skitter *supra*. The forms, derived from
various parishes adjoining, are presented together for convenience.

ULCEBY SKITTER, *Skyter* 1327 *SR* (p), *Ulseby Skittere* 1375
Works, *the Skitter* 1677 LH ii, 8, *Ulceby Skitter* 1739 *BPD*, 1830 Gre,
Skitter 1828 Bry, cf. prec.

ASHDALE HO, cf. *Ash Dale* 1795 *Yarb*. BRICK KILN (lost),
1828 Bry. BROCKLESBY OX, 1842 White. CHURCH LANE, *the
Churche waye* 1606 *Terrier*. COTE PITS, *Coat Pits* 1762 *BM*.
CROFT HO. CROSS RD. DOCKHOLE RD, cf. *Dock Hole*

Marfurr 1795 *Yarb, Dockhole Marfurr* 1833 *MiscDep 118* (*v.* **marfur**), *Dock-hole Close* 1826 *Yarb,* perhaps 'the hollow where docks grow', *v.* **docce, hol**[1]. FOX (P.H.), 1842 White. GRANGE WINDMILL, cf. Ulceby Grange *infra.* HILL GARTH FM, *Hill Garth(s)* 1826 *Yarb* and *ad montem* Hy3 *HarlCh, del Hull' de Vlseby* 1294 *Ass, del Hill'* 1332 *SR, i' the Hill* 1343 NI, *del Hill' de Vlseby* 1366 *FF, del Hille de Vlseby* 1371 *ib,* atte *Hille de Vlceby* 1374 Peace, *Hille de Wlseby* 1383 *ib, of the Hill' de Vlceby* 1398 *FF* all (p), self-explanatory. LADYPITS PLANTATION, cf. *Lady Pit* 1762 *BM.* MANOR HO is *Hall Garth* 1828 Bry, 1826 *Yarb, y*[e] *hall-garth* 1707 *Terrier, v.* **hall, garðr** 'an enclosure'. MARK COOPER'S WOOD is perhaps named from *Mark Cooper* 1842 White or a member of his family with the same name. MARTIN LANE, cf. - *Close* 1826 *Yarb,* presumably from a surn. MODEL FM. NORTH FIELD, *in aquil' campo de Vlseby* e13 (Ed1) *Newh, in North campo de Vlseby* c.1240 (Ed1) *ib, camp' borial'* ... *de Ulseby* l13 *NCot,* (*the*) *North Field* 1626 *Yarb,* 1758, 1762, 1766, 1786 *BM,* 1795 *Yarb,* 1797, 1816 *BM,* 1833 *MiscDep 118,* one of the great fields of the village, *v.* **norð, feld,** and cf. the ... South Fields in f.ns. (a) *infra.* SPRUCE LANE. SPUR PLAT WOOD (partly in Kirmington), cf. *Great -, Little Spur plat* 1832 *Yarb.* SWEETBRIER FM. ULCEBY CARR, 1824 O, 1830 Gre, (*the*) *Carr* 1677 LH ii, 8, 1758, 1766, 1786, 1797, 1816 *BM,* cf. *Carr Beck* 1762 *ib,* and *Carre dyke* 1559 *Anc.* CARR LANE, the *Carr Gate* 1762 *ib, v.* **kjarr, bekkr, dík, gata.** ULCEBY CHASE is *Newsham Chase F.*[m] 1828 Bry, 1830 Gre, from Newsham in Brocklesby *supra.* ULCEBY FIELD (lost), 1762 *Terrier,* 1824 O, *in campis Ulesbi* a1147, - *de Ulesbi* c.1150 both Dane, - *de Vlseby* e13 (Ed1) *Newh, la chaump de Vlseby* e14 *HarlCh, in campo de Vlseby* 1312 *ib, Ulcebie fe(i)lde* 1577 *Terrier, Vlcebeie feild* 1587 *Yarb, Ulsebe felde* 1601, - *feild* 1631, *Ulcebie feild* 1662, *Housby Field* (sic) 1690, *Ulseby field* 1707, *Ulceby feild* 1769 all *Terrier* (Croxton), self-explanatory, *v.* **feld.** ULCEBY GRANGE, *The Granges* (sic) 1766 *BM,* cf. *the Grange Side* 1762 *ib,* apparently a late example of the use of **grange,** for which cf. Croxton Grange in Croxton *supra.* ULCEBY MILL (lost), 1828 Bry, *molendino de Ulseby* 1190 (1301) Dugd vi, *y*[e] *Winde Milne* 1671, *a Mill calld Crofton Mill* 1700 (the same as prec.) both *Terrier,* cf. *Old Mill Hill, Mill Close* 1826 *Yarb,* the last two may not refer to the same mill. ULCEBY WOLD (lost), 1824 O, *Ulceby Wold or Newsham Chase* 1828 Bry, 1830 Gre, *Wold* 1795

Yarb, 1833 *MiscDep 118, Vlsby wald* 112 (Ed1) *Newh, le Walde* e13 (Ed1) *ib, Hulsebiwald* m13, Ed1 *HarlCh, une place qe est appelle le Wald* 1303 *ib, une place qest appellee Vlseby Wald'* e14 *ib, Wold* 1626 *Yarb*, cf. *the Wold Hedge* 1762 *BM*, self-explanatory, *v.* **wald.** VALE FM. VALE HO. WEST END RD. WESTFIELD WINDMILL, cf. *West Field* 1626 *Yarb, the ... and West Fields* 1758, 1766, 1786, 1816 *BM, Ulceby West Field* 1824 O, one of the great fields of Ulceby, *v.* **west, feld.**

Field-Names

Principal forms in (a) are 1833[1] *MiscDep 118.* Spellings dated 1587, 1625, 1708, 1779, 1794, 1795, and 1826 are *Yarb;* 1677 are LH ii, 8 (checked from MS); 1730, 1745, and 1788 are *Terrier;* 1758, 1762, 1766, 1770, 1786, 1797, and 1816 are *BM;* 1833[2] are *Lamb.*

(a) Abbey Hill 1762 (presumably the reference is to Thornton Abbey); Acre dike Cl 1826 (*the Acerdike* 1677, *v.* **æcer, akr, dik** and cf. *y*[e] *acredikes* in Barnetby le Wold f.ns. (b) *supra*); Allenby Nook 1795, 1826, Allonby - 1833[1] (cf. *Suer from Allamby greene* (sic) 1677, named from the *Allanby* family, frequently mentioned in *BT*s and cf. Richard *alanby* m16 *Cragg*); the Ash plant[n] 1779; Beck 1826 (*v.* **bekkr**); Berrin Garth 1826 (presumably named from the family of Nicholas *Beron* m16 *Cragg*); Booth ends 1762 (probably named from the family of *Mr Richard Booth* 1783 *LTR*); Bramah Close Leys 1794, 1795, 1833[1], - leys 1795; Brentywell 1762, Brentwell 1795, Brentewell 1833[1]; Brig Gate 1766, Brigg gate 1795, - Gate 1833[1] ('the road to Brigg', *v.* **gata**); Bristow Cl 1826 (named from the family of Dorcas *Bristow* 1726 *BT*); Lt Butts 1795, Butt Cl 1826 (*v.* **butte**); Caistor Rd 1762 (*castregat* c.1240 (Ed1) *Newh, Castergate* 13 (Ed1) *ib,* 'the road to Caistor', *v.* **gata**); Calf Cl 1826, Gt -, Lt Calf Hill 1794, Calf Hill 1795, 1826, 1833[1]; Carr (Flg) 1795, 1833[1], (Far) Carr Hill 1794, 1833[1] (*v.* Ulceby Carr *supra*); Collo Furze 1794, - furrs 1833, Collofurs 1795 (the second el. is from the pl. of **furh** 'furrow'; the first needs early forms to determine its etymology); Common Marfur 1794, - Marfer 1833[1] (*v.* **marfur** 'a boundary furrow', as elsewhere in the parish); Cony Garth Dale 1795, 1833[1] (*v.* **coni, garðr** with **deill**); Coney-hill 1762, Coney Hill 1794, Cony - 1833[1] (*v.* **coni, hyll**); Cow gate Marfurr 1795, - Gate Marfar 1833[1] (*v.* **cow-gate, marfur**); Daniel Cl 1826; Dinas Cl 1826; Dovecote Cl 1826; Drury Marrs 1762 (named from the family of George *Drury* 1762); the East Fd 1762; Ellerby Hedge 1762, Elerby - 1766 (named from the family of Edward *Ellerbye* 1613 *Inv*); Eshdale; Farker - Hill

1762; Feather hill 1795, Featherhill 1833; Fields Head Lane 1795 (*v. Ulceby Field supra*); The Folly 1826 (this is a small piece of land only 22 perches in area); Fools Hill 1794; Foul farr (sic) 1795, Foulfurr 1833[1] ('dirty furrow', *v.* fûl, furh); Fox Cover 1826; Frema-Close, Freemer Cl 1762, Free Moor 1795, Freemoor 1833[1]; Gated Garth 1826 (*v.* garðr); Gillyott close End 1795, Gillot Cl - 1833[1] (named from the family of William *Gilliot* 1745 *BT*); Gowdimarr 1795, Goudimar 1833[1]; Gowt Pce (the first el. is gotu 'a water-course, a channel'); goos crofts 1766; Great Cl 1826; Green gate Bottam 1766, - Gate Btm 1795, 1833[1], Greengate - 1794 (probably 'the road to the green', *v.* grêne[2], gata, with botm, cf. *atte Grene* 1327, 1332 *SR, del Grene de Ulseby* 1380 *FF* all (p), *the grene* 1587); Messuage or Tenem[t] ... known by the name of ye Greyhound 1770; The Hagg (this is the name of a field and probably from ON hǫgg 'a cutting, a cutting of trees'); Hall's Orchard 1762, 1788 (1745, *Halls Orchard* 1730, named from the family of Robert *Hall* 1687 *BT*); Highthorns 1795, 1833[1]; Home cl 1826; Hooks 1795, - Cl 1826; Howstead Hill 1826 (early forms are needed to suggest an etymology for Howstead); Hunco Btm 1794; Ickledam 1762, Ickledom 1795, Ickel dome 1833[1] (cf. *vlsebi dam* Hy3 *HarlCh, atte Dam* 1327, *atte Dame* 1332 *SR* both (p), *v.* dammr 'a dam', ME damme 'a pond'); Lees Cl 1779, Lea Cl 1826 (perhaps from the surn. *Lee* or *Leigh*, cf. Alexander *Leighe* 1599 *BT*, Richard *Lee* 1615 *ib*); Leethy Hill 1795, 1833[1]; Lever Moor 1795, Levermoor 1833[1], Leven Mere Cl (sic) 1826 (*levermarr* 1677, perhaps 'the rushy boundary land', *v.* læfer, (ge)mære); Long Rooe Furs 1762 (*v.* furh); Long Tofts 1795, Longtofts 1833[1] (*v.* lang, toft 'a curtilage', and cf. Short Tofts *infra* in f.ns. (a)); Middle Cl 1795, 1833[1]; Mill Flg 1795, 1833[1], Mill Hill, the Mill Steigh 1762 (*v.* stîg, stîgr and cf. *Ulceby Mill supra*); Ulceby Moor 1779 (*ad moram de Ulesbi* l12 Dane, cf. *the Mooredyke* 1677 and *Ulseby Wast* 1708, *v.* môr[1], dîk, weste); New Cl 1826; North Fd 1826; Ogeamehole 1762; Old Garth 1826 (*v.* garðr); Owsard-hill (sic) 1762; Pellit-Pit 1762 (named from the family of Robert *Pellit* 1641 *LPR*); Phillipian (sic) 1826; Pitmire 1795, 1833[1] (*Pitmer* 1677, *v.* pytt; the second el. is uncertain); the Rawside 1762, Row Side 1795, Rowside 1833[1], the - 1833[2] (*Rawside* 1677), Row Cl 1826 (perhaps from vrá 'a nook, a corner' or a derived surn., cf. *in Le Wraa* 1327 *SR* (p), *the Rawhouse land* 1653 WillsPCC); Rooks-Hill 1762, Rooks Hill 1795, Rookshill 1833[1] (*v.* hrôc, hyll); Rumley Mere 1794, Rumley Marsh Cl 1826; The Rundle-Gate 1762, ye Rone!s 1766, Runnel Mdw 1794 (*the Randles* (sic) 1677, probably from rynel 'a small stream'); Sandhill-Mare (*v.* (ge)mære), Sandhill Steig (*sic*) 1762 (*v.* stîg, stîgr), (Far) Sandhills 1795, Sandhills 1833[1]; Segmare-Steigh 1762 (*v.* stîg, stîgr), Segmar 1833[1] (Segmar(e) may be 'the boundary land where sedge grows', *v.* secg[1], (ge)mære, with the first el. in a Scandinavianised form; the same first el. is apparently to be found in *segwelle* e13 (Ed1) *Newh, Seggewelle dayle* 1303 *HarlCh* (*v.* deill), *v.*

wella 'a spring'); Shag Foal (sic) 1826 (probably a piece of land thought to be haunted by hobgoblins, for *shag foal* 'a hobgoblin', *v.* NED 1, 6 s.v. *shag*); Shorne Dale 1762, Shorndale 1833[1]; Short tofts 1795, - Tofts 1833[1] (cf. Long Tofts *supra*); Sinnerigs 1794, Seven Ridges 1795, - Riggs 1794, 1833[1] ('seven strips in the open field', *v.* **seofon, hrycg, hryggr,** cf. Ten Ridges *infra*); Snisnips 1762, Snisnip 1833[1], -Flg 1795; Sod Cl (*Sod* here may have the sense 'turf, peat'); South Cl 1795; the ... South Fds 1758, 1766, 1786, 1797, 1816, - Fd 1762, 1826, 1833[1], Ulceby South Fd 1794 (*in australi campo de Vlseby* Hy3 *HarlCh*, 13 (Ed1) *Newh, in Suth campo* c.1240 (Ed1) *Newh, per campum australe de Ulseby* l13 *NCot, le Suth chaumpe de Vlseby* 1303 *HarlCh, Vlcebie South feild* 1587, cf. North Fd *supra*); Southam Cl 1826, 1833[1] (*Southam* 1677); Squire Headland 1762, 1795 (*v.* **hēafod-land**); Stephenson Cl 1826 (named from the *Stevenson* family, cf. Alice *Stevenson* 1587 *Inv*); Sting Ground, Meadow Sting Ground (*v. ac' medowe called Stange Grounde* 1587, *v.* **stong** 'a pole', also used as a measure of land); Stone Croft Hill 1795, 1833[1]; Stone pitts 1795, - Pits 1833[1] (cf. *Steyngrafgate* in f.ns. (b) *infra*); Stooks; Swilton Btm 1795, 1833[1], - Side 1795, 1833[1]; Sykes 1795, 1833[1] (*v.* **sík**); Ten Ridges 1795, - Riggs 1833[1] ('ten strips in the open field', *v.* **tēn, hrycg, hryggr,** such measures were used when the stated number of adjoining holdings were consolidated and, usually, enclosed, cf. Sinnerigs *supra*); Tepsall Stones 1794, 1833[1]; Thorn Dale 1795; Thorre More 1762, Tor Moor 1795, Tormoor 1833[1]; Thornton Intack 1762 (named from the neighbouring parish of Thornton Curtis, *v.* **inntak**); Three Acres Flatt; Tibb Cl 1826 (probably from the surn. *Tibb);* Town end Cl 1826; Waley -, Warley Furrs 1794 (*v.* **furh**); Walkers Headland 1795 (from the surn. *Walker*, cf. Robert *Walker* 1637 *BT*); the Watery furs 1762, Watery Furrows 1795, Wat'ry furrs 1833[1] (self-explanatory, and note *fur(r)s* for *furrows* as elsewhere in north L); Wells Cl 1794 (*v.* **wella**, cf. *ad fontem* 1327, 1332 *SR* both (p)); West Cl 1795, West-end Cl 1826; West Fd 1826; West Pit Dale 1795, - Pitt Dale 1833[1]; White Cros 1766, - Cross 1795, 1833[1] (cf. *terram Hugonis ad crucem* Hy3 *HarlCh*, *v.* **hwīt, cros**); Wildgoose Flg 1795, Wildgoose Hill 1833[1]; Wold Gare 1794 (*v.* **geiri** 'a triangular plot of land' and *Ulceby Wold supra*); Wooton Mear 1766 (*v.* **(ge)mǣre**); Wootton Hedge Flg 1795, Wootton Hedge 1833[1] (all named from the adjoining parish of Wootton).

(b) *Bechmar'* c.1240 (Ed1) *Newh* (perhaps 'the stream forming a boundary', from **bekkr** and **(ge)mǣre**, with -*ch* for -*ck*); *Beck* 1626 (*v.* **bekkr**); *brachenhau* l12 (e13) *NCot* ('the bracken-covered hill', *v.* **brakni, haugr**, probably a Scand. compound); *brademar'* e13 (Ed1) *Newh* (*v.* **brād, (ge)mǣre**); *Broad Fen* 1587, *Bradfyn* 1677 ('the broad fen', *v.* **brād, fenn**); *Bymergrene* 1677; *Cokeryngton fee* 1431 FA (*Johanna de cokeryngton* was assessed in Ulceby in 1332 *SR*);

Corelgraues 13 (Ed1) *Newh* (obscure); *the Cornefeild* 1677; *the Cowpaster, - Cowpastor of Ulceby* 1677; *the Eae or the kings comman dreane* 1677 (*Eae* is from ēa 'a stream, a watercourse', cf. L dial. *eau* used of fenland drainage channels); *Fox Cover* 1626; *Gepsihow* e13 (Ed1) *Newh* (*v.* **haugr**, the first el. being obscure); *Grenehil* e13 (Ed1) *Newh* (self-explanatory, *v.* **grēne**[1], **hyll**); *Hassocmar'* 13 (Ed1) *Newh* (*v.* **hassuc, (ge)mǣre**); *Henepcroft* a.1147 Dane ('the hemp croft', *v.* **hænep, croft**, often applied to a small enclosure near a dwelling-place); *lamb'mar'* e13 (Ed1) *Newh* (perhaps 'the boundary land where lambs are reared', *v.* **lamb** (gen.pl. *lambra*), **(ge)mǣre**); *Langefurlanges* 13 (Ed1) *Newh* (*v.* **lang, furlang**); *langhemar'* e13 (Ed1) *Newh* (*v.* **lang, (ge)mǣre**); *licthelau* 1143-47 (Ed1) *Newh*, a.1147 Dane (the form from *Newh* appears to be from a copy of the charter in Dane; more early spellings are needed); *Linkemare* 112 Dane (perhaps from **hlinc** 'a ridge, a bank', in a Scandinavianised form, and **(ge)mǣre**); *Luthestrete* c.1150 (Ed1) *Newh*, *magnam uiam que dicitur* - c.1150 Dane, *super Lude stratam*, *Ludhestrete* 112 (Ed1) *Newh* ('the road to Louth', *v.* **strǣt**); *ad la mar'* de *Vlseby* 13 (Ed1) *Newh*, *atte mare de ulseby* 1271-72 *Ass*, *Attemare* 1294 *ib*, 1327 *SR, atte Mare* 1332 *ib, Ate Mare* 1343 NI, all (p) (from **(ge)mǣre** 'a boundary, land on a boundary'); *le marefure Will'i fil' Walt'i* 13 (Ed1) *Newh* (note the early example of **marfur** 'a boundary furrow'); *Nelthinge, Nelthouse* 1589-91 *MinAcct, Neale house land* 1653 WillsPCC (presumably named from the *Neal(e)* family, cf. Geoffrey *Nele* 1332 *SR*, Richard *Neale* 1608 *BT*, with **þing** 'property, premises', ModE *house* and **land**); *a via de Neuh'* e13 (Ed1) *Newh* ('the road to Newsham in Brocklesby'); *Normanholm'* 1312 HarlCh (it is impossible to know whether this is 'the island of land, raised land in a low-lying area of the Norwegians' or 'of a family called *Norman'*); *Northiby* c.1240 (Ed1) *Newh* (p) ('north in the village', *v.* **norð, í, bȳ**, cf. *Suthiby infra*); *the Parke nowke by Newsam* 1677 (i.e. by Newsham in Brocklesby parish); *Plumer thinge* 1554 Pat (from the surn. *Plum(m)er* and **þing** 'property, premises'); *Punhage* 13 (Ed1) *Newh* (the second el. is probably **haga**[1] 'an enclosure', the first being obscure; it is very likely that this is the same name as *punthou-*, etc. in *punthoumarisdayl* in Immingham f.ns. (b) *supra*); *Sandholm* a.1147 Dane, (*v.* **sand, holmr**); *the sinke Hoale* 1677 (for *sinke v.* Sinks covert in South Killingholme *supra*); *atte Slade* 1327, 1332 *SR* both (p) (*v.* **slæd** 'a valley'); *a Crofte called Stevens cloase* 1587 (from the surn. *Steven(s)*); *Steyngrafgate* Hy3 HarlCh (the same name occurs in Croxton f.ns. (b) *supra* and no doubt refers to the same road); *Suthiby* c.1240 (Ed1) *Newh* (p) ('south in the village', *v.* **sūð, í, bȳ**, cf. *Northiby supra*); *Thomas dalle* 1587 (held by *Thomas Wells*); *þwerthemar'* e13 (Ed1) *Newh* (the reading of the first letter is probably correct and perhaps represents **þverr, þvert** 'athwart, lying across' and **(ge)mǣre** 'a boundary, land on or forming a boundary'); *Bercherie qest appellee West cote* e14 HarlCh (*v.* **west, cot**).

Wootton

WOOTTON
>   *Udetune, -tone, Vdetone* 1086 DB, *Wodeton'* 1202 Ass (p), *-tone*
>   1306 *HarlCh, Wodton'* 1386 Peace
>   *Witchona* (with *-tch-* for *-tth-*) 1095-1100 AC, *Withtun* (2x)
>   c.1155, c.1160 all Dane (p), *-ton'* 1218 Ass, *Witthun* (sic) R1
>   Dane (p)
>   *Wittuna* c.1115 LS, *-ton'* 1166 P (p), 1200 Cur, 1242-43 Fees,
>   *-ton* 1190 (1301) Dugd vi, 1550 Pat, 1653 *ParlSurv, -tonne*
>   1562-67 LNQ v, *Wytton* 1190 (1301) Dugd vi, 1291 Tax, 1535
>   VE iv, 1539 LP xiv, 1552 Pat, *-ton'* 1242-43 Fees
>   *Wituna* c.1115 LS, *-tona* 1148-52 LAAS vii (p), *-ton* Hy3 (1301)
>   Ch, 1653 *ParlSurv, Wyton'* 1242-43 Fees
>   *Uttuna* c.1115 LS, *Wttuna* c.1115 ib, *-tona* c.1150 TYR, *-tun*
>   1238-43 Fees, *-ton'* 1212 ib, 1254 ValNor, 1272, 1273 DC,
>   *- iuxta Thornton'* 1296 *Ass*
>   *Wutton'* 1200 Cur, 1209, 1210, 1211 P all (p), 1211 FF (p),
>   1212 P (p), 1213, 1214 Cur, 1218, 1219 Ass, 1223 Welles,
>   1242-43 Fees, 1296 RSu, *-ton* 1238 RRG, 1244 Ipm (p),
>   1255 Pat, *Wuton* Ipm
>   *Wotton(')* Hy2 LN (p), 1185 Templar, 1202 Ass, 1210, 1213
>   Cur, John Abbr, 1218 Ass (p), 1242 Pat, 1255-58 RA ix
>   (p), 1259 Pat, 1268 Ch, 1275 Pat, 1287 *Ass*, 1296 *FF*, 1301
>   Ch *et freq* to 1642 *Yarb, - iuxta Vlceby* 1329 *FF, - in
>   lyndesey* 1414 *AddCh, Wotton* "or" *Witton* 1597 SP iv,
>   *Wotton als Witton* 1612 *Yarb, - als Wytton* 1648 *MiscDon 251*
>   *Wooton als Witton* 1609, 1636, 1682, 1711 *Yarb, Wootton* 1674
>   *Terrier,* 1699 *Yarb,* 1724 *Terrier,* 1736, 1737, 1745 *Foster et
>   passim*

'The farmstead or village in a wood or a tract of woodland', *v.*
wudu, tūn. Forms in *Wi-, Wy-* are from early OE **widu,** while those
in *With-,* if they belong here, may well represent a replacement of
wudu by ON **viðr** 'a wood'. The village is situated on Boulder
Clay.

DUNKIRK FM, *Dunkirk ... F.^m* 1828 Bry. DUNKIRK WOOD,
Dunkirk Cover c.1823 *Yarb,* 1824 O, 1828 Bry, 1830 Gre (c.1823 says

"*needs Planting*"), "alluding to the Duke of York's unsuccessful siege
of Dunkirk in 1793, with overtones of remoteness and difficult
management" Field 68. It is one-half mile from the parish
boundary. GLEBE FM. GRAVEL PIT. HOWE HILL, *How Hill*
1824 O; the form is late, but Howe may be from **haugr** 'a mound,
a hill'. LITTLE FM. LONG CLOSE PLANTATION, also in
Croxton *supra*, where the early forms are given. LOW FURZE
PLANTATION (lost), 1824 O, 1830 Gre; it is mainly in Wootton,
but a part is in Thornton Curtis. THE PARK, perhaps cf. *de
parcis* 1332 SR (p), *v.* **park**. RACE LANE, 1824 O, 1828 Bry, 1836
Yarb, *the race road* 1768, *the Race Road* 1774, 1804 all *ib*, cf. *Race
Lane Plat* 1817 *ib*, - *Platt* 1827 *Brad*, - *Close* 1824 *Yarb*, the same
lane as in Thornton Curtis; the etymology of *race* is uncertain.
WOOTTON DALE, 1824 O, 1828 Bry, 1830 Gre, *Wotton Dale*
1635 (c.1900) *LindDep* 78, *The Dale Farm* c.1823 *Yarb*, cf. *Dale
Bottom* 1810, 1817 *ib*, 1827 *Brad*, from the valley in which the farm
is situated, *v.* **dæl, dalr**. WOOTTON GRANGE is *New F.^{m}* 1828
Bry, but note "the Rectory and Grange of *Wotton* alias *Wytton*"
1572 Pat. The document concerns former Thornton College land in
Wootton. WOOTTON GROVE. WOOTTON HALL, 1824 O,
1828 Bry, 1830 Gre, cf. *The Hall Close* c.1820 *FLMisc*.
WOOTTON LAWN. WOOTTON LODGE. WOOTTON
PLANTATION, 1824 O, 1828 Bry, 1830 Gre, cf. *Plantation Close*
a1805 *FLMisc*. WOOTTON WINDMILL, *Wind Mill*, *Mill Hill* 1723
Yarb, *Windmill* 1772 *ib*, *Wootton Mill* 1824 O. WOOTTON WOLD
is *Wold Fm*. 1824 O, - *Farm* 1828 Bry, cf. *ye Wold* 1702, - *Woold*
1719, *Wold* 1760, 1810, c.1823, *the wold of Wootton* 1768, - *Wold of
Wootton* 1774, 1826, 1836 all *Yarb*, self-explanatory, *v.* **wald**.

Field-Names

Principal forms in (a) are a1805 *FLMisc* (Plan); forms dated 1609, 1612, 1636,
1640, 1642, 1670, 1682, 1683, 1696, 1702, 1719, 1720, 1721, 1726, 1728, 1733, 1760,
1768, 1774, 1792, 1804, 1810, 1817, c.1823, 1824, 1833, and 1842 are *Yarb*; 1601,
1606, 1662, 1697 (Thornton Curtis), 1707, 1709 (Thornton Curtis), 1718, 1724
(Thornton Curtis), 1730, 1745 (Thornton Curtis), 1762, 1822, and 1825 are *Terrier*,
1827 are *Brad*.

(a) Barn plot 1810, - Plat 1817, 1827, The - 1824 (*v.* **plot, plat**^{2} 'a small piece of ground', as elsewhere in this parish); Barton-lane Plat (*v.* plat^2 and Barton upon Humber *supra*); First -, Second Brats 1833 (*v.* brot 'small piece (of land)'); Brick Kiln Plot 1792, 1810, Brickiln Cl 1833 (cf. *the Kilnehouse Yard* 1682); Far -, Nr Bride gate, Bride gate Lane plat (*v.* plat^2); Brigg Road Platt 1827 ('the road to Glanford Brigg', with plat^2); Short Bulls; Burnham Gate platt 1817, - Plat 1824 ('the road to Burnham', with plat^2); Caistor-lane Plat ('a lane to Caistor', with plat^2); Captain's garth 1768, Captains Garth 1774, Captain - 1810, 1824 (*v.* garðr 'an enclosure, a small plot of ground', as elsewhere in this parish); Cinquefoin Plat (*v.* sainfoin (of which *cinquefoin* is a common variant), the leguminous plant, *Onobrychis viciifolia*, though the confusion with *cinquefoil, Potentilla* spp, may be significant, *v.* further Field 190. The name is common in north L. The second el. is plat^2 'a small plot', as elsewhere in this parish); Clay Pits (on Thornton boundary); Clay Lane; the Cornfield 1760 (*Corn feild* 1702, *ye Corn field* 1719, *ye Cornfield* 1733); Cottagers Garth 1810 (*v.* garðr); Cowpasture or Intack (*v.* inntak); Dale Btm 1810, 1817, - Plat 1824; Dam (Hill) a1805, Dam Cl 1810, 1824, 1827 (*atte Dam* 1327 *SR*, 1361 *Cor* both (p), from ME damme 'a body of water, e.g. a pond' (ON dammr)); the Plan, a1805, shows that this is the name of the pool in the centre of the village); East Bank (part of the lane leading east from the village towards the boundary with Ulceby); East-end Plat 1824 (cf. *the East end* 1648 *MiscDon 251, ye Eastend Close* 1662, *v.* east, ende[1]); East Fds; the Eastlanes 1768, the East Lane, the East Lanes of Wootton 1774, East Lane Clo (sic) a1805, the East Lane Paddock 1827 (cf. *ye East lanes of Wooton* 1702; the pl. form Lanes suggests that this may be the pl. of ME leyne, lain 'a layer, a tract of arable land', but the Plan, a1805, shows the close to be a small piece of land of less than two acres, lying immediately south of East Bank, itself the name of part of the road leading east of the village towards the Ulceby boundary); Eighteen Acres 1833; Fallow-heads (*v.* fealu, hēafod); Feeding Cl 1833; Fifty Acres 1833; Foot Road Fd; Forty Acres 1833; Forty Eight Acres 1833; Forty five Acres 1833; Fox Cover 1810, 1833, Fox Cover Plat a1805, 1824, Foxcover - 1817, First -, Second Fox Cover Cl 1822 (*v.* cover(t)); Great Cl (*the Great close* 1721); Home Cl a1805, 1810, 1827, 1833, Home Plat 1817, 1824; Homestead Cl 1792, 1810, Horse Cl 1833; King Hedge (on the Thornton boundary); Michael Hills; Middle Plat 1824 (*v.* plat^2); Mill Hill Plot 1792, - hill Plot 1810 (cf. Wootton Windmill *supra*); Narrow Cl a1805, - Pce 1810, 1824; First -, Second Noon Laves 1833 (possibly from the surn. *Noon*); North Crofts (*v.* croft); the North fd 1760, Wootton North Fd 1825 (*north field* 1604 LNQ x, *the north feildes* 1609, *the North Field* 1720, - *north field* 1726, *Wootton north field* 1697, - *Northfield* 1709, - *North Field* 1724, 1745, *ye Northfeild hedge* 1662, one of the open fields of Wootton, cf. the South fd *infra*); Pear-tree Garth 1762 (*pearetree garth* 1606, *Peartree-garth* 1707, *Pear tree Garth* 1709,

Pear-tree-garth 1718, *Peartree Garth* 1724, *Peartree-garth* 1730, *Pear-tree Garth* 1745, *v.* **pertre, garðr**); *Pelham Plat* 1833 (probably named from the family of William *Pelham* of *Brocklesby* (later Earls of Yarborough) 1608 *Yarb*); Peter Plat; Plantation Cl; Pond 1824; Rose Cl 1810, 1824; Sand Pit Plat 1817, 1824 (*v.* **plat²**); Gt -, Lt Seed Pce 1792, 1810; Far -, Nr Smallers; the South fd 1774 (*south field* 1604 LNQ x, *the south feildes* 1609, *the South Field* 1720, one of the open fields of the parish, cf. the North fd *supra*); South lane end 1768, - Lane End 1774; the South Wold 1774 (cf. Wootton Wold *supra*); Stackyard; Stone Pit, Stone-pit Plat; Stripe 1810 (*v.* **strīp** 'a narrow piece of land'); the Stubble fd 1760; Thirty Acres 1833; Thorntree Plat a1805, Thorne Tree - 1817, Thorn Tree - 1824 (a thorn-tree is drawn in the field on the Plan a1805); Timothy Plat (*v.* **timothy** 'meadow cat's tail grass', **plat²** and cf. Timothy Cl in Bigby f.ns. (a)); Ulceby Lane 1822 ('the lane to Ulceby (the neighbouring parish)'); the Warren 1810, 1827, Warren 1817, Old - c.1823, the Conies Warren House 1792 (*v.* **coni, wareine**); Warrick Tenᵗ (sic) 1810, Warricks Cl 1833 (named from the family of Richard *Warwick* 1702 *Yarb*); West-end Plat 1824 (cf. *The West End farme* 1682, *the west end Close* 1721, from **west, ende¹**, with **plat²** and **clos(e)**, cf. East-end Plat *supra*); First -, Middle -, Second Wold 1833, the South Wold 1774, the West Wold 1804, 1842, the Wold Lane 1822 (from Wootton Wold *supra*); Wood Cl 1768, 1774, 1810, 1824, - Pasture 1792 (*the Great -, the Little Wood* 1682); Wootton Plat a.1805, 1827, 1833, - plot 1810 (*v.* **plat²**).

(b) *Barnards Farme* 1682 (named from the *Barnard* family, frequently mentioned in local documents, cf. Roger *Barnard* 1609); *Berryes Farme* 1682 (named from the *Berrie* family, cf. William *Berrie* 1633 *BT*); *Burke Close* 1682 (from the surn. *Burke*); *the burying Garth* 1732 *LindDep* 67 (self-explanatory, *v.* **garðr**); *the coman* (sic) 1726; *Doughties Farme* 1612, 1682 (from the *Doughtie* family, frequently mentioned in local documents, cf. Richard *Doughtie* 1612); *the East close* 1682; yᵉ *feild* 1702; *Attehill'* 1287 *Ass* (p), *de monte* 1332 *SR* (p) (cf. *Hill Garth* 1682, *v.* **hyll, garðr**); *Locker Close* 1682 (probably from the surn. *Locker*); *the marfers* 1726 (*v.* **marfur** 'a boundary furrow' in the pl.); *Markhames Farme* 1612 (named from the family of Richard *Markham* 1612); *Old Garth Farm* 1682 (*v.* **garðr**); *a close cauled the personage* 1606; *lez Shepegates* 1589-91 *MinAcct*, *de duabus les Sheepgates* 1605-7 ib (*v.* **shep-gate** 'pasturage for sheep, and for a 13th century example *v.* Nettleton f.ns. (a) *supra*); *Smyths Farme* 1682 (the home of the *Smith* or *Smyth* family, frequently mentioned in local documents, cf. W. *Smyth* 1587 *BT*, John *Smith* 1713 *Yarb*); *the Southen Farme* (sic) 1636, *Southend Ferme* (sic) 1640, *the South end Farme* 1642 (cf. East-end Plat, West-end Plat, in (a) *supra*); *Ulsbie Close* 1682 (from the adjoining parish of Ulceby); *the Wash Garth* 1682 (*v.* **garðr**); *Wentford alias Wentworth House or Toft* 1682 (presumably

from a family name or names); *the West streete* 1682; *campum de Wtton'* eHy3
(m13) *NCot, in Campis de Wotton'* 1589-91, *- de Wotton* 1605-7 both *MinAcct, the
feilds of Wootton* 1607, *Wootton Feild* 1670, *Wootton fyeld'* 1626 *Terrier* (Thornton
Curtis), *Wooton feilde* 1638 *ib, Wotton feild* 1683, *Witton Feild* 1696, *Wittonfield*
1728, y^e *feild* 1702 (self-explanatory, *v.* **feld**).

Worlaby

WORLABY
>   *Uluricebi, Vluricebi* 1086 DB
>   *Wirichebi* 1086 DB
>   *Wulfrichesbi* c.1115 LS, *Wolurikesbi* 1202 Ass, *Wulurikesbi* 1209
>   P
>   *Wlfriohebi* (sic) c.1115 LS
>   *Wlfrechebi* c.1115 LS
>   *Wulurikebi* 1202, 1219 Ass
>   *Wulfrikeby* Hy2 (l13) *Stix,* 1209-35 LAHW, 1231 FF, *Wlfrikeby*
>   1229 Cur (p), 1268 Ch, *vulfrikeby* 1301 FF, *Wulfrichebi* Hy3
>   *HarlCh*
>   *Wlfricbie* 1148-52 LAAS vii, c.1150 *TYR, -bi* 1212 Fees, *-bia*
>   1212 ib
>   *Wlrikeby* eHy2 (e13) *NCot,* 1254 ValNor, 1271 RRGr, 1289
>   HMCRutl, *Wlrykeby* 1291 Tax, *Wolrikeb'* 1185 Templar, *-by*
>   1271-72 *Ass,* 1298 Ass, 1328 Banco, 1335 Pat, *Wolrykeby*
>   1271 *Ass, Wolrickeby* 1287 *ib, Wulrikeby* 1226 FF, 1242-43
>   Fees, 1282 *FF,* 1289 Cl, 1338 Pat, *Wolrekeby* 1291 Tax
>   *Wolrickby* 1314 Ipm, *Wolricby* (*iuxta Bondeby*) 1314 *FF,* 1343
>   NI, 1346 FA, 1373, 1375, 1376 Peace, *Wolrikby* 1315 Ipm,
>   1316 FA, 1332 *SR,* 1354 *Cor,* ("by Elsham") 1360 Cl, 1362
>   Pat, 1387 Peace (p), *Wolrykby* 1327 *SR,* 1431 FA, 1534 *AS,*
>   *Wolrichby* 1315 Cl, *Wolrekby* 1428 FA, 1534 *AS, Wlricbi*
>   1238-43 Fees, 1289 Ipm
>   *Wolrigby* 1303 FA, 1335 Pat, 1346 FA, 1354 Fine, 1412 *AS,*
>   1428 FA, 1448 *Ass*
>   *Wolriby* 1354 Orig, 1354 Ipm, 1373, 1381 Peace, *Wolryby* 1328
>   FA, *Wulryby* 1338 Misc, *Wlreby* 1402 FA
>   *Worleby* 1395 Peace, (*iuxta Elsham*) 1420-21 *AD,* 1449-53 ECP
>   xii, ("by Saxby") 1460, 1461 Pat, 1494 Ipm, 1526 Sub *et
>   passim* to 1664 *Terrier, -bie* 1553 Pat, 1562-67 LNQ v, *-bee*

1695 Pryme, *Worleyby* 1538-39 Dugd vi, *Worlyby* 1542 *AS*,
Wurleby 1502 Ipm
Worlaby 1478 *FF*, (*al's Worletby*) 1636 *AS*, 1668, 1674, 1678
Terrier et passim, (*alias Worletby*) 1717 *LCC*, (*otherwise
Worletby*) 1764 *ib*, -*bie* 1552 Pat, -*bey* 1574 *AS*, -*bye* 1576
Saxton, 1610 Speed, 1638 *Monson*, 1724, 1730 *Terrier*,
Worelaby 1535 VE iv
Werliby 1402 Cl
Wirlaby 1491 Ipm, *Wirleby* 1519 DV i
Worletby 1546, 1577, 1619 *AS*, 1638, 1690, 1697, 1703 *Terrier*,
-*bye* 1539 LP xiv, (*alias Worlebye*) 1594 *AS*, -*bie* 1573 *ib*,
1579, 1601, 1606, 1612 *Terrier*, *Worlettbie* c.1580 *AS*
Wollerby 1402 *AS*

'Wulfrīc's farmstead or village', from the OE pers.n. *Wulfrīc*
and Scand. **by**, identical with Worlaby in Hill Wapentake LSR. The
two DB spellings in *Ulu-* presumably are Scandinavianised forms. It
is noteworthy that only a bare handful of spellings with the OE
gen.sg. -*es* has so far been noted for this name. On the other hand
forms in medial -*e*- are very common from DB to the late 13th
century and probably represent the ODan gen.sg. in -*a*, as suggested
by Ekwall, IPN 62, rather than being a svarabhaktic vowel between
-*c*- and -*b*-. It is sometimes described as near Bonby, Elsham and
Saxby All Saints.

CASTLE FM. CLARKSON'S CARR FM, named from the
Clarkson family, cf. *John Clarkson, farmer* 1937 Kelly. CLOUGH
PLANTATION. THE GRANGE. GRAVEL PIT. HILLSIDE
PLANTATION, cf. *Hill Side Close* 1832 *Yarb*. HOSPITAL (lost),
1830 Gre, cf. *An hospitall erected in the towne of Worlaby for the
habitacons of four poor widows* 1717 *LCC*. LADYSMITH
COTTAGE, no doubt commemorating the siege of Ladysmith
during the Boer War. MIDDLEGATE LANE, *Middle Gate* 1843
TA, 1860 *FLMisc*, on which *v.* this name in Bigby *supra*. THE
PARK, 1717 *LCC*, *Park* 1843 *TA*, 1860 *FLMisc*, cf. *Old Park* 1860
ib. SOUTH WOLD FM, *South Wold* 1832 *Yarb*, *v*. **wald**.
TURNPIKE TOP FM, cf. *Turnpike* 1843 *TA*, with a farm marked
on the map and an adjacent field called *Barn Close*. VICARAGE,
cf. *the vicarage plat* 1664, *Vic: Carrs* 1707, *Vicarage Carrs* 1724, 1745,

the Vicarage Carr 1730, *Vicars Carrs* 1748, (*the*) *Vicarage Carr* 1808, 1822, *v.* plat² 'a plot of ground', kjarr 'a marsh, marshy ground', both found elsewhere in this parish. WATER INGS (lost), 1824 O, 1843 *TA*, 1860 *FLMisc*, cf. *Worlaby Ings* and Worlaby New Ings *infra.* WORLABY CARRS, *the Carre of worlibe* 1537 *Nelthorpe, the Carr* c.1580 *AS, the common car(r)* 1606, 1612, *Worleby Car* 1664, *the Carres of Worletby* 1671, *yᵉ Carres of Worlaby* 1674, *Worlaby Carres* 1679, *the Carres* 1690 all *Terrier, the Carrs of Worlaby* 1832 *Yarb, v.* kjarr, and note that in *TA* many fields there are simply called *Carr.* WORLABY CAUSEWAY, *yᵉ Carre lane called yᵉ Causeway* 1674, *yᵉ common Causy through yᵉ Carres* 1679, *the Carre Causey* 1690, *yᵉ Cawsy* 1697, *the Causey* 1707 all *Terrier, Causeway* 1875 *Holywell,* self-explanatory, *v.* caucie, and cf. *Carr Lane* 1860 *FLMisc.* WORLABY FOX COVERT. WORLABY HALL, 1717 *LCC,* 1860 *FLMisc* and note "The old Hall at Worlaby was pulled down in or about 1807" LNQ xviii. WORLABY INGS (lost), 1696, 1728 *Yarb,* 1830 Gre, *Worlebye Ynges* 1546 LP xxi, *Warlebye Inges* 1547 Pat, *Worlebyeinges* 1550 ib, *the Inges* c.1580 *AS, Worlaby Inges* 1670 *Yarb, Worleby Ings* 1683 *ib, the inges* 1791 LNQ xviii, 'the meadows, the pastures', *v.* eng in the pl, as elsewhere in this parish. WORLABY MILL (lost), 1824 O, 1830 Gre, *the Wind Mill* 1717 *LCC, a Wind mill* 1730 *Terrier, Mill* 1828 Bry, cf. *Mill Flatt* 1843 *TA,* the position of the mill being shown on *TAMap.* WORLABY NEW INGS, 1824 O, 1830 Gre, *New Engs* m16 *Cragg, the newe ynges* 1574 *AS, the new Inges* c.1580 *ib, New Ingge* 1635 (c.1900) *LindDep* 78, *the new Ings* 1717 *LCC, New Inges* 1767 *Stubbs, New Ings* 1843 *TA,* 1860 *FLMisc,* cf. *Worlaby Ings supra.* WORLABY PLAINS (lost), 1824 O, being the name of the low-lying land west of the New River Ancholme and the parish boundary, each of the fields there being called *Carr* in *TA.*

Field-Names

Forms in (a) dated 1843 are *TA,* transcribed by Mr Rex C. Russell; spellings dated 1860 are *FLMisc;* those found in both documents are marked with an asterisk. Forms dated 1553¹, 1573, 1577, c.1580, and 1631 are *AS;* 1553² are Pat; 1579, 1601, 1606, 1612, 1638, 1664, 1671, 1674, 1679, 1690, 1707, 1724, 1730, 1745², 1748, 1808 and 1822 are *Terrier;* 1717, 1745¹, and 1764 are *LCC;* 1746, 1762, 1768, and 1791 are LNQ xviii.

YARBOROUGH WAPENTAKE   305

(a) Armstrong Carr* (named from *Armstrong* family, cf. *Mr William Armstrong* 1783 *LTR*, and **kjarr**; note that all the f.ns. in - *Carr* are individual fields in Worlaby Carrs *supra*); the Bank House 1764 (alluding to the bank of R. Ancholme, cf. *Anckholme Bank* 1717); Barn Cl* (*v.* Turnpike Top Fm *supra*); Baynes Carr* (from the surn. *Baynes* and **kjarr**); Brick Garth 1860 (*v.* **garðr** 'an enclosure', as elsewhere in the parish); Brick Kiln Cl* (*Brick kiln Close* 1745^1); Bull Hill*; Butcher Cl, Butchers Cls 1843, Butcher's Cl, Butcher Cl Plantn 1860 (from the occupational name or surn. *Butcher*); High - 1843, Low Butts Cl* (*v.* **butte**); First -, Second Carr Cl 1843; Chalk Pit 1860; ye Church Lane 1808, the - 1822 (*the church lane* 1579, 1612, *y^e* - 1679, *the Church Lane* 1601, 1730, 1745^2, 1748, - *lane* 1606, *church lane* 1690, *a comon lane to ye Church* 1707, *ye North Church Lane* 1671, 1674, cf. *ad ecclesiam* 1327, *atte Kirk'* 1332 *SR*, *atte Kirk* 1354 *Cor* all (p), note that the early references are from ON **kirkja**); Cliff adjoining Bonby 1843, - Bondby 1860, - South of Wootton Road 1843, First -, Middle Cliff 1843 (*v.* **clif**); Close*; Close adjoining Lincoln Rd 1843 (i.e. the modern A15); Cottager's Carr 1860, - Pasture 1843 (divided into small strips, lettered *a* to *i*) (*v.* **cottager, kjarr, pasture**); Cow Platt* (*v.* **plat**^2 'a piece of ground', as elsewhere in this parish); Cowpers Carr* (from the surn. *Cowper* and **kjarr**); Crockendale Cl* (*Crockerdale Close* (sic) 1717); Cross Carr* (*v.* **cros, kjarr**); Lt Dale* (*v.* **deill**); Dinsdale Carr* (named from the *Dinsdale* family, cf. John *Dinsdel* 1675 *BT*, Joseph *Dingsdale* 1764, with **kjarr**); Eight Acres*; Elsham Cl & Corn Cl, Elsham Side Cls 1843, - Cl 1860 (from the adjoining parish of Elsham); Falding -, Faulding Carr 1791, Folding Carr* (probably from the *Fa(u)lding* family, cf. John *Faulding* 1717, John *Falding* 1745^1, and **kjarr**); Fifteen Acres & 17 Acres (sic) 1843, - and Seventeen Acres 1860; First Platt (*v.* **plat**^2); Flagg Carr* (*v.* ME **flegge, flagge** 'iris' or 'rush', **kjarr**); (Nr) Flotters*, Flotters Cl 1843 (the last-named is separate from Flotters and Near Flotters, and abuts on the Causeway) (*Flotters* c.1580; the fields so named are in the Carrs, where there are a number of drainage channels, so *flotter(s)* may be from OE **flodor* (ME **flod(d)er*), discussed by Kristensson, SMETT 27, s.n. Flodre, for which he suggests a meaning 'channel', the word itself surviving as dial. *flother* 'swamp', cf. Flathers Meadow PN Wa 368. The development of *-d-* to *-t-* would not be unusual, cf. e.g. Cotterstock PN Nth 200-1. A meaning 'the channels' or 'the swamps' would have been topographically appropriate); Fore Platt* (*v.* **fore** 'in front of', **plat**^2); Far 4 Acres; 14 Acres; Frankish Carr* (presumably from the surn. *Frankish* and **kjarr**); Garth 1860 (*v.* **garðr** 'an enclosure', as elsewhere in this parish); Great Carr* (*v.* **kjarr**); Hemp Garth, Hemplands 1860 (cf. *Francis Taylers hempgarth* 1679, 'hemp plot(s)', small pieces of land, often adjacent to dwelling places, *v.* **hemp-garth, hemp-land**); Far -, Fore -, Middle Hill Cl 1843, (Far) Hill Cl, Fore Hill Garth 1860 (*v.* **hyll, garðr**); Intack*, Far -, Middle

Intack*, East of Intack Lane 1843, Intack Lane 1860 (*v.* inntak); Jacklins Cl* (1717, named from the *Jacklin* family, cf. Thomas *Jackling* 1614 *BT*); (Far -, Nr) Kings Carr* (probably from the surn. *King*, with kjarr); Lath Carr*, - Cl* (*v.* hlaða 'a barn', kjarr); Lawrence Cl*; Gt -, Lt Lawyer Cl*; Ling Cl* (*v.* lyng); Long Garth 1860 (*v.* garðr); Low Carr* (*v.* kjarr); Low Garth* (*v.* garðr); Manis Cls 1843, - Cl 1860 (probably from a surn.); Markham Cl 1860 (named from the *Markham* family, cf. Edward *Markham* 1687 *BT*, Richard *Markham* 1717); Marshall Carr* (named from the *Marshall* family, cf. Robert *Marshall* 1717, with kjarr); Mason Carr* (named from the *Mason* family, cf. Richard *Mason* 1621 *BT*, Thomas *Mason* 1745[1]); May Cl*; Middle Dale 1860 (*v.* deill); ye new intack next to Bonby field 1762 (*v.* inntak), East of Middlegate Addjoining Bonby (sic) 1843 (*v.* Middlegate Lane *supra*); North Cl* (2x), North close E. of Middle Dale (*sic*) (adjoins North Close, across Middlegate Lane); Ogleby Cl* (named from the *Ogleby* family, cf. Robert *Ogleby* 1717); Orchard; (Gt) Parkinson Carr 1843, Gt Parkinson's - 1860 (named from the *Parkinson* family, cf. Thomas *Parkinson* 1702 *BT*, William *Parkinson* 1717); Parlington Garth (sic) 1860 (*Portington Garth* 1717, named from the *Portington* family, cf. Robert *Portington* 1615 *BT*, Thomas *Partington* 1617 *Inv*, Thomas *Portington* 1647 *ib*, with garðr); Pasture Carr* (*v.* pasture, kjarr); Pingle 1860 (*v.* pingel 'a small enclosure'); Plump Platt* (*v.* platt[2]); Quaker Carr* (*v.* kjarr); Richardsons Grd 1843, Richardson's - 1860 (named from the *Richardson* family, cf. William *Richardson* m16 *Cragg*); Far -, Nr Rise Cl* (*v.* hris 'brushwood'); Rundall Platt* (*v.* plat[2]; Rundall is probably from rynel 'a small stream'); Sandhill Plantn 1860; Far -, Nr 16 Acres*; South Cl* (cf. North Cl *supra*); Sutton Carr* (named from the *Sutton* family, cf. John *Sutton* 1702 *BT* and kjarr); (Nr) 10 Acres 1843, Near Ten - 1860; Thirteen Acres*; Thirty Seven Acres 1843, Thirty-seven - 1860; Three Gaits 1860 (*v.* gata); Todds Cl 1843, Todd's Cl 1860 (named from the *Todd* family, cf. Thomas *Todd* 1738 *BT*, 1745[1]); Far-First Water Grds*; Wilkin Carr* (named from the *Wilkin* family, cf. Richard *Wilkin* 1616 *BT*, Richard *Wilkin* 1745[1] and kjarr); Far -, First -, Middle Wold*, Far Wold Cl, East of First Wold adjoining Turnpike (*v.* wald and cf. South Wold Fm *supra*); Worlaby Dale in Carr 1843, - or Carr 1860 (*v.* deill, kjarr).

(b) *bleaching garth* 1671 (*v.* garðr); *Both dale* 1577 (held by Thomas *Booth* 1577, *v.* deill); *Burneham dale* 1640 *Monson* (named from Burnham (in Thornton Curtis) and deill 'a share of land'); *the Comon meadowe* c.1580; *the farther Carr* c.1580; *forby land* m16 *Cragg*, *Forby Lande* 1553[1], *Forbie land* 1553[2] ('land cultivated separately from the common field in which it lay', *v.* forbyland and *Forby Lande* in Elsham f.ns. (b), while *Forbyland* 1502 is recorded in PN YW 4 250 without comment; *forbyland* is noted in NED s.v., with only two quotations, where the meaning is given as '?extra land', relating the word to the prep. *forby* 'hard by, near' and *land*. The term is discussed by Adams 87, s.v. *forland*, who defines it as 'An odd piece of land that did not fit into the normal arrangement and was taken out for rent, but the title was different. These pieces of land usually became pasture closes and were outside the area in the township subject to a strictly regulated agrarian regime'); *Frees Farme alias Frows Farme* 1717 (occupied by *the heirs of William Frow* 1717); *Frith Carr* c.1580; *the Furth Carr* c.1580, *the furth carr* 1601, *the firth* - 1606, 1612, *Furth-carr-part* 1638 (*v.* fyrhð 'a wood, woodland', **kjarr**, with **part**, occasionally used in the area apparently with the sense 'portion of land, allotment'); *del Grene* 1327 *SR*, "- of" *Wolrikeby, atte Grene* 1328 Banco all (p) (*v.* **grene**^{2}); *Holow* 1289 HMCRutl (*v.* **hol**^{1}); *horsecarr* c.1580, *horse Carre* 1671 (*v.* **kjarr**); *Jays Farme* 1717 (probably from the surn. *Jay*); *the Low Farme* 1717; *the Mannor howse of Worlaby als Worletby* 1631; *the north feilde* 1573, *the north feild* c.1580 (one of the open fields of Worlaby, cf. "the south field" *infra*); *Pilegate* 1289 HMCRutl (perhaps, as Dr John Insley suggests, from ON **pill** 'a willow' (rather than OE **pil** 'a spike, a stake') and **gata**); *Reynold Platt* 1717 (*v.* **platt**^{2}); *South Carr* c.1580, - *Carre* 1635 (c.1900) *LindDep* 78 (no doubt part of Worlaby Carrs *supra*); "the south field" 1289 HMCRutl, *the southe fielde* 1573, *the South field* c.1580 (one of the open fields of Worlaby, cf. *the north feilde supra*); *Southyby* 1327, *Southiby* 1332 *SR* both (p) ('south in the village', *v.* **suð, i, by**); *Taggetoft* 1289 HMCRutl (perhaps from **tagga** 'a young sheep' and **toft**); *Warlett close* 1717, *Warlots* 1745^1 (*v.* **warlot**, discussed s.n. Waterhill Wood in Brocklesby *supra*); *Atte Welle* 1327, *atte Well'* 1332 *SR* both (p) (*v.* **wella**); *Wotton dale* 1640 Monson (named from Wootton, an adjoining parish, and **deill** 'a share of land'); *in campis de Worleby iuxta Elsham* 1420 *AD*, *Worlebye fieldes* 1576 *BPD*, *Worletby field* 1638 (Elsham) (*v.* **feld**).

Wrawby

WRAWBY

   Waragebi (2x) 1086 DB

   Wragebi c.1115 LS, *-by* 1276 RH

   Wragheby c.1200 HMCRutl, 1234 Welles, 1289 *Foster*, 1316 FA, 1327 *SR*

   Wrahebi 1212 Fees, *-by* 1298 Ass

   Wrakebi 1238-43 Fees

   Wraghby 1328 Banco, 1330 Ipm, 1330 Cl, 1343 NI, 1372 Orig, 1382 Cl, 1386 Peace

   Wraughby 1332 *SR*, 1371, 1410, 1441 Pat

Wraby 1242-43 Fees, 1317 Ch, 1494, 1502 Ipm, 1554 InstBen,
  -bie 1557 ib, *-bye* 1576 LNQ iii
Wraweby 1276 Ipm, 1281 QW, (*iuxta Glaunfordbrigg*') 1320 *FF*,
  1328 Banco, 1328 Ch, 1368 Pat, 1379 Fine, 1395 Pat, 1409
  FF, 1438 Cl
Wrauby 1301 Ch, 1303 FA, 1306 Cl, 1321 Misc, 1328 Ch, 1328
  Banco, 1345 *FF*, 1345 Pap, 1354 Ipm *et freq* to 1577 *Terrier*,
  -bye 1576 Saxton, 1610 Speed
Wrawby 1375 Works, 1405 Pat, 1428 FA, 1432 Fine, 1462 Pat
  et passim, (*als Raby*) 1655 *Elw*, *-be* 1639 LP xiv, *-bie*
  1562-67 LNQ v, 1576 LER, 1606 *Terrier*, (*alias Wrabie*)
  1634 *Elw*
Wrowby 1428 FA
Wragby 1242-43 Fees

The best discussion of Wrawby is by Kristian Hald, *Personnavne
i Danmark 1. Oldentiden*, Copenhagen 1971, p. 68, who suggests that
this is 'Wraghi's farmstead or village', from the ODan pers.n.
Wraghi and *by*, as Dr John Insley points out. The development to
[au] is normal in ME, *v.* Jordan, paragraph 186. The run of
spellings is quite different for Wragby LSR, the first el. of which is
the Scand. pers.n. *Wraggi*. There is no need to consider as an
alternative an appellative *vragi 'a bollard', on which *v.* SSNEM 79,
and there seems little doubt that the etymologies of Wrawby and
Wragby are indeed different.

THE BACKS, situated on the boundary with Elsham. BISHOPS
BARN (lost), *Bishops B.^{n}* 1828 Bry; it is shown on the 6" map, but
is not named. BOTANY BAY, no doubt a nickname of remoteness
being close to the boundary with Elsham. BRICKYARD LANE.
CARR DRAIN, 1805 *EnclA*, 1824 O, 1828 Bry, 1830 Gre, leading
to Wrawby Carrs *infra*. CATCHWATER DRAIN, 1824 O, 1830
Gre, *Catch Water Drain* 1805 *EnclA*, self-explanatory. COMMON
LANE (lost), 1828 Bry. GALLOWS FM is *Fox Hall* 1828 Bry,
perhaps from the *Fox* family, cf. James *Fox*, Mrs *Fox* 1767 *Stubbs*,
the modern form being named from Melton Gallows in Melton
Ross *supra*. GREAT MOOR, cf. Little Moor *infra*, both being part
of Wrawby Moor. LITTLE CARR DRAIN, 1824 O, 1828 Bry, -
Car Drain 1805 *EnclA*, cf. *little Carr feild* 1662, 1664, - *feildes* 1668,

- *feilde* 1671, *Littlecarr Field* 1690, 1693, 1697, *Little carr Field* 1703, *Litlecarfield* 1724, *Little Carfield* 1762 all *Terrier, Little Car* 1795 *LLHS, v.* **kjarr** and cf. Wrawby Carrs *infra.* LITTLE MOOR is *Moor Cover* 1828 Bry, cf. Great Moor *supra.* LITTLE MOOR DRAIN forms part of the boundary with Elsham. LOW MOOR DRAIN, 1805 *Encl4,* 1824 O, 1828 Bry, cf. *Low Moor* 1832 *Yarb,* on the boundary with Elsham. MELTON ROAD FM, self-explanatory. MILL LANE, cf. *Mill Field* 1795 *LLHS.* MOOR LANE, *Moor Road* 1805 *Encl4,* 1828 Bry, cf. *Moor F.* 1824 O, - *Ho* 1828 Bry, named from Wrawby Moor *infra.* PELHAM BRIDGE (lost), 1828 Bry, named from the *Pelham* family, Earls of Yarborough, which owned land in the parish, e.g. *C.A. Pelham, Esq,* 1767 *Stubbs* and *v. Yarb* 5/1/66, 1832. REDHOLME. SPRINGFIELD, named from a spring there. STAR CARR LANE, *Star Car Road* 1805 *Encl4,* cf. *starre carre* 1577, *one care called storcare* 1601, *Starre carre* 1638 all *Terrier,* - *Carre* 1635 (c.1900) *LindDep 78, a Carr(e) called Starr Carr* 1662, 1664, 1668, 1671, *Starr carr* 1679, 1693, *Star Carr* 1690, *Starrcar* 1697, *Starcarr* 1700, 1707, 1724, *Starrcarr* 1703, *Star Carr* 1745 all *Terrier,* 1768 (1791) *LindDep Plans,* 1790 *Monson, Starcar* 1767 *Stubbs, Star Car* 1795 *LLHS,* 'the marshy land where sedge grows', *v.* **storr**^{2}, **star, kjarr,** a Scand. compound. The use of *carr* as an appellative is noteworthy, though this is fairly common in north L. Part of Star Carr Lane is *Carr Lane* 1828 Bry. TIMARU FM is a transferred name from Timaru, New Zealand, and is close to the boundary with Elsham, and so is a nickname of remoteness. VICARAGE, *ye viccaridge* 1662, - *vicarige* 1664, *the vicarige* 1668, 1671, - *Vicaridge* 1679, 1707, *Vicarige House* 1700, cf. *ye Vicaridge dale* 1679 all *Terrier (v.* **deill** 'a share of land'). WEST MOOR RD is *School Ho Lane* 1824 O. WHITE HILLS, - *Hill* 1824 O, cf. *White Hill Fox Cover Plantation* 1828 Bry, 1830 Gre, *White Hill Plantation* 1832 *Yarb.* WRAWBY CARRS, 1767 *Stubbs,* 1824 O, *Carrs* 1830 Gre, *v.* **kjarr** 'a marsh'. WRAWBY MOOR, 1820 *MiscDep 204,* 1824 O, 1830 Gre, *the more* 1606 *Terrier, Wraby moore* 1635 (c.1900) *LindDep 78, the Common moor* 1679, 1693, *the common* - 1707, *Wrawby Comon Moor* 1724, *the common Moor* 1745, *the Common Moor* 1762 all *Terrier,* cf. *ye Moore bank(e)* 1662, 1664, 1671, *the moor banck* 1703 all *ib* and *Moor Farm* 1830 Gre, marked on the 6" OS map, but not named. WRAWBY WINDMILL, *windmill* 1675 *Elw, Wind Mill* 1868 *ib, Wrawby Mill* 1824 O, 1830 Gre.

Field-Names

Principal forms in (a) are 1832 *Yarb*; forms dated 1354 are *BR*; 1577, 1601, 1606, 1638, 1662, 1664, 1668, 1671, 1679, 1690, 1693, 1697, 1700, 1703, 1707, 1724, 1745, 1762, 1822 are *Terrier*; 1675, 1682, 1704 are *Elw*; 1790 are *Monson*; 1795 are *LLHS*; 1805 are *EnclA*; 1828 are Bry; 1832 and 1850 are *Yarb*.

(a) First -, Second Ash Hill 1832, 1850; Benjamin Tofts 1790 (from the pers.n. or surn. *Benjamin* with **toft**); Brig Fd 1762, Brigg - 1795 (*Brigg Field* 1693, *Brigg Field Stowe* 1690 (**stow** is recorded in EDD, only from L, in the sense 'a sheep-hurdle', probably earlier 'a place made of hurdles, where sheep were herded', *v.* further Sandred 36-37 and EPN s.v. **stōw** (3)), *the Cald Brigg field* 1697), Brigg Pits 1790 (*v.* **pytt**), Brigs Wood Side Fd 1795 (*Brigg Side* 1679, from the adjacent parish of Glanford Brigg); Brown Hills 1832, 1850; Bull Pce 1767 *Stubbs*, 1790 (cf. *Bull-Marrfare* 1690, *the Bull Marfar* 1693, *Bull Marr fra* (sic) 1697, *- Mar fray* (sic) 1700, *the bull-marfurrow* 1707, *Bull Marfarr* 1724, *the Bull marfurrow* 1745, *v.* **bula**, **marfur** 'a boundary furrow'); Common Carr 1790 (belonging to sundry proprietors, cf. *yᵉ Common deale* 1693, *v.* **kjarr**, **deill**)); the Cottagers part 1762 (*betwixt yᵉ Husbandes Carr and the Cottagers* 1662, 1664, 1668, 1671, *ye Cottagers partes* 1679, *the Cottchers parts* 1690, *betwixt the Husbandmens parts & Cottagers* 1693, *betwixt the Husband men and Cottagers parts* 1697, *the Cottagers parts* 1703, *- part* 1724, *yᵉ Cottagers part* 1745, *v.* **cottager**, **kjarr**, **part**, cf. the Husbandman's part *infra;* note the use of **part** in this parish, as in *Furth-carr-part* in Worlaby f.ns. (b) *supra*); Croft; East Fd 1795, the field formerly called the East field 1822 ("the east field of Wraughby" 1322 HMCRutl, *in campo orientali* 1354, *yᵉ eastm' felde* (sic) 1577, *the east feeld* 1601, one of the great fields of Wrawby, cf. North Fd, Far -, Nr West Fd *infra);* Far Cl; Btm -, Middle -, Top Goose Cl, Goose Tongue (*v.* **gōs**, **tunge**, probably in the sense a tongue of land); Far Hall 1828; Hemp Pits (Head) 1795; High field Rd 1805; the Husbandman's part 1762 (*yᵉ husbandes -* 1662, *the Husbandes -* 1664, 1668, *yᵉ Husbandes Carr* 1671, *ye Husbandmans partes* 1679, *the Husband mens parts* 1690, *betwixt the Husbandsmens parts & Cottagers* 1693, *betwixt the Husband men and Cottagers parts* 1697, *the husbandmens part* 1703, *Husbandmans part* 1707, *the husbandman's part* 1745, *the Farmers part* 1724, *v.* **husbandman**, **kjarr**, **part**, cf. the Cottagers part *supra*; **husbandman** here seems to have the sense 'customary tenant', in contrast to the *cottager*, the 1724 form referring to the same piece of land); one entire Deal called Kirkdale 1762 (*Kirkedayle* 1354, *Kyrkedalle* 1577, *one dale ... called Kirkdale* 1601, *the deal called Kirk dale* 1707, *Kirks dale* 1724, *one intire Deal called Kirkedale* 1745, 'the church allotment', *v.* **kirkja**, **deill**, a Scand. compound); Knee Pasture 1832, 1850 (probably from the surn. *Knee*); Longland

Stile (y^e *pathe called Langlande Stighe* 1577, *the pathe called longland stigh* 1638, *Longland stile* 1693, *v.* stīg, stigel, cf. *the Lands called long lande* 1606, *long lands* 1679, *v.* lang, land); low moor 1850 *Elw*, Meadow Cls 1795; Middle Cl; High Moor Drain 1805, High Moor 1832, 1850 (all named from Wrawby Moor *supra*); North Fd 1795 (*the north Field* 1690, - *North Field* 1697, - *field* 1700, *the Northfield* 1693, cf. East Fd *supra*); the Ox Pasture 1795; 1/3 Foot Carrs (sic) 1790 (*v.* kjarr; the implication of the measurement is not clear, but it *may* represent the thickness of the peat here); Second Pasture; Toll Dale 1795; Far -, Nr West Fd (*in campo occidentali* 1354, y^e *west felde* 1577, *the west feelde* 1601, *the West feilds* 1638, one of the great fields of Wrawby, cf. East Fd, North Fd *supra* and Brig Fd *supra*).

(b) "manor called" *Archemanere* 1441 Cl (cf. Gilbert *de Arcubus* 1242-43 Fees, "Robert called" *de Arcubus* of *Wraby* 1317 Ch, John *Darche* 1328 ib); *the Bailiffs deale* 1700, - *Bailiffsdale* 1707, - *Balifs dale* 1724, *the Bailiffs Dale* 1745 ('the bailiff's share or portion of land', *v.* baillie, deill); *the Brigs* 1638; *Brotdale* 1354, *Wrot dall'* 1577, *one Dale called Wrot dalle* 1601 (a Scand. compound of brot 'a small piece' and deill 'a share, a portion of land'; the 1577 *Terrier* refers to the 1354 documents, and Dr Nicholas Bennett, who checked the three spellings, agrees that it is likely that the initial *W*- of the former is an error for the *B*- of the 14th century form); *the Cantch* 1675, 1682, 1704 (cf. *The Canch* in Thornton Curtis *supra*); y^e *common* 1679, *the Common* 1697, - *common* 1700, 1707); y^e *com: field* 1679; *in campo de Wrageby* 1276 RH, y^e *feeldes* 1577 (*v.* feld); *the Furth Moore* 1638; *the headland* 1690 (*v.* hēafod-land); *Henneacredayle* 1322 HMCRutl ('the plot of arable land where wildfowl abound', *v.* henn (gen.pl. *henna*), æcer, with deill); *de Holbeck* 1300 HMCRutl, *de Holbek'* 1327, 1332 *SR*, *de Holbek* of *Wrauby* 1359 HMCRutl all (p) (*v.* hol[1], bekkr, but this may well not be a local surn.); *the Intack Parke* 1693 (*v.* inntak); y^e *lande dyke* 1577, *the Land Dike* 1635 (c.1900) LindDep 78, 1638, (*v.* land, dīk); *the Little Close* 1675, 1682, 1704; y^e *lower ende* 1577, *the lower end* 1638 (self-explanatory, cf. y^e *upper ende infra*); *in foro de ... Wrauby* 1374 Peace ('Wrawby market'); *middleforth* 1635 (c.1900) LindDep 78 (*v.* middel, ford); *Mitchill wood* 1662, 1664, 1668, 1671 (named from the family of Ann *Michell of Wrawbie* 1625 *Inv*); Nowoods 1635 (c.1900) LindDep 78; y^e *pyttes* 1577, *the pittes* 1638, ye Pittes 1662, 1671, *the* - 1664, 1668, *the Pitts* 1697 (*v.* pytt); y^e *pryeur dyke* 1577, *prye dike* (sic) 1690, *the Prior Dike* 1638 (*v.* prior, dīk); *the Sheep Walkes* 1675, - *sheep walkes* 1682, - *Sheepwalkes* 1704 (*v.* shepe-walk); *the South Field* 1693, - *field* 1700 (cf. East Fd, North Fd and Far -, Nr West Fd *supra* in (a)); *Stone hill* 1659; *one Carr called Stormire* 1606 ('the sedge marsh', *v.* storr, mýrr); *the Three Oxgangs* 1675, - *Oxganges* 1682, *the three* - 1704 (*v.* oxgang); *the Towne feeld* 1606, *the Townfield*

1693, *the towne Field* 1697 (cf. y^e *feeldes supra*); y^e *Towne streete* 1577, *the towne street* 1606, *the Towne Street* 1690, 1703, *the Town* - 1693, *Towne streete* 1697, *the Towns Street* 1707, *the Town street* 1724; *the Twoe Oxgangs* 1675, *the Two* - 1682, - *Oxganges* 1704 (*v.* **oxgang** and cf. *the Three Oxgangs supra*); *Vbbole landes* 1354; y^e *upper ende* 1577, *the upper* - 1638 (cf. y^e *lower ende supra*); *Westiby* 1327, 1332 *SR*, *Westyby de Wrauby* 1340 HMCRutl all (p) ('west in the village', *v.* **west, í, by**); *Wrawbydik* Ed1 HMCRutl (*v.* **dík**); *Wrawby Dale* 1745.

INDEX

This index is based on the following principles:

(a) It includes all the place-names in the body of the work.

(b) It covers only the main reference to each place and no cross-references are noted.

(c) Street-names are included, but only those of Barton upon Humber have been treated separately in the body of the text.

(d) "Lost" names are printed in italics.

(e) In grouping names together no distinction has been made between those written in one word or two, e.g. Windmill and Wind Mill have been grouped together.

(f) Only very few field-names (of special historical or philological interest) have been included.

Abbot's Lodge 281
Acredike 13
Acridge, East & West 36
Adlumsty 36
Alder Carr Wood 66
Alder Wood 66
Allens Wood 125
Almshouses 250
Ancholme Tavern 118
Angel Hotel 118
Angel 89
Anthony Corner 221
Anthony's Clump 221
Ashdale Ho 292
Ash Holt 239
Ash Holt 50
Audleby 88
Audleby Low Covert 96, 136
Audleby Square Wood 89
Audleby Top 90

Bacchus 118
Back Lane 10, 165

Backs, The 308
Back Wood 90
Barff, Low 78
Barff Vale 181
Barnby Ho 17
Bardney Hall 32
Barnetby, New 10
Barnetby le Wold 8
Barnetby Mill 10
Barnetby Wold Fm 10
Barrow Ferry 17
Barrow Grange 17
Barrow Hall 17
Barrow Hann 17
Barrow Hann Cover 17
Barrow Haven 17
Barrow Hawk 17
Barrow Ling 181
Barrow Mere 17
Barrow Mills 17
Barrow Rd 36
Barrow upon Humber 15
Barrow Vale 18

Barton Cliff 32
Barton Field Fm 32
Barton Grange 32
Barton Haven 32
Barton Hill Fm 32
Barton Lane 18
Barton Lodge 32
Barton upon Humber 30
Barton Vale 32
Barton Waterside 32
Barton Wold Fm 32
Bass Garth 150
Baysgarth, - Park 32, - Fm 150
Beacon Hill 33
Beaumontcote Fm 33
Beck, The 18
Beck Hill 36
Becklands 239
Beck Lane 18
Beck Plantation 239
Beck's Patch 269
Beech Grove 33
Beggarthorn 77
Bellows Pipe 221
Bell Pit 66
Belt Plantation 181
Bennett's New Covert 255
Bentley Fm 50, - Ho 136
Betty Holmes Wood 216
Bigby 48
Bigby Common 50
Bigby Hill 50
Bigby St. 118
Big Wood 239
Bishops Barn 308
Black Bank 77
Black Bull (Hotel) 33, 118, 150
Black Bull 239
Black Mills 221
Blacknall Cover 221

Black Swan 90
Black Wood 250
Blow Wells Plantation 33
Blue Bell Inn 33
Blue Coat Charity Fm 33
Bluegate Wood 66
Bodebi 280
Bonby 56
Bonby Carrs 57
Bonby Ings 57
Bonby Lodge 57
Bonby Wold Fm 57
Botany Bay 308
Bowmandale 36
Brandicarr, - Covert 77-8
Bratlands 250
Brick Kiln(s) 90, 292
Brick Lane 150
Brick Yard 106
Brickyard Lane 308
Bridge End 118
Bridge Fm 50
Bridge St. 118
Brigg 117
Brigg Rd 36, 90
Broad Piece 165
Brocklesby 61
Brocklesby Hall 66
Brocklesby Ox (Inn)
118, 292
Brocklesby Park 66
Brompton Dale 221
Brook Hill 126
Brow Hill 181
Bruff Fm 181
Bull House Fm 261
Burgate 36
Burkinshaw's Covert 196
Burnham 280
Burnham Beeches 281

Burnham Grange 281
Burnham Lodge 281
Burnham Manor 281
Burnham Park 281
Burnham Plantation 281
Burnham Rd 37
Burnham Warren 281
Burnt Wood 78
Butchery 37, 118
Butforth Drain, - Lane 18
Butter Market 90
Butters Wood 126
Butt Lane 269
Butts Rd 37
Bygott's Covert 196

Caddle Beck, - Head 175
Cadney 75
Cadney Bridge 78
Cadney Carrs 78
Cadney Causeway 78
Cadney Grange 78
Cadwell 111
Caen Hill 222
Caistor 87
Caistor Moor 90
Caistor Rd 37
Caistor Soke 88
Camp Covert 233
Canada, - Lane, - Wood 90
Canch, The 281
Candley Beck 50
Capham Hall 181
Carfax Ho 18
Carr Drain 308
Carr Fm 78, 181
Carr Gutter 126
Carr Lane 57, 159, 269, 293
Carr Leys Wood 66
Carr Side Plantation 106

Cartwright Moor 265
Castledyke 37
Castle Fm 303
Castle Hill 90
Castles, The 18
Catchwater Drain 308
Catherine St. 37
Catholic Moor Screed 265
Catta Furze 233
Cawber Fm 199
Chalk House Bottom 222
Chantry Lane 37
Chapel Field Rd 121
Chapel Fm 33, 126
Chapel Lane 37
Chase Hill Fm, - Wood 197
Cherry Lane 18
Chowder Ness 33
Church Garth Holt 106
Church Lane 165, 292
Church Lane 106
Church Side 197
Church St. 269
Cissplatt Lane 175
Clarkson's Carr Fm 303
Clay Pit 33, 159
Cliff Ho 32
Clixby 94
Clixby Lodge 96
Clixby Manor 96
Clough, The 165
Clough Plantation 303
Coach & Horses 118
Coal Dyke End 118
Coatham Nunnery 63
Cold Harbour 181
College Bridge, - Fm 281
College Rd 18
Common Lane 308

Coneygreen Wood 222
Conygarth 44
Cornhill 90 - Fm 33
Coskills 10
Cote Pits 292
Cotham, Nun 63
Coton, Nun 63
Cottagers Dale Wood 66
Course 287
Court Close 106
Cow Fm 199
Cowgate 162
Craven Close Cover 58
Creek Drain 181
Croft Ho 292
Cross Keys 136
Cross Keys 118
Cross Lane 181
Cross Rd 292
Crown, The 118
Crow Wood Plantation 255
Croxton 98
Croxton Grange 100
Croxton Plantation 100
Croxton Wold 100
Cutley Beck, - Bridge 181

Dam Bottom 66
Dam Lane 282
Dam Rd 38
Dawson's Covert 265
Decoy Ho 181
Deepdale 33
Deepdale Plantation 106
Dockhole Rd 292
Dodd's Lane 175
Doll Lane 106
Donkey Park 50
Dovecote Fm 181

Down Hall 18
Drabbles Hill 182
Draycotes 237
Dudmandale 33
Dunkirk Fm, - Wood 298
Dying Gladiator 118

Eastfield Fm 33
East Field Rd 197
Easthall Fm 182
East Halton 148
East Halton Beck 150
East Halton Grange 150
East Halton Skitter 149
East Hann Fm 17
East Marsh 122, - Rd 126
East Middle Mere Rd 198
East Moor Fm 182
East Plantation 106
Edlington Ho 78
Eleven Acre Plantation 255
Ellmore Fm 182
Elm Tree Ho 18
Elsham 105
Elsham Carr Fm 106
Elsham Carrs 106
Elsham Hall 106
Elsham Hill 106
Elsham May Bank 106
Elsham Top 106
Elsham Wolds 106
Elsham Wood 106
Epham's Lane 269

Falconer's Arms 90
Faraway Drain 78
Far Fm 90
Far Ings Lane 38
Farrishes Lane 110

Ferriby, South 109
Ferriby Bridge 110
Ferriby Hill 110
Ferriby Rd 38
Ferriby Sluice 110
Ferry 33
Ferry Boat 110
Ferry Fm, - Rd 126
Ferry Gate Bottom 265
Field Fm 34
Field Ho 34, 110, 126
Field House Fm 255
Finkle Lane 38
Fir Lane 182
Fitties 153
Fleece Inn 90
Fleet Gate 38
Folly Lane 182
Fonaby 88
Fonaby, Low 90
Fonaby Top 90
Forby Land 306
Forth Carr Plantation 255
Four Acre Clump 255
Fox 293
Fox Covert 78, 197, 282
Fox Covert Plantation 255
Fox Dale 90, 224
Fox Hills 106
Foxhole Wood 165
Frauncherey 71
Freehold Lane 269
Froghall, - Carrs 78
Frogmore Fm 282
Fulches Drain 111
Fulsoar Drain 111

Gallows Covert 10, 233
Gallows Fm 308
Gascrick 31

Gatehouse Fm 165
George & Dragon 118
George Hotel 34, 90
Glanford Brigg 117
Gleadow Plantation 10
Glebe Fm 10, 34, 141, 239, 299
Golden Fleece 90
Gorbet Bridge 78
Gorse Cover 58
Gorse Covert 255
Goultons Cover 58
Goxhill 119
Goxhill Hallands 122
Goxhill Haven 126
Goxhill Rd 18
Grammar School, - Rd 118
Grange, The 111, 282, 303
Grange Fm 255
Grange Windmill 293
Grange Wold Fm 250
Granny Wood 66
Grasby 135
Grasby Bottom(s) 136, 222
Grasby Top 136
Grasby Wold Lane 136
Gravel Pit 282, 299, 303
Gravelpit Fm 182
Gravel Pit Rd 38
Great Drift 136
Great Limber 219
Great Limber Covers 222
Great Limber Grange 222
Great Moor 308
Green Gate 34
Greengate Rd 199
Greenland Fm 222, - Top 269
Green Lane 38
Green Man 269

Green Pit 250
Griffin 90
Grove Ho 19, 90
Guilicar Lane 182
Gurnels Barn 269

Habrough 139
Habrough Grange 141
Habrough Marsh 141
Halfway Ho 223
Halland's Field 122
Hall Cross 96
Hall Fm 58
Halliday Hill 223
Halton, East 148
Halton Marshes 150
Hammer-in-Hand 118
Hanging Dales 250
Hann Fm, - Lane 17
Harding's Wood 261
Hardwick 237
Hawthorn Lane 38
Headings 14
Head Lane 223
Healing Covert 269
Hendale Lodge, - Wood 221
Hermitage Wood 250
Highfield Plantation 182
Highfields 182
Highfield Wood 175
High Sadney 184
High St. 19, 39, 239
Hill Garth Fm 293
Hill Side Plantation 255, 303
Hoe Hill Brick Works 34
Holydyke 39
Home Fm 239
Honey Close Plantation 96
Hope 118
Hope & Anchor 111

Hope Yard 118
Horns Wood 216
Horsegate Field Rd 123
Horse Market 90
Horse Pasture 250
Horkstow 158
Horkstow Bridge 159
Horkstow Carrs 159
Horkstow Grange 159
Horkstow Hall 160
Horkstow Rd 39
Horkstow Wold 160
Hospital 303
Houlton Fm 199
Houlton's Covert 199
House of Industry 90
Howe Hill 299
Howe Hill 239
Howe Lane 126
Howsham 76
Howsham Barff 78
Howsham Grange 78
Hundon Manor 89
Hundon Walk Ho 90
Hungate 39
Hudsons Gorse Cover 216
Hunger Hill Wood 250

Immingham 163
Immingham Dock 165
Immingham Grange 165
Immingham Haven 165
Immingham Lough 165
Ingold Toft 196
Ings Fm 182
Ings Ho 19
Ings Ho 182
Ings Lane 165
Ings Lock 182
Ington 198

Irongate Wood 66
Island Carr 118
Ivy Ho 261

John James' Screed 265
Joiner's Arms 90

Keelby 174
Keelby Grange 175
Kelsey, North 178
Kettleby 49
Kettleby Beck 50
Kettleby Carrs 50
Kettleby Covert 50
Kettleby Parks 50
Kettleby Thorpe 49
Keyholme 19
Killingholme 193
Killingholme, North 195
Killingholme, South 198
Killingholme Marshes 197
Kiln Lane 270
King's Arms 90
Kingsforth 34
King's Head 175
King's Head 90
Kirmington 214
Kirmington Hall 216
Kirmington Vale 216
Knab's Crossing 233
Knab's Hill 10

Ladypits Plantation 293
Ladysmith Cottage 303
Lamb 118
Lambert Hill Cottage, - Pond 66
Land Drain 182, 255
Langleys 123
Langmere Covert 150
Lawns, The 19

Lawrence Fm 96
Leys Fm 19
Limber, Great 219
Limber, Little 64
Limber Folly 223
Limber Hill 223
Limber Ho 223
Lincolnshire 1
Lindsey 2
Lion Hotel 118
Little Carr Drain 308
Little Fm 299
Little Lane 118
Little Limber 64
Little Limber Chapel 66
Little Limber Grange 67
Little London 270,
        - Fm 182
Little Marsh 34
Little Moor, - Drain
        309
Littleworth 126
Littleworth Fm 106
Long Close Plantation
        100, 299
Long Holt 106
Long Lane 270
Long Plantation 266
Long Screed 78
Long Strip 165
Long Wood 239
Lopingham 149
Lord Nelson Hotel 118
Lord's Lane 19
Low Barff 78
Low Fm 10, 197, 282
Low Fm 136
Low Fonaby 90
Low Furze
        Plantation 299

Low Moor Drain 106, 309
Low Risby Ho 126
Low Wood 10
Luxmore Fm 165

Major Wood 67
Maltby Lane 39
Malthouse 10
Maltkiln Lane 106
Manby Ho 19
Manby Rd 165
Manor Fm 175, 240, 282
Manor Fm 141
Manor Ho 10, 126, 151, 182, 197, 255, 261, 270, 293
Manor Wood 240
Manslot 208
Marfur 12
Mark Cooper's Wood 293
Market Lane 39
Market Place 39, 90, 118
Marquis of Granby 91
Marshall's Covert 106
Marsh Cottages 165
Marsh Fm 19, 34, 199
Marsh Lane 19, 39
Martin Lane 293
Mausoleum 67
Mausoleum Woods 223
Maux Hall 223, 270
Meergate Hedge 151, 197
Melton Gallows 233
Melton Hall 234
Melton High Wood 234
Melton Road Fm 309
Melton Ross 232
Mere Hill 67
Mere Plantation 34
Mickle How Hill 216
Micklemere Hill 151

Midby 19
Middle Drain 270
Middlegate Lane 50, 58, 106, 111, 160, 255, 261, 303
Middle Gate Lane 198
Middlegate Rd 234
Miller's Wood 67
Mill Fm 126
Mill Hill 182, 199
Mill Hill Ho 166
Mill Lane, 118, 175, 309
Minnitt's Fm 183
Model Fm 293
Moldefang 145
Monument 266
Moor Ho 96
Moor Lane 309
Moor Plantation 106
Moors, The 216
Mount Ho 34
Mount Pleasant 19, 175
Mount Pleasant 34, 255

Navigation Lane 91
Neatgangs Fm 124
Nelsons Fm 223
Nelthorpe Arms (Hotel) 111, 118
Ness End Fm 34
Nettlebush 277
Nettleton 236
Nettleton Beck 239
Nettleton Bleak Ho 239
Nettleton Bottom 239
Nettleton Gap 239
Nettleton Grange 239
Nettleton Hill 240
Nettleton Ho 240
Nettleton Lodge 240

Nettleton Manor 240
Nettleton Moor 240
Nettleton Rd 91
Nettleton Top 240
Nettleton Wold Fm 240
Nettleton Wood 240
New Barnetby 10
New Barns 19
New Beck Drain 67, 175
New Close Wood 223
New Fm 141, 240
New Holland 16
New Inn 223
Newland Hill 106
New Plantation 107
Newport St. 39
Newsham Abbey 64
Newsham Booth 141
Newsham Lodge 64
Newstead Drain 78
Newstead Priory 76
Nicholson's Yard 119
North Beck Drain 166
North Carr Bank 78
North Carr Lane 255
North End 127, 175
North Field 293
Northfield Lane 282
North Field Wood 216
North Garths 198
North Grange 111
North Kelsey 178
North Kelsey Beck 183
North Kelsey Carrs 183
North Kelsey Grange 183
North Kelsey Mills 183
North Kelsey Moor 184
North Killingholme 195
North Killingholme Haven 198
North Moss Lane 270

North Riding 7
Nun Cotham 63
Nun Coton 63
Nun's Creek 142
Nursery, The 67
Nut Hill 34

Oak Holt 250
Oaks, The 270
Oak Wood 79
Old Belt Plantation 255
Oldfleet Drain 269
Old Hall 10
Old Inn Fm 223
Old Knot, The 250
Old Lane Holt 107
Old Park Hill 250
Old Stone Pit 58
Old Vicarage 91
Old Windmill 91
Ostler's Lane 160
Owmby 259
Ownby Lane 184, 261
Owmby Mill 261
Owmby Mount 261
Owmby Top 261
Owmby Vale 262
Owmby Wold Lane 262
Oxford Grange 19
Oxgangs 240
Oxley 19
Oxmarsh Fm, - Lane 19

Paddocks, The 67
Palmer Lane 19
Paper Mill 91
Paradise Place 119
Park, The 299, 303
Park Fm 19
Park Wood 79

Pasture Rd 40
Pelham Bridge 309
Pelham Rd 166
Penny Carrs 79
Peplo Lane 19
Pepperdale Fm, - Covert 79
Pikendale Plantation 255
Pimlico 223
Pinfold Ho 51
Pingley Fm, - Lane 51
Plough 91
Pond Close Wood 100
Pool End 51
Poolthorne, - Covert 79
Poplar Holt 166
Poplar Walk 107
Preston Lane 40
Priestgate 40
Primrose Hill 67
Priory 127
Prospect Ho 10
Providence Cottage, - Place 20
Pye Ho 79

Race Lane 234, 282, 299
Read's Island 111
Rectory, (The) 51, 111
Redcar 79
Redcombe Rd 119
Red Hill 91
Redholme 309
Red Ho 184
Red Lion 119
Red Lion Hotel 91
Reeds Meer 166
Rein Deer 91
Rennison's Carr Fm 106
Riby 249
Riby Gap 250
Riby Grange 250

Riby Grove, - Grove Fm 250
Riby Park 250
Riby Slings Meer 250
Riby Wolds 250
Robinson Row 40
Robinson's Row 119
Rookery 107
Roscar Dike 79
Rosper Rd 198
Rough Pasture Wood 67
Round Clump 255
Rowland Hill 20
Roxton Fm 165
Roxton Wood 166
Royal Oak 20
Ruard Rd 124
Rye Hill Fm,
    - Plantations 199

Sadney, - Plantation 184
Sadney, High 184
Sainfoin 13
St Chad 20
St Chad's Well 111
St Helen's Well 119
St James Cross 34
Salt Marsh 127
Sandbraes 91
Sandham Plantation 127
Sand Hills 79
Sand Pit 175, 240,
        - Fm 20
Saner's Cottages 20
Saxby All Saints 254
Saxby All Saints Bridge 255
Saxby All Saints Carrs 255
Saxby Hall 255

Saxby Windmill 255
Saxby Wolds 255
Scales 69
Scrub Lane 151
Scrub Wood 270
Searby 259
Searby cum Owmby 259
Searby Hill 262
Searby Moor Fm 262
Searby Top 262
Searby Wold Lane 262
Setcops 184
Seventy Acre Lane 223
Shadwells 31
Shaw Wood 91
Sheepcote Hill 184
Sheepgate 244
Sheep Lane Plantation 107
Sheepwalk 286
Shepherds Ho 107
Ship 119
Ship, The 270
Shooters Dale 91
Sinks Covert 199
Six Bells 20
Skegger Beck 10
Skipworths Fm 270
Skitter Beck 292
Skitter Ness 127
Skitter Rd 151
Slack 27, 132
Sloop 91
Sloughts 258
Smallthorne Fm 184
Smithfield Fm 180
Smith's Piece 107
Smithy Lane 20, 51
Soft Lane 127
Somerby 264
Somerby Dolter 266

Somerby Hall 266
Somerby Low Fm 266
Somerby Top 266
Somerby Wold Lane 266
Sour Hill 35
Soutergate 40
South Bank 79
South Carr 184
South Cliff 35
South Cloister Covert 282
South End 127, 175
South Ferriby 109
South Ferriby Cliff 111
South Ferriby Hall 111
Southfield 35
Southfield Rd 184
Southgate 40
South Killingholme 198
South Killingholme Grange 200
South Killingholme Haven 200
South Marsh Rd 270
South Moor 240
South Plantation 255
Southside Plantation 107
South View 96
South Wold Fm 303
Sparrow Clump 223
Spa Spring 91
Springfield 309
Sprothorns, The 270
Spruce Lane 293
Spur Plat Wood 67, 293
Stackstead 248
Stallingborough 268
Stallingborough Grange 271
Stallingborough Hall 271
Stallingborough Kiln Ferry 271

Stallingborough Rd 166
Stallingborough Windmill 271
Star Carr Lane 309
Starham 184
Steep Hills 107
Stepney 175
Stingraves Ho 184
Stintings 14
Stonecliffe 10
Stonecroft Ho 10
Stope Hill Fm, - Grange 240
Strawberry Cottage 20
Street Lane 185
Suddell Ho 91
Suddle Spring 175
Summercroft Fm 20
Summerdale 35
Sun 119
Swallow Mill Quarter 124
Swallows Low Wood 160
Swan Hill 35
Sweetbrier Fm 293
Swiss Cottage 223
Sykes' Lane 127
Sykes Pond 250

Talbot Hotel 91
Tarrygarth Quarter 16
Temperance Hotel 119
Thirty Foot Drain 79
Thomas Wood 67
Thorn Covert 79
Thorney Bottom Wood 91
Thorney's Field 20
Thorns, The 216
Thornton Curtis 279
Thornton Hall 282
Thornton Moor 282
Thornton Rd 20
Timaru Fm 309

Tofts Rd 40
Top Barn 240
Topper Lane 175
Totney Hill Fm 127
Tugdale Wood 240
Tunnards 282
Tup Close Plantation 266
Turnpike Top Fm 303
Turton's Covert 160
Tweedmoor Plantation 107
Twelve Month Fm,
      - Hill Wood 185
Tyrwhitt Hall 35

Ulceby 291
Ulceby Carr 293
Ulceby Chase 293
Ulceby Field 293
Ulceby Grange 293
Ulceby Mill 293
Ulceby Skitter 292
Ulceby Wold 293
Utware 72

Vale Fm, - Ho 294
Vicarage (The) 10, 58, 107,
    128, 138, 151, 160, 175,
      185, 282, 303, 309
Victoria 91

Walk Ho 282
Walk Lane 223
Walmer Ho 200
Walnut Ho 175
Warlot 67
Warnoth 104
Warren Fm 35
Warren Hill 240
Washdyke Ho 185
Washdyke Lane 107, 166

Washdyke Wood 67
Watercress Beds 20
Water Hills 91
Waterhill Wood 67
Water Ings 304
Water Mill 91
Waterside Rd 40
Waterslacks Rd 40
Wear Dyke 255
Weir Dike 160
Welbeck Spring 234
Welham 16
Wellholmes Holt 51
Wentworth's Cottage 271
Westaby Lane 20
Westcott Fm 20
West End Rd 294
West Field 151
West Field 271
Westfield Ho 35
Westfield Rd 40, 185
Westfield Windmill 294
West Hann Fm 17
West Hills 223
West Holmes 185
Westland Lane 185
West Lane 175
West Marsh 20
West Marsh Lane 125
West Middle Mere Rd 198
West Moor Fm 91
West Moor Rd 309
Westrum 51
Wheat Sheaf 119
Whitecross St. 40
Whitegate, - Hill 91
White Hall Fm 51
White Hart 91, 119
White Hills 309
White Horse 119

White Horse 91
White House Fm 185
White Lion 36
White Swan 36
Whiting Mill Bottom 36
William IV 119
Willow Holt 68
Willow Plantation 255
Willowtree Lane 40
Winding 173
Windmill 20, 36, 91
Winship Rd 40
Wire Platt Plantation 107
Woodbine Cottage 119,
    185, - Ho 185
Wood Fm 240
Woodlands 198
Woolpack Hotel 119
Wootton 298
Wootton Dale 299
Wootton Grange 299
Wootton Grove 299
Wootton Hall 299
Wootton Lawn 299
Wootton Lodge 299
Wootton Plantation 299
Wootton Windmill 299
Wootton Wold 299
Worlaby 302
Worlaby Carrs 304
Worlaby Causeway 304
Worlaby Fox Covert 304
Worlaby Hall 304
Worlaby Ings 304
Worlaby Mill 304
Worlaby New Ings 304
Worlaby Plains 304
Worth 17
Wrawby 307
Wrawby Carrs 309

Wrawby Moor 309
Wrawby St. 119
Wrawby Windmill 309
Wykeham 238
Wykeham Well 240

Yarborough Camp 100
Yarborough Wapentake 7